WHAT IS AN
Aspen RoadMap?

Aspen RoadMaps™ are comprehensive course outlines that lead you, ster ˙ courses—helping you prepare for class and study for exams. With a cle to use as it is visually appealing, you'll be guided from the "big picture"

WHAT MAKES THE ASPEN ROADMAP™ FOR WILLS, TRUSTS, AND E⸱ ⸱⸱⸱ THE BEST?

The Aspen RoadMap™ for Wills, Trusts, and Estates:

- Guides you through the maze of terminology, rules, and policies for wills, trusts, and estates law.
- Covers all of the major subjects of a typical wills, trusts, and estates course and traces the organization of the leading wills, trusts, and estates casebook.
- Offers additional material on its dedicated Internet Website: charitable trusts, the Rule Against Perpetuities, fiduciary administration, taxation, and more! See Wills, Trusts, and Estates on www.aspenpublishers.com for links to more information on these topics.
- Addresses the relevant statutory and common law rules and policies for resolving wealth transfer disputes.
- Gives you keys to successful estate planning and strategies for avoiding wealth transfer disputes in practice.

THE PRACTICAL COMPONENTS OF YOUR ASPEN ROADMAP™

- ***The Casebook Correlation Chart*** helps you match sections of your casebook to this RoadMap™.
- ***The RoadMap*™ *Capsule Summary,*** cross-referenced to the outline text, provides a "big picture" view anytime you need it.
- ***Chapter Overviews,*** each no more than two pages long, highlight key concepts.
- ***Hypotheticals*** are interwoven throughout to help further clarify important concepts.
- ***Examples***—complete with accompanying analyses—are included in each chapter to provide lively and memorable illustrations of key points.
- ***Chapter Review Questions***—complete with answers—test and reinforce your knowledge.
- ***Exam Tips*** help you to target what you need to know, maximize your study time, and do well on exams.
- ***Sample Exam Questions and Answers*** help you prepare for the final exam.

ASPEN LAW & BUSINESS Educational Division

Dear Student,

Your course in wills, trusts, and estates will focus on family wealth transfers by will, by intestacy, and by a variety of other means that collectively are referred to as "will substitutes" (such as joint tenancies with the right of survivorship, life insurance and deferred compensation beneficiary designations, and revocable trusts). This RoadMap supplements your course by guiding you through the maze in which wealth transfer issues, terminology, rules, and policies are framed, analyzed, and resolved.

In concise and clear language, the RoadMap covers all of the major subjects of typical wills, trusts, and estates courses: how property passes when a decedent dies without a will; requirements to validly execute a will; grounds for contesting a will; revocation, interpretation, and construction of wills; will substitute property transfers; limits on the freedom of property owners to dispose of property; the creation and operation of trusts; powers of appointment; and future interests as used in wills and trusts. In addition, we have created an Internet Website with materials on additional subjects that your course may cover: charitable trusts, the Rule Against Perpetuities, duties of fiduciaries who administer estates and trusts, planning for incapacity, ethics, wealth transfer taxation, and the income taxation of trusts, estates, and beneficiaries.

Because some students find that concrete examples help them understand abstract legal doctrines and the analytic process of applying them, we also have included numerous hypothetical illustrations, with analysis. Further, each chapter ends with a series of review questions, with answers. Finally, to help you tie it all together and prepare for your exam, many exam tips are offered throughout the book and sample exam questions and responses appear at the end of the RoadMap.

In most instances we address the relevant statutory and common law rules and policies for resolving wealth transfer disputes, along with the planning implications these controversies raise. We specifically discuss affirmative planning responses because learning how to address or avoid these kinds of issues helps to better understand them. In addition, pointing out planning considerations helps to introduce you to estate planning, which is a practice specialty that, for many lawyers, is one of the most personally and professionally rewarding fields in which an attorney can practice. We each found it to be so.

Your coursebook will include many compelling cases of family disputes involving wealth transfers. Don't lose sight of the human drama being played out in these controversies. This RoadMap will guide you to understanding the substantive rules and policies of the law of wills, trusts, and estates, and it will help you appreciate and enjoy your study of this subject.

Good luck.

Jeffrey N. Pennell

Richard H. Clark Professor of Law
Emory University School of Law

Alan Newman

Associate Professor of Law
University of Akron School of Law

Aspen Publishers, Inc. A **Wolters Kluwer** Company

1185 Avenue of the Americas, New York, NY 10036
www.aspenpublishers.com

Wills, Trusts, and Estates

Jeffrey N. Pennell
Richard H. Clark
Professor of Law
Emory University School of Law

Alan Newman
Associate Professor of Law
The University of Akron School of Law

ASPEN LAW & BUSINESS
A Division of Aspen Publishers, Inc.
Gaithersburg   New York

3 4 5 6 7 8 9 0

Printed in the United States of America

Library of Congress Cataloging-in-Publication Data

Pennell, Jeffrey N., 1949-
    Wills, trusts, and estates / Jeffrey N. Pennell, Alan Newman.
      p.   cm.
    Includes index.
    ISBN 0-7355-1248-5
    1. Wills—United States. 2. Trusts and trustees—United States. 3. Estate planning—United States. I. Newman, Alan, 1951-
KF755.P46 2000
346.7305′2—dc21

                                             99-059611

SUMMARY OF CONTENTS

*Information is available on the following topics at our Website at
www.aspenpublishers.com.*

**Planning for Incapacity: Durable Powers of Attorney and Living
  Wills**
Rule Against Perpetuities
Fiduciary Administration
Charitable Trusts
Wealth Transfer Taxation Basics
Income Taxation of Trusts, Estates, and Beneficiaries
**Ethics, Professionalism, and Malpractice Issues in Estate
Planning and Administration**

CONTENTS

1   INTRODUCTION TO PROPERTY TRANSFERS AT DEATH

2 INTESTACY

3   TESTAMENTARY CAPACITY, WILL CONTESTS, WILL FORMALITIES, AND RELATED TOPICS

4   REVOCATION

5 WILL CONTRACTS

6 WILL SUBSTITUTES

7 INTERPRETATION: WHAT THE DECEDENT INTENDED

8   CONSTRUCTION: LAPSE AND CLASS GIFTS

9   CONSTRUCTION: ADEMPTION, ABATEMENT, ACCESSIONS, AND EXONERATION

RESTRICTIONS ON THE POWER OF DISPOSITION: STATUTORY FORCED HEIR SHARES AND COMMUNITY PROPERTY

11   INTRODUCTION TO TRUSTS

12   TRUST CREATION

13 TRUST OPERATION

14 POWERS OF APPOINTMENT

15 FUTURE INTERESTS: CLASSIFICATION, CHARACTERISTICS, AND CONSTRUCTION

Information is available on the following topics at our Website at www.aspenpublishers.com.

PLANNING FOR INCAPACITY: DURABLE POWERS OF ATTORNEY AND LIVING WILLS

A. The Need for Planning
    1. If No Planning
    2. Terminology
    3. Determination of Incapacity
    4. Ongoing Court Supervision
B. Planning for Property Management
    1. Outright Transfers
    2. Transfers in Joint Tenancy
    3. Revocable Trusts
    4. Durable Powers of Attorney
    5. Advantages of Revocable Trusts Over Durable Powers
    6. Durable Powers of Attorney Are Easier
C. Planning for Health Care
    1. Health Care Powers of Attorney
    2. Living Wills
    3. The Constitutional Right to Die
    4. Organ Donation

Rule Against Perpetuities

A. Statement of the Rule
B. Reasons for the Rule

Wealth Transfer Taxation Basics

CASEBOOK CORRELATION

li

CAPSULE SUMMARY

This Capsule Summary is intended for quick review at the end of the course. It is no substitute for mastering the material in the main outline.

1 INTRODUCTION TO PROPERTY TRANSFERS AT DEATH

A. TERMINOLOGY

1. Potential Heirs

Because heirs are determined at the designated ancestor's death, a living person has only potential heirs, which may be **heirs apparent** (certain to take if they survive the designated ancestor) or **heirs presumptive** (first in line presently but could be displaced).

2. Lineals

Ancestors and descendants in the blood line, including both natural born, adopted, and in most cases nonmarital and half-bloods.

3. Collaterals and Consanguinity

Nonlineal blood relatives, including natural born, adopted, and in most cases nonmarital and half-bloods.

4. Affinity

Relatives by marriage, generally not heirs unless married to the designated individual.

5. **Intestate**

Probate property not validly disposed of by a will.

6. **Testate**

There is a valid will.

7. **Testator**

The maker of a will.

8. **Will**

Handwritten by the testator (**holograph**), oral (**nuncupative**), or otherwise, this statement of the testator's wishes is revocable and **ambulatory** (it does nothing until death).

9. **Probate**

Admitting a will to probate is the process of proving a will is valid after the testator's death.

10. **Probate Administration**

The process of marshalling assets, paying debts, expenses, and taxes, and distributing a decedent's probate property, performed by a **personal representative (an executor or an administrator).** The personal representative's duty is to protect estate assets and the interests of beneficiaries and other claimants (such as creditors, who must receive actual notice if ascertainable, following reasonably diligent efforts to ascertain their identity).

11. **Probate Property** is any property not validly disposed of by a will substitute and passes under the terms of a decedent's will or by intestate succession.

12. **Nonprobate Property** passes by operation of law pursuant to various will substitutes.

13. **Will Contest**

Action challenging a will's validity for fraud, undue influence, lack of testamentary capacity, or lack of intent.

14. **Escheat**

The estate of an intestate decedent who has no living heirs passes to the decedent's domiciliary state.

15. **Succession**

The division of property among heirs, **per stirpes, per capita,** or **per capita at each generation.**

16. **Trust**

Legal entity that separates legal from equitable title, the former being held by a trustee as fiduciary for beneficiaries who own the latter.

17. **Settlor**

The creator or **grantor** of a trust.

18. **Beneficiary**

The owner of the equitable interest in a trust.

19. **Trustee**

The individual or corporation charged with the fiduciary duty to administer property for trust beneficiaries.

B. TESTAMENTARY FREEDOM

The right to devise property at death is statutory, not constitutional, and the government may limit it in a reasonable manner that is only as restrictive as necessary to affect a legitimate state interest.

C. PUBLIC POLICY limits a decedent's ability to control enjoyment of wealth after death in light of public policy prohibitions against encouraging illegal conduct or imposing certain unreasonable or immoral restrictions.

 2 INTESTACY

A. INTESTATE SUCCESSION is the statutory estate plan that applies to all probate property that is not validly disposed of by will.

1. **Jurisdiction**

The law of a decedent's state of residence governs distribution of all intestate personalty, and the law of the state in which realty is located governs intestate distribution of all intestate realty.

2. **Surviving Spouse**

The intestate share of a surviving spouse varies from state to state and may depend on which other heirs survived the decedent. Some laws give a surviving spouse a fixed dollar amount plus a fraction of any balance of the probate estate. Nonprobate property that passes to a surviving spouse is not considered in determining the spouse's share of intestate property.

3. **Survivorship** may be established by the **Uniform Simultaneous Death Act:** if there is insufficient evidence of the order of death between the decedent and a prospective heir. UPC §2-104 requires an heir to survive the decedent by 120 hours to be regarded as entitled to inherit.

4. **Descendants**

   That portion of the probate estate that does not pass to a surviving spouse usually passes to surviving lineal descendants, to the exclusion of all other relatives, by **right of representation,** which may take one of several different forms:

   a. **Classic per stirpes** makes the first division of property at the child level, creating one share for each child who is alive and one for each child who is deceased but survived by descendants who represent the child. Those representatives take the deceased child share, following the same pattern of division within each blood line separately.

   b. **Per capita** makes the first division of property at the first level below the decedent at which a descendant is alive, creating one share for each descendant at that level who is alive and one for each descendant who is deceased but survived by descendants who are alive, with a per stirpes distribution of the shares for the descendants of deceased descendants at that first level.

   c. **Per capita at each generation** also makes the first division at the first level below the decedent at which a descendant is alive, creating one share for each descendant at that level who is alive and one for each who is deceased but survived by descendants who are alive. Instead of a per stirpes distribution of the shares of the descendants who represent a deceased descendant at that first level it combines the shares of any deceased descendants at that first level and, among the representatives of only these deceased descendants, divides the combined shares equally again at the next level, again creating one share for each descendant at that level who is alive and one for each who is deceased but survived by descendants who are alive. And so on.

   d. **Modified per stirpes** divides the decedent's property equally among descendants in the same degree of relation to the decedent if they are the only takers. For example, if only grandchildren survive the decedent and no deceased grandchild is represented by descendants, the division would be equally among those living grandchildren.

5. **Ancestors and Collaterals**

   That portion of the probate estate that does not pass to a surviving spouse or lineal descendant is distributed among living ancestors and, to the extent necessary, to their descendants—collateral relatives—usually following the same form of representation applied to lineals. If the decedent has no surviving descendants, parents, or descendants of parents, some states distribute the estate under the **parentelic system** and others follow the **degree of consanguinity** approach.

B. **PARTIAL INTESTACY** occurs if a decedent has a will that does not validly dispose of the entire probate estate.

   1. **Residuary Clauses** dispose of property not specifically transferred under preresiduary provisions of the will. Absence an effective residuary clause the property passes by intestacy.

   2. **Negative Wills**

   A few states permit a decedent to expressly disinherit an heir, allowing that disinheritance to prevent the heir from taking by intestacy.

C. **QUESTIONS OF DEFINITION AND STATUS**

   1. **Spouse**

   The decedent's surviving spouse is an heir in most states, and may receive the entire probate estate under proper circumstances. A divorce or annulment prior to the decedent's death renders the former spouse ineligible.

   2. **Posthumous Heirs**

   A child conceived before the decedent's death is treated as alive at the time of conception if the child subsequently is born alive.

   3. **Half-Bloods and Step-Siblings**

   Most states do not discriminate against adopted or nonmarital children, although some states provide different intestate shares for relatives sharing one ancestor (half-bloods). Few states regard step-siblings as relatives at all.

   4. **Aliens**

   Most states do not discriminate against noncitizens, although **retention statutes, reciprocity statutes,** and **alien land laws** may govern the circumstances in which, or the property that, a noncitizen may inherit.

   5. **Adoption**

   Adoption statutes regard adopted children as natural born, and allow children to inherit from and through their adoptive parents only (and vice versa).

     a. Special rules usually apply if an adopting parent is married to a natural parent, preserving the natural parent line and, in some states, *both* natural parent lines for the child, although the parent may still be cut off and unable to inherit from the child.

b. Intestacy rules regarding adoption also may apply to determine whether a person qualifies as a member of a class under the provisions of a will, trust agreement, or other dispositive instrument.

6. **Virtual Adoption** permits a person who was not formally adopted to be treated as adopted in fact.

7. **Nonmarital Children** may inherit from and through their mother (and vice versa). In most states they inherit from and through their father if **paternity** was established prior to the father's death or other protections are met.

8. **Children of the New Biology**

A child conceived using a donor's sperm or egg is not necessarily that person's child. Instead, most statutes provide that the birth-mother and her husband are the natural parents, even if there is positive proof that either is not in fact the biological ancestor.

D. LIMITATIONS ON INHERITANCE

1. Homicide

Slayer statutes generally follow one of three approaches: the slayer may receive the property in constructive trust to be held for the decedent's other heirs, the slayer may inherit the property unconditionally, or the slayer is deemed to predecease the decedent—this third approach being the most common. A slayer statute may not apply if the slayer successfully pleads insanity as a defense or otherwise there was no intent to kill the decedent. A slayer is not divested of property the slayer owned before the killing and concurrent ownership may be regarded as if the slayer died first or may cause treatment as tenancy in common.

2. Disqualification for Other Misconduct

Abandonment of a child may preclude the parent from inheriting from or through that child.

3. Advancement

Property received from an ancestor who subsequently dies intestate may be considered as part of the heir's ultimate inheritance. Advancements are deducted from the heir's share in **hotchpot.** If the decedent dies testate the similar concept is **ademption by satisfaction.**

4. Release and Assignment; Expectancy

A release allows a potential heir to receive early distribution of a share of a property owner's estate, in exchange for a release of the potential heir's expectancy. An assignment allows a potential heir to transfer an expectancy to a third party for consideration. A release binds the heir's entire blood line; an assignment does not.

5. Disclaimer

An heir disclaims by refusing to accept property. Certain requirements apply under the Internal Revenue Code for federal gift tax purposes but state law governs disposition of disclaimed property—usually as if the disclaimant predeceased the decedent.

6. Survivorship

The UPC imposes a 120 hour survivorship requirement for an heir to be treated as having survived the decedent.

3 TESTAMENTARY CAPACITY, WILL CONTESTS, WILL FORMALITIES, AND RELATED TOPICS

A. INTRODUCTION

1. Will Validity Issues

To be valid a will must be executed with the requisite formalities by a testator with testamentary capacity and intent. The will must not be the product of undue influence, fraud, duress, or mistake, and it must not have been revoked.

2. Burdens of Proof on Validity Issues

The proponent of the will usually has the burden to prove that the will was validly executed. Will contestants then have the burden of proving invalidity.

3. Probate vs. Contest

Issues regarding execution or revocation affect whether the will is admitted to probate. Issues relating to the testator's capacity, intent, etc. are addressed in will contest proceedings.

B. TESTAMENTARY CAPACITY

1. Elements of Capacity

The testator must be a certain age and mentality to execute a will.

2. Minimum Age

The statutory minimum age requirement to execute a will usually is 18 years (although this is not uniform and may be lower in some states for married testators).

3. **Mentality**

Usually "of sound mind," mental capacity is presumed to exist if the will is properly executed and attested by witnesses.

4. **Test of Mental Capacity**

Mental capacity usually requires that the testator had the capacity to understand (i) the nature and extent of her property, (ii) the natural objects of her bounty, (iii) the disposition of the property made by the will, and (iv) the interaction of (i)–(iii) with each other, all when the will was executed.

C. LACK OF MENTAL CAPACITY

1. **In General**

Two forms of mental incapacity may affect validity of a will: deficient capability and derangement.

   a. Deficient capability means the testator cannot understand those elements required for proper execution of a will.

   b. Derangement affects only those portions of the will that are the product of paranoia, dementia, or delusions.

2. **Insane Delusions**

invalidate a will only if they affect a particular disposition and the conclusion drawn by the testator—the product of the delusion—was one that no rational person would draw.

D. TESTAMENTARY INTENT

1. **Raising the Issue**

Lack of testamentary intent may suffice to contest a will or deny probate to a will; it and forgery are the only grounds that may be asserted in either context.

2. **Presumptions of Testamentary Intent**

If a will is properly executed the presumption is that the testator had the requisite testamentary intent, placing the burden on a contestant to prove otherwise.

3. **Letter to Attorney**

A letter written by a decedent requesting production of a will and articulating the decedent's intentions does not constitute a will because the decedent did not intend the letter to be a will.

4. Effect of Lack of Testamentary Intent

The entire document is invalid if the decedent lacked the requisite testamentary intent.

E. UNDUE INFLUENCE

1. Common Contest Ground

Undue influence is the most frequent contest ground, and often is combined with a claim that the decedent lacked mental capacity.

2. "Unnatural" Dispositions may support a claim of undue influence, but do not necessarily prove undue influence. Some courts require an "injustice" to prove the existence of undue influence.

3. What Influence Is Undue?

Three requisites must be satisfied before influence is undue.

a. There must be a causal connection between the influence and the will, operating at the time of execution.

b. The influence must direct a disposition in favor of someone the influencer wishes to favor (the influencer personally or someone the influencer wants to benefit).

c. The testator must have been unable or unwilling to resist the influence.

4. Proving Undue Influence

The contestant usually has the initial burden of proof. Because the evidence required is difficult to procure, proof of three elements may shift the burden from the contestants to the proponent of the will:

a. The testator's condition made her susceptible to undue influence,

b. The influencer had an opportunity to exercise control over the testator, and

c. The influencer was disposed to exercise control over the testator.

5. Undue Inflence Invalidates only that portion of the will affected.

6. Presumptions of Undue Influence

In two circumstances the burden of proof shifts to the proponent of the will to disprove a presumption that undue influence was exerted over the testator:

a. The drafter of the will benefits personally (or benefits objects of their bounty).

b. A person having a confidential or fiduciary relation with the testator participated in preparation of the will.

7. Bequests to Attorneys

A bequest to a drafting attorney raises the presumption that the attorney exerted undue influence. Nominating the drafting attorney as personal representative or attorney for the personal representative does not raise a presumption of undue influence (although it might raise ethics concerns).

F. FRAUD

1. Definition

Fraud as a will contest ground consists of a trick, device, or deception intended to deceive the testator and to induce execution of a will or codicil (or revocation of a will or codicil) that benefits the perpetrator of the fraud.

2. Two Kinds of Fraud are actionable: **Fraud in the execution** involves deception as to the provisions or character of the document the testator signed. **Fraud in the inducement** involves deceit with respect to the testator's formulation of intent, which affects the testator's beliefs and causes the testator to knowingly execute the document containing provisions informed by the fraud.

3. Effect of Fraud

A **constructive trust** may be imposed or either part or all of the will may fail.

G. NECESSITY FOR EXECUTION FORMALITIES

1. Purposes of Execution Formalities

The trend is to relax the formal will execution requirements.

2. Essential Requirements include that the will be in writing (unless it is holographic), signed (unless nuncupative), and attested.

3. Signed by the Testator

Usually a testator must sign the will in the presence of witnesses, although in some states an acknowledgement of a previously executed signature will suffice. Almost any form of signature or mark will suffice as a signature.

   a. A testator who is unable to sign may receive assistance. Some states require the testator to request assistance; others respect the will if the assistance was not unwanted by the testator. **Signature by proxy** is valid if done in the testator's presence.

   b. A few states require a testator's signature to be at the end of the will.

4. Publication is a declaration by the testator at the time of execution that the document is a will. Only a few states require publication as well as execution.

5. **Attestation and Acknowledgement by Witnesses**

The will must be attested by at least two witnesses who are competent to understand and relate events and, in a few states, who are of a minimum age.

6. **Interested Witnesses**

Most states allow a witness to attest notwithstanding they are a beneficiary under the will and, therefore, their credibility is questionable. Renunciation of an interest after witnessing the execution will not purge the interest, but state law may purge the witness' interest and permit the witness to testify regarding execution.

7. **Order of Signing**

Cases have invalidated wills if one or more witnesses signed the will before the testator, or a long time after the testator, but the bulk of authority regards the order of signing as irrelevant.

8. **Self-Proving Affidavit**

Self-proving affidavits are in the nature of a deposition in which the witnesses affirm all the things to which the witnesses would testify, and may be admitted in lieu of a personal appearance by the witness if a will is uncontested.

H. MISTAKE IN EXECUTION

1. **Intentional Misconduct vs. Innocent Mistake**

Although will contest remedies may apply if wrongdoing occurs in the production or execution of a will, the traditional rule is that there is no remedy for an innocent mistake.

2. **Substantial Compliance**

In re Will of Ranney held that "close is good enough" to allow a court to ignore defective execution of a will if the requisite intent is apparent and no facts indicate a potential abuse or impropriety.

3. **UPC Dispensing Power** allows an instrument to be probated regardless of noncompliance with formalities if the proponent establishes the testator's intent by clear and convincing evidence.

I. WILL CONTEST STANDING exists if a person will be adversely affected by the will (usually taking more under a prior will or by intestacy).

J. TORTIOUS INTERFERENCE WITH AN INHERITANCE

1. **Tort**

A person who intentionally interferes with an expected inheritance may be accountable in tort for influencing the decedent to make, revoke, or modify a will.

2. Not a Will Contest

Tortious interference is not a will contest ground or a ground for denying admission of a will to probate. Unlike a will contest, suit may be brought before the testator's death.

3. Six Elements

The plaintiff must have had an expectancy. The defendant's conduct must have interfered, and was tortious. The defendant must have intended to interfere, the plaintiff would have received the inheritance but for the defendant's conduct, and there were damages.

K. HOLOGRAPHIC WILLS

1. Handwritten by the Testator

A will that is entirely handwritten by the testator may be valid without attestation by witnesses.

2. "Entirely" in the Testator's Handwriting

Two theories are followed by states if the will is not entirely in the testator's handwriting: the **surplusage theory** (anything not essential to the will simply is ignored) and the **intent theory** (anything not intended to be part of the dispositive provisions of the will is ignored).

3. Must Stand Alone

Under any approach, the document must be able to stand on its own if material not in the testator's own hand is ignored; if the will depends on the nonhandwritten material it will fail.

4. Date

Most states require holographic wills to be dated.

5. Signature Requirement

Typically a testator may sign a holograph by mark or with assistance, but not by proxy.

6. Testamentary Intent

Holographs must be made and executed with the requisite testamentary intent. This may be the most difficult requirement to prove.

L. CONDITIONAL WILLS

1. Effect of Condition on Testamentary Intent

If a testator states a condition that did not occur (e.g., "If I do not recover from surgery") the issue is whether the disposition was the testator's unconditional intent. Most courts construe the statement as merely descriptive of the impetus that prompted the testator to make the will, and allow the will to be admitted to probate even if the condition was not satisfied.

2. Extrinsic Evidence

There is no uniform rule regarding admission of extrinsic evidence to show whether a conditional statement was one of inducement or one of true condition.

M. NUNCUPATIVE (ORAL) WILLS

1. Limited Usefulness

Only a few jurisdictions allow testators to make oral wills in limited circumstances, such as when the testator is in the military or suffering her last illness.

2. Oral Instructions to Make a Will are not admissible as a valid will because the requisite testamentary intent is lacking.

N. INTEGRATION

1. Multiple Pages

Wills consisting of multiple pages need not be prepared all at one time. Thus, proof is required to show that all the pages of the will were present at execution, and were intended to be included.

2. Additional, Revised, or Retyped Pages

Pages that are added, revised, or retyped after execution of the will are not valid unless the will is re-executed with all the requisite formalities. If a revised or retyped page is invalid the original page may remain a part of the will under **dependent relative revocation,** the will may be invalidated, or the will may be validated without either the old or new page.

3. Two Versions of a Page at Execution

If two versions of the same page exist at execution, only the one proven to be the decedent's intent is valid.

4. Integration Proof

There is a presumption that the document as found at death is the same as the one that was executed.

5. Multiple Wills

Multiple valid wills are integrated as one dispositive instrument to the extent the provisions are consistent. If any provisions are irreconcilably inconsistent, the last in time governs.

O. INCORPORATION BY REFERENCE

1. Operation

Incorporation by reference allows another document to be treated as if it were part of the will, even though it is not a physical part of the will, nor was it present at the time of the will's execution.

2. Elements

The testator's intent to incorporate the document must be apparent from the face of the will. The incorporated document must be in existence before execution of the incorporating will (except for handwritten lists disposing of tangible personal property in UPC jurisdictions). The incorporating will must refer to the incorporated document as being in existence. And the incorporating will must describe the incorporated document with reasonable certainty.

3. Same Document

The incorporated document must be identifiable as being, and conforming to, the document described in the will.

4. Incorporation by Holograph of Typed Document

Only a few courts allow holographs to incorporate typewritten documents or material not in the testator's handwriting.

P. THE DOCTRINE OF INDEPENDENT LEGAL SIGNIFICANCE allows a testator to describe property or identify beneficiaries by reference to acts, circumstances, or documents that are extraneous to the will and that have a substantial significance apart from their impact on the will.

1. Control by Others

The act, circumstance, or document that has independent legal significance need not be subject to the testator's control.

2. Pour Over to Trust

The doctrine validates a will that pours over to a trust that may be altered at any time, even after execution of the will and even if the trust was not in existence when the will was executed. The pour over works if the trust is in existence when the testator dies.

3. Dispositions of Tangible Personal Property

Traditional wills doctrine does not allow a writing separate from the will to dispose of tangible personal property unless it is executed and attested in compliance with the requisite will formalities or it is a valid holograph or a valid incorporation by reference. UPC §2-513 specifically allows writings that are separate from the will, which list the disposition of tangible personal property, without other formalities.

Q. REPUBLICATION BY CODICIL

1. Codicils

A codicil is executed with the requisite will formalities to add, delete, modify, or otherwise change provisions in the will referred to in the codicil.

2. Validation of Invalid Will

A codicil may validate an otherwise invalid will, or revive a once valid will that subsequently was revoked, if that will remains physically in existence.

3. Effect of Republication

Republication restores the underlying will, all prior valid codicils not inconsistent with the reviving codicil, and all invalid or inconsistent codicils that are specifically identified by the reviving codicil.

4. Timing Issues

A codicil is generally treated as republishing a will on the date of execution of the codicil. Typically, changes of circumstance between execution of the underlying republished will and the republishing codicil become part of the parol evidence.

4 REVOCATION

A. THREE WAYS TO REVOKE A WILL

The Statute of Frauds permits partial or complete revocation of a will by **physical act,** by **subsequent instrument,** or by **operation of law.**

B. REVOCATION BY PHYSICAL ACT

1. Multiple Documents

There is a presumption that revocation of a will is a revocation of all codicils to that will, although revocation of a codicil is not a revocation of the underlying will or of other codicils to the underlying will unless that intent is specified.

2. Partial Revocation by Physical Act

Partial revocation of a will by physical act is permitted only in some jurisdictions.

a. There is a presumption that none of the will was revoked if the testator performs a revocatory act on only part of a will in a jurisdiction that does not recognize partial revocations by physical act.

b. If the testator performs a revocatory act on only part of a will in a jurisdiction that *does* recognize partial revocation by physical act, the issue is what to do with the property that was subject to the revoked provision.

3. Proxy Revocation by Physical Act

Most states permit proxy revocation by physical act, if the physical act occurred in the testator's presence, at her direction, and (in some states) in the presence of witnesses.

4. Form of Revocation by Physical Act

Revocation by physical act is a **mutilation** of the paper on which the will is written or an **obliteration** or **cancellation** of the words on the paper. A mutilating act need not touch the words on the paper, but it must be on the will itself—it cannot be on the blueback of the will, on the self-proving affidavit, or on a cover of the will. Some states require an obliteration or cancellation to touch the words to be obliterated or cancelled.

5. Stapled Wills

The mere act of removing a staple (or otherwise unfastening) a will may be an act of physical revocation.

6. Act and Intent Required

A physical revocatory act is ineffective if done by mistake, to the wrong document, or if the testator changed her mind before the full act intended was completed. In addition, the physical act is ineffective if the testator lacks the capacity to form the intent to revoke the will.

7. **Extrinsic Evidence** may be admitted to prove that a physical act was not done by the testator, that the testator did not possess the requisite intent to revoke the will, or that the testator had no reason to revoke the will.

8. Presumption of Revocation by Physical Act

There is a presumption that the testator destroyed the will with the intent to revoke it if the will cannot be found, the testator was the last person to possess the will, and there was a diligent search (by someone with no incentive *not* to find it) to find the will.

9. Duplicate Original Wills

Destruction of one duplicate executed original with the intent to revoke the will usually revokes all copies.

C. REVOCATION BY SUBSEQUENT INSTRUMENT

1. Form of Subsequent Instrument

The testator may revoke a will, in whole or in part, by a subsequent instrument, which may be a will, codicil, or any other instrument executed with the requisite formalities of a will.

2. Revocation by Inconsistent Subsequent Instrument may be by express provision or by inconsistency. If the subsequent instrument is a codicil, there is a presumption that the testator did not intend to revoke the underling will in its entirety, but if the subsequent instrument is a will the presumption is that it revokes prior wills in their entirety.

D. REVOCATION BY OPERATION OF LAW

1. Usually Limited to Divorce

In most states, only divorce operates to revoke a will by operation of law, although in a few states marriage revokes an earlier will as well. In at least one state the birth or adoption of a child also may revoke a prior will.

2. Revocation by Divorce

Some statutes treat a former spouse as predeceased or as having disclaimed any bequest under the will, others deem all provisions in favor of the former spouse as revoked, and some treat the entire will as revoked.

3. Need for Statute

Revocation by divorce requires a statute to that effect, because the common law did not recognize divorce.

4. Common Problems with Divorce Statutes

Many states do not address the issue whether remarriage to a former spouse revives or revalidates the will, or whether a provision favoring a former spouse's relatives also is revoked.

E. REVIVAL

1. Physical Revocation

Revocation of a subsequent will cannot revive a prior will that was revoked by physical act.

2. Revival in America

Whether a will is revived is based on the testator's intent. Some courts distinguish between revocation by inconsistency and by express provision, holding that the former permits revival if the second will subsequently is revoked but do not permit revival if the revocation was express, even if the second will subsequently is revoked.

F.   DEPENDENT RELATIVE REVOCATION

1.   Contrasted with Revival

Dependent relative revocation ignores the revocation of a will and treats the will as never revoked. The prior revoked will need not be physically in existence if dependent relative revocation applies, whereas revival requires the prior will to be physically in existence.

2.   Dependent Relative Revocation Cures Mistakes

Dependent relative revocation may provide relief for a mistake, in that it allows a previously valid will to be effective if the subsequent will is invalid due to mistake.

 ## 5   WILL CONTRACTS

A.   INTRODUCTION

1.   Terminology

A **joint will** is one document that is executed by more than one testator. It is the separate will of each. A **mutual will** is the separate will of one person that contains mirror image or reciprocal provisions to those in another person's will. A **joint and mutual will** is one document, signed by more than one testator, with reciprocal provisions and a single residuary provision, which operates on the death of the last to die.

2.   **Some States Presume** that a joint will is contractual and cannot be revoked unilaterally. UPC §2-514 is the antithesis of such a presumption for either a joint or a mutual will.

B.   PROVING A WILL CONTRACT

1.   Reciprocal or Mirror Image Provisions Are Not Enough

Similarity of dispositive provisions is not sufficient to substitute for positive proof of a contract not to revoke mutual wills.

2.   Written Proof

State law may require that the contract be proven if the will states the existence of a contract, if there is express reference in the will to a contract, or if there is a written contract signed by the decedent.

C. REMEDIES FOR BREACH OF A WILL CONTRACT

1. Revoking or Altering the Will

Anyone may alter or revoke her own will, regardless of a valid will contract. The issue is what remedies are available for breach of that contract.

2. Failure to Make a Promised Will, or if the promised will was executed and later revoked, does not permit probate of the contract or the will as anticipated. There is no specific performance for breach.

3. Action for Breach of Contract

The only available remedies for breach of a contract to execute or not to revoke a will are those available under contract law for damages, restitution, or the like.

4. Anticipatory Breach

Remedies available for *anticipatory* breach if a testator intends to breach the contract may include recovery of any consideration given, an injunction against conveyance of certain property in violation of that contract, or imposition of a constructive trust.

5. Breach at the Promisor's Death

The remedies for breach of a will contract are limited to damages, restitution, imposition of a constructive trust, or quantum meruit.

 6   WILL SUBSTITUTES

A. NONPROBATE TRANSFERS IN GENERAL

1. Nonprobate Property does not pass under a will or by intestacy. Rather, it passes in accordance with the particular will substitute.

2. A Blockbuster Will, if recognized, would dispose of all property—probate and nonprobate alike. Under current law will provisions generally are not effective to alter beneficiary designations in will substitutes unless the decedent's will complies with the terms for change in the will substitute.

3. Will Substitutes May Be Challenged to the extent they look like testamentary dispositions that lack the formalities required of a will.

B. LIFE INSURANCE, ANNUITIES, AND INTERESTS IN DEFERRED COMPENSATION PLANS

1. Testamentary Characteristics of Life Insurance

The owner of an insurance policy designates a beneficiary to receive the policy proceeds at the insured's death. This beneficiary designation is by a form provided by the insurer, not by the insured's will. The arrangement is both ambulatory and revocable, but no fiduciary or other duties are created.

2. Insurance Proceeds Not Controlled by Insured's Will

Policy proceeds may be payable to the owner of the policy (or the policy owner's estate) and, as such, pass under the owner's will or by intestacy, but only in the absence of a valid beneficiary designation.

   a. The designated beneficiary may be the insured or owner's estate, in which case the proceeds are paid to the estate and then pass with the rest of the insured or owner's probate estate.

   b. To mirror the law that revokes a will or provisions of a will in favor of a former spouse, some state statutes revoke insurance beneficiary designations that name a former spouse following a divorce.

3. Annuities

In pure form a straight life annuity pays the annuitant a fixed amount per month/quarter/year for life, with no further rights at death. It is common to find annuities with refund or survivorship features that benefit others after the annuitant's death and resemble insurance as nonprobate transfers not subject to the Wills Act.

4. Deferred Compensation Death Benefits similarly are payable to designated beneficiaries, typically in annuity format, after an employee's death and also are valid will substitutes.

C. PAYABLE ON DEATH CONTRACTS

1. What They Are is contractual agreements under which benefits are payable when the account owner dies to a beneficiary named in the contract.

2. POD Bank Accounts are the most common form of POD arrangement owned by one person but payable on her death to another. A majority of states authorize these accounts.

3. Testamentary Challenge

The more common payable on death arrangements routinely are viewed as not testamentary. Less common payable on death contracts have been held to be unenforceable because of their testamentary characteristics and failure to conform with Wills Act formalities.

D. JOINT TENANCY

1. Ownership of Property During Concurrent Owners' Lives

Joint tenants are treated as if each owns the whole property, subject to the coterminous equal rights of the other joint tenants. *Joint tenancy bank accounts,* however, are different because a concurrent owner does not own the deposit of another cotenant until a withdrawal is made. In addition, joint tenancy *safe deposit boxes* do not make the *contents* of the box joint tenancy property—they only permit either tenant to access the box.

2. Effect of Divorce

Traditionally a former spouse becomes the sole owner of property held as joint tenants with the right of survivorship if the other joint tenant dies without changing ownership of property held in joint tenancy with that former spouse. Some state statutes sever joint tenancies with former spouses when they divorce and convert the ownership to a 50/50 tenancy in common.

3. Validity of Survivorship Feature in joint tenancy is not subject to challenge as testamentary.

4. Convenience Joint Tenancies

A joint tenancy created solely for convenience (for example, so one tenant can deal with the property of the other, such as to write checks on a bank account) can be defeated as not constituting a conveyance at all. The creation of a joint tenancy generally gives rise to a *rebuttable* presumption that a "true" joint tenancy is intended.

E. DEEDS

1. Invalid as Testamentary?

Labeling a testamentary instrument as a deed, and using language usually found in deeds, will not ensure the effectiveness of the conveyance if nothing is conveyed until death.

2. Delivery

The instrument is deemed ineffective or invalid as testamentary if the instrument conveying the property is unconditional on its face but the property is not delivered until after the transferor's death.

F. REVOCABLE TRUSTS

1. Introduction

Revocable trusts are arrangements by which one or more trustees hold legal title to property for the benefit of one or more beneficiaries. The settlor may revoke the arrangement prior to death or until the power of revocation is relinquished. Revocable trusts are not testamentary or invalid merely because they are revocable.

2. Validity of Trusts

An inter vivos revocable trust must own some trust assets before it will be regarded as a valid will substitute.

a. No physical delivery or transfer typically is required to a self-trusteed declaration of trust, although a documentary transfer usually is required and may be satisfied by a change of title on a document of title, or by a bill of sale if there is no document of title.

b. Assets that do not yet exist may become trust assets upon springing into existence if the promise to entrust them is enforceable, although the trust must be valid (that is, it must own some other assets) prior to these assets springing into existence.

3. Revocable Trusts Are Not Testamentary

Lifetime retention by the settlor of enjoyment and control is normal and permissible. Revocable trusts generally are not regarded as testamentary if immediate fiduciary duties attach to the trustee and an equitable interest passes to a third party.

4. Revocation of a Revocable Trust

Because inter vivos trusts are regarded as valid will substitutes, Wills Act principles generally are not applicable to trusts. Thus, an effective revocation of a trust must comply only with those means specified in the trust instrument.

5. Creditors' Rights

A settlor's creditors typically have a right to reach the trust assets during the settlor's life. A settlor's creditors usually cannot reach trust assets post-mortem, in the absence of the settlor's fraud in establishing the trust or transferring assets to it.

6. Totten Trusts are bank accounts opened in the name of the settlor "as trustee" for herself for life, remainder to another. They are created by signing the appropriate signature card when opening a bank account, usually with no other formalities. Totten trusts are valid will substitutes.

G. EQUITABLE ELECTION

1. Election

If a will bestows interests on a beneficiary and also attempts to dispose of property owned by that beneficiary, the will constitutes an offer or option:

the rightful owner of the property must elect to allow the testator's will to govern and, in return, receive the testamentary bequest, or must deny the effect of the will on the asset and also forgo the testamentary bequest.

2. Effect of Election

A beneficiary's election to receive property under a will serves to relinquish any interest in the nonprobate property. If the beneficiary elects to retain rights in the nonprobate property, the disappointed beneficiary of that property under the will may be compensated with the rightful owner's designated interest under the will.

H. INSURANCE TRUSTS

1. Testamentary Trust

The proceeds from an insurance policy may be payable to the decedent's estate, and then distributed to beneficiaries under the terms of the decedent's will, such as a testamentary trust. A better alternative is to pay the proceeds directly to the trustee of a testamentary trust.

2. Other Trusts may receive insurance proceeds, including funded or unfunded revocable or irrevocable insurance trusts.

3. Attack by a Surviving Spouse

Under the 1990 version of the UPC a surviving spouse may elect to receive a portion of the decedent's augmented estate, which includes both the probate estate and nonprobate assets, particularly including insurance on the decedent's life.

I. POUR OVER WILLS

1. What They Are is an opportunity to leave part or all of a decedent's probate estate to a freestanding trust, rather than using a testamentary trust.

2. Independent Legal Significance

Pour over wills are valid under the doctrine of independent legal significance. Amendments to a trust instrument after execution of the pour over will are valid and the pour over is to the trust as amended. The recipient trust need not exist when the will is executed: it is sufficient if the trust exists and is able to receive assets when the pour over occurs at the testator's death.

3. Effect of the Pour Over

The recipient trust is not made testamentary by virtue of the pour over, nor is it subject to probate court control or local law restrictions on who may be trustee of a testamentary trust. Likewise, the recipient trust is not incorporated by reference into the will.

7 | INTERPRETATION: WHAT THE DECEDENT INTENDED

A. INTRODUCTION

1. **Compared with "Construction"**

    Interpretation refers to what the testator or settlor said. Construction refers to what the testator or settlor *meant* to say.

2. **Plain Meaning**

    Interpretation seeks to uncover the "plain meaning" of a word, phrase, or entire provision from within the "four corners" of the document. Extrinsic evidence typically is not admissible to prove that intent when the issue is interpretation, as opposed to construction.

3. **Testator or Settlor's Intent** is the guiding principle in the interpretation of wills and trusts, looking at the pattern of the entire document, comparing uses of the same or related terms elsewhere in the document, considering special usage, and evaluating the facts and circumstances known at execution.

4. **Gaps or Omissions**

    If there clearly is a gap or omission in a document, interpretation should not allow the court to insert what it *thinks* the testator or settlor would have wanted. But **implied gifts** that fill gaps or omissions appropriately are "interpretation" to the extent it is clear that the testator or settlor intended the provision implied by the court.

B. ABSENCE OF AMBIGUITY: MISTAKE

1. **The General Rule** applied to ambiguity is that a court may not use extrinsic evidence to alter, limit, or extend unambiguous provisions in a will, and that there is no remedy for mistake.

2. **Mistakes** come in a variety of forms: **mistakes of law, in the inducement, of omission,** and **of fact.**

3. **Extrinsic Evidence of Lack of Intent** to execute a will may be admissible by some courts as a reasonably limited deviation from traditional principles.

C. AMBIGUITIES AND INACCURACIES

1. **Patent and Latent Ambiguities: Patent ambiguities** involve errors that are apparent on the face of the document. Historically no extrinsic evidence was admitted to alter or clarify the meaning of the written provisions.

Latent ambiguities involve errors that become apparent only when the document is applied to the facts, and typically extrinsic evidence is admitted.

2. **Latent Ambiguities Take Three Forms: Equivocations** are accurate descriptions of more than one item or person, **misdescriptions** are inaccurate descriptions that arguably apply to more than one item or person, and **inaccuracies** are inaccurate descriptions that arguably apply to only one item or person.

3. **Resolving Ambiguity** often requires a court to either ignore or excise language that causes an ambiguity, if doing so resolves the issue in a manner consistent with what the court determines to be the testator or settlor's intent. Often all relevant extrinsic evidence is admitted to resolve equivocations, but not so often with respect to misdescriptions and inaccuracies.

4. **The Fictional Eraser** approach is used by some courts to resolve inaccuracies and sometimes may be used to create and then resolve misdescriptions.

5. **Reformation and Extrinsic Evidence in Will Substitutes**

   In many jurisdictions extrinsic evidence is admissible to prove a mistake in an unambiguous will substitute. The remedy often used is reformation to preserve the decedent's intent and prevent unjust enrichment of an unintended beneficiary.

6. **Mistake in the Inducement**

   Generally extrinsic evidence is inadmissible if there is a **mistake in the inducement** but no ambiguity.

D. **IMPLIED GIFTS**

1. **To Effect Intent** of the testator or settlor, implied gifts may be used by a court if the document is incomplete or ineffective (e.g., an incomplete disposition or a time gap) if the intent is clear, or to avoid unintended results or multiple generations of income beneficiaries at one time.

2. **Unanticipated Contingencies**

   Sometimes a court will provide for **unanticipated contingencies** that did occur in the same way that the testator or settlor provided for an anticipated contingency that did *not* occur.

8   CONSTRUCTION: LAPSE AND CLASS GIFTS

A. **LAPSE** refers to a gift that fails because the named beneficiary predeceased the testator or a later distribution.

1. **Implied Condition of Survivorship**

    The common law implies a condition of survivorship for wills: regardless of whether such a condition is stated in the document, the beneficiary must survive the testator to be entitled to take.

2. **Common Law Lapse Rule**

    According to the common law, a lapsed gift fails. If the lapsed disposition is preresiduary the traditional rule is that the property falls into the residue. If the lapsed disposition is part of the residue, the property passes by intestacy.

3. **Antilapse Statutes** in most states prevent failure of lapsed gifts. Many of these statutes apply to both lapsed and to **void gifts** (the named beneficiary predeceased execution of the will). These statutes apply to the extent the testator's will does not specify what happens to a lapsed gift.

    a. Antilapse statutes typically do not apply to transfers made by will substitutes, although they may apply to *testamentary* trusts.

    b. Most antilapse statutes apply only to gifts to certain beneficiaries, typically to certain relatives of the testator. Most antilapse statutes do not apply to gifts to spouses.

4. **Substituted Gifts Other Than Under Antilapse Statutes**

    A well drafted document will provide an alternative taker for a gift that the intended devisee cannot or should not receive because predeceased.

5. **Survivorship**

    Under common law there is no lapse if the devisee survives the testator, which is to say there is no required survivorship for future interests. Because it is not always easy to determine survivorship, a provision in a governing instrument or statute such as the Uniform Simultaneous Death Act may provide a presumption in certain circumstances.

6. **Lapse and Class Gifts**

    At common law, if a class member predeceased distribution, the remaining members of the class took the entire gift. If all class members were deceased, the gift property fell into the residue or passed by intestacy. Most antilapse statutes apply to class gifts, effectuating a transfer of the deceased beneficiary's share to her representatives.

    a. The order of priority applicable to class gifts is any survivorship condition is applied first, then any alternative gift is honored, then any antilapse statute is applied, followed by crossing the deceased member's "share" over to surviving class members if no antilapse statute applies, and finally lapse of the gift.

b. A class gift exists if it is to a group of takers defined by one or more common characteristics and the donor was "group minded." The size of the class and therefore the size of each member's share typically is subject to change until distribution of the gift.

B. MORE ON CLASS GIFTS

1. Composition of the Class

A class is "open" if it can get larger. No one born or adopted or otherwise made to qualify for class membership may become a member of the class after the class "closes." Afterborns in gestation are deemed to be alive when conceived.

2. Survivorship

An interest passes to a deceased class member's estate if being alive was not required and the class member dies before distribution of the gift. If survivorship *is* required, however, the interest of a class member who fails to survive the specified event fails entirely (unless the document provides for a substitutionary gift).

3. General Principles

The three basic presumptions with respect to the intent of the donor to make a class gift are that the donor wants: to benefit as many members as possible, to avoid failure or lapse, and to make distribution as early as possible. These three preferences may conflict.

4. The Rule of Convenience
modifies these three presumptions. Required is that a class receiving a per capita gift must close when the fund must be established. Otherwise the class closes when the first mandatory distribution of principal to a class member is required.

5. Exceptions
to the rule of convenience provide that afterborns in gestation when a class closes are deemed alive when conceived if they subsequently are born alive, and the class remains open if, when distribution is required, there are no class members and the gift is not a per capita gift, in which case the class will remain open and distribution will be delayed until no class members could be born or adopted.

6. Class Gifts of Income
are treated as if each income distribution was a separate gift: the class closing rules apply at each independent income distribution date.

CONSTRUCTION: ADEMPTION, ABATEMENT, ACCESSIONS, AND EXONERATION

Classification of gifts is critical to application of the following rules. Dispositions come in **specific, demonstrative, general,** or **residuary** format.

A. ADEMPTION BY EXTINCTION

1. Applicable Only to Specifics

Ademption by Extinction applies if the subject of a specific gift of real or personal property does not exist at death.

2. Theory of the Doctrine

If the subject of a specific gift is not owned by the testator at death, it must fail. Extinction of the property need not have been voluntary, although the testator should have had the ability to alter the will after extinction of the item. A minority of states allow the devisee of an extinguished specific devise to receive other property, unless there is actual proof of an intent to adeem.

3. **Partial Ademption** usually is applicable if only a portion of the subject matter of a specific gift is extinct.

B. ADEMPTION BY SATISFACTION

1. Distinguished from Advancement

The concept of advancements only applies in *completely* intestate estates. **Ademption by satisfaction** applies to testate estates (including partially testate estates) if the testator makes an inter vivos gift after execution of a will that amounts to acceleration of the beneficiary's devise.

2. **Generally Inapplicable to Specific Gifts** unless it is shown that a gift of one asset is meant to satisfy a specific bequest of another asset.

3. **Satisfaction of Residuary Gifts** is not likely to occur if there is only one residuary beneficiary because that would result in a partial intestacy, which generally is disfavored. However, ademption by satisfaction may apply if there is more than one residuary taker and less than all have received inter vivos transfers that should count against them.

4. **Satisfaction of Demonstrative Gifts** requires that, to be fully adeemed, the bequest must be adeemed both by satisfaction and by extinction.

5. **Generally Inapplicable to Gifts of Land** because these gifts generally are specific and the inter vivos gift would cause ademption by extinction.

6. **Proving Satisfaction**

At common law no proof was required to establish an intent to satisfy. UPC §2-609 reverses this rule, requiring a statement in the will or a contemporaneous written declaration by the testator or acknowledgement by the devisee when satisfaction occurs. Some non-UPC states also require proof and allow admission of extrinsic evidence to prove intent to adeem by satisfaction.

C. **ABATEMENT** applies to the extent an estate has more obligations than assets available to satisfy them.

1. **An Issue of Priority**

The standard priority of abatement is: intestate assets, any fund specified for payment, the residue, general gifts, demonstrative gifts, and specific gifts. However, the standard order may be modified by statute, by a specific provision in the will, or by a showing of the testator's overall intent as shown by the distribution scheme. Abatement usually is pro rata within each class.

2. **Payment of Taxes,** federal and state, estate and inheritance, may have a significant effect on the distribution of assets among beneficiaries.

a. Beneficiaries often are responsible for the payment of state inheritance taxes, although this obligation customarily is shifted to the probate estate by most decedents' wills.

b. Federal estate taxes often are paid out of the residue of the probate estate, with the personal representative being personally liable for any unpaid taxes. This obligation also may be altered by the terms of the will and by several exceptions, such as **apportionment** of the tax burden under state and federal law.

3. **Spousal Election and Pretermitted Heir Shares** also may be so large as to require abatement, although many states require a spouse's elective share to be taken in lieu of other provisions made for the spouse under the will and that alteration of entitlements frees up property for the residuary takers.

D. **ACCESSIONS**

1. **Premortem** accessions attributable to assets not specifically devised become a part of the general estate. Premortem accessions attributable to assets specifically devised also do not pass to the recipient of the underlying asset, unless the accession is not paid before death or is not separated from the underlying asset.

2. **Postmortem** accessions attributable to assets specifically devised pass with the underlying asset. Postmortem accessions attributable to assets generally or demonstrably devised do not pass with the underlying asset; instead,

the beneficiary of such a gift usually receives a statutory rate of interest from the time of entitlement, often one year after death. Postmortem accessions that become part of the residue and are not otherwise distributed pass with the residuary estate.

E. **EXONERATION** requires that, unless altered by statute or the governing document, debts are accelerated and must be paid from the estate at death.

1. **Three Requirements** must be met: the decedent must have been personally liable for the debt, the debt must encumber realty or specifically devised personal property, and a contrary intent must not be expressed in the will.

2. **Source of Funds** to pay exonerated debts is from the residue or from intestate personalty, if there is any.

3. **Intent**

The common law rule to exonerate (and the contrary UPC rule not to exonerate) may be overcome by proof of a contrary intent.

 RESTRICTIONS ON THE POWER OF DISPOSITION: STATUTORY FORCED HEIRS AND COMMUNITY PROPERTY

A. **SPOUSAL RIGHTS: INTRODUCTION**

1. **Exempt Property**

Most states provide a surviving spouse with a **homestead** right and certain tangible personal property of the decedent. Property passing in this manner is exempt from the claims of the decedent's creditors and may not be defeated by the decedent's will.

2. **Family Allowance**

A **family allowance** also may be provided to a surviving spouse or dependents to provide support during estate administration.

3. **Dower and Curtesy**

At common law, widows were entitled to **dower** and widowers were entitled to **curtesy.** Most states have abolished both.

4. **Protecting the Surviving Spouse**

There remain two significant forms of protection for a surviving spouse: community property or a surviving spouse's right to elect a statutory portion of the decedent's probate estate.

B.   COMMUNITY PROPERTY

1.   **Each Spouse Owns Half** of the couple's community property (generally, property acquired by onerous activity by either spouse in a community property jurisdiction during marriage—which is everything acquired other than by gift, devise, bequest, or inheritance), with ownership being 50/50 from the moment the property is acquired.

2.   **Rights of the Surviving Spouse**

     Typically a surviving spouse has no right to a statutory share of a decedent's separate property in a community property jurisdiction. However, some states recognize quasi-community property: separate property brought into the state may be treated as community property if it would have been community property had it been acquired while living in the community property jurisdiction.

3.   **Forced Election Estate Plans** permit a decedent to control the final disposition of all the couple's community property after the death of the surviving spouse. These are not a function of state law and can be employed in noncommunity property states if the surviving spouse owns property with which to engage in the decedent's proposal.

C.   NONCOMMUNITY PROPERTY: ELECTIVE SHARES

1.   **Statutory Forced Heir Shares** are available in all noncommunity property jurisdictions except Georgia.

2.   **ERISA Rights**

     The federal Employee Retirement Income Security Act entitles a surviving spouse in both community and noncommunity property jurisdictions to a survivor annuity following the death of a plan participant.

3.   **Size of Spouse's Forced Heir Share** varies among the states, and may be limited to a portion of the decedent's *probate* estate in non-UPC jurisdictions.

4.   **Effect of Election on Spouse's Rights to Other Property**

     A surviving spouse who elects to take a forced heir share rejects the decedent's estate plan. The choice is between a prescribed share of the probate or augmented probate estate and whatever the decedent's will provides. Typically **equitable election** applies, although homestead, exempt personal property, and family allowances are not lost when the spouse makes a forced heir share election. In addition, the election usually means a forfeit of any share in intestate property, but nonprobate property entitlements generally are not affected.

5.   **Incompetent or Deceased Surviving Spouses** usually may be represented by a personal representative, who may make the election on behalf of

the spouse. Some states restrict the circumstances in which a personal representative of a spouse who survived the decedent but then died before the election period expired may make an election, and some require a showing of need to elect on behalf of an incompetent surviving spouse.

6. Effect of the Election on Other Beneficiaries

Other beneficiaries' entitlements must abate when a surviving spouse elects against the will. Property destined for the spouse under the will is allocated in some cases to those beneficiaries who suffer abatement, as a form of compensation.

7. Effect of Nonprobate Transfers

Jurisdictions differ as to whether nonprobate assets are considered in awarding the surviving spouse's elective share.

8. The UPC Augmented Probate Estate regards inter vivos transfers made to third parties in excess of the gift tax annual exclusion amount and made within two years of death, and virtually all will substitute transfers to third parties as part of the **augmented probate estate** used to compute the spousal entitlement. It also regards nonprobate transfers *to* the spouse and the spouse's own marital property as part of the spousal entitlement already received by the spouse.

9. Modifications Pursuant to Prenuptial and Postnuptial Agreement

In most jurisdictions the validity of marital property agreements is measured by looking to the sufficiency of consideration, as well as other badges of fraud, duress, and overreaching.

D. PRETERMITTED HEIRS

1. Pretermitted Spouses

Some statutes provide that a surviving spouse may be entitled to an intestate share if the spouse was not provided for in the decedent's will, the will was executed before the marriage, and the omission of the spouse was unintentional. The UPC does not provide a share if the estate was left to descendants born prior to the marriage, not in common with the surviving spouse. In either case the elective share remains available (but it may be smaller).

2. Pretermitted Descendants (usually limited to children, but in some cases more remote descendants) in most states are entitled to a share if born or adopted after execution of the will (or, in far fewer jurisdictions, whenever born or adopted) if they are not mentioned or provided for in the will. Proof of an intent to omit a descendant will preclude any entitlement, although the burden of proving intent and evidentiary presumptions vary by state.

3. Negative Wills

In most states an heir may not be disinherited as to testate property unless the decedent effectively disposed of the entire estate to others. Only a few states recognize a **negative will** in which the decedent may alter intestate distribution simply to explicitly exclude an heir.

4. Beware Effect of Codicils

Execution of a codicil can bar pretermitted heir status if a marriage, birth, or adoption occurs after execution of the will but before execution of the codicil.

 ## 11 INTRODUCTION TO TRUSTS

A. CREATION

Trusts are created by a settlor, who transfers trust corpus to a trustee for the benefit of beneficiaries. There can be one or more settlors, trustees, and beneficiaries, and each role may be played by different people or by the same person—the settlor can be trustee and one of the beneficiaries.

B. UNIQUE

The three respects in which trusts differ from other legal entities are: bifurcation of title, the required fiduciary duty of undivided loyalty to all the beneficiaries, and enforceability of the trust is exclusive to the beneficiaries.

C. VARIETIES

Among the types of trust are business, public, charitable, implied, and private express trusts. The most common are **private express trusts,** which may include **inter vivos (or living) trusts, testamentary trusts, divorce trusts, damage settlement funds,** and **employee benefit trusts.**

D. IMPLIED TRUSTS are of two varieties:

1. Resulting Trusts

are created for the benefit of the settlor when an express trust fails, in whole or in part, or when the purchase price for property is paid by one person and legal title to the property is transferred to another.

2. Constructive Trusts

are created by equity to avoid unjust enrichment and may arise in many situations, such as when a transfer is induced by fraud, undue influence, mistake, or duress, when there is a breach of a confidential relation, or when retention of property would be unjust.

E. TRUST PURPOSES

1. Invalid Purposes

Trusts may be created for any legal purpose to do anything the settlor could do outright. Invalid purposes usually involve an attempt to do what the settlor could not do outright, such as violate the Rule Against Perpetuities, encourage or reward unlawful conduct, disfranchise a surviving spouse, create unreasonable restraints on marriage, or accomplish any other prohibited result.

2. Violate Public Policy

Trusts may be invalidated to the extent they offend public policy, and may not unreasonably interfere with familial relations or encourage or require waste or destruction of trust corpus.

3. Consequence of Invalidity

An invalid trust provision or purpose may be ignored or deemed satisfied, or the trust may be regarded as invalid and deemed a resulting trust in favor of the settlor.

 12   TRUST CREATION

A. INTRODUCTION

1. **Required for Trust Validity** generally are a legal purpose, an intent to impose active duties on a trustee, a corpus (and a settlor with the requisite capacity to convey that property), one or more beneficiaries, and a written instrument if the trust will own land.

2. **Not Required for Trust Validity** is a trustee (although a trustee is needed, one will be appointed in all but the most unusual cases), consideration, or notice to the trustee or acceptance by the beneficiaries.

B. INTENT AND CAPACITY

1. Form of Expression of Intent

The intent to create a testamentary trust must appear in a valid will. Inter vivos trusts require intent expressed in a written instrument if the trust holds land and in writing, orally, or by conduct for trusts that hold any other property.

2. Capacity

Testamentary trusts require that the settlor have the capacity required to execute a valid will. Inter vivos trusts require that the settlor have the higher capacity to make a valid gift free of trust.

3. Questions of Intent rarely arise unless the trust is poorly drafted or is an oral or secret trust.

C. THE TRUSTEE

1. Capacity to Serve

A trustee must have the capacity to administer assets and hold legal title. Special rules may prevent the appointment or cause the removal of minor or mentally incompetent trustees and some corporate trustees.

2. Requirement of a Trustee

Although a trust must have a trustee, a court can appoint a trustee unless it is clear that only one trustee was contemplated or appropriate and that one is not willing and able to act.

3. Cotrustees

Multiple trustees must act unanimously to bind the trust unless otherwise provided in the instrument and permitted by the jurisdiction.

4. To Serve or Not to Serve

No one can be forced to serve as a trustee, although the named trustee may be deemed to have accepted the position if it is not timely declined. Resignation thereafter can be effected only if the instrument or state law permits it, or by court order, and only upon a complete transfer of trust property to a successor trustee.

5. Removal of Trustees

A trustee may be removed for cause, such as upon incompetence or any breach of trust, or for no cause at all if the trust document grants someone the authority to remove and replace trustees.

6. Liability of Trustees

Unless the trust instrument provides otherwise, cotrustees have joint and several liability and successor trustees are liable for the failures or improper acts of their predecessors (and, thus, must sue their predecessors to redress wrongs or suffer liability for them instead).

7. **Sole Beneficiary as Sole Trustee**

The doctrine of merger applies if the sole trust beneficiary is the sole trustee, causing the legal and beneficial titles to combine and the trust to fail. This would not occur if multiple trustees are the only beneficiaries because joint trustees take title as joint tenants but multiple beneficiaries are like tenants in common.

D. TRUST PROPERTY

1. **From Active to Passive to Dry**

A trust that has completed its purpose becomes a passive trust. The trust assets are then distributed and the trust ceases to exist by virtue of becoming a dry trust.

2. **An Ascertainable Corpus** is required, although the value, duration, and the extent of the property need not be ascertainable.

3. **Nature of the Corpus**

An interest held as trust property may be present or future, vested or contingent, legal or equitable ownership, in real or personal property. The settlor's expectation of owning property in the future generally cannot constitute the corpus of the trust unless it constitutes an enforceable promise that constitutes a contract right to future property.

4. **Unfunded Life Insurance Trusts**

Most courts validate unfunded life insurance trusts because the policy beneficiary designation is sufficient to create a present interest, constituting the trust corpus.

5. **Trustee's Debt Obligation as Trust Corpus**

A trustee cannot hold its own debt obligation as trust corpus because, as both debtor and creditor, the debt would be extinguished under the doctrine of merger. Special authority is granted to corporate trustees by the Comptroller of the Currency to hold their own debts.

E. NECESSITY OF A TRUST BENEFICIARY

1. **Anyone May Be a Trust Beneficiary** if they have the capacity under law to hold equitable title, although a trust cannot be valid unless the beneficiaries are ascertainable and legally able to enforce the trust.

2. **Honorary Trusts** do not require an ascertainable beneficiary—but only to the extent the trustee voluntarily complies with the trust.

3. **If Ascertainable Beneficiaries Are Not Named** the trust fails and a resulting trust is established for the settlor. There may be an exception to the failure of a trust if the sole beneficiaries are unborn and their birth still is possible

or if the trustee refuses to select beneficiaries from a definite and reasonably small class of potential beneficiaries and a court may make the selection based on ascertainable criteria.

F. ABSENCE OF NOTICE OR ACCEPTANCE

1. **Beneficiary**

   A beneficiary of a trust need not be notified of the trust creation, unless the settlor is the trustee. However, a third party trustee may be in breach of fiduciary duty if the beneficiary is not notified of the trust existence.

2. **Disclaimer** of a beneficial interest will cause acceleration of the trust provisions or trigger applicable state law dispositions. A resulting trust may be required to distribute the trust corpus back to the settlor if the only remaining beneficiary disclaims.

G. ORAL TRUSTS

1. **Testamentary Trusts** cannot be created orally; required is a validly executed will.

2. **Inter Vivos Trusts** of personalty may be validly created orally, although the Statute of Frauds requires a writing to create an inter vivos trust of realty.

3. **The Writing Requirement** mandates that the trust identify the trust corpus, purposes, and beneficiaries. Extrinsic evidence is admissible absent fraud, duress, undue influence, mistake, or the like, but only to the extent it does not contradict express terms of the written trust.

4. **Validity**

   There are several situations in which an oral trust of realty may be valid, such as if the trustee complies even without a writing, waives the writing requirement while still holding legal title or agrees to convert the realty into other trust investments, or when a beneficiary acts in detrimental reliance on the trust.

5. **Remedy**

   Either a constructive trust or a resulting trust will be created if a trustee refuses to comply with an oral trust of realty.

H. SECRET AND SEMI-SECRET TRUSTS

1. **Secret vs. Semi-Secret Trusts**

   A secret trust is created when a gift that appears on its face to be outright to one person is made subject to a separate agreement that the property will be held for the benefit of another. A semi-secret trust is created when it is clear that a gift is made in trust, but the beneficiaries or other terms are secret.

2. **Extrinsic Evidence** may be admitted to prove the intent to create a secret trust and then to prove the terms and beneficiaries of that trust. In a semi-secret trust extrinsic evidence is not needed to prove the intent to create a trust and generally is not admitted to prove the terms or beneficiaries either.

3. **Effect of Invalid Secret or Semi-Secret Trust** is creation of a resulting or constructive trust to dispose of the property and avoid unjust enrichment of the alleged trustee.

 TRUST OPERATION

A. DISCRETIONARY TRUSTS

1. **Single or Multiple Beneficiaries or Trustees**

    A **discretionary trust** may have one or more beneficiaries, one or more trustees, or any combination of them.

2. **Standards Governing Discretion**

    A discretionary trust may provide the trustee with no standards to guide or limit its discretion over distribution, in which case a "best interests" standard will be imposed. In the alternative a discretionary trust may provide specific or even general guidelines for the trustee.

3. **Nature of a Trust Beneficiary's Interest**

    Trust beneficiaries own their own equitable interests, which are assignable, attachable, devisable, descendible, and protectible against waste, fraudulent transfer, trustee malfeasance, and the like.

4. **Effect of Trustee Discretion on Beneficiary's Rights**

    Although a discretionary trust need not provide guidelines and limits for a trustee in the exercise of discretion, trustee actions are subject to judicial review. Nevertheless, a trustee's accountability may be curtailed by express provision in the trust instrument.

5. **Giving the Trustee Broad Discretion** is appropriate because it provides flexibility, imposes some degree of control over beneficiaries, and precludes

creditor attachment. Alternatively, the imposition of more definite standards may protect a trustee from beneficiary claims by expressing what the settlor intended.

6. **Consider Beneficiary's Other Resources**

A common law trustee may not consider a beneficiary's other resources in exercising discretion, but a provision in the instrument may authorize such consideration. In any event, the trustee may consider the beneficiary's ability to support herself, the family's other needs, and tax factors.

7. **Beneficiary's Transferable Interest**

Unless the trust instrument provides otherwise, a beneficiary's interest may be transferred by renunciation (disclaimer) or by an affirmative assignment. If an interest is assigned to a creditor, most states require that the creditor exhaust the beneficiary's other assets before attaching a trust interest. If an interest is renounced in accordance with state law requirements the beneficiary is treated as having predeceased creation of the interest.

B. **SUPPORT TRUSTS,** absent language in the trust instrument, generally provide for the beneficiary's support in her accustomed standard of living.

C. **CREDITORS' RIGHTS AND SPENDTHRIFT PROVISIONS**

1. **Forms of Spendthrift Restrictions**

Spendthrift trusts come in a variety of forms: support trusts, **forfeiture** (or cessure) **provisions,** discretionary trusts, in-hand-payment, and pure spendthrift provisions.

2. **Creditors of the Settlor**

A spendthrift provision in even an irrevocable trust generally does not protect the trust from claims of the settlor's creditors. Additionally, trust assets subject to the settlor's retained general inter vivos power of appointment are not protected from the settlor's creditors. However, typically creditors cannot force the settlor to exercise a power to revoke a trust.

3. **If the Beneficiary Is Not the Settlor**

In most states, if the beneficiary of a spendthrift trust is not the settlor, creditors of the beneficiary cannot reach the beneficiary's interest in the trust, although creditors can reach trust assets after they have been distributed to the beneficiary. Likewise, a bankruptcy proceeding will not defeat the protection of a spendthrift provision.

4. **Limitations on Spendthrift Provisions**

Some states limit the effectiveness of spendthrift provisions, for example, against the provider of necessaries, or to prevent collection of governmental or tax claims.

D. MODIFICATION AND TERMINATION

1. **By the Settlor**

At common law a trust was irrevocable unless an express power to revoke was reserved. Any irrevocable trust is nevertheless revocable to the extent the settlor is the sole beneficiary, all the beneficiaries consent, the trust is invalid due to incapacity, duress, undue influence, or fraud, or the power to revoke was inadvertently omitted due to scrivener's error. Some state statutes provide that a trust is revocable unless otherwise expressed and a new Uniform Trust Act and the Restatement (Third) of Trusts will so provide as the modern rule.

2. **By the Trustee**

Absent express authority in a trust instrument, trustees generally have no power to modify or terminate a trust. An implicit power to revoke may be found in the form of a **small trust termination** provision or to the extent a trustee has the discretion to distribute as much corpus as is deemed appropriate for a beneficiary's needs.

3. **By the Beneficiaries**

Trust beneficiaries acting alone may modify or terminate a trust if all interested parties consent and there is no unfulfilled trust purpose. However, the settlor's dead hand may control only for the period of the Rule Against Perpetuities; a beneficiary entitled to an annuity may ask for the cash that would be used to purchase that annuity; property directed to be sold and the proceeds distributed may be distributed in kind; and merger of several interests may produce a termination. The Uniform Trust Act and the Restatement (Third) of Trusts will expand even further the power of beneficiaries to terminate a trust.

4. **Judicial Power to Modify Trust** administrative provisions may permit alteration of the time or manner of a beneficiary's enjoyment, but not the beneficiary's entitlement (unless the beneficiary consents).

 14 POWERS OF APPOINTMENT

A. TERMINOLOGY

1. **The donor** creates a power of appointment.

2. **The donee** may exercise the power of appointment. The Restatement (Third) of Property—Wills and Other Donative Instruments will refer to this as the **powerholder.**

3. **An object** or **permissible appointee** of the power is any person or entity in whose favor the power may be exercised.

4. **A taker in default** of exercise or a default beneficiary takes the property to the extent the power is not validly exercised.

5. **Powers may be general** or **nongeneral,** and exercisable inter vivos or at death (testamentary).

B. POWERS OF APPOINTMENT are granted to provide flexibility, to pay attention to the particular needs of the permissible appointees in lieu of mandatory distribution provisions, to permit distribution to a beneficiary who has fulfilled a qualification for distribution, and for tax purposes.

C. CLASSIFICATION OF POWERS

1. **Time of Exercise**

    An inter vivos power is presently exercisable by deed or other written instrument (as specified by the grant of the power) delivered to the trustee. A testamentary power is exercisable by a valid will (or perhaps another document that is effective only at death).

2. **Scope of Exercise**

    A general power, defined for tax purposes, is exercisable in favor of the powerholder, the powerholder's estate, or creditors of either. Any other permissible appointees are irrelevant to the classification of the power but may be allowed. A nongeneral power, defined for tax purposes, is any other power, including a **statutory power** that is exercisable in favor of anyone in the world except the powerholder, the powerholder's estate, or creditors of either.

3. **Nongeneral Powers** may be **exclusive** or **nonexclusive,** and may be **powers in trust, imperative powers,** or trigger an **implied default** provision.

D. CREDITORS' RIGHTS

1. **Donor-Powerholder**

    Generally, creditors of a donor who also is the powerholder may reach the appointive property to the extent the donor is insolvent, regardless of whether the power is general or nongeneral, exercised or just available for exercise.

2. **Third Party as Powerholder**

    If the powerholder is anyone other than the donor, property subject to a nongeneral power is immune to claims of the powerholder's creditors. Property subject to a general power may be reached by the powerholder's creditors to the extent the power is exercised and the powerholder is insolvent. Some states allow creditors to reach assets subject to an *unexercised* inter vivos general power to the extent the powerholder is insolvent.

3. **The Surviving Spouse** of a powerholder who is not the donor may reach the appointive property only to the extent the powerholder exercised a general power in favor of the powerholder's estate or the doctrine of capture applies.

E. CONTRACTS TO EXERCISE

Most jurisdictions permit a powerholder to contract to exercise an inter vivos power, but a contract to exercise a testamentary power is not enforceable.

F. RELEASE OF A POWER is permissible and acceptable unless there is no default provision.

G. EXERCISE IN FRAUD OF A POWER

An attempt to benefit individuals who are not objects of a power is a fraud on the power and usually results either in invalidation of the improper exercise and allowance of the remainder (if any) of the exercise, or invalidation of the entire appointment. Such an exercise also is void if it is clear that the power would not have been exercised if not for the invalid objective.

H. CAPRICIOUS OR ARBITRARY EXERCISE

A powerholder may exercise a power capriciously or arbitrarily to the extent the power is exercised in favor of permissible appointees.

I. CAPACITY TO EXERCISE POWERS: FORMALITIES

1. **Capacity** to exercise a power is that applicable to the relevant medium for exercise (e.g., to execute a will).

2. **Formalities** may be imposed by the donor in addition to any required for execution of the relevant medium for exercise. This usually is done by requiring the donee to make specific reference to the power.

J. CONFLICT OF LAWS

The law of the donor's domicile typically governs exercise of a power, although some courts apply whatever conflicts rule is needed to find a valid exercise. The trend is to apply the law of the powerholder's domicile.

K. APPLICATION OF LAPSE STATUTES

Generally, lapse statutes do not apply to powers of appointment, although some courts will apply a different rule to a general power and the UPC allows application of its antilapse rule to all powers of appointment.

15 FUTURE INTERESTS: CLASSIFICATION, CHARACTERISTICS, AND CONSTRUCTION

A. INTRODUCTION

1. Legal vs. Equitable Interests

Today the vast majority of future interests are created in trust, not in land.

2. Rules of Law vs. Rules of Construction

A rule of law controls without regard to intent, whereas a rule of construction is used to aid in the resolution of an issue not addressed clearly in the controlling instrument. Future interest law contains some of each, the rules of law falling more into disfavor than the constructional preferences.

3. ''Future Interest'' Is a Misnomer

A **future interest** may be contingent or vested but the property interest exists presently. Future interests are transferable, enforceable, protectible, and the interests of unborns are supported by a **relation back doctrine.**

4. Classification in General

Executory interests and **contingent remainders** are substantively the same. They both have the possibility of becoming possessory if the required condition occurs, although an executory interest becomes possessory by divesting a preceding estate whereas a remainder becomes possessory at the natural termination of a preceding estate without divesting that estate. Moreover, the Rule Against Perpetuities applies to each, only with different consequences of a violation. Transfer tax results may vary, although in all likelihood not by enough to care.

B. FUTURE INTERESTS OF THE TRANSFEROR

1. Possibility of Reverter

A transferor retains a **possibility of reverter** when a **fee simple determinable** is conveyed. If a third party were named, that interest would be a **shifting executory interest.**

2. Power of Termination

A transferor retains a **power of termination** for condition broken when a fee simple subject to a condition subsequent is conveyed. If a third party were named, that interest also would be a shifting executory interest.

3. Possibility of Reverter vs. Power of Termination

When the transferor retains a possibility of reverter, occurrence of the divesting condition causes expiration of the fee automatically, but retention of a power of termination requires an affirmative act for the transferor to reacquire possession.

4. Reversion

A transferor retains a **reversion** if less than all the transferor owns is conveyed, the interest that is retained follows a present interest, and it cannot be a possibility of reverter or power of termination. Reversions are always regarded as vested interests.

C. FUTURE INTERESTS OF TRANSFEREES

1. Remainders must be created by the same instrument that created the present interest in another person. The remainder must follow a particular estate (life estate or term of years) and must become possessory immediately upon the natural expiration of the preceding particular estate.

2. Vested

A **vested remainder** may be **indefeasibly vested, vested subject to open** or **to close,** or **vested subject to divestment.**

    a. A remainder becomes vested if its holder is an ascertained person and the only condition precedent to it becoming possessory is termination of one or more preceding estates.

    b. A contingent remainder becomes possessory subject to a condition precedent.

3. Executory Interests are future interests that are not remainders, and as a rule become possessory by divesting a prior vested estate in fee. Executory interests may be classified as **shifting** or **springing.**

D. ORIGIN AND CHARACTERISTICS

1. Transferability

Absent spendthrift prohibitions, both vested and contingent future interests are transferable during life and at death. The possibility of reverter and power of termination were not alienable at common law, although they were attachable by creditors. Today both are alienable in most jurisdictions.

2. Acceleration

Acceleration of a future interest into possession may be caused by disclaimer, homicide, or election of a surviving spouse's statutory forced heir share.

3. Protection

Holders of future interests may avail themselves of many protections, including: the sale and investment of proceeds, the prevention of waste, or the provision of security if personal property is subject to a legal life estate.

E. THREE ANCIENT DOCTRINES

1. Destructibility of Contingent Remainders

At common law a contingent legal remainder in land was destroyed by operation of law if it did not vest any later than termination of the preceding estate. Most states have abolished this rule, replacing it with a construction of a life estate, a reversion subject to divestment in the transferor, and a springing executory interest.

2. The Rule in *Shelley's Case* is a rule of law and applies if there is a conveyance of realty for life, remainder in the life tenant's heirs. If applicable, the rule converts the life estate to a fee simple by regarding the remainder in the life tenant's heirs as a remainder in the life tenant, which then may merge with the life estate. The Rule in *Shelley's Case* has been abolished in most states.

3. The Doctrine of Worthier Title is a rule of construction and applies to an inter vivos conveyance of personalty or realty for a term of years, as a defeasible fee, or a life estate, remainder to the transferor's heirs. If applicable, the doctrine converts the remainder in the transferor's heirs to a reversion in the transferor. The Doctrine has been abolished in many jurisdictions and is disfavored most everywhere else.

F. PROBLEMS OF CONSTRUCTION

1. Survivorship.

If the governing instrument does not address a survivorship requirement for future interests, the law traditionally will not imply a condition of survivorship. The UPC deviates from this traditional principle.

a. Lapse traditionally applies only if a named beneficiary under a will predeceases the testator. Few courts have applied the lapse rule to inter vivos trusts.

b. The rules in *Clobberie's Case* are as follows: If words of futurity are annexed to the substance of the gift, the traditional approach is to treat the recipient's interest as contingent, to require survivorship to the specified age, and to postpone vesting. If the words of futurity are not annexed to the substance of the gift but instead to enjoyment, the gift is not conditioned on survivorship—it is vested with a postponement of possession. If the words of futurity are annexed to the subject of the gift but the transferee also is given income from the gift, this hybrid is regarded as vested under the rule that "income vests the principle."

c. The general rule with respect to class gifts of future interests is that the class is subject to open until distribution, but is not subject to close unless survivorship expressly is required. This rule usually does not apply to classes whose members are multigenerational.

d. If the time to which survival is required is not specified, the general rule is that the beneficiary must survive all prior interests, or until the time for distribution, if later. Deviations from this general rule may occur if the income beneficiary also is a remainder beneficiary, if the condition of survivorship is expressed in a different way than a similar condition elsewhere in the document, or if surviving the life tenant was too unlikely to have been the settlor's intent.

2. Gifts to Heirs

A determination of an individual's heirs raises difficult issues, such as whether a surviving spouse is considered an heir and when the determination of who are the heirs is made.

3. Gifts to Descendants, Issue, or Children

There are a few methods of distributing a gift made by will or trust to a person's descendants, issue, or children.

a. In many jurisdictions such property is distributed according to the rules of intestate succession. Under the Restatement (Second) of Property—Donative Transfers and the UPC such property is distributed according to the per capita method, unless the gift expressly is made "per stirpes."

b. Historically the **stranger to the adoption rule** prevented an adopted child from sharing in a class gift to descendants, issue, or children unless the transferor was the adopting parent. Today, a minority of jurisdictions also do not allow a person adopted as an adult to share in a class gift to descendants, issue, or children.

c. Most jurisdictions allow nonmarital descendants to share in a class gift made by will or trust instrument.

4. **The Rule in *Wild's Case*** was an interpretation of a devise by T "to A and A's children," resolving that if A and A's children are alive at T's death, they take as equal tenants in common to the exclusion of afterborn children. Alternatives to this interpretation include treating the gift as half to A and a class gift of the other half to A's children, and the **Pennsylvania rule,** which is to A for life, remainder to the class of A's children.

INTRODUCTION TO PROPERTY TRANSFERS AT DEATH

CHAPTER OVERVIEW

- This chapter introduces you to the study of wills, trusts, and estates, including much of the terminology you need and the distinction between probate and nonprobate property.

- Also addressed are sources and limitations on the power to dispose of property at death.

A. OBJECTIVES AND EMPHASIS

Before you outline your course materials and integrate your class notes, try to determine your professor's objectives and emphasis in the course. Knowing where your professor is coming from almost always will help you know where she is heading in the course. For example, we practiced estate planning prior to becoming professors, and we tend to teach on the assumption that our students are going to practice law in this area. As a result, while we teach the substantive rules, we emphasize how to do certain tasks and what problems to avoid.

1. Estate Planning Considerations

Because lawyers prepare wills and trust agreements to accomplish personal, family, tax, and other objectives, and because of our backgrounds, we look closely at estate planning uses and tend to focus on alternative thinking: from a case or note involving an instrument that resulted in a serious dispute, often attributable to a lawyer's mistake, comes a study of how to do it right to avoid that and similar kinds of problems.

2. Policy Considerations

We also tend to think in terms of policy: the topics and rules that needlessly frustrate the intent of clients. Even in that context, our focus is on how the law might be reformed and on how wise practitioners avoid those applications under the law as it is.

3. Probate and Administration Procedure

Little emphasis is devoted in this material to probate and administration procedure, because the probate of wills and the administration of estates are particularly jurisdiction specific endeavors. There are, however, certain principles of fiduciary administration, many of which are equally applicable to trusts and estates, that are relatively universal in their formulation and application, and those are discussed in the Website.

4. Taxation

In addition, unless your school's curriculum does not offer a separate course on the tax laws that impact this practice specialty, it is unlikely that your wills and trusts course will delve much into the tax elements of this substantive area of the law. We therefore discuss those laws only in broad brush and mostly just at the Website.

5. Trusts and Estates Practice

Many lawyers who practice in the trusts and estates area find it a particularly rewarding practice. It is a family oriented practice and, although family disputes can be more bitter than most others, for many practitioners in this area such disputes account for a small portion of their practice, which for the most part is cooperative, constructive, and nonadversarial. For clients of some wealth, estate planning offers the opportunity to do sophisticated and creative tax planning work, and for those clients who own interests in closely held businesses, the estate planner also may have the opportunity to engage in related business planning (e.g., deciding who will run the business when Mom or Dad dies).

6. The Future of Estate Planning

The future of estate planning as a specialty is likely to be influenced by a number of predominant trends. Perhaps the most important is demographics and the aging of America: people are growing older and living longer, many of them will be concerned about wealth transfer planning for many years before their deaths, and most of them will be as much concerned with planning for the rest of their lives as they will be about planning for their successors.

a. **Second and subsequent marriages.** It appears that the trend of high divorce and remarriage rates will continue. Note the large number of cases that arise in the context of second and subsequent marriages, particularly if there are children from prior marriages. Those circumstances, with their potential for serious disputes, present difficult challenges in both planning and postmortem administration, for clients and lawyers alike.

b. **Increasing wealth.** Many Americans have become wealthy, particularly as a result of the stock market, and a greater number of those are seeking estate planning help.

c. **Nonprobate property.** A huge factor is the increase in the amount of property that does not pass under a decedent's will or by intestacy. Such property, typically referred to as nonprobate property, includes such assets as property held in trust, joint tenancy, or other contractual ownership forms that pass at a person's death by operation of law, and assets that pass pursuant to a beneficiary designation like an insurance contract, employee benefits, and other annuities.

d. **Role of the fiduciary.** In connection with all of this, and the increasingly litigious nature of our society, fiduciary roles and administration will become more important, both as you draft documents that employ trustees, executors, guardians or conservators, and others charged with administration of property for the benefit of others, and as you consider acting as the fiduciary yourself.

e. **Malpractice risks.** There is an unfortunate amount of malpractice being committed in this area, predominantly by lawyers who are not adequately educated or experienced and who believe that "anyone can draft a simple will." You will learn that there is no such thing as a *simple* will anymore: there are short wills, and lawyers who think about wills in simple ways, but no simple wills. Even straightforward drafting jobs can hold substantial risk of liability. This means that some of you will be successful litigators who specialize in knowing enough about this area of the law to spot and then seek redress for other lawyers' mistakes, or in defending against such claims.

B. TERMINOLOGY

Historically, different terms have been used to deal with realty and personalty, and to the passage of property at death.

1. Intestacy: Real and Personal Property

Descent is the intestate entitlement of *heirs at law* to realty. *Distribution* is the intestate entitlement of *next of kin* to personalty. These days most people refer to statutes of descent and distribution and to heirs (rather than heirs at law or next of kin), and most laws no longer distinguish between realty and personalty.

a. **Potential heirs.** Heirs cannot be determined until the death of the designated ancestor. Thus, a living person does not have heirs. Rather, we refer to *potential heirs*, and they fall into several categories: *Heirs expectant*, or *prospective heirs*, are those persons who might prove to be entitled to the wealth. *Heirs apparent* are those in the closest degree to the designated ancestor: these persons definitely will inherit if they survive the designated ancestor. *Heirs presumptive* are those individuals who presently are living and who are in the closest degree of relationship to the designated ancestor, but who can be preempted if a closer heir is born or otherwise qualifies.

 # EXAMPLES AND ANALYSIS

Your parents are your heirs presumptive if you have neither a spouse nor children, but they are not your heirs apparent because they could be supplanted if you marry or have descendants before you die.

2. *Lineals* are ancestors and descendants in the blood line, such as parents, grandparents, children, grandchildren, and such (including individuals who were adopted rather than natural born). Note that descendants are sometimes also referred to as "issue," although we will avoid that term because it sometimes is thought to mean only children.

3. *Collaterals* are non-lineal relatives who are related by blood (*consanguinity*), and also may include adopteds. By contrast, *affinity* is relation by marriage. Thus, your aunt who is the sister of your parent is related to you by consanguinity; your aunt's husband (who most of us would refer to as your uncle) is related to you by affinity. The husband of your spouse's sister is your spouse's brother-in-law (a relationship by affinity) but is not related to you.

  a. **Relatives by affinity excluded as heirs.** As we will see in Chapter 2, relatives by affinity generally are not heirs. As a result, in the example above, if you died without a will your aunt could be your heir, but your aunt's husband could not.

  b. **Relative.** Note that the term *relative* usually includes persons related by affinity or by consanguinity. Thus not all "relatives" can be heirs.

4. **Intestate Property** is any property of a decedent (other than nonprobate property, defined below) that is not validly disposed of by a will. A person who dies without a will is said to have died intestate.

5. *Escheat* is the term that applies if the decedent's estate passes to the state, usually because there are no heirs.

6. *Succession* is the term that applies to the division of an intestate decedent's estate among her heirs.

7. *Testate* means a valid will is applicable:

   a. *Testator* (or, if you still are living in the dark ages in which gender-based distinctions in terminology were popular, testat*rix*) refers to the person who makes a will. Assuming the will is valid, such a person is said to have died testate and, to the extent the will does not dispose of all the testator's property, the testator can be partially intestate.

   b. **Kinds of wills.** *Attested* wills are wills that are witnessed. Depending on the jurisdiction, *holographs* are unwitnessed wills that are signed by the testator and entirely handwritten by the testator, or the material portions of which are handwritten by the testator. *Nuncupative* wills are oral wills.

   c. **Gifts under a will.** A *devise* is a gift of realty under a will; the recipient is called a *devisee*. A *bequest* is a gift of personalty under a will, while a *legacy* is a gift of cash under a will; in each case the recipient is called a *legatee* (there is no such thing as a *bequeathee*). Because of the lack of symmetry in this terminology, the Uniform Probate Code, discussed below, has determined to call all gifts of either realty or personalty "devises" and all beneficiaries of these gifts "devisees." Because of older case law that still distinguishes between these, you probably should learn and remember the separate designations.

   d. **Ambulatory.** To be a will, the document must be both revocable during the testator's life and *ambulatory*—which means that it has no legal effect before the maker dies. So, a will *ain't nothin' 'til you die*. Documents that have legal effect, or that are irrevocable, before the maker meets her maker are not wills. This is important when we study the law of wills in Chapter 6 and its impact on instruments and arrangements, called *will substitutes*, under which property passes at a person's death other than under the terms of a will or the statutes of descent and distribution.

   e. *Codicils* are documents executed with all the formalities of a will (either a traditional attested will or, if the jurisdiction permits them, a holographic will) which add, delete, or otherwise change provisions in a will referred to in the codicil.

8. *Probate* is the process of proving after a testator's death that her will is valid (signed in the right place, by the right persons, and such), meaning that it is "admitted to probate."

9. *Administration* of an estate (which often is mislabeled as probate because this is "probate administration" under the auspices of a probate court) is the process of marshalling and distributing the decedent's property and is performed by a personal representative, of which there are several flavors:

   a. *Executor* (not execut*rix*, unless you're stuck in the dark ages) refers to a personal representative who is appointed by the will.

   b. *Administrator* (not administrat*rix*) refers to a personal representative who is appointed by the court, sometimes because there was no will, or it did not designate a personal representative, but sometimes because the executor designated by the will is unable or unwilling to act (or continue to act). *Administrator CTA* (cum testamento annexo – there is a will) means an administrator who is serving for an estate that is testate. *Administrator DBN* (de bonis non – of goods not administered) is a successor to some personal representative (executor or administrator) that began but did not finish administration. *Administrator CTA DBN* means a successor to administer a testate estate.

   c. **Personal representative.** In many jurisdictions, including those in which the UPC has been adopted, the fiduciary charged with administration of the estate is simply referred to as the *personal representative*, without regard to gender or whether the appointed fiduciary was designated under a probated will of the decedent.

10. *Will Contests* may be a third separate judicial proceeding (probate and administration being the other two), brought to challenge the validity of a will, not for lack of formalities of execution that would preclude its admission to probate (although challenges to the probate of a will also are sometimes inaccurately referred to as will contests), but for things like fraud, undue influence, lack of testamentary capacity, and so forth. This proceeding can take place at the same time the estate is being administered, with only the ultimate distribution being delayed until the contest issues can be resolved.

C.   TESTAMENTARY POWER

1.   Historical Sources

The modern law of wills in the United States is derived in large part from three English statutes: the Statute of Wills (1540), the Statute of Frauds (1677), and the Wills Act (1837). Historically, different rules applied to testamentary gifts of personal and real property. Today, the same requirements apply to each.

2.   The Uniform Probate Code, promulgated in 1969 and often simply referred to as the UPC, is a comprehensive statute dealing with the law of wills

and trusts, and with other areas of the law such as intestacy, nontestamentary transfers (such as life insurance, trusts, and bank deposit arrangements) that are testamentary in effect, future interests, guardianships and conservatorships, and powers of attorney. The UPC has been adopted in whole or in part by about one third of the states. The UPC has been amended on numerous occasions, including a substantial substantive amendment in 1990. Although most states have enacted at least some part or section of the UPC, its influence is not limited to those provisions of the various states' laws that have been taken directly from the UPC. Rather, it also represents a statement of modern policy that is relied on by courts in construing non-UPC statutes and the common law.

3. **Restatements of the Law** are comprehensive statements of the law in particular areas that influence courts and legislatures. Restatements are promulgated by the American Law Institute, the members of which include practicing lawyers, judges, and law professors. There are two Restatements that directly apply to wills and trusts, the Restatement (Third) of Property—Wills and Other Donative Transfers, and the Restatement (Third) of Trusts. Each is currently under revision.

4. **Constitutional Principles.** Before *Hodel v. Irving*, 481 U.S. 704 (1987), the right to transfer property at death was generally viewed as arising solely out of statute, without benefit of constitutional protection. In *Hodel*, the Court held invalid under the taking (without just compensation) clause of the Fifth Amendment to the U.S. Constitution a federal statute under which small, undivided interests in certain Indian lands could not pass on the owner's death by descent (i.e., by intestacy) or devise (i.e., by will), but instead automatically escheated to the tribe. The Court acknowledged Congress' broad power to regulate Indian lands, but held that the Constitution prohibited Congress from totally abolishing both descent and devise of the interests involved.

D.   TAXATION, IMPROVIDENCE, AND INHERITANCE

1. Taxation

One of the most common ways in which testamentary freedom is disrupted by the government is taxation of wealth transfers (through the estate, gift, and generation-skipping taxes). This form of interference is well accepted as constitutional, almost without limit.

2. Dissipation of Wealth; Improvidence

Authors argue about the relative merits of redistributing wealth, but the reality is that no system does as effective a job of redistribution as taxation and improvidence, and far and away the latter is the more efficient of the two. Far more concentrated family wealth is dissipated by heirs than is fragmented by taxation. Efficient estate planning seeks to minimize the effect of taxation or improvidence on the transmission of wealth.

3. Changes in Inheritance

Also note that patterns of inheritance are changing, particularly for the middle class. For example, a large chunk of the wealth of many Americans is held in a form that typically is not and in some cases cannot be enjoyed during life: life insurance. Further, for an increasing number of Americans, a sizeable portion of their accumulated wealth is invested in a form that cannot be squandered during their lives: annuities, particularly in the form of deferred compensation retirement benefits from employment. In addition, a substantial portion of accumulated wealth will be divested during life in the form of education provided to children and health care expenses.

E. COMPETING INTERESTS

Any course in wills, trusts, and estates will involve classic tensions, often between living beneficiaries and decedents who had certain objectives and desires with respect to the disposition of their wealth.

1. Taxation

One form of this tension is direct taxes on wealth transfers. Federal wealth transfer taxes generate only about a little more than 1% of the money raised by taxes in any given year. With increased frequency, there are calls for the repeal of the wealth transfer taxes.

2. Tensions Among Beneficiaries

A second form of tension found in this course is among beneficiaries, most commonly involving life income recipients who are adverse to the interests of remainder beneficiaries, but also involving the conflict between those who receive more than might seem "normal" or predictable.

 ## EXAMPLES AND ANALYSIS

D died survived by a spouse (S), and by two children (C1 and C2). D devised her estate to T, in trust, income to S for life, remainder to C1. There is a potential for conflict between S and C1 because it is in S's interests for the trust assets to be invested to maximize income; C1 would prefer investments that result in growth of principal. (See the Internet for a discussion of the trustee's duty of impartiality with respect to the administration of the trust for S and C1.) There also is a potential for conflict between both S and C1, on the one hand, and C2, who is disinherited, on the other. (See Chapter 3 for a discussion of will contest grounds.)

3.   Claims by Third Parties

A third form of tension involves "predators" who seek to tap into the wealth of decedents. Depending on the decedent's views, these might include creditors of beneficiaries, spouses of beneficiaries, greedy children, and even charities or others with their hands out. Many estate plans are drafted with an eye to minimizing the exposure to outsiders.

4.   Control from the Grave

A fourth form of tension is the "dead hand" desire of some decedents to control the lives of their beneficiaries (or at least the beneficiaries' enjoyment of the decedent's wealth) from the grave, typically through restrictive provisions in the dispositions that benefit those individuals. The Rule Against Perpetuities, discussed in the Internet, is the essential limitation imposed by the law of most jurisdictions on the duration of this form of control, but it may surprise you that, as discussed in Chapter 13, for the most part the dead hand is respected in this area of the law.

   a.   **Conditioning a gift on marriage.** For example, in *Shapira v. Union Nat'l Bank*, 315 N.E.2d 825 (Ohio Ct. Com. Pleas 1974), a father's will conditioning his son's inheritance on the son being married to (or marrying within seven years of the father's death) a woman who was Jewish and whose parents both were Jewish was upheld. If the condition had been that the son not marry at all, it would have been void as against public policy; reasonable restrictions on marriage, however, are valid. The hard issue in a case like *Shapira* is what constitutes a "reasonable" restriction. For example, it would be regarded as too restrictive if the son had been required to marry a Jewish woman whose birthday was an even numbered Tuesday in a leap year, but what if the restriction had been an Orthodox Jewish woman? The dividing line between too restrictive and permissible dead hand control always is a question of fact and degree. And what if the son had strong religious, but non-Jewish, convictions? According to the Restatement (Third) of Property—Wills and Other Donative Transfers §6.2, the test of reasonableness is whether a marriage within the religion is likely to occur. Thus, the type and strength of the transferee's religious beliefs may affect whether a condition to marry within a religious faith is reasonable.

5.   Elective Share Rights

A fifth tension is between the desires of some testators and the rights of certain individuals to a portion of a decedent's estate in the form of an elective share, by which a surviving spouse in most states (and in rare cases a child or other descendant) may reject the decedent's dispositive provisions in favor of a guaranteed portion of the decedent's wealth, typically based on concepts of fairness and the perceived need to prevent certain individuals from becoming wards of the state while others enjoy a decedent's largess. (See Chapter 10.)

F. PROBATE AND NONPROBATE TRANSFERS

1. Nonprobate Transfers: Will Substitutes

Much of a person's wealth may not pass under the terms of her will (if she died testate) or under the laws of intestate succession (if she died without a will). Examples of such property, which will be discussed in greater detail in Chapter 6, include the following:

a. **Life insurance.** The owner of a policy of life insurance (usually the insured, but often a trust or other third party so that the proceeds will escape estate taxation at the insured's death) may designate a beneficiary (and one or more contingent beneficiaries) to receive the proceeds of the policy on the insured's death. Upon the death of the insured, the proceeds are payable to the designated beneficiary without regard to the terms of the insured's will (or the intestate succession statutes, if the insured died intestate).

b. **Retirement plan interests.** The participant/employee in an employer's retirement plan and the owner of an individual retirement account (an IRA) usually may designate one or more persons to receive benefits from the plan or IRA. The designated beneficiary will receive the benefits without regard to the terms of a will or the governing intestacy laws.

c. **Joint tenancy property.** Property the decedent owned with one or more others as joint tenants with rights of survivorship will pass on the decedent's death by operation of law to the surviving joint tenant(s) without regard to the terms of the decedent's will or the applicable intestacy statute.

d. **Other payable on death (POD) arrangements.** Many states allow bank accounts, and some states allow securities such as stocks and bonds, to be owned by one person, but payable on that person's death directly to one or more designated other persons. The designated beneficiary will become its new owner without regard to the owner's will or the laws of intestacy.

e. **Property held in trust.** The decedent may have been the beneficiary of a trust that she or another person created for her benefit. Depending on the terms of their agreement, the decedent may or may not have the right to affect who will benefit from the property following the decedent's death. The trust property will pass to, or continue in trust for, persons designated in the trust agreement without regard to the decedent's will or the laws of intestate succession.

      i. Exception for testamentary power of appointment. An exception might apply if the decedent had and exercised a testamentary power of appointment (discussed in Chapter 14) over the trust property, in which case it would pass on the decedent's death in accordance with the exercise of that power. Even then, however, the property will not pass as a part of the decedent's probate estate, but will instead pass directly from the trustee of the trust to the persons named to receive the trust property in the decedent's exercise of the power.

    f. Estate planning implications. It is critical to consider carefully nonprobate property when doing estate planning for a client. An all too common problem is for a client to have a well drafted will that fails to accomplish the client's objectives because beneficiary designations, survivorship arrangements, and powers of appointment were not considered and coordinated with the terms of the will during the planning process.

  2. Probate Property passes under the terms of the decedent's will or under the laws of intestate succession (to the extent a will did not dispose of that property). To say that probate property consists of property titled in the decedent's individual name is not entirely accurate. For example, life insurance policies often are owned by the insured, individually, yet the policy proceeds are not probate assets: they usually pass to designated beneficiaries outside of probate.

EXAM TIP

The distinction between probate and nonprobate property cannot be overemphasized, either for purposes of this course or in practice. A decedent's nonprobate property will not pass under the terms of her will, if she died testate, or under the jurisdiction's law of descent and distribution, if she died intestate. The distinction also can be critical with respect to the application of many of the ancillary rules of the law of wills (e.g., lapse, discussed in Chapter 8). Nonprobate property, which is said to pass by "will substitute," is discussed in some detail in Chapter 6, but it is important to distinguish it from probate property from the outset of your study of the law of gratuitous transfers and certainly for exam purposes.

---

  3. *Probate Administration* (which sometimes is referred to as "probate" but better is called "administration" if a shorthand expression is needed) is the process by which title to probate property of a decedent is transferred to her heirs, if she died intestate, or to her devisees, if she died testate, in each case after payment of all legitimate charges against the estate (typically taxes, debts, and costs of administration itself).

a. **Probate vs. probate administration.** "Probate" is the streamlined process of validating the will by establishing that it was validly executed and constitutes the last will of the decedent. A will usually can be admitted to probate in less than a month. By contrast, probate administration almost always will extend for a period of months and, depending on the circumstances, can continue for years.

b. **Necessity of probate administration.** A common question is whether a probate administration is necessary. If the decedent died owning no probate property—having arranged for all of her property to pass by will substitute—a probate administration will not be needed. In addition, in some circumstances the estate of a decedent who died owning probate property will not need to be administered.

   i. **Tangible personalty.** For example, (i) if the decedent's probate property consisted only of tangible personal property, such as household furnishings, (ii) if there is no dispute among the decedent's surviving family members and other beneficiaries, if any, and (iii) if the claims of any creditors of the decedent can be resolved without dispute, an administration probably would not be required.

   ii. **Realty.** If the decedent's probate property included real estate, however, a probate administration probably will be necessary without regard to the beneficiaries being harmonious and all creditors' claims being resolved, because in most states the devisees of a testate decedent or the heirs of an intestate decedent will be unable to prove clear title to the real estate (so that it could be sold or encumbered in the future) without administration.

   iii. **Third parties.** Similarly, if the decedent's probate property included an asset controlled by a third party, such as cash in a bank account or securities in a brokerage account, the third party may require a probate administration to release the asset; otherwise, if the third party released the asset to the person who appeared to be entitled to receive it and it later turned out that the decedent had a will leaving the property to others, in many states the third party could be held liable to the devisees of the property under the will.

c. **Probate administration procedure.** If a probate administration is required, the form it takes will vary widely depending on the nature and extent of the probate property owned by the decedent and the probate laws and procedures of the jurisdiction in which the administration takes place. At one time the probate administration of an estate in most states was cumbersome, time consuming, and expensive, but today in most states extensive reforms have simplified administration so that it is not particularly time consuming or expensive.

i. **Court supervision of personal representative.** The administration of an estate is the responsibility of a personal representative. Traditionally, the personal representative was appointed by the probate court, which also closely supervised administration of the estate. For example, personal representatives were required to file and have approved by the court an inventory and accountings; sales of assets were required to be approved in cumbersome proceedings involving various notices and hearings; and the payment of creditors' claims required court approval.

ii. **Probate administration under the UPC.** The UPC is illustrative of the more streamlined and flexible approach many states now take to probate administration. Probate of the will, appointment of a personal representative, and administration of the estate can occur without prior notice and without formal judicial involvement, if no one interested in the decedent's estate requests formal proceedings.

d. **Choosing the personal representative.** Common choices clients make in designating personal representatives of their estates include individual family members, banks, trust companies, and business associates, such as accountants.

i. **Role of the attorney.** Although the personal representative is charged with the administration of the estate, it is common for inexperienced personal representatives to delegate much of that work to the attorney, and it also is common for attorneys who practice regularly in the estates and trusts area to have professionals on their support staffs to do much of the administration for personal representatives they are hired to represent.

ii. **Creditors of the decedent.** The personal representative serves the beneficiaries of the estate and its creditors. To facilitate the prompt administration of a decedent's estate, most states have special statutes ("nonclaim statutes") of limitation that require creditors of a decedent to submit their claims to the personal representative within a relatively short period of time to prevent those claims from being barred. In *Tulsa Professional Collection Services, Inc. v. Pope*, 485 U.S. 478 (1988), the Supreme Court held unconstitutional under the due process clause of the Fourteenth Amendment a state statute requiring only publication notice of the decedent's death and the operation of the nonclaim statute. Rather, due process requires actual notice to known or reasonably ascertainable creditors to provide them with an adequate opportunity to file their claims.

    iii.   **Other potential claimants.** There may be a similar constitutional duty to notify potential claimants against the estate, in the form of beneficiaries (either under intestacy or under prior wills that may be valid) who may have an interest in or a cause of action against the estate.

REVIEW QUESTIONS AND ANSWERS

Question: D died intestate. D was not survived by a spouse, by any descendants, or by any ancestors. D was survived by a brother (B), by B's spouse (X), and by the sister (Y) of D's predeceased spouse (S). Assuming that D's estate is to be divided among her siblings, who takes?

Answer: B will receive the entire estate by consanguinity (i.e., B is a blood relative of D). X and Y (D's sisters-in-law) were related to D by affinity (i.e., by marriage) and are not heirs.

Question: D devised her estate to "A's heirs." D was survived by A, by A's spouse (S), by A's child (C), and by A's brother (B). Who will take at D's death?

Answer: A living person can have no heirs. Rather, a *decedent*'s heirs are those persons who are entitled to receive the decedent's probate property if the decedent died intestate. Accordingly, A's heirs who are entitled to receive D's estate cannot be determined until A dies. Until then, S, C, and B are only potential heirs of A.

Question: D's will provided: "I give all of my real and personal property of any kind to A." At death, (i) D owned an insurance policy on her life, the designated beneficiary of which was X, (ii) D and Y owned Blackacre as joint tenants with the right of survivorship, (iii) D had an individual retirement account (an IRA), the beneficiary of which was designated "50% to C and 50% to D's estate," and (iv) D owned a checking account and miscellaneous tangible personal property. To whom will these assets be distributed as a result of D's death?

Answer: The insurance policy, Blackacre, and 50% of the IRA are nonprobate assets that will pass outside of D's estate to X, Y, and C, respectively, without regard to the terms of D's will. D's probate assets are 50% of the IRA payable to D's estate (for a variety of reasons it usually is not good planning to have either retirement benefits or life insurance payable to the participant/insured's estate; see Chapter 6), the checking account, and the miscellaneous tangible personal property, all of which will pass to A.

2   INTESTACY

✦ CHAPTER OVERVIEW

- Probate property of a decedent who dies without a will passes to heirs by intestate succession. A decedent's heirs include a surviving spouse, who may be entitled to receive the entire estate. The decedent's descendants take what the spouse does not and, if there are no descendants, other heirs include parents, descendants of parents, and other ancestors or collaterals.

- It is possible for a decedent to be only partially intestate.

- Intestate succession necessarily raises questions of status, such as whether the claimant was a spouse or child of the decedent.

- In limited circumstances (e.g., misconduct), a person who is an heir is barred or chooses not to benefit from the estate.

A.   INTESTATE SUCCESSION IN GENERAL

Intestate succession is the statutory estate plan: it is the legislature's guesstimate of what the average decedent would want done with her probate property—applicable to the extent a valid will does not apply. As the "every-person" estate plan, ready-made, off-the-rack, anyone may employ it by doing nothing to overcome it (i.e., by dying without a will).

1.   Property Subject to Intestate Succession

A decedent's *probate property* (see Chapter 1) passes under the governing jurisdiction's statute of descent and distribution by intestate succession to her heirs. Nonprobate property is not subject to intestate succession.

    a. Abolition of dower and curtesy. Most states have abandoned *dower* and *curtesy* (common law rights of a widow or widower, respectively, to a life estate in part or all of a decedent's realty). For easy understanding here, we assume that they are not the law or that the portion of the estate subject to dower or curtesy has been peeled off the top and that we are dealing with the balance of the estate.

    b. Net probate estate. Furthermore, an intestate decedent's probate property that is subject to distribution by intestate succession is the net probate estate, reduced by such items as taxes, debts, administrative expenses, funeral expenses, and the family allowances (see Chapter 10).

 # EXAMPLES AND ANALYSIS

D died intestate. At her death, D owned an insurance policy on her life, the death benefit of which was $100,000, and an interest in a retirement plan, the value of which was $200,000. The beneficiary D designated for each was S, her surviving spouse. D also owned investment assets of $150,000, and had debts of $20,000. The administration expenses for D's estate were $5,000, and the cost of her funeral was another $5,000. S's family allowance was $15,000. D's net probate estate that will pass by intestacy is $105,000, the difference between her probate property (the $150,000 of investment assets) and the sum of her debts, the funeral and administration expenses, and the family allowance ($20,000 + 5,000 + 5,000 + 15,000 = $45,000).

2. Governing Law

    A state statute of descent and distribution is applicable to all intestate personalty of a deceased resident of the state, no matter where that personalty is located, plus all the decedent's realty located in the state, no matter where the decedent was a resident. On occasion state law defers to the law of the decedent's domicile with respect to realty as well, but usually the law of the situs governs.

    a. Differences in state law. As we study the rules governing intestacy (and a wide variety of other issues affecting wills, trusts, and estates), you will see that they differ—sometimes substantially and sometimes in very fine and hard to discern ways—from state to state, making conflict of laws and plain old malpractice serious and omnipresent concerns.

B. SURVIVING SPOUSE

The share of a surviving spouse of an intestate decedent varies significantly from state to state. In many jurisdictions, the spouse's share depends on who else survived the decedent.

1. Under the UPC

The surviving spouse's intestate share under the Uniform Probate Code (the UPC) generally is greater than the share of a surviving spouse under most non-UPC intestate succession statutes.

a. Fixed dollar amount. UPC §2-102 gives a surviving spouse a fixed dollar amount (the exact amount is set by each state and the UPC only makes a recommendation), plus at least a fraction of any balance in the estate, notwithstanding the existence of other potential beneficiaries (such as children) of the decedent's bounty. This off-the-top fixed amount effectively gives many small estates entirely to the surviving spouse, superseding all other rules announced in the statute.

   i. Support theory. The fixed dollar amount under the UPC reflects a support theory notion that the surviving spouse will need a certain minimum amount to avoid becoming a ward of the state. Notice that the spouse is entitled to receive this amount regardless of the spouse's own resources and regardless of the amount of nonprobate property the spouse received as a result of the decedent's death.

b. Remaining estate under the UPC. Dealing only with the balance after the fixed amount is distributed to the spouse, UPC §2-102 gives the surviving spouse the entire remaining estate if (i) there is no surviving descendant or parent of the decedent, or (ii) if all of the decedent's descendants also are descendants of the spouse and there are no descendants of the *spouse* who are not also descendants of the decedent (which is to say that the spouse is not likely to divert the decedent's property to objects of the spouse's bounty the decedent would not necessarily favor).

 EXAMPLES AND ANALYSIS

D died intestate and was survived by neither parent, a spouse, and two children who also were the spouse's children. Under UPC §2-102 D's spouse inherits the entire probate estate, unless the spouse had descendants from another relationship who survived the decedent.

EXAM TIP

The UPC approach of giving the surviving spouse the entire estate of an intestate decedent who also was survived by at least one descendant—provided the surviving spouse is an ancestor of all of the decedent's descendants and no descendants of the surviving spouse from another relationship survived the decedent—is a significant departure from traditional intestate succession law under which the surviving spouse shares the decedent's intestate estate with the decedent's descendants. This change, made in 1990, is a good candidate for coverage on an exam.

    i. Descendants by another relationship of the decedent or spouse. UPC §2-102 limits the entitlement of the surviving spouse if there are living descendants of the decedent or of the spouse by another relationship. In that regard, notice that the fixed dollar amount also varies: if the decedent had descendants from a prior marriage, the fixed dollar amount would be the first $100,000; by contrast, if the spouse has descendants from a prior marriage (and all of the decedent's descendants also were descendants of the spouse), the spouse's recommended share would be the first $150,000, in either case plus ½ of the balance.

    ii. Spouse's UPC share if no descendants. If the decedent is survived by a spouse, but by no descendants, the spouse receives the entire estate if the decedent also was not survived by a parent. But if the decedent was survived by one or both parents, the spouse's UPC share is the first $200,000, plus ¾ of the balance—considerably more, as you would expect, than it would be if the decedent was survived by one or more descendants of another relationship.

2. Surviving Spouse's Share in Non-UPC States

The UPC provisions for a surviving spouse are more generous than those found in the statutes of most non-UPC states, many of which limit the spouse's share to ⅓ or ½ of the decedent's probate estate (typically depending on whether the decedent was survived by descendants and, in some cases, how many).

    a. Decedent not survived by descendants. If the decedent was not survived by any descendants, some states would give the entire estate to the surviving spouse; many others do not alter the spouse's share.

3. Decedent's Probable Intent

Is your state's entitlement for a surviving spouse what most decedents would want? Consider which rule you would prefer if this were your estate, and whether the law of intestacy is likely to be the intent of you or your typical client. If not, a will is required.

a. **Entire estate?** By way of prediction, unless there are children by a former marriage (or perhaps substantial property the decedent received from her family), most decedents (at least those whose estates are not large enough to warrant estate tax planning—generally, requiring over $675,000 in 2000, increasing to $1,000,000 after 2005) probably want the surviving spouses to take the entire estate.

4. Nonprobate Property Ignored

The surviving spouse's intestate share is limited to the probate estate. The surviving spouse may also receive nonprobate property (see Chapter 1) that passes under contract provisions or a right of survivorship, meaning that a surviving spouse may benefit to a much greater extent than the intestate statute anticipates. This especially is true in this age in which nonprobate property (e.g., life insurance, annuities, and joint tenancy) is so common.

a. **Nonprobate property to others.** The decedent would effectively disinherit the spouse to the extent the decedent owned little or no probate property, and most or all of the nonprobate property was arranged to pass to persons other than the surviving spouse. This possibility raises the subject of the spousal elective share, which is discussed in Chapter 10. Although the surviving spouse's intestate share might be reduced, in most jurisdictions such a plan of casual disinheritance will not work.

5. Survivorship

The question necessarily arises in this context (and it also arises with respect to testate decedents and nonprobate property passing by will substitute) whether an heir, devisee, or designated beneficiary *survived* the decedent.

a. *Janus v. Tarasewicz,* 482 N.E.2d 418 (Ill. App. Ct. 1985), is illustrative. Stanley and Theresa (spouses) died after having taken cyanide-laced Tylenol. Stanley was pronounced dead that evening but Theresa, who was placed on life support, was not pronounced dead until two days later. A policy of insurance on Stanley's life named Theresa as the primary beneficiary and his mother as the contingent beneficiary. The insurance company paid the proceeds to Theresa's estate and, after a close review of the medical evidence, the court agreed that Theresa did survive Stanley.

b. **Uniform Simultaneous Death Act.** Unless the decedent's will contains an explicit survivorship condition, in most jurisdictions (including Illinois, the law of which applied in *Janus*) the question of survivorship is determined under the Uniform Simultaneous Death Act: the prospective recipient of property is treated as having predeceased the property owner if there is no sufficient evidence as to the order of deaths. The Act does not apply when, as in *Janus*, there is adequate evidence otherwise.

c. **UPC 120 hour survivorship condition.** To avoid litigation over the order of deaths in cases like *Janus*, UPC §2-104 requires an heir to survive an intestate decedent by 120 hours. (Under UPC §2-702, a similar condition that a beneficiary survive the property owner by 120 hours is imposed when the gift is being made under a will or other dispositive instrument that does not address the survivorship issue.)

6. Common Disaster Clauses

Survivorship provisions should be used to plan for the possibility of multiple deaths that occur in rapid succession. Too often, however, the planning is in the form of a "common disaster" clause that produces more problems than it solves.

a. *Ogle.* For example, in *Ogle v. Fuiten*, 466 N.E.2d 224 (Ill. 1984), the wills of the husband and wife left the estate of the first to die to the other, if the other survived by 30 days, and provided that the estate was to be divided equally between two nephews if the spouses died in a common disaster. The husband died from a stroke; the wife died 15 days later from cancer. Because the wife did not survive the husband by 30 days and they did not die in a common disaster, their estates passed by intestacy to their heirs, who were not the nephews.

i. **Malpractice action.** Predictably, the nephews sued the drafting attorney, who unsuccessfully moved that the claims be dismissed for failure to state a cause of action due to a lack of privity. According to the court, an intended will beneficiary may assert a cause of action for negligence and for breach of contract against an attorney who drafts a will that does not carry out the decedent's intent to benefit the intended beneficiary.

C. DESCENDANTS: REPRESENTATION

If a decedent died intestate and was survived by one or more descendants, the portion of the estate that does not pass to a surviving spouse typically passes to the decedent's descendants, to the exclusion of other relatives such as parents and siblings. For the discussion below on how the share for the decedent's descendants is divided among them, we assume application of a basic rule giving half of an intestate decedent's estate to a surviving spouse, and the other half to the decedent's descendants. (For this example, and all others in these materials, persons represented in parentheses are deceased; all others are living.)

(D) — SS ¹/₂
|
C ¹/₂

Here, if our decedent, D, were survived by a spouse, SS, and one child, C, the division would be half and half between them.

1. Representation

```
(D) —— SS  1/2
 |
(C)
 |
GC  1/2
```

Alternatively, if C were deceased but survived by a descendant, GC, the half C would have received if living would pass down by representation to GC. This illustrates the "right of representation" by which C's descendants stand in C's shoes—represent C—to take what C would have received if living.

a. Equal shares #1

```
        (D) —— SS  1/2
      ┌─────┴─────┐
 1/4  C1          C2  1/4
```

As anyone would predict, two children taking what the surviving spouse did not receive under state law receive in equal shares.

b. Equal shares #2

```
      (D) —— SS  1/2
    ┌───┴───┐
   C1  C2  C3
   1/6  1/6  1/6
```

And here the three children split the half equally among them again. No surprises yet.

c. Representation with equal shares #1

```
        (D) —— SS  1/2
          |
         (C)
      ┌────┴────┐
 1/4  GC1       GC2  1/4
```

Equality applies at every level, in this case among the grandchildren who stand in the shoes of the deceased child.

d.   Representation with equal shares #2

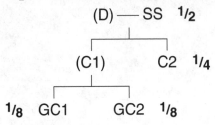

Different here is the combination of equality at the child level—division as if both children were alive—with the concept of representation among the children of C1 (with equality among them as well).

2.   Classic Per Stirpes #1

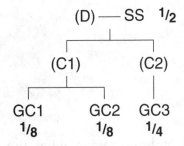

Here, the notion of equality appears to be violated, because three grandchildren are sharing in unequal amounts.

a.   Equality with representation. The logic of this approach (sometimes referred to as "classic" or "strict" per stirpes) is that division occurred at the child level as if both children were alive, and their respective shares then pass to their respective representatives, with equality within each blood line. So, C1's ¼ goes in equal shares to the two representatives of C1, and C2's ¼ goes entirely to the one representative of C2. This is equality with representation as opposed to some form of equal distribution.

b.   Division at child level. Notice the most important factor: division into equal shares at the child level, regardless of whether any children are living.

c.   Equality among blood lines. Notice also that under this approach, each child's blood line will receive the same aggregate share of D's estate regardless of whether a child survived D and subsequently left her share to her descendants or predeceased D and it went to those descendants by the right of representation.

3. Classic Per Stirpes #2

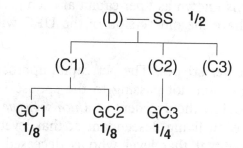

This example just rounds out a notion only implied in the discussion above that, if C3 is deceased and has no representatives who are alive, no share is created for C3 and the distribution is exactly the same as in the prior illustration. This is true if C3 never had descendants, or if all of C3's descendants also predeceased D.

4. Per Stirpes: Equal Division and Representation

With shocking frequency among poorly drafted documents you find the language "in equal shares, per stirpes." As the last two examples reveal, per stirpes distribution is not a system that produces equality. It is based on the two concepts of equal division and representation, but it does not guarantee equality among what appear to be similarly situated beneficiaries.

a. **"In equal shares, per stirpes."** What drafters of this language probably mean is "in equal shares, with the right of representation." But because per stirpes means more than just the principle of representation, the phrase "in equal shares, per stirpes" has led to all sorts of judicial interpretations trying to ferret out the decedent's intent (which is to say the intent of the drafter of the document, who usually was not the decedent).

b. **Definition of classic per stirpes.** A traditional definition of "per stirpes" in its classic sense entails two concepts: division into equal shares at the level of the decedent's children—regardless of whether anyone is alive at that level—with one share created for each person at that level who is alive and one share for each person at that level who is deceased with descendants who are alive, coupled with distribution employing the right of representation.

5. The 1969 UPC: Per Capita (Sometimes Mislabeled as "Modern Per Stirpes")

The 1969 version of UPC §2-103(1) altered the classic per stirpes approach to give each of the three grandchildren in the last two examples ⅙, providing equality among the three grandchildren. This is a "per capita" division (sometimes referred to misleadingly as "modern per stirpes" or, more accurately, as "per capita with representation") and it was meant to guarantee equality at more remote levels of descent. It did not achieve equality in the sense that the drafters anticipated, and it was changed in the 1990 version of the UPC to what is known as "per capita at each generation." However, many states still have the old version of the UPC with its per capita system.

a. **Compared with classic per stirpes.** The per capita approach of the old UPC divided the portion not passing to the spouse into equal shares at the first level below the decedent *at which someone was alive*, creating one share for each living descendant at that level and one share for each descendant at that level who is deceased but with descendants who are alive. Thus, the difference from classic per stirpes is at what level the stirps begin: under the old UPC per capita system it is at the first level at which you find a living descendant, while under classic per stirpes it is at the child generation, regardless of whether any of the decedent's children is alive.

b. **Effect of order of deaths.** Notice that, under the per capita system, the grandchildren can receive different sized shares based on the "accident" of the order of deaths.

EXAMPLES AND ANALYSIS

D died intestate survived by a surviving spouse (SS). D had two children (C1 and C2). C1 had two children (GC1 and GC2); C2 had one child (GC3). C2 predeceased D. If the per capita system were applicable and C1 died one day after D (or six days after D, if the jurisdiction has a 120 hour survivorship requirement like UPC §2-104), C1's share would be ¼, and if C1 died intestate and GC1 and GC2 were C1's only heirs, they would receive ⅛ each, while GC3 would receive ¼. By contrast, if C1 died one day before D (or within five days after D in a UPC §2-104 state), the per capita distribution result would obtain, and the three grandchildren each would receive equal ⅙ shares.

i. **Order of deaths.** We will see momentarily that the fortuitousness of the order of deaths can affect the size of shares under the "per capita at each generation" approach of the 1990 UPC. So it is a problem in all but the classic per stirpes approach.

ii. **Intent of the average decedent.** Surveys of lay individuals indicate that they want their grandchildren to share equally if the only takers are grandchildren, which supports the per capita result when a decedent is survived by grandchildren, but not by any children. The problem with those surveys is that they did not ask the respondents whether they would want different sized shares based on the fortuitousness of the order of deaths. Would you? Does your answer depend on whether—in your family—you are on the C1 or the C2 side of the family tree?

6. **Comparison of Classic Per Stirpes, Per Capita (1969 UPC), and Per Capita at Each Generation (1990 UPC)**

a. **Classic per stirpes.** In the next illustration the essential question is where do the stirps begin? Under a classic per stirpes distribution they begin (i.e., the first division is made) at the child level, regardless of the fact that no children are living. The size of each share is illustrated, and again the lack of uniformity among ostensibly similarly situated beneficiaries is apparent.

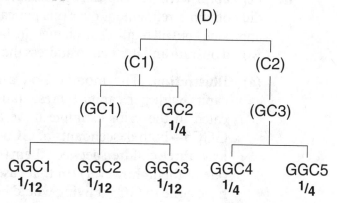

b. **Per capita.** A per capita distribution like that provided for by the 1969 UPC starts the division at the first level at which a descendant is living, which is the grandchild level here. Under that approach, the division is into three shares at the grandchild level, one for each who is alive and one for each who is deceased with descendants who are alive. The curious thing is that, under per capita, the two shares created for representatives of deceased grandchildren in this example would pass by representation in the same manner as in the classic per stirpes distribution, meaning that the great grandchildren still receive unequal shares. To illustrate:

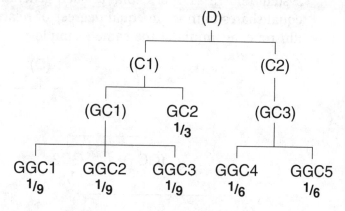

i. **After first division, same as classic per stirpes.** Here the ⅓ shares created at the grandchild level pass to representatives of deceased grandchildren just like in a classic per stirpes distribution, which produces inequality at the next generation down the ladder: equal shares among grandchildren, but not among great grandchildren. This is because the only change per capita made was in dividing the estate the first time: the stirps begin at the first level at which someone is alive, rather than at the first level below the decedent. But after making that one change, everything else remains the same. If the object is to treat similarly situated beneficiaries (i.e., the great grandchildren in this example) alike, this system does not accomplish that result.

ii. **Per capita with per capita representation.** The old (1969) UPC did contain a refinement over this per capita with representation approach, but it requires a change in facts to illustrate when it would operate and it failed to address the inequality shown above.

(a) **Illustration.** The modification can be referred to as per capita with per capita representation and would be implicated in the prior example if we assume that GGC4 and GGC5—both descendants of GC3—both are deceased and leave three children between them (not all the children of just one of them, however). In that case the ⅓ share that would have gone to GC3 if living would be divided equally among these three great, great grandchildren in equal shares of ⅑ each (rather than ⅙ to one of them and 1/12 to the other two) as a per capita distribution among GC3's grandchildren.

(b) **Reliability of lay surveys.** If you're having a little trouble with all this, consider again those surveys of lay individuals that "informed" these statutory reforms: how reliable are they if the respondents did not consider all these permutations?

c. **Per capita at each generation.** New (1990) UPC §2-106 adopted a system known as "per capita at each generation," which guarantees equal shares to those in equal degrees of relation to the decedent. To illustrate, again under the same example:

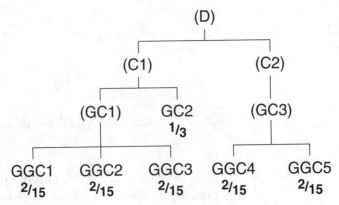

i. **Equality at each generation.** What happens here is that, as with the per capita approach of the 1969 UPC, the division is first made at the level at which someone is alive—the grandchild level here—with one share for each who is living and one for each who is deceased with descendants who are living. The difference is that the shares created for descendants of deceased grandchildren are distributed differently. Here their ⅔ of the estate is distributed in equal shares among the great grandchildren who stand in the shoes of deceased grandchildren (that is, any children of GC2 are excluded), which creates five equal shares of the ⅔ that is available. Now you find equality within each generation.

ii. **Effect of order of deaths.** Again, the intended equality is subject to the death lottery: in the example above, if GC3 had survived D by a day (or by 6 days, if a 120 hour survivorship requirement like UPC §2-104 applies), then ⅓ would have gone to GC3 and only the remaining ⅓ would be distributed to the three great grandchildren representing GC1, giving them each ⅑ rather than ²⁄₁₅. The order of deaths still can make a difference. Only the classic per stirpes approach avoids that issue, and one more: per capita at each generation, like original per capita, rewards the more prolific blood lines because the more children represented, the more a bloodline benefits.

EXAMPLES AND ANALYSIS

To focus better on the difference between the two UPC per capita distribution systems (per capita [1969 UPC] v. per capita at each generation [1990 UPC]), consider another example. Because under both systems the stirps begin at the first level at which a descendant is living, we consider only the number of living grandchildren and grandchildren who are deceased with descendants who are alive. We exclude the child level because we assume all children are deceased.

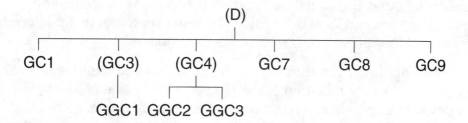

In this example (which assumes GC2, GC5, and GC6 predeceased D and that none of their descendants survived D), six equal shares would be created, four of which would be allocated to the living grandchildren.

Under the per capita system of the old UPC the remaining two shares would pass by representation and the distribution will vary based on whether GC3 and GC4 had the same or different parents: if they were children of the same parent the three great grandchildren would share equally but, if they had different children of D as parents, GGC1 would take one share as GC3's only child, and the other would pass in equal shares to the two children of GC4. Thus, under the old UPC per capita with per capita representation, GGC1's share might be twice as large (⅙) as the shares of GGC2 and GGC3 (1/12 each). The new UPC per capita at each generation approach would take the two unallocated shares and divide the ⅙ shares of GC3 and GC4 equally among the great grandchildren who stand in their shoes, giving each of those three great grandchildren an equal ⅑ share.

7. Modified Per Stirpes

There is one other modification that deserves mention. In some per stirpes states, if all the takers are in the same degree of relation (e.g., all are grandchildren, because no children are alive and because there are no great grandchildren representing deceased grandchildren) the traditional per stirpes division is abandoned and the takers receive equal shares. Usually this "modified per stirpes" approach does not apply if there is *any* taker who is not in the same degree as the rest, so it is not the same as either the 1969 UPC per capita or the 1990 UPC per capita at each generation approach. And because of the factual requisite, it also is not very likely to apply.

EXAM TIP

In thinking through a representation question, make sure your answer is consistent with the following:

1. Under the classic per stirpes system, each line of descendants receives, in the aggregate, an equal share of the intestate estate. Thus, if D had two children, A and B, and if D is survived by A or any descendant of A, and by B or any descendant of B, half of D's estate will pass to A or A's descendants and the other half will pass to B or B's descendants.

2. The only difference between the classic per stirpes and traditional per capita systems is the determination of the level at which equality among the lines of descent occurs. Under classic per stirpes, equality occurs at the child level regardless of whether any children survive the decedent. Thus, if D's two children, A and B, both predeceased D (and each was survived by at least one descendant who survived D), A's descendants will share half of the estate

and B's will receive the other half regardless of how many descendants of each survive D. By contrast, under the traditional per capita system, the generational level at which lines of descent of the decedent take equal shares is not necessarily the child level; rather, it is the level closest to the decedent at which there is a living descendant. After that determination is made, traditional per capita operates exactly like classic per stirpes. Thus, if D's two children, A and B, each predeceased D and if at least one grandchild of D survived D, the distribution of D's estate under a per capita system would be at the grandchild level the same as with the rest of the distribution under classic per stirpes.

3. Only the per capita at each generation system ensures that all members of each generation of descendants who are entitled to receive a share receive equal inheritances. Thus, under per capita at each generation all grandchildren who are heirs always will receive equal shares of the estate, as will all great grandchildren, all great, great grandchildren, etc. That is not necessarily the case under the other systems.

D. ANCESTORS AND COLLATERALS

If an intestate decedent is survived by descendants, typically whatever does not pass to a surviving spouse will pass to the descendants (with the representation questions discussed above). If there are no descendants, but a spouse survives, in some states the spouse will receive the entire estate. In others (e.g., under UPC §2-102(1)) that will be the case only if there also is not some other heir, such as a surviving parent or descendant of a parent. If the decedent is not survived by any descendants, the portion of the estate, if any, that does not pass to a surviving spouse is divided among ancestors and collaterals.

1. Parents

If one or both parents survive, in most states the estate of an intestate decedent who is not survived by descendants and that does not pass to a surviving spouse passes to the parents in equal shares or, if only one parent is alive, then all to that parent.

a. **Limitations on the right to inherit.** Under the law of several states a parent who abandoned the decedent as a child is precluded from benefitting. This might include a parent who divorced the decedent's parent who had custody, and then failed to satisfy any obligations of support. In some jurisdictions, the law might go farther to exclude a parent who stopped being a parent to the decedent. For example, the UPC allows a parent to inherit from an intestate child only if the parent openly treated the decedent as a child and did not refuse to support the child. UPC §2-114(c).

    b. **If no surviving parent.** If there is no living parent (and no descendants of the decedent), some jurisdictions (e.g., UPC §2-102(1)(i)) would leave the entire estate to the surviving spouse, while others would leave the share the parents would have received to descendants of the parents.

2. Parents' Descendants

If a decedent dies intestate not survived by any descendant, whatever the spouse and parents do not take will pass to descendants of the decedent's parents, by representation under the per stirpes, per capita, or per capita at each generation system.

3. More Remote Heirs: The Parentelic System

If there is no descendant, and no parent or descendant of a parent alive to take, some states follow the "parentelic system" under which whatever property the spouse does not take goes up and back down the family tree again. Assuming no grandparents or other ancestors of the decedent are living, the estate is given per stirpes to the living descendants of the nearest lineal ancestor of whom descendants are living.

    a. **To grandparents or their descendants.** If the decedent is survived by one or more grandparents or one or more descendants of deceased grandparents, the estate would be divided among them, with half to the maternal grandparents (or their descendants, with rights of representation, if neither maternal grandparent is living) and the other half to the paternal grandparents (or their descendants, with rights of representation, if they are not living).

    b. **To more remote ancestors or their descendants.** If the decedent is not survived by any descendant, parent, descendant of parents, grandparent, or descendant of grandparents, in states that follow the parentelic system the estate would be distributed to great grandparents, or their descendants by right of representation, and if none, to great, great grandparents, or their descendants by right of representation, etc. The UPC, however, does not recognize as heirs relatives who are more remote than grandparents and their descendants.

4. More Remote Heirs: The Degree of Relationship System

If an intestate decedent is not survived by any descendant, parent, or descendant of parents, some states do not follow the parentelic system of determining the decedent's heirs by passing up and down the family tree but instead abandon representation and distribute the portion not passing to a spouse (the entire estate if there also is no surviving spouse) to more remote family members, with distribution typically in equal shares to all who fall within the nearest degree of consanguinity, with no right of representation. Degrees of consanguinity are determined by adding (1) the number of steps from the decedent up to the nearest common ancestor of the decedent and the relative to the number of steps down from the common ancestor to the relative.

5. **Illustration #1**

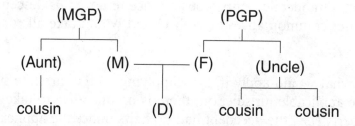

a. **Application of the degree of the relationship method.** Under the degree of relationship method, the cousins are all in the fourth degree of consanguinity, determined by counting the number of steps up to the common ancestor (in each case a grandparent) and then down to the cousin. Here the three of them would share the estate in equal ⅓ shares.

b. **Application of the parentelic method.** Under the parentelic method, we would look for the nearest lineal ancestor of the decedent of whom any descendant is alive and distribute the property per stirpes to that ancestor's descendants. Here again, the three cousins would take, but in this case the cousin on the maternal side would take half and those on the paternal side ¼ each because division is on a per stirpes basis.

6. **Illustration #2**

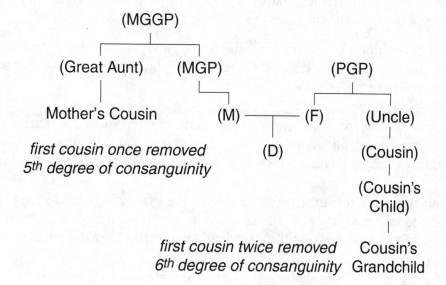

    a.   Application of the degree of relationship method. In this illustration, under the degree of relationship method, Mother's Cousin, as a first cousin once removed in the fifth degree, would take all.

    b.   Application of parentelic method. But under the parentelic method, Cousin's Grandchild, a first cousin twice removed, is descended from the closer common ancestor with D and would take all.

7. Escheat

Escheat is what would apply if, after applying all the intestate succession rules of the applicable jurisdiction, there is no one alive to take the decedent's property (i.e., the decedent had no heirs under the applicable set of rules), in which case the estate would escheat to the state.

    a.   "Laughing heirs." In some states, the statute of descent and distribution limits the extent to which ancestors and collaterals of remote degree are considered heirs (e.g., UPC §2-103 limits heirs to grandparents and their descendants). This so-called "laughing heir" limitation is designed to preclude property passing to someone who is so removed from the decedent as not to be personally affected by the decedent's death, but who would, if allowed to take, laugh all the way to the bank.

EXAM TIP

Intestate succession varies from state to state; the answer to a particular question will depend on the intestacy statute of the governing jurisdiction. In analyzing such questions, though, consider the following approach:

1. First determine the surviving spouse's share; depending on what other relatives survive the decedent and the governing law, the surviving spouse may receive the entire estate.

2. If not, or if there is no surviving spouse, next consider the shares of the decedent's descendants and the representation issue. In most jurisdictions whatever the surviving spouse does not receive will pass to descendants.

3. If no descendants survive the decedent, the governing statute may dictate that the entire estate pass to the surviving spouse; if not, or if there is no surviving spouse, usually the decedent's parents are next in line.

4. If the decedent also is not survived by either parent (or if the surviving parent or parents do not take the entire estate), next in priority are siblings of the decedent and descendants of deceased siblings, by representation.

5. If the decedent is not survived by a spouse, any descendant, any parent, any sibling, or any descendant of a sibling, the estate will pass to more remote family members, generally either under the parentelic or degree of relationship system.

6. If there still are no takers, the estate will escheat. Remember that under the UPC a relative who is not a grandparent of the decedent, or a descendant of a grandparent of the decedent, cannot be an heir.

E. PARTIAL INTESTACY

A decedent may die testate, but with a will that does not effectively dispose of her entire estate. In such a case, the decedent died partially intestate.

 # EXAMPLES AND ANALYSIS

D's will left $1,000 to the Red Cross and the residue of her estate to her friend, F. D's will did not provide an alternative devisee in the event F died before D. If that occurred, D's will still would be valid. The Red Cross would receive $1,000, and the residue of the estate would pass to D's heirs under the jurisdiction's intestate succession statute. (The devise to F is said to "lapse," or fail; it would not pass to F's successors. In many states, "anti-lapse" statutes prevent devises from lapsing, and instead result in the property passing to the devisee's descendants, by representation, but such statutes usually only apply to devises to specified relatives. See Chapter 8 for a discussion.)

1. Failure of Part of Residuary Gift

If the testator's will left half of her estate to her friend, A, and the other half to her friend, B, and if A predeceased the testator but B survived, the old common law rule was that the half left to A would pass to the testator's heirs by intestacy. In the majority of states today the entire estate would go to B. (See UPC §2-604(b)). Would you guess that to be the intent of most testators if they thought about this occurrence?

2. Negative Wills

Assume that a testator expressly disinherits a family member—let's say a child—with language in the will stating that the child will take nothing under the will or by intestacy. What if the testator then dies partially intestate? If the child otherwise would be an heir of the testator's estate, will the child take an intestate share or will the provision in the testator's will, sometimes referred to as a "negative will" with respect to the child, preclude the child from taking?

a. **Intestate succession statute controls.** In most states, the partial intestacy will result in the child taking under the intestate succession statute despite the will provision specifically disinheriting the child. The theory is that the property undisposed of by the will passes outside of its terms to the decedent's heirs as determined solely by the jurisdiction's intestacy statute.

b. **UPC §2-101(b)** allows the testator to override application of the intestate succession statute by use of a negative will. If the testator then dies partially intestate, the part of the estate that otherwise would have passed to the disinherited heir passes as if the heir had disclaimed the intestate share. (See pages 50-53 as to disclaimers.)

F. QUESTIONS OF DEFINITION AND STATUS

Difficult questions may arise as to whether a person is related to the decedent within the meaning of the jurisdiction's intestate succession statute to be an heir of the decedent.

1. Spouse

In all states the spouse of a decedent is an heir. Marital status also is critical for a variety of other reasons, including determining whether the survivor is entitled to receive an elective share, or has homestead and family allowance rights (see Chapter 10). Also, a will, insurance policy, or retirement plan may designate the decedent's "spouse" as a beneficiary.

a. **Divorce or annulment.** If the decedent and her spouse were divorced prior to her death, the former spouse will not be treated as a spouse for intestate succession purposes. (See Chapter 4 for a discussion of the effect of divorce on provisions for the former spouse in a will, trust agreement, or other dispositive instrument.) A similar result may obtain if a marriage is annulled. See, e.g., UPC §2-802(a).

b. **Formal separation.** If the parties enter into a decree of separation that does not terminate their relationship as husband and wife, they will not be treated as divorced and, upon the death of one, the other will be treated as his or her surviving spouse. This might change if an order issued purporting to terminate all marital property rights. UPC §§2-802(a) and (b)(3), and 2-213(d).

c. **Desertion or adultery.** Generally, desertion or adultery will not affect the marital status of the parties, or otherwise bar the offending party from exercising rights as a surviving spouse on the other's death.

d. **Common law marriages.** In a minority of jurisdictions persons who live together as husband and wife and hold themselves out to the public as such, but who have not participated in a formal marriage ceremony, will be treated as being married to each other.

2. Posthumous Heirs

A posthumous child is one who is conceived before, but who is born after, the decedent's death. Usually such a child can take as an heir of the parent, because posthumous children are treated as born at conception if they subsequently are born alive. This may be limited to children of the decedent and not apply with respect to other representatives, depending on state law.

3. Children of Aided Conception

The question of status as a child will take on new significance with respect to children of aided conception, but most state laws probably will follow the Uniform Status of Children of Assisted Conception Act and treat those whose birth is engineered (e.g., artificial insemination with the frozen sperm of a long deceased "father") as not the children of the gamete providers, meaning that these advances should not alter traditional estate planning concepts. We return to this concept on pages 42-43.

4. Half-Bloods and Step-Siblings

Most states no longer discriminate against adopteds or nonmarital children, but some still provide different shares for half-bloods (meaning relatives who share only one common ancestor):

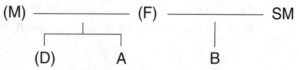

a. **Majority rule for half-bloods.** A is a full-blooded sibling of D but B is a sibling of the half-blood. In most jurisdictions (e.g., UPC §2-107) A and B would share equally in D's estate. In a few states half-bloods receive half the share received by a whole-blooded relative or the whole-blooded relative is favored to the exclusion of a half-blood.

EXAMPLES AND ANALYSIS

Child A and children B and C are half-bloods, related through a common mother but with different fathers:

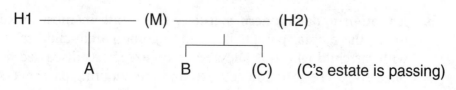

If C's estate were passing to M's descendants, it would go in equal shares to A and B in most states. UPC §§2-103(3) and 2-107. In states that provide the half-blood with only half the share of a whole-blood, C's full sibling B would take ⅔ and half-sibling A would take ⅓ of C's estate. *Beware* the math: some students would say that B takes ½ and, because A should receive half of that amount, would give ¼ to A. That leaves the final ¼ undisposed of, which is wrong. The easy way to figure this out is to count noses: two shares for B and one share for A makes three shares into which the estate is to be divided, with allocation of two to B and one to A to dispose of all C's property.

---

b. **Step-siblings.** With half-bloods, compare *step*-siblings, who share no common blood:

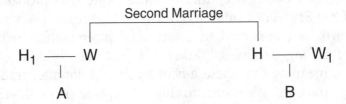

A and B have parents who are married, but A and B have no common ancestors between them.

  i. **Step-siblings are not heirs.** Although most states do not discriminate between siblings of the whole and the half-blood, few states would regard step-siblings as related at all.

5. **Aliens**

Most modern statutes have no discrimination against aliens (i.e., non-U.S. citizens). See, e.g., UPC §2-111. In some states, however, aliens are discriminated against, although the nature of the special treatment varies.

6. **Adoption**

Adoption statutes since the 1950s in most jurisdictions generally treat adopted children as natural born.

a. **Common law stranger to the adoption rule.** Under the common law adopteds inherited *from* both their natural and adoptive parents, but only inherited *through* their natural parents. Adopteds did not inherit *through* their adoptive parents due to the "stranger to the adoption" rule.

b. **Adoption under modern statutes.** By statute in most jurisdictions today, the natural parents have no ongoing parent-child relationship with the child who was adopted away (except, as discussed below, in the step-parent adoption context) and the adopting parents take their place for all purposes, making the adopted child the same as a natural born for all purposes, even to inherit through the adopting parents from the adopting parents' relatives. See, e.g., UPC §2-114.

  i.   **Summary chart.** The following chart compares the effect of adoption on the right to inherit by intestate succession under the common law and under most modern statutes:

Common Law			Modern Statutes	
Natural	*Adoptive*		*Natural*	*Adoptive*
Yes	Yes	Adopted Inherit From?	No	Yes
Yes	No	Adopted Inherit Through?	No	Yes
Yes	No	Parents Inherit From and Through?	No	Yes

 ii.   **Adoption by a relative.** In some jurisdictions there are additional statutory provisions, like UPC §2-113, directed at cases such as grandparent (or other relative) adoptions, in which the intent is to limit the beneficiary to only one share of the decedent's estate.

 # EXAMPLES AND ANALYSIS

If child (C) bears a child (G) and then dies, leaving G to be raised by C's parents, who adopt G, the question is whether, if C's parents die intestate, G should inherit from the adopting parents as a child, as a grandchild representing C, or as both. Adoption statutes typically would cause G to inherit only as a child of the adopting parents.

iii.   **Adoption by a step-parent.** Typically a special rule also applies if a natural parent is married to an adopting parent. See, e.g., UPC §2-114(b).

  (a)   **Inheritance from and through natural parents.** Unlike the statute in *Hall v. Vallandingham*, 540 A.2d 1162 (Md. Ct. Spec. App. 1988), in which adoption by a step-parent cut a child off from inheriting from ancestors of a deceased natural parent, many of the most thoughtful statutes provide that adoption in this context does not cut the child off from either natural parent or their ancestors. Such statutes allow the child to "triple-dip" in the sense that the child could inherit from and through both natural parents and the adopting step-parent as well.

(b)   **UPC** §2-114 follows this approach of allowing a child adopted by a step-parent to inherit from and through both natural parents and the adopting parent. With respect to the converse situation and only with the natural parent who is not the spouse of the adopting parent, however, the parent/child relationship is terminated by the adoption, thus precluding that natural parent from inheriting from or through the child. In addition, the UPC more broadly disallows either natural parent, or their kin, from inheriting from or through the child, unless the natural parent has openly treated the child as her own and has not refused to support the child.

 ## EXAMPLES AND ANALYSIS

Father and Mother, natural parents of Child, divorce. Mother remarries and her new husband, H, adopts Child. (Note that, under most state adoption laws, such an adoption effectively terminates the parent/child relationship between Father and Child and could only occur if Father either consents to the adoption or has his parental rights terminated, such as for refusal to pay child support.) The inheritance issues are whether Child may inherit from or through Father, and whether Father may inherit from or through Child. Under the UPC, Child—and Child's descendants—may inherit from and through Father, but neither Father nor his relatives may inherit from or through Child.

    iv.   **Adoption following natural parents' deaths.** Application of these rules can yield inappropriate and inequitable results when the adoption follows the deaths of the natural parents.

 ## EXAMPLES AND ANALYSIS

Father and Mother die in an automobile accident. Mother's sibling adopts Child. The unfortunate reality is that, in many states (and under UPC §2-114(b)), this will cut off the child from Father's family and they from the child, which probably is an unintended result and thoroughly inappropriate. Further, had the adoption been by someone not related to Mother, in most states (including those that have adopted the UPC) the child would be cut off from *both* natural lines and they from the child.

---

c. **Effect of adoption on class gifts under wills, trust agreements, and other dispositive instruments.** Most of the adoption discussion above addresses inheritance issues involving adopteds in the intestacy context. Absent a provision in a will, trust agreement, or other dispositive instrument to the contrary, those rules may also apply to the question of whether a person qualifies as a member of a class to whom a gift is made under a will, trust agreement, or other dispositive instrument. For example, if a will gives $10,000 to each of the testator's nieces and nephews, will an adopted child of a sibling of the testator take? Under the old "stranger to the adoption" rule, the answer would be "no," while under the law of many states and the UPC the answer would be "yes." UPC §2-705(a).

7. **Virtual Adoption**

Virtual, or equitable, adoption is a doctrine under which someone who has not been formally adopted may, in certain circumstances, nevertheless be treated for inheritance purposes as having been adopted. It is a creature of equity, designed to protect a child against the consequences of reliance on an adoption that was not (properly) performed, the concept being that the child should not be punished just because the purported parent never did what she alleged she would to adopt the child.

a. **Requirements.** Under Georgia case law (and it is Georgia that has pioneered the concept), a person is virtually adopted despite there having been no formal adoption if (1) there is an agreement for adoption between the person's natural and adopting parents, (2) the natural parents give up custody, (3) the child lives with the adopting parents, and (4) the adopting parents treat the child as a natural child.

b. *O'Neal.* The concept is not universally recognized and, even where it is, it may not be totally effective. For example, in *O'Neal v. Wilkes*, 439 S.E.2d 490 (Ga. 1994), the child was not acknowledged by her natural father, her mother died, and she was placed with the couple who raised her as their natural child by another family member. When the putative father died intestate, the child claimed an intestate share as an equitably adopted child. The court denied virtual adoption because no one with authority to consent to the adoption did so. The dissent argued— persuasively, in our view—that this turns equity and the object of the virtual adoption rule on their head, because it certainly was not the child's fault that this lack of authority existed.

   c. **Virtual adoption parents and their relatives are not heirs of the child.** *Estate of Riggs*, 440 N.Y.S.2d 450 (1981), properly held that equitable adoption does not apply to let the alleged adopting parents' relatives inherit through those parents from a deceased "virtually adopted" child, making it clear that virtual adoption is a one-way street: the child may rely on what should have been done but the parents and those claiming through them cannot.

   d. **Other virtual adoption issues.** May a virtually adopted child of A inherit through A? The cases go both ways.

8. **Common Adoption Issues**

Two major issues involving wills and trust agreements exist under most adoption statutes.

   a. **Retroactivity.** First, are adopteds treated as natural born under documents that were in existence or in effect before a statute treating adopteds as natural born was enacted (e.g., a testator dies before enactment with a will that creates a trust as to which it is necessary to determine in the future if an adopted child is a beneficiary of the trust)? Many statutes did not provide for retroactive application to pre-existing documents and typically the law in effect at a decedent's death will govern for all purposes in the future construction and interpretation of that decedent's will. Thus, in many such instances the old stranger to the adoption rule would apply. *Some statutes, however, have been amended to allow full retroactivity.*

   b. **Applicability to class gifts.** Second, many statutes appear on their face to apply only to intestate distribution, leaving open the question of their effect on a class gift (such as to "grandchildren" or "nieces and nephews") made in a will or inter vivos trust. UPC §2-705 covers all three situations, but many statutes are silent regarding applications other than under intestacy. Because the common law stranger to the adoption rule is not favored even without a statute, the predictable result is that courts will search for a way to apply the intestacy adoption statute in cases involving dispositive instruments, but the failure of such a statute to address such circumstances can be seen as an indication that the state legislature did not so intend.

9. **Nonmarital Children**

Nonmarital (out of wedlock, illegitimate, or bastard) children were *filius nullius* (the "child of nobody") at common law: they simply did not exist and had no inheritance rights or other status under the law.

   a. **Prevalence in the United States.** The scope of the issue of how nonmarital children are to be treated should not be underestimated in America today: in recent years, of total births, approximately 30% are nonmarital and, of the total American population under the age of 18, more than a quarter were nonmarital. Nonmarital children cut across all racial and economic lines, as illustrated by the "Murphy Brown" episode made famous by Dan Quayle in the 1992 presidential campaign, and by many famous wealthy individuals (such as Mick Jagger, Sting, Mike Tyson, Jerry Hall, Steve Garvey, Jessica Lange, Ryan O'Neill, and Farrah Fawcett, to name just a few) who have nonmarital children.

b. **Nonmarital children under intestate succession statutes; mother and child.** The typical intestacy statute today will allow a nonmarital child to inherit from its mother and vice versa. Although they also may inherit *through* each other in most states, in a few states they may not.

c. **Nonmarital children under intestate succession statutes; father and child.** *Trimble v. Gordon*, 430 U.S. 762 (1977), held unconstitutional under the equal protection clause of the Fourteenth Amendment an Illinois statute prohibiting a nonmarital child from inheriting from her father who died intestate and whose paternity had been established in a paternity suit during the father's lifetime.

   i.   **Permissible disparate treatment.** Only legitimate state interests may be effected by statutes that limit the rights of nonmarital children and, in the process, discriminate against those children. For example, states may address concerns regarding the orderly administration of estates and subsequent proof of title by a nonmarital child claiming parentage after the purported parent no longer is alive and able to defend against the charge. Thus, a year after its decision in *Trimble*, the Supreme Court held valid a New York statute that precluded a nonmarital child from inheriting from an intestate father unless the father had married the mother or his paternity had been established in a proceeding during his life. *Lalli v. Lalli*, 439 U.S. 259 (1978).

   ii. **Proof of paternity.** States may treat nonmarital children differently than marital children, if done in a rational way to further a legitimate state interest, such as efficient administration of estates and protecting against unfounded claims of paternity. Thus, the focus of statutes dealing with the rights of nonmarital children is how paternity is established. Statutes usually include one or more of the following as acceptable means: (i) litigation resulting in a judicial determination of paternity; (ii) subsequent marriage by a man to the child's mother—sometimes with the additional requisite of acknowledgement of the child or failure to reject the child (notice that, if a man and a woman are married to each other when a child is born, in many states there is a conclusive presumption that the man is the child's father, even if it can be proven that he is not); (iii) simple acknowledgement, although what constitutes an adequate acknowledgement that the child is the person's child will vary from state to state; and (iv) a determination of paternity made after the father's death during the probate administration of his estate, such as by DNA evidence.

d.   Inheritance from the nonmarital child. Remember that these issues can work in reverse. UPC §2-114(c) addresses the question of a parent inheriting from a nonmarital child, with only proof of abandonment (i.e., failure to openly treat the child as her own or refusal to support the child) serving to preclude the parent from benefitting from the child's death.

10.   Children of the New Biology

Hecht v. Superior Court, 20 Cal. Rptr. 2d 275 (Cal. Ct. App. 1993), is illustrative of the kinds of cases that may arise with increasing frequency because of the growing trend towards artificial insemination, embryo and gamete transplants, and surrogate motherhood, often without benefit of formal adoption, filiation, or (in some cases) knowledge or a record of what has occurred. In *Hecht* the court upheld a devise to the decedent's girlfriend of sperm that he had stored with a sperm bank. Such cases raise the question of whether a child conceived after the death of a sperm donor can inherit as an heir of the donor, and the difficulties such a result could pose to the timely administration and distribution of the donor's estate. The Uniform Status of Children of Assisted Conception Act provides that the donor in this kind of situation will not be treated as the parent of a child conceived after the donor's death.

a.   Artificial conception statutes. In some jurisdictions statutes have been adopted under which an artificially conceived birth is treated as natural, and the husband of the mother is treated as the natural father—even if there is positive proof that his paternity is a biological impossibility.

b.   Sperm or egg donor. Moreover, in a case like *Hecht*, under the developing law the man who provided the sperm or the woman who provided the egg would not be the parent of the resulting child unless the woman carried the child and the man was the mother's husband.

c.   Surrogate motherhood. With respect to surrogate motherhood, the wife of the natural father may not be the mother without a formal adoption, and the law will need to wrestle with the historical notion that motherhood is the easy side of most questions of status (because, at least in "the old days," the natural mother typically could prove the parent/child relationship). Historically it was the natural father that was uncertain of proof, and that issue has not been made any easier in cases of assisted conception involving implants or transplants of embryos. But today the risk of multiple "mothers" exists and raises questions of status that historically were reserved for fathers.

G. LIMITATIONS ON INHERITANCE

1. Homicide

Homicide is a pervasive bar to inheritance rights under intestate succession statutes (as well as under a will or other dispositive instrument), based on the equitable maxim that "no one may profit by a wrong committed."

a. **Judicially imposed bar.** Although many questions can arise even in the majority of jurisdictions that now have statutes addressing the subject, the more difficult cases are those in states in which there is no governing statute. For example, *In re Estate of Mahoney*, 220 A.2d 475 (Vt. 1966), presented the Vermont Supreme Court with the question of what to do about a wife who killed her husband (who died intestate), was convicted of manslaughter, and was his sole heir under Vermont's intestate succession statute. In holding that legal title to estate assets descended to the wife under the intestacy statute, to be received by her in constructive trust (see Chapter 11) for the decedent's other heirs, the court rejected the alternatives of (i) allowing the slayer to take without restriction on the ground that disqualification would be an improper added form of punishment, or (ii) disfranchising slayers by treating them as having predeceased the victim.

b. **Slayer statutes.** Several illustrations show that, although most states now have statutes prohibiting at least some killers from inheriting, there is great disparity among approaches and there are many glitches in the statutes that apply from state to state.

   i. **Who takes if the slayer does not?** If A kills D and is thus barred from sharing in D's estate, the issue is who should receive the part of D's estate that A would have received (either as an heir of D, if D died intestate, or as a devisee, if D died with a will that devised property to A) if A had not killed D? There are at least three approaches that states take to this issue. First, some statutes (e.g., UPC §2-803) provide that the slayer's share passes as if the slayer had disclaimed it. Second, in some states the slayer's share will pass as if the slayer had predeceased the victim. (As illustrated below, that approach will not always yield the same result as the disclaimer approach.) Third, some statutes provide that property that would have gone to the slayer passes to the victim's other heirs.

   ii. **Slayer's descendants.** Difficult policy questions arise if, for example, P leaves property to C if living, otherwise to C's descendants who survive P, and C kills P; should C's descendants profit from the wrong committed by C—or should they be punished along with C?

EXAMPLES AND ANALYSIS

Assume a slayer statute provides for the decedent's property that would have passed to the slayer to go instead to the decedent's other heirs. How would such a statute be applied in the following case, if B murdered P and P's will left P's estate to B?

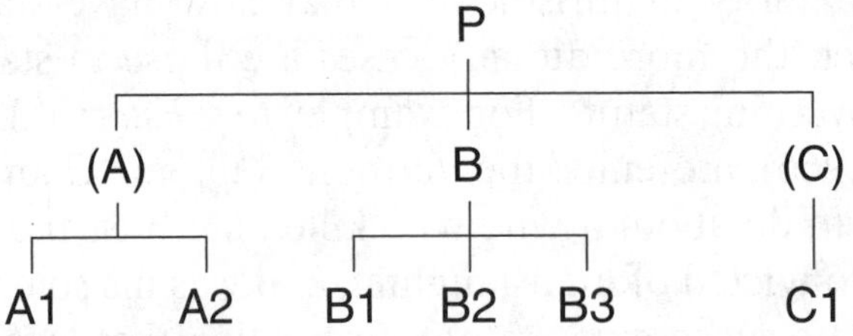

The issue here is whether a per stirpes or per capita distribution is applicable and, if the latter, whether B is treated as predeceased for purposes of determining the size of the shares to be distributed or only for purposes of preventing B from taking the share B otherwise would inherit. If a per capita distribution is applicable and B is treated as actually having predeceased P, then B1, B2, and B3, as well as A1, A2, and C1, each would receive $\frac{1}{6}$ of P's estate. If instead B is treated as having predeceased P only for purposes of preventing B from taking the share B otherwise would inherit, then B1, B2, and B3 each receive $\frac{1}{3}$ of B's $\frac{1}{3}$, or $\frac{1}{9}$ each.

To avoid this kind of question, an enlightened statute would specify (as does UPC §2-803) that B is not treated as predeceased but, rather, as having disclaimed the share to which B otherwise is entitled, in which case B1, B2, and B3 each would receive $\frac{1}{9}$, A1 and A2 each would receive $\frac{1}{6}$, and C1 would receive $\frac{1}{3}$ under a per stirpes or a per capita approach. Under a per capita at each generation system A1, A2, and C1 each would receive $\frac{2}{9}$.

In the above illustration, what would happen if P's will left $\frac{1}{3}$ of P's estate to B (or if P died intestate)? If the governing statute provides that the share the slayer would have received passes by intestacy as if the slayer had predeceased the victim, would B's descendants share the portion B would have received with A1, A2, and C1, or would A1, A2, and C1 take it all? *Misenheimer v. Misenheimer*, 325 S.E.2d 195 (N.C. 1985), held the descendants of B took all of B's share. In doing so, the court stated: "While it may be true that 'the gods visit the sins of the fathers upon the innocent children,'. . . this Court will not do so."

iii. Crimes covered; proof required. Typically, only felonious and intentional killings trigger application of the slayer bar. Thus, a successful insanity defense will prevent operation of most statutory bars, as may conviction of an offense that does not establish intent. Moreover, many statutes require a conviction for the slayer to forfeit an inheritance, meaning that the slayer's death before adjudication of guilt may prevent operation of the bar. If there is no conviction, some more enlightened statutes (e.g., UPC §2-803(g)) permit the probate court to adjudicate the question.

iv.   **Effect of killing on slayer's property interests.** Because the purpose of slayer statutes is to prevent a slayer from profiting from the crime, rather than to impose an additional punishment in the form of a forfeiture, no statute should divest the slayer's own property interests.

 # EXAMPLES AND ANALYSIS

Assume that the slayer is a remainder beneficiary following a life estate in the victim. One way to address the slayer bar issue is for the life estate to be sequestered—paid to the victim's estate or beneficiaries, but to allow the slayer to take the remainder when the victim's life expectancy would have expired—if the slayer still is living. Alternatively, the discounted present value of the life estate could be computed and paid to the victim's estate or beneficiaries—it would be "commuted"—with the remaining property (the value of the remainder) to belong to the slayer.

v.   **Joint tenancies between slayer and victim.** Similarly, assume that the slayer was a joint tenant with the victim, with the right of survivorship. The Restatement of Restitution §188(b) position is that, when the slayer dies, she is deemed to have died first; the slayer therefore is entitled to receive only income and only from half of the property, for the balance of the slayer's natural life. UPC §2-803(c)(2) treats the killing as a severance of the property and a transformation of the interests of the decedent and killer into tenancies in common. (In *Estate of Garland*, 928 P.2d 928 (Mont. 1996), the court held that, if the victim's estate could prove the victim had made more than half of the contributions towards acquisition of the property, the estate's tenancy in common interest in the property would be greater than 50%.) Under both approaches, the policy result is that improvement of the slayer's position is precluded by statute, but the slayer is not punished by a relinquishment of property already owned by the slayer.

    vi. **Life insurance.** Some slayer statutes specifically apply to bar a slayer who is the designated beneficiary from receiving the proceeds of an insurance policy on the victim's life, and insurance contracts typically are more comprehensive than state law, precluding any beneficiary from benefiting if that person caused the insured loss in any way.

2. Disqualification for Other Misconduct

Although relatively rare, in limited circumstances other than homicide a person who engages in wrongful conduct and otherwise would be entitled to share in a decedent's estate will be precluded from doing so.

    a. **Marital misconduct** (adultery or desertion), however, typically will *not* bar inheritance.

    b. **Refusal to support or treat as a child.** Refusal to support or to openly treat a child as such may preclude a parent from inheriting from a child (e.g., UPC §2-114(c)), but this too is not common.

3. Advancements

If P gives child C $10,000, and P then dies intestate, the question is whether the $10,000 gift is an advancement that will operate to count against C's right to an intestate share of P's estate.

    a. **Partial intestacy.** The concept of advancements generally applies only to a *fully* intestate estate. (UPC §2-109, however, applies the concept to partially intestate estates as well.) The logic behind inapplicability to a testate estate is a presumption that a testator would state any intent regarding the effect of prior transfers on dispositions under a subsequently executed will, or was aware of the provisions in an existing will when a gift was made and determined to make the gift anyway. Because the concept of ademption by satisfaction (see Chapter 9) under a will may serve the same purpose for a testate estate as advancement treatment in an intestate estate, be certain to consider application of that theory if the decedent died testate and advancement is not applicable.

    b. **Heirs subject to application of the doctrine.** Historically advancement treatment was applicable only for transfers to children and was based on an assumption—that an intestate would want to treat all children equally—that was not thought to apply in other situations. Nevertheless, many advancement statutes now apply to all descendants, or even to all heirs (see, e.g., UPC §2-109), but frequently *not* to a spouse (the UPC is unusual in that it does apply to a spouse).

    c. **Application to descendants of a deceased donee.** Also at issue is whether descendants of a donee who received an advancement and then predeceased the decedent are charged with those advancements and, conversely, whether an ancestor should be charged with advancements made to the ancestor's descendants.

 ## EXAMPLES AND ANALYSIS

If P made an advancement to C, who predeceased P leaving GC surviving, should GC's entitlement as C's representative be reduced by the advancement to C? Conversely, if P gave the advance to GC but C survived to take, would C's share be adjusted because of the gift to GC? The UPC does not charge advancements down to representatives of an advanced party unless the decedent indicated an intent to do so (§2-109(c)) and fails to even consider charging advancements up to ancestors of recipients.

d. **Proof of intent.** At common law, lifetime gifts to children were presumed to be advancements. Because the doctrine of advancements is not favored, especially with respect to small amounts (think of the administrative difficulties of proving the amounts of gifts made by a parent who died intestate at, say, age 80 to several children over their lifetimes), statutes in most states have reversed the presumption and now require some proof of intent to treat a gift as an advancement.

   i. **Contemporaneous writing.** Usually required is a contemporaneous written declaration by the decedent or an acknowledgement by the donee that the transfer counts against the donee's ultimate distributive share of the transferor's estate. (E.g., UPC §2-109).

   ii. **Change of intent.** If, as under the UPC, the declaration must be contemporaneous with the transfer, the intent that the gift constitute an advancement must exist at the time of the transfer. A subsequent change of heart cannot convert an outright gift into an advancement, although an intent to advance can later be abandoned, making the transfer a gift that will not be charged against the donee's intestate share. A donor can get generous in the future, but not parsimonious. Therefore, a donor who wants to convert an outright gift into an advancement must do so by executing a will that takes the gift into account.

e. **Hotchpot.** "Hotchpot" is the mechanism by which advancements are charged against the recipient's ultimate distributive share. To illustrate, assume that: (1) Decedent's probate estate is $100x; (2) inter vivos advancements (all declared in contemporaneous writings by Decedent) included an outright transfer of $40x to Child A, placement of $60x in joint tenancy with Child B, and an $80x insurance beneficiary designation of Child C; and (3) Child D received nothing.

i. **Calculating the amount of the charge against the donee's inheritance.** Computation of any advancement is at the fair market value when the transfer was made, computed without interest. Note the unfairness in that approach: the recipient receives—but is not charged in the hotchpot process for—the use of the money from the time of the gift to the decedent's death, along with any appreciation.

ii. **Dividing the probate estate.** In this illustration, if all the recipients of lifetime transfers participate in hotchpot (which they likely will not do in this case), each child's share of the probate estate would be determined as follows:

Probate estate at death......................	$100x
Add advancements:	
to Child A.................................	40x
to Child B	60x
to Child C.................................	80x
Total...................................	$280x

divided by four would give each child $70x, which would be reduced by their respective advancements.

(a) **Applicable to insurance?** If it were, would we count the insurance as an advancement at the value of the policy at the time of the beneficiary designation, or at the higher face amount of the proceeds payable at death?

(b) **"Opting out" of hotchpot.** For now, let's assume state law is clear and that the latter is the case. On the basis of that assumption, C cannot benefit from P's probate estate (because C already received $80x, which is more than C's $70x share under hotchpot) so C probably will "opt out" of hotchpot—no one can be forced to participate.

(c) **Calculation.** With C and C's advancement out of the picture, the hotchpot would be recomputed at only $200x, and it would be divided by three to give each of the other three children $66,666x. To reflect amounts that A and B already received, the distribution of P's probate estate would be made as follows:

Child A receives $66.666x - 40x = $26.666x
Child B receives $66.666x - 60x = 6.666x
Child D receives $66.666x - 0x = 66.666x
Total distributions $99.998x

iii. Calculation if insurance is not a part of hotchpot. If C's insurance is not charged as an advancement, the hotchpot would be:

Probate estate at death......................	$100x
Add advancements:	
to Child A...............................	40x
to Child B	60x
Total...................................	$200x

$200x total, divided by four, would give each child $50x. Because B's $60x advancement is greater than the $50x B would receive under hotchpot, B would opt out, leaving:

Probate estate at death......................	$100x
Add advancement to A	40x
Total...................................	$140x

$140x ÷ 3 = $46,666x.

Thus, A would receive $6,666x and both C and D would receive $46,666x, for a total of $99,998x.

4. Release and Assignment; Expectancy

The doctrines of release and assignment relate to the concept of expectancy. Assume that parent, P, who is single, has two children, A and B, and that all three are living. A and B are potential heirs of P; although they have no property rights in P's assets, they each are said to have an "expectancy" with respect to P's assets in that, if P dies intestate, A and B may share in P's estate.

a. **Release.** A release is an agreement between a potential heir and the property owner—sometimes called a "liquidated" or "negotiated" advancement—by which, to continue the example, A could ask for early distribution of A's share of P's estate in exchange for a release of A's expectancy.

b. **If potential heir predeceases.** If, after the release, A dies before P, and P is survived by children of A, those grandchildren of P will be barred by A's release so that B will take the entire estate. An exception to this general rule may apply, however, if B also predeceases P, in which case some jurisdictions will allow A's children to share in P's estate.

c. **Assignment.** An assignment is the transfer for consideration of an expectancy by a potential heir to a third party. In the United States, assignment is not common because the assignee receives only what the assignor is entitled to receive, which is zero if the assignor is disinherited by or predeceases the decedent. Because a prospective assignee of an expectancy has no way to protect the "right" to benefit from the expectancy when the prospective decedent dies, an assignee generally will not be willing to pay much for the assignment (unless the prospective decedent becomes involved in the transaction and contracts or otherwise commits not to take any action that would defeat the assignee's expectancy).

   i. **Effect on predeceased assignor's descendants.** Although a release usually will bind descendants of the releasing potential heir, an assignment will not. Although it is easy to find fault with the distinction, it is said to be based on the fact that a release is an agreement with the decedent—a "negotiated" disinheritance—while an assignment is a contract with a third party to which neither the decedent nor the assignor's representatives were parties.

d. **Consideration.** As a general rule, both releases and assignments are honored only if supported by full and adequate consideration, meaning that what the beneficiary receives is a fair reflection of what she would receive at the decedent's death.

5. **Disclaimers**

A disclaimer, sometimes called a renunciation, is a refusal to accept an inheritance or other property interest. Disclaimers of intestate property were not recognized at common law, but statutes typically now permit them.

 EXAMPLES AND ANALYSIS

P is not married and has one child, C, who also has one child, GC. C could disclaim any inheritance, causing C to be treated as having predeceased P (or, under the UPC approach, the disclaimed interest passes as if C had predeceased P). Thus, if P died intestate, the estate would descend to GC, as C's representative. If P died testate and the will provided for any property disclaimed by C to go to an alternate taker, the will provision would control. If P died testate but the will did not address the possibility of a disclaimer, the devise to C would pass under the terms of P's will as if C had predeceased P. Thus, if P's will or state law provided that the devise to C would go to GC if C died before P, as usually would be the case, a disclaimer by C again would result in GC receiving the property.

a. **Why disclaim?** People most typically disclaim for federal tax reasons or to preclude their creditors from reaching the disclaimed property.

   i. **Tax motivated disclaimers.** In the example above, if the disclaimer is "qualified" under the rules of Internal Revenue Code §2518, it is not regarded as a gift by C to GC; rather, the property disclaimed would be treated for tax purposes as having passed directly from P to GC, meaning that C would have no adverse gift tax consequences.

   ii. **Avoiding creditors.** Generally, disclaimers are effective to preempt most creditors of the disclaimant from reaching the disclaimed party. Courts differ, however, on whether that result applies to the state's claim for reimbursement of a disclaimant's nursing home expenses paid for by Medicaid. According to the court in *Troy v. Hart*, 697 A.2d 113 (Md. App. 1997), it is "ludicrous, if not repugnant, to public policy" for a Medicaid recipient to be able to disclaim an inheritance that would allow the disclaimant to become financially self-sufficient. By contrast, *In re Estate of Kirk*, 591 N.W.2d 630 (Iowa 1999), held that public policy did not allow the state to reach disclaimed assets to satisfy its claim for reimbursement of Medicaid paid nursing home expenses. *Drye v. United States,* — S. Ct. — (1999), held that disclaimer cannot preclude attachment of a federal tax lien.

b. **Qualified disclaimers.** Under Internal Revenue Code §2518 there are a number of technical requirements that must be met for the disclaimer to be qualified for tax purposes (we know you're not surprised—or amused), but the most important aspect of making a qualified disclaimer is being timely, meaning that the disclaimer must be made within nine months of the transfer by which the disclaimant becomes entitled to the property.

   i. **No benefits accepted.** In addition, for the disclaimer to be qualified the disclaimant cannot accept any benefits from the disclaimed property prior to making the disclaimer. Thus, to some extent the nine month period within which to decide whether to disclaim is misleading, particularly for nonprobate property (such as life insurance, retirement plan interests, and joint tenancies with the right of survivorship) that passes directly to the recipient as a result of the decedent's death.

c. **Qualified disclaimers: UPC vs. tax.** In UPC states, beware the fact that the UPC §2-801(b) nine month timing requirement for disclaimers differs from the federal Internal Revenue Code requirement because the UPC measures the nine month period from vesting or the event determining the taker, whereas federal law measures it from the transfer that created the interest, even though it may not be clear who will take the property until many years later when all elements requisite to vesting occur.

 ## EXAMPLES AND ANALYSIS

If the agreement for a trust created in Year 1 provided "to A for life, then to B, if B survives A, otherwise to C," and if B died in Year 20, survived by A and C, the UPC would allow C nine months from the date of B's death in Year 20 to disclaim, while a disclaimer by C generally would not be qualified under the Internal Revenue Code unless it were made within nine months after creation of the trust in Year 1.

    d. Effect of a disclaimer. UPC §2-801(d) provides that the "disclaimed interest" passes as if the disclaimant had predeceased the decedent, rather than providing for the decedent's entire estate to pass under that presumption. The rationale for this carefully drafted provision is to be certain that a disclaimer under the UPC per capita system of representation does not alter the size of other shares of the estate.

 ## EXAMPLES AND ANALYSIS

Assume A disclaims in the following hypothetical:

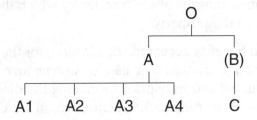

The UPC dictates that A's half interest would pass to A's descendants as if A predeceased O, and not that the entire estate would pass as if A (as well as B) predeceased (in which case C would receive ⅕ rather than half of the estate, and A would be able to increase the size of her children's inheritances from ½ to ⅘).

e. Disclaimers by personal representatives. The 1990 version of UPC §2-801(a) makes clear what the prior UPC and many state statutes do not, that a disclaimer is permissible by a personal representative for a deceased beneficiary. Often the decision to disclaim occurs because the taker dies quickly after the decedent whose estate is passing and an analysis of the tax consequences reveals that such a disclaimer will reduce taxes.

   i. Effect on deceased beneficiary's creditors. Although it is clear that the federal estate tax liability may be reduced in such a manner, state law in many jurisdictions remains unresolved as to whether other creditors may be disfranchised by disclaimers made by personal representatives for deceased beneficiaries. *In re Estate of Heater*, 640 N.E.2d 654 (Ill. App. Ct. 1994), disallowed such a disclaimer because a personal representative must act for the benefit of all parties interested in an estate, including creditors.

6. Survivorship

The UPC imposes a 120 hour survivorship condition on the ability of an heir to inherit from an intestate decedent (and on the ability of a devisee under a will or a beneficiary under another dispositive instrument to take, if the will or other instrument does not address the survivorship issue). Thus, under the UPC, if P dies intestate, survived by an heir (C) who dies within 120 hours after P's death, C will not share in P's estate.

a. Joint tenancy property. What if P and C in the example above owned Blackacre as joint tenants with the right of survivorship, and they died within 120 hours or each other?

   i. Simultaneous deaths. If they died simultaneously (i.e., there was insufficient evidence to determine who died first), the result under the Uniform Simultaneous Death Act would be to treat each as having predeceased the other as to half of the property. Thus, the property would pass as if it had been owned by them as equal tenants in common, with each treated as having survived the other.

   ii. Deaths not simultaneous. If one died after the other, but within 120 hours, the Uniform Simultaneous Death Act would not apply, the survivor would take the entire property, and it would then pass to the survivor's heirs (if the survivor died intestate) or devisees (if the survivor died testate). By contrast, in a UPC jurisdiction, the same result as would be reached under the Uniform Simultaneous Death Act if they died simultaneously would be reached even if one clearly died after, but within 120 hours of the death of, the other. UPC §2-702.

REVIEW QUESTIONS AND ANSWERS

Question: D died intestate. The UPC governs. D was survived by a spouse (S), by one child (C1) from D's marriage to S, by one child (C2) from another relationship, and by one step-child (SC) who is a child of S. D's net probate estate was $250,000. To whom is it distributable and in what amounts?

Answer: S receives the first $100,000, plus half the balance, for a total of $175,000. (D was survived by a descendant of S who was not a descendant of D (SC), and she was survived by a descendant who was not a descendant of S (C2). Accordingly, S's off-the-top amount under the UPC is $100,000. Even though S is more likely to leave property received from D to C1 than to C2, the remaining $75,000 is divided equally between C1 and C2, each receiving $37,500. (That is the case SC is not an heir of D and does not share in the distribution of D's estate.)

Question: How would D's intestate estate be distributed among the following descendants under the three systems for dividing intestate property?

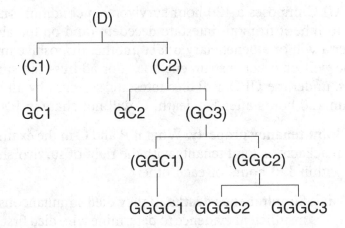

Answer:

	Classic Per Stirpes	Per Capita	Per Capita with Per Capita Representation or Per Capita at Each Generation
GC1	½	⅓	⅓
GC2	¼	⅓	⅓
GGGC1	⅛	⅙	1⁄9
GGGC2	1⁄16	1⁄12	1⁄9
GGGC3	1⁄16	1⁄12	1⁄9

Question: D died intestate, survived for more than 120 hours by her spouse, S; by one child, C; and by her father, F. The UPC governs. To whom is D's net probate estate distributable?

Answer: S might receive the entire estate, but we need additional information. First, if C is not a descendant of S, S's share of D's estate is the first $100,000, plus half the balance; C takes the remainder, if any. Second, even if C is a descendant of S, does S have any other descendant who is not a descendant of D and who survived D by at least 120 hours? If so, S's share is the first $150,000, plus half the balance; C takes the remainder. In either case, because D was survived by a descendant, F will not share in D's estate.

Question: D died intestate, not survived by a spouse, by any descendant, by either parent, or by any descendant of a parent. D was survived by one maternal grandparent, by an uncle (her father's brother), and by two cousins (children of her father's sister). To whom is D's net probate estate distributable?

Answer: It depends on the jurisdiction's law for dividing intestate property among ancestors and collateral relatives. Under the UPC (which follows a parentelic system but does not include as heirs relatives more remote than descendants of grandparents), the maternal grandparent would take half; the other half would be divided among the descendants of D's paternal grandparents by representation (D's uncle would receive ¼; each of D's cousins would receive ⅛). If the jurisdiction employed a degree of relationship system, D's maternal grandparent would receive the entire estate.

Question: If D died intestate, is it more likely that her surviving spouse would receive more of her estate if she died in a UPC or in a non-UPC jurisdiction?

Answer: D's surviving spouse probably would receive more of her estate if the UPC governed than if it did not. Under the UPC, the surviving spouse will receive at least the first $100,000, and half of the balance of the net probate estate. Further, in the still relatively common situation of a decedent being survived by a spouse and by one or more descendants all of whom also are descendants of the spouse, and the spouse not having any descendant from another relationship who survives the decedent, the spouse will receive the entire intestate estate under the UPC. By contrast, in most non-UPC jurisdictions, if the decedent was survived by any descendant the spouse will receive only ⅓ or ½ of the net probate estate.

But under the UPC, if the decedent was not survived by a descendant, the spouse's share is the first $200,000, plus ¾ of the balance, if the decedent was survived by one or both parents; in at least one state (Ohio), the spouse receives the entire estate under that scenario.

Question: Father and Mother had twins, Son and Daughter. Subsequently, Mother married Husband, who adopted Son and Daughter (either with Father's consent, or after Father's parental rights had been terminated, such as for failure to pay child support). Son died intestate, unmarried, and survived by Father, but not by any descendant. Thereafter, Father died intestate, unmarried, and survived by Daughter. Under the UPC, is Father an heir of Son? Is Daughter an heir of Father?

Answer: Under the UPC, the adoption of Son and Daughter by Husband does not terminate the right of Son and Daughter to inherit from (and through) Father because of the step-parent adoption exception to the general rule that adopteds are children of their adopting parents but not their natural parents. Accordingly, Daughter is an heir of Father. The rule does not work in reverse, however; the adoption by Husband of Son and Daughter cuts off the rights of Father (and those who would inherit through Father) to inherit from Son and Daughter. Accordingly, Father is not an heir of Son.

Question: S lived with her elderly unmarried parent, P. S and P owned Blackacre as joint tenants with the right of survivorship. S and P were found in their home by a neighbor; P was dead; S died at the hospital a week later. A police investigation determined that S shot P and then shot herself. A note determined to have been written by S was found near their bodies; the note read: "I am going to kill P and myself. This is our only hope for escape before they take us for their experiments." P died intestate. S died testate; her will named her friend, F, as the personal representative of her estate, and left her entire estate to F. Discuss the issues raised by the question of whether F, as S's successor, will receive part or all of Blackacre and P's probate estate.

Answer: Because a person should not be able to profit from her wrongdoing, most states have "slayer statutes" that, if applicable, preclude a slayer from inheriting from her victim. Generally, those statutes are designed to prevent the killer from profiting from the killing, not to impose an additional punishment on the killer. Accordingly, if the slayer statute is applicable, F should not be able to receive P's interest in Blackacre as S's successor, but should be able to receive S's interest in Blackacre. That result is accomplished under the UPC by the joint tenancy being converted to a tenancy in common, if the UPC slayer statute is applicable. The Restatement approach, however, would treat S—at S's death after P—as having predeceased P, in which case no part of Blackacre would pass to F as S's successor, if the slayer statute is applicable. Most slayer statutes do not apply unless the killing was intentional; here, the note appears to raise a question as to S's sanity and thus S's ability to form the requisite intent to kill P. Further, some slayer statutes (but not the UPC) apply only if the slayer is convicted of an intentional killing; there will be no such conviction here because of S's death. If the statute is not applicable, Blackacre and S's share of P's estate would pass to F as S's successor, subject to a possible civil claim being made against S's estate by P's successors for the killing by S of P.

Question: At the dinner table following a family celebration, Parent told her child, A, and A's spouse, that she was giving A $25,000 to help them buy a house, and that the $25,000 was to come out of A's share of Parent's estate when Parent died.

Parent made the gift to A and died a month later, intestate. A and another child of Parent, B, were Parent's only heirs; Parent's net probate estate was $175,000. How is it divided between A and B?

Answer: If the $25,000 gift is treated as an advancement, hotchpot results in the $175,000 being divided $100,000 to B and $75,000 to A; if not, each receives $87,500. At common law the gift would be an advancement. In many jurisdictions today, including those that have adopted the UPC, a gift is not treated as an advancement unless there is a contemporaneous writing evidencing either the donor's intent to that effect, or the donee's acknowledgement that the gift was an advancement.

Question: D died intestate, survived by one child (A); by two children of A (GC1 and GC2); and by GC3, who was the only child of D's other child (B), who predeceased D. D's estate consisted of Blackacre, located in a UPC jurisdiction, and Whiteacre, located in State X. A timely disclaimed A's interest in D's estate. The law of State X provides that if someone disclaims an inheritance they are treated as having predeceased the decedent; State X also divides an intestate's property among her descendants under the per capita method. How are Blackacre and Whiteacre to be distributed?

Answer: GC1 and GC2 each receive ¼ of Blackacre; GC3 receives the other ½. Whiteacre probably is divided equally among them. Under the UPC, which governs the disposition of Blackacre because it is real estate located in a UPC jurisdiction, the property A would have received but for the disclaimer—a ½ interest in Blackacre—instead passes to A's descendants by representation as if A had predeceased D. Thus, GC3, as B's representative, receives the ½ B would have received if living, and the ½ A would have received had A not disclaimed it passes ¼ to each of GC1 and GC2.

By contrast, A's disclaimer will cause Whiteacre to pass under the law of State X as if A had predeceased D. If A had predeceased D, the heirs of D would have been D's three grandchildren (GC1, GC2, and GC3). Because State X follows the per capita approach for distributing intestate property among descendants, each of GC1, GC2, and GC3 will receive ⅓ of Whiteacre.

TESTAMENTARY CAPACITY, WILL CONTESTS, WILL FORMALITIES, AND RELATED TOPICS

CHAPTER OVERVIEW

- This chapter addresses will validity issues: (i) whether execution complied with required formalities, and (ii) whether the will is invalid due to undue influence, fraud, duress, or mistake.

- Also covered are several related topics—the doctrines of: (i) integration (multiple pages constitute the decedent's will, even if only the last of them was executed); (ii) incorporation by reference (documents outside the will but referred to in it that are treated as part of the will although not executed as a will); (iii) independent legal significance (matters extraneous to the will considered in interpreting the will because they have significance independent from the testator's testamentary wishes); and (iv) republication by codicil (an earlier revoked or invalid will or codicil revived or validated by execution of an amendment to the will).

A. TESTAMENTARY CAPACITY

1. Elements of Capacity

Historically several classes of persons lacked capacity to execute wills in some jurisdictions (e.g., married women, aliens, and certain convicted criminals). Today, anyone who is of requisite age and mentality may execute a will. Thus, lack of testamentary capacity can be of two types; the testator is too young or lacks mental capacity. Most capacity issues question the latter.

2.   Minimum Age

A minimum age to execute a will is a statutory requisite in all states. The required minimum age typically is 18, but variations exist. For example, the minimum age requirement is waived in some states for married testators.

3.   Mentality and Presumption of Capacity

The requisite mentality usually is articulated as something like "of sound mind." Usually this is presumed to exist if the will properly was executed and attested by witnesses, whose attestation usually says something like "we the witnesses whose signatures are affixed below swear that we saw X sign the will and believed X to be over the age of * and of sound mind and memory. . . ."

4.   Test of Mental Capacity

Most statutes do not address the mentality necessary to meet the statutory requisite; this is determined by case law.

- **a.   Four part test.** Generally, courts hold that being of sound mind means the testator had the ability to understand: (i) the nature and extent of the testator's property; (ii) the natural objects of the testator's bounty (i.e., those persons—usually family members—who the testator "ought" to have in mind when deciding to whom to leave her property); (iii) the disposition being made; and (iv) how these three interact with each other.

- **b.   Actual knowledge not required.** It is not necessary that the testator *actually* understood these things; it only is necessary that the testator had the *capacity* (i.e., the ability) to understand them.

- **c.   Understanding the disposition being made.** The capacity to understand the disposition the testator is making does not require an appreciation of all the technical aspects of the plan; the testator needs to be able to comprehend only the general pattern of the dispositive provisions. Boilerplate, technical tax jargon, and such need not be within the ken of the average individual.

- **d.   Understanding the natural objects of the testator's bounty.** The testator can know and understand the natural objects of her bounty without providing for them. The key is whether the testator knew that the dispositive provisions were out of the ordinary (such as leaving her estate to a friend or caretaker, instead of to her children, or leaving the entire estate to one child to the exclusion of others) if that was the case.

  - **i.   Normal disposition not sufficient.** That the dispositive provisions are "normal" will not prove capacity, nor is capacity belied by an unjust or unnatural disposition; a person with capacity may make as eccentric, injudicious, and unjust a will as caprice, frivolity, or revenge may dictate.

e. **Understanding the nature and extent of the testator's property.** The testator need not know with any precision what property she owns; she need only have the ability to understand the kinds and values of property she owns. It may be that a marginally competent testator would have the requisite mental capacity to dispose of a small, simple estate, but lack the capacity to dispose of a large, complex one.

5. **Capacity for Other Tasks**

Although cases refer to a testator's ability to perform other tasks as indicative of testamentary capacity, it is not determinative whether testator could contract, transact normal business, or manage the normal affairs of living. A greater level of capacity generally is required to enter into a contract or to conduct normal business affairs than to execute a will.

a. **Capacity to create a trust.** Curiously, the capacity to enter into a trust relationship (under which all of a person's property could be transferred) is higher than to execute a will. Thus, a marginal case may create problems if both a will and a trust are involved.

b. **Wards may have testamentary capacity.** Being declared incompetent or having a guardian or conservator appointed will not prove incapacity to execute a will, especially if appointment of a guardian or conservator was to ease the burdens of property administration for a testator who was late in life, ill, or just did not want to be bothered.

6. **When Capacity Is Necessary**

Capacity is tested at the moment of execution; losing it thereafter, or lacking it before execution, will not affect validity. Incapacity may be fleeting; the impairment may be temporary (a chronic alcoholic may execute a valid will while sober) or testators with serious mental impairments may enjoy a "lucid interval."

B. LACK OF MENTAL CAPACITY

1. **Two Forms of Mental Incapacity** can affect the validity of a will: (i) deficient capability, meaning that the testator simply was unable to understand those things discussed above that are required for a proper execution, in which case the entire will is invalid, and (ii) derangement, which may be paranoia, general dementia, or a delusion, each of which generally affects the validity of only those portions of the will that are the product of the derangement.

a. **Either results in lack of capacity.** A person will lack mental capacity to execute a will if she either is deranged or has deficient capability, or both. Evidence of mental derangement may show that the testator had deficient capability. For example, *In re Hargrove's Will*, 28 N.Y.S.2d 571 (1941), involved a decedent who allegedly suffered from an insane delusion that two children born to his wife during their marriage were not his, and that he therefore had deficient capability because he was not able to know the natural objects of his bounty.

2. Paranoia

In re Strittmater, 53 A.2d 205 (N.J. 1947), illustrates that derangement cases are unpredictable. The testator left her entire estate to the National Women's Party, for which she worked as a volunteer and of which she was a member. In holding the will invalid, the court noted that the decedent's doctor diagnosed her as suffering from paranoia and considered, among other things, that the decedent wrote that her "father was a corrupt, vicious, and unintelligent savage, a typical specimen of the majority of his sex." According to the court, the evidence showed "incontrovertably her morbid aversion to men," and that "[s]he regarded men as a class with an insane hatred."

a. **Questionable decision.** For all we know, the decedent in *Strittmater* may have been raped, sexually abused by her father, or subjected to discrimination that would inform her judgment. Although the testator's reaction might be too severe, the degree of her response to factors that we all understand is not relevant. We doubt this will would fail today, or that it would have failed in 1947 if the facts were a man leaving property to the JAYCEEs or a white supremacist to the Klan.

3. Insane Delusions

An insane delusion is a belief to which the testator adhered without knowledge or evidence that a sane person would believe. To be an *insane* delusion, the delusion must affect the disposition(s) under the will, and the conclusion(s) the testator drew from the delusion must be such that no rational person would draw. Some states also require that the falsity of the testator's conclusions were pointed out to her and the testator continued to believe them nevertheless.

a. **Credible evidence.** It is not an insane delusion if the testator's belief is based on evidence a rational person could believe. In most jurisdictions, however, if the testator drew a conclusion from the evidence that no rational person would draw, the delusion will invalidate any portion of the will affected by it.

b. *In re Honigman,* 168 N.E.2d 676 (N.Y. 1960), illustrates that the equities of a particular case may influence the application of these rules. In *Honigman*, the decedent substantially disinherited his wife, who had participated in the business from which the wealth was accumulated, because he believed she was fooling around with another man. Her challenge of the will for lack of mentality was successful—despite evidence that the decedent allegedly hid outside his home and saw the other man enter the home while his wife was inside. If the evidence was believable, then the conclusions he drew might be different or more paranoid than those that might be drawn by others. The decedent's conclusions, however, were not based on a lack of evidence and probably were not such that no rational person could draw. So a finding of insane delusion sufficient to invalidate the will probably was improper. Trial was to a jury, however, and it ruled that the decedent suffered from an insane delusion when the will was executed. The appellate court viewed this as demonstrating that the jury simply did not believe the evidence.

EXAM TIP

A person may have basic mental capacity but still lack the mentality to execute a will. In *Strittmater* and *Honigman*, for instance, the question was not whether the testators had the ability to understand the nature and extent of their property, the objects of their bounty, the disposition they were making of their property, and the relationship among these three. Rather, the questions were whether they suffered from a derangement and whether any part of their wills was a product of the derangement. If a question raises a derangement issue, it may be appropriate to begin your analysis by noting that testators who can meet the four part test of mental capacity nevertheless may suffer derangement sufficient to invalidate all or part of the will.

---

4. Other Mental Characteristics

Eccentricities, peculiarities, exaggerated personality traits, religious beliefs, or beliefs in the supernatural typically will not invalidate a will on grounds of insanity.

C. TESTAMENTARY INTENT

1. Intention Required

To be a valid will the decedent must execute the document with the intent that it be her will.

2. Lack of Testamentary Intent may serve as a will contest ground or a ground to deny probate to a will. (See the discussion below of contests and probate.) It is unusual in that respect: contest grounds usually are not adequate to deny probate of a will. The usual remedy if there are grounds to contest a will is to admit the will to probate and then challenge its validity in a contest action.

3. Presumption of Testamentary Intent

Proper execution of a will raises a presumption that the testator knew the contents of the will and understandingly executed it with the requisite intent. The burden is on the contestant to rebut the presumption of testamentary intent raised by proper execution.

4. Letter to Attorney

A common source of a challenge based on lack of testamentary intent is a client who writes a letter to an attorney asking for the preparation of a will, spelling out the client's testamentary objectives. This cannot constitute a will even if it otherwise meets the statutory requisites for execution of a will, because the client did not intend the *letter* to constitute a *will*; it is obvious the client knew the difference between them and that the client wanted the letter to result in the production of a will.

5. Nontestamentary Purpose

Occasionally, a decedent's duly executed will is challenged on the ground that it was executed to accomplish a purpose other than disposition of the testator's property and thus was invalid due to a lack of testamentary intent. For example, in *Lister v. Smith*, 164 Eng. Rep. 1282 (1863), the decedent's codicil was invalid for lack of testamentary intent because the testator did not intend it to have testamentary effect: it revoked a bequest to a family member to induce the family member's mother to move out of a house she was occupying. Note, though, that some courts will not admit extrinsic evidence to make such an argument (see 176-177).

D. UNDUE INFLUENCE

1. Common Contest Ground

Undue influence probably is the most frequent contest ground, particularly if lack of capacity cannot be proven. Frequently contestants attack a will on both grounds and, in some cases, the same evidence (e.g., a weak and feeble minded testator) may be relevant to both claims.

2. Distinguishable from Fraud

Undue influence often is confused with fraud because both terms are used to describe undue influence. Fraud as a separate will contest ground is discussed below.

3. What Influence Is Undue?

A will beneficiary can exert influence on a testator that affects the testator's dispositive provisions without that influence being *undue*. For influence to be undue, it generally must satisfy three requisites.

a. **Relates to execution of will.** First, the influence must be directly connected with execution: required is a causal connection between the influence and the will, operating at the time of execution (although the influencer need not be present at the time of execution). Thus, general influence unrelated to execution of the will is not undue influence.

EXAMPLES AND ANALYSIS

Assume Child A and Child B do not speak or otherwise communicate with or see each other. Child A prevails upon Parent to cut Child B out of Parent's life, leaving nothing to Child B. There is no undue influence if Parent later executes a will if Child A had nothing to do with creation or execution of that will.

b. **Improper purpose.** Influence directed at dispossessing someone else is not undue influence, although it might be actionable fraud or deceit. So, second, the influence must be directed toward procurement of a disposition in favor of the influencer or someone the influencer wishes to favor. For example, *In re Estate of Maheras*, 897 P.2d 268 (Okla. 1995), involved a testamentary gift to the testator's church that was found to be the product of undue influence by the testator's spiritual advisor.

EXAMPLES AND ANALYSIS

Assume T's will left ¼ of T's estate to her nephew. There is no undue influence if T's child prevails upon T to leave the nephew's share to T's alma mater, to which T's child had no connection.

c. **Substitution of desires of influencer for free will of testator.** Third, and perhaps most important, to be undue influence the influence must destroy the testator's free will and result in a will that reflects the wishes of the influencer instead of the testator. The testator's independence must be overcome so that she is unable or unwilling to resist the influence.

    i. Susceptibility of testator. Thus, in many jurisdictions a factor bearing on the question whether influence was undue is the susceptibility of the testator to influence. As a result, undue influence claims—which are difficult to prove in any case—are most likely to succeed with respect to elderly, dependent, and weak-willed testators.

    ii. Effect on testator. To prove undue influence it is necessary to show what *this* testator thought and whether *this* testator was influenced; it won't suffice to show what the average individual in the testator's circumstances would have done or thought in the face of an alleged influence.

d. Coercion; duress. Undue influence frequently is said to involve an element of coercion—the influencer so overcomes the will of the testator as to coerce the testator into executing a will that reflects the influencer's wishes rather than the testator's. Duress is not common as a will contest ground, but it relates to undue influence because a will executed by a testator under duress may produce—not reflect—the testator's testamentary desires.

    i. Lawful vs. unlawful threats. If a testator signs a will because a gun is held to her head, the will is invalid because signed under duress. But it is not universally true that only unlawful threats constitute duress. See, e.g., *In re Sickles' Will*, 50 A. 577 (N.J. Prerog. Ct. 1901), in which a threat to abandon a paralyzed elderly testator was held to be undue influence.

4. Effect of "Unnatural" Dispositions

Unjust or unnatural provisions in a will may *support*—but will not *prove*—a case that the testator was prevailed upon to do something that she otherwise would not have done, and that this influence was undue. Some courts improperly state that influence is not undue if it does not result in an injustice; that conclusion is wrong, although it might be hard to make the case and it depends on what the court would consider an "injustice." To illustrate, consider a will leaving an equal share to a child who exerted undue influence to overcome the testator's antipathy toward the child that resulted in a previous will that cut the child out completely.

5. Proving Undue Influence

The initial burden of proof with respect to undue influence is on the contestant. This burden requires evidence of the testator's subjugation to the will of the influencer, which could be next to impossible to produce: proof of undue influence usually is scant, often only circumstantial and lacking in verifiability, because the influence usually occurs in private.

a. **Shifting the burden of proof.** Consequently, in many jurisdictions proof of three elements suffices to shift the burden of proof from the contestant to the proponent of the will. As a practical matter, it typically is the burden shifting that is most important to winning an undue influence case. To shift the burden of proof, typically it is necessary to show three things:

   i. **Testator's susceptibility.** First, that the testator's condition or state of mind made the testator susceptible to undue influence; the more feeble minded the testator, the easier will be the proof of this element.

   ii. **Influencer's opportunity.** Second, there must be proof of the influencer's opportunity to exercise control over the testator, with special scrutiny if the alleged influence came from the testator's attorney or other advisor.

   iii. **Influencer's disposition; motive.** Third, that the alleged influencer was disposed to exercise control over the testator (i.e., there was a motive); proof of actual activity exercising such control or of advantage to be obtained by the influencer usually will suffice and frequently is shown by a testamentary gift to the influencer (or someone she wanted to favor) in an amount that is greater than would have passed without the alleged influence.

b. **Inadequate proof.** Proof that will not establish undue influence is argument, persuasion, advice, assistance, affection, kindness, or solicitude; normally, for influence of this type to be undue, it must rise to the level of violence, abuse, litigation, or abandonment.

 EXAMPLES AND ANALYSIS

T's child cares for T in T's home. With the intent of procuring a will that leaves all of T's estate to the child (to the exclusion of T's other children), the child threatens to move T to a nursing home and files litigation to declare T incompetent and have the child appointed as T's conservator. If T executes a new will in exchange for the child abandoning the litigation and allowing T to remain in the child's care, that will is infected by undue influence.

c. **Standard of proof.** Given the nature of the proof required and the elements that must be proven, the level of persuasion is very important. Typically only a preponderance of the evidence is required, but in some jurisdictions, clear and convincing evidence is the standard applied.

d.   **Presumptions of undue influence.** In two circumstances a presumption of undue influence will shift the burden of proof to the proponent.

   i.   **Drafter/beneficiary.** First: a drafter of a will that benefits the drafter or a natural object of the drafter's bounty is presumed to have exerted undue influence over the testator. For a case in which the presumption was not applied—we think improperly—see *Lipper v. Weslow*, 369 S.W.2d 698 (Tex. Civ. App. 1963), in which an attorney child of the testator drafted her will that left her estate equally to her two children by her second marriage. Had the burden shifted, the child who was the proponent of the will would have been required to prove that the will was not the product of undue influence.

   ii.   **Confidential relationship.** More common is the presumption of undue influence arising if there is a confidential or fiduciary relation with the testator, if the dominant party participated in procurement of the will. In this case the relation is not enough; there must be proof of participation in preparation of the will.

      (a)   **Relations covered.** Relations that allow application of this presumption include clergy, attorney, physician, nurse, trustee, conservator, or close business partner; usually insufficient would be a parent, spouse, or child (although a child who cares for and manages the finances of an aged parent may be held to occupy a confidential relationship with the parent).

      (b)   **Drafting attorney/beneficiary.** If, as was the case in *Lipper*, the drafter/beneficiary is also the testator's attorney, the presumption of undue influence would arise both because the will drafter was a beneficiary and because of the confidential attorney-client relationship.

e.   **Rebutting the presumption.** In many jurisdictions if a presumption of undue influence arises, it may be rebutted by a direct showing that the testator was strong willed and made her own decisions, or by a showing that the testator received independent legal advice. If the testator's attorney also represents the influencer, however, this showing likely could not be made.

> # EXAM TIP
>
> Distinguish between what constitutes undue influence (conduct by the influencer that is directly connected with execution of the will, that is designed to produce a provision benefiting the influencer or someone the influencer wishes to favor, and that so overcomes the free will of the testator as to substitute for it the desires of the influencer) and what is required to shift the burden of proving undue influence from the contestant to the proponent (e.g., depending on the jurisdiction, (i) susceptibility, opportunity, and disposition or motive, or (ii) a confidential relationship and participation in procurement of the will). In some jurisdictions, a presumption of undue influence can be overcome by a showing that the testator received independent legal advice; that showing also will tend to negate that the testator's free will was overcome by the influencer, but not necessarily. The will proponent also can introduce direct evidence tending to negate that the testator's free will was overcome by the influencer. For example, a testator may be elderly, infirm, and dependent on others for physical care, but still be strong willed, with a mind of her own that is not malleable to the influence of the influencer.

6. Effect of Undue Influence

A finding of undue influence will vitiate only the affected parts of the will; only if the remaining portions cannot stand alone, or the court concludes that the whole must fail to best implement the testator's intent, will the entire plan fail.

    a. Invalidating revocation of a will. If a testator revoked her will pursuant to undue influence the revocation may not be effective and the allegedly revoked will can be admitted to probate.

7. Bequests to Attorneys

If a testator's will includes a gift to her attorney, or to objects of the attorney's bounty, a presumption of undue influence arises if the attorney either drafted the will or participated in preparation of the will.

    a. Natural bequests. A "natural" bequest no larger than if another drafter were involved (such as a single testator with two children and no descendants of deceased children leaving half of her estate to her child who is the attorney/drafter) *may* be permissible, without contest concerns, although a bequest to the drafter in a will always raises eyebrows and presents the potential for a contest. (See page 66 as to the possibility of undue influence even if there is not an "unnatural" disposition.)

    b. Model Rules of Professional Conduct. Rule 1.8(c) of the Model Rules of Professional Conduct provides that a gift to the drafting attorney (or a close relative of the drafting attorney) is copacetic if the testator and attorney are "related." The question of how closely they must be related (aren't we all related somehow, if we go back far enough?) isn't addressed.

  i.   **Insubstantial gifts.** In addition, a gift to an unrelated drafting attorney is permissible under Rule 1.8(c) if it is not "substantial." Although the rule seems to indicate that the gift must be nominal in value to be insubstantial, *In re Tonken*, 642 P.2d 660 (Or. 1982) held that a $75,000 gift to the drafting attorney from a decedent who had a $6,000,000 estate did not warrant disciplinary action.

  ii.   *Lipper.* The parent/child relationship between the testator and the drafting attorney might justify the result in *Lipper* upholding the will. Even so, consider the time, expense, and hassle the family suffered because of the son's involvement in drafting the will (and whether his sister could have recovered litigation expenses from him).

c.   *In re Will of Moses,* 227 So. 2d 829 (Miss. 1969), illustrates the lengths some courts will go to prevent attorneys from being beneficiaries under their clients' wills. In *Moses*, the testator was a widow who was sexually involved with her attorney, to whom she devised the bulk of her estate. The attorney/beneficiary did not draft the document and apparently did not participate in the decedent obtaining other counsel to do so. The court held that the attorney-client relationship between the beneficiary and the testator when the will was executed, and their sexual relationship, gave rise to a presumption of undue influence, even though the attorney/beneficiary apparently played no role in preparation of the will.

  i.   **Finding of no independent legal advice.** In another questionable part of the opinion, the court held that the drafter (who met with the testator, ascertained that she was not married and had no children, discussed her property with her to consider possible tax issues, learned from her what she wanted done with her property at her death, and then drafted her will accordingly) did not provide any "meaningful independent advice" relating to her decision to leave her estate to her attorney rather than to her blood relatives. As a result, the presumption of undue influence was not overcome and the will was held invalid.

  ii.   **Understanding the decision.** One way to read *Moses* is to conclude that an attorney simply cannot ever be a beneficiary under a client's will, at least if the attorney is not related to the client. That, however, probably is reading too much into the case. It appears more likely that the sexual relationship between the attorney and his client (and perhaps that he was 15 years her junior), and that the case was decided by a southern court in 1969, explain the result.

    (a) *Kaufmann.* Another case involving a nontraditional relationship between a wealthy testator and his same sex partner in which undue influence was found is *In re Kaufmann's Will,* 247 N.Y.S.2d 664 (1964), aff'd, 205 N.E.2d 864 (N.Y. 1965). The relationship lasted for approximately 10 years prior to the testator's death. Over the last eight of those years the testator executed numerous wills benefiting his partner. The court effectively struck all of them by a finding that undue influence was exerted when the first of them was executed. We question the legitimacy of that decision.

d. **Drafting attorney as fiduciary distinguished.** A will nominating the drafting attorney as personal representative, or as attorney for the personal representative, does not create the same kinds of problems as a will devising property to the drafting attorney (because the nominations are not binding, and an attorney who serves in one or both of those capacities will provide services for which compensation will be received, rather than receiving a gift under the will). Neither is the attorney signing the will as a witness a problem, but overreaching or solicitation is an ethics concern and writing the drafter's name into a document for any purpose raises questions of propriety. Even so, for an attorney to serve as a fiduciary for an estate or trust of a client is not unethical and should not raise serious will contest concerns if proper precautions are taken.

E. FRAUD

1. Definition

Generally speaking, fraud as a ground for a will contest is a trick, device, or deception, typically involving a misrepresentation to the testator, intended to deceive the testator and to induce execution of a will or codicil that benefits the perpetrator of the fraud.

a. **Preventing revocation of a will or execution of a new will.** It may also be fraud to prevent revocation of a prior will, or to prevent execution of a new will (although these are not nearly as common). In *Latham v. Father Divine,* 85 N.E.2d 168 (N.Y. 1949), for example, the plaintiffs alleged that the defendants, by misrepresentations, undue influence, physical force, and murder, prevented the testator from revoking her will and executing a new one in the plaintiffs' favor. In agreeing with the plaintiffs that the allegations stated a cause of action, the court held that, if the allegations were proven, the defendants (who would then be devisees under a will that was not revoked due to their wrongful conduct) would hold the estate in constructive trust for the plaintiffs.

2.   Two Kinds of Actionable Fraud

Fraud usually takes either of two forms: fraud in the execution or fraud in the inducement.

3.   Fraud in the Execution

Fraud in the execution is a deception as to the provisions of the document the testator intended to sign, or as to the character of the document itself. It is more likely with someone who is unable to read (poor eyesight, illiteracy, or the testator speaks only a foreign language and was relying on a true translation).

EXAMPLES AND ANALYSIS

A testator is told by her niece that the will she is about to sign leaves her estate to her church, which she intends, but the instrument actually leaves her estate to the niece; or the testator is asked to sign a document that is presented to her as a lease agreement for her apartment, but in fact it is a will.

4.   Fraud in the Inducement

Fraud in the inducement occurs when the testator knowingly executed the document, with provisions that she intended to include, but the will or its provisions resulted from a deception worked upon the testator in forming that intent.

   a.   Elements of fraud in the inducement. Six elements must be proven to establish fraud in the inducement: (i) false statements or material omissions of fact that prevented the testator from recognizing the truth (e.g.: "Dad, brother Billy is bankrupt—a spendthrift"); (ii) if false statements are involved, they were made with knowledge that they were false; (iii) the statements or omissions were with intent to deceive—innocent misrepresentations or omissions are not actionable; (iv) the statements or omissions were material; (v) the statements or omissions actually deceived; and (vi) causation, being a link between the misrepresentation or omission and production or execution of the will or affected provision.

   b.   Causation tests. The tests applied to determine causation vary, including a "but for" approach (requiring only that fraud was a link in the chain resulting in a given provision), a "sole motive" test (requiring that fraud was the operative reason for the provision), and a "would have made" standard (requiring proof that the testator would have done something different had the truth been known).

5. Effect of Fraud

If fraud is established, the remedy will depend on the circumstances.

a. Constructive trust. As illustrated by *Father Divine*, fraud after execution that prevents the revocation of a will results in the imposition of a constructive trust (discussed in Chapter 11), not in denial of admission of the will to probate or invalidation of the will in a contest.

b. Failure of will. If the entire will is the product of fraud, the entire will fails.

EXAMPLES AND ANALYSIS

If fraud in the execution occurs and the testator did not know that the instrument she signed was her will, testamentary intent will be lacking and the will can be denied admission to probate or it can be successfully attacked in its entirety in a contest. Similarly, if X fraudulently induces the testator to leave her entire estate to X, the entire will may be challenged successfully in a contest.

c. Partial invalidation. If fraud taints only some provisions of the will, only those provisions will be invalidated; the entire will does not fail unless the entire will was the product of the fraud or it is impossible to separate the portions of the will procured by fraud from the others.

EXAMPLES AND ANALYSIS

By fraud, Child persuaded the testator to provide a life estate to Child, with a remainder to charity. Absent the fraud the charity would have received the estate immediately. The remedy will be to invalidate the life estate and accelerate the remainder so the charity takes the estate immediately. If the will had failed entirely the estate may have passed by intestacy, maybe even to Child and certainly not to the charity. If the facts were that Child would have received the entire estate had it not been for a fraud committed by charity, invalidation of the charitable remainder would cause the remainder to pass by intestacy following Child's life estate. If Child is the testator's sole heir who will receive the remainder by intestacy, the rest of the will can remain valid (a preferable result if, for example, the will contains other provisions for innocent beneficiaries such as a preresiduary gift to a beneficiary who would not be an intestate heir).

F. PRACTICALITIES

1. Burdens of Proof on Validity Issues

States differ on how the burdens of proof are allocated between proponents and contestants of a will. In many states (see, e.g., UPC §3-407), the *proponent* of the will is required to prove (i) the will was validly executed (i.e., in accordance with the jurisdiction's required formalities) and (ii) the fact of the testator's death. Assuming those proofs are made, the *contestants* then have the burden of proving lack of testamentary intent or capacity, or undue influence, fraud, duress, mistake, or revocation.

   a. Proving testamentary capacity or incapacity. Although this division of the burden of proof is fairly common even among non-UPC states, in some jurisdictions the proponent also bears the burden of proving testamentary capacity, rather than the contestant having to establish a lack of such capacity.

2. Probate vs. Contest

Although the distinction is blurred in many jurisdictions, issues related to due execution generally affect whether the will is *admitted to probate* (i.e., determined by the probate court to have been executed in accordance with the required formalities), while issues related to capacity, undue influence, and so forth are addressed in *will contest* proceedings. In some jurisdictions probate and contest proceedings are separate, while they are combined in others. Testamentary intent often may be raised in either context.

3. Standing

A person generally has standing to contest a will if she has an interest or right that will be adversely affected if the will is allowed to control disposition of the testator's estate.

   a. Heirs and devisees. For example, an heir who receives nothing under the will clearly has standing to contest it. On the other hand, an heir who receives at least as much under the will as she would if the will fails cannot contest it. Similarly, a person who is a devisee under both a prior and a subsequent will may not contest the subsequent one unless it leaves her less than did the prior one.

   b. Creditors of heirs and devisees. The cases are divided on whether a creditor may contest a will. For example, if A is a devisee under Will

#1, but not under subsequent Will #2, or if A is an heir of a testator whose will disinherits A, in some jurisdictions a general, unsecured creditor of A may not bring the contest, but a secured creditor may.

c. **Personal representative.** If Will #1 appoints B as personal representative of T's estate, and T then executes Will #2, which appoints someone else, B may have standing to contest Will #2, but the cases are divided.

4. Contests Usually Fail

Because will contests often are brought after a will has been admitted to probate (because there often is no question as to the due execution of the will), it is predictable that most cases will not be successful: the prevailing presumption usually favors validity, which is consistent with the court's determination in admitting the will to probate that the will is the final validly executed expression of the testator's intent.

5. Planning in Anticipation of Contest

A variety of steps can be taken to minimize, if not eliminate, the possibility of a successful contest.

a. **Contract with potential contestant.** The testator could contract with a potential contestant to not contest the will.

b. **Estoppel** also may bar a person from challenging a will if that potential contestant accepts benefits under the will. So, if the client anticipates a challenge from a particular individual, a second approach is to include a bequest in the will to that individual that is sufficiently attractive that the contest will be discouraged because, if the contest is successful, the contestant's bequest is defeated as well.

c. **No-contest clauses.** The will also might include a valid no-contest clause, which also often is referred to as an *in terrorem* provision.

   i. **Intended effect.** A no-contest clause (which typically would provide that a devisee who contests the will forfeits the devise to her) will not preclude a contest, but it will eliminate the bequest for a contestant under the challenged will if the contest fails and the will is upheld. As a result, the contestant must decide whether to accept the sure thing of a devise under the will, or to challenge the will and lose all if the contest fails.

   ii. **No effect if contest succeeds.** If the contest *succeeds*, the will fails and with it the *in terrorem* clause also fails.

   iii. **Enforceability.** In addition, even if the contest fails and the will is upheld, some courts regard an *in terrorem* provision as valid only to the extent the contest was frivolous, vexatious, not in good faith, or based on no reasonable grounds. If the contest was deemed to be in good faith (even if unsuccessful), many courts will not allow the *in terrorem* provision to apply. For example, UPC §§2-517 and 3-905 provide that a no-contest clause will not be enforced in the case of an unsuccessful contest for which there was probable cause.

iv.   **Characterization of challenge.** A court that is reluctant to enforce a forfeiture against an unsuccessful contestant may avoid the *in terrorem* result—depending on the language of the no-contest clause and the form of the plaintiff's claim—by construing the action brought by the "contestant" as other than a "contest." As a result, "contestants" of wills that include devises to them and no-contest clauses frequently make claims in forms other than traditional will contests. For example, a claimant might bring an action to construe the will in her favor, or to be treated as a pretermitted heir (see Chapter 10), or to have a subsequent instrument with more favorable provisions for her admitted as the decedent's last will, or to have the devise to the claimant be free from estate taxes, etc.

d.   **Living probate.** A small number of jurisdictions authorize the premortem validation of a will, allowing the testator to appear while alive to be interviewed by the court to determine whether any contest grounds are valid.

e.   **Using trusts to avoid contests.** Often, the answer to the question of how to avoid contests is to use inter vivos trusts, which substantially reduce the likelihood of a contest being brought or, if one is, of it being a success. There are a number of reasons why this may be the case (for example, because there may be a third party trustee involved who knew the testator and can vouch for her competence, because the plan was effected while the testator was alive and could alter it—indicating that it was not the product of undue influence—and because trusts are not frequently challenged and are even less often defeated).

6.   **Predicting Contests**

Common circumstances under which it is likely that a will contest might result include a testator who (i) has children by a prior marriage and intends to favor a surviving spouse who is not their other parent, (ii) treats similarly situated descendants differently, (iii) has no close relatives who might be inclined to accept a unfavorable will rather than to contest the will, because they don't want to tarnish the testator's reputation with a will contest action, or (iv) enjoyed an "alternative" lifestyle or made an "unusual" disposition (e.g., a dedicated Hare Krishna, an open homosexual, or a donor to an "extremist" organization).

G. TORTIOUS INTERFERENCE WITH AN INHERITANCE

1. Tort

Closely related to a will contest is an action in tort for intentional interference with inheritance. It is a separate cause of action—not a will contest ground or a ground for denying admission of a will to probate.

a. Remedy. A successful will contestant shares in the decedent's estate. A successful tort action results in a judgment against the tortfeasor. If the estate has few assets the tort action may be preferable.

2. Timing for Action

A will contest cannot be brought until after the decedent's death. A tortious interference with inheritance might be actionable prior to the property owner's death, when the property owner as well as others may testify. See, e.g., *Plimpton v. Gerrard*, 668 A.2d 882 (Me. 1995). In *Brown v. Kirkham*, 926 S.W.2d 197 (Mo. Ct. App. 1996), however, the court held a tort claim filed before the decedent died was premature because the plaintiff had no vested interest—only an expectancy—and thus had no damages yet.

3. Elements

The elements of the cause of action are: (i) plaintiff had an expectancy (see page 49 for a discussion of expectancies); (ii) conduct by the defendant interfered with it; (iii) defendant intended to interfere with it; (iv) defendant's conduct was tortious, such as fraud, duress, or undue influence; (v) but for defendant's interference, plaintiff would have received the inheritance; and (vi) damages.

H. ATTESTATION AND EXECUTION FORMALITIES

1. Purposes of Execution Formalities

In many jurisdictions to validly execute a will requires strict compliance with a variety of very specific rules (*formalities*).

a. Formalities have abated. Although some of the traditional formalistic requirements for valid execution remain in place in many states, in others they have been relaxed considerably and the trend is in that direction. The most clear example of this trend is the so-called "dispensing power" of UPC §2-503, adopted in 1990, under which a document not executed in compliance with the execution formalities required for a traditionally valid attested or holographic will nevertheless will be treated as a valid will if the proponent establishes by clear and convincing evidence that the testator intended the document to be her will. See the discussion on pages 91-92.

b. Testator's intent vs. compliance with execution formalities. In many cases the clearly expressed intent of the testator is thwarted by noncompliance with technical execution (or revocation) formalities. In many cases, the trend towards liberalizing will execution formalities recognizes the fact that the foremost objective should be to effect the testator's expressed intentions.

c.   **Why be picky?** Will execution formalities have been a part of the law for centuries; the relatively recent changes liberalizing them in some jurisdictions are the product of careful and deliberate consideration and a study of empirical evidence regarding the abuses to which the formalities were directed. Among the questions raised are why the execution formalities arose in the first place, and why they have persisted for so long? Four functions of execution requirements can be articulated:

i.   **The ritual function.** Did the property owner really mean it? To illustrate, assume D writes a letter to A stating: "When I die, I want you to have Blackacre." Because the transfer of a decedent's property to successors is a significant event about which the decedent will be unable to speak, we want to have a relatively high degree of certainty that the decedent really intended that the transfers be made. The various execution formalities make it unlikely that a document not intended by the testator to have testamentary effect will do so, and that a will not be a casually considered document.

ii.   **The evidentiary function.** How do we know that a writing or other communication offered after a decedent's death is in fact the decedent's will? To take an extreme example, if oral wills were allowed (and, as discussed on page 95, they are in a few jurisdictions, in very limited circumstances), think of the difficulties and uncertainties that would arise in trying to prove the existence and terms of such a will. Although those kinds of issues are not as pronounced for writings, the many cases dealing with the question of whether an offered document is the will of the decedent demonstrate that they also exist for writings, even with will execution requirements in place. Without such requirements, presumably there would be more of those cases. Thus, compliance with execution formalities results in documents that courts and persons interested in decedents' estates can rely on with some confidence.

iii.   **The protective function.** To be valid it is necessary that execution of a will be the free act of the testator, and not the result of undue influence, fraud, or duress. The execution formalities (e.g., requiring the will to be witnessed by two disinterested witnesses) reduce, at least to some extent, the possibility of a will being executed under those kinds of circumstances.

> **iv.   The channeling function.** The will execution formalities contribute to wills providing testators with a routine, accepted, and thus fairly reliable means of disposing of property.

2.   Essential Requirements

Essential requirements for the valid execution of a will are statutory and are virtually identical everywhere.

a.   In writing. The will must be written (unless, as discussed on page 95, a nuncupative will statute is applicable, which today is quite uncommon). Almost anything will do to satisfy the writing requirement if it is readable. Your casebook probably has notes about valid wills written on the fuselage of an aircraft that crashed, or on the wall of a flop house, or in the drawer of a dresser, on postcards, in books, and such. In ink, chalk, blood, with a knife blade, awl, ice pick, you name it.

b.   Signed. Unless the will is nuncupative, it must be signed by the testator.

c.   Attested. Witnesses, if any (i.e., the will is not holographic), must attest (under most statutes, in the testator's presence, and often in each other's presence too).

3.   Conflict of Laws

Testing the validity of an execution usually follows the maxim that "valid anywhere is valid everywhere," meaning that courts apply the law of a state that will produce an execution procedure that validates the will. Generally, if it was valid when executed under the law of the jurisdiction in which it was executed, it is valid. Similarly, it is valid if it was valid under the laws of the jurisdiction in which testator was domiciled at death, either under the laws of the domicile at the time of execution or at the time of the testator's death.

4.   Signed by the Testator

Numerous issues have arisen involving the seemingly straightforward requirement that a valid will (other than a nuncupative one) be signed by its testator. Generally, the testator signs immediately after the *testimonium clause* of the will (e.g., "In witness whereof, I have signed this will on the __ day of _____, ____, at Hometown, Anystate.")

a.   In the presence of the witnesses. Usually the testator must sign the will in the presence of witnesses (unless it is holographic, in which case witnesses are unnecessary and actually may be harmful). If not, in most states it may be valid if the testator *acknowledges* to the witnesses that the signature on the will is the testator's (or, in some jurisdictions, that the will is the testator's, which is deemed to include an implicit acknowledgement of the signature by the testator; see, e.g., UPC §2-502(a)(3)). This "presence" requirement is discussed further below.

b.   **What constitutes a signature?** Almost any form of signature or mark (e.g., "X") will suffice, if it is the full act intended for validation of the will by the testator. There are cases in which a thumbprint or similar mark was accepted as the testator's intended signature.

c.   **Signature with assistance.** Assistance is permissible if the testator cannot complete the full act intended. In most states no request for assistance is required. So if the testator starts to get the vapors during the execution and literally runs out of gas before the full signature is completed, there are plenty of cases allowing an observer to seize the testator's hand or arm and "help complete the act."

 # EXAMPLES AND ANALYSIS

Extraordinary amounts of assistance have been held to be permissible; for example, there are cases in which someone wrote the testator's name with the testator merely touching the top of the pen, or the assistor guided the testator's hand in making the signature or mark. No doubt, there is contrary authority as well. See, e.g., *In re Estate of Dethorne*, 471 N.W.2d 780 (Wis. Ct. App. 1991) (grasping dying testator's hand and making signature was rejected). The key in *Dethorne* was that the testator never requested the assistance. Unusual about the case is that in most states a request is not required. It is essential, though, that the testator intend to execute the will, and in *Dethorne* concern about a lack of such intent may have influenced the decision.

d.   **Signature by proxy.** Distinguish between signature with assistance, as to which the testator is signing but needs help to do so, and signature by proxy, which occurs when someone else signs for the testator, who does not physically participate in the signing. To illustrate, if Professor Newman signed Professor Pennell's will for him, the signature would be by proxy and might be: "J. Pennell, by A. Newman"—the way you often see a letter signed by the writer's secretary. Here the testator must request the proxy to sign for the testator, and the signature made by the proxy must be in the testator's presence.

e.   **Location of signature.** A few states require all this signature business at the *physical* end of the document. Presumably the notion is that it is too easy for forged additions to the will to be made after the signature. But questions may arise with respect to where the "end" of the will is. For example, to avoid invalidating wills, several cases have held that the "end" of the will is the "logical" end, which is not necessarily the physical end.

EXAMPLES AND ANALYSIS

Imagine a will written on foolscap, like a greeting card, in which the cover is written first, then the right hand inside page facing you when you open it, then the inside page that is the backside of the cover, and finally—if needed—the back cover; if the will ended on the inside page that is the backside of the cover, courts in some jurisdictions would uphold the will because—even though it was not signed at the physical end—it was signed at the logical end of the document.

      i. Provisions after the testator's signature. If signature at the end is required and there are provisions after the testator's signature, the first question is whether the offending provisions were there when the will was executed or were added after execution. If the latter, the additional provisions likely constitute an unexecuted and thus invalid attempted codicil to the will that will not affect its validity. If the former, the consequence of having provisions after the testator's signature may depend on the nature of the provision. Nondispositive provisions (e.g., a provision naming a personal representative) typically would be ignored, without affecting the validity of the will. Dispositive provisions may cause the purported will to be invalid. Alternatively, if the nonoffensive provisions of the will can be interpreted and make sense, they may be allowed to stand on their own. Only if they do not produce a comprehensible dispositive scheme for the testator's estate, the document will not be given effect as the testator's will.

5. Publication

Publication (a declaration by the testator at execution that the document is the testator's will) is required in a decreasing number of jurisdictions; it was designed merely to impress all parties involved in the execution with the nature and import of the act of execution. The preferred method of satisfying a publication requirement is simply for the testator to state to the witnesses that the instrument before them is her will, such as by answering "yes" to a question to that effect posed by the attorney who is supervising the execution. There are, however, many cases to the effect that the testator can publish the will other than verbally, such as by conduct that clearly indicates the testator's understanding that the document being executed is her will.

6. Attestation and Acknowledgement by Witnesses

Only two witnesses are required to attested wills in virtually all American jurisdictions. Even so, use of a third is common, and good practice to protect against one witness being unavailable at probate (e.g., has died, is disqualified by interest [discussed below], is incompetent, or cannot be located). In most jurisdictions, qualification to be a witness to a will requires only that the person be competent to understand and relate events (i.e., is able to "attest"); in others, witnesses must have attained a minimum age.

a. **Interested witnesses.** A significant witness issue involves persons who are "interested" in the estate acting as witnesses. At common law, a person "interested" in the estate simply could not serve as a witness; if there were an insufficient number of disinterested witnesses, the will was not validly executed. The approach today, in most jurisdictions, is to allow the interested witness to serve as a competent witness to the will; in such a case, the question is not whether the will is valid, but is instead what effect, if any, the witness' interest will have on the devise to the witness.

b. **What constitutes interest?** In most jurisdictions in which an interested witness is of consequence, a witness is "interested" in the estate if she takes more under the will than without it. Absence of interest usually does *not* necessarily mean the witness is not a devisee under the will; rather, it usually means the person takes no more under the will than if it is not admitted. The minority view is that a person is an interested witness if she is a beneficiary under the will regardless of what she would have received from the testator's estate in the absence of the will—under a prior will or by intestacy.

 # EXAMPLES AND ANALYSIS

If T has a will leaving A one third of T's estate, and T executes a new will that, among other things, leaves A one third (or less) of T's estate, in most jurisdictions A can serve as a witness to the new will without being an "interested witness." The result is the same if A is an heir of T and T executes a will, witnessed by A, that leaves A no more than A's intestate share.

c. **Spouse or potential heir of a devisee.** In some states a devisee's spouse is an interested party (the devisee's interest taints the spouse, as if the spouse and the beneficiary were a single individual) but the potential heirs of a devisee usually are not themselves tainted.

d. **Renunciation of interest.** Purification of interest by renunciation of the interest left to the witness typically is not permitted; quaere: why not? For example, in *Estate of Parsons*, 163 Cal. Rptr. 70 (1980), a decedent's will was witnessed by Nielson, who was left $100 under the will; Gower, who was left certain real property; and Warda, who also served as notary and who was not a devisee under the will. California's disinterested will statute voided gifts under the will to interested witnesses in excess of what they would have received without the will, unless the will was witnessed by two other disinterested witnesses. Nielson, who would not have taken anything in the absence of the will, disclaimed the $100 gift to her. The court held that Nielson's disclaimer did not cause her to be treated as a disinterested witness, because the purpose of the statute was to protect the testator from fraud and undue influence and the interest determination therefore is determined at the time of execution. The result was that Gower, who also would not have taken anything without the will, was unable to take the real property.

e.   **Gifts that do not make a witness interested.** Devises that do *not* constitute interest include a bequest to a church—the minister is permissible as a witness. Similarly, it is not an interested witness problem if the will names the drafting attorney as personal representative and the attorney witnesses the will. If the attorney serves as personal representative of the estate, the benefit the attorney receives will be compensation for services and not a gift.

f.   **Presumption of undue influence.** The approach taken by some states is to treat a devise to a witness as creating a presumption of undue influence by the witness that will result in the devise (or at least the portion of the devise in excess of what the witness would receive in the absence of the will) being forfeited unless the witness can rebut the presumption.

  i.   **Purge: If the witness is needed.** Still another approach is to consider interest in judging credibility and to purge the interest by statute, but only if the witness is needed to testify to admit the will; if so, the witness is forced to testify and is left with only that amount (if any) the witness would have received if the will were not admitted.

  ii.   **Rationale.** Why is purge appropriate to protect against fabrications but disclaimer/renunciation is not? Perhaps because other beneficiaries of the will might pay the witness to disclaim or renounce so that the remaining beneficiaries could take under the will, so there remains the opportunity and even an incentive to lie. The purge statute operates automatically, so the thought is that there is not the same risk of skullduggery.

iii.   **UPC** §2-505(b) goes further and is representative of state laws that avoid the problem altogether, without purge, by simply declaring that interest is not a disqualification. Thus, in a state that has adopted UPC §2-505(b), a devisee can serve as a witness without affecting either the validity of the will (except to the extent, if any, that the devisee being a witness is a factor leading to a finding of undue influence) or the devise to the witness.

 # EXAMPLES AND ANALYSIS

T is eccentric and hermetic; the only people T will allow to be near enough to act as witnesses are interested because they all are devisees under T's will. Can the will be validly attested? Consider having witnesses A and B attest will number 1, in which they are not beneficiaries. Then will number 2 is executed, attested by witnesses C and D, who take no more under will number 2 than they do under will number 1. Will number 2 includes witnesses A, B, C, and D as devisees, as T intended. It should be valid.

g.   **Notary as witness.** Allowing the proponents of a will to count the notary as a witness, as was done in *Parsons*, is not common but it also is not unique. See, e.g., *Estate of Price v. Price*, 871 P.2d 1079 (Wash. Ct. App. 1994).

h.   **Request by testator that witnesses attest.** In a minority of jurisdictions, statutes require that the testator ask the witnesses to witness the will. As with the publication requirement, this requirement usually can be satisfied by conduct, as well as by words, of the testator.

7.   **Presence**

Discussed at page 79 is the requirement that the testator sign the will in the presence of the witnesses (or, if she does not, that she acknowledge to the witnesses that the will or the signature on the will is hers). Many statutes also require the witnesses to sign in the presence of the testator, and some in the presence of the other witnesses as well. The presence requirement in each of these contexts has generated considerable unnecessary litigation.

a.   **Witnesses present at the same time.** For example, *In re Groffman*, 2 All E.R. 108 (1969), involved a testator who signed his will outside the presence of the witnesses, before asking them to witness it. The testator acknowledged his signature on the will to each of them separately. Because the governing statute required the testator to sign or acknowledge the will in the presence of two or more witnesses "present at the same time," the will was denied probate.

    i.   Equities in *Groffman*. The court admitted that the will reflected the testator's intent. The intestate beneficiary was the testator's widow (who was a second spouse, and there were children from a prior marriage in the picture) who received the entire estate, rather than a life estate in the testator's property left to her under the will. Quaere whether the court was engineering a result it thought more equitable.

    ii.   Policy. The reason for the requirement that the witnesses be present together when the testator signs or acknowledges the will is that, if the validity of the will is challenged, the witnesses will be testifying with respect to what happened, and the testator's capacity, at the same time. Without this requirement, a testator could sign or acknowledge her signature, in the presence of witness A in Year 1, and then wait years to acknowledge her signature to witness B. Because the benefits of this requirement are marginal at best, most states, and the UPC, have done away with the present-at-the-same-time requirement.

b.   Witness attestation in testator's presence. Although many statutes do not require witnesses to sign in their collective presence, most require that each witness sign in the testator's presence.

    i.   UPC reasonable time. The UPC, however, requires only that each witness sign within a "reasonable time" after witnessing the testator's execution of the will or acknowledgement of the signature or the will. UPC §2-502(a)(3). *In re Estate of Royal*, 826 P.2d 1236 (Colo. 1992), refused to allow the witnesses to sign after the testator's death even though there was a showing that it was impossible—or nearly so—for the witnesses to sign before the testator died. The UPC "reasonable time" within which to sign was deemed to end with the testator's death. By contrast, *In re Estate of Peters*, 526 A.2d 1005 (N.J. 1987), indicated that the witnesses might be able to sign after the testator's death in a proper case, but did not allow it in that case because the witnesses did not sign until 15 months after the testator's execution of the will, which the court held was too long.

c.   What is "presence"? Historically, the presence requirement was said to be a way for the testator to be sure that everyone did what they needed to do to make the will valid. Given that this knowledge had to be provided in a different way if the testator was blind, alternative tests for presence developed, and that development has supported a relaxation of the requirement. Today, there are two tests for compliance with the presence requirement: the line of sight test and the conscious presence test.

i. **Line of sight test.** The more strict line of sight test requires proof that the testator either did or could have (without great physical effort) seen the witnesses sign (and, if needed, that they could have seen each other sign). You wouldn't believe some of the case law that developed under this approach, with testimony from experts about where the testator was lying and how much contortion would have been required to view the witnesses signing at a table, and such.

 # EXAMPLES AND ANALYSIS

T, who is very ill, executes a will while in bed; the witnesses are in the same room and attest while sitting at a table in a corner of the room. In a strict line of sight jurisdiction, if the evidence was that T could not see the witnesses without moving, and could not move or could not move without great difficulty or danger, the witnesses would not be deemed to have attested the will in T's presence. Similarly, the court in at least one old case held that if the testator could see only the backs of the witnesses, and not their hands and the will itself, the presence requirement was not satisfied. *Graham v. Graham*, 32 N.C. 219 (N.C. 1849).

ii. **Conscious presence test.** The more liberal conscious presence test, which is followed by the UPC, requires only that the testator had a conscious awareness that the witnesses were attesting, that the testator was capable of understanding what they were doing, and (unless blind) could have seen the attestation if she had wanted (either by moving or requesting the witnesses to move closer). To illustrate, if the testator is in a bedroom next to the kitchen, and the witnesses attest the will at the kitchen table while carrying on a conversation with the testator, the line of sight test would inquire into whether the door between the rooms was open (unless the door was glass or otherwise could be seen through), whether the testator's position in the bedroom was such that she could see through to the kitchen table, and so forth. By contrast, it would be sufficient under the conscious presence test that the testator could hear the witnesses and was generally aware that they were signing the will.

> # EXAM TIP
>
> In a will execution question, consider whether, under the applicable jurisdiction's governing law, a presence issue exists in one or more of the following contexts:
>
> - If the testator's signature was made by a proxy for the testator, many statutes require that the testator request the proxy to sign for the testator, and that the proxy do so in the testator's presence.
>
> - Many execution statutes require that the testator sign, or acknowledge her signature, in the presence of the witnesses. Notice that UPC §2-502(a)(3) does not expressly require that the testator sign or acknowledge in the witnesses' presence, but instead requires that the witnesses must have "witnessed" the testator's signing the will or the testator's acknowledgement of the signature or the will. To "witness" a signature or an acknowledgement, the witness must be in the testator's presence.
>
> - As illustrated by *Groffman*, some statutes require that the testator sign or acknowledge in the collective presence of the witnesses (i.e., that the witnesses be in the presence of each other when the testator signs or acknowledges).
>
> - Most execution statutes require that the witnesses sign in the presence of the testator.

8. Witness Signatures

In jurisdictions requiring that the witnesses sign in the testator's presence, a witness cannot sign the will outside of the testator's presence and then acknowledge the witness' signature to the testator in the testator's presence (although you have to wonder why not). Proxy signature or the witness signing by mark or with assistance ought to be permissible, but this is not clear in most states either. (Quaere: if an able person is available to serve as proxy or to assist another who has trouble writing, why would you ask the person who has trouble writing to attest instead of simply having the person who is able to write to act as witness? The answer is in the interested witness statutes.)

9. Effect of Attestation

Attestation is the witness' certification that the testator signed the will. Technically, "attestation" is bearing witness to the proper execution of the will by the testator; "subscription" occurs when the witness signs the will, which serves as the certification by the witness that the will was executed by the testator. Although some execution statutes require witnesses to both attest and subscribe, the term "attestation" in many jurisdictions generally is understood to include both bearing witness and signing.

a.   **Proof of compliance with formalities.** The witness' signature is regarded as proof that the testator signed (and declared, if necessary), or acknowledged after having signed earlier, in the witness' presence, and that the witness signed in the testator's presence and at the testator's request (if necessary), and so forth.

b.   **Attestation clause.** It is good practice to include in a will an *attestation clause*, which recites compliance with required execution formalities. As an example:

> We, the undersigned persons, of lawful age, have on this day, at the request of T, witnessed T's signature to this instrument which T declared to be T's will in the presence of each of us, and we have, at the same time in T's presence and in the presence of each other, subscribed our names hereto as attesting witnesses, and we each declare that we believe T to be of sound mind and memory.

c.   **Forgetful or absent witnesses.** If the witnesses cannot remember the execution of the will, or are unavailable, an attestation clause along with the witnesses' signatures provides prima facie evidence of due execution. At least one court has held that a will cannot be admitted to probate if the witnesses cannot remember enough to establish compliance with execution formalities and the will does not contain an attestation clause, *Young v. Young*, 313 N.E.2d 593 (Ill. App. Ct. 1974).

d.   **Witness bound by attestation.** Generally, a witness cannot recant by later alleging that the attestation is not true, unless the witness proves that her attestation was made without the required intent to validate the will.

10. Order of Signing

Is the will validly executed if the witnesses sign before the testator? How can a witness who signs first be attesting to the testator's signature (or acknowledgement)? Although there would appear to be a risk of the will being held invalid if signed by one or more witnesses before the testator, there is good authority upholding such wills when the testator and witnesses were all together when they signed, regardless of the order. *Waldrep v. Goodwin*, 195 S.E.2d 432 (Ga. 1973).

11. Self-Proving Affidavits

Most states now permit self-proving affidavits for attested wills. These affidavits are signed by the testator and the witnesses and state that the requisites for valid execution in the jurisdiction were followed. Although good drafters regard a self-proving affidavit as a necessary part of the execution process (because it facilitates the admission to probate of an uncontested will), it is not essential to a valid will.

a. **Effect of self-proving affidavit.** The self-proving affidavit is like a deposition: in most cases the witnesses need not appear at probate to certify that the signatures that appear are theirs and that they really saw the testator sign, etc.; instead, if the will is not contested, the affidavit affirms all the things to which the witnesses would testify and may be admitted in lieu of their personal appearances. The UPC goes a step further—according to the comment to UPC §2-504, a self-proved will may not be contested as to signature requirements.

12. **Procedure for Validly Executing a Will**

The following recommended procedure from 1 Casner & Pennell, Estate Planning §3.1.1 (6th ed. 1995), should result in a valid will execution in any American jurisdiction.

- First, the testator should examine the entire will and understand all its substantive provisions.

- The testator, three observers who will witness the will (and who are not "interested," as discussed beginning on page 82), the person conducting the execution, and a notary public (if required with respect to a self-proving affidavit and the person conducting the execution does not meet this requirement) should be in a room from which all others are excluded and from which no one will depart until the execution is completed.

- The person supervising the execution should ask the testator: "Is this your will, do you understand it, does it express your wishes regarding disposition of your property after your death, and do you request these observers to witness your execution of it?" The testator's affirmative response should be audible to the three observers.

- The observers should witness the testator date and then sign the testimonium, which should appear at the end of the will. In addition, it is desirable to have the testator initial or sign each prior page of the will.

- The person conducting the execution should instruct the three observers that, "your signature as witness attests that (1) [the testator] declared to each of you that the document is [his/her] will, (2) [he/she] dated and signed the will in your presence, and (3) [he/she] asked you to witness the execution. You are attesting that you signed in the presence of [the testator] and the other witnesses, believing [the testator] to be of sound mind and memory." If the observers agree, then in the presence of the testator and of each other, they should witness the will by signing the attestation provision and writing their addresses for future identification.

I. MISTAKE IN EXECUTION

1. *In re Pavlinko's Estate,* 148 A.2d 528 (Pa. 1959), is representative of a classic execution mistake; all the requisite formalities for execution were met, but each spouse signed the will intended for the other. Acknowledging that the result dictated by the applicable Wills Act—failure of the will because it was not signed by the testator identified as such in the document—was "very unfortunate," the court followed the traditional approach of refusing to correct mistakes in the execution of a will and denied probate of the will. By contrast, if wrongdoing (fraud, undue influence, etc.) occurs in the will production and execution process, the result under the will that the testator did not really intend will be corrected. The interesting issue is why not when an innocent mistake is involved.

   a. **Rationale for not correcting mistakes.** In a case like *Pavlinko* there is no uncertainty about the mistake or the intent of the decedent; nevertheless, a majority of courts would deny relief. Most of the mistake cases in which relief is denied cannot be explained by some notion of a lack of intent or issues of credibility (fraud, forgery, and such); there simply is an historical "aversion" to correcting mistakes that takes the form of requiring strict compliance with the formalities for execution.

   b. **Protecting against fraudulent claims.** According to the court in *Pavlinko,* if courts ignore the requirements of the jurisdiction's will execution statute "to accomplish equity and justice in that particular case, the Wills Act will become a meaningless . . . scrap of paper, and the door will be opened wide to countless fraudulent claims which the Act successfully bars." We cannot agree.

   c. *In re Snide,* 418 N.E.2d 656 (N.Y. 1981), involved similar facts as *Pavlinko,* and thus presented the same issue. Unlike the *Pavlinko* court, however, the *Snide* court admitted the will to probate that purported to be the will of the decedent's spouse but that was signed by the decedent, relying on the fact that the instruments contained identical dispositive provisions and were executed at the same time in compliance with the required formalities. The court found there was no risk of fraud; thus, to deny probate of the will would "unnecessarily expand formalism" and produce an "unjust result." For a similar holding in a case involving wills of sisters, see *Guardian, Trust & Executors Co. v. Inwood,* [1946] N.A.L.R. 614.

2. Substantial Compliance

In re Will of Ranney, 589 A.2d 1339 (N.J. 1991), adopted a "substantial compliance" approach to rectify or ignore the defective execution of a decedent's will. In *Ranney*, the witnesses signed the self-proving affidavit that was attached to the will, but failed to sign the will itself in the attestation provision. Other cases with similar facts have held such signatures to be adequate by regarding the affidavit as part of the will proper. The *Ranney* court correctly held that the affidavit is not part of the will, and may be the first court to hold that close is good enough when the requisite intent is apparent and there are no facts indicating a potential abuse or impropriety.

3. UPC Dispensing Power

A 1990 amendment to the UPC goes even further than the substantial compliance approach to dealing with execution mistakes. UPC §2-503, referred to as a "dispensing power," allows an instrument to be probated as a decedent's will regardless of noncompliance with execution formalities if the proponent establishes with clear and convincing evidence that the testator intended the instrument to be her will.

a. **Expected circumstances for application.** The comment to UPC §2-503 states an expectation that it will be applied most often (i) when a will is not properly witnessed and (ii) when a testator attempts to change a previously executed will with, for example, an interlineation that is not executed in compliance with required formalities.

b. **Proof of intent.** In many jurisdictions the will proponent bears the burden of proof as to due execution; if that burden is met, there is a presumption of capacity and the burden of proof on that issue is on the contestant. In *Estate of Brooks*, 927 P.2d 1024 (Mont. 1996), the court held that no such presumption exists when the proponent seeks to have an instrument that does not comply with the execution formalities admitted under the UPC dispensing power; rather, the proponent bears the burden of proving testamentary capacity as a part of her burden of proving the testator intended the instrument to be her will.

c. **Reach of the dispensing power.** UPC §2-503 applies to "a document or writing added upon a document"; oral wills and, arguably, video-taped wills therefore should not be validated by the dispensing power. It does not require the document or writing to be signed, and it is clear that an addition or change to a previously executed will may be valid under the dispensing power even though the addition or change is not signed. If an instrument never signed by the decedent is offered as her will, however, it likely will be very difficult to establish by clear and convincing evidence that the decedent intended the instrument to be her will.

d. Other applications of the dispensing power. UPC §2-503 by its terms also applies to an instrument offered as (i) an addition to or change of a will, (ii) a partial or complete revocation of a will, and (iii) a partial or complete revival of a formerly revoked will (see Chapter 4).

EXAM TIP

The UPC dispensing power dispenses with defects in the execution of testamentary instruments if there is clear and convincing evidence that the testator intended the instrument to have testamentary effect. It does not cure other kinds of problems, such as a defective revocation by physical act (see Chapter 4), the execution of a will by a testator who lacks testamentary intent, or a testator validly executing an instrument under a mistake of fact or law.

---

4. Consequences of Requiring Strict Adherence to Execution Formalities

A case demonstrating how serious the consequences of requiring strict compliance with will execution formalities can be is *In re Estate of Peters*, briefly discussed on page 85. In *Peters* a wife left all her property to her husband, who died 126 hours after she did. He left all of their collective property to her son, which clearly would be her intent. His will, however, was invalidly executed and the court refused to relax the requirements, notwithstanding that the decedent's intent was clear; there was no suggestion of impropriety and imposition of the requirements resulted in the property escheating. In that respect *Peters* is a clear illustration of how far the law has yet to go.

a. Reality. Formalities often provide grist for the litigation mill. Many cases find ways to admit wills that lack formalities, to work the appropriate equities, and the movement towards relaxing the execution requirements shows that courts and legislatures are troubled by these realities—and by the frustration of testators' intentions. We expect further changes as more states adopt the UPC dispensing power or otherwise embrace, directly or indirectly, the substantial compliance doctrine.

J. HOLOGRAPHIC WILLS

1. Handwritten by the Testator and Unattested

About half the states recognize holographs: a will that is handwritten by the testator and valid without attestation by witnesses. See, e.g., UPC §2-502(b).

2.   "Entirely" in the Testator's Handwriting

Most states that recognize holographs require them to be *entirely* in the testator's handwriting. Under the surplusage theory followed in some jurisdictions, a will that contains some material not in the testator's handwriting may be a valid holographic if the nonholographic provisions can be ignored and the balance of the will administered without them. By contrast, under an intent theory only those nonholographic items that are not intended to be an operative part of the will are ignored; substantive nonholographic material invalidates the will.

3.   UPC Material Portions Requirement

The UPC requirement for a valid holograph is only that the "material portions" (and the signature) be in the testator's handwriting. That approach should allow more valid holographs than does even the surplusage theory, but questions will arise as to whether the handwritten portions constitute the "material portions."

a.   *In re Estate of Johnson,* 630 P.2d 1039 (Ariz. 1981), for example, involved a preprinted will form with only the fill-in-the-blanks portion of the will being in the testator's handwriting. In holding that the handwritten portions did not establish the necessary testamentary intent, and thus that the material portions of the instrument were not in the testator's handwriting, the court found the handwritten words "To John M. Johnson 1/8 of my Estate," with a handwritten list of other devisees and fractions, inadequate to establish the decedent's testamentary intent. UPC §2-502(c) addresses the *Johnson* problem and provides that portions of a holographic will that are not in the testator's handwriting may be considered to establish testamentary intent.

4.   Date

Many states (but not the UPC) require a holographic will to be dated, even though most do not require an *attested* will to be dated. Presumably, the different treatment is attributable to an expectation that the witnesses to an attested will can testify as to the execution date. Holographs have no witnesses to provide that information.

5.   Signature Requirement

The state law signature requirement also may differ for a holograph: typically a testator may sign a holograph by mark or with assistance, but usually not by proxy. This might be relevant if the will was written (but not signed) before the testator became ill or lost the ability to make a signature. Remember that a will need not be prepared all at one time; indeed, many holographs give the appearance that they were prepared over a period of time, perhaps in multiple sessions.

6.   **Testamentary Intent** questions most often arise with respect to holographs. For example, *In re Kimmel's Estate*, 123 A. 405 (Pa. 1924), involved a letter from a father to two sons that was held to be a holograph—based primarily on language essentially stating that the father might come to visit the sons; that, if he did, he would bring some valuable papers he wanted the sons to keep for him so that, if anything happened to him, various listed assets would go to named persons; and that the sons should keep the letter because it might help them out.

K.   CONDITIONAL WILLS

1.   Effect of Condition on Testamentary Intent

To be valid a will must be made with testatmentary intent. If the will states a condition that did not occur, the issue that arises is whether it nevertheless was intended by the testator to be her all-events will. Generally, that depends on whether the statement was intended by the testator to be a true condition, or whether it was instead merely a statement of what induced the testator to make her will. Examples of language raising the issue are: "if anything happens to me," "if I do not return from my trip," or "if I do not recover from surgery."

a.   **The favored construction** is that the statements were merely a gratuitous expression of the inducement for writing a will that would apply under all circumstances, thus allowing a finding of intent to make the will and for it to be applicable in all events.

2.   Conditional Wills and Extrinsic Evidence

Throughout the law of wills is the question whether extrinsic evidence of facts or circumstances outside of the will itself can be considered to explain what a testator meant by a provision in a will. (See Chapter 7.) With respect to conditional wills, the question is why extrinsic evidence should be admissible to show that the statement in the will was a mere statement of inducement and not a statement of true condition, if such evidence is rejected in other cases involving pure mistake in execution. Extrinsic evidence almost certainly would be rejected if offered to show that a will that is absolute on its face actually was meant to be conditional. The extrinsic evidence issue is one of the least definable in the entire law of wills.

a.   **Conditional wills and latent and patent ambiguity.** Historically, extrinsic evidence has been admitted only with respect to "latent" ambiguities (those that are not apparent on the face of the will). Extrinsic evidence has not been permitted with patent ambiguities (those in which it is clear from the provisions of the will that something is not clear or complete) to explain what the will meant. See Chapter 7. Because the condition in a conditional will is apparent from the face of the will, consideration of extrinsic evidence is fundamentally inconsistent with this historical position.

L. NUNCUPATIVE (ORAL) WILLS

1. Limited Use

In narrowly defined circumstances, testators may in some jurisdictions make their wills orally. Generally, such wills are valid only if the testator was in the military, or in a last illness, and typically can pass only a small amount of personal property. They are rarely used.

2. Oral Instructions to Make a Will

A question that comes up occasionally is whether oral instructions given to an attorney can be a valid will if the document is not prepared and executed before the intended testator dies. The answer is that the oral instructions were not meant to be a will (remember the testamentary intent issue even with a letter written to the attorney) and therefore intent is lacking because a written will was intended.

M. INTEGRATION

1. Multiple Pages

Wills typically consist of many pages that not be prepared all at once. Thus, there must be proof of the pages that were present at execution and that were intended to be included (i.e., "integrated") in the will, because only those can constitute the testator's will and be given testamentary effect.

2. Additional, Revised, or Retyped Pages

Pages added, changed, or even retyped after execution cannot be a valid part of the will, unless the formalities for execution of a valid codicil (an amendment to a will) are met, because those pages were not present at execution of the will in its final form—and thus were not integrated into the validly executed will.

a. **What happens if a revised page is invalid?** If changes made after execution are not a validly executed codicil (in that regard, keep the dispensing power of UPC §2-503 in mind), the original, unaltered page *might* remain a valid part of the will, if it still is identifiable, under a dependent relative revocation theory.

b. **Effect of invalid change on rest of will.** If the original, unaltered page does *not* remain a valid part of the will the question may be whether removal or substitution of even one page invalidates the entire will. If the pages are separable (not physically, but in substance, because the provisions on the pages are sufficiently independent of each other), the will may be able to stand on its own without either the original or the invalid page, unless the revision, addition, or replacement shows indications of fraud or forgery in the execution, a lack of testamentary intent at the time of execution, or an implied revocation of the whole will.

 # EXAMPLES AND ANALYSIS

Page 2 of T's holographic will contains a single provision that leaves $10,000 to X. After the holograph is executed, T destroys the original page 2 and inserts a new one providing for the $10,000 to go to Y. New page 2, however, is not validly executed. The balance of the will stands on its own as a valid will; the $10,000 is not devised to anyone, but will instead pass with the residue of the estate to the residuary beneficiaries. If page 2 also left the residue of T's estate to Z (and the new page 2 attempted to do the same), the pages are not separable and the will would fail unless saved by doctrine of dependent relative revocation.

3.   Two Versions of a Page at Execution

If there were two versions of a certain page at the time of execution (e.g., because the decedent had not decided which to include), only the one proven to be intended at execution by the decedent to be part of the will can be valid. If one of the two pages is inserted in the proper order in the will, and the pages of the will were stapled or clipped together, that page presumably was the one intended by the testator. On the other hand, it may not be possible to prove which the testator intended if the two versions of the page were kept together with the other pages of the will. In that case, neither is valid and the will can stand only if that page is separable.

4.   Integration Proof

In the suggested procedure for execution of an attested will the witnesses were not asked to examine the will or count its pages. (In many states it is not even necessary that the witnesses know the document is a will, to say nothing of seeing what is written on any page or how many pages there are.) Moreover, some drafters intentionally place the attestation clause (after which the witnesses sign) on a separate page to prevent the witnesses from seeing any of the will provisions. Moreover, integration often is an issue for holographs, for which there typically are no witnesses.

a.   Integration presumption. So, usually the only way to prove that all the pages were present at the time of execution is a presumption, in this case that the condition of the document at death was its condition when it was signed. In that regard physical attachment of the pages at death implies that all pages were together at the time of execution.

b. **Initials or signature on each page.** Addition of initials or the testator's full signature on each page is only as reliable as the handwriting analysis procedures employed. *In re Estate of Beale*, 113 N.W.2d 380 (Wis. 1962), shows that this can be flawed: the decedent's initials appeared on pages of his will that clearly were typed after he died.

c. **Relationship of pages.** An internal connection or flow of the provisions one to another (e.g., page 4 ends in the middle of a sentence that continues on page 5) also is taken as indicative of presence and intent at execution, but modern word processing equipment can make this appear to be the case even if a page was revised after execution.

d. **Extrinsic evidence.** Extrinsic evidence typically is admissible to show any facts and circumstances at execution that might indicate the presence of all pages at that time, but statements relating to the substance of any provision or the intent of the decedent regarding the presence of any particular page or provision typically would not be admissible.

5. Multiple Wills

Wills that lawyers draft typically include clauses expressly revoking all prior wills. Persons who prepare their own wills, often holographs, however, may die with more than one will, none of which expressly revokes any of the others. Multiple wills that each are valid documents standing on their own all are entitled to probate.

a. **Judicial integration.** In such a case judicial integration applies to the extent the wills are not inconsistent. Each document is considered alone to determine whether all its pages were present at the time of its execution. To the extent each is separately valid, then the several valid documents are considered in terms of their effect on each other. To the extent they are not inconsistent, the multiple valid documents are integrated to form a single dispositive plan. Only to the extent the documents are irreconcilably inconsistent will any provision be regarded as ineffective: the last of the inconsistent wills to be executed prevails.

N. INCORPORATION BY REFERENCE

1. Incorporation by Reference Planning

Incorporation by reference probably serves only two planned functions. Most common is to facilitate laziness. Second, in jurisdictions in which the incorporated document is not made part of the public record in probate, incorporation may allow an added degree of privacy. If this were the concern, however, the most appropriate answer is to use a form of transfer that is not a public record, such as a trust.

2.   Operation

Incorporation by reference says "treat this other writing as if it were a part of the will," even though it is not—and usually was not physically present at execution. Nevertheless, the other writing may be treated as if it was physically part of the will.

3.   Elements

The basic requisites for incorporation by reference are:

a.   **Intent** to incorporate another writing into the will, which must be apparent from the face of the will.

b.   **Existence of incorporated document** before execution of the incorporating document.

    i.   **Tangible personal property.** Handwritten lists disposing of tangible personal property (e.g., mementos, furniture, jewelry, and the like) often fail to be incorporated on this ground. As a result, UPC §2-513 authorizes such a list, which need not be handwritten, without regard to its existence at the time the will is executed, if the list is signed by the testator as if it were a valid holograph. Under the UPC, the only kind of tangible personal property that cannot be disposed of by such a list is money. See page 105.

    ii.   *Clark.* In *Clark v. Greenhalge*, 582 N.E.2d 949 (Mass. 1991), the notebook clearly was not in existence at execution—although republication by codicil saved the day.

c.   **Reference to existence of incorporated document.** Third, the incorporating instrument must refer to the incorporated document as being in existence.

    i.   **Existence at execution uncertain.** The cases that deny incorporation on this ground may just be situations in which the court believed, but could not be sure, that the document to be incorporated was not in existence when the will was executed. For example, words of futurity (e.g., "I give my ABC Co. stock to my children and grandchildren as set forth on a list I *will* prepare") can disqualify what otherwise might be a valid incorporation.

    ii.   *Clark* **and** *Simon.* In *Clark v. Greenhalge* it was not clear whether this requirement was satisfied, but in *Simon v. Grayson*, discussed below, this requirement probably was not met, as the will directed the $4,000 to be distributed ". . . as shall be directed in a letter that will be addressed to . . . and will be dated. . . ."

d.   **Identification of incorporated document.** Fourth, the incorporating document must describe the incorporated document with reasonable certainty. Required is a clear, definite, explicit, and unambiguous reference—to make clear what document is being incorporated and avoid concerns of fraud.

   i.   *Simon v. Grayson,* 102 P.2d 1081 (Cal. 1940), involved a testator's 1932 will, republished by a 1933 codicil, which directed distribution of $4,000 in accordance with a letter also dated 1932. At testator's death, a 1933 letter, but not a 1932 letter, was found with instructions for the distribution of the $4,000. The July 1933 letter was held to be the one referred to in the will and thus was incorporated by reference into it. It is not clear but entirely possible that there was a 1932 letter, which later was replaced with the 1933 letter, in which case the 1933 letter should not have been incorporated into the will (because it was not referred to by the will at all). In any case, it is difficult to conclude that the reference in the will to a letter dated 1932 clearly identified the 1933 letter.

   ii.   *Clark.* Similar difficulty is encountered in *Clark v. Greenhalge,* in which the court held that the will's reference to a "memorandum" referred to the notebook.

e.   **Conformance of document with will description.** Fifth, the incorporated document must be identifiable as being the document described in the will. Any alteration to the incorporated document after the will is executed precludes incorporation of the new provisions and might prevent incorporation of the original provisions as well.

   i.   *Simon.* In *Simon,* if there was a 1932 letter and, instead of replacement with the 1933 version, it had been altered or amended, it still would fail because the amended letter would not be the one that was in existence at the time the will was executed. The unaltered original version might be admitted notwithstanding the amendment, unless the amendment is treated as a revocation. Even then the concept of dependent relative revocation might apply to preserve validity of the unaltered original version. See Chapter 4.

   ii.   **Parol evidence.** Parol evidence may be admissible to prove that the document produced conforms to the description in the will.

4.   *Clark v. Greenhalge,* 582 N.E.2d 949 (Mass. 1991), involved a testator's will, executed in 1977, which included a provision for her personal representative to distribute tangible property "among such persons as I may designate by a memorandum left by me and known to him . . . ." The testator

left a document prepared in 1972 and amended in 1976, entitled "Memorandum," that disposed of certain items of tangible property. The dispute was over a painting listed in the testator's notebook with a designation that it was to go to the plaintiff. The testator executed two codicils to her will in 1980, and the court found that the notebook was in existence when the codicils were executed. Under the doctrine of republication by codicil, discussed below, the notebook was treated as being in existence when the will was executed, thus allowing the court to apply incorporation by reference and award the painting to the plaintiff. Note that the issue should be whether the notebook was in existence when the will was republished by the codicils in 1980, and whether the entry in the notebook was made before the second codicil was executed.

5.   *Clark* **and** *Simon*

Could the notebook in *Clark* or the letter in *Simon* themselves be valid holographic codicils to the wills? In *Simon* the letter was written, dated, and signed. In *Clark*, however, there apparently was no signature on the notebook. Further, any reference to a will in *Simon* is sketchy—the 1933 letter referred to "my will" and the two were found together. But to be a codicil to the will, the reference probably should be more positive. The notebook in *Clark* may not have referred to the testator's will at all. And in either case quaere whether there was the requisite testamentary intent—neither the letter nor the notebook was meant to be a will.

6.   *Johnson v. Johnson,* 279 P.2d 928 (Okla. 1954), illustrates use of incorporation by reference as a fall back argument, rather than an affirmative estate planning tool, to validate a will that was not executed in the usual fashion. The decedent, a lawyer who had prepared many valid wills for clients, died leaving a single, unsigned typewritten sheet of paper stating that it was his will and providing for various devises. At the bottom of the page, in his handwriting and signed by him, were the words: "To my brother James I give ten dollars only. This will shall be complete unless hereafter altered, changed, or rewritten." The court admitted the will to probate.

a.   **Republication by codicil.** According to the court, the typed portion was a "will" (even though it was not validly executed), and the bottom portion was a validly executed codicil to the will that republished it (see pages 105-107). Did the testator intend the typewritten page to be his will and the handwriting at the bottom of the page to be a codicil or, as the dissent persuasively argues, did the testator intend the entire document to be his will? Not all jurisdictions allow a validly executed codicil to republish a will that was not validly executed (Compare *Hogan v. Sillers,* 151 So. 2d 411 (Miss. 1963); *Everett v. Everett,* 309 S.W.2d 893 (Tex. Ct. App. 1958), with *In re Brown's Will,* 160 N.Y.S.2d 761 (1957)).

b.   **Incorporation by reference?** Could the handwritten portion constitute a holographic will—not a codicil—that incorporated the typed portion into it by reference?

   i.   **Testator's intent?** Again, is that what the testator intended or did he intend the entire page—the typed and handwritten portions—to be his will? If the latter it cannot be valid as a holograph because not even the material portions were handwritten, and it clearly was not executed in compliance with the formalities required for attested wills. Even if somehow the entire document was valid as a holograph, in many jurisdictions the non-handwritten portion would be excised as surplus (which it clearly wasn't, as substantially all of the dispositive provisions were contained in the typed portion).

   ii. **Reference to typed portion.** If the handwritten portion is a holographic will, does it adequately refer to the typed portion to incorporate it by reference (assuming there was an intent to incorporate)? The only possible reference to the typed portion in the handwritten portion is the "This will . . ." sentence; arguably that reference, along with the placement of the handwriting on the bottom of the typed portion, adequately identifies the typed portion to satisfy that requirement for application of incorporation by reference. That sentence, however, seems to indicate that the testator viewed both portions of the page as a single will, rather than that the typed portion was to be incorporated into the "separate" handwritten holograph.

7.   Incorporation by Holograph of Typed Document

In a state allowing holographs, arguably, a holograph should not be permitted to incorporate a typewritten document by reference because the verification function of a holograph (written in the testator's handwriting) is lacking with respect to the typewriting. (On the other hand, the verification function of an attested will is the attestation by the witnesses, which also is lacking for incorporated typed documents—yet incorporation routinely is allowed for them.) Even if the typed document is treated as being incorporated into the holograph, it should invalidate the holograph (because it is not in the testator's handwriting), or at least be excised from the holograph as surplusage. Nevertheless, some courts allow holographs to incorporate typed documents.

O.   THE DOCTRINE OF INDEPENDENT LEGAL SIGNIFICANCE

1.   Importance of the Doctrine

Like insurance, if we didn't already have this concept, we would need to invent it. Independent legal significance is the heart of the doctrine underlying the pour over will, which is an absolute mainstay in estate planning.

2.   Operation of the Doctrine

The doctrine allows a testator to describe property or identify persons who will be beneficiaries under her will by reference to acts, circumstances, or documents that are extraneous to the will, if they have a "substantial significance apart from their impact on the will."

EXAMPLES AND ANALYSIS

Identifying Beneficiaries. To "my mother-and-father-in-law" or "my spouse" or "my employees at the time of my death" all are valid because we assume marriage and employment have significance independent from the will. As a consequence, if your will gave $10,000 to every employee of yours at the time of your death, an individual could be added as a beneficiary merely by putting them on the payroll rather than by amending the will.

Describing Property. Disposition of "my car" or "my household furnishings" or "the contents of my safety deposit box at ABC Bank" or "the contents of my top desk drawer" all would be valid, and a larger or smaller bequest could be effected by buying or selling, adding to or deleting from, and such.

---

a. **Assumption that changes have independent significance.** Although a person might marry/divorce, hire/fire, or move assets around, we assume those acts would not be done solely for testamentary disposition—they presumably have a significance apart from their testamentary effects.

b. **List of gifts.** Invalid under independent significance is a gift to the "persons listed on the paper to be found with my will" because this has the sole objective of a testamentary disposition and therefore has no independent legal significance. (Such a disposition might be valid, however, under incorporation by reference or, for tangible personal property, under UPC §2-513, discussed at page 105.

c. **Control by others.** Notice that the act, circumstance, or document that has independent legal significance need not be subject to the testator's control.

EXAMPLES AND ANALYSIS

"To the person married to X at my death" or "to each grandchild of mine who survives me" or "to each grandchild who is married at my death" all would be valid, even though it gives X or each child or each grandchild the power to alter the testator's bequest. Similarly, "to the persons named as beneficiaries in the will of X as in effect at my death" also would be valid notwithstanding that X may name beneficiaries with no significance independent from X's testamentary objective: the point is that naming beneficiaries in X's will does have significance (the disposition of X's property) independent from the *testator's* testamentary purpose.

3.   Pour Over to Trust

Most importantly, the independent legal significance doctrine makes valid a gift "of the residue of my estate to the acting trustee of the trust executed by me on [date], to be added to and administered as a part of the trust estate held under that trust as in effect at my death." This is what a typical *"pour over will"* would provide, pouring the residue of the decedent's estate into the trust and allowing the trust document to govern its disposition.

a. **Alteration of trust after execution of will.** A valid pour over relies on the doctrine of independent legal significance and permits the trust to be altered after execution of the will.

b. **Existence of the trust.** Historically some states required that the trust instrument be executed prior to execution of the testator's will. Under the UPC and the Uniform Testamentary Additions to Trusts Act, it is required only that the trust be in existence and able to accept the pour over when the testator dies. This could include a trust created under the will of someone else, provided that they die before the testator.

c. **Incorporation by reference distinguished.** Pour over wills do not rely on incorporation by reference, unless the drafter has been inept, and would not qualify in many cases as an incorporation by reference because frequently the trust is amended after execution of the will, making the independent legal significance doctrine critical to this common planning approach.

i. **Advantages of independent significance.** Thus, unlike incorporation by reference, (i) the pour over concept does not require republication of the will each time the trust is amended, and the amendments will govern if the pour over will does not provide otherwise, (ii) the trust is not made testamentary (meaning it need not be executed in accordance with will formalities to be valid), nor is it subject to probate, and (iii) the trust is not made subject to creditors' claims nor to the claims of a spouse under the statutory share concept addressed in Chapter 10 (although the trust assets may be subject to claims of both creditors—see Chapter 6—and a surviving spouse).

d. Uniform Testamentary Additions to Trusts Act. UPC §2-511, which also is the freestanding Uniform Testamentary Additions to Trusts Act, permits pour overs to trusts that have not been funded during the decedent's life. Under traditional trust law there cannot be a trust without trust property; see Chapter 12. Indeed, UPC §2-511 permits a pour over to a trust initially funded by the devise itself. Because substantially all of the ultimate dispositive provisions for the testator's property usually are in the trust instrument, this result really turns fundamental notions of wills and their effect on their head.

i. Additional flexibility. In addition, under UPC §2-511 (i) the trust terms may be contained in an instrument executed before, after, or concurrently with execution of the will, (ii) the pour over is permissible if the terms of the trust permit the devised property to be administered in accordance with the terms of the trust as amended after the testator's death (provided that the will does not specifically provide against such postmortem changes), and (iii) the testator's will may provide that the devise does not lapse (see Chapter 8) even if the trust is revoked or terminated prior to the testator's death (for example, by incorporating by reference the terms of the trust as a part of the pour over will if the trust is not in existence to accept the pour over—which might be useful if the pour over is to the trust of someone else and they might revoke it without the testator's knowledge or at a time when the testator lacks the ability to change the testator's will).

ii. Far reaching effect. The Uniform Testamentary Additions To Trusts Act has been adopted in all states, either as part of the UPC proper or as a freestanding enactment. This is so contrary to so much traditional wills doctrine that it has contributed to the modern trend of courts moving toward ever greater flexibility in their interpretation of the formalities for execution.

4. Dispositions of Tangible Personal Property

Clark v. Greenhalge, discussed above, is illustrative of the kinds of disputes that arise over the disposition of a decedent's tangible personal property. Under traditional wills doctrine, such property is subject to the same rules as are applicable to the testamentary disposition of other kinds of property. Thus, a writing separate from a will purporting to dispose of tangible personal property would not be valid unless it was executed and attested in compliance with required will formalities, or unless, for example, it satisfies the requirements for a holographic will or codicil, or is valid under incorporation by reference.

a. **UPC §2-513.** Because it is so common for testators to attempt to dispose of tangible personal property by writings separate from their wills, because such property typically is not of substantial value, and because such attempted dispositions so often were invalid under traditional wills doctrine, UPC §2-513 provides a special dispensation: a will can refer to a list or other statement to dispose of any item of tangible personal property other than money.

i. **Other rules don't apply.** The list or statement need not be valid as a holograph (e.g., it can be typed), and it need not comply with incorporation by reference requirements (e.g., it can be prepared or revised after the will is executed).

ii. **Special application of independent legal signifiance.** In some respects, UPC §2-513 is a special application of the doctrine of independent legal significance, deeming the written statement or list to have a sufficient independent existence from the testator's testamentary disposition to validate it (a true fiction, but allowed because usually—although not always, and it does not matter—the amounts involved are de minimis and havoc wreaked by invalidating this common planning technique just is not worth the damage that purists might regard as done to traditional wills doctrine).

iii. **Signed writing required.** Note, however, that UPC §2-513 requires that the list or statement be in writing and that it be signed by the testator. Because many homemade attempts to dispose of tangible personal property in writings separate from wills probably are not signed—as appears to have been the case in *Clark v. Greenhalge*, for example—problems likely will continue to be encountered in this area even in jurisdictions that adopt UPC §2-513.

P. REPUBLICATION BY CODICIL

1. *Codicils* are documents executed with all the formalities of a will (either a traditional attested will or, if the jurisdiction permits them, a holographic will) that change provisions in a will referred to in the codicil. It may supplement, explain, modify, add to, subtract from, qualify, alter, restrain, or revoke provisions in the will.

2. Validation of Invalid Will

Important here is that, in some circumstances a codicil may in the first instance validate an otherwise invalid will, or may revive a once valid will that subsequently was revoked.

EXAMPLES AND ANALYSIS

- T executed a will in Year 1 under undue influence (or when T lacked testamentary capacity), and the will therefore was not valid. In Year 2—when T is not under undue influence or incapacitated—T validly executed a codicil to the will. The codicil is said to "republish" the will, meaning that for many purposes the will is treated as having been re-executed on the date the codicil is executed, making the will valid.

- T executed a document intended to be a will in Year 1, but it was not valid as a holograph (material portions were typed), it was not properly attested, and the jurisdiction has not adopted the UPC dispensing power or the substantial compliance doctrine. If T validly executed a codicil in Year 2, it may republish and thus validate the will. See the discussion of *Johnson* above.

- T executed Will #1 in Year 1. T executed Will #2 in Year 2, expressly revoking Will #1. In Year 3, T executed a codicil to Will #1, specifically referring to it and making no mention of Will #2. The codicil republishes, and thus validates (i.e., "*revives*"), Will #1. (Note: assuming both wills dispose of T's entire estate, the republication of Will #1 by the codicil may operate as a revocation by inconsistency of Will #2. See Chapter 4.

---

3. **Analogy to Incorporation by Reference**

    It may help you to understand the concept of republication to think about it as if, in effect, a codicil incorporates the underlying will by reference. But be careful, because in republication analysis we don't technically follow the incorporation by reference approach, all the formalities of incorporation by reference are not required, and timing issues and interpretation of the documents may differ from what you might expect under traditional incorporation doctrine. More importantly, republication may apply in states that do not recognize incorporation by reference.

4. **Requisites for Republication by Codicil** and thus validation of a will, include:

    a. **Physical existence of will.** Just as the incorporated document must be in existence when a will incorporating it is executed, a validated or revived will must be physically in existence when the codicil republishing it is executed; physical revocation of the will (such as by having burned it) precludes its republication by codicil.

    b. **Intent** to validate or revive.

    c. **Identification.** A sufficient description of the will to be validated or revived. Physical attachment of the codicil to that will probably will suffice. Finding both together in the same physical location (an envelope, box, or drawer, for example) may suffice if the codicil refers to "my will" and no other will is found.

5. **Effect of Validation Through Republication** is restoration of the underlying will, plus (i) all prior valid codicils to that will that are not inconsistent with the reviving codicil (even if those codicils are not specifically identified in the reviving codicil), and (ii) all invalid or inconsistent codicils that are specifically identified by the reviving codicil. The general rule is that "republication comprehends republication of all codicils." So look for an expansive interpretation of the effect of a valid codicil.

6. **Timing Issues**

The general treatment of a codicil as republishing a will (and other codicils) on the date of execution of the codicil raises a number of questions.

   a. **Interpretation.** For interpretation of a will or earlier codicil, if circumstances at execution are relevant, should we look to circumstances at original execution of the will or prior codicil, or those on the later date of validation/revival by codicil? Typically changes in circumstances between execution of the will and execution of the codicil become part of the parol evidence available for interpretation.

   b. **Application of statutes.** For purposes of statutes that refer to the date of execution, would that be the date of original execution of the will or the date of republication of the will by the codicil? Frequently it will be the date of original execution of the will, although this is not certain. See *Azcunce v. Estate of Azcunce*, 586 So. 2d 1216 (Fla. Dist. Ct. App. 1991) and its discussion in Chapter 10 for an example dealing with a pretermitted heir statute when the date of the republishing codicil was used, yielding an unfortunate and inequitable result.

REVIEW QUESTIONS AND ANSWERS

Question: D was an 84 year old widow when she executed her will; she died six months later, survived by two children, C1 and C2. D's will left her entire estate to C1. During the last several years before her death, D's mental faculties declined. At times she was confused and disoriented; occasionally, she would not recognize or remember people she had known for years. Three years before her death, D turned over the management of her property to a local bank trust department. D received an inheritance from a sibling two years before her death, but she had that property delivered directly to the bank to manage for her. Although the bank trust officer who handled D's account attempted to communicate with her about it, D had no interest in the management of her property and did not know what property she owned when she executed her will. Did D have testamentary capacity to execute her will? Discuss.

Answer: A person can lack testamentary capacity to execute a will because of a derangement (no evidence indicates this) or because of the lack of the requisite mental ability to satisfy the four part test of mentality that D had the ability to understand (i) the nature and extent of her property, (ii) the objects of her bounty, (iii) the disposition she was making of her property by her will, and (iv) the way in which these three factors interrelate. The fact that D did not know the property she owned when she executed her will is not necessarily determinative; the issue is whether she had the *ability* to understand the nature and extent of her property at that time. D's deteriorating mental condition would be admissible and relevant evidence with respect to whether she had the requisite mental capability when she executed her will, but it also is not determinative. The question is whether, at the time of will execution—perhaps during a "lucid interval"—D had the ability to meet the four part test; that is a question of fact, not of law, and we do not have enough information from the question to answer it.

Question: D's first will, executed in 1990, left her estate equally to her children, A and B. D's second will, executed in 1998, left nothing to A. D died in 1999. How might A contest will #2 by alleging undue influence by B?

Answer: Normally the burden of proving undue influence is on A. What must be proven to meet that burden varies by jurisdiction. Generally, A may prove undue influence by B directly, or by raising a presumption of undue influence by B that B is unable to rebut. Direct proof of undue influence by B would require that A prove (i) that the influence exerted by B was directly connected to D's execution of her will, (ii) that the influence exerted by B was intended to result in D's will favoring B or someone B wished to be benefited by it, and (iii) that the influence was such as to result in D's free will having been destroyed so that her will reflects B's desires rather than her own.

Because of the great difficulty of directly proving undue influence, most contestants attempt to "prove" their case either by shifting the burden of proof to the alleged influencer or by raising a presumption of undue influence that the alleged influencer is unable to rebut. In some jurisdictions the former can be accomplished by showing that the testator was susceptible, that the influencer had the opportunity to exert significant influence over the testator, and that the influencer had a disposition or motive to exert undue influence.

A presumption of undue influence may be raised by a showing that the influencer drafted the testator's will, which benefits the influencer or a natural object of the influencer's bounty. Alternatively, a contestant can raise a presumption of undue influence by showing that the influencer had a confidential relationship with the testator and participated in the preparation or execution of the testator's will, or that such a confidential relationship existed and that there were other suspicious circumstances. The most common means of rebutting a presumption of undue influence is for the influencer to show that the testator had the benefit of independent legal advice.

Question: In the previous question, what if the evidence is that on many occasions B truthfully told D about aspects of A's lifestyle that B knew D would find objectionable, and that as a result D changed her will to leave her entire estate to B?

Answer: That evidence alone should not be enough to establish undue influence. Was B's influence directly connected with D's execution of her will, or was it more general influence? The facts given are not enough to establish the former. Because of the truth of B's statements, A also could not prove fraud.

Question: In the previous question, what if the evidence is that B also repeatedly told D that because of A's objectionable lifestyle, D should disinherit A and leave A's share of D's estate to a favorite charity of D and that, as a result, D did just that?

Answer: Here, B's influence is directly connected with the execution of D's will, but it was not directed at securing a benefit for B or an object of B's bounty (unless B is somehow associated with the charity). This is not undue influence.

Question: D wrote the following letter to a friend, F: "I've been giving my estate a lot of thought. You were right. When I die I want it all to go to X. I'm counting on you to make sure that happens. D." D died the next week. Can the letter be admitted to probate as D's will?

Answer: The primary issue is whether D executed the letter with testamentary intent (i.e., when D signed the letter, did D intend it to be D's will)? Usually testamentary intent is not present in letters that express what the author intends to do with respect to a will. There are, however, cases in which letters have been held to be testamentary instruments; this one clearly expresses what D wants done with her estate at her death and the language, "I'm counting on you to make sure that happens" arguably indicates that D believed the letter would effect her testamentary wishes.

If testamentary intent is found to be lacking, the letter will have no testamentary effect.

Even if testamentary intent is found, the letter clearly cannot be admitted to probate as an attested will. But if the jurisdiction has adopted the dispensing power of UPC §2-503, the letter might be admitted to probate if the proponent can establish with clear and convincing evidence that the letter was intended to be D's will. If the dispensing power is not applicable in the jurisdiction, the letter might meet the requirements for a valid holograph.

Question: D died domiciled in State X, the will execution statute of which is:

No will shall be valid unless it is in writing, signed by the testator, or by someone else in his presence and by his direction; and such signature shall be made or acknowledged by the testator in the presence of two or more witnesses, each of whom shall attest and subscribe the will in the presence of the testator.

(a) D signed an instrument purporting to be a will at D's home, took it to D's office, showed it to two co-workers, A and B, and asked them to sign it. Before they did so, the telephone rang. D took the call; the conversation lasted several minutes. During the entire conversation D gazed out the window, which was located behind her desk, with her back to A, B, and her desk. While D was on the telephone, A and B signed the instrument at D's desk and left. D died in a car accident on the way home from work that day. Was the will validly executed?

(b) What result if (i) D called A and B into her office and asked them to witness her will, (ii) A left D's office before D signed it to confer with someone about something, (iii) D, and then B, signed the will while A was absent from D's office, (iv) B left D's office, (iv) after which A returned to D's office and signed the will?

(c) What result if the facts were: D took the will to A's office, signed it while A looked on, and asked A to witness it, which A did; D then took the will to B's office. Because B was not there, D left the will on B's desk and went back to D's office. A few minutes later, D called B on the telephone and said, "I put my will on your desk. A and I already have signed it. Please sign it and I'll pick it up when I leave for lunch." B signed it during the telephone conversation with D.

Answers:

(a) Because D did not sign the will in the presence of witnesses, the first issue is whether D's signature was acknowledged by D in the presence of A and B. It should suffice that D showed A and B the will and asked them to sign it, although arguably the statute requires that A and B see or at least physically have been able to see D's signature. Here we are not told whether D showed A and B the page of the will on which D had signed it. A more liberal interpretation of the statute would treat D's acknowledgment of the *will* as an acknowledgment of D's *signature* on it without regard to whether A or B saw or had the physical ability to see D's signature on the will. The second issue is whether A and B attested and subscribed the will in D's presence. Under the line of sight test, they did not; under the conscious presence test they probably did as D likely was conscious of their presence and witnessing of the will even though D was not looking at them and was talking on the telephone to someone else.

(b) The issue is whether D acknowledged D's signature in A's presence. Was D in D's office when A returned to sign the will? If so, what, if anything, did D say to A? Did A see, or at least have the ability to see, D's signature on the will? Note that the statute does not require that D sign or acknowledge in the collective presence of A and B, or that A and B witness the will in each other's presence.

Under a dispensing power or substantial compliance standard this execution should suffice.

(c) There are two related problems with the execution of D's will. The statute requires that D sign or acknowledge in B's presence, and that B attest and subscribe in D's presence. D's acknowledgement was by telephone; was it in B's presence? Similarly, did B attest and subscribe in D's presence? If the line of sight test is applied, clearly the execution of the will fails to comply with the statutory requirements on both counts. If the conscious presence test applies, an argument can be made that D and B were in each other's presence during the telephone conversation, but it almost surely would not succeed.

Question: D's 1993 will left her friend, F, $2,500. D executed a second will in 1997 that revoked the 1993 will, left $10,000 to F, and $20,000 to a religious organization of which D was a member. The jurisdiction requires two witnesses; the will was witnessed by F and X, a cleric of the religious organization. D died in 1998. What effect does the 1997 will being witnessed by F and X have on its validity and on the bequests to F and the religious organization?

Answer: F is an interested witness (unless D had executed another will that would be admitted to probate if the 1995 will is not, and it bequeathed property with a value of at least $10,000 to F); in most jurisdictions X's relationship with the religious organization would not make X an interested witness. In most jurisdictions, an interested witness can attest a will—D's will should not be invalid because of F's status as an interested witness. Instead, in most jurisdictions an interested witness is purged of gifts under the will in excess of what the witness would have received in the absence of the will. In such a jurisdiction, F would lose $7,500 of the $10,000 bequest under the 1997 will.

Question: D's will provided: "I will leave in my safe deposit box an envelope for A which will have in it a list of paintings A is to receive from my estate. I leave the rest of my estate to X." Following D's death, an envelope addressed to A was found in D's safe deposit box. Inside the envelope was an unsigned list of paintings D owned at D's death. Are the paintings on the list distributable to A or to X?

Answer: Probably X. For the list to be incorporated by reference into D's will it must have been in existence when the will was executed and referred to in the will as being in existence at that time. Here, D's will does not indicate whether the list was in existence when D executed the will. If extrinsic evidence is sufficient to prove that the list was in existence at execution, however, a court might relax the requirement that the will refer to the list as already being in existence.

The list will not be given testamentary effect under the independent legal significance doctrine because the list had no significance independent of the disposition of the paintings listed on it at D's death. (By contrast, if the bequest were of valuable coins located in an envelope addressed to A in D's safe deposit box, A likely would receive the coins: the independent legal significance doctrine typically is liberally applied; here, the storage of the coins in the safe deposit box has significance independent from their disposition at D's death.)

Even if the jurisdiction has adopted UPC §2-513 A would not receive the paintings. That section allows tangible personal property to pass pursuant to the terms of a writing separate from the will that is not in existence at execution, but the writing must be signed by the testator. This was not.

4 REVOCATION

CHAPTER OVERVIEW

- Wills may be revoked by physical act, by subsequent written instrument, or by operation of law.

- Revocation by physical act requires the act (e.g., tearing the will) and the intent to revoke (not merely the intent to perform the act). The physical act must be performed by the testator, or by a proxy in the testator's presence. In some states, the act must be performed in the presence of witnesses.

- Revocation by subsequent instrument can be by a will, a codicil, or an instrument executed in compliance with will execution formalities that does nothing more than revoke the will. The subsequent will may expressly revoke the prior will or codicil, or it may do so by inconsistency.

- Revocation by operation of law generally constitutes only a partial revocation and occurs if the testator's circumstances have changed such that it is presumed that she would want certain provisions revoked (e.g., divorce resulting in revocation of provisions in favor of the former spouse).

- Certain wills that were revoked can be "revived." For example, if Will #1 was revoked by Will #2, which then was revoked by physical act.

- Revocation of a will may be ineffective under the doctrine of dependent relative revocation because it was conditioned on the existence of facts or law that were not as the testator thought.

A. REVOCATION BY PHYSICAL ACT

1. Form of Revocation

Physical revocations normally take either of two forms: mutilation of the paper on which the will is written, or obliteration or cancellation of the words on the paper.

a. Mutilation includes tearing, cutting, burning, or other forms of destroying the paper. Total destruction is not required, but the issue will arise whether the testator intended a partial or complete revocation if the will is only partially mutilated. If partial revocation by physical act is not valid in the jurisdiction, the question is how much of an act is needed to constitute a total revocation vice none at all. With partial mutilations, there always are questions of fact about what the testator intended.

EXAMPLES AND ANALYSIS

If the pages were singed rather than the entire will being destroyed by fire, a court might assume that the testator changed her mind and pulled the will out of a fire intending not to revoke, or merely acted under the assumption that holding a match to the pages is enough to revoke the will, or ran out of matches before one caught the will on fire and burned it up.

---

   i.   Practice consideration. To avoid such uncertainties with respect to intent, physical act revocations should be of the entire will.

   ii. Words of the will. Unlike the law in many states for revocations by obliteration or cancellation, mutilation acts—tearing, burning, cutting, or otherwise—need not touch the words on the paper of the will.

   iii. Will must be mutilated. The mutilation must affect the will proper and not just a backing, a self-proving affidavit, or a cover.

b. Obliteration or cancellation. The second form of physical revocation is a physical act done to the printed words on the paper. Obliteration renders the words unintelligible: for example, if T tapes strips of paper over or completely blacks out words of the will. Cancellation involves writing over or marking through words.

    i. Cancellation need not touch every word. Under the traditional view, however, writing only in the blank spaces, margins, or on a cover will not suffice. By contrast, UPC §2-507(a)(2) expressly provides that a cancellation need not touch *any* words to revoke the will.

EXAMPLES AND ANALYSIS

In *Thompson v. Royal*, 175 S.E. 748 (Va. 1934), the attempted revocation was made by the testator's lawyer writing on the back of the will's cover that it was null and void. The statement was dated and the testator signed it. When she died, the will was admitted to probate over objections that it had been revoked, because the writing on the back cover did not touch the words of the will. Had UPC §2-507(a)(2) been in effect, the revocation would have been valid. (The attempted revocation also was ineffective as a revocation by subsequent instrument because the writing was not attested and not in the testator's handwriting, and thus not made in compliance with the formalities for will execution.)

    ii. Cancellation by words or marks. Writing "canceled" or "revoked" across the printed page is a cancellation by physical act (and *may* be a revocation by subsequent instrument as well). Similarly, making an "X" over one or more provisions of a will is a cancellation. Among the questions raised by such an act are: (1) did the testator intend to revoke the will in whole or in part (or perhaps not at all); (2) if a partial revocation was intended, are partial revocations by physical act valid in the jurisdiction; (3) if a partial revocation was intended and respected, which provisions were revoked; and (4) if a partial revocation occurred, will it increase devises to others and, if not, with what result (see pages 117-119)?

2. Act and Intent Required

Any physical revocation will be unsuccessful lacking either the proper act or intent to revoke. Thus, physical acts do not revoke if they were done by mistake, to the wrong document, or the testator's intent changed before the full intended act was completed. A physical act will not suffice if the testator was incapable of forming the requisite intent, or if it was not done by the testator (unless it was a valid proxy revocation).

    a. Strict compliance. *Thompson v. Royal*, discussed above, is representative of cases that require strict compliance with specific statutory provisions for revoking wills. By contrast, the dispensing power in UPC §2-503 validates instruments that attempt to revoke wills but that are not duly executed, if the intent to revoke is established by clear and convincing evidence.

3. Presumption of Revocation by Physical Act

There is a presumption of destruction by the testator with the intent to revoke if a will cannot be found, or is produced in a mutilated, obliterated, or cancelled condition, provided that (i) the testator was the last person to have possession of the will, (ii) possession was not available to others, and (iii) if the will is lost, there was a diligent search for it.

a. Possible access to will by others. The presumption of revocation may be rebutted if the will is not discovered but someone who would benefit if it was revoked had access to the place where the testator kept the will. Compare *Estate of Travers*, 589 P.2d 1314 (Ariz. 1991), with *Lonergan v. Estate of Budahazi*, 669 So. 2d 1062 (Fla. Dist. Ct. App. 1996).

b. Lost will and presumption not raised. Admission is possible by proof of the will if it is not found but the presumption of revocation is rebutted. For example, in most jurisdictions, an unexecuted or conformed copy will suffice. "Conformed" means that an unexecuted will is made to show by typewritten entries what appears in handwriting on the signature and date lines. For example, a document with a signature line that appears like *"/s/ John Doe 1/1/96"* means that John Doe signed and dated the original in his handwriting.

c. *Harrison v. Bird,* 621 So. 2d 972 (Ala. 1993), saved the intended revocation by the presumption of destruction with intent to revoke. The testator had executed duplicate original wills, one kept by the drafting attorney and the other by the named beneficiary/personal representative. When the testator decided to revoke the will, she called the attorney who tore it up (or had his secretary do so) and advised the testator in a letter that he had revoked the will for her and was sending her the pieces. The pieces of the will, however, were not found after the testator's death. The duplicate original of the will was denied probate.

i. No physical revocation by proxy. The governing statute imposed the usual requirement that a proxy physical revocation be performed in the testator's presence. Thus, the act of tearing up the will did not revoke it.

ii. Presumption of revocation by physical act. Because the pieces of the will had been sent to the testator and were not found following her death, however, the presumption that she destroyed the will with the intent to revoke it applied and was not rebutted.

 EXAMPLES AND ANALYSIS

If the testator in *Harrison* had thrown the pieces of the will in a trash basket by her desk, but the testator died and the pieces were recovered, the testator did not tear, burn, cut, obliterate, or mutilate the will, nor was it subjected to such an act by her proxy in her presence. If the governing statute allows physical revocation by "destruction," perhaps the testator's disposal of the pieces in the trash was a "destruction" of the will. If the jurisdiction had adopted UPC §2-507(a)(2), which allows a will to be revoked by a "revocatory act" to the will, which is defined to include burning, tearing, canceling, obliterating, or destroying it, the UPC philosophy of relaxing technical wills-related requirements in favor of giving effect to the intent of testators arguably would result in the term "revocatory act" being held to include the act of throwing the will away. If not, and if throwing the will away did not constitute a "destruction" of it, the will likely would not have been revoked.

4. **Extrinsic Evidence**

Because revocation is so difficult, extrinsic evidence usually is admissible to prove lack of possession by the testator (and thus that a physical act may not have been done by the testator and therefore is invalid as a revocation), declarations by the testator regarding intent (which might explain the significance of a physical act), and circumstances showing reasons (or the lack thereof) for the testator to revoke (which might help understand the testator's intent or ascertain the consequences of a revocation).

5. **Partial Revocation by Physical Act**

Some jurisdictions permit partial revocation by physical act if less than all of a will is torn, burned, obliterated, cancelled, or made subject to another act that can revoke it. Many others do not.

a. **If invalid under state law.** If partial revocation by physical act is not allowed, and the testator performs a revocatory act on only a part of the will, the presumption is that none of the will was revoked, as opposed to the attempted partial revocation resulting in a revocation of the entire will. The partial revocation necessarily will be effective, however, if the attempted partial revocation obliterates provisions of the will such that they cannot be read (and there is no extrinsic evidence, such as a copy of the will, that can prove what the obliterated language said).

b. **If valid under state law.** If partial revocations by physical act are allowed, the next issue is what becomes of the property that was subject to the revoked provision?

i. **Revocation vs. change.** The property that was subject to the revoked provision necessarily passes to someone else. The question is whether the partial revocation is effective to make a new bequest. The issue is really one of formalities for a *change* as opposed to an effective revocation. The act of deleting a devise may not suffice to change the devisee. In some jurisdictions a partial revocation results in the property passing by intestacy. In others, a partial revocation may increase a residuary gift but not a preresiduary gift.

 ## EXAMPLES AND ANALYSIS

T's will provided: "I give Blackacre to A, B, C, and D. I give the residue of my estate to E." Under a law that allows partial revocations by physical act, T crosses out "B" in the devise of Blackacre and also revokes the residuary provision. The residue will pass to T's heirs as intestate property. The attempted partial revocation of B's share of Blackacre might increase the gifts to A, C, and D, it might cause ¼ to become part of the residue, or it might be wholly ineffective.

D's will provided: "I give Blackacre to X; I give the residue of my estate to A." If D crossed out the gift of Blackacre the effect would change the beneficiary of Blackacre from X to A. The rationale for this result is that A already was entitled to the residue, and the residue of any estate always is subject to change. Indeed, A probably would take Blackacre notwithstanding this change if X simply did not survive the testator (unless an antilapse statute were applicable, as discussed in Chapter 8).

c. **Proxy revocation by physical act.** Most states permit proxy revocations by physical act, but typically only if the proxy performed the act in the presence of the testator, at her direction and, in some states, in the presence of witnesses. The same presence issues discussed for execution apply to the proxy revocation. See pages 84-87.

i. **Invalid revocation; "lost" wills.** The will should be admitted to probate if the presence requirement is not met but the will was destroyed by the proxy. The difficult aspect is proof of the provisions of the will, again resolved if state law has a "lost" will provision.

ii. **Proxy revocation under UPC §2-507** must be in the testator's conscious presence and at her direction, but does not require witnesses.

6. Multiple Documents

When revocation is by physical act the intent of the testator may not be clear, as it normally would be if revocation was by a writing (which presumably states or reveals the testator's intent). This can raise problems if there are multiple documents that make up the estate plan.

a. **Effect of revocation by physical act of one document on other documents.** Assume there is a will and several codicils to it. If the revocation is by physical act to the will the presumption is that it also revokes all codicils to that will. Revocation of a codicil, however, is not regarded as a revocation of the underlying will or of other codicils to it. This rule is not necessarily intuitive, given that a codicil must be executed with all the formalities for execution of a valid will, meaning that a codicil really is a freestanding document that could be probated as a will. Such a codicil, however, probably would not dispose of the entire estate and may not make sense without reference to the underlying— and now revoked—will.

b. **Compare invalid partial revocation by physical act.** Even in a state that does not recognize partial revocations by physical act, revocation of just a codicil and not the underlying will or other valid codicils, is not regarded as an invalid partial revocation.

7. Stapled Wills

Most wills consist of multiple pages held together with a staple. The problems that can arise when a staple is removed are illustrated by *Estate of Goldey*, 545 N.Y.S.2d 464 (1989), in which a probate petition was filed to remove the staple in a final will to permit separation and inspection of the pages—all to explain the fact that there were excess holes in the pages that could be seen (on the top and bottom of the stack). Suspected in a case like *Goldey* is that some pages in the middle have only one set of holes, indicating that they were not part of the original will and therefore were added after execution of the will. Those pages not present for the execution are not valid (see the discussion of integration in Chapter 3) and the pages they replaced may have been revoked by the physical act of their removal and disposal.

8. Duplicate Original Wills

Duplicate executed originals are neither necessary nor advisable. With duplicate executed originals, notwithstanding extensive misconceptions on this score, revocation of one typically (although not always) revokes all.

 ## EXAMPLES AND ANALYSIS

T executed duplicate originals at the recommendation of her attorney, who explained that it would reduce the likelihood of "inadvertent" revocation by destruction of the will. One copy was left with the attorney for safekeeping; T took the other home. At T's death, her copy cannot be found. Extrinsic evidence supports a motive for revocation. The general rule is that all originals must be produced to avoid a presumption that destruction of one was a revocation of that one, and that revocation of the one is a revocation of all.

a. **Multiple originals in testator's possession.** This presumption of revocation is weak or nonexistent, however, if the testator had multiple copies and retained at least one executed copy of the will. The notion is that, if revocation was intended, all copies in the testator's possession would have been destroyed. That is the key: if all copies in the testator's control are missing the existence of other copies in someone else's possession is not adequate to frustrate the testator's intent to revoke. That being the case, there is no sense in using duplicate original executed wills.

B. REVOCATION BY SUBSEQUENT INSTRUMENT

1. Any Subsequent Instrument

The second way to revoke a will is by a will, a codicil, *or any other instrument* executed with the formalities of a will.

 ## EXAMPLES AND ANALYSIS

T wrote a note to the custodian of T's will, requesting destruction of the will by the custodian; two witnesses attested the note. At T's death, the will had not been destroyed and the note does constitute a sufficient subsequent instrument to revoke the will. Often these letters are not attested and state law does not recognize a holograph. A more important issue is the same as regards letters requesting the production of a will (see page 64): there is no intent to revoke by the letter; the intent is to solicit a physical revocation by proxy, not to accomplish a revocation by subsequent instrument. (Thus, the dispensing power of UPC §2-503, which can cure execution defects, would not save the "revocation.") Also significant is that, if the custodian complied with the request, the resulting "revocation" would fail as a physical revocation (because the presence requirement for a proxy revocation would be unmet). The naked request should not suffice if the act requested itself would not. See *In re McGill*, 128 N.E. 194 (N.Y. 1920).

2. **Writing on the Will Itself** may act as a revocation by subsequent instrument even though at first blush it looks to be a revocation by the physical act of writing on the document (i.e., a cancellation). The point is that a subsequent instrument need not be on a separate piece of paper (although usually it is).

EXAMPLES AND ANALYSIS

T writes across the middle of the first page of her will, intending to revoke it: "This will is void." She then dates and signs the writing. The writing constitutes a revocation by subsequent instrument if the jurisdiction recognizes holographs. It also constitutes a revocation by the physical act of cancellation. But the intended revocation would be ineffective if the writing was in the margin and did not touch the words of the will, and the jurisdiction required a touching for a cancellation, and if holographs were not recognized.

3. **Revocation by Inconsistent Subsequent Instrument**

A subsequent instrument can revoke a prior one even if it does not say it is doing so. Revocation by subsequent instrument may be by inconsistency rather than by an express provision. In some cases the inconsistency is such that there is little question that the testator intended the subsequent instrument to revoke the prior one. In other cases, the subsequent instrument raises difficult questions as to whether the testator intended it to revoke any part of a prior will.

a. **If the subsequent instrument is a codicil.** If the subsequent instrument is a codicil, the presumption is that the testator did not intend to revoke the underlying will, because codicils normally operate to amend wills, not revoke them. As a result, in the revocation by inconsistency context a codicil generally is presumed to be only a partial revocation of the will, if a revocation at all, meaning that the issues would be whether and to what extent an inconsistency exists.

EXAMPLES AND ANALYSIS

Assume a will left the testator's property all to X and a subsequent codicil devised Blackacre to Y. The presumption is that the codicil overrides the will only with respect to Blackacre. Y therefore takes Blackacre but X takes the residue of the testator's estate.

   b.   Subsequent wills that do not address prior instruments. Hard cases can arise when a subsequent will does not include an express statement of revocation.

   i.   Disposition of entire estate. The issue would be moot if the later will effectively disposed of all assets in an inconsistent manner. Integration of the two documents would honor the last in time first, trumping all inconsistent prior documents, and it effectively would override—and thus revoke—all earlier documents. Thus, if Will #1 gave all the testator's property to X and Will #2 devises Blackacre to Y, Greenacre to Z, and the residue to A, Will #1 would be totally revoked by inconsistency.

   ii.   Extent of inconsistency uncertain. If the multiple documents are not clearly inconsistent, however, integration may work unintended results.

 EXAMPLES AND ANALYSIS

(all without express indication of intent)

- "100 shares of IBM stock to A" in a will, "Blackacre to A" in a later codicil. The gifts would cumulate. The fact that A is the beneficiary in each document creates no inference that the later gift is meant to replace the earlier.
- "100 shares of IBM stock to A" in a will, "50 shares of IBM stock to B" in a later codicil. Again, these would cumulate, or at least there is no reason on the face of the documents to suggest inconsistency. If, however, the testator owned less than 150 shares, would these be inconsistent or would the estate just acquire more shares? It might matter if the gifts were of *my* shares of IBM stock" as opposed to any shares available for purchase in the open market. It also might matter that at no time did the testator own more than

100 shares, although extrinsic evidence of this type might not be admitted. The point here is that, unless there are added facts and a court finds them to be relevant and admissible, there is no reason to read these documents as creating an inconsistency at all, and therefore no reason to regard the codicil as a revocation of the will. At most, this may raise an abatement issue of what to do when the testator is more generous than the estate can accommodate (see Chapter 9).

- "100 shares of IBM stock to A" in a will, "50 shares of IBM stock to A" in a later codicil. This is not as easy a case as the prior two, but the same result ought to obtain: there simply is no more reason to suspect that the gift in the codicil—absent some express admissible statement otherwise—was meant to substitute for the disposition in the will rather than cumulate with it.

- "100 shares of IBM stock to A" in a will, "100 shares of IBM stock to B" in a later codicil. Although this might look more like a substitution because the gifts otherwise are identical, in fact this is an even easier case than the last, with the same nonrevocation result: the testator has made a total gift of 200 shares.

- "Blackacre to A" in a will, "Blackacre to B" in a later codicil. Unlike IBM stock, Blackacre is not fungible, which most courts would assume to mean that the codicil supersedes the will. It could be that A and B should take as tenants in common, just as the gifts of stock cumulate and both A and B would take. We think that most courts would regard this last case as an inconsistency and regard the codicil as superseding the will, so that B would take Blackacre to the total exclusion of A. As the progression in examples is meant to indicate, however, this is not necessarily intuitive.

---

     iii.   **Subsequent instrument: will or codicil?** Some opinions suggest that, in each of the prior examples, it might make a difference if the second document were called a will instead of a codicil, because of the presumption that a codicil amends while a will replaces a prior will. We suggest that you not succumb to such overbroad formulations.

C. REVOCATION BY OPERATION OF LAW

1. Divorce (or Annulment)

Certain changes in a testator's circumstances can result in a revocation of the testator's will by operation of law. In most states, only divorce (with or without a property settlement) or annulment still operates to revoke a will (in whole or in part, as discussed below) by operation of law.

    a. **Marriage.** In some states marriage also revokes an earlier will, or results in the surviving spouse being entitled to an intestate share of the decedent's estate, unless the will contemplated the marriage (e.g., by bequeathing something to the testator's intended spouse, who was identified as an intended) or the testator provided for the spouse to receive nonprobate assets in lieu of a testamentary gift. See, e.g., UPC §2-301, discussed in Chapter 10. If marriage does not revoke a prior will the surviving spouse is protected by elective share statutes or by community property regimes. See Chapter 10.

b.   Birth of a child. In at least one state (Georgia) the birth of a child revokes a will. More states do not regard births as a revocation because their pretermitted heir statutes protect children born after execution of a parent's will. See Chapter 10.

2.   Revocation by Divorce

Various statutes provide for divorce in different ways. For example, some statutes treat the former spouse as predeceased, or as having disclaimed any bequest under the will. (See page 52 for a discussion of the difference between these two approaches.) In these states, the will is not actually revoked; rather, the will is valid and may be admitted to probate, but the former spouse cannot take. Other state statutes deem all provisions in favor of the former spouse as having been revoked; the rest of the will remains valid. Finally, some state statutes regard the entire will as revoked.

3.   Common Problems with Divorce Statutes

A variety of problems may be encountered with revocation by divorce statutes. For example, if the testator remarries the former spouse, UPC §2-804(e) revalidates the will provisions for the spouse; most non-UPC states do not address the issue.

a.   Former spouse's family. Treating a former spouse as predeceased or having disclaimed, or revoking all provisions in favor of the former spouse, may work unintended results. For example, if the testator's will provided for the former spouse for life, remainder to the spouse's child by a prior marriage, or bequeathed property to the former spouse if living, otherwise to a child of the former spouse by a prior marriage, exclusion of the spouse may merely move the former spouse's child into immediate possession.

    i.   What did testator intend? In most cases it is arguable (and in many it is likely) that the testator would have preferred other contingent beneficiaries under the will, or that she be treated as having died intestate, rather than having anything pass to the former spouse's family. But this is not universal.

ii. **Judicial solution.** In some cases courts have ruled that the former spouse's child is entitled to the interest only if the child actually survives the former spouse (rather than being alive when the former spouse is treated as having predeceased the testator). Thus, if the former spouse survives the testator, the child of the former spouse cannot take because the condition had not occurred. Clearly courts sometimes work equity as they see it.

iii. **UPC** §2-804 provides that divorce results in both the former spouse and relatives of the spouse being treated as if they disclaimed all devises to them under the will.

b. **Nonprobate property.** Although this discussion does not address will substitutes (see Chapter 6), these revocation by operation of law situations also impact nonprobate property, such as a beneficiary designation under a life insurance policy or employee benefit annuity contract. The only real solution is legislation—such as UPC §2-804—that applies the revocation by divorce statute to all wealth transfer situations.

D. REVIVAL

1. The Situation

A will that is revoked may be made valid again without a new execution. If Will #1 is revoked by Will #2, which itself is later revoked, the revocation of Will #2 might restore (i.e., "revive") Will #1. Some states do not treat Will #1 as revived. The rationale for the no-revival result is that Will #2 revoked Will #1 immediately upon execution of Will #2. As a consequence, revocation of Will #2 could not revive Will #1. By contrast, the theory underlying the revival result is that wills are ambulatory, meaning that Will #2 had no legal effect until the testator's death. Thus, revocation of Will #2 prevented it from revoking Will #1 because Will #2 had no legal effect during the testator's life.

2. Physical Revocation

If Will #1 was physically revoked, redrafting and execution of a new will is a virtual necessity—the later revocation of Will #2 cannot revive Will #1 if it is not physically in existence.

3. Testator's Intent

Some courts purport to decide the revival question based on their perception of the testator's intent. It probably is fair to say that the assumption is that Will #2 immediately revokes Will #1, so that a later revocation of Will #2 does not revive Will #1, unless there is some evidence of an intent otherwise.

a. **Revocation of Will #1 by inconsistency.** If Will #2 revoked Will #1 only by inconsistency ("to make room" for the Will #2 provisions), some cases hold that Will #1 is revived by revocation of Will #2 because there was no explicit expression of intent that Will #1 be revoked. Under this approach, a codicil would revoke only by inconsistency, if at all. Thus, a subsequent revocation of the codicil likely would revive those provisions of the will the codicil had revoked.

b. **Express revocation of Will #1.** But if Will #2 revoked Will #1 expressly, the intent is clear that Will #2 should be deemed to be an immediate revocation of Will #1, with the result that Will #1 cannot be revived by the subsequent revocation of Will #2.

c. **UPC §2-509** abandons this express/inconsistency distinction; under it, the effect on Will #1 of a revocation of Will #2 depends on whether Will #2 was a total or only a partial revocation of Will #1. If Will #2 is *physically* revoked (i) UPC §2-509(b) presumes revival if the revocation of Will #1 by Will #2 was partial, but (ii) UPC §2-509(a) presumes against revival if Will #2 completely revoked Will #1. By contrast, if Will #2 is revoked by Will #3, Will #1 is revived only if that intent is shown in Will #3.

E. DEPENDENT RELATIVE REVOCATION

1. Introduction

Dependent relative revocation addresses a revocation that was brought about by mistake of fact or law.

2. Contrasted with Revival

If, for example, Will #1 was physically revoked in connection with the execution of Will #2 and it turns out that Will #2 was not validly executed, dependent relative revocation ignores the revocation of Will #1.

a. **Physical existence of the will.** Unlike revival, if dependent relative revocation is applicable the prior will need not be physically in existence. Dependent relative revocation does not restore the purportedly revoked will; rather, its revocation never occurred. Dependent relative revocation is a "never revoked" concept and the fact that the will is not *physically* present is not an impediment if its terms can be proven.

3. Conditional Revocation

"Dependent relative" revocation means that revocation implicitly was dependent—conditioned—on the existence of certain facts or legal results to which the revocation related. Thus, if the facts or the law were not as the testator thought, the revocation that was conditioned on them is deemed not to have occurred.

a.   **Circumstances in which dependent relative revocation can apply.**
Dependent relative revocation most often is applied when a testator
revokes a will or codicil in connection with an alternative disposition
that fails. It also can apply if the revoking instrument recites the
mistake. For example, "I revoke the $50,000 devise to B because B
has just won $1,000,000 in the lottery," when in fact B won only
$100 in a $1,000,000 lottery. Dependent relative revocation is broadly
applicable any time a revocation is made because of a mistake of fact
or law that can be established by clear and convincing evidence. Thus,
if the testator lined through B's $50,000 bequest with the intent to
revoke it, but clear and convincing evidence shows that the revocation
was made because of the mistaken belief regarding B's lottery winnings,
the revocation would be denied effect even without a recital of the
mistake in the instrument making the revocation.

b.   **Doctrine of presumed intent.** Dependent relative revocation is a doctrine of presumed intent: if the testator revokes Will #1 in connection
with executing Will #2, which for whatever reason is invalid, it is
presumed that the testator would have preferred that Will #1 remain
in effect rather than intestacy. If that presumption can be rebutted,
dependent relative revocation will not apply.

c.   *Carter v. First United Methodist Church,* 271 S.E.2d 493 (Ga. 1980),
illustrates the role of the presumption in dependent relative revocation.
The decedent's 1963 will was found with pencil marks through the
dispositive provisions, folded with a 1978 handwritten but unsigned
document that was labelled her will and that included dispositive
provisions different from those in the 1963 will. Because the two
documents were found folded together, the purported revocation of
the 1963 will was deemed conditioned on the unsigned 1978 document
taking effect as her will. Dependent relative revocation was applied
because the 1978 document was not valid, raising a presumption that
the testator would not have wanted the 1963 will revoked if the 1978
document was not effective.

  i.   **Rebutting the presumption.** The presumption might be rebutted
with evidence that intestacy would come closer to accomplishing
the testamentary objectives of the 1978 document than would
the 1963 will. In such a case it is likely that the testator wanted
the 1963 will revoked regardless of whether the 1978 document
was effective.

4.   *Estate of Alburn*

The usual factual context for application of dependent relative revocation is
illustrated by *Carter*: a revocation of Will #1 in connection with an ineffective
making of Will #2. *Estate of Alburn,* 118 N.W.2d 919 (Wis. 1963), differs
because Will #2 (the Kankakee will) was revoked in the mistaken belief that

Will #1 (the Milwaukee will) would be revived. Because that belief proved to be wrong, the revocation of Will #2 was ignored by dependent relative revocation. Ignoring the revocation prevented the perceived injustice of intestate takers receiving the estate. We know the testator would have preferred Will #2 over intestacy because the beneficiaries under Will #1, which the testator wanted to revive, were very similar to the beneficiaries under Will #2 and both were very different from her heirs.

5. **Dependent Relative Revocation Cures Mistakes** notwithstanding statements that "there is no remedy for mistake" in the law of wills. One explanation for the dissonance in result is that dependent relative revocation returns the testator to a previously valid will rather than curing a mistake—typically one that prevented validity of a will in the first instance. The law with respect to substantial compliance and harmless error in execution has taken longer to develop than in revocation.

6. **Dependent Relative Revocation and Amendments**

   A frequent application of dependent relative revocation involves a testator who tried to make a change by physical alteration without the benefit of proper execution.

 # EXAMPLES AND ANALYSIS

Assume that T's will included a bequest of $1,000 to B, and that T crossed out the "$1,000" and wrote above it "$1,500." If that increase is not effective, because it was not accompanied by the formalities required to execute a codicil, dependent relative revocation should cause the act of physically revoking the $1,000 gift to be ignored, because the testator clearly would want a bequest of $1,000 if $1,500 could not pass. If the change was from $1,000 to $500, however, it probably is impossible to predict how a court would rule. Given that the attempted change to $500 cannot be given effect, the only options are for B to receive the original $1,000, if dependent relative revocation is applied, or nothing, if the revocation stands.

The dispensing power of UPC §2-503 may apply if the change from $1,000 to $1,500 is ineffective and the proponent can establish by clear and convincing evidence that the change was made by the testator with testamentary intent.

EXAM TIP

Students sometimes attempt to apply dependent relative revocation to cure revocation mistakes that are not within its reach. For example, dependent relative revocation cannot save defective revocations in cases like *Thompson*—there, the revocation was one that failed for lack of compliance with the requirements to revoke a will, not one that met those requirements but was conditional.

7. Other Doctrines May Apply

Dependent relative revocation often is considered in contexts in which other doctrines also would produce the same results.

a. Lack of intent to revoke. A prior revocation may not be effective if, for example, it was performed by mistake and the requisite intent was lacking (watch for the issue whether extrinsic evidence to prove the mistake would be admissible). *Carter* may fall in this category: arguably, when the testator pencilled through the dispositive provisions of her will, she did so not intending to revoke the will (which she intended to do when her new will was in place), but simply in connection with thinking through the changes she wanted to make to it, as set forth on the unsigned document she was working on as her will. In that regard, there are cases that treat pencilled marks differently than marks made in ink, the theory being that pencilled marks do not indicate finality of intention.

b. Lack of intent or capacity to execute new will. Will #2 might be invalid because the testator lacked either the intent or the capacity to execute a new will. If Will #1 was not physically revoked, but was instead "revoked" only by Will #2, there would be no revocation of Will #1 at all, without reliance on dependent relative revocation.

c. Failure of condition. The revocation of Will #1 may have been expressly conditional such that failure to meet the condition causes the revocation to be a nullity, again without regard to dependent relative revocation.

EXAM TIP

Interlineation questions may raise both execution and revocation issues. If the interlineation attempts only to add one or more devises, only execution issues are raised—the fact that such a devise will reduce the residue is not viewed as a partial revocation of the residuary gift. Such interlineations constitute attempted codicils; to be valid they must be executed in accordance with the required formalities (unless the dispensing power of UPC §2-503 or the substantial compliance doctrine is applicable).

Execution and revocation issues should be addressed if the interlineation includes an attempted change to or elimination of a devise. Start with the execution issues; if the change is executed in accordance with the required formalities for an attested or holographic codicil (or the dispensing power or substantial compliance doctrine is applicable), then the change will be given effect and the revocation issues need not be considered (except to note that the codicil partially revoked the will by subsequent written instrument).

If an interlineation that attempts to change or eliminate a dispositive provision codicil is not a validly executed codicil, it is necessary to consider the revocatory effect of the interlineation. First, does the jurisdiction recognize partial revocations by physical act? If not, the interlineation has no effect (unless it evidences an intent to revoke the entire will). If so, dependent relative revocation must be considered. Would the testator have wanted the revocation to take effect had she known the change could not? Compare how the property will be distributed if the revocation is effective with how it will be distributed if it is not, and consider which is closer to the change the testator attempted in the interlineation.

REVIEW QUESTIONS AND ANSWERS

Question: T, who was single, had two children, A and B, but she was estranged from A. T asked her lawyer to prepare a will for her leaving her entire estate to B. She executed the will at her lawyer's office and took the original and a copy of the will. She told her lawyer that she was going to put the original in her safe deposit box and keep the copy at home for her reference. A month later she called her lawyer and said that A was going to come for a visit in a week or so and she was worried that A would find out about the will. Her lawyer asked her where the original and the copy of the will were; she replied that she had the copy at home and that the original was in her bank safe deposit box. Her lawyer told her that if she was concerned A would find the copy, she could destroy it or take it somewhere else. T replied that she didn't really need the copy and would just throw it away. The next day, T died of a heart attack. The original of her will was never found; the copy was found in her safe deposit box. The bank's records establish that T had not been in her safe deposit box since the day she executed her will. Should T's property pass under the will or by intestacy?

Answer: Because T had possession of the original will, and assuming that no one else did, the inability to find it following her death raises a presumption that she destroyed it with the intent to revoke it. The question is whether that presumption can be rebutted. From her conversations with her lawyer and the fact that T had not been in her safe deposit box, it appears likely that T deposited the copy of her will in the safe deposit box and took the original home by mistake. B's argument would be that even if T is presumed to have destroyed the will, she did not do so with the intent to revoke it; rather, she believed she was destroying the copy and thought the original was in her safe deposit box. To revoke a will by physical act requires both the act and the intention to revoke the will by the performance of the act. If the will was not revoked, it will be treated as a "lost" will with its terms established by reference to the copy.

Question: After T's death her will was found in a stack of papers on her desk. In the margin of the first page was written: "Revoked. 10/7/98. T." Was T's will revoked?

Answer: There are two possibilities for T's will to have been revoked: by physical act (cancellation) or by subsequent instrument. Traditionally, a cancellation had to touch the words on the will; writing in the margin would not revoke the will. Under the UPC, a cancellation need not touch the words of the will and T's will would be revoked by cancellation. In that regard, finding the will with T's papers on her desk would raise a presumption that she had made the writing in the margin; however, if it could be established, such as by a handwriting expert, that T had not done so, there would be no revocation even in a UPC jurisdiction, unless it could be proven that the proxy revocation rules of the jurisdiction had been complied with (e.g., that someone else had made the writing on the margin of the will at T's request and in T's presence).

Whether the writing revoked the will by subsequent instrument would depend on whether the jurisdiction recognizes holographic wills and, if so, whether the writing would be sufficient to constitute a holographic revocation. See Chapter 3.

Question: T's will left Blackacre to A and the residue of her estate to B. It was found with the word "Blackacre" stricken through; above it T had written "Whiteacre." T owned Blackacre and Whiteacre, each of which represented about 10% of the value of T's estate. To whom will they pass?

Answer: The attempted change will be given effect if the jurisdiction has adopted the dispensing power of UPC §2-503 and it can be proven by clear and convincing evidence that T made the change and intended it to be a modification to her will. A will receive Whiteacre and B will receive Blackacre along with the residue of T's estate. (See Chapter 3 for a discussion of UPC §2-503.)

If the jurisdiction has not adopted UPC §2-503, or the requisite proof cannot be made, the next question is whether the jurisdiction permits partial revocations by physical act. If not, the attempted change will be ignored; A will receive Blackacre and B will receive Whiteacre with the residue. (T's attempted change would not completely revoke the will by cancellation; the attempted cancellation was with respect to a single devise representing only about 10% of the value of the estate. If the jurisdiction recognizes partial revocations by physical act but the attempted gift of Whiteacre to A cannot be given effect, dependent relative revocation should save the devise of Blackacre to A: the presumption is that, had T known that the attempted gift of Whiteacre to A would fail, T would not have wanted to revoke the gift of Blackacre to A. On these facts, dependent relative revocation probably should apply.

Question: T executed duplicate originals of her will; she put one in her bank safe deposit box and her attorney kept the other. Later, her attorney discontinued the practice of safekeeping wills for clients and delivered that original to T. At T's subsequent death, the original in her safe deposit box was found but the other original was not. Can the will be probated?

Answer: Probably so. The inability to locate one of the originals at T's death, combined with the fact that it was last in T's possession, would create a presumption that T destroyed it with the intent to revoke it, but the presumption would apply only if the other original was not in T's possession. Here T controlled the safe deposit box and the will in it likely would be treated as in T's possession. Because one of the originals in T's possession was found at her death, the presumption of destruction with intent to revoke would not arise.

Question: T's will included specific devises of $2,500 to A and $5,000 to A's sibling, B; the residue of T's estate was left to C. In a validly executed holographic codicil T wrote: "I leave $5,000 to A"; no mention was made in the codicil of the gift to A under the will. How much will A receive?

Answer: The question is whether the gift to A under the codicil revokes the gift to A under the will by inconsistency. On these facts, there is nothing to indicate that the $5,000 gift under the codicil was intended to be a substitute for the $2,500 gift under the will; it is likely that the gifts would cumulate so that A will receive $7,500. An argument to the contrary would be that the two gifts to A raise an ambiguity, the resolution of which should permit the admission of extrinsic evidence. T's inheritance would be $5,000, not $7,500 if such an argument were successful and there was sufficient extrinsic evidence that T intended A to receive a single $5,000 gift to match B.

Question: D created a revocable trust (see Chapter 6) in 1990; the instrument directed the trustee to distribute the trust assets to D's spouse, S, if living and, if not, to S's child, SC. In 1995, D and S were divorced. In 1997, D and S remarried. D died in 1998, survived by S and SC, without having revoked or amended the trust. To whom should the trustee distribute the trust assets?

Answer: The first question is whether there is an applicable statute with respect to the effect of the divorce on the distribution of trust assets. If the UPC is in effect, S is entitled to the trust assets: although UPC §2-804 applies to revoke provisions in favor of former spouses under will substitutes as well as wills, it also provides that the revoked provisions are revived if the spouses remarry. The divorce/revocation statutes of many non-UPC jurisdictions do not address remarriage, but also do not apply to nonprobate assets; thus, in such a jurisdiction it is likely that S would be the proper distributee of the assets.

Question: T executed a will in 1995 leaving T's entire estate to A; in 1998, T executed a second will leaving half of T's estate to A and the other half to B. The 1997 will made no mention of the 1995 will. In 1998 T destroyed the 1997 will with the intent to revoke it. At T's subsequent death can the 1995 will be admitted to probate?

Answer: The 1997 will revoked the 1995 will by inconsistency; it also may have been revoked by a physical act. If so, it cannot be revived by revocation of the 1997 will. Assuming that the 1995 will was not revoked by physical act, the question is whether revocation of the 1997 will revived the 1995 will.

Under the UPC, the physical revocation of the 1997 will is presumed to revive the 1995 will if the revocation of the 1995 will by the 1997 will was partial; if the 1997 will revoked the entire 1995 will, the subsequent revocation of the 1997 will by physical act is presumed not to revive the 1995 will. In either case, the presumption is rebuttable by extrinsic evidence. In a non-UPC jurisdiction, the likely result is that the 1995 will is revived by revocation of the 1997 will because the 1997 did not expressly revoke the 1995—it did so only by inconsistency.

Question: D's first will left D's estate to D's spouse, S, if living, and to D's child from a prior marriage, C, if S did not survive D. Because S filed a petition for divorce, D tore up the first will and, on the same day, executed another one leaving D's estate to C; the new will, however, was not validly executed. D died shortly thereafter (while the divorce was pending). Does D's property pass to S, C, or D's heirs?

Answer: D's heirs. Unless the doctrine of dependent relative revocation applies, the first will was revoked by D tearing it up. Because the revocation of the first will was made in connection with the attempted but ineffective execution of the second, there is a presumption that revocation of the first will was conditioned on the second will being validly executed. Thus, unless the presumption is rebutted, dependent relative revocation would treat the first will as if it had not been revoked. (Note that the question is not whether the first will is revived; rather, it is whether the first will never was revoked. Accordingly, it is not a problem that the first will was physically destroyed.)

Dependent relative revocation in this case presumes that D would not have revoked the first will if D had known that the second will would not be given effect (i.e., that D would prefer the first will to intestacy). Here, because the first will was revoked in response to S filing a petition for divorce, because the divorce was pending at D's death, because the second will attempted to leave D's estate to C, and because C almost certainly will be an heir of D, the presumption of dependent relative revocation is overcome. Revocation of the first will stands and D's estate will pass by intestacy to S, C, and D's other heirs, if any.

(Note that any divorce/revocation statute likely would not apply to cause D's estate to pass to C as the contingent beneficiary under the first will; such statutes typically do not apply if a divorce proceeding merely was pending at the first of their deaths.)

5 WILL CONTRACTS

CHAPTER OVERVIEW

- Persons may contract for any of them to make a will, to not make a will, to revoke a will, or to not revoke a will.

- This chapter addresses whether a will is contractual and, if so, the effects of a breach of the contract.

- Contractual wills are the same as any others: a breach of contract spawns contract remedies but does not affect the will or intestacy.

- Contracts to make a will (or not to make a will, which is much less common) or to revoke (or, more likely, not revoke) a will are litigation breeders. Knowledgeable estate planners eschew their use.

A. TERMINOLOGY

Remember that a will is revocable during the testator's lifetime and ambulatory, meaning that it has no legal effect until the testator dies.

1. *Joint Will:* one document that is executed by more than one testator. It is the separate will of each and is entitled to probate on each testator's death. Even if the will so provides, probate cannot be denied until the death of the survivor. (However, often the testators of joint wills own everything in joint tenancy, meaning that their will often need not be produced until the survivor's death.)

2. *Mutual Will:* the separate will of one person, containing provisions that mirror the will, or that are the reciprocal of those in the will, of another person. *Reciprocal* typically means leaving everything to the other testator(s).

Mirror image means that each will does the same thing on the death of the last to die.

EXAMPLES AND ANALYSIS

Husband leaves his estate to Wife if she survives, Wife leaves her estate to Husband if he survives, and each leaves everything to their children in equal shares on the death of the survivor of the two of them. These mutual wills are reciprocal (he to her and her to him) and mirror image (to the children on the second death in each document).

3. ***Joint and Mutual Will:*** one document signed by more than one testator (most commonly two, a husband and wife) with reciprocal provisions and a single residuary provision operating on the death of the last to die; the phrase often is used with reference to a joint will with reciprocal and mirror image provisions made pursuant to a contract between spouses under which each spouse agrees not to revoke the will after the first of their deaths, and not to revoke it during their joint lives without the other's consent. A joint will that also is a mutual will usually is not referred to as a ''joint and mutual will'' unless it is contractual.

EXAMPLES AND ANALYSIS

Husband and Wife, each of whom has children from a prior marriage, agree to execute, and not revoke, a joint and mutual will under which, on the first of their deaths, the decedent's estate will pass to the survivor and, on the survivor's death, his or her estate will pass to their children equally as if their children were common to the marriage.

4. **Not Necessarily Contractual**

Neither joint wills nor mutual wills are necessarily contractual; mutual wills—at least those that are not also joint wills—usually are not. In some states, however, execution of a joint will gives rise to a presumption that it is contractual and cannot be revoked (without breaching the contract) unilaterally. Under UPC §2-514, no such presumption is created by the execution of either a joint will or mutual wills.

B. PROVING A WILL CONTRACT

1. Reciprocal or Mirror Image Provisions Not Enough

In the last example, if the survivor died after changing the will to cut out the step-children, the step-children would need to prove the existence of the contract not to revoke the will. Mere similarity of dispositive provisions does not make wills contractual. So the existence of either reciprocal or mirror image provisions, or both, would not suffice to prove a contract not to revoke.

2. Joint Will Not Enough Either

Similarly, the existence of a joint will, even one with reciprocal or mirror image provisions, does not necessarily mean the will is contractual (although some states presume that a joint will is contractual).

3. Written Proof

There ought to be written evidence of any contract. UPC §2-514 deals exclusively with the issue of proof, not with questions of validity or enforceability of these contracts. Under it the contract may be proven *only* by a writing in one of the following forms: (i) the will itself states the terms of the contract, (ii) the will expressly refers to the contract and the terms of the contract are proved by extrinsic evidence, or (iii) a written contract is signed by the decedent.

4. Oral Contracts and the Statute of Frauds

Even in a jurisdiction without a statute like UPC §2-514, proof of an agreement is made difficult by application of the Statute of Frauds, which typically requires that contracts to sell land be in writing, and which also has been held applicable to contracts to dispose of land by will.

 # EXAMPLES AND ANALYSIS

Testator orally promised to devise Blackacre to Caregiver. Testator's will leaves Blackacre to someone else. Whether Caregiver can enforce the contract depends on whether it is excepted from the Statute of Frauds.

    a. Exceptions to Statute of Frauds relative to oral contracts to make wills disposing of realty include:

        i. Part performance. Caregiver's performance of services for Testator constitute part performance sufficient to avoid the Statute of

Frauds. In the mutual will context, death of the first to die with a will that complies with the agreement constitutes part performance that avoids application of the Statute of Frauds.

ii. **Estoppel** may bar reliance on the Statute of Frauds by someone who has accepted benefits under the mutual will of the first mutual testator to die. Thus, if Wife dies first and her mutual will leaves property to Husband, which he accepts, he and those claiming through him may be estopped from relying on the Statute of Frauds to defend against a subsequent breach of the contract.

b. **Documenting the agreement.** Because proof is a severe issue for contractual wills, an estate planner who chooses to draft contractual wills should avoid the Statute of Frauds problem by documenting the agreement.

C. AVOIDING WILL CONTRACTS

1. Problems Beyond Proving the Contract

The difficult problem of proving there was a will contract can be solved by documenting the agreement. But will contracts typically present other substantial problems, so wise planners typically solve the issue that informs the use of a contractual will with some other mechanism and avoid the will contract altogether.

2. Mutual Wills for Spouses

The contract obligation can cause reduction of the federal estate tax marital deduction, so contractual mutual wills are not a wise plan for spouses whose estates are large enough to make marital deduction planning important. Using a so-called Qualified Terminable Interest Property (QTIP) trust is far easier and certain.

3. Mutual Wills Among Nonspouses

 # EXAMPLES AND ANALYSIS

Two siblings, neither of whom has descendants, inherit property from their parent. Each wants the other to have the property on the first of their deaths, and for it to go to another designated family member on the second death. Contractual mutual wills are not a good idea in this situation. Let's say one sibling survives the other by 15 years; during that period, may the survivor consume the principal as well as the income from the property? If so, for what purposes? May the survivor make gifts of the property? Or give away the survivor's own assets and consume the inherited family property for the survivor's own uses? Sell it and reinvest the proceeds? Must the survivor provide accountings to the designated family member? Does the survivor have any obligations to that family member with respect to maintenance of the property? Questions of what the surviving mutual testator may do with the property show that contractual mutual wills typically are not a good idea; a trust would serve the client's objectives better.

>   **a. Joint trusts.** In the example above, the siblings could place the property they inherit from their parent in a single trust during their joint lives, with the trust to become irrevocable on the first of their deaths. Such trusts may involve a gift tax on the death of the first settlor to die, difficulties in the event of divorce (if the two settlors are spouses), and questions concerning the management and use of the property during their joint lives. If prohibiting disposition of the property is not their objective, a better approach is for each individual to create their own trust for the benefit of the survivor for life, with the remainder passing in the agreed manner.

> **4. ''Widow's Election'' Estate Plan**
>
> A ''widow's election'' estate plan typically provides for a surviving spouse for life if the surviving spouse agrees to leave property to designated beneficiaries on the second death. For a number of tax and other reasons, these are not common outside the community property jurisdictions and may not be good planning in taxable situations even there. Again, the preferable approach is a trust.
>
> **5. Will Contracts Not Involving Mutual Wills**
>
> Will contracts are used—and often create serious problems that lead to litigation—in a variety of situations in which mutual wills are not involved.

 # EXAMPLES AND ANALYSIS

Testator, who is elderly and in need of care, promises to leave half of Testator's estate to Caregiver if Caregiver will live with and care for Testator for the rest of her life. What happens if Testator is not satisfied with Caregiver's care or Caregiver dies or becomes incapacitated before Testator? If Caregiver satisfactorily cares for Testator until Testator's death, should Caregiver receive the same property regardless of whether Testator lives one or twenty years? What limits, if any, are placed on Testator's use of her property by entering into the contract?

D. REMEDIES

1. Breach of a Will Contract

Even if a valid contract is proven, any party may alter or revoke her will (even if it is a joint will).

 ## Examples and Analysis

A agreed to make (and not revoke) a will devising A's property to B. A made such a will and the contract for the will is valid. Nevertheless, A later revokes the will and executes Will #2 devising A's property to C. The revocation of Will #1 and the execution of Will #2 are unaffected by the contract. Will #1 is revoked and Will #2 will be admitted to probate. B's remedy is not in probate; it is for breach of contract.

2. Failure to Make a Promised Will

Similarly, a contract to make a will is not the same as the will it anticipates, meaning that there can be no probate of the contract if the promised will is not executed, nor can the promised will be treated as if it were executed: there is no specific performance available in this context.

3. Action for Breach of Contract

The only available remedy when a promisor fails to make a promised will or revokes or alters a will she promised not to revoke or alter is for breach of the contract, with typical contract law requirements relating to consideration, ascertainability of provisions, and so forth. For example, some property, dollar amount, fractional share, or other identifiable portion of a decedent's estate that is subject to the contract must be spelled out in a manner that would allow a court to enforce the contract. Lacking some specific promise, at best the recovery will be for something like quantum meruit.

 ## Examples and Analysis

Testator's promise to Caregiver was: "If you care for me for the balance of my life, I *will take care of you* under my will." If Testator's will does not provide for Caregiver, the likely remedy, if any, is only for the fair value of the services rendered.

a. **Consideration.** Consideration exists in mutual will cases once the first to die has complied with her end of the bargain by dying with the anticipated mutual will. Otherwise, consideration often takes one of the following forms.

    i. Services. Caring for the testator, living with the testator, or supporting the testator (assuming there was no obligation to do so and that services provided were not provided gratuitously). Close family members are presumed to provide care for free, and one spouse may have a legal obligation to care for the other spouse, meaning that this care may not qualify as consideration for an alleged contract to make a will.

    ii. Marriage. Marriage to the testator (or, conceivably, to someone, like a child, who the testator wanted to be married). Thus, a promise in a premarital agreement to devise $X to the spouse-to-be if she survives the promisor will be supported by consideration (assuming the marriage takes place).

    iii. Property transfer. Conveyance of property to a third party, or payment of an annuity or similar amounts to the testator for life.

    iv. Forbearance. Forbearance of suit or of a contest of a will.

b. Public policy. If the object of the agreement was to perform acts that violate public policy or that are illegal or immoral (e.g., divorce someone, commit adultery, or commit a crime at the decedent's request), that consideration likely will not support litigation for breach.

4. Anticipatory Breach

A will contract promisor may breach the contract prior to her death. If so, one or more of the following remedies may be available for the anticipatory breach: (i) recovery of any consideration already given to the breaching promisor; (ii) restitution for property conveyed in reliance on the contract; (iii) maybe an injunction against a threatened conveyance to a third party of property subject to the contract; or (iv) a constructive trust imposed on the transferee if property promised under the contract is conveyed to a third party (unless, perhaps, the third party is a bona fide purchaser for value); (v) but an injunction against revocation or specific performance ordering execution of a promised will are out of the question.

 # Examples and Analysis

Testator does not have sufficient liquid funds to pay her ongoing living expenses and is unable to continue managing Blackacre. Testator agrees to leave half of Blackacre to Manager, if Manager will pay to Testator $X per month, and manage Blackacre, for the rest of Testator's life. Testator gives Blackacre to Child after Manager has complied with the contract for two years. Manager may bring an action during Testator's life for breach of the contract. If Manager wants to continue with the contract, she may have available as a remedy the imposition of a constructive trust on half of Blackacre. If Manager does not want to continue the contract, she should be able to recover amounts paid to Testator under the contract and probably the fair value of her services in managing Blackacre for the two year period. If instead of giving Blackacre to Child, Testator continues to own it but simply does not execute the promised will, or after having done so revokes it, Manager has no actionable claim unless and until Testator dies without the promised will.

5. Breach at Promisor's Death

Any action to recover for breach of the contract at the death of the contracting party is not in probate. Again, a promised will cannot be restored after the decedent revoked it and cannot be regarded as executed if the contracting party never signed it. Entitlement probably will be limited to damages, specific performance in the form of a constructive trust, restitution, or quantum meruit, all in the local court that decides contract actions.

 # EXAMPLES AND ANALYSIS

Husband and Wife, each of whom has one child from a prior marriage, execute a joint and mutual will under which each agrees to leave his or her property to the other spouse, or equally to the two children if the other spouse is not living. Husband dies and leaves his estate to Wife, and Wife later changes her will to leave her entire estate to one of the children. Although the omitted child has no actionable claim prior to Wife's death, upon her death the omitted child could assert a claim for a constructive trust to be imposed on half of the property left by Wife to the other child.

6. Contractual Wills and the Surviving Spouse's Elective Share

The spouses in *Via v. Putnam*, 626 So. 2d 460 (Fla. 1995), executed contractual mutual wills providing for the estate of the first to die to pass to the survivor, and for the survivor's estate to pass to their children. Joann died first, after which Edgar married Rachel. When Edgar died Rachel claimed a pretermitted spouse's ½ share of Edgar's estate (see Chapter 10). The court held that the children's claim under the contractual wills lacked priority over Rachel's claim. The same issue arises when a surviving spouse in Rachel's position asserts a claim to an elective share (see Chapter 10), and cases go both ways; *Putnam* held for Rachel on the basis of the strong public policy in favor of a surviving spouse's pretermitted heir status.

a. **The equities.** In some cases involving contractual mutual wills between spouses, the first spouse to die would have left less to the second to die were it not for the contract. Thus, without the contract, the second of the spouses to die would have less property. If the surviving spouse remarries, denial to the new surviving spouse of a share of property subject to the contract in such cases isn't inequitable—the decedent's net worth is greater just because of the life estate received in the property of the first spouse to die. In such a case, equity doesn't favor a claim by the new surviving spouse against the property subject to the contract.

EXAM TIP

The law of wills treats contractual wills like noncontractual wills. The question whether a decedent died testate or intestate, or which will was the testator's valid last will, should be analyzed under the usual execution and revocation rules without regard to whether the testator was under a contractual obligation to die intestate or testate with a will containing specified provisions.

Thus, for example, assume that T entered into a contract with A under which T agreed to devise A half of T's estate if A would serve as the president of a company T owned for the rest of T's life. T executed the required will. Later, A breached the agreement and terminated A's employment relationship with the company. A is entitled to half of T's estate if T dies without having revoked the will. The breach of the agreement by A does not cause a partial or complete revocation of T's will (although T or the company may have separate breach of contract claims against A). Similarly, if A had complied with the contract and T had executed a will devising T's entire estate to someone else, the will would control the disposition of T's estate. T's breach of the contract would not affect the validity of the will; A's remedy would be a breach of contract claim against T's estate, or perhaps a claim for a constructive trust to be imposed on ½ of T's estate left to the devisees under the will.

---

b. **Election against the will.** If D and S, spouses, enter into a contract to execute and not revoke wills leaving property of the first to die to the other, and property of the survivor to named beneficiaries, the survivor may renounce the will and elect to receive a statutory share of the decedent's estate unburdened by the contract. (See Chapter 10.) See *Bauer v. Piercy*, 912 S.W.2d 457 (Ky. Ct. App. 1995) (the contract precluded a revocation by the survivor, but not a renunciation).

EXAM TIP

For contractual wills questions, consider employing the following analysis:

- If there is a decedent, determine how her property will pass under the law of wills without regard to whether disposition of the testator's estate is subject to a contract.

- If there is a contract purporting to affect the disposition of the decedent's property, consider whether the contract is enforceable. In some jurisdictions (e.g., UPC §2-514), the contract must be evidenced by a writing. In others, an oral contract may be enforced if it can be proven with clear and convincing evidence.

- Even if the jurisdiction generally enforces oral will contracts, consider application of the Statute of Frauds (e.g., if the contract is with respect to the disposition of real estate).

- If oral will contracts generally are enforceable but there is a Statute of Frauds issue, consider whether the part performance or estoppel exceptions to application of the Statute of Frauds bar are available.

- If the contract is enforceable, consider what remedies are available for its breach. Specific performance of the contract is not an option.

REVIEW QUESTIONS AND ANSWERS

Question: T entered into a valid contract under which T agreed to revoke her will (which left her entire estate to a charity) and to execute a new will leaving her entire estate to A. Subsequently, A learned that T had not done either. What recourse does A have?

Answer: None during T's lifetime. If, at T's death, the first will remains unrevoked and T has not executed the second one, A then may sue the personal representative of T's estate for breach of contract. A may not have the first will treated as revoked and the contract admitted to probate as T's will. T's will may only be revoked in accordance with the jurisdiction's governing law (generally, by a duly executed subsequent writing or by a physical act; see Chapter 4). Similarly, a will is not valid unless executed with testamentary intent in accordance with the required formalities (see Chapter 3). Thus, the first will was not revoked, nor was the second executed; A's remedy is provided by the law of contract, not the law of wills.

Question: D and D's spouse, S, executed a joint will providing for the property of the first to die to pass to the survivor, and for the survivor's property to be divided equally among their children from prior marriages (the descendants of a deceased child of D or S to take the child's share, by representation). D died first, after which S executed a will leaving S's property to S's descendants only. What recourse do D's descendants have?

Answer: The threshold question is whether the will was contractual. In some jurisdictions, the execution of a joint will raises a presumption that it is contractual. Generally, mutual terms in the wills of two or more persons will not alone cause the wills to be contractual. Under UPC §2-514, wills are not contractual unless the will sets forth the contract terms, the will references the contract and its terms can be proven, or there is a writing signed by the decedent evidencing the contract. In a state without a similar statute, it may be impossible due to the Statute of Frauds to prove the existence and terms of the contract, if there was an oral contract and it provided for the devise of property, such as land, subject to the Statute of Frauds. The part performance of the contract—D's death with the will in effect and property passing under it to S—may avoid the Statute of Frauds issue, and S's estate (S having received property under the will at D's death) may be estopped from relying on the Statute of Frauds to bar the claims of D's descendants. In this case, more information is needed to determine if the joint will would be treated as contractual.

If so, D's descendants may assert a breach of contract claim against D's estate, and may be able to impose a constructive trust on S's descendants for half of S's estate.

Question: D is elderly and infirm. C moves in with D and cares for D for the rest of D's life so that it will not be necessary for D to go to a nursing home. At D's death, C asserts that D promised to leave C half of D's estate if C would move in with and care for D. Neither D's will nor any other writing evidences such a contract. What result?

Answer: In some states (e.g., UPC §2-514), a contract to make a will only may be proven by a writing. In such a jurisdiction, C likely would have a claim in quantum meruit for compensation for the value of the services rendered to D. If C were D's spouse, however, such a claim would be barred because of C's obligation to support D. Similarly, if C were a close family member of D, such as a child, in many states there would be a presumption that the services rendered by C to D were gratuitous.

If the jurisdiction allows oral contracts to make wills, the Statute of Frauds should not bar C's claim even if D's estate consists of real property because C's performance of services should constitute part performance under the contract sufficient to avoid the Statute of Frauds.

6 WILL SUBSTITUTES

 CHAPTER OVERVIEW

- A substantial part of this topic involves the law of intestacy, wills, and decedents' estates. However, much—or even all—of what a person considers to be her property may not pass under the terms of her will (if she dies testate) or by intestacy. Rather, it is "nonprobate property" and passes pursuant to the terms of the particular instrument or rules—sometimes called a "will substitute"—that governs it.

- Common forms of nonprobate property include joint tenancies, life insurance, retirement plans, annuities, and trusts.

- A common theme addressed here is the extent to which the law of wills governs will substitutes.

A. COORDINATING NONPROBATE PROPERTY WITH THE ESTATE PLAN

1. The Best Laid Plans . . .

Even the "perfect" will has no effect on the disposition of nonprobate property.

 EXAMPLES AND ANALYSIS

Your client is a single parent with one small child. You work through all of the questions she must answer for you to draft her will with a trust for the child (who should be trustee, how long should the property stay in trust, may the trustee expend trust funds for the child, what if the child dies before the trust terminates, etc.). You draft the will, your client executes it, and she dies in a car accident a month later. The value of her probate estate—net of debts—is $25,000; she had a $500,000 insurance policy on her life, the beneficiary of which was her child and it pays double indemnity due to the accidental death. The $25,000 net probate estate passes under the terms of the will to the trust for the child; the $1 million of insurance proceeds are paid to a court appointed guardian for the child, to be distributed outright to the child at age 18, subject to cumbersome and expensive court supervision until then. The estate plan failed because the life insurance beneficiary designation was not coordinated with the will.

B. WIDESPREAD USE OF WILL SUBSTITUTES

Most wealth is in nonprobate form (see Chapter 1). Even with improvements that facilitate probate administration, several common purposes for using will substitutes explain their popularity.

1. Avoiding Probate

Some states still lack independent (i.e., not subject to court supervision) probate administration, making avoidance of the cost, publicity, and delay of probate important.

2. Tax Planning

Minimizing wealth transfer and income taxation is possible through lifetime gifts that "mature" at death, such as gifts made to irrevocable life insurance trusts.

3. Planning for Incapacity may utilize lifetime management and protection of the assets with a trust. For more information, see the Website.

4. Life insurance (The Instant Estate) is used to provide liquidity to pay death taxes and debts, and to augment the estate. With proper planning, the insurance proceeds can be received free of federal income and estate tax.

5. Avoiding Claims

Finally, some transfers are employed to minimize the rights of predators, such as creditors and surviving spouses who may exercise elective share rights (see Chapter 10).

C. VALIDITY OF WILL SUBSTITUTES

Nonprobate transfers are subject to challenge to the extent they look like testamentary dispositions but lack the formalities of a will. Litigants who make such challenges include surviving spouses, creditors, and an occasional disappointed heir, all seeking to reach nonprobate property through a claim against an estate they hope to augment: if the nonprobate transfer fails and the property that would have been subject to it instead becomes a part of the probate estate, those with claims against the probate estate benefit.

1. Trend

The clear trend, coincident with the increased use of will substitutes, is to uphold them. Still, two conflicting factors sometimes create chaos in this arena. First, some courts appear to decide these cases with at least one eye on the equities involved (claimant versus potential beneficiary of the nonprobate disposition). Second, courts seem to uphold the more common nonprobate transfers more often than they uphold the more unusual.

2. General Principles

Among the few identifiable generally applicable principles in this area, consider the following.

a. Wills compared to will substitutes. Wills are both ambulatory (they have no legal effect until the testator's death) and revocable during the testator's life. The challenger of a will substitute should at least show that the decedent did nothing irrevocable and parted with nothing during life.

b. Interest in beneficiary. To be valid, a will substitute should operate during the decedent's life to create some interest in a beneficiary. Enjoyment of the interest may be deferred, provided that the interest is created presently. It is adequate that the interest is contingent, provided that an interest actually is created presently.

c. No guarantees. Showing that the will substitute is ambulatory and revocable, and that no interest was created in the beneficiary of the will substitute until the decedent's death, does not guarantee a successful challenge; several of the most common will substitutes (e.g., life insurance) look like wills under these standards but are treated universally as not invalid—indeed, they rarely are challenged.

D. LIFE INSURANCE, ANNUITIES, AND INTERESTS IN DEFERRED COMPENSATION PLANS

1. Testamentary Characteristics of Life Insurance

Most notable among the nonprobate transfers that do nothing until a decedent's death is insurance on the decedent's life. In the typical case a person owns insurance on her own life for which she has designated a beneficiary to receive the proceeds at her death. That arrangement is both ambulatory and revocable:

a.   **Ambulatory.** No interest in the policy is created by the beneficiary designation (unless you really stretch and treat the beneficiary designation as creating an expectancy that counts as an interest in the policy; but no fiduciary or other duties are owed by the policyholder to the beneficiary, and a beneficiary has no more of an interest in the policy than a devisee under a will has in the property of a living testator).

b.   **Not testamentary.** Thus, life insurance would seem to be a good candidate for a successful attack as being a testamentary arrangement that does not comply with required will formalities. Nevertheless, life insurance is clearly and consistently regarded as not being testamentary in nature.

2.   Insurance Proceeds Not Controlled by Insured's Will

Cook v. Equitable Life Assurance Society, 428 N.E.2d 110 (Ind. Ct. App. 1981), illustrates the corollary to insurance being nontestamentary: when a beneficiary of a policy is named, the insured's will has no effect on disposition of the proceeds. In *Cook,* the insured named his wife as beneficiary before they were divorced. Without changing the beneficiary designation, the insured executed a will that purported to leave the proceeds of the policy to a new spouse and child. At the insured's death, the court awarded the proceeds to the ex-spouse. *Cook* is a dramatic example that rules that apply with respect to wills would be useful with respect to will substitutes (in this case, the rule causing a revocation by operation of law of the will or a bequest under a will in favor of a former spouse; see Chapter 4). Indeed, many states have addressed the *Cook* problem with statutes that revoke insurance beneficiary designations naming the insured's ex-spouse. See, e.g., UPC §2-804.

3.   Control of Insurance Proceeds by Will

In limited circumstances the will of the insured policyholder controls the disposition of the proceeds on the insured's death. For example, if the beneficiary of the policy is the insured's estate, the proceeds will be payable to the estate for disposition with the rest of the insured's probate estate under the terms of the insured's will (or the jurisdiction's intestacy statutes, if the insured died intestate). However, for reasons discussed on page 163, it generally is not a good idea to name the insured's estate as the beneficiary of a life insurance policy; rather, it is preferable to coordinate the disposition of the insurance proceeds with the disposition of the rest of the insured's estate in another manner.

4.   Annuities

In their purest form, annuities pay a person a fixed amount per month for life; at death, there are no further rights under the annuity arrangement to pass on to others, and the question of validity as a will substitute does not arise. Annuities with refund or survivorship features, however, provide benefits to others after the annuitant's death, typically by beneficiary designation as a nonprobate transfer by will substitute. Although such annuities, like life insurance, are revocable and ambulatory and thus would appear to be vulnerable to attack for lack of compliance with will formalities, they are enough like insurance that they also are not regarded as testamentary.

5. Deferred Compensation Death Benefits

Similarly, deferred compensation plan benefits (e.g., IRAs and employee retirement plans) payable after the employee's death to designated beneficiaries generally are not regarded as invalid will substitutes, again without regard to their appearing to be testamentary in nature and often not creating any interest in a beneficiary upon designation as such.

E. PAYABLE ON DEATH CONTRACTS

1. What They Are

Payable on death (POD) contracts include a wide variety of contractual arrangements under which, on the death of a party to the contract, benefits are payable to one or more beneficiaries named to receive them in the contract, without regard to the terms of the decedent's will or the jurisdiction's intestacy statutes. Theoretically, POD contracts include life insurance, annuities, and deferred compensation plans. But the term more commonly is used to refer to bank accounts owned by one person and payable on death to another, stock ownership arrangements (sometimes referred to as transfer on death (TOD) accounts), and other contracts such as employment agreements, partnership agreements, depository agreements, and so forth.

2. Testamentary Challenge

The more common POD arrangements routinely are viewed as nontestamentary—and thus not subject to successful challenge for failure to comply with will formalities—without regard to their testamentary characteristics. Other less common POD contracts have been held unenforceable on that ground.

   a. *Wilhoit v. Peoples Life Insurance Co.,* 218 F.2d 887 (7th Cir. 1955): the beneficiary of a life insurance policy (B) deposited the proceeds with the insurance company under an arrangement that differed in minor respects from the payout option under the policy itself. The court held that the deposit arrangement was not covered by the protection from a testamentary attack afforded life insurance. Noteworthy is that (i) B had designated her own beneficiary (DB) to receive any funds remaining at B's death, (ii) DB predeceased B, and (iii) B then executed a will that devised the funds to a devisee under B's will. Arguably, giving effect to B's intent for disposing of the funds influenced the court's conclusion that the deposit arrangement was invalid (i.e., testamentary without having been executed in compliance with will formalities).

b.   Current treatment of payable on death contracts. UPC §6-101 broadly authorizes POD arrangements in all contracts, as well as in a variety of other instruments that are not usually viewed as contracts, such as promissory notes, bonds, conveyances, deeds of gift, and trusts. Most states have followed the UPC approach.

    i.   Trend. *Estate of Hillowitz,* 238 N.E.2d 723 (N.Y. 1968), shows that courts have not rejected will substitutes merely for failing to comply with the execution formalities of the Wills Act. The decedent was a partner in a partnership that called for his interest to be paid to his wife on his death. The personal representative of the decedent's estate challenged the agreement and the court held for the widow because it deemed the partnership agreement a third party contract for her benefit, not an invalid testamentary disposition.

    ii.   Quaere. If the trend illustrated by UPC §6-101 reflects a determination that formalities are not necessary to protect against abuse, why do formalities prevail with respect to wills?

3.   POD Bank Accounts

Many banks permit accounts owned in the name of one person, payable on her death to another. These are pure will substitutes: the depositor has unrestricted ownership—and the payee-to-be has no interest—in the funds until the depositor's death. Consequently, POD accounts are vulnerable to attack as testamentary and lacking compliance with required will formalities. Statutes in a majority of states, however, authorize such accounts. See pages 159-160 for a discussion of the very similar Totten trust bank account form of will substitute.

F.   JOINT TENANCY

1.   Ownership of Property During Tenants' Lives

Each joint tenant is treated as owning the whole property, subject to the equal rights of the other joint tenants. Thus, if A owns Blackacre and transfers ownership to A and B as joint tenants with the right of survivorship, A is treated as having made a gift of an interest in Blackacre to B.

2.   Joint Tenancy Bank Accounts

Joint tenancy bank accounts are different. Generally each tenant has full access to the funds in the account during their joint lives, and the survivor becomes the sole owner on the death of the other tenants. In the event of a dispute, however, most jurisdictions treat the funds as owned in proportion to the respective depositors' net contributions to the account. See, e.g., UPC §6-211.

3. Stock

Blanchette v. Blanchette, 287 N.E.2d 459 (Mass. 1972), addressed the lifetime ownership of joint tenancy stock in the context of a divorce. Husband bought the stock and took title in the joint names of Husband and Wife. Under the traditional joint tenancy rule Husband made a gift of the stock to Wife. Husband testified and the court found, however, that no gift was intended because Husband took title in joint tenancy solely so that Wife would be the beneficiary at his death. Consequently, upon their divorce, the stock was deemed to be his and not theirs.

4. Safe Deposit Boxes

A joint tenancy safety deposit box is only that; it does not make the contents of the box joint tenancy property.

5. Death of Joint Tenant Following Divorce

Assume in *Blanchette* that ownership of the stock had not been changed in connection with the divorce and Husband then died. Although state statutes revoke provisions in a will in favor of an ex-spouse (see Chapter 4), many do not apply to nonprobate assets. Thus, Wife would have become the sole owner by the right of survivorship. By contrast, UPC §2-804 would sever the joint tenancy and convert it to a tenancy in common.

6. Validity of Survivorship Feature

The survivorship feature in a joint tenancy is not testamentary, even if all tenants have a unilateral right to terminate the tenancy until death. This result is more defensible than the nontestamentary treatment afforded life insurance, annuities, deferred compensation plan interests, and many POD contracts because each joint tenant is viewed as owning the whole property, subject to similar ownership rights of every other tenant, from inception of their concurrent ownership.

7. Convenience Joint Tenancies

However, a joint tenancy created solely for convenience can be defeated as not constituting a conveyance at all. Such cases typically arise with respect to bank accounts.

a. *Franklin v. Anna Nat'l Bank,* 488 N.E.2d 1117 (Ill. App. Ct. 1986), for example, involved an individual who established a joint tenancy bank account with his sister-in-law when she began caring for him. When he changed caregivers he unsuccessfully attempted to substitute his new caregiver as the other joint tenant on the account. At his death, the personal representative of his estate and the sister-in-law both claimed the funds. Based on the facts, the presumption that the depositor intended a "true" joint tenancy with survivorship was successfully rebutted and the funds in the account were deemed part of the decedent's probate estate because no gift was intended and no true joint tenancy with right of survivorship was meant to be created.

    b. Surviving joint tenant often takes. Although *Franklin* may yield the "right" result, the presumption of a true joint tenancy with ownership rights often means that the surviving joint tenant takes in cases in which that result seems questionable. Thus, *Franklin* illustrates a danger with such accounts: without intending the right of survivorship, many people create them for convenience or to solve a property management problem to which an inter vivos trust or a durable power of attorney would be better answers.

8. Tax Considerations

Without going into detail, joint tenancies produce adverse tax results in various cases.

9. Creditors' Rights

Generally a creditor of a decedent may not reach assets the decedent owned in joint tenancy with one or more cotenants. If the joint tenancy is a bank account, however, the creditor may reach it under UPC §6-215. (Note also that a creditor of one joint tenant can reach a portion of the joint tenancy property during the debtor/joint tenant's life.)

G. DEEDS

1. Invalid as Testamentary?

Labelling an instrument as a deed, and using language usually found in deeds ("I grant, bargain, sell and convey . . ."), will not ensure that a purported conveyance is effective.

 EXAMPLES AND ANALYSIS

Grantor executed a deed that conveyed Blackacre to Grantee with the proviso: "this deed to be effective only at Grantor's death." The deed is testamentary and invalid if it did not presently convey an interest and was intended to pass nothing until the grantor's death. See *Butler v. Sherwood,* 188 N.Y.S. 242 (1921) (the deed was invalid even though it was delivered to the grantee). There are cases that hold the deed nontestamentary and valid, with the grantor viewed as having conveyed a vested remainder subject to a retained life estate.

2. Delivery

No completed gift was made if the instrument on its face is an unconditional conveyance but it was not delivered until after the grantor's death—delivery, actual or constructive, is required. Absent delivery, there is no lifetime conveyance of an interest and the instrument—not executed with Wills Act formalities—does not pass the property at the grantor's death.

H. REVOCABLE TRUSTS

1. What They Are

A trust is an arrangement by which one or more trustees hold legal title to property for the benefit of one or more beneficiaries. (See Chapter 11.) The settlor may revoke a revocable trust, in which case the trust property is transferred back to the settlor (or her designee).

2. Basic Structure

Settlors usually create revocable trusts for their own benefit. The settlor often is the sole beneficiary during her life. After the settlor's death, the trust property is administered for—and sooner or later distributed to—beneficiaries named by the settlor in the trust instrument, much like probate property owned by a decedent is administered in her estate and distributed to the devisees under her will (or to her heirs, if the decedent died intestate).

3. Why Settlors Create Revocable Trusts

Revocable trusts have become extremely common for a variety of reasons: To minimize the rights of a creditor or spouse, which may not be achieved; to prepare for the settlor's incapacity (although that objective usually can be accomplished more simply by use of a durable power of attorney); to secure management assistance (although in many cases a durable power of attorney can accomplish that more efficiently); to avoid a will contest; and to avoid probate. None of these objectives entail giving up ultimate control over the trust assets. In addition to being the sole beneficiary of the trust for life, often the settlor serves as its sole trustee or, if a third party is named as trustee, the settlor typically reserves a right to remove and replace the trustee.

4. Fundamental Requirement for Validity

Revocable trusts are valid as will substitutes without regard to execution formalities, because there is a present declaration of trust as required and a transfer of property to the trust. Thus, validity turns on whether the trust is valid. See Chapter 12.

5. **Corpus Requirement**

To be valid, the trustee must presently become the owner of some trust assets. Almost anything will do and many trusts are created with a de minimis amount (e.g., $10).

a. **Self-trusteed trusts.** A self-trusteed declaration of trust requires no physical delivery or transfer of property (how would you deliver assets to yourself as trustee?). This makes it look like there has been no real change in ownership, which then supports the charge that the trust is testamentary because it is revocable and has not accomplished anything prior to the settlor's death.

b. **Formal transfers of assets.** The easy solution is to cause assets that are represented by a document of title (such as the deed to realty, or the title to your car) to be reregistered to show trust ownership. With respect to any asset that lacks a document of title, we merely use a bill of sale to prove delivery: "I, Irene Nixon, hereby sell to Irene Nixon as trustee of the Irene Nixon trust dated _____ all of my tangible personal property, including all household goods and furniture, clothing, and articles of personal use. . . ."

c. **Assets not yet in existence** (for example, royalties from books that we may write): (1) these may become trust assets upon springing into existence if there is an enforceable promise to entrust, which is a matter of contract law, but (2) the trust must be valid prior to their springing into existence.

   i. **Enforceable promise.** The consideration needed for a trust to attach to a promised asset once it comes into existence is the consideration normally needed to support either (i) a promise to create the trust, or (ii) a contract right of the trust to receive assets not yet in existence. Beware: the promise must be held by someone who has both the right and the ability to enforce it—the settlor cannot be the trustee of her own promise, because there is no one to enforce that promise; merger of the obligation and the right to enforce it would cause its extinction.

   ii. **Validity of trust.** In *Estate of Brenner*, 547 P.2d 938 (Colo. Ct. App. 1976), the settlor executed a trust declaring that he held real property described in an attached exhibit; he also attached a dollar bill to the trust instrument. He did not own the real estate when he executed the trust, but acquired it—taking title in the name of the trust—five days later. On the settlor's death, the validity of the trust was challenged on the basis, among others, that he did not own the real property when the trust instrument was signed. Although the trial court held that the dollar validated the trust, the appellate court upheld the trust without addressing that issue, holding that conveyance of the real property to the trust five days after execution of the trust instrument validated the trust. The theoretical issue raised by *Brenner* is whether a trust can be made valid in the first instance by funding with future assets when they come into existence, allowing the trust then created to be a valid receptacle for those assets themselves. In a sense this is a metaphysical question whether the trust can receive the assets and thereby become valid if the trust is not yet valid by virtue of owning some asset. The easy answer is to avoid the question by funding the trust at its inception.

d. **Incomplete transfer.** A transfer usually is effective if the settlor does all that she must do to make the conveyance, even if the trustee has not yet received the property.

 # EXAMPLES AND ANALYSIS

If the settlor has signed stock powers (which are instruments for the transfer of stock) and placed them and the underlying certificates (which typically would be mailed in a separate envelope for security purposes) in the mail, but dies before the trustee receives them, the black letter rule is that the settlor's acts validated the trust as if the stock already was a part of the trust corpus, notwithstanding that delivery was not immediate because of incomplete administrative steps that were beyond the settlor's control.

6. **Are Revocable Trusts Testamentary?**

The second issue with respect to the validity of an inter vivos revocable trust is whether it is testamentary in nature.

a. **Retained rights and powers.** Lifetime retention by the settlor of enjoyment and control is normal and permissible, and includes (i) rights to receive income and principal, (ii) powers of appointment, (iii) powers over investment and administration, (iv) even powers as trustee, and (v) powers to amend or revoke the trust.

b. **Revocable trusts are not testamentary** for two fundamental, interrelated reasons:

   i. **Fiduciary duties.** The fiduciary relation between the trustee and the beneficiaries creates fiduciary duties, and exposure for breach, that are not present with respect to property the settlor owns outright. That makes the ownership of property under a trust indenture different from holding assets that will be subject to probate and the Wills Act.

    ii. Beneficial interests of others. Creation of equitable interests in a third party—for a revocable trust, typically a remainder beneficiary—validates the trust and constitutes something more than a purely ambulatory will would accomplish during the testator's life. Even if those beneficial interests are contingent, defeasible, or remote, their existence impairs alienability at least to some extent and allows enforceability of the trust. Unlike a will, which is of no legal effect until the testator's death (i.e., it is ambulatory), present rights in others are created by even the most naked trust.

  c. *Farkas v. Williams,* 125 N.E.2d 600 (Ill. 1955), is a wonderful case to showcase these elements. The settlor named himself as trustee, retaining a life estate and the power to amend or revoke the trust. The trust provided for the assets to be distributed at the settlor's death to a named beneficiary. The court relied on both the elements of impaired alienability and fiduciary responsibility, essentially holding that the settlor accomplished something during life that was sufficient to distinguish the trust from a purely testamentary disposition.

  d. When might a revocable trust be testamentary? Although it is difficult to envision why a settlor might do so, and how a challenge might result, a revocable trust might be vulnerable to a testamentary attack: if the settlor is trustee and sole lifetime beneficiary, and if the only remainder beneficiary is the settlor's estate.

EXAM TIP

If the validity of a revocable trust is at issue, consider the following:

- If the settlor lacked the requisite capacity (see Chapter 3) to create a trust, it will be invalid. Similarly, undue influence, fraud, and duress also are grounds for attacking the validity of a trust.

- There can be no trust without trust property; the exception to this rule is if the unfunded "trust" is the devisee under the settlor's pour over will, the Uniform Testamentary Additions to Trusts Act validates the trust—and the pour over to it—without regard to whether the trust otherwise had a corpus.

- If the Act is not applicable (e.g., the trust is not a devisee under a pour over will), and the trust has property, the trust will be invalid if it is testamentary and the formalities required for the valid execution of a will were not met.

- The most likely circumstance for a testamentary challenge is if the settlor is the sole beneficiary for the settlor's life and serves as the sole trustee. Even then, however, if there is a remainder beneficiary a testamentary attack will fail because the trust creates present rights in the remainder beneficiary; the trustee has fiduciary duties to the remainder beneficiary and the settlor's ability to alienate the trust property has been impaired.

7.   Revocation of a Revocable Trust

In re Estate and Trust of Pilafas, 836 P.2d 420 (Ariz. Ct. App. 1992), raised the issue of how a settlor of an inter vivos trust who retained the power to revoke may exercise that power. (1) The trust authorized the settlor, who also served as trustee, to revoke the trust by a written instrument delivered to the trustee and (2) the original trust was in the settlor's possession but was not found following the settlor's death. The court refused to apply the presumption of revocation by destruction that would apply to a will in that circumstance (see Chapter 4). The trust specified the means of revoking the trust and it could not be revoked by physical destruction of the trust instrument, even if the settlor was presumed to have performed that act. *Pilafas* thus illustrates that, trusts are valid will substitutes and will principles generally do not apply to trusts.

8.   Creditors' Rights

State Street Bank and Trust Co. v. Reiser, 389 N.E.2d 768 (Mass. App. Ct. 1979), illustrates the nature of an inter vivos revocable trust vis-a-vis the outside world. The issue was whether a creditor of the settlor may reach trust assets after the settlor's death. The court held that it could.

    a.   Effect of settlor's death. The creditor could have reached the trust assets during the settlor's life. See Chapter 13. In *Reiser* the settlor was deceased, but if there had been no trust and the settlor had owned the assets at death, they would have become part of the probate estate, and the creditor could have reached them. The court concluded on policy grounds that the creditor could bank reach trust assets after the settlor's death, as it could estate assets, because of the settlor's retained powers over the trust assets. That holding is not necessarily ''wrong,'' but it is contrary to Restatement (Second) of Trusts §330, which provides that creditors usually cannot reach trust assets postmortem, in the absence of fraud (which did not exist in *Reiser*).

9.   Totten Trusts

Many banks permit customers to open savings accounts in the name of the settlor "as trustee" for the settlor for life, remainder to another. Called

"Totten trusts" (after *In re Totten*, 71 N.E. 748 (N.Y. 1904), which held them valid), these "savings account trusts" are only barely legitimate trusts, created simply by signing the appropriate signature card when opening a bank account, usually with absolutely no formalities that anyone could even argue rise to the level of protection of the Wills Act.

a. **Purpose.** Totten trusts were developed as a will substitute for bank accounts before the advent of POD accounts to pass to the designated beneficiary without the need to comply with the Wills Act formalities and to avoid probate.

b. **Validity.** Totten trusts are valid in most states, either by court decision or, more commonly, by statute. See, e.g., UPC §6-201 et. seq., which treats them the same as POD accounts. This is the case even though (i) they have virtually no terms or formalities, (ii) fiduciary obligations are nonexistent, and (iii) beneficial interests are tentative during the settlor's life.

c. **Trustee's ownership of funds.** Absent an indication that the settlor intended otherwise, during the settlor's life the account belongs to the trustee, who may spend or give away the funds for any purpose the trustee chooses.

d. **Revocability.** The general trust rule is that a trust is irrevocable unless expressly made revocable by the creating instrument. Totten trusts, however, are revocable, absent an indication that the settlor intended otherwise. Delivery of the passbook or giving notice of creation to the beneficiary may, but will not necessarily, make a Totten trust irrevocable; it is a question of the settlor's intent. Unless a Totten trust is irrevocable, partial revocations (by withdrawal) are possible.

e. **Death of settlor.** On the settlor's death, any funds remaining in the account belong to the beneficiary, unless the settlor's will provides otherwise—unlike most will substitutes, the beneficiary of a Totten trust traditionally can be changed by the settlor's will. There is, however, a presumption against a will acting as a revocation. However, UPC §6-213(b), applicable to Totten trusts, POD accounts, and joint bank accounts, provides that the right of survivorship under any of these accounts cannot be changed by the depositor's will.

f. **Creditors' and spouse's rights.** Consistent with the almost complete and unrestricted control a settlor has over funds in a Totten trust, creditors (and usually a surviving spouse) cannot be disfranchised by creation of such an account, because it is just too "thin" for the purposes of diminishing these legitimate interests. (Restatement (Second) of Trusts §58(d)).

I.   THE ''BLOCKBUSTER'' WILL

1.   Controlling Nonprobate Transfers by Will

The blockbuster will concept suggests that a single document—a will—should be adequate to alter any beneficiary designation with respect to any property—nonprobate as well as probate—held during life and passing at death, including insurance proceeds, employee benefits, or POD contracts and accounts (excluding joint tenancies).

2.   Current Law

Under the law today, however, usually a will provision is not effective to alter a trust or other beneficiary designation. A will may do so, however, if it meets the terms for a change of the nonprobate asset.

 ## Examples and Analysis

Settlor created a revocable trust, retaining rights to income and principal for life and providing for distribution of the trust assets to Trust Beneficiary on Settlor's death. The trust instrument provides that any revocation must be written and delivered to the trustee during life. Settlor's will leaves the trust assets to Will Beneficiary. On Settlor's death, Trust Beneficiary and Will Beneficiary claim the trust assets. If a third party served as trustee, the revocation provision in the trust would prevent any argument that the will constitutes an effective revocation of the trust. But if the settlor was serving as trustee when the will was executed, *perhaps* the settlor as trustee could be deemed to have received the will, which arguably constitutes a revocation or amendment of the trust.

---

3.   Making Wills Law Applicable to Nonprobate Transfers

The law of wills addresses many issues that are not addressed by the rules applicable to separate forms of nonprobate property. The UPC, which does not recognize the blockbuster will concept, does address many of these kinds of issues, bringing many concepts that traditionally have applied only to wills and probate property to bear on nonprobate assets. Most states do not so provide. Among the rules that apply to a decedent's will and probate estate but often fail to apply to nonprobate transfers are those that address: divorce, adoption, pretermission, survivorship, lapse, tax apportionment, and creditors' rights. Chapter 10 addresses the rights of a surviving spouse with respect to nonprobate transfers. Many state statutes also do a poor job in this respect, which again argues for an integrated approach to all of a decedent's wealth transfers.

J. EQUITABLE ELECTION

1. Hypothetical

Decedent created certain rights in a beneficiary by a will provision but also attempted to dispose of that beneficiary's interest in nonprobate property (such as the proceeds of insurance on the decedent's life) by another provision in the will.

    a. Ignoring will provision vs. election. Normally a will cannot control the disposition of nonprobate property. But the rightful owner of that property is put to an election to either take under the will and allow the will to operate in all respects (i.e., to dispose of the nonprobate property), or to deny the effect of the will on the nonprobate asset and, in the process, relinquish all beneficial interests under the will.

2. Life Insurance and Joint Tenancy

Equitable election is particularly common with both life insurance and joint tenancy because decedents often do not know that a will cannot control the devolution of those assets, so they put the beneficiary to an unintended election.

    a. Can a mistake be corrected? Typically, there is no remedy for mistake under the law of wills. This means that the beneficiary cannot argue that the will provision attempting to dispose of the nonprobate property is invalid but not the balance of the will. Thus, the will either applies in toto, due to the election, or it fails with respect to the nonprobate assets, and the beneficiary who was put to the election; reformation is not customarily available as a remedy.

    b. Expressed intent of the testator. Because of the possibility that a testator will devise property to a beneficiary and also attempt to devise nonprobate property to others without knowing that the testator could not do so, some jurisdictions apply the doctrine of equitable election only if the testator expresses an intention to put a devisee to an election. In *Williamson v. Williamson*, 657 N.E.2d 651 (Ill. App. Ct. 1995), for example, the testator and a son owned real property in joint tenancy. The testator's will devised 2/3 of the property to five other children and the residue of his estate to all six children. The son accepted a distribution from the residue and his siblings claimed he therefore was required to convey to the father's estate 2/3 of the joint tenancy property. The court held for the son, refusing to apply the equitable election doctrine to joint tenancy property without an express indication that the testator so intended.

3. Election by the Beneficiary

An effective, binding election by the beneficiary requires acceptance of benefits under the will, with knowledge that the effect of doing so is relinquishment of the beneficiary's interest in the nonprobate property. If the election is not made, and the rightful taker of the nonprobate asset retains its ownership, the disappointed taker under the will might be compensated with the rightful taker's designated interest under the will (although this kind of equitable rearrangement is not predictable).

 # EXAMPLES AND ANALYSIS

T's will leaves Blackacre to A and Whiteacre to B; T owns Blackacre outright but T and A own Whiteacre in joint tenancy with the right of survivorship. A must elect either to accept Blackacre and have Whiteacre pass to B, or keep Whiteacre and give up Blackacre. If A decides to keep Whiteacre, part or all of Blackacre may go to B.

K. INSURANCE TRUSTS

1. Why Entrust Insurance Proceeds?

It often is advisable for a variety of nontax and tax reasons to place insurance proceeds on the death of an insured in trust. For example, the insurance may provide for minor beneficiaries, or a surviving spouse for life, remainder to children. The object may be to exclude the proceeds from estate tax.

2. Estate as Beneficiary

The insured could name the insured's estate as beneficiary under the policy, with the proceeds being distributed to devisees under the will, such as a testamentary trust. This rarely is advisable. Naming the estate as beneficiary subjects the proceeds to claims of the decedent's creditors; by contrast, in most states insurance proceeds paid to a trust as the designated beneficiary are not subject to that risk. Also, if the estate is the beneficiary, the proceeds are part of the probate administration, which means added delay and expense. And the proceeds will be subject to federal estate tax (if the estate is taxable) and probably any state transfer tax as well.

3. Testamentary Trust as Beneficiary

In many states it is possible for the proceeds to be paid to the trustee of a testamentary trust without subjecting them to creditor claims. That approach also should exclude the proceeds from probate administration. It will, however, cause some delay in the beneficiaries' access to the proceeds (because the will creating the trust must be admitted to probate before the trust can be put into operation and then claim the proceeds) and the proceeds will be subject to estate tax. A surviving spouse's elective share rights may extend to a testamentary trust and, if the insured wants to change the terms of the trust, a validly executed codicil is required, as opposed to a simple trust amendment. As a result, this alternative, although preferable to naming the estate as beneficiary, also is not advisable.

4. **Other Trust Alternatives** are available: funded or unfunded, revocable or irrevocable insurance trusts. Funded insurance trusts are not common, and most unfunded trusts are revocable.

   a. **Irrevocable insurance trusts.** Unless part of a divorce property settlement or an estate tax minimization plan, irrevocable insurance trusts normally are unattractive because of the loss of control and because any transfer of the policy or other funds to the trust may generate a gift tax. Ongoing premium payments must be considered and they also increase the gift tax exposure. Problems also exist in using insurance proceeds from irrevocable trusts to provide estates with liquidity to pay estate taxes and other obligations.

   b. **Funded trusts are expensive.** Trustee fees during the insured's life (if a third party acts as trustee) often discourage creation of a funded insurance trust. However, funded revocable trusts can receive insurance proceeds without problems if avoidance of estate tax is not an object and the insured or someone else who will not charge a fee for serving (such as a spouse or adult child) serves as trustee. This might suit a client who uses a self-trusteed revocable trust for probate avoidance and names the trust as beneficiary of insurance to accomplish nontax objectives.

5. **Unfunded Revocable Insurance Trusts**

   Most clients use the unfunded revocable insurance trust, in which there may be little or no fees during the insured's life because there are no trust assets. Further, there are no taxable gifts because there are no transfers to the trust, and the trust is revocable. Flexibility is maintained through the ability to change the beneficiary of the policy and the terms of the trust. And full liquidity may exist at death because there was no effort to keep the proceeds out of the insured's taxable estate.

   a. **Testamentary issue.** Given these results, however, an unfunded revocable insurance trust may be challenged as being testamentary. The argument is not usually based on the control retained by the settlor, nor on lack of terms during the insured's life. Instead, if the trust is only named beneficiary of the policy but is not funded and does not own the policy, the concern is lack of a corpus during the insured's life. (A trust usually fails if it lacks a corpus.)

   b. **Not testamentary.** Validity usually is justified on at least two grounds. First, the trust is no more testamentary than the insurance policy itself; insurance policies are not treated as testamentary, and the unfunded revocable insurance trust merely provides for the administration of the proceeds following the insured's death. Second, an unfunded revocable insurance trust as the designated beneficiary of insurance possesses either a vested right with respect to the insurance (subject to divestment on change of beneficiary), or only an expectancy? The vested right constitutes a sufficient corpus to validate the trust, and some courts say that the expectancy means the trustee has made a promise to create a trust of the proceeds when received, which is supported by consideration (being made beneficiary of the policy) that makes it enforceable. Restatement (Second) of Trusts §84(b) says the trustee's interest is more than a mere expectancy but it does not go so far as to say it is a vested interest. So the answer is: courts have finessed the question to avoid the alleged invalidity of an unfunded revocable insurance trust.

L. POUR OVER WILLS

1. Validity

A *pour over* will leaves the residue of a decedent's estate to a trust in existence at the testator's death. Pour overs are valid under state statutes or the doctrine of independent legal significance. See Chapter 3. Most states have adopted the Uniform Testamentary Additions to Trusts Act, which relies on the independent legal significance doctrine to permit a pour over to either an inter vivos or a testamentary trust.

2. Creation of Trust

Under the Uniform Testamentary Additions to Trust Act the trust need not be in existence when the will is executed; it is required only that the trust be in existence and able to receive the assets when the pour over occurs.

3. Amending the Trust

Under the Act, amendments to the trust instrument after execution of the will are valid. If the trust was created by another person, or otherwise is subject to amendment, it can be changed after the testator's death. The most common use of pour over wills is with revocable trusts that are used to avoid probate and provide for incapacity. These trusts typically prohibit amendment after the testator's death. But the pour over may be to a trust that can be amended by a third party after the testator's death, which creates problems only if the pour over will did not anticipate and authorize those changes.

4. Unfunded Trust

Under the Act, the pour over is permitted even to a trust that was not funded by the settlor during life. In the absence of the Act, the failure to fund the trust would result in there being no trust into which the decedent's assets could pass under the pour over will, but the Act finesses this issue: The recipient trust is not made testamentary by virtue of the pour over, nor is it subject to probate court control or local law restrictions on who may be trustee under a testamentary trust.

a. **Not incorporation by reference.** *Miller v. First Nat'l Bank & Trust Co.,* 637 P.2d 75 (Okla. 1981), involved a decedent who had divorced his former spouse, but who had not substituted another beneficiary for her under a revocable trust that was the beneficiary of insurance on his life. A state statute provided that, upon divorce, provisions in a will of one spouse in favor of the other were automatically revoked; the statute did not apply to trusts. The court held that the will incorporated the insurance trust by reference by virtue of a pour over provision in the will. In that respect the holding was aberrational and almost certainly equity driven; although it may have produced the right result in *Miller* it was wrong in the manner in which the court accomplished that result and, therefore, is dangerous precedent for spousal and creditors' rights cases.

b. **Compare former spouse as insurance beneficiary.** Compare the result in *Miller* to the available alternatives: If the proceeds were payable to the decedent's estate, and the decedent's will left them to the former spouse, the former spouse would be excluded. But if the former spouse were directly named as beneficiary under the policy she would have taken. Which result is more appropriate? Like UPC §2-804, state law should cover the effect of divorce in all these cases, but most states' statutes are not that sophisticated yet.

5. *Clymer v. Mayo,* 473 N.E.2d 1084 (Mass. 1985), illustrates a different approach courts have taken when a decedent's revocable trust named a spouse as beneficiary, the spouses divorce, the trust is not amended after the divorce, and the state divorce/revocation statute applies only to wills. In *Clymer,* the court held that the divorce terminated the ex-spouse's interest in the trust, not because it was incorporated by reference, but because the statute was deemed to reflect or presume the settlor's intent to revoke. According to the court, the wills/divorce statute was indicative of the intent of the average citizen with respect to this kind of trust as well as a will.

EXAM TIP

Will substitutes raise a variety of issues:

- Who takes? For example, generally, proceeds of insurance pass to the designated beneficiary, as does a decedent's interest in a retirement plan or IRA, without regard to the terms of the decedent's will. A joint tenancy bank account will pass to the surviving tenant(s) unless it is established that the account was an agency account that was made joint for the owner's convenience, such as to allow the other tenant(s) to pay bills for the owner if the owner is unable to do so.

- Is the will substitute testamentary? If so, it fails unless will execution formalities were met. Revocable trusts generally are not testamentary if there is a remainder beneficiary following the settlor's death, even if the settlor was the sole trustee and the sole beneficiary for life. POD bank accounts and Totten trust savings account trusts are allowed by statute or judicial decision in most states.

- If capacity is at issue, a higher standard of capacity may be imposed for a will substitute than for a will.

- Do the subsidiary rules of the law of wills apply? For example: (a) If the person named to receive the nonprobate property on the decedent's death dies before the decedent, does that person's estate or descendant take? (See lapse, discussed in Chapter 8.) (b) If the named beneficiary is the decedent's ex-spouse, does the spouse nevertheless take? (See Chapter 4.) (c) May creditors of the decedent reach the nonprobate property? (d) What if the named beneficiary killed the decedent? (See Chapter 2.) (e) May the decedent by will change the recipient of nonprobate property?

- May mistakes be corrected? (See Chapter 7.)

- Does a surviving spouse's election against the will reach nonprobate property? (See Chapter 10.)

REVIEW QUESTIONS AND ANSWERS

Question: T's will included the following provisions: "I give the proceeds of the ABC Life Insurance Company policy on my life to A, Blackacre to B, my account at XYZ Bank to C, my retirement plan interest through Employer, Inc. to D, and the residue of my estate to E." At T's death, the designated beneficiary of the ABC insurance policy was E, Blackacre was owned in joint tenancy by T and S, the XYZ account was styled "T, payable on death to S," and S was the designated beneficiary of T's retirement plan interest. A, B, C, D, E, and S survived T. How will the assets devised by T's be distributed?

Answer: The life insurance policy, Blackacre, the XYZ account, and the retirement plan interest are nonprobate assets, the disposition of which are established by the terms of the instruments (i.e., the "will substitutes") governing them. Accordingly, at T's death the insurance proceeds are payable to E, Blackacre is owned by S as the survivor of the joint tenancy, and S is entitled to receive the funds in the POD bank account and will succeed to T's interest in the retirement plan. None of these assets will pass under the terms of T's will, except perhaps the insurance proceeds. This is because the devise of the residue of T's estate to E, combined with the devise of the proceeds of the insurance policy to A, put E to an election whether (i) to accept the devise of the residue of T's estate under the will, in which case E will be required to forgo receipt of the proceeds of the insurance policy and allow them to pass to A under the terms of the will, or (ii) to accept the proceeds of the insurance policy, in which case E will forgo receipt of the residue of T's estate under the will. If E elects to accept the proceeds of the insurance policy, the residue of T's estate will pass to T's heirs by intestacy, unless the court allows A to take in lieu of the insurance proceeds.

Question: D was the promisee of a note payable to D by Maker. The note included a provision that "if D dies before this note is paid in full, the amounts due under it shall be payable to X, provided that D may change the identity of the person to whom the note shall be payable at D's death by notifying Maker; neither X nor any other person named by D to receive payments under this note at D's death shall have any rights under this note until D's death." D also owned a policy of insurance on D's life, the named beneficiary of which was X. D died intestate survived by one heir, H. Assuming there are no questions of lack of capacity, undue influence, fraud, misrepresentation, duress, or mistake, on what basis might H claim the note or insurance proceeds; would you expect H to succeed?

Answer: A potential basis for a claim by H to the note and insurance proceeds is that the arrangements for them to pass to X on D's death are testamentary in nature and thus invalid (assuming the note and insurance policy were not executed in compliance with the formalities required for the valid execution of a will). The terms of the note and insurance policy have the essential characteristics of a will (i.e., they are ambulatory, meaning they create no rights in their designated beneficiaries and have no other legal effect until D's death, and they are revocable by D). Life insurance policies, however, have been immune to such attack and there is no realistic possibility of H successfully attacking X's rights to the insurance proceeds by arguing the insurance policy is a testamentary arrangement. The possibility of successfully attacking the note is greater, as POD arrangements are not as widely sanctioned as insurance beneficiary designations. If the governing jurisdiction has adopted the UPC, X will receive the note because the UPC broadly permits POD arrangements.

Question: P, age 80 and in failing health, had two adult children, A and B. P and A lived in the same community; B lived 2,000 miles away and visited P and A infrequently. P did not live with A, but A helped P on a regular basis in a variety of ways, including paying P's bills. P's will, executed several years before P's death, left P's estate equally to A and B. Two years before P's death P changed the ownership of a bank account from P's name to P and A, as joint tenants with the right of survivorship. At P's death, A claims ownership of the funds in the bank account; B claims the funds are estate assets that pass equally to A and B under P's will. What result?

Answer: In most states there is a rebuttable presumption that funds in a joint tenancy account at the death of a tenant belong to the surviving tenants by operation of law. In such a jurisdiction, the bank account funds belong to A unless B is able to rebut the presumption. To do so B must establish that the joint tenancy was not established by P with the intent that A become the owner of the funds at P's death, but was a matter of convenience to allow A to pay P's bills in the event of P's inability. Extrinsic evidence will be admissible with respect to P's intent. Without more evidence than is found in the question, B will not rebut the presumption.

Question: D executed an instrument that purported to create a trust of which D would be the initial trustee and the sole beneficiary during D's life. The trust also was revocable by D during her lifetime; at her death, the trust assets were to be distributed to the Red Cross. At the same time D executed the trust instrument, she also executed a pour over will under which D's probate estate was devised, in trust, to the trustee of the revocable trust. D did not transfer any assets to the trust during her life. At her death, D's heir, H, argues that the trust is invalid and that D's estate therefore passes to H by intestacy. What result?

Would your answer differ if the trust had been executed by D as trustee as well as settlor, and recited that D had created the trust by transferring to the trustee "$10 and other good and valuable consideration, the receipt of which is acknowledged by the trustee"?

Answer: Assuming there are no issues of lack of capacity, undue influence, fraud, duress, etc., H's argument if the trust was not funded is that the trust fails for lack of a corpus. This argument will not succeed if state law includes the Uniform Testamentary Additions to Trusts Act or a similar statute, because it is not necessary for a trust that is the recipient of assets under a pour over will to be funded before the testator's death. In the absence of such a statute H's claim that the trust fails for lack of a corpus would succeed: in the absence of a statute to the contrary, to be valid a trust must have property for management by the trustee on behalf of a beneficiary. If this problem is not solved by statute and the trust fails for lack of a corpus, the residuary gift under the will would fail and D's property would pass by intestacy.

If the trust instrument recited creation of the trust by the transfer of property to the trustee, the corpus requirement likely would be satisfied without regard to proof of an actual transfer. In that case, H's argument would be that the trust fails because it is testamentary and was not executed in accordance with the formalities required for the execution of a will. That argument also would fail, possibly for two reasons. First, the pour over would be valid under the Uniform Testamentary Additions to Trusts Act. Second, even in the absence of that Act, self-trusteed revocable trusts of which the settlor is the sole beneficiary for life are held nontestamentary because the trust has lifetime legal effect, unlike a will that is ambulatory, in two respects: (i) fiduciary duties are owed by the trustee to the remainder beneficiary, and (ii) the remainder beneficiary has received an interest in the trust assets, which impairs their alienability by the settlor.

Question: You represent UC, an unsecured judgment creditor of D, who recently died. At the time of D's death, (i) D owned a policy of insurance on D's life, the beneficiary of which was D's niece, N; (ii) D and N owned Blackacre and a checking account as joint tenants with the right of survivorship; (iii) N was the beneficiary of a revocable trust D created for D's sole benefit during D's life; and (iv) there were funds in a savings account styled "D as trustee for the benefit of N" that D established and funded. Which, if any, of these assets may UC reach?

Answer: In most states life insurance proceeds payable to a designated beneficiary are not reachable by the insured's creditors. If the beneficiary of the policy were the insured's estate, however (or the personal representative of the estate in its fiduciary capacity), the proceeds are subject to claims of the insured's creditors. Similarly, creditors of a deceased joint tenant usually cannot reach the property in the hands of the surviving tenant(s); for joint tenancy bank accounts, the UPC creates an exception and allows the deceased joint tenant's creditors to reach the decedent's interest in the funds. Traditionally, a creditor of a deceased settlor of a trust that was revocable by the settlor immediately before death could not reach the trust assets following the settlor's death. However, at least in part because revocable trusts now are so commonly used as will substitutes, some recent cases have allowed the creditors of a deceased settlor of a revocable trust to reach the trust assets following the settlor's death, just as they could reach the assets in the settlor's estate if the settlor had used a will rather than a funded revocable trust as her primary dispositive instrument. The savings account is a Totten trust; because of the almost complete and unrestricted control the settlor of a Totten trust retains over the funds in the trust, they can be reached by the creditors of a deceased settlor.

7 INTERPRETATION: WHAT THE DECEDENT INTENDED

CHAPTER OVERVIEW

- Interpretation is searching for the "plain meaning" of the language used from within the "four corners" of the document; absent an ambiguity, evidence extrinsic to the will or trust typically is inadmissible in this search for the decedent's intent.

- Most courts admit extrinsic evidence to interpret an ambiguous will without regard to the kind of ambiguity. Some jurisdictions treat patent and latent ambiguities differently and some courts will not admit extrinsic evidence in the form of the testator's declarations.

- Much difficulty flows from the fact that courts use a variety of ways to avoid harsh and inequitable results attributable to the traditional rejection of extrinsic evidence offered to correct alleged "mistakes."

- In many jurisdictions, extrinsic evidence is admitted to correct mistakes made in will substitutes.

A. INTERPRETING WILLS AND TRUSTS

1. Interpretation vs. Construction

"Interpretation" is reading the lines. "Construction" (see Chapters 8 and 9) is reading *between* the lines. Interpretation determines what the testator or settlor (for ease we will just say "decedent" because we usually could ask what was meant of the settlor of a trust who still was living) meant by the words used. Construction is closer to ascertaining what the decedent *meant* to say and supplies rules to resolve questions raised by gaps in the document if there is no indication of what the decedent actually intended. These distinctions, however, are not always observed; some courts refer to interpretation and construction interchangeably and the line between the two is not always clear.

2.   Plain Meaning

When we "interpret" a will or trust, we attempt to determine what the decedent meant by the words used in the instrument. Often interpretation is a search for the "plain meaning" of a word, phrase, or entire provision from within the "four corners" of the document; typically evidence extrinsic to the will or trust is inadmissible in this search of the document for the decedent's intent. (As discussed below, however, if the document is ambiguous, or if an ambiguity arises in attempting to apply the document to the facts existing outside of the will or trust, extrinsic evidence may be admitted to resolve the ambiguity and ascertain the decedent's intent.)

3.   Interpretation Methodologies

Thus, interpretation in the classic four corners sense limits itself to methodologies that do not involve the admission of extrinsic evidence, such as (i) viewing the pattern and logic of the gifts made, in toto, as providing meaning about the decedent's overall intent; (ii) looking to understand terminology used that may be unclear or inconsistent with other indications of intent, by comparing other uses of the same or related terms elsewhere in the document; (iii) considering special usage—nicknames, abbreviations, slang, or even concepts used in nontraditional or informal ways—when it appears that the decedent did not intend a common or technical meaning to apply (e.g., using the term "heirs" in a context that reveals that the intent was "children" or "lineal descendants"); and (iv) perhaps considering facts and circumstances known to the decedent at the time of execution—probably meaning when signed, and not at a later date if a will was republished [see Chapter 3])—to assist in determining what the document says; notice, however, that even this little deviation from the four corners approach is a relaxation of the no-extrinsic-evidence rule.

4.   What this Decedent Actually Said and Meant

Intepretation is not an effort to determine what a decedent *should* have said, or what the average person *would* have meant by the words used, although courts often do just this, notwithstanding protestations otherwise. Rather, the effort is to determine what this decedent meant by the words used. Consider the difficulty of interpretation without reliance on what you personally mean by language, or your experience or expectations based on what the average individual would mean by certain language.

EXAMPLES AND ANALYSIS

T's will provides: "I leave all my personal property to A." Do you regard "personal" as juxtaposed with "real" property or as expressing some sense of ownership: is it all of T's property other than T's real property, or is it all property of T, including real property (that T considers "mine personally" as opposed to shared or jointly owned)? If you answered the former, what would you have thought before enrolling in a law school property course? The presence of other provisions in the will may affect our interpretation of "personal." For example, if the will included another provision leaving "everything else" to B, that may mean T intended for B to receive only her real property and A to receive all of her tangible and intangible personal property. Perhaps T meant for A to receive only assets such as jewelry and clothing (personal effects), with B to receive such "impersonal" assets as cash, stocks, bonds, and real property.

Try another one: If T's will left $1,000 to "my sister-in-law," would she mean her brother's wife, her husband's sister, or the wife of her brother-in-law? Most people would answer "all three," but by now you know that your brother-in-law's wife is not *your* sister-in-law—she is your spouse's sister-in-law, but is nothing to you, notwithstanding common usage of the term. The will or trust interpretation question, however, is what T meant, not what most people would have meant and not what *you* know to be correct.

5. Gaps or Omissions

If there clearly is a gap or omission in the document—a paragraph or a disposition missing or a contingency not addressed—interpretation is not supposed to be a process by which a court may insert what it thinks the decedent would have wanted to provide. Implied gifts that fill such gaps is a difficult concept to characterize but we think it properly is regarded as "interpretation," because it is premised on a notion that it is clear from what is said in the document that the decedent intended the gift that the court implies. In that sense construction fills in gaps based on fixed rules only if there is no indication of intent, and interpretation determines what this particular decedent intended, based on indications in the instrument (or extrinsic evidence if there is an ambiguity).

  a. **Implied intent;** *Engle v. Siegel.* Notwithstanding our effort to distinguish these concepts and draw boundaries around their proper application, beware a court "interpreting" a document based on an "implied" intent generated under rules of construction. For example, *Engle v. Siegel*, 377 A.2d 892 (N.J. 1977), involved wills of spouses who provided that each of their mothers would take half of their respective estates if the spouses and their children died in a common disaster. The husband's mother died after the wills were written; the spouses and children later died in a common disaster. The issue was whether the wife's mother would receive all of both estates, or whether other blood relatives of the husband (siblings, in this case) should receive the half that the husband's mother would have received if living.

    i.   **Applicable statute.** Under the controlling law, if a testator's will provides for multiple residuary beneficiaries, at least one of whom died before the testator (and if the antilapse statute does not apply—see Chapter 8—as it did not in *Engle*), the surviving residuary beneficiaries take the entire residue. Application of that statute would have excluded the husband's family. Extrinsic evidence (testimony of the drafter), however, made it clear that this was not the testators' intent.

    ii.   **Probable intent.** The court applied a "doctrine of probable intent" to imply a provision that did what the antilapse statute would have done if it were applicable and that effected the "obvious" intent of the testators. As a result, half of each estate was distributed to the husband's siblings. *Engle* was not copacetic interpretation jurisprudence, although the result was equitable; this is *reformation* without admitting it.

    iii.   **Extrinsic evidence.** The *Engle* court considered extrinsic evidence in interpreting the testators' wills. Doing so was a departure from the tradition of not considering extrinsic evidence in interpretation except to reveal special usage or circumstances at the time of execution, or to resolve ambiguities.

  b. **Construction cases** (see Chapters 8 and 9) seek to determine not what the decedent meant by what she said, but what she meant to say, and we *do* fill gaps, based on notions of whether we believe the decedent considered the issue and formulated an intent.

B. ABSENCE OF AMBIGUITIES; MISTAKES

Issues of interpretation typically arise in the context of ambiguities or mistakes and involve questions of whether and to what extent extrinsic—outside the terms of the document—evidence is admissible.

  1. **Two General Rules** commonly are professed about ambiguities and mistakes in wills (as we will see, trusts and will substitutes traditionally have been treated differently). First, a court cannot use extrinsic evidence to alter, limit, or extend unambiguous provisions in a will that can be applied without problem to the facts and circumstances existing outside of the will. Second, there is no remedy for mistake. These rules can produce harsh and inequitable results, and many courts use a variety of techniques to avoid them.

2. **The Traditional Approach** is illustrated by *Mahoney v. Grainger*, 186 N.E. 86 (Mass. 1933). The decedent left the residue of her estate to her "heirs at law . . . to be divided among them equally, share and share alike . . . ." (Remember that "heir" refers to someone who is entitled to receive the estate of an intestate decedent.) Although the decedent had 25 or so first cousins, her sole heir was an aunt.

    a. **Extrinsic evidence** was admitted that the testator's lawyer asked her who her nearest relatives were and who she wanted to receive the residue of her estate, and the testator responded that she wanted 25 of her first cousins to split the residue of her estate. This evidence was admitted, however, only to establish the circumstances that existed when the will was executed; it was not admissible to contradict the plain meaning of the residuary clause of the testator's will and establish a contrary intent for disposition of the residue of her estate.

    b. **No ambiguity.** According to the court, if the will was ambiguous, when applied to the facts existing at the testator's death (i.e., if there had been a *latent* ambiguity in the will), extrinsic evidence of the testator's intent would have been admissible to resolve the ambiguity. The court held there was no ambiguity. Accordingly, the aunt received the residue. The result would have differed if the will had contained language indicating that the testator meant her cousins when she used "heirs." The will contained no such language, so there was no basis for such a finding—the extrinsic evidence to that effect was not admissible because the court determined that the will was not ambiguous.

3. **Mistakes** affecting wills raise interpretation and extrinsic evidence issues; they come in many forms.

    a. **Of law.** Thinking that only one witness was needed instead, that "heirs" means children or, in *Mahoney*, that it meant the testator's cousins, are examples of mistakes of law. Generally, extrinsic evidence to prove and correct such a mistake is not admissible. See *Estate of Taff*, at page 184, for an exception.

    b. **In the inducement** mistakes occur under various circumstances. These innocent misrepresentations or self-induced mistakes also generally cannot be proven by extrinsic evidence. For example, the testator may have included a provision based on misinformation innocently provided by others. Or the testator may be mistaken about such things as whether she made prior loans, gifts, or advances; the extent of a beneficiary's poverty or property; or a person's relation to her (e.g., a reference to "my cousin first removed" when the person is really a second cousin, or a reference to "my sister-in-law" when the person is the wife of the testator's brother-in-law).

    c. **Mistakes of omission or of fact** are those that courts seem most willing to correct. For example, in cases involving execution of the wrong mutual will—which now might be rectified (see Chapter 3)—or typos (courts may be willing to include or excise material that was improperly omitted or included by mistake—assuming there is clear proof of the original intent and of the mistake).

        i. *Wilson v. First Florida Bank,* 498 So. 2d 1289 (Fla. Ct. App. 1986), illustrates gaps or omissions caused by errors of drafting attorneys. The will made several specific devises, after which appeared language "[t]o the University of Georgia" in trust for a scholarship fund. The will did not state what property was left to that trust. The will otherwise did not contain an effective residuary clause, and the heirs argued that the residue therefore passed to them by intestacy. The court found the will to be ambiguous, admitted extrinsic evidence and determined on the basis of it that the testator intended the residue to pass to the trust. It corrected the mistake, essentially by inserting the omitted but intended language into the will.

        ii. **Scrivener errors.** Cases like *Wilson*—that involve mistakes in documents caused by the drafter's error—seem to be more likely candidates for relief than cases involving other kinds of mistakes, but many courts apply the same rules to cases of mistakes caused by a scrivener as to other mistakes.

    d. **Mistaken revocation** of a testamentary instrument may be proven by extrinsic evidence and corrected under the doctrine of dependent relative revocation; the kind of mistake is not determinative in that context. See Chapter 4.

C. LACK OF INTENT TO EXECUTE A WILL

This chapter is mostly about extrinsic evidence used to determine what the decedent intended by the words used in a document. Occasionally a contestant will argue that a document that appears to be a will and that was executed in accordance with required execution formalities nevertheless should not be admitted to probate because the maker did not intend that it make a testamentary disposition, but instead executed it to serve another purpose. Such a challenge necessarily relies on extrinsic evidence of the "testator's" intent. The question is whether extrinsic evidence of intent is admissible.

    1. *Fleming v. Morrison,* 72 N.E. 499 (Mass. 1904), admitted extrinsic evidence that the testator executed a will leaving his estate to Mary Fleming, not because he intended to make a testamentary disposition of his estate, but to induce her to sleep with him. On the basis of that evidence, the will was denied probate because the testator lacked the requisite testamentary intent. Although extrinsic evidence would not be admissible to interpret the document, it was admitted to show that the document was not valid. *Lister v. Smith*, 164 Eng. Rep. 1282 (1863) (see Chapter 3), similarly admitted extrinsic evidence to show the intent of the maker of a document purporting to be a will.

2.   **Compare** *Estate of Duemeland,* 528 N.W.2d 369 (N.D. 1995). The testator's two children were involved in a business dispute. With the testator's encouragement, his son made a settlement offer to his daughter. When his daughter refused to accept the offer, the testator threatened to disinherit her, and then executed a new will that did so. The testator died less than three months later and the daughter claimed the will was invalid because it lacked testamentary intent. She offered extrinsic evidence that the testator was "merely bluffing," executed not to dispose of property but to encourage settlement of the dispute. The court refused to allow the evidence and admitted the will to probate.

D.   AMBIGUITIES AND INACCURACIES

The most common illustrations of courts admitting extrinsic evidence involve ambiguities or inaccuracies, traditionally classified as either patent or latent, with the classification dictating whether extrinsic evidence was admissible.

1.   **Patent Ambiguities** involve errors that appear on the face of the document. *Historically*, courts professed that no extrinsic evidence is allowable to alter the meaning of the written provisions (except facts and circumstances at execution) for patent ambiguities. Today, most courts admit extrinsic evidence to resolve patent ambiguities.

 EXAMPLES AND ANALYSIS

T's will provides: "I leave my IBM stock to my friend John Doe, my ATT stock to my partner John Smith, and my Coca-Cola stock to John." This is a patent ambiguity because we know from reading the document that we don't know which John is to receive the Coca-Cola stock. Under the traditional approach extrinsic evidence was not admissible to resolve the ambiguity; in most jurisdictions today extrinsic evidence would be admitted.

---

2.   **Latent Ambiguities** are those that appear only when the document is applied to the facts at hand. Typically extrinsic evidence is allowed in these cases, although sometimes declarations of a decedent are not admitted.

3. **Rationale for Different Evidentiary Rules**

The professed logic behind the historic inconsistent treatment of patent and latent ambiguities was that extrinsic evidence is required in the latent ambiguity case just to discover that an ambiguity exists—it is not apparent from the face of the document—and, once the door is open, the courts may as well admit extrinsic evidence of all sorts for all purposes, including resolution of the ambiguity. But in the patent ambiguity situation, because the glitch is apparent on the face of the document and no extrinsic evidence is needed to raise the issue, courts historically said that the door should be kept shut.

4. *Mahoney* illustrates the traditional approach. The testator's sole heir was her aunt but her will left the residue of her estate to her "heirs at law . . . to be divided among them equally, share and share alike. . . ." Was "heirs" (in the plural) a latent ambiguity or just good drafting (because the testator likely would have multiple heirs if the aunt died first)? The court held there was no latent ambiguity and refused to consider extrinsic evidence of an intent to benefit her cousins.

5. *Estate of Russell,* 444 P.2d 353 (Cal. 1968), discarded the distinction between patent and latent ambiguities and reflects the modern trend that allows extrinsic evidence to resolve any form of ambiguity. The decedent's holographic will included specific bequests to her sole heir and left the residue of her estate to "Chester H. Quinn and Roxy Russell." Chester was a friend of the testator; Roxy was the testator's dog. Because dogs may not own property, the issue was whether Chester received the entire residue or whether half of the residue passed by intestacy to the heir. The lower court admitted extrinsic evidence that (i) the testator and Chester had discussed his caring for Roxy after the testator's death and (ii) the testator did not want her heir to receive more than the specific bequests, and held that the testator intended Chester to receive the entire residue. According to the lower court, including Roxy in the residuary clause was only to express the testator's desire—not intended to be legally enforceable but only *precatory*—that Chester care for Roxy.

   a. **Lower court reversed.** The Supreme Court confirmed that extrinsic evidence is admissible to resolve ambiguities without regard to whether they are patent or latent. But before using such evidence, it is necessary to determine if there *is* an ambiguity. Considering the extrinsic evidence, the question is whether the language is reasonably susceptible to more than one meaning: if so, extrinsic evidence is considered to determine the testator's intent; if not, it is not admissible to controvert the only reasonable meaning of the language in the will. In a questionable decision, the court held the language of the residuary clause, even interpreted in light of the extrinsic evidence that Roxy was a dog, was not reasonably susceptible to the interpretation that Chester was to take the entire residue or that the provision for Roxy was precatory. Rather, the court held the language "to Chester H. Quinn and Roxy Russell" could only be interpreted to mean that Chester and Roxy were intended by the testator to share the estate equally. The devise to Roxy failed, and the heir took Roxy's half.

b. **Failure of residuary devise.** *Russell* involved the common law rule that a failed portion of a residuary devise passes by intestacy. In jurisdictions that have adopted UPC §2-604(b), or a similar statute, the failed portion of a residuary devise passes to the other residuary devisees; there is no intestate property unless there are no other residuary devisees. See page 199. Had the Uniform Probate Code (UPC) rule applied Chester would have received the entire residue without regard to whether the testator intended a flawed gift of half the residue to her dog.

6. **Three Types of Latent Ambiguities**—apparent only when applying a seemingly clear provision to the facts:

a. **Equivocations.** Language that is *accurate* with respect to more than one person or asset. For example, "my antique car to X"; Testator owned several. Or, "my car to my cousin Jim"; Testator has two cousins named Jim. (Note: it is not uncommon for a single family to have multiple individuals with the same name.)

b. **Misdescriptions** involve language that is *inaccurate* with respect to more than one person or asset. For example, "my antique Lincoln automobile to X"; the testator had an antique Ford and a new Lincoln. Or a gift "to my cousin John" when the testator has only one cousin, named Jim, but also has a nephew whose name is John. And finally, "to Erma's daughter, Irene" would be a misdescription if Erma has twin daughters, one Aileen and the other Arleen.

c. **Inaccuracies** involve language that is *inaccurate* but arguably applicable only to one person or asset. For example "my house in Atlanta on Decatur Street"; Testator's house is on Atlanta Street in Decatur or on Decatur Street in Marietta. Or, "to Erma's daughter, Irene"; Erma's only daughter is Aileen.

7. **Admitting Extrinsic Evidence: Latent Ambiguities**

Extrinsic evidence traditionally has been admissible in cases of latent ambiguities; the process involves two steps. First, in attempting to apply the will to the facts existing at the testator's death, the court will examine proffered extrinsic evidence to determine whether an ambiguity exists. Second, if a latent ambiguity is found, the court then determines whether to consider the same extrinsic evidence (and perhaps more, if there is any) to resolve the ambiguity. Quaere how a court performs the second step objectively, or how it objectively resolves the case if it sees the evidence, determines there is no ambiguity, and thus chooses to decide the controversy without admitting it.

EXAMPLES AND ANALYSIS

The testator's will includes a devise of "my house in Atlanta on Decatur Street." If the extrinsic evidence shows that the decedent owned a house on Decatur Street in Atlanta when an earlier will was executed but sold it before executing a later will, the court might conclude that an ademption by extinction should result (see Chapter 9), even though the decedent replaced the house with one on Atlanta Street in Decatur and either the testator or the drafter was confused in drafting the decedent's final will.

8. Inconsistent Results

Because many courts are unwilling to ignore the equities in cases involving mistake, cases in this arena are difficult to predict—there are results clearly not informed by the stated rules regarding interpretation, the four-corners approach, or traditional limitations on the admission of extrinsic evidence. See, for example, *Engle*, discussed above, and *Gibbs Estate*, discussed below.

9. Resolving Ambiguities

After extrinsic evidence is admitted to identify an ambiguity and to determine the testator's intent, courts often will either ignore or excise the offending language, if doing so will resolve the ambiguity in a manner consistent with what the court determines—with the help of extrinsic evidence—to be the testator's intent.

  a. Inaccuracies. With a latent ambiguity in the form of an inaccuracy—only one person or asset arguably meets the disposition—courts are prone to use this "fictional eraser" method as a relatively easy and non-invasive method of resolving the ambiguity without "rewriting" the decedent's will by inserting clarifying language.

EXAMPLES AND ANALYSIS

In the examples of inaccuracies above, a court might use a fictional eraser to eliminate the bracketed language. (i) "My house [in Atlanta] on Decatur Street," if the testator's house was on Decatur Street in Marietta, or "My house in [Atlanta on] Decatur

[Street]," if the testator's house was on Atlanta Street in Decatur. (ii) "To Erma's daughter [Irene]," if Erma had only the one daughter.

---

       b. Misdescriptions. With latent ambiguities that are misdescriptions and more than one person or asset that could be referred to by the disposition, some courts will follow the same fictional eraser tactic to excise the language creating the misdescription, if doing so will resolve the ambiguity in a manner consistent with what the court determines is the testator's intent.

 # EXAMPLES AND ANALYSIS

The misdescription was "My antique Lincoln automobile to X" when the testator owned an antique Ford and a new Lincoln. The ambiguity could be remedied by erasing either antique or Lincoln, depending on what the extrinsic evidence showed to be the testator's intent. Similarly, if the bequest were "to my cousin John," when the testator had only one cousin, named Jim, and a nephew named John, the ambiguity could be resolved by striking either "my cousin" or "John," depending on the testator's intent.

---

      i. *Ihl v. Oetting,* 682 S.W.2d 865 (Mo. Ct. App. 1984), illustrates that the fictional erasure technique won't work in many misdescription cases. The testator left property to "Mr. and Mrs. Wendell Richard Hess, or the survivor of them, presently residing at No. 17 Barbara Circle." Wendell was married to Glenda when the will was executed, and they resided at No. 17 Barbara Circle; before the testator died, however, Wendell and Glenda divorced, No. 17 Barbara Circle was sold, and Wendell married Verna. The issue was whether Glenda or Verna should receive the property.

      (a) Ambiguous? There was an ambiguity because wills are deemed to speak at death even though they are written and executed only with knowledge of facts and circumstances at an earlier time. At the testator's death, Glenda was not "Mrs. Wendell Richard Hess," and Verna was not residing—and never resided—at 17 Barbara Circle. The result was a latent ambiguity of the misdescription type; extrinsic evidence was admitted to determine that the will was ambiguous and that the testator intended to benefit Glenda.

(b) **Remedy.** The fictional eraser approach to resolve the ambiguity was not appropriate, because using it—to erase "No. 17 Barbara Circle"—would have given the devise to Verna as the only Mrs. Hess at the testator's death. As a result, the court "resolved" the ambiguity by simply holding that Glenda was to receive the devise.

    ii. **Erma's two daughters.** Similarly, in the devise "to Erma's daughter, Irene" when Erma had two daughters, Aileen and Arleen, the erasure approach would not work because eliminating "Irene" would leave two persons who could claim and an unanswered question of intent. However, a court might engage the tactic anyway because "Irene" does not identify either daughter; with the name removed, the fictional erasure would create an equivocation and extrinsic evidence most often is admitted to resolve these cases.

    c. **Equivocations.** Latent ambiguity cases involving equivocations (e.g., "my antique car to Fred" when the testator owned several; or "my car to my cousin Jim" when the testator had two cousins named Jim) were among the first in which courts admitted extrinsic evidence to determine a testator's intent to resolve an ambiguity. Such cases frequently result in admission of all relevant extrinsic evidence, including oral declarations by the testator, in search of the true intent.

 # EXAMPLES AND ANALYSIS

Assume the testator had eight houses in DeKalb County and the will provision read "My seven houses in DeKalb County to A." The quoted language is not ambiguous until it is applied in the context of the extrinsic evidence that, at the time of the testator's death when the will speaks, the testator owned eight houses in DeKalb County. The result is a latent ambiguity. Extrinsic evidence would be admissible to determine whether the testator intended A to receive all eight houses, or only seven houses (and which of the eight to exclude). In the absence of extrinsic evidence that the testator intended A to receive only seven houses, a court likely would resolve the ambiguity by striking "seven"—resulting in a devise of "my houses in DeKalb County to A"; doing so would allow all eight to pass, and spare the court of trying to figure out which was not meant to be given. If there was extrinsic evidence that the testator intended A to receive only seven houses, but no evidence of which seven houses, it is unclear how a court would resolve the issue. If the testator owned only seven houses at execution, perhaps that would be sufficient extrinsic evidence to indicate an intention that A was to receive only those seven. (Although the will speaks at the testator's death, most courts consider facts and circumstances existing at the time of execution in interpreting the will.) Alternatively, that evidence might convince the court that the testator intended A to receive all of the testator's houses, now totalling eight.

---

10. Correcting Mistakes Absent an Ambiguity

A few courts have been persuaded to abandon the traditional rule that, in the absence of an ambiguity, extrinsic evidence is not admissible to correct mistakes in wills.

a. *In re Gibbs,* 111 N.W.2d 413 (Wis. 1961), is illustrative. The wills of the decedents (spouses) included a bequest "to Robert *J.* Krause, now of 4708 North 46th Street, Milwaukee." There was a Robert J. Krause who lived at that address. Although he did not know the testators, he speculated that he had been named in their wills because he was a taxi driver and an elderly woman passenger—who he assumed to be one of the testators—had expressed sympathy and asked his name when he told her of his wife's illness and his need to take a second job. If allowed, extrinsic evidence would show that a Robert *W.* Krause was an employee of one of the testators (and a friend of both of them) and that he lived quite close to the address of Robert *J.* Krause.

   i. **No ambiguity.** This testators' wills were not ambiguous: this was an accurate description of one person—it just happened to be a mistake. (The lesson for drafters is that someone—the drafter, a secretary or legal assistant, or maybe the testators themselves—apparently looked up "Robert Krause" in the telephone book and found a listing for one in the general neighborhood as the intended Robert Krause).

   ii. **Mistake.** *Gibbs* involved a mistake, not an ambiguity, and the traditional law of wills is not to correct mistakes (except, in the context of revocation, under the doctrine of dependent relative revocation; see Chapter 4). The judge acknowledged that there was no ambiguity but still ruled in favor of Robert W. Krause and against the Robert J. Krause named in the will. According to the court, identifying details, such as street addresses and middle initials, are particularly subject to error and should not frustrate the "clearly demonstrable intent" of the testator "when the proof establishes to the highest degree of certainty that a mistake was, in fact, made." The court essentially reformed the will to correct the mistake.

b. **Similar results elsewhere.** The court in *Gibbs* candidly acknowledged that there was no ambiguity in the testator's will; it granted relief anyway by carving out an exception for cases involving details of identification from the usual rule denying the admission of extrinsic evidence in the absence of an ambiguity. In *Estate of Taff*, 133 Cal. Rptr. 737 (1976), the court was not so forthright.

   i.   **Mistake of law.** The *Taff* will left the residue of the decedent's estate to her sister and provided that, if her sister did not survive her, the residue was to be distributed to the testator's heirs under the California intestate succession statute. The testator's sister predeceased her and the residue of the estate should have been distributed under California law half to the testator's blood relatives and half to blood relatives of the testator's deceased husband. The court admitted extrinsic evidence to show that the testator misunderstood California law because she intended only her blood relatives to take. The court therefore held that her relatives were entitled to the entire residue of the estate, to the exclusion of her husband's relatives.

   ii. **Rationale.** According to the court, the evidence was admissible to create an ambiguity and then to resolve the ambiguity so created. In essence, the court admitted extrinsic evidence to prove a mistake that it then corrected by implicitly reforming the will, even though there was neither a patent nor a latent ambiguity.

c. **Scriveners' errors.** A few courts have relaxed the traditional rule to admit extrinsic evidence to correct mistakes attributable to scrivener error. To illustrate, the testator in *Erickson v. Erickson*, 716 A.2d 92 (Conn. 1998), executed his will two days before his marriage and devised his estate to his bride-to-be. Because it did not expressly provide for the contingency of his marriage, however, the testator's children claimed that the will was revoked by Connecticut's pretermitted spouse statute (see Chapter 10). The court remanded the case for a new trial, at which the surviving spouse would be permitted to introduce extrinsic evidence that, if clear and convincing, could be used to establish and correct the mistake.

d. **Restatement.** Consistent with the rules applicable to will substitutes, discussed below, a tentative draft of §12.1 of The Restatement (Third) of Property—Wills and Other Donative Transfers provides that *any* mistake in any donative transfer (including a will) may be corrected, without regard to whether there is an ambiguity, if the mistake and what the testator or donor intended are proven by clear and convincing evidence.

11. **Will Substitutes: Reformation and Extrinsic Evidence**

In many jurisdictions, the rules prohibiting the admission of extrinsic evidence in the absence of an ambiguity, and the refusal to correct mistakes when there is no ambiguity, apply only to wills and not to will substitutes, such as trusts, life insurance beneficiary designations, and so forth. In these jurisdictions mistakes in an unambiguous will substitute can be proven by extrinsic evidence and the document may be reformed.

a. **Unjust enrichment: reformation and constructive trusts.** Reformation in these cases is viewed as appropriate to effectuate the decedent's intent and to prevent the unintended beneficiary of the mistake from being unjustly enriched. If simple reformation of the document cannot correct the mistake, then a constructive trust may be imposed on the recipient of the property, obligating that beneficiary to convey legal title to the intended beneficiary.

b. **Different treatment for wills.** Wills were treated differently, probably because the issue of mistake in a will typically only arises after the testator's death, when the testator is unable to address whether a mistake was made. Precluding admission of extrinsic evidence was viewed as the best means of ensuring that the testator's intent is carried out rather than subverted by fabricated or mistaken evidence that the testator intended something other than what the will specified. Thus, unless there is intentionally wrongful or fraudulent conduct, constructive trusts typically are not imposed in wills cases to remedy mistakes when there is no ambiguity.

   i. **Exception.** In at least one case, however, a court imposed a constructive trust to correct a mistake involving a will when there was no intentionally wrongful conduct. *In re Estate of Tolin*, 622 So. 2d 988 (Fla. 1993), involved a testator who wanted to revoke a codicil to his will. He showed a photocopy of the codicil, which he mistakenly thought was the original, to a lawyer, who also thought it was the original; the lawyer told him he could revoke the codicil by tearing it up. Intending to revoke the codicil, the testator tore up the copy, believing it to be the original; at his death, the original was offered for probate. The court held that revocation of a copy of a testamentary document is not a valid revocation and admitted the codicil to probate. Because of the mistake, however, the court imposed a constructive trust on the beneficiary under the codicil in favor of the person who would have received the property if the codicil had been revoked properly.

c. **Reformation of wills?** The increasing use of will substitutes, combined with the increasing acceptance of the UPC philosophy to unify the law of probate and nonprobate transfers and to subordinate strict compliance with formalities to effectuate the testator's intent (see, e.g., the dispensing power in UPC §2-503 in Chapter 3), may lead to a further relaxation of the traditional no extrinsic evidence/no reformation rules of the law of wills.

EXAMPLES AND ANALYSIS

T's will left $50,000 to each of two grandchildren, A and B, and nothing to a third grandchild, C. About the same time T executed the will, T bought a $100,000 insurance policy on her life, and named A and B as the sole beneficiaries. T died later that year. Extrinsic evidence would show that T believed that C was wealthy as a result of the success of a business that C owned, and that T's belief of C's business success was the only reason T did not treat C the same as A and B. In fact, C's business was insolvent throughout the year in which T executed the will and bought the insurance policy, and C's financial condition was no better than A or B's. If C attempts to share on an equal basis with A and B, the extrinsic evidence may be admitted in connection with the insurance policy but not the will, and C has a better chance to receive a third of the insurance proceeds than she does to receive any of the property passing under T's will. This disparate treatment is difficult to justify and the probate result might gravitate toward the nonprobate result during your career.

12. **Mistake in the Inducement** (occasioned by someone's innocent misrepresentation or by the testator's own misconception) is sometimes regarded as a special case in which relief may be given from the no–extrinsic-evidence or no reformation rules applicable to wills. Generally, however, that is not the case and the usual rules apply: no extrinsic evidence will be admitted if there is only a mistake in the inducement and no ambiguity. An exception may permit extrinsic evidence to be admitted to correct a mistake in the inducement in the rare case in which the will itself reveals both the mistake and what the testator would have done if the truth had been known. See, e.g., *Gifford v. Dyer*, 2 R.I. 99 (1852) (dicta).

EXAMPLES AND ANALYSIS

T's will leaves her alma mater, City University, $100,000. A codicil to the will provides, "because City University has been left $10,000,000 by A. Phil Anthropist, I revoke my $100,000 bequest to it." In fact, Mrs. Anthropist left the $10,000,000 to City *College*, not City *University*. Under the *Gifford v. Dyer* dictum, extrinsic evidence would be admissible to correct the mistake and reinstate the $100,000 bequest to City University. Although the codicil does not expressly state what T would have done if she had known City University did not receive the $10,000,000 bequest from Mrs. Anthropist, it implicitly does and that likely would be sufficient to correct the mistake.

Consider another example: T's will provides, "because my son is dead, I leave my estate entirely to my daughter." In fact, T's son was not dead and actually survived

T. Extrinsic evidence that T's son is not dead may be admissible notwithstanding that the *Gifford v. Dyer* exception is not directly applicable because the will does not state what T would have done had she known that her son was living. In a case such as this—in which a will mistakenly states that nothing is left to a child because the child is dead—it may not be necessary that the will state what the other disposition would be: absent evidence that the testator would have cut out the son anyway—as was present in *Gifford v. Dyer*—the son and daughter likely would share the estate equally because the law generally presumes an intent to treat all children equally. Such a result would be reached in a jurisdiction that has adopted UPC §2-302(c), under which a child who is not provided for in a testator's will solely because the testator believes the child is not living may receive a share of the estate as an after-born or after-adopted pretermitted heir (see Chapter 10).

EXAM TIP

In analyzing questions that raise interpretation issues, consider the following framework:

- If the document involved is a will substitute, extrinsic evidence may be admissible to correct a mistake by reforming the document without regard to whether there is an ambiguity.

- If the document is a will and there is a patent ambiguity the traditional approach was not to admit extrinsic evidence, but most courts today will allow extrinsic evidence without regard to the type of ambiguity.

- If the document is a will that is not ambiguous on its face, but the ambiguity arises in trying to apply the terms of the will, extrinsic evidence probably is admissible to determine the existence of and then resolve this latent ambiguity. In some jurisdictions, however, declarations of the deceased testator will not be admitted, except perhaps in the case of an equivocation.

- If there is an ambiguity, consider whether it can be resolved by use of the fictional eraser method. If not, the court still may ignore the ambiguity in ordering the estate distributed in accordance with what the court determines to be the testator's intent, based on extrinsic evidence admitted to establish the ambiguity and what the testator intended.

- If there is neither a patent nor a latent ambiguity, at best there is a mistake. Generally, in the absence of an ambiguity, if a will is involved extrinsic evidence is not admissible to prove the testator meant something different than what was said in the will (i.e., mistakes in wills usually go un-corrected).

- Courts have created a variety of exceptions to avoid the harsh results of not correcting will mistakes when there is no ambiguity. First, the mistake may be corrected if the mistake is apparent from the will itself, and the will states what the testator would have done if there had been no mistake. Second, if the mistake involves a detail of identification (such as a street address or a middle initial), a small minority of courts may be willing to admit extrinsic evidence to correct the mistake. Third, in rare cases the court may admit extrinsic evidence to create an ambiguity when none otherwise existed and then resolve it. And if the mistake resulted in a revocation of a will or codicil, dependent relative revocation may be available to correct it. See Chapter 4.

E. IMPLIED GIFTS

Implied gifts are a legal fiction, employed to provide what a court perceives to be the decedent's intent in cases in which the document is incomplete or ineffective in disposing of the decedent's assets. We cover implied gifts here because interpretation is the process of determining what the decedent intended by words used in the instrument, and because gifts are implied when a court determines from the language of the instrument (and extrinsic evidence) that doing so is necessary to effect the decedent's intent.

1. Unanticipated Contingencies

The *Engle* case discussed at pages 173 and 174 illustrates the operation of this totally unpredictable theory. Recall that there was no ambiguity in *Engle*; there was not even a gap in the dispositive plan that would have caused part of the estates to pass by intestacy. Rather, not allowing the wife's mother to receive the entire residue and implying a gift to the husband's family to effect probable intent amounted to a reformation of the will to correct a mistake in the form of an unanticipated and thus unplanned for contingency that occurred. *Engle* shows how far the court was willing to go to give effect to the testators' probable intent, which it determined from extrinsic evidence. It is not representative of the law in this area; in most cases extrinsic evidence would not be admissible to contradict the intent of the testators as evidenced by unambiguous terms in their wills, and the wife's mother would have taken the entire residue of their estates.

2. The "Rule" of Implied Gifts for Unanticipated Contingencies (if it can be elevated to that status) in a case like *Engle* is that a court will provide for an *un*anticipated contingency that *did* occur the same way the testator

provided for an *anticipated* contingency that did *not* occur. The assumption—absent other evidence addressing the issue in the document or otherwise—is that the decedent would want the same result under either contingency. Again, this remedy clearly is a deviation from the traditional rule that says there is no relief for mistakes in wills, even if the glitch was the failure to anticipate all possible contingencies.

3. Implied Gifts on Incomplete Dispositions

Failure of a dispositive provision (for example, due to violation of the Rule Against Perpetuities, renunciation, or lapse) may create a gap in the distribution plan for the decedent's estate. The question is how to cure this dispositive gap. Implied gifts are more likely in this kind of situation than in a case like *Engle*, in which the will was not ambiguous and disposed of the entire estate.

 ## EXAMPLES AND ANALYSIS

Assume that a trust provided for X for life, remainder to X's descendants by representation, and that X renounced the life estate or otherwise is precluded from enjoying it (e.g., because X killed the decedent and the slayer statute is applicable (see Chapter 2), or because X was a surviving spouse who renounced the plan in favor of an elective share of the decedent's estate (see Chapter 11)—in either case causing X to be deemed to have predeceased the decedent). How should the balance of the plan be implemented—is X's life estate eliminated so that X's then living descendants take the property, by representation, immediately; if not, what happens to X's life estate during X's remaining life?

If X is precluded from taking the life estate in connection with an action that adversely affects another beneficiary, some cases will sequester X's life estate for the benefit of the other, disappointed beneficiary. For example, if X were to take ⅓ of the residue of the decedent's estate under a forced share election (see Chapter 10), the residuary beneficiaries who suffer that invasion of "their" residue might receive the life estate X otherwise would have received. More common is acceleration of the remainder, as if the person who otherwise would take were deceased, unless there is an obvious reason to delay distribution. For example, if X renounced the life estate and the remainder goes to X's then living descendants immediately, there is a possibility of afterborns of X who would be cut out if the remainder is accelerated. In such a situation, the life estate might be sequestered. That would not be the case if the gift were to X for life, remainder to Y's descendants who survive X, and Y already is deceased; in such a case acceleration to Y's descendants would be the likely result. (See the discussion of the *Gilbert* case in Chapter 15.) If these approaches do not solve the dilemma, we will soon learn that gaps are filled with a reversion to the decedent.

4. "Time" Gaps

Assume that a trust provides for its "income to be equally divided between A and B until the death of the survivor of them." If A dies first, the question unanswered by the quoted language is what should be done with A's equal share of the income after A's death, pending the death of B. Should we assume that B is to receive all the income during this period, or should it go to the remainder beneficiaries or to A's estate? There are cases reaching each result.

5. Testator's Clear Intent

Implied gifts sometimes are used to fill a gap if the intent of the testator is clear.

EXAMPLES AND ANALYSIS

T's testamentary trust provided separate shares of the residuary estate for T's children, A and B, with distribution on a child's death to the child's living descendants by representation or, if none, then to the child's sibling. Child A died survived by descendants who took A's share. Child B then dies with no descendants. To whom does B's share pass? A is not alive and no provision gives B's share to A's descendants. Our choices are A's estate, A's descendants, a reversion to the testator's estate to pass by intestacy, or B's other siblings, if any. Note that the takers of A's estate—A's heirs, if A died intestate, or A's devisees, if A died testate—may be different than A's descendants and T may have other children.

Did A need to survive B to take B's share? Traditional future interests law (see Chapter 15) does not impute a survivorship requirement in such a gift, in which case A's estate would receive B's share. Assuming, as likely is true, that the testator intended A's descendants to take under these facts, allowing A's estate to take may not be the "right" result, because A's estate may not pass to A's descendants. (UPC §2-707, discussed in Chapter 15, changes the traditional future interests rule that survivorship is not required; under it, A's estate would not take under this example.) In this case, some courts likely would find the testator's intention clear that A's descendants should take B's share, and imply a gift to A's descendants to reach that result.

A third approach would be to treat the right to receive B's share as retained by the testator (i.e., a reversion). Because disposition of that reversion would not be provided for under the will, it would pass by intestacy, which the law normally abhors in a testate estate, so this would not be our first choice. It might, however, be the preferred result if it generates the same result (all to A's descendants, because A and B *were* T's only children) without resort to the implied gift remedy.

6.   Implied Gifts to Avoid Unintended Results

Likewise, if a gap results in a disposition that the testator obviously did not intend, a court likely will imply a gift that appears consistent with the testator's intent and that avoids the unanticipated and unintended consequence.

EXAMPLES AND ANALYSIS

T's will specifically disinherits T's child, C, who is T's only heir, and leaves T's estate: "To my grandson, GS, if he graduates from college before he reaches age 25 with a grade point average of 2.5 or better on a 4.0 scale. If GS does not graduate from college with a grade point average of 2.5 or better on a 4.0 scale, I give my estate to my granddaughter, GD." T dies; GS subsequently graduated from college with a 2.6 grade point average, but he was 27 years old. To whom should T's estate be distributed? The choices: (i) GS, but he did not graduate from college before he reached age 25, and thus did not satisfy the clearly expressed condition for taking; (ii) GD, but GS did not graduate from college with a grade point average of less than 2.5, and thus the clearly expressed condition for her taking also was not satisfied; (iii) C, as T's heir, because T did not make an effective disposition of T's estate (assume that the jurisdiction has not passed a "negative will" statute like UPC §2-101(b); (see Chapter 2). It is not likely that GS would take; he was the primary residuary beneficiary, but his devise was expressly conditioned on graduating from college before he reached age 25, which he did not do. It appears that the testator intended GD to take the estate if GS did not satisfy the condition to receive it; expressing GD's gift as subject only to the condition that GS graduate with a GPA of less than 2.5, rather than also being payable to GD if GS did not graduate before reaching age 25, appears to be an oversight by the drafter. An implied gift to GS under that condition is a likely alternative to allowing the property to pass by intestacy to T's disinherited child, C.

7.   Implied Gifts to Avoid Multiple Generations of Income Beneficiaries

An implied gift also may be useful to keep multiple generations from being income beneficiaries at the same time. For example, if a testamentary trust provided "to H and W for life, and on their deaths to their descendants," the question is what happens on the death of the first of H and W to die: does the survivor continue to enjoy all the income, or do their descendants share income with the survivor, which is not likely the intent of most donors? Many courts would imply a gift to the survivor of all the income after the first death. But if the gift was income to siblings A and B rather than to spouses, with half the remainder to each of their descendants, the implied gift of half the income on the first sibling's death might well be to those descendants.

8. Implied Gifts for Similar Contingencies

If two similar contingencies are possible, and one is provided for but the other occurs, the presumption is that the same result is intended under each. For example, "To W for life, then to A and B in equal shares; if A dies without descendants, to B, and if B dies with descendants, to those descendants." What if A dies and B already is dead: do B's descendants take A's share the same as they took B's original share? And what if A dies with descendants; should A's descendants take as provided with respect to B and B's descendants, or does A have a vested share that passes through A's estate if A does not die without descendants? Absent evidence that the testator for some reason intended otherwise (which might not be admissible, because the document really is not ambiguous), the likely result is that a gift would be implied to A's descendants, if any, and if there were none, that B's descendants would take the share.

EXAM TIP

Distinguish between cases involving ambiguities or mistakes and cases in which a gift may be implied. Ambiguity cases are those in which the decedent provided a devise in an unclear way (e.g., "$100 to my cousin Jim" when the decedent had two cousins named "Jim"—a latent ambiguity—or "$100 to John Smith, $100 to John Jones, and Blackacre to John"—a patent ambiguity). Implied gift cases involve a gap in the dispositive scheme; the court's alternative usually is to fill the gap with a reversion to the settlor's estate, in the case of a trust, or with the property falling into the residue, in the case of a gap in a preresiduary testamentary gift, or with the property passing by intestacy, in the case of a gap in a residuary testamentary gift. In the right circumstances some courts will imply a gift to avoid these alternatives. In one sense, of course, a "mistake" occurs if there is an ambiguity or the need to imply a gift, but the pure mistake cases involving wills or will substitutes occur when there is no ambiguity and no gap to be filled. Rather, the allegation is that the gift of the specific property to the specific beneficiary was made by mistake and does not reflect what the decedent really intended.

REVIEW QUESTIONS AND ANSWERS

Question: T's validly executed 1993 will provides: "I give my property to my heirs, who practically raised me and who I love dearly." T was survived by a spouse, S, from whom T was estranged since 1990, by no descendant, and by an older brother and sister. Under the applicable intestate succession statute, T's sole heir is S; if T had been single, her heirs would have been her siblings. If admissible, extrinsic evidence would show that T and S were estranged and that T's sister and brother had assumed significant responsibilities in caring for T when T was a child. How should T's estate be distributed?

Answer: T's estate should be distributed to her siblings. Although T's will leaves her estate to her "heirs" and "heirs" has a precise legal meaning—the person or persons who would inherit T's estate if T died intestate (here, S)—the task of interpreting T's will is to determine from the words of the will what T meant. Had T's will simply left her estate to her heirs, S probably would have inherited T's estate. (Compare *Mahoney v. Grainger* and *Estate of Taff*, both discussed above.) But T's will left her estate to her heirs who she loved dearly and who practically raised her. This is not a simple case of the testator having made a mistake of law—in thinking "heirs" meant her siblings when in fact it meant S. Rather, in addition to such a mistake there is a latent ambiguity, because when we apply the will to the facts existing outside of it, we will find that T's heir, S, did not practically raise her and that T and S were estranged, indicating that S was not "dearly loved" by T. The extrinsic evidence (of T's history with her siblings and her relationship with S) would be admitted first to establish the ambiguity and then to resolve it; that evidence would show that T meant her siblings by use of the term "heirs," and they should take.

Question: A document intended to be Jane Remington's will left her estate to her sister, Maude Remington, for life, remainder to R; a document intended to be Maude Remington's will left her estate to her sister, Jane Remington, for life, remainder to R. Jane signed the will intended for Maude; Maude signed the will intended for Jane. Jane died. Is the will signed by Jane admissible to probate? If so, to whom is the life estate in Jane's property distributable?

Answer: These were the facts in *Guardian, Trust & Executors Co. v. Inwood*, [1946] N.Z.L.R. 614. Unlike the court in *Pavlinko* (see Chapter 3), the New Zealand court in *Guardian, Trust* found that Jane had testamentary intent in executing the document she signed, and admitted it to probate as her will. That document, however, provided for the testator's property to be distributed to "my sister, Jane Remington." The court resolved the ambiguity—arguably a latent one, because it was necessary to consider the extrinsic evidence that Jane's sister was named Maude, not Jane, to ascertain that the will was ambiguous—by the fictional eraser approach (eliminating the name "Jane" from the will). The result was language in Jane's will leaving a life estate to "my sister [Jane] Remington," and Maude could take.

Question: Testator's will left the residue of her estate "to my nephew Jack and his wife Beth." At the testator's death, and at the time the will was executed, Jack's wife was named Ann; the testator and Ann were close. Beth was Jack's former wife who had not seen the testator for 12 years prior to the testator's death, or for several years before the testator executed the will. Jack receives half of the residuary estate; to whom is the other half distributable?

Answer: Ann. On its face the will is not ambiguous; the ambiguity is a latent one (a misdescription) that results from Jack's wife at the time of the testator's death (at which time the will speaks) being named Ann and not Beth. Extrinsic evidence of Jack being married to Ann at the time of the testator's death would be admissible to establish the ambiguity. The next step is to determine who the testator intended to receive that half of her residuary estate. The same extrinsic evidence of Jack being married to Ann at the testator's death would be admissible to determine the testator's intent, as would the facts that Jack was married to Ann when the testator's will was executed, that Jack had been married to Beth, that Beth had not seen the testator for 12 years before the testator's death or for several years before the testator executed the will, and that the testator and Ann were close. After considering the extrinsic evidence, the court likely would determine that the testator intended Ann to receive half of the residuary estate. That result could be accomplished by striking the name "Beth" from the devise; the gift would then be "to my nephew Jack and his wife [Beth]." As Jack's wife at the time of the testator's death (and at the time of execution), Ann would take half of the residue. (See *Breckheimer v. Kraft*, 273 N.E.2d 468 (Ill. App. Ct. 1971)).

Question: Testator's will included a devise "to my friend Richard H. Simpson." At the testator's death, the personal representative of the estate learns that the testator had a friend named H.R. Simpson; a person named Richard H. Simpson is found, but he was not known by the testator. Which Simpson receives the devise?

Answer: H.R. Simpson would receive the devise. This is a misdescription—a latent ambiguity—because it was not clear on the face of the will that the devisee named was not a friend of the decedent. Extrinsic evidence that the testator had a friend named "H.R. Simpson" and that the testator did not have a friend named "Richard H. Simpson" would be admissible to determine both that a latent ambiguity existed and that the testator intended the devise for "H.R. Simpson." The remedy would be to strike the "Richard H." so that the devise would read "to my friend Simpson." (Notice that this case is not as difficult as *Gibbs*, discussed above, because in *Gibbs* there was no ambiguity at all.)

Question: D provided for her assets to be distributed equally between two of her children (A and B); no provision was made for a third child (C) solely because of D's mistaken belief that C had died. At D's death, to whom are D's assets distributable?

Answer: If UPC §2-302(c) is in effect and D's disposition is by will, C will share the estate equally with A and B. If UPC §2-302(c) is not in effect and D's disposition is by will, C nevertheless may receive a third of the estate if the will recites the mistake (e.g., "Because C is not living, I leave my estate equally to my children who are living, A and B"). If D's disposition is by will and it does not recite the mistake, A and B probably will share the estate equally: because there is no patent or latent ambiguity, extrinsic evidence will not be admitted to cure the mistake. Even though that result is an inequitable one—assuming there is extrinsic evidence that C was disinherited solely because D mistakenly thought C was dead—there likely would be no remedy. (Note that, if the dispositive language were "to my living children, A and B," a court might find a latent ambiguity when extrinsic evidence established that C also was a living child of D, in which case the fictional eraser technique might be employed to strike "A and B" from the devise and allow C to take an equal share.) If the disposition is by will substitute, in many jurisdictions extrinsic evidence would be admissible to establish and correct D's mistake.

8

CONSTRUCTION: LAPSE AND CLASS GIFTS

CHAPTER OVERVIEW

- Rules of construction are needed when a document does not provide for the disposition of property under a contingency that occurs.

- Devises to beneficiaries who predecease the decedent lapse. The devise fails unless the document addresses that contingency or an antilapse statute applies to send the devise to the beneficiary's descendants.

- A class gift (e.g., "to my children" or "to my siblings") is made to persons who constitute members of the class. Among the many issues that arise for class gifts are whether the gift *is* a class gift or a gift to individuals; how the lapse and antilapse rules apply; and when the class closes to exclude afterborn or afteradopted persons as members of the class.

A. CONSTRUCTION AND INTERPRETATION

It is not uncommon for a decedent's will to lack answers to all questions that arise after the decedent's death about how the decedent's property is to be distributed. Interpretation is the process of answering those questions involving the decedent's intent from the language of the document (see Chapter 7). It is necessary to resort to a rule of "construction" to resolve questions that must be answered for which there is no indication of the decedent's intent.

1. Intent of Decedent Controls

Rules of construction apply only if the document does not address the issue to which the rule of construction is applicable; there is no gap and no need to resort to a rule of construction if the instrument answers the question.

If the decedent has expressed her intent (or it can be determined through interpretation), it controls; if not, rules of construction may be called on to provide answers.

2. Compare Rules of Law

In a few circumstances, even the clearly expressed intent of a decedent will not be given effect; rather, issues raised in these circumstances are governed by rules of law. The Rule Against Perpetuities is an example: if the common law rule is applicable in the jurisdiction and a dispositive instrument violates it, the offending devise fails without regard to the decedent's intent. See the Website for further information.

B. LAPSE

If a gift lapses, it fails. Lapse applies if a named beneficiary predeceases the testator: if T's will leaves $100 to A, and A dies before T, the bequest to A is said to lapse.

1. Implied Condition of Survivorship

Lapse results even if survivorship is not a stated condition because the common law implies a condition of survivorship on a beneficiary taking a bequest at the transferor's death—even if the document is silent regarding the need for the beneficiary to be alive to inherit. Thus, if the testator's will provides ''Blackacre to A,'' without specifying whether A must survive the testator to take, the common law interprets the will as if it read ''Blackacre to A if living at my death'' or ''Blackacre to A if A survives me,'' and *not* as if it read ''Blackacre to A, or to A's heirs or devisees if A does not survive me.'' If A does not survive the gift lapses. The drafting alternative usually is to give the gift to A's descendants, by representation, or to an alternate devisee.

2. Twofold Issue

In a lapse case the share of a beneficiary who predeceases the testator fails: the issue is whether it passes to someone else or as a part of the decedent's residuary or intestate estate.

a. **Drafting to address the contingency.** A well drafted document will specify whether survivorship is required and, if so, what happens if the devisee does not survive. If survivorship is not required, the will may preclude lapse—the interest then would pass to the devisee's estate and through it to the devisee's own heirs or devisees. Most wills require survivorship and direct disposition of the devise if the devisee predeceases.

b. **Rules of construction.** The lapse rules are rules of construction that apply only if the instrument does not adequately address the contingency of a devisee predeceasing the testator. Especially under the Uniform Probate Code (UPC), the adequacy of a provision addressing the lapse issue is not easy to predict.

EXAM TIP

In any question involving the death of a devisee before the testator, the initial consideration should be whether the instrument addresses the question with an alternative disposition to a devisee who survives the testator. If so, that provision controls. If not, the lapse rules apply to resolve the issue.

---

3. Common Law Lapse Rule

The normal common law implied condition of survivorship and lapse rules do not provide for an alternative distribution, meaning that a lapsed gift simply fails. Thus, if a devise is to A and A dies before the testator, under the common law the gifted property does not pass to A's estate or to A's descendants. Instead, the devise fails and the property remains a part of the transferor's estate.

a. Preresiduary gift. If the disposition precedes the residue, the traditional rule is that the lapsed gift falls into the residue. Thus, if T willed "Blackacre to A, residue to B," and A dies before T, Blackacre would be distributed to B as a part of the residue.

b. Residuary gift. If the lapsed gift is part of the residue, the property becomes intestate. Thus, if T's will read "I leave my entire estate to A," and A died before T, under the common law T's estate would pass by intestacy to T's heirs. This is a result the law traditionally abhors for a testate decedent.

    i. Lapse of a part of the residue. If T willed "the residue of my estate to A and B in equal shares," and A died before T, under the common law A's half would pass by intestacy to T's heirs, not to B. (See the discussion of *Russell* in Chapter 7 for an application of this "no residue of the residue" rule.) Most state statutes, including UPC §2-604, have reversed that rule. In those jurisdictions, if A predeceased T and the antilapse statute did not apply (discussed below), B would take the entire residue.

4. Antilapse Statutes

Most states have "antilapse" statutes to prevent failure of gifts. If applicable, they dispose of a lapsed gift—usually to the predeceased beneficiary's descendants by representation.

a. **Void dispositions.** At common law, a devise to someone who was not living when the will was executed was "void"; technically such a gift did not lapse (although it too failed). Many antilapse statutes expressly apply to void dispositions as well as to lapse (which occurs if the beneficiary was alive when the will was executed but died before the testator), and these statutes uniformly are referred to as antilapse statutes without added reference to void dispositions. So their application is easy: regardless of whether the beneficiary died before or after execution of the will, the antilapse statute will apply if the other conditions of the statute are satisfied.

b. **Usually not applicable to will substitutes.** Typical antilapse statutes do not apply to transfers under will substitutes, even if distribution occurs at the testator's death. This is subject to exceptions, the most notable being UPC §§2-706 and 2-707, which generally treat will substitutes the same as wills for antilapse purposes.

   i. **Testamentary trusts.** Antilapse statutes typically apply to testamentary trusts. Thus, if T's will provides for T's estate to be held in trust for A and A dies before T, the antilapse statute may apply (assuming the will does not address the contingency and the other conditions for application of the antilapse statute are met). If so, A's descendants would be substituted for A as beneficiaries of the testamentary trust. The reason this makes sense is because the trust is created by T's will and therefore is subject to the Wills Act and the antilapse statute. An inter vivos trust, however, would be a different story unless state law is like the UPC in its reach.

   ii. **Will substitute gifts may not lapse.** The common law implied condition that the beneficiary must survive the decedent and that the gift lapses if the beneficiary does not typically does not apply to gifts made by will substitute. Thus, there is no lapse upon which an antilapse statute could operate and the deceased beneficiary is entitled to the property.

 ## EXAMPLES AND ANALYSIS

The AB Partnership agreement provides that upon D's death, D's interest in the partnership passes to D's spouse, S. S dies a year before D's death. Assuming the arrangement does not fail as being testamentary and not executed in compliance with the will execution formalities (see the discussion of *Hillowitz* in Chapter 6) and that the contingency of S dying before D is not addressed, in many jurisdictions D's partnership interest will pass as a part of S's estate to S's heirs or devisees. No condition of survivorship is implied or imposed on S, there is no lapse, and there is no application of an antilapse statute.

c. **Required relationship.** An important limitation on the application of antilapse statutes is that the beneficiary must be within a designated group—typically relatives of the testator, sometimes lineal descendants. UPC §2-603 is broader than most antilapse statutes: it applies to beneficiaries who are grandparents or descendants of grandparents of the testator. It even includes step-children. Most antilapse statutes (including the UPC) do *not* apply to spouses. And most antilapse statutes do not apply to persons who are not related to the testator. Thus, the implied condition of survivorship still applies and the gift may fail.

EXAMPLES AND ANALYSIS

T's will leaves $10,000 to her sister, S, $20,000 to child A, and the residue ¼ to friend F, ¼ to charity, and ½ to child B. S, A, F, and B all predecease T. S's descendants who survive T will take the $10,000 by representation if the applicable antilapse statute includes a testator's sibling. Otherwise, or if no descendants of S survive T, the $10,000 will fall into the residue. The $20,000 left to A will pass under every antilapse statute we know to any of A's descendants who survive T, by representation; only if there are none will the $20,000 fall into the residue. (Note that, either way, the $20,000 will not pass as a part of A's estate to A's heirs or devisees.) Any descendants of B who survive T will take B's share of the residue by representation, but the ¼ of the residue left to F probably will lapse because most antilapse statutes do not apply to gifts to non-relatives. If the jurisdiction follows the approach of UPC §2-604, rather than the common law no residue of the residue rule (see discussion above), F's ¼ would simply remain a part of the residue to be divided pro rata between B's descendants and the charity. Thus, if any of B's descendants survive T, the residue will be divided ⅔ to B's descendants and ⅓ to charity. If no descendant of B survives T, the charity will receive the entire residue. If, on the other hand, local law still adheres to the no residue of the residue rule, F's ¼ would become intestate property in T's estate and pass to T's heirs. T's will could provide for the possibility of one or more of the named beneficiaries not surviving T, in which case the will would govern and the antilapse statute would not apply.

d. **Default rules.** Antilapse statutes dictate default results that apply only if the testator's will does not say what happens to a gift to a beneficiary who is not alive. There is no lapsed gift on which the statute can operate if the will addresses that possibility with a gift over to another beneficiary. Thus, if T's will provides: "$10,000 to A if living, otherwise to A's spouse B, if living, and if neither A nor B survive me, to charity C," the antilapse statute will not apply regardless of whether A or B survives T.

e. **Requirement of survivorship.** An antilapse statute may not apply if T's will makes a gift to a devisee who is covered by the antilapse statute and the will expressly requires the devisee to survive T, but does not expressly provide an alternative disposition if the devisee does not survive. For example, assume T's will provides "Blackacre to my Child C if C survives me, residue to X," and that C dies before T, survived by a descendant of C who survives T.

   i. **Most antilapse statutes.** The will expressly conditioned the gift to C on survivorship; because C did not survive, the condition is not satisfied and there is no bequest on which the antilapse statute may apply. Thus, the condition of survivorship overrides or negates the need for the antilapse statute. Put another way, antilapse statutes can apply only if a testator devises property to a beneficiary who predeceases the testator and the will does not provide for that possibility. In most states, an express survivorship condition is an adequate provision to negate application of the antilapse statute. In such states, the devise to C would fail by its own terms and not by virtue of the lapse rule, the antilapse statute would not apply, and Blackacre would pass as a part of the residue of T's estate.

   ii. **UPC.** A different result may be reached under UPC §2-603(b)(3), which specifies that a survivorship condition alone does not override the antilapse statute, absent additional sufficient indications of a contrary intent (such as an alternative disposition in the event of a devisee not surviving the testator, or extrinsic evidence—such as testimony of the drafter—that the testator did not intend the devisee's descendants to take the devisee's share). This UPC provision is quite controversial; even in a UPC jurisdiction, be certain to ascertain whether the legislature adopted this rule.

   iii. *Allen v. Talley,* 949 S.W.2d 59 (Tex. Ct. App. 1997), illustrates that it is difficult in some cases to determine whether a will states an intent that an antilapse statute should not apply. The testator's will left her estate to "my living brothers and sisters: John . . . , Claude . . . , Lewis . . . , Lera . . . , and Juanita . . . share and share alike. John, Lewis, and Juanita were living when the testator executed the will but predeceased the testator; their decendants claimed their parents' shares. The court instead held that Claude and Lera received the entire estate because the quoted language was deemed to impose a condition of survivorship, thereby expressing the testator's intent that the antilapse statute not apply.

EXAMPLES AND ANALYSIS

T's will bequeathed her estate "to my siblings, A and B, share and share alike, or all to the survivor of them." A died, then B died, and then T died. One child of A and two children of B survived T, who also was survived by another sibling, C; T died unmarried, survived by no other relatives.

The alternatives for distribution of T's estate are: (i) half to A's child and the other half in equal shares to B's children, under the antilapse statute, (ii) the entire estate in equal shares to B's children by virtue of the antilapse statute, leaving the entire estate to B's descendants because B survived A, or (iii) by intestacy, with the relative shares of C and the descendants of A and B depending on the jurisdiction's system of representation (see Chapter 2). The antilapse issue is the same as in *Allen*: does the survivorship language in T's will reflect T's intent that the antilapse statute not apply? Because the survivorship condition expressly applies only if one of A or B survives T, the will states no intent with respect to the contingency of both A and B predeceasing T. Accordingly, and because of the presumption against intestacy, the antilapse statute probably would apply. Further, because the will speaks at death, at which time the testator's survivors are determined, and because there is no indication that T would prefer the descendants of B over the descendants of A, all the children of A and B would share under the antilapse statute without regard to B having survived A. (Note, however, that if B had survived A and T, the antilapse statute would not have applied and B would have taken the entire estate.)

Note also that the antilapse statute gives A's child half of the residue while B's children, who are similarly situated (all being nieces or nephews of T) split the other half; even under the UPC antilapse statute, the share of a named beneficiary who predeceases a testator passes to the beneficiary's descendants, by representation—there is no per capita at each generation system for property distributed under antilapse statutes to descendants of multiple predeceased beneficiaries, as there is under the UPC for intestate property. No reason is articulated in the UPC for this inconsistent treatment. For a case with facts similar to those of this example, see *Early v. Bowen*, 447 S.E.2d 167 (N.C. Ct. App. 1994).

---

    f. **Survivorship conditions: the UPC** reverses the longstanding rule that a survivorship condition in a gift negates application of the antilapse statute. Thus, assume that T's will leaves "$1,000 to A if she survives me," that the will does not otherwise address the possibility of A dying before T, that A does not survive T, and that there is no extrinsic evidence that T would not want the antilapse statute to apply; despite the survivorship condition, if A is within the required relation to T, the UPC antilapse statute will apply and A's surviving descendants will take the $1,000 by representation.

5. Substituted Gifts

If a devisee dies before the testator, the first question to consider—before application of an antilapse statute—is whether the will provides for an alternative taker for the gift. If so, the alternative taker receives the devise; there is no lapse and the antilapse statute is not an issue. On occasion courts stretch to find an alternative taker under a will if the antilapse statute would not apply to save a gift, because failure to do so would cause the devise to lapse.

   a. ***Jackson.*** For example, in *Jackson v. Schultz*, 151 A.2d 284 (Del. Ch. 1959), the testator's will provided, "I give . . . to my beloved wife, Bessie . . . all my property . . . to her and her heirs and assigns forever." Bessie predeceased the testator. Three of Bessie's children from a prior relationship survived the testator, who had not adopted the children (although he had helped raise and support them). The testator died without heirs and, if his property did not pass to Bessie's children under his will, it would have escheated (the antilapse statute not being applicable to gifts to spouses). The court held for Bessie's children, finding that the testator intended that his estate would pass to Bessie's heirs if she predeceased him. This construction avoided both intestacy and escheat to the state.

      i. **"To A *or* her heirs" v. "To A *and* her heirs."** If the gift had been to "Bessie *or* her heirs and assigns," the result the court wanted to reach would have been easy—a gift over to the children if Bessie predeceased. In *Jackson*, however, the gift was to "Bessie *and* her heirs and assigns." This language generally is construed to mean only that the devisee receives a fee, not that heirs and assigns take an alternative gift if the devisee predeceases the testator. Nevertheless, the court held that "and" can be read as "or" if, as in this case, doing so will carry out the testator's intent.

   b. **Compare *Hofing v. Willis,*** 201 N.E.2d 852 (Ill. 1964). In *Hofing* language similar to that employed in *Jackson* was used—"to A *and* her heirs and assigns"—and the same argument was made that "and" should be read as "or" to allow the heirs of A, who predeceased the testator, to take. The court held that construction to be unreasonable because it would allow A to assign the right to receive the devise to whomever A chose. The *Hofing* analysis probably is preferable to the construction in *Jackson*, although *Jackson* is revealing in how ardent the law is about avoiding a lapse (especially when it would cause property to pass by intestacy or, worse in *Jackson*, to the state by escheat).

6. Survivorship

Lapse occurs if a devisee predeceases the testator and the will does not name an alternative taker. There is no lapse if the devisee or the alternate survives the testator. In some circumstances (e.g., an automobile crash in which the testator and the devisee are killed) it may not be possible to determine if a devisee actually survived the testator. Further, the devisee may be treated as having predeceased by statute or by the will even if it is clear that the devisee actually survived the testator. See, e.g., UPC §2-702 (120 hour survival requirement).

a. **Addressed by the governing instrument.** A provision in the governing instrument controls if it addresses the question whether a beneficiary named in the instrument survived another person, such as the testator or another devisee.

EXAMPLES AND ANALYSIS

T's will leaves $10,000 to T's friend, F, if F survives T. The will defines "survives" to require survival by at least 30 days. T dies; 20 days later F dies. Despite having actually survived T, F will not take under T's will. If the will does not provide an alternative taker the devise will lapse (unless the governing antilapse statute applies to non-relatives, which is not likely) and the devise will fail.

b. **Not addressed by the governing instrument.** Survivorship that is not addressed by the governing instrument is resolved by statute in most cases. The original Uniform Simultaneous Death Act (USDA) applied if deaths occurred under such circumstances that it was not possible to prove the order of deaths. Because of litigation that avoided application of the original USDA by proving the order of deaths (see *Janus v. Tarasewicz* in Chapter 2), the USDA and the UPC were revised to require a beneficiary to survive a decedent by 120 hours to be treated as a survivor. Although a statutory survivorship requirement will not apply if the document addresses the survivorship issue, the document must do so explicitly.

EXAMPLES AND ANALYSIS

A comment to both the revised USDA and the UPC includes the following example. G's will leaves her estate to her husband, H, and provides that, "in the event he dies before I do, at the same time that I do, or under circumstances as to make it doubtful who died first," G's estate goes to her brother, Melvin. G dies; H dies about 38 hours later. Under the USDA and the UPC, Melvin takes G's estate. Although G's will addressed survivorship, the provision is not operable because G and H did not die at the same time or under circumstances that make it doubtful who died first. Further, G's will did not explicitly override the 120 hour statutory survivorship requirement. Accordingly, it applies; H is treated as having predeceased G because H did not survive G by that period.

---

   c. **Operation of survivorship statutes.** The USDA and UPC §§2-104 and 2-702 provide rules for the disposition of property on the death of a decedent when a beneficiary does not survive the decedent by at least 120 hours.

   i. **Will beneficiaries.** As between two individuals whose wills benefit each other, the rule is that each is treated as the survivor with respect to his or her own property, thus preventing double administration of any of their property.

   ii. **Life insurance.** With respect to a life insurance beneficiary designation, if the statute applies the insured is treated as surviving the designated beneficiary.

   iii. **Joint tenancies.** If the statute applies to joint tenancy with the right of survivorship, each joint tenant is treated as the owner of an equal share of the property and regarded as surviving for purposes of disposing of his or her share.

   iv. **Beneficiaries dying simultaneously.** Not addressed by statute in most states is the order of deaths among beneficiaries, neither of whom is the transferor (e.g., "to Child for life, remainder to Grandchild" and Child and Grandchild die under circumstances such that the order of their deaths cannot be proven). In some states that do address this subject the oldest is deemed to die first.

   d. **Survivorship planning.** When two persons die within a relatively short time, survivorship conditions in a document (and the survivorship provisions of the USDA and the UPC) serve two purposes. First, they cause each decedent's property to pass to her designees (usually her relatives), rather than her devisee's designees (usually the devisee's relatives). For example, G's will leaves her estate to her husband, H, but if he predeceases her, to her brother. If H fails to survive G by the requisite period, G's property will pass to her brother instead of to H's estate, from which it might pass to H's relatives. Second, survivorship conditions prevent double administration costs because property does not pass from one estate to another.

7. Lapse and Class Gifts

In the context of lapse, class gifts raise two issues: is a particular gift a "class gift" and, if so, how do the lapse and antilapse rules apply, if at all? The second question is easier. For example, "to my children in equal shares" is a class gift; the issue is what happens if one or more of the children predecease the donor.

a. **Common law rule.** The common law provided no protection to the descendants of a member of a class gift who predeceased the testator. For example, assume that (i) T's will devises property to her children, equally, making no provision for the possibility of a child predeceasing; (ii) T's child A predeceases T; and (iii) A's only child, GC, survives T. At common law GC would not take the share of the class gift that A would have received if living. Rather, the common law rule is that the remaining class members take the entire class gift; there is no share for a predeceased class member. If no child survived T the gift would fail, meaning that the property would become residuary (if the class gift was preresiduary) or intestate (if the class gift was of the residue).

b. **Class gifts and antilapse statutes.** Most antilapse statutes apply to class gifts. Accordingly, if (1) there is a class gift, (2) a member of the class dies before the testator, (3) the instrument does not include a gift over, and (4) there is an antilapse statute that applies to class gifts and it is applicable (e.g., because the predeceased class member is within the proper relation to the testator) then the deceased class member's descendants take the share the deceased class member would have received if living. As in any antilapse situation, the descendants take directly from the testator, not through the deceased class member's estate. In every respect, it is as if they were members of the class, meaning that the deceased class member's creditors and surviving spouse (see Chapter 10) have no claim against the descendants' share.

c. **Priority rules.** There are a number of rules that could apply in any given case, necessitating a rank ordering of the rules if a will contains a gift to a class and a member of the class fails to survive the testator. Here is their priority:

    i. **Survivorship condition.** Any survivorship condition—either expressly stated in the document or under an applicable statute regarding survivorship (such as the UPC 120 hour rule)—applies first. A class member who does not survive by the requisite period has no entitlement and, unless an antilapse statute then kicks in, neither do her representatives.

ii. **Alternative gift.** A gift over in the event of nonsurvival specified in the document applies. (E.g., "to my siblings, but if any does not survive me, her share to the Red Cross.")

iii. **Antilapse statute.** If there is no alternative disposition provision or if it is not effective (e.g., "to my children, equally; if any do not survive me, to his or her spouse who survives me," and the testator's child predeceases with no surviving spouse), then an antilapse statute that applies to class gifts may apply to cause the deceased class member's descendants to take the share. (An antilapse statute would not solve the problem if, for example, the deceased class member is not within the required relationship to the testator or no descendant of the deceased class member survives the testator.)

iv. **Survivorship within the class.** If no antilapse statute is applicable, then the deceased class member's "share" crosses over to the other class members, if any—meaning the surviving class members—take everything.

v. **Lapse.** Finally, if the cross-over cannot apply (e.g., because no class member survives) and the gift is not caught by any of the prior rules, then the gift lapses and falls into the residue or, if it *is* the residue, passes by intestacy.

 # EXAMPLES AND ANALYSIS

T's will leaves $60,000 to "my nephews who survive me by 30 days." T is survived by 30 days by two nephews, A and B. T had a third nephew, C, who predeceased her. C's only child, X, survived T by 30 days. In most states, the survivorship condition would negate application of the antilapse statute (even if nephews are within the category of devisees to whom the antilapse statute otherwise would apply), in which case A and B each would take $30,000. (Under the UPC the survivorship language, in the absence of other sufficient evidence of the testator's intent, would not negate application of an antilapse statute that otherwise is applicable. As a result, and because the UPC antilapse statute applies to devises to descendants of the testator's grandparents, A, B, and X each would receive $20,000 under the UPC.)

Let's look at another one. T's will left her estate to "my first cousins, equally, and if any of them are not living, to their spouses." Assume T had four first cousins (A, B, C, and D); A and B survived T; C and D predeceased T; C was survived by a spouse

(S) who also survived T; D was single when she died but D's only child (X) survived T. Because the will included a gift over to the spouse of a first cousin who predeceased T, S will take C's share without regard to the jurisdiction's antilapse statute. Depending on whether the applicable antilapse statute applies to class gifts and, if so, whether first cousins are within its reach, D's share may pass to X or there will be no share for D. In the latter case the entire residue will be divided among A, B, and S. If the UPC were in effect, X would take ¼ of the residue (as would each of A, B, and S), because the UPC antilapse statute applies to class gifts (as do most) and because it applies to devises to descendants of the testator's grandparents, which would include first cousins.

8. What Is a Class Gift?

The second class gift/lapse issue is whether the gift is to a class in the first place. Usually this question should be addressed first, although we deferred it here because it is the more elaborate concept to digest. A "class gift" is one to takers who are defined by one or more common characteristics. For example: to my "children," "grandchildren," "employees," "former spouses," "siblings," "nieces and nephews," "first cousins," or such. When the recipients of a gift are identified as a group, the assumption is that the donor was "group minded" and intended the gift to be shared by those persons who were members of the group at the appropriate time (more on that shortly). Thus, a fundamental characteristic of a class gift is that the number of persons who are to receive it can increase or decrease, as changes in composition of the class occur.

a. **Size and number of shares subject to change.** In a class gift the size of each member's share is subject to change as the number of shares changes (increasing while the class is "open" and decreasing *if* a member dies and survivorship is required). The important point is that the number of takers and the size of their respective shares is uncertain until a determination is made at some definite time as to who is included in the class. For example, a devise in equal shares to grandchildren who survive the testator may fluctuate as grandchildren are born or die between the time the will is executed and the time the testator dies.

b. *Dawson.* In *Dawson v. Yucus*, 239 N.E.2d 305 (Ill. App. Ct. 1968), the testator's will left an interest in a farm half to Stewart and half to Gene, both of whom were nephews of her predeceased husband. Gene died before the testator; Stewart claimed that the devise of the farm was a class gift, in which case he would take the entire interest as the only survivor of the class. (The antilapse statute did not apply to Gene, who was related to the testator only by marriage and not by blood.) The court held that, because the devisees were designated by name and the size of their shares was fixed, the devise was not a class gift. As a result, Gene's gift lapsed; because it was a preresiduary gift, it fell into the residue and passed to the residuary beneficiaries.

   i. Class gift language. For a devise to be a class gift the will should have said something like "in equal shares to such members of the class consisting of my husband's nephews, Stewart and Gene, as survive me." There can be a class that is as small as two potential takers, and all persons who could qualify as class members need not be included in the class (e.g., the quoted language would constitute a class gift even if there were other nephews of the testator's husband who survived her, which was the case).

 # EXAMPLES AND ANALYSIS

T's will includes a gift of "the residue of my estate ⅓ to A, ⅓ to B, and ⅓ to C." The gift is not a class gift, even if A, B, and C share a common characteristic that would allow them to be described as a class (e.g., if they were siblings). This would be the case even if C predeceases T, the antilapse statute is not applicable and, in the absence of class gift treatment, C's ⅓ would pass by intestacy. (Note that intestacy would result in that circumstance if the jurisdiction follows the traditional no residue of the residue rule, rather than the approach of UPC §2-604, under which A and B would share C's ⅓ even without class gift treatment.) In *Sullivan v. Sullivan*, 529 N.E.2d 890 (Mass. App. Ct. 1988), the court improperly deemed such a disposition to be a class gift to avoid intestacy. The preferable means of achieving class gift treatment in such a situation would be for the will to say something like "to my siblings who survive me" or, if there were more siblings than A, B, and C but only those three were meant to benefit, "to such members of a class consisting of my siblings A, B, and C as survive me."

   c. "To A and the children of B." *In re Moss*, 1899 2 Ch. 314 (Eng. C.A.), addresses the question whether a gift—in *Moss*, of a remainder—"to A and the children of B" is a single class gift, or an individual gift of a part of the property to A and a class gift of the balance of the property to the class of B's children. The cases are divided; the *Moss* court held the gift to be a single class gift, perhaps because to have done otherwise would have resulted in the lapse of the gift to A, which would have caused part of the remainder to pass to the life tenant, whom the testator clearly intended to receive only a life estate.

   d. Presumption. When the issue whether there is a class gift is in doubt, there is said to be a slight presumption in favor of the gift being to individuals rather than to a class. Thus, drafters cannot be too explicit in describing a gift as to a class if that is the intent.

C. MORE ON CLASS GIFTS

Class gifts raise various construction issues, in addition to the threshold question whether a class gift has been created and the lapse and antilapse problems. These issues arise only if a contrary intent is not clearly expressed: resort to the class gift rules of construction is not necessary if all of the various contingencies concerning class membership, the deaths of class members, and distributions are clearly addressed in the document.

1. Composition of the Class

Central to class gift issues is the question of who comprises the class and thus who shares in the gift to the class. The key questions are when is membership in the class determined and under what conditions may someone who shares the common characteristic for class membership nevertheless be excluded from the class. These questions require an understanding of open and closed classes.

a. **An "open" class** means that it can get larger. For example, if the class is my grandchildren, and my children are still alive, the class is open (unless treated as closed under the rules described below) because my children can have more children who will be my grandchildren.

b. **"Closing" a class** means that no one born or adopted or otherwise made to qualify for class membership (e.g., by marriage) after the class has closed can become a member of the class, even if they otherwise share the class characteristics.

   i. **Exception.** Afterborns in gestation are deemed to be alive when conceived; thus, a child conceived before a class closes, but born after, is a member of the class. Being alive but not yet adopted will not suffice—the adoption does not relate back to birth for class closing purposes.

   ii. **Impossibility.** The class closes no later than when it is physiologically impossible for a person to be born into a class. For example, if T left Blackacre in trust for A for life, remainder to B's children, the class will close no later than on B's death during A's life. Some classes close even sooner than that, as we will see.

2. Survivorship

A different question is whether survivorship of a future event, such as the death of a person, is required to become a class member in the first instance, or to share in a distribution of the class gift after the death of the class member.

a. **If survivorship is not required** but the class member dies before distribution occurs, the interest of the class member is an asset that passes through the class member's estate to her heirs, if she dies intestate, or to her devisees, if she dies testate.

 ## EXAMPLES AND ANALYSIS

T's will left Blackacre in trust, with income to be paid to A for life, remainder to B's children. A and two children of B, C and D, each survive T but C predeceased A. At A's death, what disposition is to be made of Blackacre? At common law, and in most jurisdictions today, the remainder beneficiary is not required to survive the life tenant: C's remainder interest in Blackacre vests upon C's survival of T. Thus, at A's death, half of Blackacre passes to D and the other half to C's estate to be distributed to C's heirs or devisees. Notice that this rule, with respect to *future* interests, differs from the common law rule that a devisee must survive the testator to avoid a lapse. Although it might seem that a consistent survival rule should apply, we will see that these two cases are very different at common law. (As discussed in Chapter 15, a recent change in the UPC reverses this traditional treatment, requires that C survive A to take, and injects an antilapse concept into future interest law, all of which is a major change in the law of future interests.)

b. **If survivorship is required** the interest of a class member who predeceases the specified event fails.

 ## EXAMPLES AND ANALYSIS

T's will left Blackacre to her children, equally. T had three children, A, B, and C. A predeceased T but B and C survive T. At common law, the gift to A fails; class membership for an immediate gift at the death of the testator is determined at the testator's death and the common law survival requirement at T's death is applicable even in this class gift. Because A did not survive T, A was not a member of the class and had no interest in Blackacre. Thus, at T's death A's estate will not share in the gift of Blackacre. In most jurisdictions antilapse statutes apply to class gifts, and gifts to children are covered by antilapse statutes. As a result, in most states any descendants of A who survive T will stand in A's shoes to take the share of Blackacre that A would have received if living. If no descendant of A survives T (or if the gift was to a class whose members are not covered by the applicable antilapse statute, or if the applicable antilapse statute does not apply to class gifts), Blackacre would pass to B and C, the members of the class who survived T.

3. General Principles

If a gift to a class is intended, three general principles or presumptions, and one basic rule modifying them, are found in most cases (although they may conflict):

a. **Include as many members as possible.** First, the assumption is that the donor wants to benefit as many members as possible (subject to the rule of convenience, discussed below, that closes the class when distribution is required or when a fund established currently for later distribution must be set aside).

b. **Avoid failure or lapse.** The second presumption is that the donor wants to avoid lapse. Although delayed determination of class membership is not favored, neither is closing the class *before necessary* if the effect might be to exclude possible members.

 ## EXAMPLES AND ANALYSIS

T's will left Blackacre in trust, income to A for life, remainder to B's children. T died, survived by A, B, and a child of B (X). At common law, X's interest vests at T's death even if X dies before A (in which case X's share passes when A dies through X's estate to X's heirs or devisees). The class of B's children does not close at T's death, because distribution of Blackacre is not required until A dies. Thus, if another child of B is born or adopted after T's death but before A dies, that child also will have a vested share in the gift of Blackacre. Blackacre is to be distributed at A's death and the class therefore closes *even if B is then living*; a child of B born thereafter would not share in the gift.

c. **Early distribution.** The third presumption assumes that the donor wants an early distribution.

 ## EXAMPLES AND ANALYSIS

T's will left $30,000 to A's children who reach the age of 30 years. T died, survived by A and by two children of A, W (age 10) and X (age 6). The class closes when A's oldest child reaches the age of 30 years: the presumption is that T intended distribution to A's children as they reach the age of 30, not at a later date when we would know with certainty how many children of A will reach the age of 30. If X is living when W reaches the age of 30, along with a third child of A who was born after T's death, W will receive $10,000, and the remaining $20,000 will be held for X and the third child until they reach the age of 30. If X dies before reaching the age of 30, half of X's share will be distributed to W and the other half will remain as part of the share being held for the third child (unless an antilapse statute were applicable, in which case X's descendants would be substituted, by representation, for X as members of the class). Any additional children of A born or adopted after W reaches the age of 30 years are excluded from the class because it closed when W reached the age of 30 to facilitate an early distribution.

---

4. **The Rule of Convenience** is a basic rule that modifies these three general principles.

   a. **Per capita gifts.** A gift of a fixed dollar amount (or quantity of other property) to each member of a class sometimes is referred to as a *per capita gift* and requires, under the rule of convenience, closing the class when the fund must be established (the time of "funding"). Thus, if T gave a specified amount to each member of a class, the class closes at the testator's death regardless of whether distribution of the gift is to be made at the testator's death or thereafter, or whether any members of the class survive the testator.

 # EXAMPLES AND ANALYSIS

T's will left $1,000 to each grandchild who survived her. T is survived by two grandchildren, GC1 and GC2, and by three children. The class closes at T's death; GC1 and GC2 each receive $1,000. Any grandchildren born after T's death (unless in gestation when T died, in which case $1,000 also is set aside for each of them) are excluded from the gift. If T's will had provided for $1,000 to be distributed to each grandchild when they reach the age of 30 years, the class still would close at T's death, even if GC1 and GC2 both were under 30 at T's death. Grandchildren born after T's death would be excluded from the gift regardless of whether they were born before or after either or both of GC1 and GC2 reached 30 years of age. If T had no grandchildren at T's death and the gift is a per capita affair, some states might leave the class open to admit someone and, because this violates the principle of the rule of Convenience, now would leave it open until all of T's children are dead. But most courts would close the class at T's death and the gift would fail (assuming an antilapse statute was not applicable).

---

      i.   Rationale. Per capita gifts are treated differently for class closing purposes than gifts of a fixed total sum or specified property, to be divided among members of a class, because the gifted property that is the subject of a per capita gift cannot be set aside for later division when distribution is required. With a per capita gift there is no way to know how much to set aside to fund the per capita gifts, so the rule of convenience closes the class to make distribution of T's estate possible.

  b.   First mandatory principal distribution. If per capita gifts are not involved, under the rule of convenience the class remains open until the first mandatory distribution of principal to a class member. For example, if a trust were created for T's grandchildren and the trustee could distribute income or principal to them in its discretion but must distribute corpus when each grandchild reaches the age of 35 years, the class would remain open until the first living grandchild actually reaches the age of 35, at which time a distribution must be made to that grandchild of an equal share of the trust corpus. The class closes then—so the trustee can determine how large a share to distribute.

5.   Application of the Rule of Convenience: Immediate Gifts

If T's will leaves Blackacre to X's children, the rule of convenience dictates that the class closes at T's death, at which time distribution is to be made to the children of X who survive T (or, if an antilapse statute is applicable, to descendants of any deceased child of X), without regard to X also having survived T and thus without regard to the possibility of there being additional children of X.

  a.   Rationale. To do otherwise would be unworkable. To hold the gift in T's estate until X's death would delay the distribution to children of X who survive T, and it would delay closing T's estate for what could be many years. To distribute part of Blackacre to X's children who survive T and withhold the balance for future born children entails the same ongoing estate administration problem and presents the possibility of X having more or fewer children than anticipated. Finally, to distribute Blackacre to the children of X who survive T, subject to an obligation that they convey interests in Blackacre to any children of X subsequently born or adopted raises questions of enforceability, administration, title, and such.

6. Application of the Rule of Convenience: Postponed Gifts

If a fixed sum or gift of specified property is not to be distributed until a future date, the rule of convenience closes the class when the first mandatory distribution of principal is required, even though that occurs well after the testator's death.

 ## EXAMPLES AND ANALYSIS

T's will devised Blackacre to A for life, remainder to B's children. When T executed her will, B had two children, V and W, both of whom were living. V died first, followed by T, who was survived by A, B, and W. During A's life, but after T's death, B has another child, Y, and then W died. A then died, survived by Y, after which B had yet another child, Z. Distribution is not required until the death of the life tenant, A. Accordingly, the class did not close until then. Because Z was born after the class closed, Z is not a member of the class and does not share in the distribution of Blackacre. Because Y was born before A's death, Y is a member of the class and shares in the distribution. Because V did not survive T, V is not treated as a member of the class (although V's descendants may be substituted for V as class members if an antilapse statute applies). Finally, W survived T but died before A; in most jurisdictions W's remainder would vest at T's death and would pass to W's estate to be distributed to W's heirs (if W died intestate) or devisees (if W died testate). Under the new UPC, however, W's interest would fail (see Chapter 15), unless saved for her descendants by an antilapse statute.

---

a. **Acceleration of postponed gift.** If a testator provides for a postponed gift to a class and the class closes on its own, circumstances *may* dictate that the distribution of the gift be accelerated.

 ## EXAMPLES AND ANALYSIS

T's will left $25,000 "to A's children, to be paid to them when they reach the age of 30 years." T died, survived by A and A's only child, X, who was 10 years old. X dies two years after T and A died three years after X. The interest of X in the fund vested at T's death. (Note that the gift is to A's children, "*to be paid to them* when they reach the age of 30 years," not "to A's children *who reach* the age of 30 years"; see the discussion of *Clobberie's Case* in Chapter 15.) Probably no portion of the fund was distributed to X's heirs or devisees at X's death, however, because A was still living and could have additional children before X would have reached 30. In other words, the class remained open after X's death until X would have reached 30, and any children of A born or adopted before that date would become class members. Upon A's death before X would have reached 30, however, the class closes physically, after which there is no further reason to withhold distribution of the fund to X's heirs or devisees, and the distribution of their share likely would be accelerated.

---

    b. Disclaimer by life tenant. Assume that T's gift was to A for life, remainder to A's children and that T died survived by A and by A's only child, X. If A disclaims (see Chapter 2), the class is not physiologically closed, because A could have additional children, but UPC §2-801(d)(1) provides that a future interest (the remainder to A's children) that becomes possessory after the termination of a disclaimed current interest (A's life estate) takes effect as if the disclaimant predeceased the decedent. In this example, A would be treated as having died before T and the class would close at T's death; any children of A born or adopted thereafter would be excluded from the gift. That result was reached under the UPC in *Pate v. Ford*, 376 S.E.2d 775 (S.C. 1989), even though (i) the disclaimer was by a sibling who had five children, (ii) another sibling had none but could have had children in the future who would have been beneficiaries, and (iii) the disclaimer resulted in the disclaimant's five children taking to the exclusion of any of their after born or after adopted first cousins.

    c. Postponement until youngest class member reaches specified age. In *Lux v. Lux*, 288 A.2d 701 (R.I. 1972), a grandmother's will left the residue of her estate to her grandchildren, but further provided that any realty in the residue was to be maintained for the grandchildren and not sold until the youngest reached the age of 21 years.

        i. Immediate outright gift vs. gift of future interest in trust. The first question was whether the realty passed outright to the grandchildren at their grandmother's death, in which case the class would have closed then, or whether the gift was made in trust, in which case the class would not close until the youngest grandchild reached the age of 21 years. The court held that the grandmother, recognizing the income producing nature of the real property and the young ages of her grandchildren, and providing for the realty to be maintained for them and not to be sold until a future date, intended to create a trust with principal distributions not to be made to the grandchildren until a future date. Thus, the class did not close at her death.

        ii. When the class closed. The court considered four possible dates for closing the class: (i) when the youngest grandchild living when the will was executed reached 21, (ii) when the youngest grandchild living when the testator died reached 21 (one of the five grandchildren who were living when the testator died was born after the will was executed), (iii) when the youngest of all grandchildren living at any time reached 21, or (iv) when the youngest grandchild whenever born reached 21, even if that grandchild might be born or adopted after all others were over the age of 21 years. (The testator's only son, the father of the five grandchildren, informed the court that he and his wife planned to have more children.)

(a) **Include afterborns if reasonable.** The first of the alternatives would exclude a grandchild living at the testator's death; the second would exclude grandchildren born after the testator's death but before the youngest of the grandchildren who survived the testator reached the age of 21 years. These alternatives each were rejected, presumably because they would exclude grandchildren born before any distribution of principal was required.

(b) **Early distribution; the rule of convenience.** The fourth alternative would require delaying distribution until the son's death, when the class would close physiologically, even if all of the living grandchildren had reached the age of 21 years. The court also rejected that construction and adopted the third alternative, which it viewed as representing the average testator's intent. It also is the alternative recommended in such a situation by the Restatement (Second) of Property—Donative Transfers.

7. Exceptions to the Rule of Convenience

There are two minor exceptions to the rule of convenience.

a. **Afterborns.** As stated above, afterborns in gestation are deemed to be alive when conceived.

b. **No class members.** If no class members exist when distribution is required and it is not a per capita gift, failure is prevented by admitting *all* afterborns and afteradopteds: the class does not close until no more may be born or adopted. For example, if distribution is to grandchildren when the testator dies, the testator's children are alive at that time, but there are no grandchildren yet, the class would not close until all the children die.

i. **Rationale.** Class closing rules are rules of construction designed in significant part to carry out the presumed intent of the testator. If T's will provides for an immediate gift at T's death to her grandchildren and at least one grandchild is then living, the assumption is that T wanted distribution to occur at her death. Closing the class at that time accomplishes that result, as well as avoiding the administrative problems of keeping the class open until the death of the last of T's children. But if there are no grandchildren living at T's death (and an antilapse statute does not apply to substitute as class members descendants of a predeceased grandchild), the class cannot close at that time without defeating the gift altogether.

ii.   **Implicit assumptions.** The implicit assumptions underlying this exception to the rule of convenience are that T did not want the gift to fail, that T knew no grandchildren were living at her death, and that T wanted the class to remain open after her death to benefit all members of the class whenever born or adopted. In this case T's estate probably will be kept open to hold the property until the death of her last child, but it had to be kept open beyond T's death in any event; once it is kept open beyond T's death, it is not closed at the birth or adoption of any grandchild. That approach would avoid further administrative inconvenience at the cost of excluding additional grandchildren from sharing in the gift. Afterborns or afteradopteds are excluded if there is anyone alive in the class to take at the testator's death, but not if the testator was not survived by any class members.

8.   **Class Gifts of Income**

Special rules apply to class gifts of income from a fund. Assume that A survived T and that T's will left property in trust, with income to be paid annually to A's children and the remainder to be paid to B at the death of the last of A's children to die. The class will not close at T's death; rather, income is distributable each year to those children of A who are alive at the time of each distribution. As a result, if one child of A (X) survives T and A has a second child (Y) five years after T's death, the trust income for the first five years will be paid to X; income for subsequent years will be shared by X and Y until one of them dies (in which case, assuming an antilapse statute is not applicable, income would thereafter be paid to the survivor), or until additional children of A are born (in which case they too would share in future income distributions). In a sense, each income distribution is treated as a separate gift as to which the class closing rules apply.

 EXAMPLES AND ANALYSIS

T's will devised property in trust, with the principal to be distributed to the children of A who reach the age of 30 years and the income to be distributed to them currently, as it is earned. T died, survived by A and by two children of A, W (age 15) and X (age 10). Before W reached the age of 30, A had another child, Y; after W reached the age of 30, A had a fourth child, Z.

Here, income will be distributed to A's children who will receive distributions of principal upon reaching the age of 30 years. Under the class closing rules for postponed gifts, the class will close when the oldest of A's children, W, reaches the age of 30 years. Because Z was born after that, Z is excluded from the class and will not share in income or principal. W will receive ⅓ of the principal when W reaches age 30; X will receive ½ of the remaining principal when X reaches age 30; and Y will receive all of the remaining principal when Y reaches age 30. Income will be distributed equally to the current class members. Thus, W and X will share the income from T's death until the birth of Y; income will be distributed in equal thirds among W, X, and Y from the birth of Y until W reaches age 30; X and Y will share the income from W's 30th birthday until X reaches age 30; and all income will be distributed to Y after X reaches age 30.

9. Planning for Class Gifts in Trust

Class gift rules are rules of construction. As such, they give way to a contrary intent stated in the instrument. In most cases, the preferable course is to avoid the class gift rules of construction by specifically addressing each of the various contingencies that can arise with a class gift.

REVIEW QUESTIONS AND ANSWERS

Question: T's will left $100,000 to "my siblings who survive me." T had two siblings, S and B. B died before T, who died survived by S and by the only children of B, N1 and N2. Who receives the $100,000? Why?

Answer: The gift of $100,000 is a class gift to T's siblings. At common law, S would take the $100,000 as the only surviving member of the class. Today most states have antilapse statutes that apply to class gifts. Assuming this jurisdiction has such a statute, two additional questions are raised. First, does the survivorship language negate application of the antilapse statute? In most jurisdictions it would and S would take the entire $100,000; under the UPC it would not. Second, if the antilapse statute is not negated by the survivorship language, does it apply to gifts to siblings who predecease the testator? If so (as does the UPC), N1 and N2, as the only descendants of B to survive T, would be substituted for B as members of the class, to take B's share by representation; thus, S would receive $50,000, and each of N1 and N2 would receive $25,000. If the antilapse statute does not apply to gifts to predeceased siblings, the common law class gift rule would apply and S would receive the entire $100,000.

Question: T's will left Blackacre to A's children. A had two children (W and X) when T executed her will. W died before T's death. T died, survived by X, W's only child (C), and A. A had another child (Y) six months after T's death. A had a fourth child (Z) two years after T's death. A died five years later. Who takes Blackacre? When? Why?

Answer: The gift of Blackacre is a class gift. Under the rule of convenience, the class closes at T's death, because the distribution of Blackacre is to be made at that time. At T's death the class consists of X and Y (Y presumably was conceived before T's death because Y was born within nine months after T's death). Because Z was conceived after T's death, Z is excluded from the class. Because W died before T, W will be excluded from the class, but an antilapse statute may apply to substitute C for W as a member of the class. If there is an antilapse statute that applies to class gifts and W is covered by it, Blackacre will be shared by X, Y, and C, each of whom would receive ⅓. If no antilapse statute applies to class gifts, or if W is not closely enough related to T to be covered by it, X and Y each will receive ½.

Question: T's will devised her estate "½ to A, ¼ to B, and ¼ to C." C died before T, but A and B survived T. How is T's estate distributed? Why?

Answer: The first question is whether the antilapse statute applies to save the devise to C. Most antilapse statutes apply only to gifts to devisees who were related to the testator in a specified manner. If C was so related to T, C's descendants, by representation, will share C's ¼. If C was not so related to T, or if no descendants of C survived T, at common law C's ¼ would pass to T's heirs by intestacy. Under UPC §2-604 and the law of most states, however, if the antilapse statute does not apply C's ¼ of the residue will be divided between A and B in the ratio they receive the remaining residue; thus, A would receive twice as much of C's ¼ as would B. The result is that A would receive ⅔ of the residue and B would receive ⅓.

Question: T's will devised Blackacre "in equal one-third shares to my children, A, B, and C" and the residue to charity. T had only the three children, A, B, and C. A died before T's will was executed. A's only child, GC1, survived T, as did B and C. To whom is Blackacre distributed? Why?

Answer: Because A died before T's will was executed, at common law the devise to A was void. As a result, at common law A's share of Blackacre would fall into the residue and pass to charity, unless the gift could be construed as a class gift. If so, at common law Blackacre would pass in equal shares to B and C, as the surviving members of the class. Because the devise was of specified, fixed shares (⅓ of Blackacre) to specified devisees (A, B, and C), the devise probably would not be treated as a class gift, although the fact that Blackacre was left to T's children and the residue to charity would support an argument that a class gift of Blackacre was intended even though traditional class gift language was not employed.

Most antilapse statutes apply when a devisee predeceases the testator, regardless of whether the devisee died before or after execution of the will. Assuming such a statute is applicable, and that it applies to gifts to children of the testator, GC1 would be substituted for A as the devisee of ⅓ of Blackacre. If the applicable antilapse statute applied to void dispositions but did not apply to class gifts, B and C could argue that the devise of Blackacre was a class gift and thus that they take to the exclusion of GC1. Such an argument would be less likely to succeed if the antilapse statute would apply to substitute GC1 for A, despite A having died before execution of the will, than it would if class gift treatment was necessary to avoid ⅓ of Blackacre passing with the residue to charity.

Question: T's inter vivos revocable trust provided for Blackacre to be distributed to T's brother, B, if B survived T, and for the remainder of the trust assets at T's death to be distributed to T's child, A. B died before T; B's only child, N, survived T, as did A. To whom is Blackacre distributed? Why?

Answer: In many jurisdictions antilapse statutes apply only to wills; in such a jurisdiction, Blackacre would pass with the remainder of the trust assets to A. Antilapse statutes also are applicable to trusts under the UPC and the law of some jurisdictions. In such a jurisdiction N would receive Blackacre if the antilapse statute applies to gifts to predeceased siblings and is not negated by the survivorship requirement. If not, A would take Blackacre.

Question: T's will left $100,000 in trust, to be paid to A's children who reach the age of 30 years. T died, survived by A and by one child of A (X, age 12). A had another child, Y, when X was 16; when X was 33 A had a third child, Z. How is the $100,000 distributed?

Answer: The gift to A's children is postponed; distribution is not required until a child of A reaches age 30. Under the rule of convenience the class will not close at T's death, but instead will close when A's oldest child, X, reaches 30. At that time, Y is living but Z has not been conceived. Accordingly, the members of the class are X and Y. Half of the fund is distributable when X reaches 30; the balance is distributable to Y when she reaches 30.

9 CONSTRUCTION: ADEMPTION, ABATEMENT, ACCESSIONS, AND EXONERATION

CHAPTER OVERVIEW

- Interpretation and construction focus on problems of identifying the property being devised or the devisees to receive it. This chapter addresses other issues affecting the distribution of a decedent's property that are not resolved by the testator's will: ademption, abatement, accessions, and exoneration.

- *Ademption* involves a will that devises property that the testator did not own at death.

- *Abatement* arises if the will includes devises of more property than the decedent owned at death. It may arise if the will did not address whose share bears taxes and administration expenses.

- *Accessions* issues include whether beneficiaries are entitled to receive interest on general pecuniary bequests or dividends, interest, rent, or other income earned by the estate on assets specifically bequeathed.

- *Exoneration* is relevant if the testator devised encumbered property and whether the devisee takes the property subject to the debt or the estate must repay the debt so the devisee takes the property unencumbered.

A. CLASSIFICATION OF DISPOSITIONS

Most topics in this chapter are affected by the type of disposition (specific, general, demonstrative, or residuary) involved, making *classification* of a disposition critical. Recall from Chapter 1 that a "devise" is a gift of land, a "bequest" is a gift of personal property, and a "legacy" is a gift of money; the UPC refers to all three as "devises." In this RoadMap we sometimes use the traditional terms and sometimes follow the UPC approach.

1. *Specific* devises are gifts of particular assets or gifts payable from specified funds.

2. *Demonstrative* devises are specific gifts that may be satisfied from general funds if the specified funds or particular assets are exhausted. These gifts are treated as specific first but, if the asset or fund is inadequate, general estate assets are used to fund the balance of the gift. The notion is that the testator intended such a result often is a fiction to avoid ademption of a specific devise or to delay abatement of a general devise.

3. *General* devises are neither specific nor demonstrative; a gift is to be made to the devisee, but not of particular assets nor from a specific fund. General devises are satisfied out of any available assets or funds.

4. *Residuary* gifts are what remains after all specific, demonstrative, and general devises have been satisfied.

Examples

- **"My living room furniture": specific bequest.**

- **"The money that X owes me": specific legacy.**

- **"100 shares of X company stock": general bequest; maybe demonstrative if the testator owned X stock but, if there were not enough shares of X stock in the estate, the personal representative would acquire additional shares.**

- **"$100 worth of my X company stock": probably a specific bequest (because of the use of the word "*my*":** it is not just *any* shares of X stock being given).

- "$100, to be satisfied with my X company stock": specific and probably a pecuniary legacy, although it may be a specific bequest of stock. This distinction—between a gift of money or a gift of stock—probably does not matter except for income tax purposes (which are out of our league in this course). Quaere what the decedent would want if there is not enough X stock at death; should cash or other assets be used to make up the difference?

- "The greater of money and property of the value of $1 million or one-third of my estate": a general legacy or a residuary bequest, depending on which is greater.

- "$100 from my account at the X bank": specific legacy; arguably demonstrative (easier to argue if a comma appeared before "from") if the account is inadequate to satisfy the legacy and other funds are available.

- "The residue of my property": residuary.

- "All the rest of my land": residuary devise, or does "*my*" make it specific?

- "All my personal property": general bequest, residuary, specific (because of "*my*")?

> The last two examples illustrate how clarity may be elusive notwithstanding a simple, common disposition. Courts trifle with the classification rules (because they often dictate resolution of the issues addressed in this chapter) to serve their sense of equity or justice in a given case.

5. **Classifications Are Not Absolute** and may differ, depending on the substantive issue at stake and who the court wants to protect or disfranchise. (This is why the plaintiff in *Wasserman v. Cohen*, discussed below, was complaining about the court's decision to classify the gift before determining whether it adeemed.) For example, a disposition may be regarded as general for ademption by extinction purposes but specific for abatement or ademption by satisfaction reasons. Both (inconsistent) classifications would protect the taker, as we will see. So be careful with caselaw that classifies a disposition—the result may be affected by why the classification was being done.

B. ADEMPTION BY EXTINCTION

applies if the subject of a *specific* gift does not exist in the testator's estate at death. Unless the will provides otherwise (such as by making an alternative gift), generally the gift will fail due to extinction of the gifted property.

1. Applicable Only to Specifics

Ademption by extinction (often called just ademption) is applicable only to specifics, the subject of which is no longer in the estate at death; it cannot apply to general, demonstrative, or residuary dispositions because, for gifts in all three of those categories, there is not a gift of a particular identified item that can be exhausted or adeemed. Notice, however, that general, demonstrative, and residuary gifts can abate (see the discussion below) to exhaust those forms of gifts.

2. Theory of the Doctrine

Ademption by extinction is based on the assumption that a testator who intended to preserve a gift to a devisee after extinction of the subject of the specific devise would have changed her will to do so.

a. **Actual intent irrelevant.** In most states, failure to alter the will to preserve the gift is taken as conclusive proof of an intent to adeem. These states follow the "identity" theory: if the specifically devised property is not owned by the testator at death, the gift fails without regard to what the testator's actual intent may have been. For example, in *Wasserman v. Cohen*, 606 N.E.2d 901 (Mass. 1993), the settlor provided for a specific gift of an apartment building to a beneficiary. The gift adeemed when the settlor sold the building prior to death and did not amend the trust to provide an alternative gift. The court refused to consider the question whether the settlor *actually* intended the gift to adeem.

      i.   **Application of doctrine to revocable trust.** Notice that the *Wasserman* court applied the traditional wills doctrine of ademption to a revocable inter vivos trust. According to the court, "a trust, particularly when executed as part of a comprehensive estate plan, should be construed according to the same rules traditionally applied to wills." See Chapter 6.

      ii.   **Applicable to involuntary extinction.** In *Wasserman* the gift adeemed because the settlor voluntarily sold the property. Ademption by extinction traditionally applies even if the property was extinguished *without* the testator's consent. Thus, at common law and in many states today, it is not necessary to find (or even presume) that extinction of the item was voluntary.

      iii.   **Exception.** Some states (see, e.g., UPC §2-606) depart from traditional ademption doctrine by giving the devisee of a gift that was the subject of an involuntary extinction insurance proceeds (in case of a loss of the specifically devised property by fire or theft) or the proceeds from condemnation or a personal representative's sale on behalf of an incompetent or disabled individual.

  b. **Intent to adeem.** Cases allowing the devisee of an extinguished specific devise to receive other property in its stead are in the minority. And they will not apply if there is actual proof of a positive intent to adeem. Also, in some states the beneficiary may need to identify the proceeds from a particular disposition to avoid ademption.

      i.   **UPC §2-606(a)(6)** prevents ademption unless there is positive proof of an intent to adeem (and tracing is not required). In the absence of this proof, the devisee of the extinguished item receives the value of the specifically devised property from other assets in the estate.

3. Inability to Change the Will

Because the doctrine of ademption by extinction is based on the testator's presumed intent—that the testator intended the extinction because, had she not, she would have changed the will to substitute other property—the doctrine should require that the testator had the ability to alter the will after extinction of the item. Thus, the doctrine should not apply if extinction of the item occurred after the testator's death, incapacity, or if there were time or space limitations that would prevent alteration of the will. For example, if the property was destroyed in a fire or wreck in which the testator died, the intended beneficiary should receive any insurance proceeds representing or replacing the destroyed asset.

a.   Sale by agent under durable power of attorney. UPC §2-606(b) applies to any disposition of specifically devised property during the testator's life by an agent acting under a durable power of attorney (or other personal representative, such as a guardian); in the event of such a disposition, the devisee of the property under the will receives an amount equal to the proceeds of the disposition from other assets of the estate. UPC §2-606(b) is unusual in this respect.

i.   *In re Estate of Hegel,* 668 N.E.2d 474 (Ohio 1996), strictly followed ademption doctrine despite the testator's inability to change her will after a sale of specifically devised property. In *Hegel*, an agent under a durable power of attorney sold property of an incapacitated testator shortly before the testator's death. The agent did not realize that she personally was the specific devisee of the property under the testator's will. Ohio's ademption statute protected specific devisees from sales made by guardians, but not from sales made by attorneys-in-fact for incapacitated principals. The Supreme Court held the devise adeemed.

4.   Partial Ademption

Pro tanto ademption is possible in the case of a disposition or destruction of a portion of the specific devise.

 # EXAMPLES AND ANALYSIS

T's will devised an 80 acre tract of land to A. Subsequently, T sold 20 of the 80 acres to a third party. In an identity theory jurisdiction the gift is adeemed to the extent of the 20 acres; A will receive the other 60. In an intent theory or UPC jurisdiction A will receive the 60 acres plus the value of the 20 acres, unless it is established that T intended the gift of the 20 acres to adeem.

5.   Avoiding Ademption

In addition to drafting to provide for an alternative gift if specifically devised property is adeemed, ademption by extinction may be avoided in any of three ways.

a. After-acquired property. First, the specific gift is interpreted to apply to after-acquired items matching the item that was extinguished: the new property will pass in place of the asset originally owned. For example, if the will said "I give my home" to X, whatever home was owned at death would pass, even if different from that owned when the will was executed.

b. Classification of the gift. Second, if the gift is construed to be demonstrative or general. For example, assume that T's will devises "100 shares of IBM stock to each of A, B, and C." When the will was executed, T owned 300 shares of IBM stock. Subsequently, however, T sold the IBM stock and died owning none. If the gifts are specific, they might adeem (if additional shares cannot be bought); if they are general they do not. To avoid failure of the gifts, many courts would classify them as general (thus requiring the personal representative to purchase the 300 shares to satisfy the gifts). But if the devise had been "100 shares of *my* IBM stock to each of A, B, and C," the gifts likely would be classified as specific, and adeem by virtue of the sale and that classification.

c. Changes in form. Third, changes only in form do not cause ademption. For example, T's will devised "my 100 shares of ABC stock to A." Subsequent to execution of the will, ABC merged into XYZ, and T received 200 shares of XYZ stock in exchange for the ABC stock. T died owning the XYZ stock, but without having changed her will. A will receive the 200 shares of XYZ stock.

 # EXAMPLES AND ANALYSIS

T owned two pearl necklaces and executed a will bequeathing "my larger string of pearls" to A and "my other string of pearls" to B. Subsequently T combined the pearls into one string. If the combination is regarded as a mere change of form, A and B would take as tenants in common, probably with their fractions of ownership depending on the relative values of the two strands.

---

i. UPC §2-606(a)(5) expands and codifies the change in form exception. Property acquired as a "replacement" for specifically devised property passes to the specific devisee. According to the UPC comment, this provision does not introduce tracing into the law of ademption, but is intended to be a "mere change in form" principle.

EXAMPLES AND ANALYSIS

T's will devised Blackacre to A. After execution T sold Blackacre for $100,000; three months after the sale, T bought Whiteacre for $150,000. Shortly thereafter, T died. In a UPC §2-606(a)(5) jurisdiction the devise to A is not adeemed if Whiteacre was acquired as a "replacement" for Blackacre. If both were principal personal residences of T, the gift would not adeem. By contrast, if Blackacre was T's principal residence and, after selling it, T moved into a rented apartment and Whiteacre was commercial realty, the devise of Blackacre probably would adeem. If Whiteacre was a duplex and T lived on one side and rented out the other for income perhaps A would take the duplex as replacement property for Blackacre. If Whiteacre cost $400,000 and was a triplex or a four-plex, and T lived in one unit perhaps A would take an undivided interest in Whiteacre (½ if Whiteacre is a duplex, ⅓ if it is a triplex, or ¼ if it is a four-plex). If Blackacre was farmland and Whiteacre was a convenience store or if Blackacre were T's personal residence and T sold it and used the proceeds to buy investment securities, A would not take the new investment because it would not be replacement property for the personal residence. We don't know if that also would be true if Blackacre was investment real estate and its sale proceeds were reinvested in securities.

EXAM TIP

If specifically devised property is extinguished before the testator's death, under the UPC the devisee will take the value of the property from other assets of the estate unless it is established that the testator intended the devise to adeem. The devisee will take the replacement property if the change in form, replacement property exception applies. If it does not and there is not a showing that the testator intended the devise to adeem, the devisee will take the value of the specifically devised property. In either event, the devisee's gift is not adeemed.

C. ADEMPTION BY SATISFACTION

This doctrine may apply if the testator makes lifetime gifts to will beneficiaries after execution of a will; generally, it applies only if the testator made lifetime gifts to beneficiaries of general bequests under the will, but occasionally it applies to lifetime gifts to residuary, demonstrative, and even specific devisees. When it applies, ademption by satisfaction (or just "satisfaction") is the testator taking care of or accelerating the testamentary beneficence by making a gift during life. For example, if T's will gave $25,000 to a hospital, and T subsequently gave the hospital $25,000 before death, the hospital will not receive another $25,000 from T's estate at her death if the doctrine of satisfaction applies.

1. Distinguish from Advancement

Carefully distinguish terminology: this is *not* "advancement," which only applies in completely intestate estates. See pages 46-49. But the concepts operate in essentially the same manner.

2. Generally Inapplicable to Specific Gifts

Satisfaction usually does not apply to specifics, because if the specifically devised property is given away during life, the testamentary gift usually would adeem by extinction rather than by satisfaction. The net effect, however, is the same; the gift under the will fails. Note, however, that satisfaction could apply to a specific if it were shown that a gift of asset A was meant to satisfy a specific bequest of asset B, or a gift of "50 of *my* shares of IBM" (a specific bequest because of the word "my") could adeem by satisfaction if 50 shares were given during life and another 50 shares remain in the estate at the testator's death (meaning that ademption by extinction could not apply and only satisfaction would generate the "right" result of preventing the beneficiary from receiving another 50 shares).

3. Satisfaction of Demonstrative Gifts

To adeem a demonstrative gift would require both satisfaction and ademption by extinction because a demonstrative has the characteristics of both a specific and a general. That is, in theory, an ademption by satisfaction would only affect the general bequest; to affect the specific bequest in a demonstrative would require an ademption by extinction.

 ## EXAMPLES AND ANALYSIS

To illustrate, if a bequest was of "$50,000, to be satisfied first from my bank account at ABC Bank," and a lifetime gift of $50,000 was made, the general bequest might be said to be adeemed by satisfaction regardless of whether there was $50,000 or more in the account at T's death. But if the bequest was of "1,000 shares of *my* IBM stock, to be satisfied first from shares acquired in 2001 from X," the argument might be made that an inter vivos gift of *any* shares of IBM stock do not adeem by satisfaction or extinction the specific gift of those shares the testator acquired in 2001. Fortunately, demonstratives are not common and probably amount to a legal fiction in terms of what the testator intended: it would be very hard to argue that ademption was not intended in either circumstance. Our study of abatement will show why demonstrative is regarded as a useful theory notwithstanding its fictional nature.

4.   Satisfaction of Residuary Gifts

Satisfaction will not apply if there is a single residuary beneficiary, because the residuary devisee presumably was intended to receive the residue of the estate, without regard to amounts of lifetime gifts; a finding that a lifetime gift satisfied the residuary gift to the sole residuary devisee would result in partial or complete intestacy and there is a relatively strong presumption against intestacy. But there could be a satisfaction of part or all of some of the residuary devises if the residue was left to two or more devisees and lifetime gifts were made to some but not all of them, or were made to all of them in different proportions than the gift of the residue.

5.   Generally Inapplicable to Gifts of Land

Satisfaction is not customarily applicable to gifts of land because they usually are specific and because satisfaction is a form of partial revocation as to which the Statute of Frauds would apply, requiring a writing.

6.   Partial Satisfaction

Satisfaction may be pro tanto (with a presumption against total satisfaction by receipt of a lesser amount unless the beneficiary consents to a total satisfaction). Modest gifts, however, usually are not regarded as a satisfaction, even if they are great in the aggregate or over a long period of time.

7.   Proving Satisfaction

Satisfaction usually applies only if a gift made by the testator was intended to be in partial or complete satisfaction of a devise under the will. In most cases the biggest stumbling block is proving intent to satisfy. At common law, no proof was required because intent to satisfy was presumed. UPC §2-609 reverses this and, similarly to the treatment of the advancement issue by UPC §2-109 (see page 47), requires a statement in the will or a contemporaneous written declaration by the testator or acknowledgment by the devisee when the satisfaction gift occurs.

a.   **Gifts to children.** The presumption of intent to satisfy in non-UPC cases most frequently applies if the testator and beneficiary are parent and child (in loco parentis), because the law presumes that a parent wants to treat all children equally. If a gift inter vivos disrupts that presumed testamentary equality, in some non-UPC jurisdictions the intent required for ademption by satisfaction likely would be presumed.

b.   **Parol evidence.** In other non-UPC cases, parol evidence—including the testator's own declarations—may be admitted to prove the intent to adeem by satisfaction.

D. ABATEMENT

arises if there are more obligations of an estate (including "obligations" to devisees, creditors, and the government) than assets available to satisfy them.

1. Why Assets May Be Insufficient

An estate may not have enough assets to satisfy all (or any) devises under the will for such reasons as: (i) depletion (either before death or after death and before final distribution of the estate to its beneficiaries), (ii) debts, expenses, or taxes (especially when the probate estate is exhausted to pay those that relate to nonprobate assets), (iii) a forced heir or spousal share entitlement (see Chapter 10), or (iv) generosity, meaning that the testator has provided testamentary gifts with a higher priority that simply exhaust the testator's wealth.

2. An Issue of Priority

The abatement issue is which dispositions are preferred and which abate (i.e., are reduced or eliminated) if necessary to satisfy true obligations (e.g., debts of the decedent, administration and funeral expenses, and taxes), forced heir claims, and dispositions that are preferred.

    a. Order of abatement. The standard abatement priority, often statutory, is: (i) intestate assets abate first, (ii) then any fund specified for payment, (iii) then the residue (in some cases debts, expenses, taxes, and prior testamentary gifts would exhaust the estate and there would *be* no residue), (iv) then generals, (v) next, demonstratives, and (vi) finally, specifics.

    b. Abatement of demonstratives. Remember in considering the abatement of demonstratives that this category is a fiction that straddles the fence between generals and specifics. To illustrate the significance of this, consider this hypothetical: T's will leaves "$50,000 to A, to be satisfied first from my account at ABC Bank." If this was a general bequest it would *abate* with all the other general bequests, meaning that A might receive less than the amount T had in mind; as a specific bequest it might *adeem* by extinction if the ABC Bank no longer exists or if T's account in that bank was insufficient. As a demonstrative, the gift would abate with the specifics and adeem as a general, meaning that it is favored under both concepts.

    c. Abatement within a class. Within each class, abatement usually is pro rata and no longer gives any preference to devises (i.e., in the olden days, a general devise of land [e.g., an undivided ¼ of all the testator's farmland] would abate only after all generals of personalty [e.g., cash of $25,000]).

Examples and Analysis

T's will gave Blackacre to A, a painting to B, $20,000 of XYZ stock (a publicly held company in which T did not own stock when the will was executed or at T's death) to C, $50,000 to D, and the residue of her estate to E. It provides for T's debts, funeral, and administration expenses to be paid from the residue of her estate. At T's death, her estate included Blackacre (with a value of $60,000), the painting (with a value of $10,000), and other assets (with a value of $50,000). T had debts of $60,000, her funeral expenses were $5,000, and her estate incurred administration expenses of $15,000. How is T's estate distributed?

The total value of T's estate is $120,000 and the total of the debts, funeral, and administration expenses is $80,000, leaving net distributable assets of $40,000. T's will purported to make gifts of assets with aggregate date of death values of $140,000 to A, B, C, and D (with any residue going to E). Accordingly, a total of $100,000 of gifts will abate. There is no intestate property from which debts, funeral, and administration expenses can be paid and the fund designated for their payment—the residue—is nonexistent because the value of the general and specific devises under the will ($140,000) exceeds the value of the assets in the estate ($120,000). The next gifts to abate are general devises; here, there are two: the $20,000 gift of XYZ stock to C and the $50,000 gift to D. The $100,000 of gifts that must abate, however, exceeds the $70,000 of general devises. As a result, $30,000 of the specific gifts (Blackacre, with a value of $60,000, to A and the painting, with a value of $10,000, to B) also will abate. The abatement will be pro rata between them, meaning that $6/7$ of the $30,000 shortfall (approximately $25,700) will be charged against the gift of Blackacre to A and the other $1/7$ (approximately $4,300) against the gift of the painting to B.

One method of paying the debts, funeral, and administration expenses and distributing assets to A and B would be for the personal representative of the estate to borrow $25,700, secured by a mortgage on Blackacre, and $4,300 secured by the painting, and then to distribute Blackacre and the painting, so encumbered, to A and B. Another would be for A and B to use their own assets to pay their shares of the shortfall. A third would be for the personal representative of T's estate to sell Blackacre and the painting to raise the remaining funds necessary to pay the debts, funeral, and administration expenses and to distribute the remainder of the sales proceeds to A and B in the appropriate ratio.

    d. Modifications to abatement. The standard order of abatement is subject to modification by statute (such as for estate taxes, as discussed below) or by a specific direction in the will—usually in the form of a provision directing the payment of taxes and expenses from a specified source—or by an overall intent as shown by the scheme of distribution or circumstances at execution that illustrate a desire to protect certain beneficiaries.

3. Tax Payment

The way federal and state estate and inheritance taxes are borne by the beneficiaries of a decedent's probate and nonprobate assets has a significant effect on the distribution of the decedent's wealth. The apportionment of these taxes (particularly the federal estate tax, which can be as high as 60% of the decedent's taxable estate) among beneficiaries may be governed by special rules.

a. **State inheritance taxes.** State "inheritance" taxes (as opposed to state "estate" taxes) often are an obligation of the recipient of property from the estate, although it is customary for a tax clause in a will to shift this obligation to the probate estate.

b. **Federal estate taxes.** Under federal law, estate taxes on nonprobate and probate assets alike befall the residue of the probate estate and the personal representative potentially is personally liable to the extent these taxes are not paid. This burden on the residue rule may be altered by the terms of the decedent's will and several notable exceptions exist.

i. **Six Internal Revenue Code apportionment provisions** impose the tax attributable to certain nonprobate assets on the recipients of those assets (e.g., life insurance proceeds). Couched in terms of "discretion" to seek reimbursement of estate taxes paid on such assets from those nonprobate takers, the fiduciary obligation imposed on the personal representative effectively is a mandate to the extent ultimate distributions to probate estate beneficiaries will be affected. A testator may waive these rights of reimbursement, meaning the taker of the nonprobate assets receives them unburdened by federal estate taxes.

ii. **Uniform Estate Tax Apportionment Act.** Most states have adopted the Uniform Estate Tax Apportionment Act, or something similar, which governs estate taxes apportionment unless the will provides otherwise. This legislation requires that each taker of property included in the decedent's taxable estate— whether probate or nonprobate—pay a pro rata share of the estate taxes based on the value of property received by the taker relative to the value of property received by all takers. In making this calculation, property passing tax-free (such as to a spouse or charity) generally is excluded. This exclusion is referred to as "equitable apportionment."

EXAMPLES AND ANALYSIS

T's will gave $300,000 to C, her child from her first marriage, $200,000 to her brother, B, $100,000 to charity, and the residue to her husband, H. In addition, C was the beneficiary of a $500,000 insurance policy T owned on T's life. T's will did not provide for the apportionment of estate taxes. Under federal law, the devises to charity and to H are not subject to federal estate tax because of the unlimited charitable and marital deductions. Accordingly, T's taxable estate will consist of the $1,000,000 of probate and nonprobate assets passing to C and B. Because C will receive 80% of the $1,000,000 and B 20%, under an equitable apportionment approach the estate tax liability will be borne by them in that ratio.

---

    iii.   **Burden on the residue.** The common law burden on the residue rule imposes inequitable and unintended results. For instance, in the example the residue passing to H would bear the estate taxes for the property passing to C and B even though the devise to H generated no tax itself (because of the marital deduction). The taxes owed on the property passing to C and B might exhaust the residue so that H receives nothing. A tax clause in the will or trust may change the applicable rules and may be essential to effect the decedent's intent.

   4. **Spousal Elective and Pretermitted Heir Shares**

      A surviving spouse may have a right to elect against the will of the decedent to take a statutorily forced share of the estate, and certain heirs of a decedent who were omitted from the decedent's will also may have rights to take shares of the estate as defined by statute. See Chapter 10. In these cases the claims of the surviving spouse or pretermitted heirs may be so large that they disrupt the estate plan and require abatement of other gifts to fund them.

     a. **Abatement to satisfy elective share.** Most elective share statutes force a surviving spouse who elects a forced share to forgo other rights under the will. In other states the first property used to satisfy the elective share is property devised to the spouse under the will. Usually that property will not be enough to satisfy the full elective share, and the normal abatement rules (first intestate assets, then the residue, next generals, finally specifics) typically apply in satisfaction of the shortfall. As with other abatement issues, however, the instrument will override these rules and control to the extent it addresses the possibility of a spouse's election against the will and the resulting abatement issue.

b. **UPC pro rata approach.** UPC §§2-209(b) and (c) alter the traditional rules for abating devises to satisfy an elective share: abatement is pro rata among all probate and nonprobate beneficiaries alike.

 # EXAMPLES AND ANALYSIS

T's will, which is silent regarding priority and abatement, directs the following dispositions: (i) summer home to brother, (ii) specific bequests and legacies that total $100,000 to persons other than the surviving spouse, (iii) a formula bequest to the surviving spouse (designed to accomplish estate tax minimization) of "the smallest amount needed to reduce my estate taxes to the lowest possible amount," (iv) $200,000 to charity, and (v) "$200,000 plus the residue" to a trust for children.

- For federal estate tax purposes, the estate consists of $800,000: (i) the summer home, worth $50,000, (ii) a residence (in joint tenancy with the surviving spouse), worth $150,000,[1] (iii) life insurance (payable to the spouse) of $200,000, and (iv) liquid probate assets of $400,000.

- The only probate assets are the summer home and the $400,000 of liquid probate assets.

- The amount of property passing to the spouse under the formula marital bequest is zero due to the tax situation here—the charitable bequest and the nonprobate property passing to the surviving spouse are fully deductible and will reduce the taxable estate to below the amount at which no federal estate taxes need be paid. So there is no need for an additional marital bequest to zero out the taxes, and the formula bequest will therefore give the spouse nothing.

- Nothing can be done about the nonprobate property that passes automatically to the spouse, so the only issue is who will take which dispositions from the probate estate, who will pay taxes (if any), and who will suffer abatement if available assets are insufficient.

- In this case the brother will receive the specific devise of the summer home and the other specifics of $100,000 have the same first priority. After

---

[1]Notice that, under IRC §2040(b), only half of the value of the joint tenancy with the surviving spouse would be includible in the decedent's gross estate for federal estate tax purposes. Nevertheless, we are reporting it here at its full value for two reasons. One is that, whatever the value, it all qualifies automatically for the marital deduction so the amount includible also is deductible, making the valuation irrelevant for federal estate tax purposes. Second, for those of you who have not studied tax and do not care to, it simply is easier to understand what is going on by looking at the real value of the property and not the limited amount that the tax law considers.

taking them out of the estate, only $300,000 remains in the probate estate, and there are two general claims against that amount—the $200,000 to charity and the $200,000 to the children's trust—totaling $400,000. This means that there will be no residue and the children's trust and the charity both will abate pro rata, each receiving only $150,000 instead of the $200,000 specified in the will.

E. ACCESSIONS

The issue with respect to accessions is whether a gift under a will or trust instrument bears interest or receives accessions (such as dividends, interest, or rent) that accrue or are paid either before death or after death but before final distribution. For example, if T's will gave Blackacre to A and it is leased during estate administration for $10,000, with rental expenses of $2,000, does A receive the $8,000 of net rental income in addition to Blackacre?

1. Address in the Instrument

Careful drafters address such questions in the instrument because the state law rules that otherwise govern may be inadequate or unclear.

2. Before Death

If the accession occurs before death, the issue applies only to specifics: interest, dividends, rent, and other accessions received before death on assets not specifically devised become a part of the general estate available to satisfy obligations and general, demonstrative, and residuary devises. As to premortem accessions attributable to assets specifically devised: by the general rules, if an accession (i) is paid before death and (ii) is separated from the underlying asset, the accession does *not* pass to the recipient of the underlying asset. Otherwise, it does.

a. **Interest, rent, and cash dividends.** Interest, rent, or cash dividends received before death are separated from the underlying asset (i.e., the specifically devised interest bearing asset, cash dividend paying stock, or rent generating asset) and thus do not pass with the property that produced these accessions.

b. **Stock dividends.** A stock-on-stock dividend, declared in the payor's own stock, does not alter the percentage ownership of the corporation held by the estate (there are just more pieces of paper representing the same investment), so the percentage ownership of the company will be reduced (and control may be lost) if the dividend shares do not pass with the investment. Nevertheless, the majority rule is that the dividend shares do not pass with the underlying bequest, although there are courts that are changing this rule, as does UPC §2-605.

EXAMPLES AND ANALYSIS

There are 1,000 shares of stock of XYZ Corp. outstanding. T owns 10% of them—100 shares—and T's will gives "*my* 100 shares of XYZ Corp. stock" to A. After execution of T's will but before T's death, XYZ Corp. pays a 10% dividend in its own stock, which means that T receives an additional 10 shares. At T's death, she owns 110 shares (still 10% of XYZ's outstanding stock, which now consists of 1,100 shares). Under the majority rule, A receives only 100 shares and not also the dividend shares. Under the UPC/minority rule A receives 110 shares. A different result would obtain if the bequest were something like "All my shares of" XYZ Corp. stock, instead of something specific like "My 100 shares"; in such a case, A would receive the 110 shares even in a majority rule jurisdiction.

c. *In re Tase,* NYLJ, May 31, 1990, at 31, involved a decedent who, by paragraph Second of a will, made a specific bequest of "all my American Telephone and Telegraph stock" and then provided for each of six named legatees to receive 30 shares. When the will was executed the decedent owned 180 shares of AT&T stock. At death the decedent owned 621 shares of AT&T and 1,178 shares of the seven regional holding companies (the "Baby Bells") that were spun-off by AT&T for antitrust purposes. The questions presented were whether paragraph Second disposed of all of the decedent's AT&T shares or only 180 of them and whether the will carried out any shares of the regional holding companies. The court held that the reference to "all my" stock meant the entire holding at death should pass under paragraph Second. Also, the court held that all of the regional holding company shares were bequeathed under paragraph Second. We think these are proper results, but they are not predictable from the common law rule.

d. **Stock splits.** A stock split is very similar to a large stock dividend and occurs when a company issues, say, one or two new shares of stock for each outstanding share (if one new share is issued, the split is referred to as a 2-for-1 split, because the shareholder now has two shares for every share she had before the split). Unlike stock dividends, stock split shares usually *do* pass to the named taker, which is inconsistent with the stock-on-stock dividend rule.

This also is the right result, and the stock-on-stock dividend rule is changing to match it.

3. After Death

All beneficiaries of specific devises are entitled to accessions paid after they become entitled to the gifted property. With a specific devise, the beneficiary is entitled to the property as of the moment of death (subject to abatement), meaning that all receipts from the property after death pass with the property, even if the accession was earned (but not paid) before death. This rule is consistent with the premortem rules noted above: if the accession is still attached to the property, it passes with the property and not to the estate.

 ## EXAMPLES AND ANALYSIS

T's will gave Blackacre to A. As of death there are rents that accrued before death that had not yet been paid. In most states A gets these rent payments in addition to Blackacre itself. Although the rent accrued before T's death, it was not paid. Notice that, in many commercial rental situations the rent is prepaid (think about the typical apartment or house lease) so this problem would not be common. In agricultural rentals the rent often is payable after the harvest, so this example could be very common. And some commercial rents are based on sales or profits and may be payable after the term rather than before, also making the example relevant. If the rent is paid annually in advance (e.g., on December 31 for the next year) and the testator dies after the rent is paid (e.g., on January 1), the prepaid rent belongs to the estate, not to the specific devisee, even though it is rent for a postmortem period. And even if the new owner needs the rent to service a debt that encumbers the property. See Exoneration, discussed below.

a. **If no accession on a specific devise.** If no income or other accession is paid after the testator's death, but before distribution, on the subject of a *specific* devise, the taker receives nothing (other than the specifically devised property itself), even if distribution is delayed during administration.

b. **General and demonstrative devises** differ: because the taker is not entitled to specific assets, the taker is not entitled to actual accessions on the property actually distributed. Instead, interest usually is payable at a statutory rate from a statutory date of entitlement, which usually is one year after death.

EXAMPLES AND ANALYSIS

T's will gave Investmentacre to A and $100,000 to B. There are no receipts attributable to Investmentacre between T's death and the date it is distributed to A. Thus, because this is a specific devise, A receives Investmentacre, but is not entitled to interest on its value regardless of the length of time between T's death and the date Investmentacre is distributed. Assume that under the will or applicable state law, the personal representative has authority to satisfy B's $100,000 entitlement in kind (rather than in cash) and selects for distribution Farmacre, which has a fair market value of $1 million but is subject to mortgage indebtedness of $900,000. The crop grown on Farmacre was harvested just before T's death, but the debt service is at year end, just around the corner. Assume the decedent died on January 1 and that the personal representative distributes Farmacre before the following December 31—to avoid paying the debt service. B would receive no interest (because in most states a beneficiary of a general devise is not entitled to interest on it unless distribution is delayed more than one year after death) or other income but would incur the debt service. Quaere whether the impending debt service obligation would alter the fair market value of the property for purposes of determining whether B receives the full bequest to which B is entitled.

    c. Residue. By definition, the residuary takers receive whatever is left in the estate after the payment of all specifics, generals, and demonstratives, and after the payment of accessions on the specifics and interest on the generals and demonstratives. Although residuary takers are not entitled to interest, any income earned by the estate and not paid to the takers of specifics (if, for example, an interest bearing investment was specifically devised), generals, or demonstratives remains a part of the residue. Thus the residue bears the risk that interest on general and demonstrative dispositions will exceed actual earnings on estate assets not specifically devised, but the residue also benefits from investment performance in excess of statutory interest requirements on generals and demonstratives.

4. A Note About Demonstratives

In all these rules on accessions, demonstratives are governed by the rules applicable to specifics to the extent of the specified fund or asset, and by the rules applicable to generals to the extent the entitlement is satisfied from general funds because the specific is inadequate. Thus, no special rules are needed for demonstratives.

F. EXONERATION

addressed whether a devise of property that secures a debt of the decedent takes the property subject to the debt or whether the estate must repay the debt so that the devisee takes the property free of encumbrances. Unless changed by statute (as has been done in many jurisdictions), the common law requires that debts, even though not yet due, be paid out of the estate as a whole if three requirements are met.

1. Decedent Was Personally Liable

First, the debt was a personal obligation of the decedent (i.e., not just nonrecourse purchase money debt, meaning that in the event of a default the lender could have sued the testator and collected from her personally, rather than being limited to foreclosing on the property).

2. Realty or Specific Devise

Second, the debt must encumber realty or specifically devised personal property. (Notice that this is the converse of satisfaction—which typically does not apply to any gift of realty or specifics of personalty.)

3. Intent of the Testator

Third, the will must not have expressed a contrary intent. In some jurisdictions, an implied intent not to exonerate can be shown by surrounding circumstances.

 ## EXAMPLES AND ANALYSIS

T's will gave Blackacre to A. At T's death Blackacre was burdened by mortgage indebtedness of $50,000. If T was personally liable on the debt secured by the mortgage, the will does not provide otherwise, and T's intent for the debt not to be exonerated cannot be established, the common law rule results in the $50,000 indebtedness being paid from other estate assets, and A thus receives Blackacre unencumbered.

4. Source of Funds to Pay Exonerated Debts

If exoneration is required, payment comes from the residue or from intestate personalty, if there is any (perhaps also from personalty that otherwise would be used to satisfy general bequests). Because exoneration applies to realty and specifics, these classes of gifts are not used to finance exoneration. The theory is that one set of specific beneficiaries or takers of realty should not be burdened to benefit another set.

 ## EXAMPLES AND ANALYSIS

T's will gave Blackacre to A, Whiteacre to B, a valuable painting to C, and the residue to D. At T's death Blackacre was worth $60,000, but it was encumbered by $50,000

of mortgage indebtedness on which T was personally liable. Whiteacre was worth $100,000; the painting was worth $10,000; and the residue, which consisted of cash, was worth $20,000, net of administration and funeral expenses and other debts of T. At common law, the indebtedness on Blackacre is to be exonerated, but the only asset available to do the job is the $20,000 of cash. Thus, A receives Blackacre burdened by $30,000 of the mortgage debt; B and C receive Whiteacre and the painting, respectively, unencumbered; and D receives nothing.

5.   Theory of the Doctrine

The common law exoneration rule assumes that the loan creating the debt somehow benefited the personal estate (e.g., T borrowed $50,000 against Blackacre and put the funds in the bank). That rationale is nonsense today, and UPC §2-607 properly reverses the common law rule (even if the will includes a general boilerplate provision that the personal representative is to pay all of the decedent's debts; for exoneration to apply, the will must specifically so specify).

a.   Rationale of modern rule. Reversing the common law exoneration rule is appropriate because most testators don't distinguish their personalty from their realty in terms of benefits or burdens, and because most secured debt is purchase money debt anyway, meaning that the debt benefited the taker of the encumbered asset, not other property of the estate.

6.   Intent; Planning

The common law rule to exonerate and the UPC rule not to exonerate may be overcome by proof of a contrary intent. A standard debt payment clause (e.g., "I direct my Personal Representative to pay all of my just debts") typically won't prove intent because it usually applies only to debts that are currently due. To overcome the common law rule, language should specify that property passes "subject to outstanding debts." Conversely, it would be wise to specify that exoneration is intended, if that is the case, by stating that a gift of property is "free from all outstanding debts."

EXAM TIP

Keep the doctrines we've studied in this chapter straight and consider their applicability to the various kinds of gifts under a will. Ademption addresses the question of what to do if specifically devised property is not in the estate at the testator's death. It applies to specific, but not to general, demonstrative, or residuary gifts. The doctrine of satisfaction should be considered if the testator made a lifetime gift to a devisee after executing the will; it typically applies only to general gifts of personality, although in limited circumstances it can apply to specific, demonstrative, and residuary gifts of personality. Abatement answers the questions of (i) which beneficiaries' gifts bear the burden of paying the testator's debts and funeral expenses, and the taxes and administration expenses owed by the testator's estate, and (ii) what to do if the testator purports to devise more property than is in her estate at her death. All kinds of gifts can abate; the order of abatement is intestate property, the residue, general devises, and then specific devises. Exoneration of liens should be considered if the testator was personally liable on debt that is secured by realty or specifically devised personality; if it applies, the debt is paid by other assets of the estate and the takers of the realty and specifically devised personality receive their gifts unencumbered. The accessions rules establish whether beneficiaries of an estate receive interest, income, or other accessions in addition to the property devised to them. Generally, takers of specific devises can receive income earned by property devised to them; devisees of general devises can receive postmortem interest on the value of their devise; and the residuary beneficiaries take what is left.

REVIEW QUESTIONS AND ANSWERS

Question: T's will devised "my home to A, 100 shares of General Motors stock to B, and my diamond ring to C." T died in a fire that destroyed her home. Prior to her death, she had the diamond removed from her ring and placed in a necklace with other jewels. Although T had owned 100 shares of General Motors stock when her will was executed, she owned none at her death. What, if anything, will A, B, and C receive? Why?

Answer: The traditional doctrine of ademption by extinction follows the "identity theory": the devisee receives nothing if specifically devised property is not owned by the testator at death. The identity theory is based on a conclusive presumption that the testator did not intend the devisee of specifically devised but extinguished property to receive other property because, if she had, the testator would have changed her will after the extinguishment.

Because T died in a fire that destroyed her home, however, it was not possible for her to alter her will to provide an alternative devise to A. Accordingly, ademption by extinction should not apply to the devise of the home; A should receive the lot, what remains of the home, and the insurance proceeds from the fire. With respect to the bequest of the diamond ring, it will adeem unless the necklace can be viewed as a mere change in form of the ring. If so, many jurisdictions would allow C to take the necklace. The greater the value of the diamond from the ring relative to the value of the necklace, the greater that possibility. The gift of the General Motors stock will be adeemed unless it can be characterized as a general bequest rather than a specific; if so, the personal representative of T's estate will be required to acquire 100 shares of General Motors stock on the open market to distribute to B, or perhaps to pay B its fair market value. Because the gift to B was of "100 shares of General Motors stock" rather than "*my* 100 shares of General Motors stock, and because the gift to B will fail if the bequest is classified as specific, it is likely that it would be classified as general.

Question: T's will devised Blackacre to X. Prior to becoming incapacitated, T executed a durable power of attorney appointing PA her attorney-in-fact. Acting properly under the durable power of attorney, PA sold Blackacre to a third party prior to T's death. What, if anything, does X receive?

Answer: X will receive nothing at common law and in states that follow the identity theory of ademption. The disposition of Blackacre during T's life and the failure of T to revise her will to make an alternative gift to X are conclusively treated as indicating T's intention that X not receive anything. Because that result is so clearly wrong in a case like this one—in which, due to T's incapacity, it was not possible for T to provide for X to receive an alternative gift—the UPC and the law of many other states would provide X with the value of Blackacre.

Question: T's will devised Blackacre to A, all of T's stocks and bonds to B, $100,000 to C, and the residue to D. T died survived by A, B, C, and D. T's estate consists of Blackacre (fair market value of $80,000), stocks and bonds (fair market value of $120,000), and cash of $120,000. At T's death, her debts totalled $100,000, funeral and administration expenses were $30,000, and state estate taxes were $10,000. How is T's estate distributed?

Answer: The total of debts, funeral and administration expenses, and taxes is $140,000; their payment has priority over T's beneficiaries. T's will includes specific, general, and residuary devises. Residuary gifts abate first, followed by generals, and then specifics. Here, the residue consisted only of the $20,000 of cash (the total cash of $120,000 less the general legacy of $100,000 to C), as the other assets in the estate (Blackacre and the stocks and bonds) were specifically devised. The $20,000 will be used first to pay debts, expenses, and taxes, leaving a shortfall of $120,000. The general legacy of $100,000 to C will abate next, still leaving unpaid estate creditors with $20,000 of claims. The specific devise of Blackacre ($80,000 value) to A and the specific bequest of the stocks and bonds ($120,000) to B will abate pro rata: 40% of the $20,000 will be charged against Blackacre, and the other 60% against the stocks and bonds. Sales of these assets will be necessary to raise the funds necessary to pay the remaining creditors' claims, unless A and B pay the $20,000 from their own funds or otherwise make satisfactory arrangements with the estate's creditors.

Question: T's 1997 will devised a specifically described painting (with a value of $5,000) to her cousin, C; $10,000 to her nephew, N; and the residue of her estate in equal shares to her children, S and D. In 1998, T gave antiques with a value of approximately $5,000 to C; cash of $6,000 to N; and stock with a value of $25,000 to S. In 1999, T died owning the painting and other net distributable assets of $300,000. How are they distributed?

Answer: The question is whether the lifetime gifts to C, N, and S were in satisfaction of the devises to them under T's will. None of the lifetime gifts would satisfy the testamentary gifts under the UPC unless the will provides for reduction for the gifts, or there is a contemporaneous writing by T or a written acknowledgement by the donees of the lifetime gifts that they were made in satisfaction of the devises under the will. The common law presumed that lifetime gifts to persons named in the will to receive general devises were in partial or full satisfaction of their devises, particularly if the donee of a lifetime gift was a child. In a common law jurisdiction, therefore, the $6,000 gift to N likely would be treated as a partial satisfaction of the $10,000 devise to him under the will, in which case he would receive $5,000 from the estate. Although satisfaction usually does not apply to residuary gifts, in a case like this—in which there are multiple residuary beneficiaries and significant lifetime gifts are made to one of them—satisfaction likely would be applicable. If so, S would receive $25,000 less than would D. Generally, ademption by satisfaction does not apply to specific devises, and it is unlikely that the gift of antiques to C would be treated as in satisfaction of part or all of the devise of the painting to C.

10

RESTRICTIONS ON THE POWER OF DISPOSITION: STATUTORY FORCED HEIR SHARES AND COMMUNITY PROPERTY

CHAPTER OVERVIEW

- Marital property rights at the death of the first spouse to die come in two forms. In a community property jurisdiction the surviving spouse owns ½ of the couple's community property, even if title is in the deceased spouse's name. In all noncommunity property jurisdictions except Georgia the surviving spouse is entitled to receive a statutory share of the deceased spouse's probate estate (and, in many cases, nonprobate assets as well).

- Protection is afforded to certain pretermitted heirs who are omitted from a testator's will, including a surviving spouse (if the testator's will was executed before the marriage), children, and sometimes more remote descendants. Each entitlement assumes that the testator "forgot" to include the heir in the will and evidence that the omission was intentional will preclude a successful claim.

A. STATUS AS SPOUSE

Spousal rights are available only to a survivor who was a spouse at the decedent's death.

1. Common Law Marriages

Nearly ⅓ of the states recognize non-ceremonial, common law marriages in which a couple lives together and hold. . . . themselves out as spouses.

2. Same Sex Marriages are not yet recognized. See, e.g., *Baehr v. Lewin*, 852 P.2d 44 (Haw. 1993) and *Baehr v. Miike*, 1996 WL 694235 (Haw. Cir. Ct. 1996) (Hawaii had no compelling interest in forbidding same sex mar-

riages), after which Hawaii voters amended their constitution to ban same sex marriages. See also *In re Estate of Cooper*, 592 N.Y.S.2d 797 (1993) (New York refusal to allow same sex marriages does not violate the equal protection clause of the Fourteenth Amendment).

B. ADDITIONAL MARITAL RIGHTS

A surviving spouse typically has a variety of other rights in addition to elective share or community property.

1. **Homestead** is an entitlement that is free from creditor claims and cannot be defeated by the decedent's will. In some states it is a dollar amount (e.g., $15,000 under UPC §2-402); in others it is a right to occupy the family home for life without regard to its value.

2. **Exempt Tangible Personal Property** (e.g., automobiles, household furniture, appliances, and personal effects) of the decedent may be exempt from creditors' claims and cannot be defeated by the decedent's will. Most states limit exempt personal property in value (e.g., the UPC §2-403 limit is $10,000).

3. **Family Allowances** provide support during administration. In some states it is fixed (e.g., $25,000 in Ohio); in others it is set by the probate court in an amount that is "appropriate" (e.g., known as "year's support" in Georgia, the amount needed for one year). Again, this protection generally is exempt from creditors' claims and may not be defeated by the decedent's will.

4. **ERISA Rights**

    A federal form of protection of the surviving spouse is the spousal annuity requirements under the Employee Retirement Income Security Act (ERISA)—which involves retirement benefits. See Internal Revenue Code §401(a)(11). For plans subject to these rules, a surviving spouse is entitled to an annuity following the death of the plan participant. A spouse (but not a fiancee) can waive the entitlement and must do so if the participant wants to make any beneficiary designation other than the spousal annuity— even to provide a more favorable disposition to the spouse (such as a lump sum distribution at the participant's death).

5. **Social Security** also provides survivor's benefits that belong to the spouse and, therefore, are not subject to claims of the decedent's creditors, may not be defeated by the decedent's will, and may not be waived.

6. **Dower and Curtesy**

    The common law dower generally provided a widow a life estate in ⅓ of her deceased husband's real estate; curtesy provided a widower a life estate in all of his wife's real estate, but only if there were children of the marriage. Dower and curtesy have been abolished in virtually all states.

7. Protecting the Spouse

Community property protects spouses in Louisiana, Texas, New Mexico, Arizona, California, Washington, Idaho, and Nevada—and the very similar statutory community property under the Uniform Marital Property Act (UMPA) in Wisconsin. The right of a surviving spouse in a noncommunity property jurisdiction to elect a statutory share of the decedent's probate estate (and in some jurisdictions nonprobate assets as well) regardless of the terms of the decedent's will (and, in some states, notwithstanding the terms of instruments governing nonprobate property) applies in every jurisdiction except Georgia.

C. COMMUNITY PROPERTY

Each spouse in a community property jurisdiction owns ½ of the couple's community property from the time it is acquired, regardless of how title to the property is held. Generally, community property consists of all property acquired by either spouse during the marriage other than by gift, devise, bequest, or inheritance; in addition, in some states (e.g., Texas and under UMPA) the income from separate property (other than mineral interests in Texas) also is community property.

EXAMPLES AND ANALYSIS

Young Lawyer is single, successful, and engaged. When Young Lawyer and Spouse marry, Young Lawyer has assets, net of debts, of $100,000; Spouse has $50,000 of net assets. During the marriage, Young Lawyer accumulates an additional $300,000 from earned income from practicing law; Spouse accumulates $150,000 from earnings during the marriage. Also during the marriage Young Lawyer receives a gift of $75,000 and Spouse receives a $200,000 inheritance. The $100,000 of assets Young Lawyer brought to the marriage and the $75,000 gift are separate property, as are the $50,000 of assets Spouse owned when they married and the $200,000 inheritance received during the marriage. The $450,000 they accumulated from their earnings during the marriage is community property—each is treated as the owner of ½ of it regardless of the fact that Young Lawyer earned and accumulated twice as much as Spouse, and regardless of how they hold title to the $450,000. This is the economic partnership of marriage.

1. Community Property for Noncommunity Property Lawyers

Noncommunity property lawyers need to know about community property for several reasons. First, for conflict of law purposes, real estate located in a community property state may be governed by the community property laws. Second, with the migratory nature of clients, many will possess some community property because the client lived and earned property in a community property state at some time during the marriage and, generally, "once property is community property, it always is community property," unless they "partition" the property to destroy its community nature. Plus, UMPA may be the wave of the future, although there has been little interest in it for quite some time.

   a.   Separate property of deceased spouse. Typically, a community property surviving spouse has no statutory forced heir rights in the decedent's separate property (or in the decedent's share of the community property). Thus, if there is little or no community property when a spouse dies, a survivor who owns little or no separate property may be left with little or nothing—if the decedent does not provide for the survivor—regardless of the amount of separate property the decedent owned.

 # EXAMPLES AND ANALYSIS

D and S lived their entire married life in a community property jurisdiction. They owned little property when they married. During the first part of their marriage they each worked, but they accumulated little in the way of assets—they spent what they earned and assets they acquired were bought with borrowed funds and little equity. D then received a substantial inheritance, after which D and S "retired" and began enjoying the good life. When D died, the inheritance was intact (they had managed to live off its income) but they had little or no community property. Regardless of the length of their marriage and the value of D's inherited separate property, S will have no claim to any of D's separate property and will be left with only ½ of their community property, if any (and any homestead, exempt personal property, and family allowance provided by law).

   b.   Quasi-community property. Some states (California, Idaho, Louisiana, and Washington) have a "quasi" community property system that may treat some of a deceased spouse's separate property as if it was community property.

 # EXAMPLES AND ANALYSIS

Spouses D and S lived their entire working lives in Illinois, a noncommunity property state, and then retired to Arizona, a community property state that does not embrace quasi-community property. All their wealth was acquired during their marriage from their earnings, and all their wealth is titled in the name of D, who dies first. S will receive nothing from D's separate property under Arizona law, meaning that S will receive only whatever meager amount constitutes S's share of their community property from earnings received while they lived in Arizona prior to D's death. If, however, they had moved to California, which recognizes quasi-community property, D's separate property would be deemed ½ owned by S to the extent it represented earnings received while they were married.

---

      i. Death vs. divorce. Although the notion of quasi-community property generally is to treat separate property the same as if it was community property, some quasi-community property states (e.g., Arizona, New Mexico, and Texas) apply the concept for divorce only and not at death.

   c. No other entitlement. Excepting homestead, exempt personal property, and a family allowance, there is no other spousal entitlement guaranteed under state law in a community property state, and no election against the decedent's estate plan is provided if the decedent chooses to exclude the spouse.

2. Forced Election Plan

Sophisticated estate planning (even in noncommunity property states—sometimes less accurately referred to as the "common law" property states) may take advantage of a "forced election" plan that basically says to the surviving spouse: "If you agree to subject your separate and community property to the provisions of my trust, I will give you a life estate in my separate and community property and in your separate and community property, all held in the same trust." The object of the plan is for the decedent to control devolution of all the couple's property after the surviving spouse's death.

D. NONCOMMUNITY PROPERTY JURISDICTIONS: THE ELECTIVE SHARE

The other significant spousal entitlement is the statutory forced heir share (sometimes referred to as an "elective" share, because the spouse must elect to receive the forced share) found in all noncommunity property states except Georgia.

1. Size of Spouse's Forced Share varies considerably among the states. Frequently it is ⅓ of the decedent's probate estate (or of the decedent's "augmented" probate estate, which includes nonprobate property), sometimes increased to ½ if the decedent was not survived by any descendant. In some states the forced share is the same share the spouse would receive if the decedent died intestate and may be the entire estate. (See Chapter 2.)

   a. Comparison with intestate share. Generally, the surviving spouse's intestate share will be at least as large, and often larger, than the forced share. For example, under the UPC the intestate share never is less than the first $100,000 plus ½ the balance, but the forced share is ½ maximum—unless the supplemental elective share amount is larger, which would occur only in a smaller estate—and may be much less. The difference may be more subtle; for example, Illinois differs on equitable apportionment of estate taxes for intestate or forced shares, as discussed below.

i.   **Effect of nonprobate assets.** Note that the intestate share is limited to the decedent's probate estate; the UPC forced share applies to the augmented estate, which includes most nonprobate assets and may be significantly larger than the probate estate. Thus, for intestate decedents who own substantial amounts of nonprobate property and who die in a UPC augmented estate jurisdiction, the forced share may be greater than the intestate share.

 EXAMPLES AND ANALYSIS

D and S were married 20 years when D died intestate with a net probate estate of $100,000. D had a child, C, from a prior marriage; D and C owned property with an aggregate value at D's death of $400,000 as joint tenants with the right of survivorship (D provided all the consideration to acquire this property). The jurisdiction has adopted the UPC. Accordingly, S's intestate share of the probate estate is the entire $100,000 (see Chapter 2). S's elective share under the UPC, however—assuming S had no probate or nonprobate property—would be $250,000 (½ of D's augmented probate estate of $500,000; see the discussion below of a surviving spouse's elective share under the UPC).

EXAM TIP

The surviving spouse's elective share claim commonly is referred to as a right to elect against the decedent's will. Don't let that concept lull you into not considering an elective share claim in the case of an intestate decedent. As the example above illustrates, if the decedent has substantial nonprobate assets, the elective share may be greater than the intestate share. In the absence of nonprobate assets, the intestate share usually, if not always, will equal or exceed the elective share.

2.   **Effect of Election on Spouse's Rights to Other Property**

An electing spouse is allowed simply to reject the decedent's estate plan in favor of an affirmative election to take a statutorily defined share of the decedent's probate (or augmented) estate.

a. **Election precludes benefits under the will.** Typically, "equitable election" will apply when the forced share election is made, meaning that the spouse may take under the will of the decedent or may elect against the estate, but not both. (In some jurisdictions the same result is reached by statute: the spouse who elects a statutory share is treated as predeceased with respect to all provisions for the spouse under the will. Also, in some jurisdictions—e.g., UPC §2-209—the share of an electing spouse is satisfied first from property left to the spouse under the decedent's will or passing to the spouse by will substitute.)

b. **Intestate property also forgone.** Usually the spouse is entitled to share in the intestate property when a will gives away less than the decedent owned. A spouse who elects against the will, however, also elects against taking any share of intestate property, meaning that this really is an election against the estate, not just the will.

c. **Homestead, exempt personal property, and family allowance.** In many states (e.g., UPC §2-202(c)) the homestead allowance, exempt personal property, and family allowance are in addition to the statutory forced heir share, because these rights often are directed toward maintenance of the surviving spouse during administration of the estate and not to an equitable division of the marital wealth.

d. **Nonprobate property.** As we will discuss, the election does not normally disfranchise the spouse's interest in nonprobate property. The prime exception to this is under the UPC augmented probate estate concept.

3. Estate Taxes

Equitable apportionment (see Chapter 9) is a significant issue with respect to the elective share: does the spouse receive the statutory share before or after payment of estate taxes? Or, stated differently, does the spouse share in the gross estate (before tax) or the net estate (after tax)?

a. **Comparison with intestate share.** The same issue may come up under intestacy—and the answer may differ. For example, in Illinois the intestate share and the forced heir share are the same fraction but the intestate share is computed as a fraction of the gross estate and the forced heir share is a fraction of the net estate. In that state, if the estate is large enough to generate an estate tax liability, a spouse therefore would be better off challenging and defeating a will in a will contest action to cause intestacy than to just reject the will and take the elective share—all other factors being equal. Under the UPC, the elective share is calculated before estate taxes.

b. **Interrelated computation.** An interrelated computation is required if the forced share is calculated after tax—the tax cannot be calculated without knowing the spouse's share (because a marital deduction is allowed for it) and the spouse's share cannot be calculated without knowing the amount of tax (because it is a fraction of the after tax estate).

4. Incompetent or Deceased Surviving Spouse

A second question is whether a personal representative for an incompetent or later deceased surviving spouse may elect on behalf of the spouse. Not all states allow the personal representative of a subsequently deceased surviving spouse to elect (e.g., UPC §2-212(a)). Most allow the personal representative of an incapacitated spouse to make the election, but the conditions under which such an election can be made differ.

EXAM TIP

A spouse only will have a right to elect to take a statutory share of the decedent's estate if the spouse survives the decedent. As discussed in Chapter 2, the Uniform Simultaneous Death Act and the UPC require a person to survive by at least 120 hours to be treated as having survived. Consequently, if the USDA or the UPC is in effect, and if a person survives her spouse but dies within 120 hours of his death, she will not be treated as having survived him for elective share purposes and it will be irrelevant whether the jurisdiction otherwise allows the personal representative of a deceased surviving spouse to make the election.

---

a. **Need vs. best interests.** In some states the personal representative of an incapacitated surviving spouse may not make the election absent a showing of need. *In re Estate of Cross*, 664 N.E.2d 905 (Ohio 1996), involved such a statute and a disinherited surviving spouse who was living in a nursing home, the expenses of which were being paid by Medicaid. An election on her behalf was upheld because failure to make the election would have jeopardized the surviving spouse's continued qualification for Medicaid. In other states, the election can be made on behalf of an incapacitated surviving spouse if doing so would be in her best interests. *In re Estate of Clarkson*, 226 N.W.2d 334 (Neb. 1975) and *Spencer v. Williams*, 569 A.2d 1194, 1198 (D.C. Ct. App. 1990), held that "best interests" means simply that the election should be made if the monetary value of what the spouse receives is greater under the elective share than under the will.

b. **Fiduciary duty to elect?** Consistent with *Clarkson* and *Spencer*, some commentators feel the personal representative of an incapacitated or subsequently deceased surviving spouse has an overriding fiduciary obligation to elect against the will if doing so will maximize the spouse's estate, even if this is not what the spouse would have done and even though it may bastardize the decedent's estate plan.

5. Life Estate of Spouse Under the Will

Under the UPC, provisions made for a surviving spouse under the decedent's will count toward the elective share entitlement. Thus, if the will leaves the spouse $100,000 and the elective share amount is $250,000, the $100,000 bequest will be credited against the $250,000, leaving the spouse with a net elective share claim of $150,000. How to treat a surviving spouse's lifetime interest in a trust has been a controversial issue under the UPC.

 ## EXAMPLES AND ANALYSIS

Assume that the surviving spouse's elective share is $250,000, and that the decedent's will provides for $500,000 to be left in trust, with the surviving spouse entitled to all income from the trust for life. Assume also that the actuarial value of the spouse's interest in the trust (determined by current interest rates and the spouse's age and life expectancy) is $250,000. The question is whether the spouse may be forced to accept the trust interest (by counting it as part of the elective share), or whether the spouse may disclaim it and instead take the elective share outright. Until recently, the UPC position was the former; as of 1993, it is the latter. This issue is significant because, if the spouse effectively can be forced to accept a life interest in a trust in lieu of an outright elective share, the decedent can control the disposition of the assets remaining at the spouse's death.

6. Effect of the Election on Other Beneficiaries

If a spouse elects to receive a forced share, other beneficiaries usually will receive less than they otherwise would. As a result, abatement typically is required to accommodate the spousal election; under UPC §2-209(b) and 2-209(c) the obligation is a claim that is allocated pro rata among the other takers of both the decedent's probate and nonprobate assets, but in many states it is charged according to traditional abatement rules (see Chapter 9).

a. **Acceleration of remainders.** The electing spouse is treated as predeceased for the balance of the decedent's testamentary estate plan. This may accelerate any remainder interest under the will as drafted, which could create unfairness.

EXAMPLES AND ANALYSIS

D's will devised $200,000 to a preresiduary trust of which the surviving spouse S is the income beneficiary for life, remainder to Z; the residue of D's estate totals $400,000 and it is left to X. S elects against the estate plan and state law provides a ⅓ ($200,000) elective share, to be satisfied out of the residue according to normal abatement principles. Z would receive the $200,000 trust corpus early, because the election would cause S to be treated as predeceasing D, while the residuary beneficiaries suffer for having satisfied the $200,000 elective share. The appropriate remedy is to sequester S's life estate to compensate the residuary beneficiaries for this inequity (i.e., continue the trust for S's remaining life, paying the income to the residuary beneficiaries). In some cases the court will "commute" the value of that life estate (i.e., determine its discounted present value) and distribute that value to the residuary beneficiaries and the remainder of the trust to Z at D's death, instead of continuing the trust until S actually dies.

7.   Effect of Nonprobate Transfers

Nonprobate assets, such as transfers in trust, property that passes by beneficiary designation, joint tenancy, or payable on death and Totten trust accounts, may benefit the spouse or they may pass to other takers, with the potential effect of reducing the property subject to the surviving spouse's election. Whether such nonprobate assets are considered in determining and then in satisfying the elective share is a question upon which courts have gone in every possible direction.

 EXAMPLES AND ANALYSIS

D owned $600,000 of assets; the elective share is ⅓ of a deceased spouse's estate. If D died with the $600,000 in her probate estate, the surviving spouse's (S) elective share would be $200,000. But S gets nothing if D transfers the $600,000 to a revocable trust and the elective share is strictly limited to the probate estate (and S is not a beneficiary of the trust at D's death). Alternatively, if D places $300,000 of the $600,000 in joint tenancy with S—with the right of survivorship—S will keep the $300,000 of joint tenancy property and may elect against the will to take $100,000 of the $300,000 probate estate. Legislatures and courts have resolved these kinds of questions in a wide variety of ways.

a. **POD accounts.** For example, *Snodgrass v. Lyndon State Bank*, 811 P.2d 58 (Kan. Ct. App. 1991), held that the surviving spouse could not reach a POD bank account; apparently a state statute shielded the account from claims. Since *Snodgrass* was decided, however, Kansas adopted the 1990 UPC elective share provisions, discussed below, under which POD accounts are part of the decedent's augmented estate and subject to the spouse's elective share. UPC §2-205(1)(iii). Further, other courts employing an illusory transfer test, also discussed below, might subject POD accounts to the spouse's elective share because the owner of such an account typically retains complete and unrestricted control over it until death, and the payee has no interest in or rights over the account until the owner's death.

b. **Totten trusts and joint tenancy real estate and bank accounts.** Similar to *Snodgrass*, *Dalia v. Lawrence*, 627 A.2d 392 (Conn. 1993), held that a surviving spouse could not reach Totten trusts, joint tenancy real estate transferred with a retained life estate, or joint tenancy bank accounts. UPC §2-205(1) and 2-205(2)(i) would allow the survivor's elective share claim to reach all of these assets.

c. **Transfers to the spouse.** *Snodgrass* and *Dalia* illustrate that an elective share can be defeated by nonprobate transfers to beneficiaries other than the spouse in a non-UPC state. By contrast, lifetime gifts and nonprobate transfers to the spouse in a non-UPC state may cause the surviving spouse to receive *more* than the elective share percentage of the decedent's assets: the spouse is entitled to a statutory forced heir share of the decedent's probate estate in addition to receiving the gifts or nonprobate transfers.

d. **Completed gifts.** Although lifetime gifts and nonprobate transfers to the spouse effectively may increase the spouse's entitlement in a non-UPC jurisdiction, in some states complete (no strings attached) gifts to third parties, even if made close to death, generally are effective to disfranchise the spouse, as is placing property in joint tenancy with third parties. We will see that UPC §2-205(3) may bring back into the augmented estate even completed gifts made to others within two years of death, but not in every case.

8. Revocable Trusts

Depending on the jurisdiction, a person may be able to transfer assets to a trust for her own benefit and disfranchise a surviving spouse, particularly if the decedent retained no more enjoyment and control than a life estate and a power of revocation.

a. *Seifert v. Southern Nat'l Bank*, 409 S.E.2d 337 (S.C. 1991), disregarded a change in South Carolina's elective share statute that expressly limited the forced share to the decedent's *probate* estate, which was specifically defined as property passing under the will (or by intestacy), and allowed a surviving spouse's elective share claim to reach assets held in the decedent's revocable inter vivos trust. The decision illustrates the strength of the elective share policy in some states, protecting a surviving spouse from disinheritance.

b. *Johnson v. La Grange State Bank*, 383 N.E.2d 185 (Ill. 1978), in contrast with *Seifert*, shows that a trust may be used to disfranchise a surviving spouse. This consolidated case involved an inter vivos revocable trust created by the decedent for her own lifetime benefit (she was trustee and retained the income for life along with a power to revoke), and then for the benefit of several relatives—including her spouse—and various charities; a second case involved joint tenancy savings accounts created by the decedent in which the surviving spouse had no interest. Unusual, perhaps, about each case was that the plaintiffs lost in their bids to invalidate nonprobate transfers and claim a share of the assets involved as part of the statutory forced heir share, and in each case the plaintiff was a surviving husband.

c. **Assets subject to elective share.** Non-UPC elective share statutes—the law in many states—typically limit the elective share to assets in the decedent's probate estate. As we will see, the UPC augmented probate estate concept includes some nonprobate assets, including those held in inter vivos revocable trusts, in the elective share calculation.

   i. **Illusory or invalid.** Without the UPC augmented probate estate concept, the alternative for an elective share claim to reach inter vivos trust and other nonprobate asset transfers is to find them invalid or illusory as against a challenge by the surviving spouse. The question involving a trust is the degree of control that a settlor may retain without subjecting the trust to the surviving spouse's elective share. *Seifert* did not answer that question but *Johnson* did, illustrating how easy it is, at least in Illinois, to disfranchise a surviving spouse.

   ii. **Life estate and power to revoke.** On the issue of the degree of control that may be retained without making a trust subject to a spouse's forced share, you should question why retention of no more than a life estate and power to revoke will make the trust immune to challenge in some states. After all, hardly any power is more important than the power of revocation, which (because the assets are returned to the settlor on revocation of the trust) gives the settlor the ability to exercise unrestricted control over the assets at will.

d. **Remedy.** If a trust is subject to the elective share of a surviving spouse, the remedy also may differ depending on the jurisdiction.

    i. **Trust valid except for elective share purposes.** One approach, exemplified by *Seifert*, is to hold the trust invalid in its entirety. As a result of *Seifert*, however, the South Carolina legislature amended state law to clarify that the trust is not *really* invalid—other than for purposes of computing and funding the statutory share—which is really what is needed. That is, if the effort to use a trust to disfranchise the spouse is not effective, trust assets should be counted in determining the elective share and, if probate property is not adequate to satisfy that share, an invasion of the trust (or other nonprobate property) may be necessary. But the trust should not be invalidated otherwise.

    ii. **UPC and Restatement.** For example, the UPC augmented estate concept does not treat Totten trusts as invalid, but includes the trust assets in computing the size of the spouse's share.

    iii. **Problems with invalidating the trust.** Total invalidation in those states with a more blunt approach to the issue presents a number of problems: (i) it unnecessarily subjects all the property to probate; (ii) it may alter the disposition of assets not passing to the spouse; (iii) it will defeat a pour over estate plan; and (iv) it creates title problems for real estate held in revocable trusts.

9. **Testing the Validity of Nonprobate Transfers for Elective Share Purposes**

In some states (e.g., Connecticut and Ohio), revocable trusts are not subject to a surviving spouse's elective share because the forced share statutes make the election applicable only to probate assets, and the courts view it as up to the legislature whether to expand the election to nonprobate assets. Most states, however, subject nonprobate assets—including revocable trusts—to the spouse's elective share if the test for reaching such assets in the applicable jurisdiction is met in the particular case.

a. **Confusion.** Historically, a variety of tests have been used to determine the validity of a trust against a spouse's challenge. And they often have been confused. The primary reason for this is due to a misuse of terminology (e.g., "fraud" is used interchangeably in cases involving will contests, secret transfers, intent to defeat spousal rights, illusory trusts, or absence of donative intent, notwithstanding that it means different things under each). Confusion also results because in some cases courts say they are doing one thing when in fact they are responding to equities without admitting this added factor.

b. **Intent or motive.** The intent or motive test—which asks whether the establishment of the trust was a "fraud" on the surviving spouse's marital rights—is the oldest test used to invalidate a trust. It is imprecise and may be difficult to prove, but may be favored by some courts because it allows the court to weigh various equities: (i) proximity of the transfer to death; (ii) extent of the decedent's retained controls; (iii) the relative size of conveyances to and away from the surviving spouse; (iv) the relative wealth of the various parties; (v) the moral standing of the surviving spouse; and (vi) identifiable motives of the settlor (e.g., in *Johnson* the decedent's motive was to protect the surviving spouse as well as the decedent's mother and other relatives—not to disfranchise the surviving spouse).

c. **Illusory trust: Retention of control.** The illusory trust or retention of control test, used by the South Carolina court in *Seifert*, is the most predictable because the diversity of controls that may be retained is not great. The sole inquiry is whether the alleged transfer into trust was "real." Essentially a court asks whether the settlor took back as much control or enjoyment as was given and whether the settlor lost any meaningful control. (As indicated above, however, a problem with this test is that, if the settlor retains only the power to revoke, essentially the settlor has retained complete ultimate control even if no other controls or beneficial interests are retained.)

d. **Present donative intent test.** The third test, adopted in *Johnson*, is the present donative intent test. It is just the opposite of the retention of control test: it asks whether anything was given up presently rather than whether too much was retained. As we saw in *Farkas v. Williams* in Chapter 6, the same test was applied in Illinois to determine whether an inter vivos trust was a valid will substitute.

e. **General power of appointment test.** A fourth test, adopted prospectively for Massachusetts in *Sullivan v. Burkin*, 460 N.E.2d 571 (Mass. 1984), subjects trust assets to the spouse's elective share if the settlor alone had a general power of appointment, exercisable during life or at death, over the trust (i.e., a power to direct the assets for her own benefit). Because the power to revoke a trust is such a general power of appointment, this test results in all revocable trusts being subjected to spousal elections (but only, apparently, if the power is exercisable by the settlor alone, and not if the power is exercisable only with a third person, such as a child of the settlor).

f. **Test applied determines result.** *Johnson* and *Sullivan* are virtually identical on their facts; the difference in result (or at least the result the *Sullivan* court announced it would reach in such cases in the future) is just a function of the test used.

10. **The UPC Spousal Elective Share** augmented probate estate concept is designed to deal with the issue whether nonprobate transfers (by the dece-

dent to the surviving spouse or others, or by the surviving spouse) will affect the surviving spouse's entitlement. Under the UPC, the surviving spouse's elective share is a percentage not of the decedent's probate estate, but of the augmented probate estate. As we will see, property passing to the surviving spouse is included in the augmented probate estate and is applied against the elective share to satisfy or partially satisfy the spouse's claim.

EXAMPLES AND ANALYSIS

The decedent's revocable trust had $400,000 of assets at the decedent's death, all of which were to be distributed to the decedent's child from a prior marriage. The decedent had $500,000 of investment securities titled in the name of the decedent, "TOD" (i.e., transfer on death) to the decedent's spouse. Under the UPC, the spouse's elective share claim is against the decedent's augmented estate, not the probate estate; the augmented estate includes both the revocable trust assets and the securities. The securities received by the surviving spouse will be credited against the elective share claim. If there were no other assets in the augmented estate, the result is that the spouse's elective share claim would be no more than ½ of the $900,000 augmented estate, or $450,000. (As discussed below, the size of the spouse's elective share under the UPC depends on the length of the marriage, but except for the so-called "supplemental" elective share in small estates, it cannot exceed 50%.) Because the spouse received $500,000 of securities, there would be no net elective share entitlement.

a.   **Transfers by the decedent to third parties.** Inter vivos transfers away from the spouse in excess of $10,000 per donee per year, made within two years of death, and nonprobate transfers to others that essentially are not effective until death, are "brought back" into the "augmented probate estate" to compute the spousal entitlement. Thus, under the UPC a decedent's augmented probate estate generally will include the probate estate, nonprobate assets (such as joint tenancies, revocable trusts, POD accounts, and Totten trusts), and even gifts exceeding $10,000 per donee per year made within two years of death.

i.   **Life insurance.** Until 1990, the UPC did not include the proceeds of insurance on the decedent's life in the augmented probate estate, even if the decedent owned the policy. Such proceeds now are included in the augmented estate under the UPC. The insurance industry really dislikes this change and has lobbied extensively—successfully in some states—for insurance to retain its protected status, not subject to the augmented estate calculation or satisfaction of an elective share.

b.   **Transfers by the decedent to the spouse.** Nonprobate transfers *to* the spouse (which, again, are included in the augmented estate against which the elective share is calculated) are counted against the augmented estate entitlement; in most non-UPC states nothing transferred *to* the spouse counts in determining the elective share, or in satisfying it (see, e.g., the discussion of *King* above).

c.   **Pre-1990 UPC elective share calculation.** Prior to the 1990 changes discussed below, the surviving spouse's elective share under the UPC was ⅓ of the deceased spouse's augmented estate, which included (in addition to the decedent's probate estate and most of the decedent's nonprobate assets) assets the decedent transferred to the spouse during life. The surviving spouse's net elective share claim was the difference, if any, between that product and the lifetime and other transfers at death to the surviving spouse.

EXAMPLES AND ANALYSIS

D transferred $50,000 to D's spouse, S, during life. At D's death, D's net probate estate was $200,000, ½ of which D left to S and the other ½ to C, D's child. D also had a revocable trust with assets of $250,000, all of which were left to C. Finally, D had a POD account of $100,000, payable to C. D's augmented estate is $600,000; S's ⅓ share is $200,000. Credited against S's $200,000 entitlement is the $50,000 lifetime gift and the $100,000 gift from the revocable trust, leaving S with a net elective share claim of $50,000.

11.   **The UPC** elective share system was completely redesigned in 1990.

a.   **Spouse's property included.** Unique about the new spousal share is that the spouse's own property (including property the surviving spouse effectively owns in nonprobate form, such as a revocable trust), also is included in the augmented probate estate computation, regardless of how the spouse acquired that property.

b.   **Partnership theory of marriage.** This reveals an economic partnership theory of marriage under which—as with community property—all the property they accumulate during their marriage is considered, regardless of how title to their property is held.

c.   **Support theory.** An important underlying policy of traditional elective share systems was to ensure support for a surviving spouse to protect against becoming a drain on the social welfare system. The new UPC reflects the support theory for the elective share in a limited fashion by providing the surviving spouse with a supplemental elective share amount designed to ensure that, following a decedent's death, the surviving spouse will have at least $50,000 of assets (including the spouse's own property as well as property received from the decedent), excluding any homestead, exempt personal property, and family allowance—all of which are in addition to the spouse's elective share and supplemental elective share amounts.

d. Approximation system; length of the marriage. The object of the redesigned UPC elective share system is to incorporate a partnership theory of marriage. The idea is that the survivor is entitled to a share of all property the couple accumulated during their marriage from both of their earnings (i.e., a pseudo community property concept). This is accomplished not by trying to identify and divide their marital property, as is necessary in community property states, but by approximating how much property the couple acquired during the marriage. Rather than by tracing or other accounting methods, this approximation is conclusively determined by the length of the marriage.

   i. Marriage of less than one year. For a marriage of less than a year, the assumption is that none of the couple's property is marital. As a result, the surviving spouse of such a marriage has no elective share (unless a supplemental elective share is available to provide the survivor with a total of no more than $50,000).

   ii. Marriage of fifteen years or more. For a marriage of 15 years or more, all of their property is treated as marital. As a result, the survivor's elective share essentially is that amount of the decedent's property needed to leave the surviving spouse with ½ of the combined total of *all* of their property.

   iii. Marriage of between one and fifteen years. An increasing percentage of the couple's property is treated as marital for marriages of between one and fifteen years. For example, for a marriage of between 10 and 11 years, 60% of the couple's aggregate property is assumed to be marital and the surviving spouse is entitled to ½. Thus, as actually implemented, the augmented estate concept for a marriage of between 10 and 11 years gives the spouse 30% of the augmented estate. Thus, if D died with a $500,000 net estate, if there were no nonprobate assets, and if D's surviving spouse had no other property, $300,000 of D's assets would be regarded as marital property and S's elective share would be ½ of that, or $150,000. The UPC accomplishes this by giving D's surviving spouse 30% of D's $500,000 estate.

 ## EXAMPLES AND ANALYSIS

The decedent's probate estate, all left to C (a child from a prior marriage) is $100,000. Joint tenancy property (all consideration provided by the decedent) with the surviving spouse was worth $150,000, insurance payable to X (a third party) totals $75,000, a Totten trust with Y (a third party) holds $100,000, and an inter vivos trust for Z (a third party) is worth $125,000. The amount the surviving spouse receives under the UPC depends on how long they were married, and how much property the surviving spouse owns. Let's assume the marriage was for more than 15 years and that the survivor owned no other property.

$100,000   probate estate ☞ C
 150,000   joint tenancy with spouse
  75,000   insurance ☞ X
 100,000   Totten trust ☞ Y
 125,000   inter vivos trust ☞ Z
$550,000   Augmented probate estate

The spousal share of the augmented probate estate is ½ (because the marriage was for at least 15 years), or $275,000. Because the spouse already owns the joint tenancy of $150,000, the spouse will receive only $125,000 more under the UPC. (This $125,000 would come from the probate estate, insurance, Totten trust, and inter vivos trust pro rata.)

If the spouse had owned $300,000 of assets, that amount would have been included in the augmented probate estate calculation, increasing it to $850,000. The spouse's elective share would be ½, or $425,000. Credited against that would be the $150,000 of joint tenancy property and the spouse's own $300,000, for a total of $450,000. Thus, there would be no elective share (although the spouse would not need to "pay back" the $25,000 overage). The no-elective-share result would be the same even if the spouse could prove that the spouse's $300,000 was inherited from a third party and that all of the rest of the decedent's augmented estate was marital property.

In a non-UPC state, the surviving spouse would take the joint tenancy $150,000 plus a statutory share (usually ⅓ or ½) of the probate estate, the Totten trust (which would not withstand challenge in most states, despite the holding in *Dalia*, discussed above, because it is such a thin will substitute), and maybe the inter vivos trust. Nothing received by the spouse outside probate (e.g., the $150,000 joint tenancy), or owned by the spouse before the decedent died, would count against the elective share.

e. **Observations.** The 1990 UPC elective share system addresses several shortcomings with the prior system. For example, a surviving spouse of a short term, late in life marriage no longer will be entitled to ⅓ of a decedent's property; indeed, if the marriage lasted less than a year, the survivor will not be entitled to an elective share at all (unless the estate is small and the spouse is entitled to a supplemental elective share to ensure that the spouse will have at least $50,000 of assets). Similarly, consistent with the partnership theory of marriage, in a long-term (15 + year) marriage, the survivor's elective share is for ½ of the decedent's assets, not ⅓. But in some cases, the new system also will yield inequitable results. For example, in a long-term late in life marriage, all of a decedent's assets may be subject to a 50% elective share claim by a surviving spouse even if all of those assets are separate property that under the partnership theory of marriage ought not be subject to a spouse's elective share claim.

EXAM TIP

If a couple were married more than 15 years at the first of their deaths, the analysis under the 1990 UPC is as follows. First, calculate the decedent's augmented probate estate: (i) add the values of the probate and nonprobate assets of each spouse; (ii) add gifts in excess of $10,000 per donee/per year made within two years of the decedent's death by either spouse; (iii) subtract the decedent's debts, funeral, and administration expenses; and (iv) subtract the homestead allowance, exempt tangible personal property, and family allowance. Second, multiply the augmented probate estate by 50% to get the spouse's elective share amount. Third, reduce the spouse's elective share amount by the sum of the spouse's probate and nonprobate assets, gifts in excess of $10,000 per year/per donee made by the spouse within two years of the decedent's death, and probate and nonprobate assets the spouse receives from the decedent. The result is the spouse's net elective share claim. If the spouse has more property than the decedent (including for this purpose gifts made within two years of the decedent's death by each of them in excess of $10,000 per year/per donee), the spouse will receive no net elective share.

---

12. **Problems Created by Migratory Clients**

Because of the rule that once property is community property, it always is community property, there is a tracing problem in identifying community property held by a decedent dying in a noncommunity property state. Similarly, there is a need to identify separate and quasi-community property of a decedent dying in a community property state.

a. **Death in a noncommunity property state owning community property.** The spouse may receive more from a forced share than is equitable if the spouses accumulated community property while living in a community property state and then moved to a noncommunity property state before the decedent died.

 ## EXAMPLES AND ANALYSIS

Decedent died in a noncommunity property jurisdiction with $90,000 of community property and $60,000 of separate property; the statutory share is ⅓. The initial reaction that the surviving spouse will receive $50,000 (⅓ of the aggregate wealth of $150,000) is not correct. Instead, the spouse already owns ½ of the community property ($45,000) and is entitled to ⅓ of the decedent's separate property (another $20,000). Depending on state law, the spouse also may receive ⅓ of the decedent's share of the community property (another $15,000), for a total of $80,000. Notice that, at the most, the spouse's share would have been ⅓ of $150,000 if this all was the decedent's separate property. The disparity is produced because the community property share is ½ *and* we don't cut the spouse out of the decedent's separate property and may not cut the spouse out of the decedent's share of the community property.

b. **Decedent dies in a community property state owning quasi-community property.** The surviving spouse may receive less than is equitable if the decedent died in a community property state owning property accumulated from the decedent's earnings while the couple lived in a noncommunity property state.

 ## EXAMPLES AND ANALYSIS

Decedent died in a community property jurisdiction that does not recognize quasi-community property with $140,000 of separate property and $10,000 of community property. Because community property states do not have elective shares, the surviving spouse receives $5,000 only, as ½ of the community, because there is no quasi-community property entitlement. Were this a jurisdiction that applies the quasi-community property concept at death, the surviving spouse would receive ½ of the $140,000 as well, if it all was earned during the marriage, as if it were true community property. Quaere whether this $75,000 aggregate result is more appropriate than the $80,000 result in the prior example: the $75,000 is ½ of the couple's $150,000 of marital property.

13. **Is There a Better Way?**

    Commentators argue about whether there is a better way to address marital property rights than the existing elective share systems.

    a. **Follow federal estate tax rules.** One approach would mimic the federal estate tax gross estate as the decedent's true wealth (the UPC augmented estate comes close), and then base the elective share on that. Uncle Sam does not let much escape that system and the inclusion rules are pretty clear.

    b. **Divorce.** Another avenue is to look to what the surviving spouse would have received under state law had the parties divorced just prior to the decedent's death. Arguably more equitable results would result, but at the cost of delay and less predictability.

    c. **Community property.** A third approach would be to convert to community property—recognizing quasi-community property at death as well as at divorce—and abolish the elective share altogether.

    d. **Deferred community property.** A fourth would be to include only the couple's marital property in the augmented estate and establish the spouse's 50% elective share without regard to the length of the marriage, excluding their separate property from the computation. The result arguably would be more equitable, but at a cost of having to classify the couple's property as marital or separate at the first of their deaths.

14. **Pre- and Postnuptial Agreements**

    Particularly for subsequent marriages if there are children from prior marriages, it is not uncommon for spouses to modify or waive marital rights they otherwise would enjoy, using a pre- or occasionally a postnuptial agreement. (Prenuptial agreements often are referred to as "antenuptial" agreements. Some people hear ante-nuptial as if it was anti-nuptial, however, so we use "prenuptial" instead.)

    a. **Validity.** Pre- and postnuptial agreements essentially are contracts regarding entitlement at death or divorce. Historically, in many jurisdictions these agreements were subject to special rules and close scrutiny in determining their validity. For example, in some jurisdictions a prenuptial agreement was not valid unless executed more than a specified number of days, such as 10, before the wedding. Today, in many jurisdictions the validity of these agreements is measured as in any contract, looking to sufficiency of consideration, fraud, duress, and overreaching. In others, however, the nature of the relationship between prospective spouses continues to subject prenuptial agreements to special scrutiny and can, if there is a sufficient degree of inequality between the parties, result in the proponent having the burden of proving that the agreement was not procured by fraud or overreaching. See, for example, *In re Grieff*, 703 N.E.2d 752 (N.Y. 1998).

i. **Postnuptial agreements.** In some states (e.g., Oklahoma, Iowa, and Ohio), elective share rights may not be waived in postnuptial agreements.

ii. **Trend.** Otherwise, there is a growing trend in favor of upholding pre- and postnuptial agreements if (i) the agreement is based on full disclosure of the spouses' resources *or* each spouse freely signed and either did have or could have had knowledge of the other spouse's holdings, and (ii) the provisions for the complaining spouse are fair and reasonable. For example, *In re Estate of Garbade*, 633 N.Y.S.2d 878 (N.Y. App. Div. 1995), upheld a prenuptial agreement limiting the surviving spouse's rights against the $2.5 million estate of her deceased husband to the proceeds of a $100,000 insurance policy (she apparently received another $240,000 of assets at her husband's death by other means) because there was no showing of fraud and the husband made a full disclosure of his assets.

iii. **Presumption.** There is a presumption of inadequate disclosure if the amounts provided for the complaining spouse are disproportionately small, but that presumption is rebuttable with (i) proof of knowledge by the complaining spouse of the other spouse's resources (or, perhaps, lack of concealment by the other spouse), or (ii) independent representation of the complaining spouse (this part is key because, in the absence of fraud, it virtually negates a successful challenge).

iv. *In re Burgess' Estate,* 646 P.2d 623 (Okla. Ct. App. 1982), illustrates the new attitude towards marital agreements. In *Burgess*, the premarital agreement waived elective share rights and made no provision for the surviving spouse. The agreement was upheld despite conflicting evidence of whether there had been full and fair disclosure of the husband's assets because the court found the wife had a generally accurate knowledge of the husband's property. In so holding, the court stated:

> [C]ourts have tended to be rather more exacting of such contracts than of other contracts. At the root of this tendency seems to lie an attitude of paternalism toward women. For example, [one] court labeled an antenuptial contract "a wicked device to evade the laws applicable to marriage relations, property rights and divorces," which was "clearly against public policy and decency,"

and an attempt by the husband to "legalize prostitution, under the name of marriage."

* * *

Well-intentioned though this chivalrous attitude may have been in the past, times have changed. It will no longer do for courts to look on women who are about to be married as if they were insensible ninnies, pathetically vulnerable to overreaching by their fiances and in need of special judicial protection.

Moreover, there are today many policy reasons favoring the enforcement of ante-nuptial agreements. These contracts can be seen as fostering marriage since some couples, especially older ones who typically already have families and property of their own, might choose not to marry absent assurance that they will still be free to order their affairs as they wish.

b.   Uniform Pre-Marital Agreements Act. The Uniform Pre-Marital Agreements Act is the same as UPC §2-213 and presupposes validity of a pre- or postnuptial agreement unless (i) the agreement was involuntary, *or* (ii) there was (a) no disclosure to the complaining party of the other's financial condition, (b) no knowledge by the complaining party of the other's financial condition, (c) no reasonable basis for the complaining party to acquire such knowledge, (d) no waiver by the complaining party of such disclosure, *and* (e) the agreement was unconscionable (which is a subjective determination, to be made by the court as a matter of law) when executed. These are tough standards to meet and probably impossible, in the absence of fraud, if the complaining party had independent counsel.

E.   PRETERMITTED HEIRS

We focus now on all the natural objects of a decedent's bounty. Most states have pretermitted (i.e., omitted) heir statutes under which heirs who are not provided for under a decedent's will *may* be entitled to share in the estate. Heirs who may benefit from these statutes usually include children and sometimes more remote descendants or the decedent's spouse.

1.   Pretermitted Spouses

Statutes providing protection to surviving spouses, if applicable, allow a spouse to reject a will that was executed before the marriage and take an intestate share. In noncommunity property jurisdictions other than Georgia (which does not provide the spouse with an elective share entitlement), the spouse may choose whether to take an elective share or as a pretermitted spouse.

a.   Rationale; contrary intent. This election to take as a pretermitted spouse is based on an assumption that after the wedding the decedent forgot to amend (or intended but did not get around to amending) the will to include her spouse as a beneficiary; the failure to provide for the surviving spouse is presumed to be inadvertent, not intentional. A pretermitted spouse statute will not apply if the failure to provide for the spouse was intentional. The question is how to determine whether that was the case.

b. *Estate of Shannon,* 274 Cal. Rptr. 338 (1990), involved a testator's will that left the entire estate to a child and included a provision that the testator "intentionally omitted all other living persons and relatives." The testator's surviving spouse nevertheless took a share of the estate under a pretermitted spouse statute because the will—executed some 12 years prior to the testator's marriage to the spouse—did not show a specific intent to exclude the spouse. Extrinsic evidence in the form of testimony by the testator's attorney that the testator stated that the surviving spouse had more property than the testator and that the testator wanted the child to receive the entire estate did not affect the result: the controlling statute required a testator's intention not to provide for a spouse to be shown from the will itself.

c. **UPC §2-301.** The pretermitted spouse's share under the UPC is an intestate share, not of the entire estate, but only of that portion of the estate left to beneficiaries who are not descendants of the decedent born prior to the marriage. Under the UPC, a pretermitted heir entitlement is *not* available to a surviving spouse to the extent the decedent left the estate to descendants born prior to the marriage who are not descendants of the spouse, because the assumption that the decedent forgot to revise the will to provide for a new spouse is regarded as not sufficient to overcome the decedent's other testamentary objectives. In such a case the omitted surviving spouse would need to elect against the will and take the elective share of the augmented estate; note that in many cases the elective share will be much smaller than an intestate share.

   i.   **Subject to decedent's intent.** Under the UPC, an omitted spouse will receive no pretermitted heir share—and will be left only with an elective share remedy—if the testator's failure to provide for the spouse was intentional, as shown by (i) evidence that the will was executed in contemplation of the marriage, (ii) a provision in the will that it is to be effective notwithstanding a subsequent marriage, or (iii) the decedent having provided for the spouse by will substitute, with evidence that the provision was in lieu of a testamentary gift.

EXAMPLES AND ANALYSIS

T, a single person, executed a will that gave the entire estate to two favorite nephews and made no reference to the possibility of a subsequent marriage. Several years later, T, who had no descendants, married S. T died 13 months after the marriage without having changed the will or providing for S by will substitute. Under UPC §2-301, S is a pretermitted spouse entitled to receive an intestate share of T's entire estate (because no part of it passed to descendants of T). Because T had no descendants, S's intestate share will be the entire estate if T also was not survived by a parent, or the first $200,000 of the estate, plus ¾ of the balance, if T was survived by a parent. (See Chapter 2.) By contrast, if T's will had stated that it was to be given effect without regard to a subsequent marriage by T, S could not take as a pretermitted spouse, and would be relegated to an elective share. For this one year marriage the spouse's elective share percentage under the new UPC forced share system would be only 3% of the decedent's augmented estate. If T's will made no reference to the possibility of a subsequent marriage and devised the estate ½ to a child and ½ to beneficiaries who are not descendants, S's share under UPC §2-301 would be an intestate share of the ½ left to nondescendants.

---

    ii. **Nonprobate transfers.** The augmented estate concept is missing from the UPC pretermitted spouse rule. Thus, in the preceding example, if T had arranged for property to pass to the two nephews by will substitute, S's pretermitted spouse share would not reach those assets. If all of T's property passed by will substitute, S would take nothing as a pretermitted spouse and again would be left only with an elective share. On the other hand, as a pretermitted spouse S is entitled to an intestate share of probate property left to nondescendants (assuming T's failure to provide for S was not intentional), even if S has more assets than T and therefore would not be entitled to an elective share. S also is entitled to a pretermitted spouse share even if T provides for S by will substitute, unless the proof shows that these transfers were meant to be in lieu of a testamentary provision.

  2. **Pretermitted Descendants**

    The foregoing may be too much ado about nothing because there aren't many pretermitted spouse statutes and even fewer claims. But pretermitted descendant statutes are found in most states and they can be important. Some (e.g., UPC §2-302) protect only children; others also protect more remote descendants.

a. **Two categories.** Generally, these statutes fall into two categories:
(i) some protect only children (or more remote descendants) born or
adopted after execution of the will; (ii) others protect any child (or
more remote descendant) not provided for in the will, whenever born
or adopted.

b. **The pretermitted descendant's share.** The share of a pretermitted
child (or more remote descendant) varies from state to state. The
typical entitlement is the share the child (or descendant) would have
received had the estate been intestate (less any advancements). Notice
that this may be substantially more or less than what other descendants
in the same relationship to the decedent receive under the will.

   i. **Protection under the UPC** is afforded only to children, not
   to more remote descendants. The share of a pretermitted child
   depends on whether any children of the decedent were living
   when the will was executed, and often will not be as large as an
   intestate share. If no children of the testator were living when
   the will was executed, a pretermitted child will receive an intestate
   share, unless the will devises substantially all of the estate to the
   other parent of the omitted child; in that case, the pretermitted
   child takes nothing. If the testator had one or more children
   living when the will was executed, a pretermitted child will share
   on a pro rata basis with the other children in property devised
   to these children (or in trust for their benefit).

c. **Who is pretermitted: the burden of proof.** Except in Louisiana, a
parent may disinherit children (and more remote descendants); pretermitted descendant statutes do not provide forced share rights like those
provided to spouses in noncommunity property elective share states.
Rather, pretermitted heir statutes only protect from *inadvertent* disinheritance, meaning that proof of an intent to omit will preclude a claim.
For example, *In re Estate of Laura*, 690 A.2d 1011 (N.H. 1997), the
pretermitted heir statute provided protection only to children and descendants of deceased children who were not "referred to" in the will.
The court held that a provision expressly disinheriting a grandson,
but not expressly referring to his descendants, nevertheless "referred
to" the grandson's descendants for purposes of the pretermitted heir
statute, and thus barred them from taking. A significant difference
among the statutes is where the burden of proof lies on the issue
whether the failure to provide for a child (or other descendant) was
intentional.

   i. **Burden on the omitted descendant.** In some jurisdictions the
   omitted individual must prove the disinheritance was unintentional. Typically, extrinsic evidence is allowed because this chore
   is so great.

>   **ii.   Burden on the will proponents.** In other jurisdictions the propo-
>   nents of the will must prove that disinheritance was intentional.
>   Typically no extrinsic evidence is allowed in this endeavor (i.e.,
>   the intent to disinherit must be evident from the will itself).

3.   Negative Wills

A negative will states an intent to disinherit a person who is a potential
heir (remember: "heir" is a term of art, meaning those persons who take
by statute from an intestate decedent) of the testator. Usually required to
be effective is a disposition of the entire estate; in most states an heir's
entitlement to intestate property cannot be prevented by a will that states
only the decedent's negative intent regarding the heir—there must be a
valid alternative disposition. Exceptions are found in some states (e.g.,
New York and UPC §2-302(b)(1)), which permit a will to state that some
potential heirs are to receive nothing even from the intestate portion of
the estate.

4.   If Pretermitted Heir Status Is Precluded

If a decedent dies with a premarital will and a surviving spouse is precluded
from receiving a pretermitted heir share, the spouse nevertheless may elect
against the estate. By contrast, if a pretermitted heir statute is no help to
an omitted child (or more remote descendant), the only other alternative
is to bring a will contest action to defeat the will entirely. This alternative
also is available to a surviving spouse, but as we saw in Chapter 3, it is
not a very good alternative because success under contest actions is so
unpredictable.

5.   Beware Effect of Codicils

As discussed in Chapter 3, a codicil normally operates to republish a will
as of the date of the codicil. Because pretermitted heir statutes often apply
only if the testator was married after execution of the will or with respect
to descendants born or adopted after execution of the will, the execution
of a codicil can bar pretermitted heir status if a marriage, birth, or adoption
occurs after execution of the will but before execution of the codicil.

>   **a.   *Azcunce v. Estate of Azcunce,*** 586 So. 2d 1216 (Fla. Dist. Ct. App.
>   1991), involved a father's 1983 will that devised property in trust for
>   his wife and his three then living children; no provision was made for
>   afterborns. A fourth child was born in 1984. Her status as a pretermitted
>   heir was defeated by the father's execution of a codicil—which ex-
>   pressly republished the terms of the will—in 1986. There was evidence
>   the father did not intend to disinherit her—he had asked his attorney
>   to revise his will to include her—but the controlling Florida statute
>   protected only children born or adopted after execution of the will.

6.   Policy

The theories alleged to support statutes that protect a spouse or child (or other descendant) who is not provided for in a will vary. For example, some courts would say that there is a postmortem support obligation. Others would say that there is an entitlement. If either rationale was correct it should not be possible to overcome the pretermitted heir statute with a showing of the decedent's positive intent to disinherit. A third stated rationale is protection against mistake or inadvertence.

REVIEW QUESTIONS AND ANSWERS

Question: Client and Spouse lived in a community property state for the first five years of their marriage, after which they moved to a noncommunity property state. In the community property state, both Client and Spouse worked outside their home, as they did for the first three years they spent in the noncommunity property state. For the remainder of their marriage, during which time they continued to live in the noncommunity property state, Client worked outside their home and Spouse cared for their children and managed their home, but did not work for monetary compensation. Client died, testate, 20 years after their marriage. Describe in general terms Spouse's marital property rights.

Answer: Any property Client or Spouse owned at the time of their marriage is separate property. Property they accumulated from the earnings of either of them during the first five years of their marriage while they lived in the community property jurisdiction is community property and retained that character after they moved to the noncommunity property jurisdiction. Property accumulated from Client's earnings in the noncommunity property state is not community property. At Client's death, Spouse will be the owner of ½ of their community property. Spouse will be entitled to take any gifts made to Spouse under Client's will, along with any nonprobate assets of which Spouse was the designated beneficiary, surviving tenant, or other successor. Assuming the noncommunity property state is not Georgia, Spouse may elect to receive a statutory share of Client's estate, in lieu of property devised to Spouse under Client's will. Depending on the jurisdiction, Spouse's elective share rights may extend to Client's nonprobate property and, if the state has adopted the UPC, the share will depend on the length of their marriage—in this case it will be the largest share (50%) because the marriage lasted over 15 years. In addition, Spouse probably will be entitled to a homestead allowance, some exempt tangible personal property, and a family allowance.

Question: T and S have been married for 15 years and live in a noncommunity property, non-UPC jurisdiction that grants to a surviving spouse the right to elect to receive ⅓ of a decedent's estate in lieu of all other provisions for the spouse under the will. T's child, C, from a prior marriage has diminished mental capacity.

T has been diagnosed with a terminal illness and has a life expectancy of six months. At death, T wants to leave T's entire $400,000 estate in trust for C. T also wants to create a trust of which T is the trustee and to which all of T's assets will be transferred; the trust instrument would provide for T to receive all income for life and T would retain the ability to revoke or amend the trust. After T's death the trust would continue for C's benefit for C's life and provide that, in the event of an emergency involving S's support or health, if S has no other resources the trustee (a bank) may make distributions to S, or for S's benefit, to provide for S's emergency needs. T and S own their home (value of $100,000, with no mortgage) in joint tenancy with the right of survivorship. S has a $150,000 estate. Assume that T dies four months later and that S elects against T's estate plan. The issue whether S may reach the trust assets with an elective share is one of first impression in the jurisdiction. Evaluate whether S may reach the trust assets with an elective share claim.

Answer: It depends. One approach would be to hold that the elective share only can reach assets in the probate estate—that it is up to the legislature to expand the elective share rights of a surviving spouse. Assuming the court rejects that restraint, S's ability to reach the trust assets will depend on the test the court employs for deciding the issue.

Under the intent or motive test, the court may examine the equities to determine whether the trust was intended to defeat S's marital rights. Factors that support S reaching the trust include: the proximity of the creation and funding of the trust to T's death and the facts that T's assets are substantially greater than S's, T provided for S only through the joint tenancy and the trust interest, and T essentially retained unrestricted control over the trust until T's death. Factors supporting the validity of the trust against S's election include: T's motive to provide for a child with diminished mental capacity and S's needs being provided for by S's own assets, S receiving the home debt-free, and S being a beneficiary of the trust if necessary to provide for S's health or support. Our guess: under the intent or motive test, S probably would not reach the trust.

Under the illusory trust test, S likely would reach the trust assets: T retained not only a life estate and power to revoke the trust, but also complete control over the trust during T's life by serving as its sole trustee. Similarly, S could reach the trust assets under the Massachusetts general power of appointment test: T's power to revoke the trust was exercisable by T alone and constituted a general power of appointment (an unrestricted ability to use or direct the use of the trust assets for T's own benefit).

Under the present donative intent test, the question is whether T intended by present creation of the trust to confer a benefit on a third party. The instrument named C as the remainder beneficiary; C's contingent interest is enough to uphold the validity of the trust as against a testamentary challenge, and also should be adequate to protect against a surviving spouse's elective share.

Question: T died in a UPC state and S is T's surviving spouse. T's will devised T's $250,000 estate to C, a child from a prior marriage. S's assets at T's death totaled $300,000, all of which was inherited from S's parent. T had no nonprobate assets and made no transfers within two years of T's death. T and S were married for 20 years. What is the size of S's elective share claim against T's estate?

Answer: Zero. T and S have been married for more than 15 years, so S's elective share is 50%. However, S's $300,000 of assets will be included in T's augmented probate estate and then credited against S's share. Because that amount exceeds ½ the augmented estate, S has no net elective share claim. The fact that S's $300,000 was inherited is irrelevant, as is the source of T's $250,000 of assets. T's estate has no claim against S for the amount ($25,000) by which S's wealth exceeds ½ the augmented probate estate.

Question: T and S were married more than 15 years when T died a resident of a noncommunity property elective share state. T's will left T's $200,000 estate to a third party, X. In addition, T gave X $50,000 one year before T's death; $70,000 three years before T's death; and X was the beneficiary of a $100,000 policy of insurance T owned on T's life. T and S owned their home, valued at $180,000, as joint tenants with the right of survivorship. S was the settlor, trustee, and sole lifetime beneficiary of a trust that was revocable by S, the assets of which had a net value at T's death of $120,000. S owned no other assets. Would S's net elective share of T's estate be greater under a non-UPC elective share statute under which S's forced share is ⅓ of T's probate estate, or under the UPC?

Answer: Under a non-UPC ⅓ elective share statute, S's elective share would be $66,667 (⅓ of T's $200,000 probate estate); the lifetime gifts to X and the life insurance benefits received by X would have no bearing on the calculation, and neither would the home T and S owned as joint tenants or S's revocable trust.

T's augmented probate estate for elective share purposes under the UPC includes T's $200,000 probate estate, $40,000 of the $50,000 gift made to X a year before T's death (the first $10,000 of gifts to a donee in a year are not included in the augmented probate estate even if made within two years before the donor's death, and the $70,000 gift would not be included as it was made more than two years before T's death), the $100,000 of insurance proceeds, the $180,000 joint tenancy residence, and the $120,000 of S's revocable trust assets, for a total of $640,000. S's elective share percentage is 50% (because the marriage lasted longer than 15 years), for a total of $320,000, but the $120,000 of revocable trust assets and the $180,000 joint tenancy residence are credited against the $320,000, leaving S with a net elective share claim of $20,000. S would be better off with a non-UPC ⅓ elective share of the probate estate.

Question: T had two children, A and B, when T and S were married. After the wedding, T executed a valid holographic will that stated: "I give $15,000 to each of A and B, and the rest of my estate to S." Two years later, T and S had a child,

C. When C was 20, C had a child, GC; shortly thereafter, C died. At T's subsequent death, T's net probate estate was $200,000; in addition, T and S owned their home, valued at $150,000, in joint tenancy with right of survivorship, and T had a POD account with $10,000 in it, the payee of which was X, a third party. Shortly after T's death it was determined that T was the parent of a nonmarital child, Z, who was born before T's marriage to S. What rights, if any, do GC and Z have?

Answer: Some pretermitted descendant statutes protect only children; others also protect more remote descendants. If the controlling statute applies only to children, GC will have no claim to any property of T. If the statute also applies to more remote descendants, GC will be entitled to a share of T's estate, the size of which depends on state law and is limited to a share of T's probate estate—nonprobate assets are not reachable by pretermitted heirs. In many states a pretermitted heir receives an intestate share; in such a state, GC likely would receive more than the $15,000 A and B each will receive. For example, if the controlling intestate succession statute leaves ½ to a surviving spouse and the balance to descendants, by representation, GC's intestate share of T's $200,000 probate estate would be $25,000 (¼ of $100,000).

Z's status as a pretermitted heir also would depend on state law. Z's nonmarital status is irrelevant if paternity properly was established. Some pretermitted descendant statutes, including the UPC, apply only to descendants born after execution of the will. In such a jurisdiction, Z would receive nothing. Other pretermitted descendant statutes also apply to descendants born before execution of the will. In such a jurisdiction, Z would take as a pretermitted heir unless T's failure to provide for Z was intentional. If the jurisdiction requires Z to prove that T's failure to provide for Z was not intentional, extrinsic evidence likely would be admissible; extrinsic evidence likely will not be admitted if controlling state law provides that Z will take unless the proponents prove T intentionally did not provide for Z.

EXAM TIP

It is a mistake to address issues not reasonably raised by the question. The previous question states that T executed a valid holographic will. Because the validity of the holograph is a given, it is unlikely your professor would give you any credit for pointing out that holographs are valid in only about ½ of the states; or that they do not need to be witnessed; or that, depending on state law, either the entire will or at least the material portions must be in the testator's handwriting.

By contrast, the question asked about the rights of Z and GC. Z's rights will depend on whether state law protects children born before execution of the will and on whether Z's omission from the will was intentional. For that reason, addressing the burden of proof and extrinsic evidence issue would be appropriate. Although these issues also could be addressed with respect to GC's status as a pretermitted heir, they are more directly relevant for Z because Z was living when T executed the will. On the other hand, speaking to Z's nonmarital child status may justify a sentence or two, but otherwise is not the thrust of this question.

11

INTRODUCTION TO TRUSTS

 CHAPTER OVERVIEW

- This chapter reviews the background, varieties, and purposes of trusts.

- Trusts are property management arrangements that bifurcate title—the trustee holds legal title for the beneficiary, who holds equitable or beneficial title.

- Trusts facilitate creative estate planning and may be created during life or at death, may be irrevocable or revocable, and may be implied by operation of law (resulting and constructive trusts) or intentional.

A. **A TRUST IS** an arrangement by which a fiduciary—the trustee(s)—holds legal title to property for the benefit of one or more others—the beneficiaries—who hold the beneficial title to the trust property. For example, a parent might provide by will for her estate to pass in trust for the benefit of a child until the child reaches a specified age, meanwhile managing the trust property for the child's benefit.

B. **BACKGROUND**

The trust had its origins in the 1400s when it was known as a "use." Active uses, the forerunner to the modern trust, provided actual management of property; passive uses, as to which the trustee had no management responsibilities, were used to avoid feudal duties, circumvent property ownership and transfer limits, evade creditors, or minimize dower rights.

1. **Passive Uses and Dry Trusts**

A passive trust is not effective—with the exception of "land trusts," which are recognized in a few states, in which the trustee's only "duty" is to hold legal title to land. If the trustee has no duties to perform (other than not to interfere with the beneficiary's enjoyment of the trust property), that trust will be "executed," meaning that legal title passes to the beneficiaries on demand and thereby merges with their equitable title. Similarly, a "dry trust" owns no property and fails for lack of a trust corpus. Active trusts do not become passive trusts because active trusts automatically terminate on fulfillment of their stated purposes.

2. Equitable Nature of Trust Law

Trust law essentially is judicial in origin (Trust Acts in most states merely codify existing law in most respects) and equitable, arising on the Chancery side and still lodged there.

C. PARTIES AND PROPERTY

Trusts are created by a *settlor* (or *grantor*) who transfers property (the trust *corpus, principal,* or *res*) to the *trustee*—a fiduciary—for the use or benefit of *beneficiaries* (present or future interest holders).

1. Number of Parties

Typically, there is only one trust settlor, but there can be more. For beneficiaries it is the opposite: typically trusts have multiple beneficiaries (although it is common for there to be only one current beneficiary), but there can be only one. Many trusts have one trustee; some have multiple trustees.

2. Multiple Roles

Each of the three roles may be held by a different person, or one person may serve in two or even all three of them. For example, in a revocable trust the settlor often will serve as trustee and be the sole current beneficiary. (In such a case, however, to avoid merger of title and failure of the trust it is necessary that there also be at least one remainder beneficiary who is not the settlor's estate; that almost universally is the case, so that this limitation is of little practical significance. See Chapter 12.)

D. DISTINGUISHING TRUSTS

Although trusts exhibit characteristics of contracts, agencies, deeds, wills, co-ownership (such as joint tenancy or a life estate followed by a remainder interest), and life insurance, they are unlike all other legal entities in three essential respects.

1. Bifurcation of Title is the first. Legal title is held by the trustee; the beneficiaries hold equitable title or the beneficial interest. This separation of title has made trusts unacceptable under many non-Anglo systems of law.

2. Fiduciary Duty is the second unique aspect of trusts. Imposed on the trustee is the fiduciary duty of undivided loyalty to the beneficiaries, which ensures the protection of the beneficial interest. The duty of a fiduciary is

the highest recognized at common law. The trustee is barred from acting for its own benefit or from engaging in any activity that is not for the exclusive benefit of the trust and its beneficiaries. Even the appearance of impropriety, such as self-dealing (even if at terms that are entirely fair), may result in discharge, surcharge, or other liability to the trustee. A trust could not exist in the absence of this fiduciary relation.

3. **Enforceability** is the third element that distinguishes trusts. Unlike other relations in which any party may sue for enforcement, only the beneficiaries of a trust may engage the trustee in litigation to enforce the trust. Except to challenge its validity, or perhaps on contract grounds, no person who is not a beneficiary (not even the settlor) may enforce a trust. As a result, trust litigation, which most often involves either drafting glitches (i.e., construction suits) or the allegation of breach, falls into relatively few categories.

   a. **Beneficiaries sue** to enforce, to rectify any breach of fiduciary duty, or for accountings to assess whether there has been any breach.

   b. **Trustees sue** to have accounts approved (protecting them from liability for any act revealed therein), to have the document construed when unclear or subject to conflicting claims (often due to deficiencies that may generate malpractice exposure to the drafting attorney), or to resign (a right that does not otherwise exist unless granted by the trust document).

   c. **Outsiders sue** to invalidate the trust, asserting defects in creation or continued existence (such as a creditor who wants to reach the trust corpus to satisfy its claim) or on policy grounds (such as a surviving spouse who seeks to reach trust assets for elective share purposes. See Chapter 10).

EXAM TIP

The trustee of a trust is charged with administering the trust to carry out the intent of the settlor as evidenced by the terms of the trust, but the rights and interests in a trust in which the settlor has not retained a beneficial interest belong solely to the beneficiaries. Accordingly, a settlor who is not also a beneficiary may not sue the trustee to enforce the trust, or for damages for breach of trust. A settlor may nevertheless play a role in the administration of the trust in a variety of ways. For example, generally a trust may not be terminated early by the beneficiaries and the trustee without the settlor's consent. Similarly, the settlor may be able to provide input concerning her intent (although the relevant intent is the settlor's if an issue of interpretation or construction of a trust instrument arises, at creation of the trust, not at a later time during its administration).

Finally, the trust may authorize the settlor to participate in administration of the trust, such as by replacing the trustee in the event of a vacancy, or removing and replacing a serving trustee.

E. TYPES OF TRUSTS

There are various types of trusts and motives for their creation.

1. Business, Public, or Charitable Trusts

Estate planners typically are not concerned with the first two and, because of the complexity required to qualify for exempt status under the federal income tax law, our treatment of charitable express trusts is limited (see the Website).

2. Private Express Trusts

Most important for purposes of this course are private express trusts. Within this category, the common forms are:

a. Inter vivos trusts. Also called living or revocable trusts (and typically—although not always and not of necessity—holding most of a settlor's assets during her life), along with the special type of living trust known as a "self-trusteed declaration of trust" in which the settlor also is the initial trustee (and, usually, the initial beneficiary too).

    i. Terminology. Literally, an "inter vivos trust" is a trust created by a settlor during the settlor's life and may include a variety of different kinds of trusts, such as revocable and irrevocable insurance trusts and trusts for the education of the beneficiaries (typically irrevocable). The common inter vivos trust is revocable and designed for more active purposes than receiving life insurance proceeds in the future.

    ii. Among other purposes, inter vivos trusts can avoid probate, provide management of the settlor's property, and preserve privacy. See Chapter 6.

    iii. Irrevocable at settlor's death. Generally, inter vivos trusts become irrevocable at the settlor's death, at which time the assets may be distributed outright to the beneficiaries—after postmortem administration of the trust is completed. Alternatively, the trust may become irrevocable and continue for the beneficiaries, similar in operation to testamentary trusts (except that in some states the latter are subject to ongoing judicial supervision while the former are not).

b. Testamentary trusts are created by a testator's will and are irrevocable (because the settlor is deceased) and funded (usually by the residue of the testator's estate). The will creates the trust, which does not come into existence and has no legal significance until the testator's death.

c. **Insurance trusts** are created to receive life insurance proceeds, typically insuring the life of the settlor. In some cases insurance trusts own the policy itself and these almost always are irrevocable as part of a plan to avoid subjecting the proceeds to federal estate tax when the insured/settlor dies. Alternatively, insurance trusts often are revocable and "unfunded," in the sense that the only "property" owned by the trustee is the designation of the trust as beneficiary of an insurance policy, typically owned by and on the life of the settlor.

 EXAMPLES AND ANALYSIS

Parent owns a policy of insurance on Parent's life. For reasons such as ensuring professional management, avoiding the costs and limitations of court supervised guardianships, and providing for children to obtain control over the proceeds only when they reach a specified age, Parent's estate plan designates a trust to hold insurance proceeds for children after Parent's death.

d. **Other.** Divorce trusts usually are used to better guarantee the settlor's obligations under a decree. Tort settlement or damage trusts usually are created by court order and held for the benefit of an injured party, often because the party is unable to manage the settlement and, perhaps, because the court does not trust their guardian or next friend with the money. Employee benefit trusts are the repositories of vast amounts of American wealth and—even more so than charitable trusts—are subject to complex tax qualification requirements and regulation. Notice that most other trusts are not subject to oversight by government agencies; courts may have jurisdiction to settle disputes if they arise, and federal and state banking and trust company examiners regulate corporate trustees—and thus indirectly the trusts they manage—but private express trusts generally are self-executing and self-governing.

3. **Implied Trusts** stand in juxtaposition to express trusts: these come in two flavors: resulting trusts and constructive trusts.

a. **Creation; duties of trustee.** Both arise by operation of law, not by actions taken by a settlor who intends to create an express trust. The trustee of a resulting or constructive trust is not charged with managing property on behalf of trust beneficiaries over time, but instead is required to convey the trust property to a rightful owner. Until that conveyance is made, the trustee's duty is to hold title to the property and preserve it for that beneficiary.

b. **Resulting trusts** are created for the benefit of the settlor (or her successors in interest) in two different kinds of situations: (i) when an express trust fails in whole or in part or (ii) when the purchase price for property is paid by one person and legal title to the property is transferred to another.

   i. **Failure of express trust.** A resulting trust may arise if a private express trust fails, is invalid in whole or in part, or to the extent the trust exceeds its original purpose and there is no disposition of the balance of the trust property. In each case the law presumes that the settlor did not intend to benefit the trustee, so a resulting trust is created in favor of the settlor or the settlor's assignees, devisees under the settlor's will, or the settlor's heirs at law.

 EXAMPLES AND ANALYSIS

D transferred Blackacre to T, in trust providing for the income to be paid to D's spouse (S) for life, remainder to D's child (C) if C survives S, otherwise to C's then living descendants, by representation. S died not survived by C or any descendant of C. T holds title to Blackacre on a resulting trust for D, if living, or D's heirs if D died intestate, or D's devisees if D died testate.

   ii. **Purchase money resulting trusts** arise in a purchase money transaction. For example, if A gave money to B to purchase Blackacre for the benefit of C (or for A, for that matter), and B completes the purchase and takes title in B's name, there may be a resulting purchase money trust even though the agreement between A and B was oral.

   iii. **Illegality.** Many purchase money trusts are oral or secret because the purpose is illegal, such as to encourage immoral or illegal acts, to defraud a spouse or creditor, or to evade alien land laws. In such cases a resulting trust likely will not be established to assist in the conduct because the resulting trust concept is equitable. Unjust enrichment to the transferee is outweighed by a policy against providing relief to anyone who enters into an illegal transaction. Thus, a trustee who refuses to perform the illegal purpose may be allowed to keep the property.

iv. **Partial resulting trusts** are possible, for example, if a testator transferred property in trust for A for life, remainder to B and C, if they survive the testator, and C predeceases the testator. There would be a resulting trust of ½ of the remainder beneficiaries.

v. **Statute of Frauds.** In no event does the resulting trust violate the Statute of Frauds (because the "trust" is not really a trust at all, it merely is a legal fiction to cover what is, in reality in many cases, the absence of a trust, as where an express trust has failed or is incomplete). Moreover, in the purchase money situation a transfer of money, not of land, was involved, making the Statute of Frauds inapplicable. In each case, Section 8 of the original English Statute of Frauds exempted these trusts from its scope.

c. **Constructive trusts** are a fiction created by equity to avoid unjust enrichment. Unlike resulting trusts, which arise on the basis of assumptions of a settlor's or payor's intent, constructive trusts are remedial.

i. **Wrongful conduct or mistake:** a transfer was induced by fraud, undue influence, mistake, or duress. Note, however, that if the transfer was by will, mistake alone usually is not a sufficient ground for relief, including imposition of a constructive trust. See Chapter 7.

ii. **Breach of confidential relation:** transfer resulted from a breach of a confidential relationship.

iii. **Retention unjust:** any other case in which retention of property by a party would be unjust. Examples include succession to property by operation of law if the successor committed a homicide that led to the succession (see Chapter 2), or wrongful interference with testation that led to the succession (see the discussion of *Latham v. Father Divine* in Chapter 3). Constructive trusts are imposed on wrongdoers and innocent parties who would benefit from the wrongdoing alike, in each case to prevent their unjust enrichment at the expense of the person with a rightful claim to the property.

Examples and Analysis

A, the owner of Blackacre, borrowed $10,000 from B. To secure the loan, A conveyed title to Blackacre to B, although there was no documentation for the loan or the "mortgage." A repaid B but B refuses to reconvey legal title to Blackacre. B holds Blackacre as constructive trustee for A.

iv. **Elements.** Constructive trusts are not common or easy to create or impose. The necessary elements for imposition usually include: (i) an express promise or an equitably implied agreement to hold the property in trust, (ii) reliance or other detriment by the injured party, (iii) unjust enrichment if the holder is allowed to retain the property, and (iv) a superior entitlement in the claimant to possession, even if that person never was legally entitled to the property.

F. **REASONS TO CREATE EXPRESS PRIVATE TRUSTS** are even more varied than the types of trusts that may be created. Common motives fall into tax and nontax oriented categories:

1. **Nontax Objectives** for using trusts probably are twice as numerous as the tax objectives, and even more likely to endure as tax laws ebb and flow.

   a. **Estate planning uses.** Trusts allow imposition of dead hand controls over future use of property, allowing the settlor, for example, to defer beneficiaries' enjoyment of property, to establish transmission that ensures accomplishment (or avoidance) of certain uses, or to reward or punish certain conduct.

   b. **Flexibility.** Coupled with judicious use of powers of appointment and trustee discretion (see Chapters 14 and 13), flexibility is inherent in trust dispositions but lacking in outright gifts.

   c. **Controls on enjoyment.** Perhaps most important, trusts make possible a sharing or bifurcation of enjoyment of property in myriad contexts. For example, a trust for a child might be designed to defer the child's control over the property until the child reaches a specified age, but to have the assets managed by someone else and available for the child's benefit in the meantime.

   d. **Group trusts.** A single fund of assets may be made available for a group, such as for children until all have received an education, followed by any remaining funds being distributed in equal shares.

   e. **Ultimate disposition.** A trust may provide benefits to one beneficiary for life, with ultimate distribution of remaining trust property to other beneficiaries. For example, trusts sometimes are used to provide for a surviving spouse for life, but guaranteeing ultimate receipt by the settlor's descendants, such as children of a former marriage. Similarly, it is possible to use a trust to provide for a son- or daughter-in-law after a child's death, while preserving principal for ultimate distribution within the blood line.

f. Benefiting multiple generations. Another common use of trusts is to provide enjoyment of benefits by successive generations without fear of dissipation through profligacy, improvidence, or inexperience.

g. Management of property. Trusts present several advantages over other property management alternatives. For example, consider the hassles of co-ownership of property by several intended beneficiaries (in operating, renting, selling, or mortgaging the underlying property, for example) as compared to having a single trustee hold title to the property for the benefit of these same beneficiaries.

   i. Management by beneficiary inappropriate. Assuming proper selection of the trustee, trust administration ensures better management if the beneficiary lacks the desire, experience, or ability to manage property given outright, or is immature or improvident and, therefore, cannot (yet) be trusted to manage the property.

   ii. Compared with agencies. Trusts permit greater flexibility and less supervision than agencies (which terminate with death in all cases, and on incapacity of the principal unless created as a "durable" power of attorney), conservatorships or guardianships, or custodianships under statutory arrangements such as the Uniform Transfers to Minors Act (which either involve court supervision or cannot be altered to fit certain needs or adapt to certain assets).

h. Protection from creditors' claims. Trusts can be used to provide funds for the use of beneficiaries without subjecting these funds to the claims of most creditors of the beneficiaries. See Chapter 13.

i. Inter vivos trusts. Finally, several additional advantages are available with respect to inter vivos trusts or declarations of trust.

   i. Probate avoidance. Most common is avoiding the inherent delay and publicity that are common in states with no form of independent probate administration, and interruption in management attendant to the public probate process in virtually all cases.

   ii. Contestability. An inter vivos trust may be invalidated or reformed on the same grounds as may other lifetime gratuitous property transfers: fraud, duress, undue influence, or mistake. But as a practical matter, successful contest of trusts is much lower than the contestability of wills.

   iii. Fees. Trustee fees often are lower than personal representative fees for performing the same functions related to death of the settlor (such as filing federal and state estate and fiduciary income tax returns, paying creditors, and distributing assets), all due to the lack of court supervision and the attendant time drain involved in probate in many jurisdictions.

    iv. **Avoiding ancillary administration.** Even if probate administration would be an easy matter, avoiding ancillary administration of out-of-state assets is desirable because it seldom is advantageous to conduct more than one probate administration.

    v. **Creditors' and spouses' claims.** Although a living trust cannot disfranchise the settlor's creditors, in some jurisdictions it is possible to disinherit a surviving spouse through creation of an inter vivos trust. See Chapter 10.

    vi. **Insurance proceeds and employee benefits.** Many astute planners recognize that insurance and receptacle trusts are an expeditious device for the receipt of employee benefits or insurance proceeds at death, permitting collection and investment before probate may begin.

    vii. **Avoiding will formalities.** Trusts are easier to execute and amend than wills (there are virtually *no* formalities in most states), permitting the use of inter vivos trusts as the primary estate planning document (coupled with a simple pour over will) to avoid the formalities of wills.

2. Tax Objectives

Tax oriented reasons for using trusts are beyond the scope of this RoadMap, but they generally entail (i) minimizing the settlor and beneficiaries' estate, gift, and generation-skipping taxes and minimizing income taxes—trusts being separate income tax paying entities that permit some income shifting.

G.   TRUST PURPOSES

Trusts may be created for any legal purpose. Assuming that no lack of capacity is evidenced by arbitrary, illogical, or capricious provisions, anything a settlor could do by an outright transfer may be done in the guise of a trust.

    1. **Invalid Purposes** usually involve attempts to do what the settlor could not do outright, such as:

        a. **Rule Against Perpetuities.** Violate limits on trust duration imposed by the Rule Against Perpetuities.

        b. **Wrongful conduct.** Encourage or reward crime, torts, or immorality.

        c. **Defraud creditors.** Property owners may create trusts that allow beneficiaries to enjoy the property free from the claims of most creditors but settlors usually cannot create trusts of their own property for their own benefit that will withstand attack by their creditors. See Chapter 13.

d. Marital rights. It is not possible to use a trust to disfranchise a surviving spouse in some states. See Chapter 10.

e. Accomplish prohibited results, such as designating impermissible appointees under a power of appointment. See Chapter 14.

2. Violate Public Policy

Trusts also may be invalid to the extent they offend public policy.

a. Familial relations. A trust may not interfere with familial relations, such as by (i) denying custody of a child (e.g., S creates a trust that will benefit P only after P agrees to grant custody of their child to S), (ii) encouraging abandonment of child support (e.g., S creates a trust that will benefit P only after P agrees to give up P's practice of paying child support to P's nonmarital child), or (iii) encouraging divorce (e.g., S creates a trust that will benefit S's child only if the child divorces her current spouse).

b. Waste. A trust may not call for destruction or waste of trust corpus. Thus, a direction to destroy trust assets would not be enforceable over the beneficiary's objection (the trustee also has standing to challenge the direction on its own motion).

3. Marriage and Divorce

Unreasonable restraints on marriage also are invalid trust purposes. The key is *"unreasonable"* restraints; the breadth and duration cannot be excessive, but some restriction is permissible. For example, a court likely would uphold a trust provision that conditioned a right to receive trust distributions on a beneficiary not being married younger than a reasonable age (e.g., 25) and a court might not invalidate a provision terminating trust benefits to a beneficiary who married outside a given faith (provided that sufficient opportunities to marry within the faith exist). See Chapter 1.

a. Divorce. Encouraging divorce might be viewed differently from providing a safety net in case thereof, the latter being valid even if the former is not. Even a skilled and careful drafter would have trouble walking the dividing line between these two objectives, and the apparent intent of the settlor likely would be significant. For example, a bequest "if X divorces _____" likely would be viewed differently from "to provide for X in the event of divorce and its effect on X's income or lifestyle": the former would fail; the latter might be valid.

b. Encouraging marriage or discouraging divorce almost certainly is copacetic, although a marriage might be abusive and the trust constitutes a financial handcuff preventing the beneficiary from breaking free, in which case it might be invalid.

c.   **Remarriage.** Restraints on *re*marriage ("in trust for S for life or until S's earlier remarriage") usually are permissible, because the trust presumably was created to support the beneficiary only while unmarried, and because there seems to be a "gigolo or golddigger" notion that the settlor should not be required to provide support to a surviving spouse (and, indirectly, a new spouse) who has found a replacement.

4.   **Restraints on Religious Freedom**

A trust conditioning enjoyment on a beneficiary changing her religion likely would be an invalid restraint on religious freedom.

5.   **Consequence of Invalidity**

The effect of an invalid trust or provision might be any of (i) a resulting trust for the settlor or her successors in interest, (ii) segregation of the invalid condition from the valid provisions to deem it met or as if it did not exist, and (iii) application of a clean hands doctrine that denies relief to anyone seeking to enforce the provision, as a way to deter future trusts of a similar variety or to punish culpability.

REVIEW QUESTIONS AND ANSWERS

Question: Parent (P) pays the purchase price for Blackacre to Seller, who conveys title to Blackacre to P's child, C. Thereafter, P manages Blackacre, leases it to a tenant, collects rent, pays insurance and taxes, and maintains it. Who is the owner of Blackacre?

Answer: C holds legal title to Blackacre. The issue is whether C is trustee for P under a resulting purchase money trust. If so, P holds equitable title to Blackacre and can demand that C convey the legal title to P. Because C is a natural object of P's bounty there is a presumption that P made a gift of Blackacre to C, which presumption may be rebutted with evidence that P intended otherwise. There may be sufficient evidence here to overcome the presumption—P's actions with respect to Blackacre, presumably taken with C's knowledge and acquiescence, appear to be those of an owner. But we need more information. For example, did P retain any net rental income or transfer it to C? Did P or C cover any shortage if the rent was inadequate to cover its expenses? Who reported the rental income and expenses for income tax purposes? What did P say when Blackacre was purchased in C's name (e.g., did P say she wanted C to have Blackacre at P's death without having to go through a probate proceeding)? Are there other natural objects of P's bounty, what other property does P own, and what provisions are in place for its disposition? What is the value of Blackacre relative to the value of P's other assets?

Question: T's will left part of T's estate in trust for T's child, C, and the balance for T's spouse, S. At T's death, C was 35 years of age and married to Inlaw; T's will provided that C may not receive distributions from the trust until the earlier of (i) C's divorce from Inlaw, (ii) Inlaw's death, or (iii) C reaching age 65. T's will also provides that S will be a beneficiary of the trust until the earlier to occur of S's death or remarriage. Are the trusts for C and S valid?

Answer: With respect to the trust for C, the issue is whether T's dominant motive for limiting C's beneficial interest in the trust was to provide for C's support if C became single, or to encourage C to divorce Inlaw. If the former, the trust provisions are valid; if the latter, the prohibition on distributions to C while married to Inlaw is invalid. Drawing the line between the two may be impossible if the settlor's motive is both. *In re Estate of Donner*, 623 A.2d 307 (N.J. Super. App. Div. 1993), upheld a similar trust notwithstanding that the testator strongly disliked the in-law.

The trust for S is valid. The provision terminating the surviving spouse's interest upon remarriage is enforceable and the public policy against discouraging marriage usually does not apply to a trust created for a surviving spouse.

12 TRUST CREATION

CHAPTER OVERVIEW

- Among the more significant requirements for the creation of a valid trust are that the settlor intended to create a trust, there is at least one ascertainable beneficiary, and the trust has a corpus.

- Although—as a general rule—trusts for realty (but not personalty) must be in writing, the exceptions to that rule are numerous enough to call it into question.

- Precatory language (e.g., hope or request) usually means that there was no intent to create a trust and the transferee takes the property free of trust.

- Except for charitable trusts, generally a trust must have at least one beneficiary who is ascertainable and able to enforce the trustee's fiduciary obligations.

A. CREATING A TRUST

The most common ways to create a trust are by a testamentary devise (a testamentary trust), an inter vivos transfer (an inter vivos or living trust), and a declaration by a property owner that she holds property as trustee (a self-trusteed declaration of trust).

1. Requisites for Trust Validity

The requisites to create a valid trust are: (i) a *legal purpose* (see Chapter 11), (ii) a manifestation of the settlor's *intent*, (iii) to impose *active duties* on a trustee, (iv) a trust *corpus*, (v) which requires a settlor with the requisite *capacity* to convey property to fund the trust, (vi) one or more *beneficiaries*, and (vii) generally, for a testamentary trust or a trust of land, a *written instrument*.

a. Capacity. Other than the writing requirement for testamentary trusts and inter vivos trusts of realty, there are virtually no formalities for the creation of a trust other than the requirements that property law imposes on the transfer of the trust corpus.

b. Settlor imposed requirements. The document itself, however, may create additional requirements to amend or revoke the trust. (See *Pilafas* in Chapter 6.)

c. Compare with will requirements. Notice how very different the trust creation rules are from the law of wills (e.g., generally, witnesses are not required for the creation of a trust).

2. Not Required for Trust Validity

A valid trust may be created without (i) a trustee (in the absence of a trustee, the court will appoint one), (ii) consideration (most transfers in trust are gratuitous), or (iii) notice to or acceptance by the trustee or the beneficiaries.

B. INTENT AND CAPACITY

A trust cannot be created unless there is a proper manifestation of intent by a competent settlor. For testamentary trusts, the manifestation of intent must appear in a valid will. For inter vivos trusts of land, the Statute of Frauds usually requires a written instrument. For other inter vivos trusts, the settlor's intent to create a trust relationship may be manifested orally, in writing, or by conduct.

1. Capacity

The capacity required to create a valid trust depends on the nature of the trust created.

a. Testamentary trust. To create a valid testamentary trust the settlor must have the capacity to execute a will. See Chapter 3. Thus, absent unusual circumstances—a derangement that affects a testamentary trust, but not the remainder of the will, for example—a testator who had the requisite capacity to execute a valid will has the capacity to create a testamentary trust under that will.

b. Revocable inter vivos trust. Surprisingly, there is not much law on the capacity required to create a revocable, inter vivos trust. Arguably the settlor must have only testamentary capacity to validly create a trust that serves as a will substitute. Inter vivos trusts, however, require a transfer of property (see the discussion of *Farkas v. Williams* in Chapter

6); accordingly, the somewhat higher capacity necessary to make a valid conveyance of property by gift may be required.

c. **Irrevocable inter vivos trust.** Required is the same capacity to make a valid gift free of trust.

2. Questions of Intent

The issue whether a trust was meant to be imposed seldom arises unless the trust was poorly drafted or an alleged trust is oral or secret or both.

a. **Substance controls.** A trust is a relationship under which trustees with fiduciary duties hold legal title to property to manage it on behalf of beneficiaries. The requisite intent is to create that relationship. Words like "trustee" or "trust" do not alone create a trust but their presence in a document may be indicative of an intent to create a trust; their absence is indicative of nothing.

   i. *Jimenez.* For example, in *Jimenez v. Lee*, 547 P.2d 126 (Or. 1976), a father was accountable to his daughter as a trustee when gifts for the daughter's education were made shortly after her birth. There was no trust instrument nor any express mention made of the creation of a trust. Trusts nevertheless were created because the transfers were made with the intent that the gifts be held for the benefit of the daughter.

b. **Incomplete gift vs. declaration of trust.** A valid lifetime gift requires delivery (actual, constructive, or symbolic delivery). If a donor expresses an intent to make a gift but never makes a delivery, most courts will not save the "gift" by recharacterizing the donor's conduct as a declaration that the donor holds the property as a trustee for the benefit of the donee. See, e.g., *The Hebrew University Ass'n v. Nye*, 169 A.2d 641 (Conn. 1961), in which a donor's public declaration that she gave a collection of undelivered rare books to a university did not constitute a declaration of trust because there was no indication that the donor intended to create a trust relationship by assuming fiduciary duties before the books were delivered to the university.

3. Precatory Language

If a transferor transfers property with a request that the transferee use the property in a specified manner, the question is whether the "request" was meant to bind the transferee. If so (and the other requirements of a valid trust are met) the transferee holds the property as trustee with fiduciary duties to do as "requested"; if not, the transferee takes the property as a donee, free of restrictions. Whether precatory language in the dispositive provisions of a will or trust (desire, hope, wish, recommend, or suggest) is binding creates perhaps the most uncertainty with respect to the intent requirement for the creation of a trust.

EXAMPLES AND ANALYSIS

- "I give the contents of my home to my daughter, with the hope and expectation that she will share them with her brother and sister." This might be meant to create a trust (it is likely the testator intended the daughter to divide the contents among the three), but it likely would be held to be a transfer to the daughter free of trust. (This form disposition illustrates another method some testators use to accomplish the results authorized by the list of tangible personal property that UPC §2-513 addresses, as discussed in Chapter 3.)

- "I give $X to my son and request that he pay my sister-in-law $208.33 per month until her death." Notwithstanding the "request," a court might read this as a "polite command" creating a trust and, given the specificity involved, it is sufficiently detailed to be enforceable. (Notice that this language also raises a question of what disposition is to be made of any funds remaining from the original gift after the sister-in-law's death; likely they belong to the son.)

- "To my wife, to be her absolute estate forever. I request that she leave the property to my siblings." This hard case probably is not a trust. The gift is absolute, in fee simple; the alleged obligation is in precatory words, and the notion might be that the spouses had discussed how things probably would go when they both were dead and this statement just reflected that planning, leaving it up to the survivor to do what he or she thought was best given any changes in circumstances between the dates of their deaths. (See also the discussion of the "rule of repugnancy" in Chapter 14.) If it were regarded as a trust, however, the surviving spouse—as both trustee and beneficiary for life—would have full power to consume the property for reasonable needs and purposes during life and would be obliged to transfer only the amount that remained at the survivor's death.

a. **Factors to consider.** In interpreting devises accompanied by precatory language, the usual inference is that the testator left the property to the devisee, unencumbered by a trust, with the intention that the devisee decide whether to follow the suggestion. Factors that may indicate an intent to create a trust include:

   i. **Identity of transferee.** Presumably there is an intent to create a trust if the precatory language is directed to an unrelated person. Directing precatory language to a natural object of a decedent's bounty presumably is a gift with no strings attached. However, the same direction to a close relation may be regarded as a polite command, with the possible imposition of a trust.

   ii. **Relative size of the purported trust.** Small amounts given to natural objects of the decedent's bounty likely are outright gifts.

Large amounts, especially if transferred to someone other than a natural object of the transferor's bounty, likely are trusts.

iii.   **Lifetime gifts.** The precatory language may extend a lifetime pattern of gratuitous transfers.

iv.   **Relative financial positions.** The relative financial positions of the purported trustee and beneficiary may indicate a trust if the former is flush and the latter is less so.

 ## EXAMPLES AND ANALYSIS

D supported an elderly and needy sibling (X) for several years before D's death. D's will devised the estate to D's spouse (S), with the "request that S continue to provide for X, as S thinks appropriate." D's estate is more than adequate to provide for X's continued care, and S has significantly more resources than may reasonably be needed for S's future support. Despite the use of the word "request," which usually is deemed to be precatory, S probably takes D's estate in trust for the combined support of S and X, with a duty to make reasonable provision for X's care.

v.   **Specificity of language.** Is the language specific enough to enforce as a trust (e.g., there are identifiable beneficiaries, specific terms, and a clearly defined property meant to be held)? If so, the intent to create a trust is more likely to be found; if not, and the requisite intent nevertheless is found, the result probably is an unenforceable semi-secret trust with a resulting trust back to the settlor's estate. (Semi-secret trusts are discussed below.)

vi.   **The equities.** The presumption against an intent to create a trust when precatory language is used may yield to equitable persuasions.

b.   **Distinguish lack of intent from lack of enforceable terms.** The precatory language issue is whether the transferor intended to create a trust; also important is whether an intended trust has terms sufficiently specific to be enforceable.

 ## EXAMPLES AND ANALYSIS

T's will provides: "I give all my personal effects to A, to be distributed as A deems would be my wish." X's will provides: "I give all my personal effects to A, to be disposed of according to the terms of a letter to be found with this will'' (and no letter exists). Each potential trust would fail for lack of enforceable terms, even if an intent to create a trust is deemed to exist. Notice, however, that if an intent to create a trust is found, the trustee would not be allowed to keep the property, as she would if there was no such intent and the language accompanying the devise is deemed to be precatory. The result would be a resulting trust, to be distributed to the residuary beneficiaries of the testator's estate.

C.   THE TRUSTEE

Trusts may have one or more trustees, who may be individuals or entities (such as a corporation).

1.   Capacity to Serve

The requisite capacity to act as trustee is that capacity required to hold legal title to property. Generally anyone who can hold legal title may be a trustee—which is not to say that just anyone is skillful enough to do the job properly and avoid liability for their inabilities.

a.   Incapacitated individual trustee. A minor or mental incompetent can hold legal title and thus could serve as trustee, but each also could be removed because of their inability to perform their duties, either permanently or until capacity is gained or restored, depending on the circumstances.

b.   Corporate trustee. Usually an entity such as a corporation may not serve as a trustee unless it has received a charter or other permission to do so from the applicable governmental agency.

c.   Foreign corporations. Foreign corporations and similar entities may have problems holding title to property as trustee due to local law limitations on ownership of land by an alien (which, for this purpose, refers to anyone not from within that jurisdiction). Thus, corporate (or similar entity) trustees from one state might not be able to serve in another. Many states have reciprocity statutes under which an out-of-state trustee may serve within their borders if their trustees may serve in the other state. Others may prohibit out-of-state trustees unless there is a resident agent for service of process (which is an easy condition to satisfy).

d.   Settlor as trustee. The settlor may serve as a trustee (e.g., in a self-trusteed declaration of trust), which is very popular with people who want to avoid probate and therefore find a trust attractive during life, but who do not want to relinquish control or incur trustee fees before they become unable to manage their own property.

     e. **Beneficiary as trustee.** Similarly, a beneficiary may serve as a trustee (although the sole beneficiary of a trust may not serve as its sole trustee).

2. Requirement of a Trustee

A trust must have a trustee, yet "no trust will fail for lack of a trustee."

     a. **Failure of a trustee.** If no trustee is named but it is clear that a trust was intended, or if the named trustee is unable or unwilling to act and the instrument does not provide for a successor, a court will appoint a trustee unless it is absolutely clear that the named trustee was meant to be the one and only—which would be quite rare.

     b. **Vacancy.** The document should provide for succession but a court will appoint a successor if a vacancy occurs because there is no appointment process designated in the document, or the named successors are unable or unwilling to act, or those who were designated to select a successor no longer are available to act, etc.

     c. **A trustee must own trust assets.** Property does not care who owns it, but it must *have* an owner, and that is no different with a trust: someone must own the legal title to trust assets at all times and, at a minimum, a duty to convey it to the next proper trustee or outright owner. Thus, if there is a complete vacancy in the office of trustee, a court must guarantee that the trust assets have an owner.

          i. **Resignation of sole trustee.** For this reason, typically any resignation of a sole trustee (a voluntary act and not an unavoidable vacancy) is effective only upon conveyance of legal title of the trust assets to a successor trustee.

         ii. **Unexpected or involuntary vacancy.** If that is not possible, because a vacancy was not avoidable or voluntary, a constructive trust may be imposed on the last predecessor trustee or successors in interest, to convey the trust corpus to the next trustee once one is appointed. Alternatively, if the trust terminated, a resulting trust would be imposed pending conveyance of the trust property to the proper remainder beneficiary.

3. Cotrustees

Multiple trustees generally must act unanimously to bind the trust, although the instrument may provide otherwise and statutes in some jurisdictions allow a majority to act on behalf of the trust.

     a. **Failure of one cotrustee.** If one of several trustees fails to become or ceases to act, the remaining trustee(s) continue to hold title to all the trust assets, but a successor trustee is required and will be appointed—unless the trust expresses a contrary intent by indicating that no successor be named. In that case a replacement is required only if there is no remaining trustee.

4.   To Serve or Not to Serve

Substantial fiduciary duties expose trustees to significant liabilities. As a result, no one can be forced to serve as trustee, and a named trustee need not act. Rather, a named trustee can decline to serve by timely filing a declination to act, which would be effective to avoid ever putting on the fiduciary mantle. But if the trustee does not timely decline, the trustee may resign only if authority to resign is granted in the document or a court expressly grants the power to resign. This is no small matter and, once undertaken, the fiduciary duty is not easily thrown off.

5.   Removal of Trustees for cause is one of several options available to a court in the wake of fiduciary malfeasance or incompetence (the others including reducing or eliminating the trustee's fees or surcharging—imposing damages on—the trustee).

a.   Cause required for removal. Often, cause sufficient to warrant removal is difficult or impossible to prove and, unless the instrument provides otherwise, a trustee generally cannot be removed without a showing of cause. Generally, cause exists if the trustee's service creates a serious risk of loss to the beneficiaries. Among grounds that have been held sufficient to remove a trustee for cause are a material breach of fiduciary duty, conviction of a crime involving dishonesty, and incapacity.

b.   Power to remove without cause. Many documents give someone (a beneficiary or a "trust protector") authority to remove and replace trustees, often based on a list of factors such as too frequent turnover in the trust officer, takeover of the trustee by another institution, excessive fees, inadequate investment performance, drug addiction or other personal problems of the fiduciary, a move out of state by the beneficiary, and so forth.

6.   Liabilities of Trustees

Unless the document provides otherwise (which it often does, particularly with respect to successor trustee liabilities):

a.   Cotrustee liabilities are joint and several. This explains why each trustee (if they understand their exposure) will charge a full fee (and maybe more), rather than split one fee: each is fully responsible—indeed each is responsible for the other's mistakes too—instead of shared responsibility.

b.   Successor trustee liabilities exist for any failure to redress improper acts of a predecessor trustee. This explains why a successor will charge a fee for accepting a trust: the successor must inspect the accounts of the predecessor to be sure it receives all it should or sues for any losses, mismanagement, etc. attributable to the predecessor.

7. Sole Beneficiary as Sole Trustee

The doctrine of merger applies if the sole beneficiary is sole trustee. A trustee cannot sue itself to enforce the trust, meaning the trust fails: legal and equitable title become one ("merge") and the trust automatically ceases to exist.

a. Self-trusteed declaration of trust. A self-trusteed declaration of trust is one in which the settlor, trustee, and beneficiary are all the same at inception, which would suggest that the trust should fail or collapse due to merger. It does not because there is at least one other beneficiary—with at least a contingent future interest at the settlor's death—and that interest is enough to preclude merger and failure.

b. Sole beneficiary as cotrustee. A sole beneficiary may be one of several cotrustees because trustees hold title as joint tenants, meaning that a total merger cannot occur even if a trustee is the only beneficiary.

c. Cobeneficiary as sole trustee. Although the legal justification is a bit hazy, a cobeneficiary may be a sole trustee because, absent a partition, the cobeneficiaries cannot purport to possess some appropriate fraction of the equitable title, so there will be no merger even with respect to an undivided fraction of the trust.

d. Cobeneficiaries as cotrustees. Cobeneficiaries may act as cotrustees because their titles as trustee (joint tenants) and beneficiary (tenants in common) differ and therefore cannot merge.

8. Trustee Tax Considerations

Depending on the powers the trustee possesses, adverse tax consequences may result from a settlor or a beneficiary serving as a trustee. These consequences cannot be avoided by naming a third party as trustee if the settlor or beneficiary may remove the third party and name herself as successor trustee.

D. TRUST PROPERTY

A trust is a relationship with respect to property; the essence of the relationship is that title to property is bifurcated with one person, the trustee, holding the legal title subject to a fiduciary obligation to manage it on behalf of another, the beneficiary, who holds the equitable or beneficial title. Accordingly, generally there must be a corpus (also called principal or *res*) and it must be ascertainable to have a valid trust; a trust can exist (temporarily) with no trustee and with beneficiaries to be identified in the future, but generally there cannot be a dry trust (one with no property).

1. From Active to Passive to Dry

In addition, a trust becomes a passive trust once it has completed its purpose and no longer has a function to serve. It must distribute its property and then cease to exist by virtue of becoming a dry trust.

 ## EXAMPLES AND ANALYSIS

D devised property to T, in trust, to provide for the education of A and B. At termination the trust is distributable equally between them. B completes law school at the age of 26. A previously completed medical school. If A and B have completed their educations, the purpose of the trust has been accomplished, T has no further duties to perform (meaning that the trust is passive), the assets will be distributed equally to A and B, and the trust will become dry and thereby terminate.

2. An Ascertainable Corpus

The ascertainable corpus requirement can be a slippery concept; the existence of a corpus must be ascertainable, but neither the value, duration, nor the extent of the property need be. The trustee must own something to prevent existence of a totally dry trust, which would terminate, but that something does not need to be much. A viable trust property interest may be a present or a future interest, with vested or contingent title, legal or equitable ownership (a trust can be beneficiary of another trust), in real or personal property. So this corpus hurdle is not particularly high.

3. The Expectation of Property

Generally, the settlor's expectation of owning property in the future cannot constitute the corpus of a trust. Thus, for example, if a child executes a trust instrument under which she purports to hold in trust for the benefit of a third party part or all of the property she expects to inherit from her living parent, there is no trust res and no valid trust. Upon the death of her parent, however, any rights of the child to a share of her parent's estate may become a trust asset and validate the trust at that time.

 ## EXAMPLES AND ANALYSIS

An author intends to write a book (but has no contract with a publisher to do so; if there were such a contract, the author's rights under it could constitute the corpus of a trust). The author agrees to hold in trust any royalties from the sale in the future of the book. The expectation of receiving royalties in the future cannot be trust property. But if the trust otherwise is valid, and if it is funded with something (e.g., $1) to support it between the time the author executes the trust and the time she actually earns a royalty, those future royalties, if any, may become trust assets when they spring into existence, *provided that* (i) a valid contract right exists, supported by consideration, between the author and the trust (which is not likely), or (ii) a reaffirmation of intent to entrust the royalties occurs when they come into existence; often inaction will suffice if the trustee treats the asset as belonging to the trust and no one objects. In our author's case she probably would need to endorse the royalty check and then hold the proceeds in a trust capacity (e.g., in a separate bank account titled in the name of the trust).

---

a. *In re Estate of Brenner,* 547 P.2d 938 (Colo. Ct. App. 1976), involved a declaration of trust by a settlor of real property that the settlor did not own at the time of the declaration. The property, however, was acquired shortly after the declaration, with title being taken in the name of the settlor, as trustee. In rejecting a challenge to the trust, the court held that acquisition of the property in the name of the trust validated the trust: "Where, as here, an individual manifests an intention to create a trust in property to be acquired in the future, and thereafter confirms this intent by taking the steps necessary to transfer the property to the trust, the property so transferred becomes subject to the terms of the trust."

b. *Brainard v. Commissioner,* 91 F.2d 880 (7th Cir. 1937), an income tax case, is consistent with *Brenner.* In *Brainard* the taxpayer orally declared a trust of any stock trading profits he might earn in the next year. Profits were earned the next year and they were reported for income tax purposes by the trust beneficiaries. The issue whether the taxpayer, instead, was taxable on the income turned on whether unearned profits expected from future stock trading could be held in trust on behalf of the taxpayer's family members. According to the court, an interest that has not come into existence cannot be held in trust; the declaration to do so for the unearned stock trading profits amounted to no more than an unenforceable—for lack of consideration—promise to create a trust in the future. The profits thus belonged to the taxpayer when earned and were taxable to him. The trust, however, did not fail.

Rather, as the profits were earned, the taxpayer credited them on his books to accounts for the beneficiaries, which was a sufficient manifestation of intent to cause the profits to become trust assets at that time.

EXAMPLES AND ANALYSIS

If the taxpayer in *Brainard* had declared that he held his stock—and not just the profits he expected to earn from the stock—in trust for others for a specified term, the trust clearly would have been valid; the stock would have constituted the corpus and the tax objective would have been achieved. (Note that *Brainard* was a 1937 case. Under current tax law, such a course of action might not succeed in shifting the income earned during the trust term to the trust beneficiaries for tax purposes.)

EXAMPLES AND ANALYSIS

A orally declares herself trustee for B of a percentage of the royalties A expects to earn on a book A is writing. A writes the book, sells it, and begins receiving royalties, but refuses to hold any of them in trust for B. If there is no delivery of a written assignment the oral statement likely would be viewed as one of intent to make a gift in the future and not a valid trust creation. There usually is no delivery requirement for declarations of trust: if A declares she holds a painting in trust for B, a valid trust is created. But when the subject of the gift in trust is property not yet in existence, a delivery requirement—in the form of a writing, may be imposed. At a minimum, there should be a valid trust if, after the book is written and there are royalties, A sufficiently manifests a reaffirmation of her intent to hold a percentage of the royalties in trust for B. But without such a manifestation of intent, made after the royalties come into existence, there probably is no trust.

4.   Unfunded Life Insurance Trusts

One of the more difficult issues in this area is how an unfunded life insurance trust (i.e., a trust is created today; no assets are transferred to it, but it is named the beneficiary of a life insurance policy) is supportable under the trust property requirement.

a.   **Contract rights.** Most courts would regard an unfunded life insurance trust as valid because the beneficiary designation under the policy is deemed adequate to create a present interest (subject to defeasance on change of the beneficiary designation or lapse of the policy) sufficient to constitute the trust corpus. The Comment to UPC §2-511, in noting that the contract right to the proceeds of the policy on the insured's death is the trust res, takes the position that the term "unfunded life insurance trust" is a misnomer: "the term 'unfunded life-insurance trust' does not refer to an unfunded trust, but to a funded trust that has not received *additional* funding.''

b. **Additional funding.** Nevertheless, many lawyers will fund an insurance trust with an EE U.S. Government savings bond (or its $25 purchase price) to guarantee that there is a corpus. It is a prudent investment and requires no administration; you just hold it until it matures (and thereafter if you want), earning interest that accrues and requires no action, so no fee and no liability is incurred during the interim waiting for the insurance to mature and pay proceeds to the trust.

5. Uniform Testamentary Additions to Trust Act

An exception to the requirement that a trust have a corpus is found in the Uniform Testamentary Additions to Trust Act. A trust named as the devisee under the settlor's will is valid—as is the pour over from the settlor's estate under the will—without regard to whether it is funded with any assets prior to the settlor's death. See Chapter 6.

6. Trustee's Debt Obligation as Trust Property

Of real practical import is the rule that a trustee cannot hold its own debt obligation without special authorization.

EXAMPLES AND ANALYSIS

S executes a trust instrument naming T as trustee for B, funded with Blackacre. Later, T sells Blackacre to S for its fair market value, S paying with S's promissory note, payable two years later. This is no problem because S's debt obligation is property that T can enforce. But if T ceased to serve as trustee and S becomes the successor trustee, S's note no longer can be trust property because S cannot sue S to enforce it.

a. **Merger.** Because a trustee cannot sue itself to collect on its own obligation, the debt is said to be extinguished by merger. This would result in an obvious unjust enrichment to the trustee (S, in our example), which would generate a resulting trust with a court appointed ''trustee to collect'' charged with the duty to force S to pay the debt.

b. **Corporate trustees** would encounter this problem regularly with respect to deposits they make of uninvested trust cash in their own banking department were it not for authority granted by a Comptroller of the Currency regulation. Required is a security deposit by the trustee of its own marketable securities or U.S. government bonds equal to the amount of the cash deposit—reduced by the amount of any deposits that are FDIC insured. Merger technically occurs, but the trust has a right to an equitable remedy in the form of the security interest, and this prevents extinguishment by merger.

E.   NECESSITY OF A TRUST BENEFICIARY

The beneficiaries are the persons or entities for whose benefit property is held in trust by the trustee(s). Although a trust may have as few as just one beneficiary (as long as that beneficiary is not the sole trustee), the great majority of trusts have multiple beneficiaries, often seriatim. A trust beneficiary may have a present interest in the trust (e.g., "income to A for life") or a future interest (e.g., "remainder to B"); the interest may be vested or contingent (e.g., "but if B does not survive A, remainder to C").

1.   Who May Be a Trust Beneficiary

Anyone with capacity to hold title (the equitable interest) may be a trust beneficiary, including minors, incompetents, entities like corporations and partnerships and, depending on their status under state law, foreign corporations and individual aliens.

2.   Beneficiaries Must Be Ascertainable

The most significant trust beneficiary issue is whether a trust *has* at least one ascertainable beneficiary—someone who is able to enforce the trust. Without at least one beneficiary there can be no bifurcation of title and no one to whom the trustee's duties run.

    a. *Clark.* For example, in *Clark v. Campbell*, 133 A. 166 (N.H. 1926), the testator devised various items of tangible personal property to his "trustees" to be distributed by them to "such of my friends as they, my trustees, shall select." Because the beneficiaries of the trust were not objectively ascertainable, the trust failed and the gift was ineffective.

    b. **Beneficiaries identified by class.** It is not necessary to specifically identify each beneficiary of a trust—beneficiaries often are described by class (e.g., "my children") and may include future-borns as well as living persons. The problem arises if a class of beneficiaries is named and it is not possible to determine objectively any members of the class. Granting discretion to a trustee to select beneficiaries from a class of members who are not objectively ascertainable is not objectionable because the trustee has discretion; it is problematic if the discretion is too broad to be enforced.

        i. **Permissible class descriptions.** Sufficiently narrow classes of potential beneficiaries include descendants, employees (at a certain time), and heirs (if the designated ancestor is deceased). "Relatives" is problematic: it may be construed to mean heirs, in which case it would be an ascertainable class, but if it is construed to mean anyone related to the settlor, no matter how remotely, the trust likely would fail for indefiniteness of beneficiaries.

ii.   **Impermissible class descriptions.** Consider also how "family," "friends," "anyone the trustee may wish to select," or "those the trustee knows the settlor would have wanted" would be enforced if the designated trustee is unable or unwilling to serve and a replacement is required to exercise this discretion. And how would a court review the exercise even by the original trustee if other individuals claim that they should have been selected? For these reasons, such classes should not be used; they invite disputes and, as in *Clark*, likely would result in trust failure.

iii.   **Enforcement.** There is no problem if the trustee selects (and no one objects); the issue arises if the trustee refuses to select the beneficiaries (typically coupled with a claim that the trustee is entitled to retain the "trust" property), or if the settlor's successors in interest—those who would take the property if the trust fails—challenge its validity. A major trust law principle is that a court will not exercise discretion on behalf of a trustee; it only will judge whether the trustee properly exercised the discretion granted. Therefore, required are sufficient guidelines or standards—in this context, for the selection of beneficiaries—for a court to exercise its review.

c.   **Trustee's discretion to select beneficiaries compared to power of appointment.** Although trustee discretion to select beneficiaries in some respects does not differ in function from a power of appointment (see Chapter 14) in a beneficiary or fiduciary powers to distribute income or corpus, the difficulty is that these powers need not be exercised while the selection of beneficiaries is imperative. (Also, with respect to a fiduciary power to distribute income or corpus, the beneficiaries to whom distributions may be made may enforce the trustee's obligation to exercise the discretion reasonably and in good faith; by contrast, if the discretion is to select the beneficiaries in the first place, there is no one to enforce the trust.)

EXAMPLES AND ANALYSIS

D devised property to T, in trust, for Spouse (S) and Child (C) for S's life. The instrument directed T to distribute income to S and authorized T to make discretionary distributions of principal to S and C to provide for their best interests. D's will also granted S a testamentary power to appoint by will the takers of the property remaining in the trust at S's death; property as to which S did not exercise the power is distributable to D's then living descendants, by representation. T is not required to exercise the discretionary power to invade principal; failure to do so simply results in the principal being preserved for distribution at S's death. Similarly, S is not required to exercise the testamentary power of appointment; failure to do so results in the property passing at S's death to D's descendants. But if D's will had devised the property to T, in trust, with distribution at S's death to those persons T believes D would have wanted to benefit, T would be required to select the beneficiaries and there would be no way for a court objectively to determine who the beneficiaries should be and thus who could enforce the trust. Accordingly, the remainder interest in the trust would fail.

---

    i. **Power coupled with a trust.** The trustees argued unsuccessfully in *Clark* that their power to select the takers of the testator's tangible personal property should be valid as a power of appointment. The court regarded the trustees as holding an imperative power to select beneficiaries—a "power coupled with a trust," which is unlike a simple power of appointment because it must be exercised. As a result, the trust principle that there must be an ascertainable beneficiary applied and the trust/imperative power failed.

    ii. **Power not coupled with a trust.** With a simple power of appointment—not coupled with a trust—a failure to appoint simply causes trust corpus to pass to "default" beneficiaries designated by the creator of the power in the document (or provided by court order, through a resulting trust; see Chapter 14). In any case the trustee would not be allowed to keep the trust property.

  d. **Ascertainable beneficiaries are not required** by the Restatement (Second) of Trusts, which provides that a trust for an indefinite class of beneficiaries is valid if the trustee chooses to act, its acts are not outside the scope of its discretion, and the class is sufficiently definite to ascertain whether any person falls within it. But this is not the majority position and the standard rule is that there must be an enforceable identification of the beneficiaries.

  e. **Charitable trusts** do not need ascertainable beneficiaries—the public is considered the beneficiary of a charitable trust, with its rights enforceable by the state attorney general. See the Website.

3. Honorary Trusts

Because their purposes are viewed as worthy of protection, honorary trusts (e.g., for the care of a pet or a grave site or for the erection of a monument, the trust being "honorary" because the trustee is on its honor to comply, there being no human who can enforce the trust) are an exception to the rule requiring an ascertainable beneficiary. The trust is valid *if* the trustee complies. Silly as this may seem, this is not a minor problem—lots of people attempt to create mechanisms to provide for their surviving "dependents" (pets—their legal dependents, if any, having grown up and become self-supporting). Indeed, this is so common that there are state and federal inheritance and income tax rulings involving these trusts.

 # EXAMPLES AND ANALYSIS

D's will devises a cat, Jake, to a friend (F) and leaves $2,500 to T, in trust, for Jake's care. The trust for Jake is an honorary trust; T may agree to serve as trustee and administer the trust for Jake. If T is not willing to do so, or attempts to use the trust funds for other purposes, a court will order a resulting trust for D's residuary beneficiaries.

a.   *In re Searight's Estate,* 95 N.E.2d 779 (Ohio Ct. App. 1950), involved two gifts by a testator—one of his dog, Trixie, to Florence, and a second of $1,000 in trust, from which Florence was to be paid $0.75 per day for Trixie's care. This trust was upheld by the court and shows how to avoid the honorary trust problem. This was not an honorary trust because Trixie was given to a person who was made the trust beneficiary and who therefore could sue to enforce the trust. That is the key. An added advantage would exist if the trustee was directed to oversee the individual's care of the pet and to place the pet with a different individual (who then would become the trust beneficiary) if necessary.

4.   If Ascertainable Beneficiaries Are Not Named

The effect if no ascertainable beneficiaries are named is a failure of the trust and a resulting trust for the settlor or his or her successors in interest. The property is returned, the sole obligation under the resulting trust being distribution of the trust corpus to the settlor or the settlor's successors in interest.

a.   **Unborns as the sole beneficiaries.** An exception to the rule that a trust will fail without an ascertainable beneficiary exists if the trust is for unborns and a possibility of birth or adoption exists that would solve the lack of beneficiary problem. A resulting trust would be maintained pending the birth of a child, probably to accumulate income while awaiting the existence of a beneficiary. Once beneficiaries are born or adopted, the trust is then held for those beneficiaries, according to the trust terms. If the possibility for births or adoptions expires without a beneficiary having been generated (e.g., if the trust is for the settlor's grandchildren and there are none, then on the death of the last of the deceased settlor's children), the resulting trust would terminate by distribution to the settlor or his or her successors in interest.

   b.   Trustee refusal to select. Another exception may apply to the rare case in which no beneficiaries are named because the trustee refuses to exercise its authority to select, but a definite and reasonably small class of potential beneficiaries exists, in which case an implied default or power in trust may cause the class from which the trustee could select to be given equal shares. See Chapter 14.

F.   ABSENCE OF NOTICE TO OR ACCEPTANCE BY TRUSTEE OR BENEFICIARY

A trust can be validly created without prior notice to any trustee or beneficiary. A court will appoint a trustee if necessary. Similarly, validity is not dependent on a beneficiary having notice of the creation of the trust or accepting benefits under it. If the settlor also is the trustee, however, the failure to notify any beneficiary of the trust may evidence the settlor's lack of intent to create a present trust.

1.   Disclaimer by a Beneficiary

If a named trust beneficiary refuses to accept the beneficial interest— usually by disclaiming it (see Chapter 2)—the interest will pass according to the terms of the instrument that created the trust, if it addresses that possibility, or under applicable state law if it does not. A resulting trust for the settlor or her successors in interest arises if the sole beneficiary refuses to accept the beneficial interest, or all beneficiaries refuse their interests.

G.   ORAL TRUSTS

The great majority of trusts are created by written instrument; in some circumstances, however, a writing is not required to create a valid trust.

1.   Testamentary Trusts

The Statute of Wills prohibits extrinsic evidence used to alter or establish a testamentary trust of *either* realty or personalty. As a result, a testamentary trust may be validly created only by the terms of a validly executed will.

2.   Inter Vivos Trusts

The Statute of Frauds only prohibits the use of extrinsic evidence to establish or prove an oral trust of *realty*. Thus, an inter vivos trust of personalty may be created orally.

3.   The Writing Requirement

Required under the Statute of Wills to create a valid testamentary trust, or under the Statute of Frauds to create a valid trust of realty, is a signed writing identifying the trust (i) property, (ii) purposes, and (iii) beneficiaries.

    a.   Extrinsic evidence. Absent fraud, duress, undue influence, mistake, etc., extrinsic evidence is admissible only to the extent it does not contradict any express terms of a trust; otherwise it cannot be used to vary the expressly stated intent. Unlike the case with a will (see Chapter 7), extrinsic evidence generally is admissible to prove a mistake in a trust and reform the document to correct it. Extrinsic evidence of fraud, duress, or undue influence is admissible; if it is proven that a trust was created under any of those circumstances, it may fail, or perhaps be enforceable without a writing that otherwise would be required. Note that a court may admit extrinsic evidence to establish whether there was a fraud or another basis for enforcing the oral trust, but then ignore it if the court determines that there was not. Quaere how well a court that has heard the evidence for the one purpose then puts it out of mind for purposes of the balance of the case.

    b.   Ambiguities. As is the case with wills, extrinsic evidence is admissible to resolve latent ambiguities in trust instruments and usually is admissible to resolve patent ambiguities as well. See Chapter 7.

4.   Enforcing Oral Trusts of Realty

There are exceptions to the general rule that a trust of realty will not be enforced in the absence of a writing. In *Hieble v. Hieble*, 316 A.2d 777 (Conn. 1972), for example, a mother who had recently undergone surgery and believed she might be terminally ill transferred real estate to her son and daughter as joint tenants subject to an oral agreement that she would remain in control of the property, and that if her condition improved they would reconvey the property to her at her request. When requested to reconvey, the daughter complied; the son, however, refused. In upholding the trust, the court avoided the Statute of Frauds by creating a constructive trust, to prevent the son's overreaching and unjust enrichment, based on the confidential relationship between the settlor and her son. (For a discussion of constructive trusts, see Chapter 11.)

a. **Compare** *Pappas v. Pappas*, 320 A.2d 809 (Conn. 1973), in which a father conveyed realty to his son in anticipation of a divorce from a second spouse, the son having agreed to reconvey after the divorce. In the divorce proceedings the father testified that the conveyance to the son was for consideration; after the divorce the father asked the son to reconvey the property. The son refused and the father's suit to recover the property was unsuccessful: he had unclean hands as a result of his misrepresentation to the divorce court of the nature of the transfer to his son, so the court refused to grant the equitable remedy of a constructive trust.

b. **Exceptions to the Statute of Frauds or Statute of Wills.** In several other circumstances an oral trust of realty may be valid despite the Statute of Frauds and the Statute of Wills.

   i. **Compliance by the trustee.** First, the absence of a writing does not invalidate the purported trust if the trustee chooses to comply, because only the holder of legal title (the trustee) may assert the defense of the Statute of Wills or of the Statute of Frauds.

EXAMPLES AND ANALYSIS

O conveys Blackacre to T, subject to an oral agreement that T will hold it in trust for B. T agrees to do so, declining to assert the Statute of Frauds; the trust is valid (assuming the other requirements of a valid trust are met). Note, however, that the trust would fail if the gift had been in the form of a devise under O's will, with no mention made in the will of the trust for B. See the discussion of secret trusts below.

   ii. **Estoppel.** The legal titleholder also may be estopped to assert the defense if a beneficiary acts in reliance on the purported trust.

   iii. **Waiver.** In all cases any waiver of the defense must occur while the legal titleholder still has the title. For example, in the last example, if T sold the property to X for its fair market value and B then sued T for breach, T could not then assert the defense of the Statute of Frauds as a bar to B's suit. Nor for that matter could T defeat the sale to X by later asserting that T could not sell because T was only a trustee or that T did not have title because the purported trust was invalid due to the Statute of Frauds.

    iv.   Agreement to convert realty to personalty. There also may be a dodge to the oral trust issue if there was an agreement by the trustee to convert realty into other trust investments, not because a promised conversion will upgrade an otherwise voidable trust, but because the promise to convert on its own may be enforceable in contract and that promise could be the valid corpus of an enforceable trust.

c.   Trustee's refusal to comply with an oral trust of realty. If a settlor attempts to create orally a trust of realty and the trustee refuses to comply:

    i.   Constructive trust for intended beneficiaries. Grounds for imposition of a constructive trust in favor of the intended beneficiaries include fraud, duress, misrepresentation, undue influence, constructive fraud, etc.: in these cases the Statute of Frauds is no bar and extrinsic evidence is admissible.

    ii.   Resulting trust for settlor or settlor's successors in interest. In other cases, a resulting trust in favor of the settlor or her successors in interest may be the relief available if it is clear that a trust was intended. Sometimes, however, a resulting trust is not the remedy of choice, because the trustee is an heir of the decedent and benefits by refusing to perform the trust, or because the heirs paid the trustee to refuse to perform the trust. Cases like these are messy and produce inconsistent results—all equity driven.

 # EXAMPLES AND ANALYSIS

S has no descendants; her sole heir is N. S creates an inter vivos trust into which she transfers Blackacre, and executes a pour over will under which her probate assets, if any, are devised to the trust. S serves as the sole trustee, but the instrument designates N as successor trustee. The trust instrument further provides that, at S's death, the trust corpus is distributable to N. Extrinsic evidence shows that S intended that Blackacre be held in trust for the benefit of third parties and that S discussed that trust with N. A constructive trust likely would be imposed if the extrinsic evidence also shows that the trust was not set out in the instrument due to N's fraud, misrepresentation, undue influence, or duress. If, however, there was no wrongful conduct by N and she instead simply refused to comply with the oral trust, the likely remedy would be a resulting trust in favor of S's estate. The problem with that result is that, under it, Blackacre would pass to N as S's heir. Note that, for these purposes, a trustee's refusal to comply with an oral trust is not fraud. Nevertheless, a court would likely impose a constructive trust, given the enrichment to N that otherwise would result from N's refusal to enforce the trust.

---

    iii.   **Trustee keeps property.** If a trustee refuses to comply with an oral trust of realty, a third alternative is for the trustee to keep the property in an individual capacity. This would be quite unusual. For example, assume that S conveys Greyacre (commercial real estate) to T, with an oral agreement that T will hold it in trust for B and lease it to X. Unbeknownst to T, the plan of S, X, and B is for Greyacre to be used for the conduct of criminal activities. T refuses to comply with the oral trust when T learns of the criminal activity being conducted on the premises, and terminates the lease to X. Because of the unclean hands of S and B, T may be allowed to retain title to Greyacre, individually.

H.   SECRET AND SEMI-SECRET TRUSTS

"Secret" trusts arise when a devise that appears on its face to be outright to one person is made subject to a separate, usually oral, agreement that the recipient will hold it for the benefit of another. By contrast, with a "semi-secret" trust it is clear from the devise itself that the taker is to receive it in trust, but the beneficiaries of the trust or its other terms are not stated. These cases often also involve elements of unenforceable discretion.

EXAMPLES AND ANALYSIS

D's will devised Blackacre to T. Before death D told T that D wanted T to hold Blackacre for B's benefit until a serious problem with B's creditors was resolved and then to distribute Blackacre to B. T agreed to do so. The trust is secret because there is no mention of a trust in D's will. The trust would be semi-secret if D's will devised Blackacre to T, "to keep until it is safe to deliver it to the person T knows I want to have it"; we can tell from the devise that it is meant to be in trust, rather than to T outright, but the will does not name the beneficiary of the trust or the terms for its administration.

---

   1.   **Extrinsic Evidence**

      Recall the discussion in Chapter 7 of the distinction between patent and latent ambiguities. In a secret trust, extrinsic evidence may be allowed to prove the alleged settlor's intent to establish a trust (and preclude the recipient from being unjustly enriched) and, once this door is open, all other extrinsic evidence needed to prove the terms and beneficiaries then may be admitted. Analogy: latent ambiguity. By contrast, in a semi-secret trust, because the intent to create a trust is clear without the need for extrinsic evidence, no extrinsic evidence would be needed to prove that intent (and to prevent the recipient from being unjustly enriched). Because the extrinsic evidence door is not opened, no other extrinsic evidence would be admitted either. Analogy: patent ambiguity.

a.   *Olliffe.* For example, in *Olliffe v. Wells*, 130 Mass. 221 (1881), the testator's will devised the residue of her estate to Reverend Wells "to distribute the same in such manner as in his discretion shall appear best calculated to carry out wishes which I have expressed to him or may express to him." The intent to entrust is clear but not the purpose or any of the specifics regarding trust beneficiaries or operation. The result was a semi-secret trust that failed; the residue went back to the decedent's heirs by resulting trust.

EXAM TIP

Distinguish between semi-secret trusts and outright gifts in which precatory language is used. With the former, the testator's intent is to create a trust—the trust fails not because of a lack of intent, but because of a lack of specified terms (usually including the identity of the beneficiaries, as was the case in *Clark v. Campbell*, discussed above). With the latter, the testator's intent is to make an outright gift—the "terms" the testator wants the recipient to follow may be set forth in the instrument, but the intent is for those terms to be only a request, not an enforceable trust. For an example, see the second review question at page 317.

---

2.   **Disposition of Property**

The trust corpus must be disposed of; to prevent unjust enrichment, clearly a court should not allow the trustee to keep it invalid. There are two options: a resulting trust for the settlor or her successors in interest or a constructive trust for the intended beneficiaries.

a.   **Traditional approach.** Secret trusts often are enforced by way of a constructive trust for the intended beneficiaries because extrinsic evidence is necessarily admissible in the first instance to prove that a trust, rather than an outright gift, was intended and to prevent the recipient from being unjustly enriched. Once extrinsic evidence is admitted for that purpose, it also is admitted to establish and allow the enforcement of the terms of the intended trust. By contrast, extrinsic evidence is not needed to prevent unjust enrichment if the trust is semi-secret—because it is clear from the document itself that the gift was not outright—and it also is not admitted to prove the terms of the trust. Thus, with a semi-secret trust that fails, there often will be a resulting trust in favor of the settlor or her successors in interest.

b. Resulting trust for both. Of the two options, Professor Scott argues that a resulting trust for the settlor or her successors in interest is more legitimate for both secret and semi-secret trusts.

    i. Resulting trust vs. constructive trust. 5 Scott & Fratcher, The Law of Trusts §462.1 at 313 (4th ed. 1989):

> Although the distinction between a constructive trust and an express trust is clear, it is more difficult to draw the line between constructive trusts and resulting trusts. It would seem, however, that a resulting trust arises where property is transferred under circumstances that raise an inference that the person who makes the transfer or causes it to be made does not intend the transferee to take the beneficial interest in the property. In the case of the resulting trust, as in the case of an express trust, the intention of the parties is of importance; but in the case of a resulting trust that intention is not so much an intention to create a trust as an intention not to give to another the beneficial interest, and it is an intention that appears from the character of the transfer rather than from direct evidence of the intention of the parties. On the other hand, a constructive trust is not based upon the intention of the parties but is imposed in order to prevent unjust enrichment.

c. Constructive trust for both. The Restatement position is that constructive trusts for the intended beneficiaries should be imposed for semi-secret as well as secret trusts, and that extrinsic evidence be admissible in each case.

d. Planning consideration. Often the solution to the desire to accomplish an intent like that of the testator in *Olliffe* is to create powers of appointment. See Chapter 14.

EXAM TIP

The question whether a trust has been created in a given situation may raise many issues. An intent to create a trust is required, but that is not enough. To have the requisite intent, the settlor must have capacity, and the degree of capacity required may depend on whether the trust is inter vivos or testamentary. Further, there also must be someone to enforce the trust; except for charitable trusts the intended trust will fail if the beneficiaries cannot be ascertained. And the intention of a settlor to create a trust for ascertainable beneficiaries is not enough to do so: as discussed in Chapter 11, the trust must have a legal purpose. If it is clear the settlor intended to create a trust for a legal purpose to benefit ascertainable persons, there also must be trust property, because a trust is an arrangement by which one or more trustees manage property for one or more beneficiaries. (The exception: an unfunded trust named as the devisee of the settlor's will is valid under the Uniform Testamentary Additions to Trust Act.) The trust will not fail if there is no trustee because the court must appoint a trustee. There must be a written instrument if the trust is testamentary or an inter vivos trust of realty; the inference is that the only permissible oral trusts are inter vivos trusts of personalty. But there are enough exceptions to that rule to warrant a warning. Among them: secret trusts; constructive trusts to prevent unjust enrichment when there has been fraud, misrepresentation, duress, mistake, or undue influence, or to prevent unjust enrichment when there is a confidential relationship; oral trusts the trustee is willing to administer; oral trusts relied on by the beneficiary; and promises by the trustee to convert realty to personalty.

REVIEW QUESTIONS AND ANSWERS

Question: A's sibling (S) helped care for A and A's children during A's extended illness. Two years after A's recovery, while A was researching a business opportunity, A sent S a letter stating that A wanted to repay S's kindness and assistance, that A planned to form a corporation to pursue the business opportunity, and that A would act as trustee of half of any stock A might receive in the corporation, all for S for life, remainder to S's children. Nine months later, A formed the corporation to pursue the business opportunity; unfortunately, however, A and S had a falling out and A refused to hold any of the stock in trust for S and S's children. S sues. What result, and why?

Answer: The question is whether a trust arose when A declared in the letter to S that A was trustee for S and S's children of half of the stock to be issued in the future. Generally, property not in existence cannot be held in trust, even if it is expected to come into existence in the future. Assuming that the agreement by A to do so was not supported by consideration, there is no trust and S loses. If, however, A's promise was supported by consideration, S may have a breach of contract claim (to be distinguished from a trust claim) against A.

Question: D's will devised $10,000 of her $400,000 net estate to her nephew, N, "with the hope and expectation that N will use this gift for the purposes we have discussed and to which we are committed." The residue of D's estate was left to R. What disposition should be made of the $10,000? Why?

Answer: The issue is intent: whether the quoted language was intended by D to be precatory only, in which case N receives the $10,000 outright (with perhaps a moral obligation on D to use it in accordance with their discussions, but no more than that) or did D intend to create a semi-secret trust, in which case the gift probably fails and a resulting trust is imposed to cause the $10,000 to pass back to D's estate, through which it will descend to R as D's residuary devisee. The word "hope" indicates D intended to let N decide whether to carry out D's wishes, but the word "expectation" and the reference to D's "purposes" for the gift and to D being "committed" to them connotes something more than a suggestion. The relative size of the gift (only 2.5% of D's net estate), and the familial relationship between D and N tend to support the gift being an outright one, although precatory words used with family members sometimes are regarded as "polite commands" (this being a particularly hard question because a nephew is not so close a relative to raise a compelling inference). It is more likely that this transfer would be construed as one in trust if another devise were made to N under the will and it was unencumbered by language of a similar ilk. Extrinsic evidence would be admitted to determine whether D's intent was for N to receive the gift outright. If that inquiry produced a finding that a trust was intended, it would be a semi-secret trust and in most jurisdictions extrinsic evidence would not be admissible to prove the terms of the trust. But without more as to what such extrinsic evidence might show (and assuming that there was not another devise to N), we expect that the usual inference from the use of precatory language—that an outright gift was intended—would be drawn. If a trust intent is found the fact that the trust would fail for lack of enforceable terms actually might influence a court to find that the gift was meant to be in trust. This especially would be true if, as between the donee and the residuary beneficiary of D's estate, the court favors the latter.

Question: D devised Blackacre to T, in trust, for T for life, remainder to R "if living and, if not, to T's estate." Is the trust valid? What if T and R survived D, but R predeceased T?

Answer: A valid testamentary trust was created at D's death: T, as trustee, holds legal title for the benefit of T and R. At R's death, however, T holds the life estate and the nonvested remainder to T's estate would likely cause T to be deemed the sole trustee and the sole beneficiary; the result would be a merger of the legal and equitable title and a failure of the trust. T would own the fee. Note that the same result would be reached even if D's gift in trust was made inter vivos and D was living when R died; the merger issue of the legal and equitable titles of the trustee and the beneficiary occurs without regard to the settlor, who plays no ongoing role.

Question: D's inter vivos trust instrument provides that, at D's death, the trust assets are to be distributed by the trustee (T) to R, except that specified property is to be held in further trust by T, "to make distributions of income and principal to those people who have contributed significantly to the successes I have enjoyed in my career and to those who were particularly helpful to me during the long illnesses of my mother, uncle, and son, such property to be distributed in full no later than 21 years after the date of my death." T began administering the trust, making distributions to several persons T determined qualify as trust beneficiaries. X made a claim to a share of the trust that was rejected by T, resulting in litigation; meanwhile, R challenged the validity of the trust and claims the trust assets. What result?

Answer: The trust for D's benefactors will fail for lack of ascertainable beneficiaries; it is not possible to objectively determine the persons intended by D to share in the trust. The trust could have continued if T had continued to administer the trust without objection, but the disputed claim by X of a right to receive distributions as a trust beneficiary demonstrates that the trust cannot be enforced—the standards for T's selection of beneficiaries are not sufficient for a court to review T's exercise of discretion. In this case when this portion of the trust fails the trust by its own terms calls for distribution to R. If the trust had been different it might yield a resulting trust in favor of D's successors in interest—beneficiaries of D's estate or D's heirs at law.

13 TRUST OPERATION

CHAPTER OVERVIEW

- Trust operational issues include the rights of beneficiaries and creditors of beneficiaries in discretionary trusts, support trusts, spendthrift trusts, and Medicaid qualifying trusts.

- Also relevant are rules governing the modification or termination of trusts, and issues peculiar to charitable trusts.

A. DISCRETIONARY TRUSTS provide for distributions of income, principal, or both—all in the trustee's discretion.

EXAMPLES AND ANALYSIS

D devised her estate: "To T, in trust, to pay income and principal to A in T's sole discretion, adding any undistributed income to principal. After A has reached 25 years of age, T shall pay the income to A and may distribute principal to A in T's sole discretion. A may withdraw any part of the trust after reaching 35 years of age. If A dies before withdrawing the full corpus, any remaining trust assets shall be distributed to the Red Cross." The trust is discretionary with respect to both income and principal until A reaches age 25, after which it is mandatory with respect to income (and discretionary with respect to principal). It would be mandatory with respect to principal if the trust required distributions to A when A attained a certain age or pursuant to some objective standard (such as for education) on any other triggering event.

---

1. Single or Multiple Beneficiaries or Trustees

A discretionary trust may have one or many beneficiaries, one or more trustees, or any combination of trustees and beneficiaries. Although not common, a trust may be discretionary with respect to one or more beneficiaries and mandatory with respect to others. For instance, in the example above, if the trust instrument also provided for a monthly distribution of $1,000 (indexed for inflation if desirable) to D's elderly dependent relative, the trust would be discretionary with respect to A and mandatory with respect to D's relative.

2. Standards Governing Exercise of Discretion

The example above illustrates a trust in which the trustee has complete discretion over distributions, with no standards to guide or limit the trustee's exercise of discretion. (Even this kind of discretion always is subject to judicial review.) Alternatively, most well-drafted trusts provide for discretionary distributions of income or principal or both for one or more specific purposes, such as for the beneficiary's best interests, health, education, maintenance, support, or welfare.

3. Trustee Discretion must be exercised reasonably and in good faith for the trust purposes. *Marsman v. Nasca*, 573 N.E.2d 1025 (Mass. App. Ct. 1991), illustrates a breach of this duty because the trustee failed to distribute principal to the settlor's husband "if necessary or desirable from time to time . . . for his comfortable support and maintenance."

4. Nature of a Trust Beneficiary's Interest

Although there was some doubt historically, it is well established today that trust beneficiaries own their equitable interests rather than merely having a chose in action to enforce them. In this respect the beneficial interest is like any other asset that a person can own, enjoy, or incur taxes on. Thus, (i) subject to any spendthrift limitation, the beneficial interest is both assignable by the beneficiary and attachable by the beneficiary's creditors, (ii) if a beneficiary's interest survives her death (which usually is not the case) it passes to her heirs or devisees, and (iii) perhaps most important, the beneficiary's interest is entitled to protection against waste, fraudulent transfer, trustee malfeasance, and so forth.

5. Effect of Trustee Discretion on Beneficiary's Rights

Although a trustee may have broad discretion over distributions to a beneficiary and it might appear that the beneficiary owns nothing that is capable of conveyance, taxation, or enforcement, trustee discretion is subject to certain constraints and cannot be excessive. For example, no amount of discretion given to a trustee exempts the trustee from judicial supervision.

a. **Trustee's overriding fiduciary obligations.** The document may exonerate the trustee from surcharge liability, but it cannot relieve the trustee from acting consistent with its overall fiduciary obligation to exercise good faith for a proper purpose without caprice or arbitrariness. As a result, a court *always* has the power to review a fiduciary's performance and, if appropriate, to impose sanctions or exact remedies for violation of the terms of the document and other fundamental fiduciary obligations. In *Briggs v. Crowley*, 224 N.E.2d 417 (Mass. 1967), for example, language in a trust purporting to relieve the trustees of the duty to account to anyone was invalid as against public policy; the trustees were required to faithfully perform their duties under the trust, which could not deprive the court of jurisdiction and the beneficiaries of standing to enforce that obligation.

6. **Beneficiary's Remedies**

A court may remedy a breach of fiduciary duty by directing the trustee to perform or desist from certain actions, removal and replacement of the trustee, surcharging the fiduciary (assessing damages), or denying the fiduciary's compensation (a lesser remedy).

a. **Exoneration or exculpation provisions.** The remedies available to a court to redress fiduciary breaches may be limited by an exoneration or exculpation provision in the trust—the former providing that the trustee will be repaid any amounts assessed against it by the trust estate and the latter essentially holding the trustee harmless for enumerated actions (or failures to act). Either protection usually will not be effective if the fiduciary is deemed to have breached its duties recklessly, or in bad faith or by dishonest acts.

   i. **Drafted by trustee.** The Restatement (Second) of Trusts §222, comment d, lists factors that may be considered in determining the validity of an exoneration provision, particularly including whether the trustee drafted the trust provision (which is not uncommon with banks that promulgate their own trust forms) and whether the settlor was independently advised (which is not always the case, some banks helping settlors create trusts without the interference, input, or assistance of an attorney).

b. **Courts will not substitute their judgment.** Somewhat difficult to reconcile with the rule that a trustee's conduct always is subject to judicial review is the principle that a court will not substitute its discretion for that of the trustee. The exercise of discretion in the administration of a trust is not a court's function, and the trustee presumably has special skills that made it appropriate for the settlor to repose discretion in the trustee. Nevertheless, although a court will not substitute its judgment for that of the trustee, a court may review what the trustee has done (or refrained from doing) and determine whether there has been an abuse of discretion that requires judicial action. That is, a court will not act affirmatively with respect to an exercise of the trustee's discretion in the first instance, but it *will* second guess the trustee in reviewing its exercise of discretion.

c. **Insufficient discretionary distributions.** In reviewing a trustee's exercise of discretion over distributions, a court may conclude that the trustee acted too parsimoniously in the past. If so, the usual remedy is merely to require it to be less so in the future, rather than to order it to distribute amounts that it would have paid out if its discretion had been exercised properly.

7. Why Give the Trustee Broad Discretion?

Given that it can be pretty close to a blank check, subject to little restraint or oversight, a settlor might grant broad discretion to a trustee because the settlor *trusts* the fiduciary to do what the settlor would do if still living; the discretionary trust provides flexibility, like an extension of the settlor's pocketbook. We will see a more devious reason when we study spendthrift trusts: discretionary trusts grant an interest that is too amorphous to be anticipated (i.e., sold or borrowed against by the beneficiary)—which imposes some degree of control over the beneficiaries and, more importantly, precludes creditor attachment.

8. What Discretionary Trust Beneficiaries Own and May Enforce

In light of these realities and this ephemeral character of the discretionary trust beneficiary's interest, it is hard to pin down exactly what the beneficiary of a discretionary trust owns and how, if at all, it may be enforced. The easier case is one, like *Marsman*, in which the trustee is given discretion to make distributions for stated purposes, such as the beneficiary's support, health, or education. In these cases the trustee is required to exercise discretion reasonably to provide for the specified needs or circumstances of the beneficiary.

a. **Absolute or uncontrolled discretion.** Courts opine that fiduciary good faith and reasonableness and the beneficiary's best interests always are implied standards that govern every relation, even if the trustee is granted "absolute" or "uncontrolled" discretion over distributions, or is simply authorized to distribute to the beneficiary such amounts as the trustee determines. Although these are the broadest standards known to the law (meaning a fiduciary has the broadest latitude in doing its job), enforcement always is available as against the trustee's bad faith or capriciousness. There *never* is unfettered discretion in a trustee.

9. **Standards Guiding Exercise of Discretion**

Some fiduciaries prefer maximum discretion—i.e., no standards—because they believe it gives them maximum flexibility with minimum exposure to second guessing by beneficiaries or courts. By contrast, some fiduciaries *want* a standard, even if only "best interests" (the broadest standard known to trust law), to which they can point in asserting that their actions were above reproach. Further, because trustees always are required to act in a fiduciary capacity (in good faith, reasonably, and for proper purposes), the objective of maximum flexibility may be elusive and unavailable even if the instrument purports to give the trustee "absolute" discretion over distributions.

10. **Considering Beneficiary's Other Resources**

A classic tension exists whether consideration of a beneficiary's other resources is proper in determining whether the trustee should exercise its discretion to make or withhold distributions to the beneficiary. From a planning perspective, allowing the trustee to consider the beneficiary's other resources may be advisable if the beneficiary has a taxable estate and the trust assets will not be taxable in the beneficiary's estate at her death. Such a provision also is appropriate if the remainder beneficiaries (e.g., the settlor's descendants from a prior marriage) may differ from the persons the beneficiary will favor with her own assets at death.

a. **Common law rule.** Normally the common law provides that (absent a trust provision authorizing or requiring such consideration), a trustee may not consider other resources of the beneficiary in exercising its discretion. In theory, if the rule was otherwise the beneficiary might be inclined not to work, which would encourage sloth while discouraging industry and frugality. Even under the common law, however, the trustee may consider the beneficiary's ability to support herself, along with the beneficiary's other family needs.

11. **Beneficiary's Transferable Interest**

Unless provided otherwise (e.g., in a spendthrift clause, which we will study shortly), a beneficiary may assign a beneficial interest and the beneficiary's creditors may attach it. Attachment is a spendthrift issue, so let's focus now on a beneficiary's transfer of the beneficial interest—either by renunciation or disclaimer (a rejection, which causes the interest to pass to someone else; see Chapter 2) or by an affirmative assignment.

a. **Multiple assignments; priority.** With respect to the affirmative act—assuming it is not precluded (most trust spendthrift provisions do preclude assignment, which is not always a good result, as we will study)—questions of priority arise if several assignments of the same interest are made. It happens, sometimes because the beneficiary is not careful (or forgets), and sometimes because something not entirely proper is happening. Restatement (Second) of Trusts §163 specifies that the first assignment in time prevails, but the trustee is protected if it has no notice of an assignment and makes payment to a later assignee.

b. **Assignment to creditor.** Notwithstanding a valid assignment, another question in a credit resolution context is whether a creditor or other assignee must exhaust the beneficiary's other assets before attaching trust interests. Because there are other beneficiaries of most discretionary trusts, most states permit the creditor to reach only the amount needed to satisfy an insufficiency in the assigning beneficiary's own assets, and then only to the extent of the beneficiary's interest in the trust and only when the beneficiary is entitled to receive it (meaning that there is no acceleration of the beneficiary's interest just because there is an assignment of it).

c. **Renunciation or disclaimer** is regarded differently than an assignment, because the beneficiary is not directing to whom the interest passes; instead, the beneficiary just refuses to accept it. Assuming that the renunciation or disclaimer satisfies applicable state law requirements, its effect is as if the beneficiary predeceased creation of the interest and, because there is no affirmative disposition of the trust interest by the beneficiary, a spendthrift clause is no restriction.

B. SUPPORT TRUSTS

A classic *"support trust"* uses an enforceable standard that provides more of a guarantee to the beneficiary (and any creditors who provide support to the beneficiary) and less discretion to the fiduciary, to insure that a certain ascertainable level of support will be provided.

1. What Is "Support"?

Absent language in the instrument providing guidance to the trustee, "support" generally is thought to mean the beneficiary's support in her accustomed standard of living. (Questions also can arise, and should be addressed in the instrument, as to the time at which the beneficiary's accustomed standard of living is determined, because there is no general rule to resolve that question, other than that intent of the settlor controls.) Thus, if the beneficiary's standard of living is modest and the transferor intends the trust to improve the beneficiary's standard of living, language to that effect should be included.

2. Health, Education, Maintenance, and Support: Ascertainable Standards

Support trusts often provide for distributions to the beneficiary for "health, education, maintenance, and support" (HEMS). These standards are said to be "ascertainable," meaning that the trustee's duty to make distributions to the beneficiary for these purposes can be objectively reviewed and enforced. (For tax purposes it may be critical that the trustee's ability to make distributions to a beneficiary is limited by such an ascertainable standard.) There are other terms that also may be ascertainable, but the HEMS standard is the most commonly recognized ascertainable standard.

3. Discretionary Support Trusts

The line between support and discretionary trusts may not be clear—transferors often provide for the trustee to make distributions to the beneficiary for support (or a combination of health, education, maintenance, and support), "in such amounts as the trustee in its absolute discretion determines" (or similar language to that effect). Such trusts are a species of discretionary trust, with the trustee's discretion being significantly more limited than a trust that provides no standards to guide or restrict exercise of the trustee's discretion in making distributions.

4. Advisability

It is not necessary to hobble a reliable fiduciary's discretion by creating a support trust and, for a number of reasons—most notably the rights of third parties (such as the state) to obtain reimbursement for necessary services provided to the beneficiary—in many cases support trusts are inadvisable.

C. CREDITORS' RIGHTS AND SPENDTHRIFT PROVISIONS

Virtually all trusts today contain some form of provision that restricts or eliminates the ability of a beneficiary's creditor to reach the beneficiary's equitable interest in the trust to satisfy the creditor's claim. The term "spendthrift trust" often refers to a trust the governing instrument of which includes a provision expressly prohibiting voluntary or involuntary alienation of the beneficiary's interest, but other trust provisions also can protect the beneficiary's interest from creditors and sometimes also are referred to as "spendthrift" provisions. We will return to the question whether automatic insertion of a spendthrift provision is wise.

1. **Spendthrift Restrictions** come in a variety of formats.

   a. **Support trusts.** For example, a trust created to provide only support or education is immune to attachment or assignment except for the support or education of the beneficiary. Attachment in reimbursement of necessaries provided to the beneficiary is thought to be consistent with the intent of a settlor who created a trust for just the support or education of a beneficiary.

 ## EXAMPLES AND ANALYSIS

B is the beneficiary of a trust that T created. The trust provides for the trustee to distribute income to B on an annual or more frequent basis. Bank loaned money to B for an investment, B defaulted, and Bank now attempts to be repaid from the trust.

The trust is not a support trust with respect to trust income because B is entitled to receive current income without regard to support needs. Bank may attach B's income interest in the trust to satisfy its claim if the trust does not include a spendthrift clause. Rather than wait until trust income is payable to B, the Bank will want to accelerate the value of that interest by commutation—meaning that the trustee would determine the discounted present value of B's life estate and distribute corpus in the amount of the lesser of Bank's claim or that amount. If the trust instrument provided for distributions of income and principal to B only for B's support, or support and education, Bank would not be able to reach the trust assets (although the landlord of a residence B rents and in which B lives could).

---

b. Forfeiture provisions are common in Great Britain but not the United States, because they are a blunt form of protecting the trust from creditor attachment or beneficiary alienation: any attempted assignment (and in some cases, a third party's levy on or attachment of a beneficiary's interest) works a termination of the beneficiary's interest. This approach may protect the trust property, but not the beneficiary. In most cases, a better alternative to a pure forfeiture provision is a provision like that in *Scott v. Bank One Trust Co.*, 577 N.E.2d 1077 (Ohio 1991), which prohibited distributions to any beneficiary who was insolvent, filed a petition in bankruptcy, or would not personally enjoy the property; in any such case the beneficiary's interest became discretionary until the beneficiary's creditor problems were resolved.

c. Discretionary trusts have a spendthrift nature because there is nothing a creditor can attach or that the beneficiary can assign unless or until the trustee chooses to exercise its discretion. Thus, for example, *United States v. O'Shaughnessy*, 517 N.W.2d 574 (Minn. 1994), held that the beneficiary of a discretionary trust had neither "property" nor any "right to property" in undistributed trust principal or income that the United States could attach in a federal tax lien enforcement action. Short of suing to force an exercise of discretion based on a breach of fiduciary duty, there is little a claimant can do to squeeze money out of a discretionary trust. Rather, in most jurisdictions, a creditor of a beneficiary of a discretionary trust must wait until the trustee has exercised its discretion and made a distribution to the beneficiary, and then attempt to collect from the beneficiary. In some jurisdictions, the creditor may obtain an order directing the trustee to pay to the creditor any amounts it otherwise would distribute to the beneficiary pursuant to an exercise of its discretion. The result is that, if the trustee properly chooses to make no distributions, neither the beneficiary nor the creditor can benefit from the trust property, which likely would lead to settlement of the claim.

i.   **Medicaid eligibility.** State law regarding discretionary trusts varies, and the ability of a state to reach the trust assets or to cut the beneficiary off from Medicaid benefits (e.g., the cost of living in a nursing home) while the trust has assets is a subject of constant change and extreme sensitivity. There is a severe tension between a settlor who wants the beneficiary to receive maximum state benefits while maintaining the trust as a safety net if state aid is insufficient, and the state that has limited resources and therefore wants to deny public funds to people who can afford to pay for their own care. The parameters of this intersection between spendthrift protection and public benefits law will continue to evolve and is too amorphous currently to define in a meaningful manner for the 51 American jurisdictions. This subject is discussed further below.

d.   **In-hand payment and pure spendthrift clauses.** Requiring the trustee to make payments directly to the named beneficiary and not to any assignee or agent, or provisions that expressly deny any attachment or assignment, are the common American creditor protection approaches. Trusts including these provisions commonly are referred to as "spendthrift trusts"; although controversial (because they allow beneficiaries to enjoy trust property that is not available to satisfy legitimate claims of the beneficiaries' creditors), spendthrift trusts are effective—to varying degrees—in the great majority of American jurisdictions.

2.   Creditors of the Settlor

A spendthrift provision in a trust in which the settlor also is a beneficiary normally does not insulate the trust from claims by the settlor's *own* creditors, even if the trust is irrevocable. Creditors of the settlor may reach the full trust if a transfer into trust initially was a fraud on creditors; required is that the settlor was insolvent at the time of, or became insolvent by virtue of, the transfer. (In such a case the settlor's creditors normally may reach the transferred assets even if the settlor is not a beneficiary.) Absent such a fraudulent transfer, creditors of the settlor may reach the full amount the trustee *could* pay to the settlor as a beneficiary, regardless of whether anything actually is paid.

 # EXAMPLES AND ANALYSIS

S created a trust with T as trustee, providing "income and principal to S, as determined by T in its discretion, to provide for S's support. On S's death, remainder to S's descendants, per stripes." The trust has a standard spendthrift provision preventing any beneficiary's interest from being alienated or attached voluntarily or involuntarily.

Later, S defaults on a debt to C. Under the traditional rule, C may reach the amount T could distribute to S. This does not necessarily mean that C can reach all assets in the trust (which C could if creation of the trust was a fraudulent transfer—but let's assume otherwise here—or if T was authorized to distribute such amounts to S as T in its unfettered discretion determines). Instead, depending on factors such as the size of C's claim, S's age and life expectancy, and the amounts T could distribute to S for S's support without violating T's fiduciary duties to the remainder beneficiaries, C may not be able to attach enough trust assets to satisfy the claim in full.

a.   **New Alaska and Delaware statutes.** Apparently in an effort to compete for trust business, several states—led by Alaska and Delaware—enacted legislation under which a settlor may transfer assets in trust (provided the transfer is not in fraud of creditors) and retain the ability to receive distributions from the trust—but only in the trustee's discretion, and not pursuant to an ascertainable standard such as for support—without the trust assets being reachable by the settlor's creditors. In effect, these laws have eliminated the special rule applicable only to self-settled trusts and regard all beneficiaries—settlors and third parties—alike. (Another anticipated objective of trusts created under the new statutes is for their assets to be excluded from the settlor's estate for estate tax purposes. Success is unlikely. A growing number of states also have abolished the Rule Against Perpetuities, making these trusts ideal for generation-skipping transfer tax trust planning.)

3.   **Other Controls Retained by Settlor**

Assets subject to a settlor's retained general inter vivos power of appointment (discussed in Chapter 14) also can be reached by the settlor's creditors, but a creditor usually cannot force exercise of a power to revoke a trust. The distinction that permits a creditor to force exercise of a general power of appointment but not a power to revoke makes no sense to us.

EXAMPLES AND ANALYSIS

G created Trust #1 for D and D's descendants and Trust #2 for S and S's descendants. G is not a permissible beneficiary of the income or principal of either trust, but G retained a general inter vivos power of appointment over Trust #1, under which G could appoint the assets in the trust to anyone, including G personally. No such power was retained in Trust #2, but G reserved the power to revoke Trust #2, in which case the assets would be conveyed back to G. Assuming transfers to the trusts were not made in fraud of G's creditors, a creditor of G could not reach the assets in Trust #2, either directly or by forcing an exercise by G of the power to revoke the trust.

But G's creditor could reach the assets in Trust #1, regardless of whether the transfers to it were made in fraud of the creditor's rights and without regard to whether G chooses to exercise the power to appoint.

4. **If the Beneficiary Is Not the Settlor** of a spendthrift trust, in most states most creditors of the beneficiary may not reach the beneficiary's interest in the trust: generally, spendthrift provisions work to protect trust assets from the beneficiary's creditors.

    a. **Trust assets distributed to the beneficiary.** This protection extends only to the beneficiary's interest in the trust; assets distributed to the beneficiary from a spendthrift trust lose their protection from creditors. As a practical matter, a beneficiary attempting to avoid paying creditors will try to spend distributed trust assets before creditors can attach them, but in many states knowledgeable creditors can simply garnish the trust—obtaining a court order requiring the trustee to make payment directly to the creditor. Many trust instruments contain facility of payment provisions that authorize distributions to the beneficiary directly or to third parties for the beneficiary's benefit. If the beneficiary is having creditor problems, the trustee of such a trust may make distributions for the beneficiary directly to third parties that the beneficiary designates (such as the mortgagee of the beneficiary's home), but again only in the absence of a garnishment order.

    b. **Bankruptcy.** In bankruptcy, the trustee of the bankrupt's estate succeeds to all the rights and interests of the bankrupt, but subject to the same limitations—such as a spendthrift clause—that apply to the beneficiary's interest. Accordingly, creditors of a beneficiary who cannot reach a trust interest directly because of a spendthrift clause also cannot do so in a bankruptcy proceeding.

5. **Competing Policies**

    The policy underlying enforcement of spendthrift clauses is protection of the transferor's property rights; as stated by *Scott v. Bank One Trust Co.*, 577 N.E.2d 1077, 1083 (Ohio 1991): "[A]s a matter of policy, it is desirable for property owners to have, within reasonable bounds, the freedom to do as they choose with their own property. That freedom is not absolute . . . . But . . . in a society that values freedom as greatly as ours, this consideration is far from trivial." On the other hand, "[t]here are many who consider it contrary to their notions of right and wrong that a person should be permitted to live on income that he does not earn and yet that is not subject to the claims of his creditors." *Utley v. Graves*, 258 F. Supp. 959, 960 (D.D.C. 1966), rev'd, 382 F.2d 451 (D.C. Cir. 1967). Other policy issues affecting the validity of spendthrift provisions include:

a. **Societal economic impact.** Disabling restraints such as spendthrift clauses arguably take property out of commerce and thus adversely affect the economy. A response with respect to spendthrift provisions in trust is that the trustee has free alienability—only the beneficiary is restricted with respect to transfers of the equitable interest. The counter response that entrepreneurial investments generally may not be made with spendthrift trust funds because of the investment limitations imposed on fiduciaries is not compelling, because that argument would apply to any trust, not just a spendthrift trust, and would not justify defeating the trust.

b. **Unfair to beneficiary's creditors.** Another is that spendthrift provisions serve to improperly mislead creditors. A legitimate response is that creditors have no right to rely on the appearance of wealth and should not extend credit without verification of the nature and extent of the beneficial interest and the debtor's ability to pay. In addition, some would argue that the transferor's property should not be subjected to the beneficiary's debts.

c. **Inherited vs. earned wealth.** A third policy argument against spendthrift protection is that spendthrift provisions tend to protect inherited wealth from creditors in ways that earned wealth cannot enjoy, which seems improper. One legitimate response may be that, by protecting against improvidence, the spendthrift provision protects those beneficiaries who were left wealth *in trust* because they were unable to earn or manage wealth on their own. Further, tax qualified retirement plan interests represent a substantial portion of many persons' earned wealth; generally, they are subject to the federal Employee Retirement Income Security Act (ERISA), which protects participants' interests from their creditors.

6. Limitations on Effectiveness of Spendthrift Protections

In an effort to balance these conflicting concerns, some states recognize spendthrift provisions but limit their effectiveness in various ways (and a few states do not enforce them at all). The law on these issues varies significantly from state to state and increasingly is governed by statute.

a. **Settlor as beneficiary.** As discussed above, in virtually all states a spendthrift provision will not protect a settlor's retained interest as a beneficiary in a trust created and funded by the settlor: generally, you cannot create a valid spendthrift trust for yourself.

b. **Restraint on assignment and attachment.** A spendthrift clause prohibiting attachment by creditors is valid only to the extent it also prohibits voluntary assignment by the beneficiary. A spendthrift clause that expressly prohibits attachment but is silent with respect to assignment may be construed to prohibit both.

c. **Tort claimants.** Although there are cases to the contrary, the trend is to allow involuntary tort claimants to reach trust assets for the full amount of a judgment; see 2A Scott & Fratcher, The Law of Trusts §157.5 (4th ed. 1987), *In re Estate of Nagel*, 580 N.W.2d 810 (Iowa 1998), and *Sligh v. First Nat'l Bank*, 704 So. 2d 1020 (Miss. 1997). The policy supporting this exception is that a tort judgment creditor did not voluntarily extend credit on the appearance of wealth and should not be barred from wealth that is available to the tortfeasor.

d. **Direct limitations.** Some states restrict the fund or the amount of income that can be protected.

e. **Support claimants.** Most states preclude application of a spendthrift restriction against the provider of necessaries. The theory is that the trust presumably was created to ensure support without dissipation by a profligate; the exception is thought to be consistent with the overriding intent of the settlor. Under such a theory, the amount available to the furnisher of necessaries should be limited to a reasonable, fair value, not any higher contracted price agreed to by a profligate beneficiary.

f. **Qualification for governmental assistance.** Most states also preclude reliance on a spendthrift clause to prevent collection of governmental claims (e.g., a state may count the trust interest in determining eligibility for Medicaid or attach the trust to reimburse it for benefits already paid). See below regarding the effect on Medicaid qualification of a trust beneficial interest.

g. **Tax claims.** Generally, a beneficiary's interest in a spendthrift trust may be reached to satisfy the claims of both federal and state taxing authorities against the beneficiary.

h. **Alimony and child support claims.** Cases are divided on whether alimony and child support claimants may reach a beneficiary's interest in a spendthrift trust, although the majority rule probably is that claims for child support may be successfully asserted while alimony claims often cannot. The Uniform Trust Act would permit a spouse, a former spouse, and children to reach the trust for support and alimony.

7. Discretionary Trusts with Spendthrift Clauses

Note that a trust may provide protection from creditors' claims both by making the beneficiary's interest subject to the discretion of the trustee, and by including a spendthrift clause. For example, in *Shelley v. Shelley*, 354 P.2d 282 (Or. 1960), the trust beneficiary (Grant) was entitled to receive current distributions of income, but principal only in the trustee's discretion, and the trust included a spendthrift clause. The court said that the alimony and child support claimants could reach Grant's interests in the trust despite the spendthrift clause but it did *not* in fact violate the spendthrift nature of the trust: they only received income that Grant was entitled to, when he was entitled to it, and could not reach principal unless and until the trustee exercised its discretion.

8. Accumulated Distributable Income

A trust in which a beneficiary is entitled to receive current distributions of all trust income ordinarily should have little or no accumulated income. If a trustee accumulates income rather than distribute it to the beneficiary, the accumulated income should be viewed as the beneficiary's property and it should be subject to the claims of *any* creditors of the beneficiary, without regard to a spendthrift clause or the nature of the creditor's claim.

9. Qualification and Reimbursement for Government Assistance raises significant issues for trust beneficiaries or for applicants who have made transfers of their assets within a relatively short period prior to applying for assistance.

a. **Long-term institutional care.** There are more elderly persons in the United States than ever and they are living longer than ever. Many are unable to care for themselves and the costs of institutional care are high. Persons who require institutional care may qualify to have these costs paid by Medicaid, which is a joint federal-state program that is the primary government program providing funds for institutional care of the elderly.

b. **Resource and income limitations.** To qualify for Medicaid assistance, a person must have nonexempt resources and income of less than specified amounts (exempt resources may include, among others, part or all of the value of a residence, household goods and personal effects, an automobile, and a burial fund); although the disqualification amounts vary from state to state, they are uniformly low. A prospective Medicaid recipient whose nonexempt assets exceed the resource threshold must "spend down" before qualifying. For married couples, complicated rules consider the assets and income of both spouses in determining the eligibility of either, but make provision for one spouse to be institutionalized and qualify for Medicaid without the other having to be totally impoverished.

c. **Qualification planning.** For some who can afford to pay for nursing home care, the idea of government assistance is offensive to their personal values and their desire not to be, in effect, "middle class welfare recipients." Many others (and often their children) are offended by the prospect of their life savings being dissipated in the last years of their lives to pay for nursing home care; sometimes their view is that they have paid taxes all of their lives and that there is nothing wrong with doing everything possible to preserve assets for their families and letting the government pay for their nursing home care. Parents of disabled children often want to provide care that is not provided by the government without having funds they set aside for that purpose disqualify their children from receiving basic government support assistance.

d. **Self-settled trusts.** Various rules and exceptions establish whether the assets and income of a trust created by a settlor for her own benefit (or by her guardian, conservator, attorney-in-fact, or even by a court out of the proceeds of a judgment or settlement award obtained on her behalf) will be counted in determining eligibility for Medicaid. Generally, consistent with the normal spendthrift rules for a self-settled trust, the maximum amount a trustee *could* distribute to the settlor from such a trust will be counted as an available resource unless an exception applies.

   i. **Trusts not covered.** In certain limited circumstances a settlor (or someone acting on her behalf) may create a "pay-back" trust for herself, the assets and income from which will not be counted in determining Medicaid eligibility. The trust must provide that the state be repaid for assistance it provided from any assets remaining in the trust at the beneficiary's death.

   ii. **Termination of settlor's interest on institutionalization** is treated as a transfer by the settlor that triggers application of the look-back rules discussed below, resulting in a period of ineligibility for Medicaid.

e. **Third party created trusts.** The rules are much more lenient if a trust was established for a beneficiary by a third party (not the beneficiary, the beneficiary's spouse, a representative of the beneficiary, or a court acting on the beneficiary's behalf). Trusts created by persons who want to provide benefits to a beneficiary over and above the basic support that the state provides, without jeopardizing that assistance ("supplemental needs" or "special needs" trusts) are not counted as available resources of the beneficiary. Trust assets *are* counted, however, if it is a support trust or to the extent it is a mandatory distribution trust.

   i. **Discretionary vs. support.** In *Myers v. Department of Social and Rehabilitation Services*, 866 P.2d 1052 (Kan. 1994), a testamentary trust provided that the trustee "shall hold, manage, invest and reinvest, collect the income [therefrom and] pay over so much or all the net income and principal to my son as my trustee deems advisable for his care, support, maintenance, emergencies and welfare." The court held this was a discretionary trust because the trustee was required to pay only amounts it deemed advisable: neither the beneficiary nor any creditor could compel the trustee to pay trust income or principal to the beneficiary (although the beneficiary could have compelled distributions if the trustee had abused its discretion in refusing to provide funds).

f.   **Asset transfers.** A person in need of institutionalized care, but who has too much property to qualify for Medicaid, may transfer assets to a third party (for example, a child) and then qualify, providing she waits long enough after the transfer to apply for benefits.

   i.   **The look-back period.** Assets transferred within a "look-back" period are considered in determining eligibility for benefits; transfers made before the look-back period are not. The look-back period is 36 months for outright transfers and 60 months if a trust is involved.

   ii.   **Disqualified transfers.** Under the look-back rule asset transfers may cause the transferor to become disqualified for a period of time (not the 36 or 60 months—it is determined by a formula).

EXAMPLES AND ANALYSIS

Assume that $120,000 was transferred. If the state's monthly cost of nursing home care is $3,000 the transferor would be disqualified for 40 months from the date of the transfer (the formula is the amount transferred divided by the monthly cost). Because the look-back period is only 36 months, the transferor in this example would have been better off to simply wait 36 months after the transfer to apply because no part of this outright transfer before the look-back period would be considered in determining the period of ineligibility.

   iii.   **Exceptions** apply to the asset transfer, ineligibility, look-back rules. For example, transfers to trusts for the benefit of the transferor are not subject to the 60 month look-back period rules; rather, these assets are counted as resources of the transferor for eligibility purposes (unless the trust is excepted). Further, residences transferred to a spouse or certain family members are excepted, as are transfers to a spouse (because each spouse's assets are considered in determining either spouse's eligibility). In addition, a transfer to or in trust for the benefit of a blind or disabled child is exempt, as are transfers in trust for the benefit of a disabled person under 65 years of age.

g.   **State reimbursement claims.** A related question to Medicaid eligibility is whether a state may be reimbursed from a trust for costs the state pays for the care of a beneficiary. If the beneficiary was the settlor the usual rule allowing creditors to reach as much of the trust assets as the trustee could have distributed to the beneficiary applies. If the trust settlor was a third party, and the trust is discretionary, the state can reach trust assets only if and to the extent the trustee exercises its discretion to make distributions; if the trust is a support trust, the state can reach it for the support the state provided.

h.   Caveat. These rules for qualifying for public assistance, a state's ability to successfully seek reimbursement for assistance provided, and the issue of asset transfers are complex: they derive from federal and state statutes and regulations; they involve sensitive questions of public policy; and they seem to be in an almost constant state of change. And there can be difficult ethical and malpractice issues.

 ## EXAMPLES AND ANALYSIS

An elderly parent transferred assets to a child to qualify for assistance at termination of the look-back period. The oral and unenforceable understanding is that the child will use the transferred assets for the parent's benefit, if needed, or return the assets to the parent if requested. Even after expiration of the 36 month look-back period, there is a difficult question whether the parent can apply for Medicaid without committing fraud. Moreover, if the parent, perhaps because her health unexpectedly improves, requests that the child return the assets and the child refuses, it probably is not possible for the parent to force the child to comply with their understanding. If that is true, the parent may attempt to hold a lawyer who was involved with the planning responsible.

10.   Spendthrift Clauses and Practicalities

If spendthrift clauses are given effect in the jurisdiction, an obvious effect of including a spendthrift clause in a trust instrument (or providing that distributions to the beneficiary are subject to the trustee's discretion) is that it will be difficult or impossible for the beneficiary to borrow against her interest or for a creditor to reach it—both of which are desirable consequences for some transferors.

a.   Not universally wise. Certainly no boilerplate should be used without thought, and on occasion, for tax purposes especially, an assignment that could *not* be made if there *is* a spendthrift provision may be very useful. Although a renunciation or disclaimer is not precluded by a spendthrift clause, the taker in the event of a disclaimer might not be the person in whose favor an assignment would be best. So in some cases spendthrift provisions that preclude an affirmative assignment to a particular recipient can be harmful. Further, because they also may preclude trust termination under the *Claflin* (unfulfilled purposes) doctrine discussed on page 341, next below, in many added cases spendthrift provisions may be harmful.

b. **Flexibility with a spendthrift clause.** If creditor protection is needed, a spendthrift clause coupled with a power of appointment may be an acceptable method to preserve flexibility, as we will see in Chapter 14.

D. MODIFICATION AND TERMINATION

For a variety of reasons, one or more trust beneficiaries may want to modify its terms or terminate it early.

1. Modification and Termination by the Settlor

Consider a hypothetical: Settlor was scheduled to receive a substantial sum of money at the age of 21 (perhaps from a Uniform Transfer to Minors Act account or a trust created for her benefit by an ancestor). Settlor's parent, trust officer, and their attorney recommended Settlor create an irrevocable trust to receive the sum, over which Settlor retained (i) generous lifetime enjoyment, (ii) with provision for a life estate for Settlor's spouse (if any) for the spouse's overlife, and (iii) payment of the remainder per stirpes to Settlor's descendants who survive the survivor of Settlor and the Settlor's spouse. The issues raised are: does the attorney have a conflict of interest in this representation, why would this trust be irrevocable, and under what, if any, circumstances may Settlor later revoke the trust?

a. **Attorney's conflict.** The attorney has a conflict of interest because the parent and trust officer are the attorney's clients and they were pushing the irrevocable trust; was it in Settlor's best interests and who did the attorney represent with respect to the trust? That conflict may be compounded by the fact that Settlor arguably was unable to give an informed and voluntary consent by virtue of the same defects of character and experience that prompted the parent and trust officer to recommend this rollover trust. Unless it is clear that the attorney represented Settlor alone—which the facts almost certainly do not support—there has been a real ethical breach here and the attorney also potentially is liable for malpractice.

b. **Why would this trust be irrevocable?** There is no tax advantage (Settlor's retained enjoyment will cause the trust to be taxable when Settlor dies). We also know from the spendthrift provision material that there is no protection from creditors to the extent the trustee may pay income and principal to Settlor. There are some potential reasons for the trust to be irrevocable, but none are likely to apply in this case. And that raises the question whether Settlor may revoke the trust.

c. Revocation of ''irrevocable'' trust is available at common law only if:

    i. An express power to revoke was reserved; if the instrument is silent on the settlor's power to revoke, in most jurisdictions the trust is irrevocable (the Uniform Trust Act would reverse this rule); or

    ii. The settlor was the sole beneficiary; the ability to revoke under this exception is relatively rare, because even if the settlor is the sole lifetime beneficiary, most trusts provide for remainder beneficiaries (as opposed to the trust assets being distributed to the settlor's estate at the settlor's death); or

    iii. The consent of all beneficiaries is obtained, which often is difficult or impossible because of, among other things, minor, unborn, and contingent or unascertainable beneficiaries; or

    iv. The trust was invalid due to incapacity, duress, undue influence, or fraud—which might exist in this case (although it is more likely that simple ignorance was exploited); or

    v. The power to revoke was meant to be included but was inadvertently omitted (assuming this could be proven, based on extrinsic evidence such as the testimony of the drafter).

    vi. A mistake of law usually won't suffice to make the trust revocable (e.g., the settlor or drafter thought the trust was revocable if it was not expressly made irrevocable). A mistake of fact might suffice (e.g., the settlor thought she was signing some other document), but again it could be hard to prove.

d. Revocability in hypothetical. In the hypothetical the settlor probably could not revoke, because there are unborns and an unknown (perhaps unborn too?) spouse who cannot consent, and none of the other exceptions to irrevocability apply.

    i. Virtual representation. In addition, although the doctrine of virtual representation—under which an unrepresented beneficiary's interest is deemed adequately represented by a similarly situated beneficiary who is a party—sometimes will surmount the obstacle of unascertained or unborn beneficiaries who cannot consent, it will not apply here because there is no one who virtually represents Settlor's unborn children or potential future spouse.

    ii. Guardian ad litem. Sometimes a guardian ad litem can be appointed to give the requisite consent, but it is not likely in this case that a consent would be given because it clearly is not in the best interests of those unborns who would be affected by a revocation.

    iii. **Wisdom of irrevocability.** As the hypothetical illustrates, irrevocability means that the terms of the instrument limit the beneficiaries' access to the trust assets, which are controlled by a trustee to whom fees must be paid, and there may be other administrative costs (e.g., accounting and legal fees). In short, irrevocability is serious business—it may be appropriate for such purposes as tax planning, creditor protection (to the extent the settlor is not a beneficiary), or resolution of a dispute (e.g., a divorce), but a trust never should be made irrevocable without careful deliberation. Although some of the adverse consequences of irrevocability can be mitigated through the use, for example, of powers of appointment (see Chapter 14), adequately drafting for unexpected changes in the future is difficult.

e. **State revocability statutes.** Some state statutes (e.g., in California, Oklahoma, and Texas) change the default rule to provide that a trust is revocable unless expressly made irrevocable, and the Restatement (Third) of Trusts and Uniform Trust Act both propose to make the same change. Reliance on them is foolish, however, because of the conflict of law principles that may apply and the significant time it will take for the Restatement position to become the law (if it ever does) or the Uniform Trust Act to be adopted.

f. **Rights of settlor's creditors.** Under the common law, creditors cannot force a settlor to exercise a power of revocation (although a creditor might set aside a trust that was created with a fraudulent transfer). On the other hand, a settlor's trustee in bankruptcy may exercise all the settlor's powers, including any retained power to revoke.

    i. **Retained inter vivos general power to appoint.** As we will see in Chapter 14 a settlor's creditors may reach a retained general power of appointment and force its exercise to the extent the settlor as the power holder is insolvent.

    ii. **Power to revoke vs. general inter vivos power.** The curious aspect of these rules is that, for all practical purposes, a power to revoke and a general inter vivos power to appoint don't differ. Yet the power to revoke is favored here. We are unable to give a good justification for the disparity in treatment.

2. Modification and Termination by Trustee

Trustees generally have no power to modify or terminate a trust absent express authority granted in the instrument. For example, an express power to revoke often is granted in the form of a provision granting the trustee the authority to terminate a trust if it becomes too small to justify its continuance. (Caution is needed in small trust termination provisions because an individual trustee who also is a beneficiary may have a taxable ownership interest in the trust if, upon termination, any portion of the trust corpus passes to the trustee as beneficiary.)

a. **Distribution powers.** An implicit power to terminate a trust also exists in the form of a trustee's power to distribute "so much or all of the principal of the trust as the trustee deems appropriate . . . ," or as the trustee deems appropriate for certain designated purposes. To the extent the trustee's exercise of the granted discretion is proper under the applicable standard, termination may occur because the trust becomes "dry," due to distribution of all the trust assets to any one or more of the beneficiaries.

b. **Tax motivated terminations.** A difficult question exists whether a trustee may terminate a trust purely for tax purposes (e.g., because the income tax rate on undistributed trust income is so much higher than it is for individuals). Most courts hold that the trustee may not, because the remainder beneficiaries' interests deserve protection notwithstanding what may be a significant diminution in wealth due to taxes if termination is not permitted. Further, investment alternatives are available to reduce adverse income tax consequences.

3. **Modification and Termination by Beneficiaries** is an extremely limited opportunity: the beneficiaries acting alone may modify or terminate a trust early (even without the trustee's consent), but only if:

a. **All interested parties consent**—required is that all interested parties be in existence or represented, and sui juris (i.e., competent adults or represented by guardians). "Interested parties" does *not* include the settlor, even if living, unless the settlor also is a beneficiary.

b. **There is no unfulfilled trust purpose.** Any unfulfilled purpose of the trust will preclude termination (this is the *Claflin* doctrine, named after an 1889 Massachusetts case). Such purposes include (i) protection of the trust corpus from the beneficiary's improvidence or creditors, as evidenced by inclusion of a spendthrift clause; (ii) postponement of possession, as evidenced by a provision delaying distribution until a beneficiary is a certain age to protect against the beneficiary's improvidence or immaturity; and (iii) more generalized objectives, such as providing management, support, bifurcation of title (providing for multiple beneficiaries seriatim), or protection against dissipation (e.g., a life estate with a testamentary power of appointment but no opportunity for a beneficiary to invade or withdraw).

i. **Multiple trust purposes.** Fulfillment of one or more trust purposes will not allow early termination if other trust purposes remain unfulfilled. E.g., *In re Estate of Brown*, 528 A.2d 752 (Vt. 1987), involved an education trust that continued for the life of a nephew and his wife. After the education aspect was accomplished the court rejected a petition to terminate the trust because, in addition to educating the beneficiaries, a material purpose was to provide for the nephew and his wife for their lives, to allow them to live in their accustomed standard of living. That purpose would have been defeated if the trust had been terminated.

ii. **The Uniform Trust Act** would permit revocation if all the beneficiaries agree, even if an unfulfilled purposes exists. This shift of emphasis from the dead hand to the living beneficiaries is controversial.

c. **Underlying policy and exceptions to the rule.** The general policy in this country with respect to trust termination and modification is to respect and protect the settlor's intent, which translates into denial of any proposed early termination or modification that is inconsistent with the settlor's intent. A few exceptions do exist, including:

i. **Perpetuities limits.** We only allow the settlor's dead hand to control for the applicable period of the Rule Against Perpetuities (if any) in the state. See the Website for further information.

ii. **Annuities.** The rule is that, if the document provides for acquisition of an annuity that can be resold, the beneficiary can ask for the cash that would be used to purchase the annuity or, if it already was purchased, for acceleration (by sale of the annuity and distribution of the proceeds). The rationale here is just that, with a resalable annuity, there is no reason to incur the costs of purchase and then resale if the beneficiary doesn't want the annuity in the first place. And because it *is* an annuity, there is no remainder beneficiary to consider.

iii. **Distribution of sale proceeds.** Directions to sell land and distribute the cash proceeds can be overridden by the beneficiary's request that the property itself be distributed in kind. This exception is based on notions that land is nonfungible and having the sale proceeds that could be used to purchase other property is not the functional equivalent of having the original property instead.

iv. **Termination by merger.** A termination may be produced by merger, if it is possible for a sole beneficiary to become the owner of both the life estate and the remainder—which would yield the power to terminate the trust. This is not easy to accomplish, however, especially because most trusts have a spendthrift provision that would preclude transfers to or acquisition of the life estate and remainder interest by the same person.

d. **Overcoming the unfulfilled purpose bar and gaining the consent of all interested parties.** So how can a beneficiary avoid the unfulfilled purpose bar? Consent of the settlor would be an estoppel to the bar of an unfulfilled purpose, but in most cases the settlor won't be alive to consent and, if the settlor *is* available, that fact alone in some cases creates a problem because additional potential beneficiaries can be born or adopted by the settlor—meaning it may be difficult or impossible to obtain the consent required from all potential beneficiaries. In addition to the presumption of the fertile octogenarian (anyone at any age can parent a child), there always is the possibility of adoption.

i. **Guardian ad litem.** Appointment of a guardian ad litem (GAL) often is suggested as the answer to needing the consent of all potential beneficiaries when some are not available. For any one of several reasons, however, that often will not suffice. For example, (i) a GAL may not be able to consent for the ward under the law of your state, (ii) some courts are reluctant to appoint GALs, (iii) in courts that are not reluctant, costs, delays, and fraud (yes, some of the abuses that occur in this realm would make your toenails curl) all may be involved in an appointment, or (iv) last but not least, consent may prove to be not in the ward's best interests, meaning that the GAL should not consent.

ii. **Construction solution.** Applicable rules of construction may eliminate an interest that stands in the way of consent. Unfortunately the Rule in Shelley's Case (remainder to the heirs of a named beneficiary is instead a remainder in the named beneficiary) and the Doctrine of Worthier Title (remainder to the settlor's heirs instead is a remainder in the settlor—known by the name "reversion") are in disfavor (the Rule in Shelley's Case having been repealed most everywhere by statute, so this alternative is not likely to bear fruit either. See Chapter 15).

iii. **Consent for consideration.** Conveyance of a quid pro quo may produce consent—that is, if ascertained but nonconsensual beneficiaries are reluctant, perhaps they can be bought off.

iv. **Virtual representation.** Short of these, in most cases virtual representation is the only answer. Under this doctrine beneficiaries who are similarly situated to unascertainable or unascertained (and therefore nonconsensual) beneficiaries may represent all beneficiaries whose interests are similar—on a theory that what is good for some is good for all and that the consent of those few should suffice. It is not unheard of, but it probably is fair to say that a trustee or other court appointed representative should not be allowed to virtually represent an unascertained beneficiary. If a court appointment is being used, it usually will be a GAL appointed for this purpose, raising the problems noted above.

v.   **Beneficiary holds a power.** A general inter vivos power of appointment might be regarded as tantamount to making the powerholder the sole beneficiary, in which case a termination by merger could occur. This is not a truly copacetic notion unless there are no takers in default of an effective exercise of the power, which is unusual. (See Chapter 14.) Further, even if this general inter vivos power of appointment solution is viable, however, a general *testamentary* power or any *nongeneral* power will not suffice, so the opportunity of a beneficiary/powerholder to terminate is limited (if useful at all).

(a)   **Required consents.** If it is a testamentary or nongeneral power, or if there are takers in default of exercise of a general inter vivos power so that termination by merger is not an option, the takers in default are beneficiaries who must consent, although permissible appointees probably are not.

vi.   **Trustee's participation.** The most fruitful source of an exception to the unfulfilled purpose bar to modification or termination is the trustee's participation in a termination made with the consent of all beneficiaries: a willing trustee simply goes along with a proposal and is estopped to object by virtue of its participation.

 ## EXAMPLES AND ANALYSIS

A trust provides for income to A for life, remainder to a charity. The trustee, A, and the charity agree to terminate the trust and to distribute the discounted present value of each interest. Some courts hold that the settlor's assurance of income to A for life or preservation of an unreduced corpus for the charity is a purpose that should prevent termination. Nevertheless, termination in cases like this occurs often—frequently because the trust fails to qualify for the federal estate tax charitable deduction as drafted but the deduction can be salvaged by an immediate termination and distribution. 4 Scott & Fratcher, The Law of Trusts §337.6 (4th ed. 1989), says this is a legitimate action if it is designed to preserve the settlor's overall intent—which may include qualification for the deduction—as opposed to being part of a scheme to defeat the settlor's intent.

    vii.   **Trustee consent.** If all the beneficiaries consent and the trustee does not object, an unfulfilled purpose does not act as a bar. So why might a trustee object to termination?

        (a)   **Protect trust business?** Contrary to your first suspicion, in most cases involving a professional trustee it is not to preserve its fee; usually a knowledgeable trustee will resign if possible if the beneficiaries are dissatisfied, because the beneficiaries are more trouble than they are worth. Indeed, many trustees make money by termination because they charge a fee that can run in the neighborhood of several percentage points of the trust value. Nevertheless, a trustee might object to modification or termination for several reasons.

        (b)   **Attorney general involvement.** In most jurisdictions the state Attorney General oversees all trusts involving charities. So there could be legal problems emanating from the Attorney General.

        (c)   **Beneficiaries' best interests.** The trustee may share a philosophy with the settlor about the beneficiaries' abilities to handle the assets responsibly—or lack thereof—and the right time to distribute the wealth.

        (d)   **Potential liability.** Conservative or prudence concerns may preclude a trustee's consent, there being exposure if not all beneficiaries (e.g., unascertained or unborn beneficiaries) have given a competent consent.

        (e)   **Professional reputation.** Professional trustees have their reputations to protect; the fiduciary obligation is to object to premature termination and other potential settlors won't likely hire the trustee in the future if it is known to be a pushover.

4. Judicial Power to Modify a Trust

Judicial restraints on modification of trusts vary depending on whether the requested modification is with respect to an administrative or a distributive provision.

a. Deviation from *administrative* provisions—not *dispositive* provisions—is the more commonplace request and, although administrative provisions may permit an indirect diversion from one beneficiary to another (e.g., reallocation of receipts or disbursements will shift some enjoyment between income and remainder beneficiaries), these changes don't normally alter substantive distributive rights.

> i. **Restatement requirements.** According to Restatement (Second) of Trusts §167, the general requirements to authorize such changes include: (i) the deviation is necessitated by a change of circumstances that was unanticipated by the settlor (it probably needs to be one that the reasonable settlor *would* not have anticipated); (ii) the change in circumstances is such that it would defeat or substantially impair the primary purpose(s) of the trust if deviation is not allowed; and (iii) deviation must be the only means to correct the problem.

 # EXAMPLES AND ANALYSIS

To illustrate an unanticipated event, consider an economic depression or other significant change in investment climate. Some trusts drafted just after the Great Depression (and many still are in existence) specifically deny the trustee power to invest in stocks. Today that prohibition would be quite unfortunate and a court might allow deviation from it. Similarly, but not very likely, a trust drafted during a bull stock market might command investment *only* in stocks—which might be unwise from a diversification perspective—and a court might allow deviation if unanticipated events showed that dictate also to be unwise. Less sudden than a depression or stock market crash but equally dramatic unanticipated changes—like run-away inflation—also might suffice to permit deviation from restrictive investment proscriptions for purposes of the changed circumstance requirement.

> ii. ***In Re Pulitzer.*** Most deviation cases involve provisions that prove to be unwise. The most common is requiring nontraditional investments or failing to consider the effects of inflation, or both. E.g., *In re Pulitzer*, 249 N.Y.S. 87 (Sur. Ct. 1931), involved an express prohibition against sale "under any circumstances whatever"; in the face of a downturn in the business the beneficiaries wanted to sell and the court allowed it. The settlor stated in the instrument that he sacrificed his health to maintain the business, and likely anticipated that it was tentative and might not succeed, which proved to be the case. The question therefore was whether the settlor's primary purpose for the trust was to preserve principal and maintain a fair income stream for the beneficiaries, or to preserve the business. The factor that probably justified the result

in *Pulitzer* was the court's conclusion that the settlor's dead hand had controlled long enough; the court chose to protect what little remained for the living beneficiaries.

iii. **Public policy.** In some cases public policy grounds may favor deviation. For example, assume that a testator devised land in the heart of a city's business district in trust for a long period and directed that no building shall be erected on it that is more than three stories high. The provision may be so harmful to the community, as well as to the trust beneficiaries, as to be unenforceable as against public policy. Similarly, trust provisions to tear down or board up a house for 20 years or throw money into the sea would be unenforceable.

iv. **Drafting considerations.** Because the requirements for deviation are not easy to meet, good drafters consider and reflect the importance of drafting for flexibility to meet changing circumstances, and usually repose a lot of discretion in the trustee to adapt to changing circumstances rather than being locked into a fixed formula for investment, allocation of principal and income, situs for trust administration, or whatever.

b. **Deviation from *distributive* provisions.** The traditional rule is that a court may alter the time or manner of a beneficiary's enjoyment to meet the beneficiary's legitimate needs, but a court may not alter or deprive a beneficiary of an entitlement unless the trustee is able to secure the consent of the beneficiaries who are affected by it, which is not always possible.

i. *Stuchell.* For example, *In re Trust of Stuchell*, 801 P.2d 852 (Or. Ct. App. 1990), involved an unsuccessful effort to modify a trust to prevent a required distribution from adversely affecting an incompetent beneficiary's receipt of public assistance. A guardian was not appointed to consent for the incompetent beneficiary, perhaps because such a consent arguably would not have been in the beneficiary's best interests and might have exposed the guardian to future personal liability. Further, virtual representation was not a viable solution because the other beneficiaries were not similarly situated (they were going to receive their shares as drafted). The result was a denial of deviation even though it might have made the trust more advantageous to the beneficiaries as a class and notwithstanding the virtual certainty that the settlor could not have anticipated this state of affairs and arguably would not object to the deviation if alive.

REVIEW QUESTIONS AND ANSWERS

Question: D created a trust naming D's child (C) as beneficiary and D's sibling (S) as trustee. The trust summarized C's troubled past (drug abuse, lack of employment, and financial irresponsibility) and granted to S the authority to distribute to C, or to third parties for C's benefit, such amounts of income and principal as S determines to be appropriate in S's sole and uncontrolled discretion. The instrument further provided that C was not to be notified of the trust unless and until S elected to do so, that C was not to receive any financial or other information regarding the trust, and that S's exercise of discretion was not subject to review by C, or by any court. What limits, if any, are there on the exercise by S of this discretion?

Answer: There is no such thing as absolute discretion of a trustee. If there were no outside review or control, there would be no trust because the essence of the trust relationship is the management of property by a trustee for a beneficiary and there would be no way to ensure management by the trustee for the beneficiary in the absence of control or review of the trustee's exercise of discretion. Accordingly, S's exercise of discretion will be subject to judicial review; generally required is that S exercise it in good faith, in a reasonable manner, and for the purposes intended by D. To permit C to enforce the trust, in most (if not all) jurisdictions C is entitled to a copy of the trust instrument as well as financial and other material information concerning the trust.

Question: B, who is the beneficiary of a valid spendthrift trust, lives in a home rented from L for $3,000 per month, which is the home's fair rental value. B is delinquent on the rent. May L enforce a claim for back rent against B's interest in the trust?

Answer: A spendthrift provision will not bar claims of a creditor who provides necessaries to a beneficiary. Housing is a necessary, but luxurious housing (B's residence might be—at $3,000 rent per month) would not constitute a necessity. An appropriate level of support for B would depend on a variety of factors, including the size and terms of the trust and B's accustomed standard of living. If a home that would rent for $800 per month was appropriate for B's support, L's claim against B's interest in the trust would be limited to that monthly amount.

Question: D devised her estate to T, in trust, income to her child (C) until C reaches 50 years of age, at which time the principal is distributable to C; if C dies before reaching age 50, the trust assets are distributable to T's friend, F, if F survives C. At D's death C, who was 30 years old, and F decide they want the trust to terminate immediately, with 90% of the assets to be distributed to C and 10% to F. Will they succeed in terminating the trust early?

Answer: Unless the trustee were to agree otherwise, under the *Claflin* doctrine beneficiaries may not terminate a trust early without the consent of the settlor if a material purpose of the trust would be defeated by doing so. The beneficiaries will be unable to terminate a spendthrift trust (that also would be true if the trust was a support trust, but this one is not). If the trust is not a spendthrift trust, D's plan to postpone C's possession until C reaches 50 years of age likely also would be deemed a material purpose that would be defeated by an early termination. Furthermore, a trust termination may not be accomplished by the beneficiaries, even if there is no problem with the unfulfilled purposes bar, unless all beneficiaries consent to the termination and the trustee does not object. Here, C and F are aboard, but D retained a reversion: T would hold the trust assets on a resulting trust for D's heirs (see pages 284–285) if C dies before reaching 50 years of age and F is not then living.

14 POWERS OF APPOINTMENT

 CHAPTER OVERVIEW

- A power of appointment permits its holder to select, within limits prescribed by the creator of the power, who will receive the property subject to the power. Powers of appointment add flexibility to an estate plan: with them the powerholder may decide how to distribute property subject to the power after considering changed circumstances.

- A general power is exercisable in favor of the powerholder, her estate, or the creditors of either. All other powers are nongeneral. The creator of a power may make it exercisable during the holder's life, at the holder's death, or both.

- Power of appointment issues include whether creditors of the powerholder may reach the appointive property; whether a power was exercised; whether antilapse statutes apply if the appointee predeceases the holder; and how property subject to a power should be distributed in default of effective exercise if the creator did not name default beneficiaries.

A. A POWER OF APPOINTMENT PERMITS a powerholder to decide who will receive property that is subject to the power. For example, if D, the owner of Blackacre, grants to P a power to appoint Blackacre, P may designate—within limits established by D—who will take Blackacre. Powers of appointment may be granted over property not in trust; more commonly, however, powers of appointment are used with trust property. Thus, the more likely scenario would be a transfer of Blackacre by D to T, in trust, for the benefit of one or more beneficiaries, one of whom also would be given a power to appoint Blackacre to others.

B.   TERMINOLOGY

1.   Donor

The person who creates the power is known as the *donor* of the power, regardless of whether the power is created by inter vivos instrument or by will.

2.   Donee; Powerholder

The person who is authorized to exercise a power of appointment is known as the *donee* of the power, even if she may not personally benefit from it. Modern literature and the Restatement (Third) of Property—Wills and Other Donative Transfers will instead refer to the donee as the *powerholder* and avoid confusion that often exists because of the donee label.

3.   Objects; Permissible Appointees

The persons in whose favor the power of appointment may be exercised are known as the *objects* or *permissible appointees* of the power. If D in the example above had provided that the power could be exercised only in favor of D's descendants, they would be the objects, or permissible appointees. Each person in the world would be an object of a power exercisable in favor of anyone.

4.   Takers in Default of Exercise; Default Beneficiaries

The persons who take property to the extent a power is not validly exercised are known as the *takers in default of exercise* or the *default beneficiaries*. If D had provided in the example above that, to the extent P did not effectively exercise the power, the property would pass at P's death to P's descendants, by representation, P's descendants would be the default beneficiaries or takers in default of exercise of the power.

5.   Kinds of Powers

Powers come in two flavors (*general* or *nongeneral*) and may be exercised at two times (inter vivos or at death); these characteristics also yield definitions, to which we turn shortly.

C.   WHY PEOPLE USE POWERS OF APPOINTMENT

The primary rationale for using powers of appointment is flexibility: they add the ability for the powerholder to take a "second look" at the facts and circumstances as they develop over the life of a trust and alter the donor's plan accordingly—as if the settlor of the trust were still alive and able to respond to changing needs and circumstances.

1.   Leverage

A second reason for their use is suggested by the title to the hit song by Tina Turner: "You Better Be Good to Me." Or, as Professor Halbach says, a power to appoint is a power to *dis*appoint, meaning that the powerholder may prevail on the class of permissible appointees to pay attention to the powerholder's needs and desires lest they be divested of their expectancy by effective exercise of the power in favor of others.

 # EXAMPLES AND ANALYSIS

D devised her estate to T, in trust, to pay income and principal for S's health and support. S also was given a power to appoint the trust assets in favor of D's descendants. To the extent S does not effectively exercise the power, the default beneficiaries are D's descendants, by representation. If a descendant of D develops significant needs, S may exercise the power to benefit that descendant to a greater degree than other objects. In addition, any descendant of D who is not appropriately attentive to S may be excluded from the property by an exercise by S in favor of other descendants of D.

2. Avoid Mandatory Distributions

A third use of powers is in lieu of mandatory distribution to a beneficiary who has reached the age or other qualification for distribution. The more appropriate drafting approach is not to force distribution of the share to that person but to allow her to withdraw her entitlement; that power of withdrawal is a general inter vivos power of appointment, as we will see shortly.

3. Tax Planning

Powers of appointment also are used to accomplish tax objectives. For example, it usually is possible to avoid present gift tax treatment on a transfer to a trust if the donor retains a testamentary power of appointment, because the transfer is not sufficiently complete to incur the tax. Depending on the tax planning involved, a completed gift on an initial transfer of property to a trust may or may not be desirable. General powers also are used to qualify for the estate and gift tax marital deduction and the gift tax §2503(c) qualified minor's trust annual exclusion. Further, efficient use of nongeneral powers may defer the incidence of generation-skipping transfer taxation, and there's the Delaware Tax Trap and other highly refined uses to select between estate tax and generation-skipping transfer tax, depending on which is cheaper.

D. CLASSIFICATION OF POWERS typically focuses on two relevant characteristics—the time and scope of exercise.

1. Time of Exercise

An *inter vivos*, or *presently exercisable*, power of appointment is exercisable by the powerholder by deed or other written instrument delivered during life to the trustee. Many statutes regard an inter vivos power of appointment as also exercisable at death, but technically and without statutory authority otherwise, an inter vivos power that is not expressly also a testamentary power ends the nanosecond before death. A *testamentary* power of appointment is exercisable by the powerholder by a valid will or, in some cases, a document *other* than a will that is regarded as effective only at death. Many powers are expressly both inter vivos and testamentary—the powerholder may exercise them during life or by will at death.

2.   Scope of Exercise

A *general* power of appointment is defined for tax purposes as one that is exercisable in favor of the powerholder, the powerholder's estate, or creditors of either; any other permissible appointee is irrelevant to classification. The key is whether the powerholder can benefit personally, directly or indirectly. For example, a trust beneficiary with a power to withdraw trust assets for her own benefit has a general power of appointment. Similarly, a transferor may convey a life estate to a transferee and authorize the transferee to consume principal if necessary to meet the transferee's needs. Such a power of consumption would be a general power of appointment.

   a.   **Nongeneral.** A *nongeneral* power of appointment for tax purposes is any other power, including *statutory powers* that are exercisable in favor of anyone in the world *except* the powerholder, the powerholder's estate, or creditors of either. (The old property law definition of "special" or "limited" powers of appointment is being subsumed by the tax definition of a nongeneral power, and the Restatement (Third) of Property—Wills and Other Donative Transfers has abandoned the old terminology in favor of general and nongeneral powers, with tax definitions to control for property law purposes.)

3.   Powers of Appointment: Sample Provisions

GENERAL TESTAMENTARY POWER
(from a Marital Deduction Trust)

> Upon the death of my spouse the principal and any accrued and undistributed income of the trust estate shall be held in trust hereunder or distributed to or in trust for such appointee or appointees (including the estate of my spouse), with such powers and in such manner and proportions as my spouse may appoint by will, making specific reference to this power of appointment. Upon the death of my spouse, any part of the principal and accrued and undistributed income of the trust estate not effectively appointed shall be distributed to . . . [insert default beneficiaries]

Notice that this is a general power because the spouse can appoint to the spouse's own estate. The second sentence is the "default" clause, which governs distribution of the appointive property to the extent the power is not effectively exercised (and note also that it is not limited in application to a situation in which the power is not exercised, because it also should apply if the power is exercised ineffectively). This testamentary power of appointment also could require exercise by an instrument delivered during life, with no effect until death, to avoid several problems noted below relating to exercise inadvertently by will.

STATUTORY TESTAMENTARY POWER
(from a Child's postponement trust)

Upon the death of a child who survives me, the child's trust shall be held in trust hereunder or distributed to or in trust for such appointee or appointees other than the child, his or her estate, his or her creditors, or the creditors of his or her estate, with such powers and in such manner and proportions as the child may appoint by his or her will making specific reference to this power of appointment. Upon the death of a child, any part of his or her trust not effectively appointed shall be distributed per stirpes to his or her then living descendants or, if none, then per stirpes to my then living descendants.

This is a "statutory" power of appointment because exercise is in favor of the broadest class of permissible appointees allowed by the tax statutory definition without being a general power. With only one exception, only general powers of appointment are taxable, so the distinction is significant.

NONGENERAL INTER VIVOS POWER
(from nonmarital trust for a surviving spouse)

My spouse may at any time or times during [his or her] life by instrument in writing delivered to the trustee appoint any part or all of the principal to or in trust for any one or more of my descendants and their respective spouses and charitable, scientific, or educational purposes as (s)he directs, and the trustee shall reimburse [him or her] from the remaining principal, if any, for the amount of any gift taxes incurred thereby.

This inter vivos power of appointment is more limited than the statutory power because the donor has allowed exercise only in favor of a limited class of permissible appointees.

4. Nongeneral Power Classifications

Two added classifications exist for nongeneral powers:

a. **Exclusive or nonexclusive** involves the question whether the powerholder may exclude any permissible appointee in exercising the power (an exclusive power) and, if not (a nonexclusive power), how much must be given to each permissible appointee. Notice that, in a statutory power of appointment and many other nongeneral powers, a nonexclusive power would be an impossibility because nonexclusivity requires a narrow class of permissible appointees and a clear intent to preclude exclusion. Under a nonexclusive power each member of the class must receive a share, so a very broad class of permissible appointees would be impossible to administer.

    i. Exclusive powers favored. Notice that the nonexclusive label also is contrary to a fundamental objective of powers (being to add flexibility), so this classification is disfavored. As a result, the intent to create a nonexclusive power must be clear; proof may include extrinsic evidence of the relation of the appointees to the donor or to the powerholder and the size of the class, and a four corners consideration of the pattern of the estate plan and the use of certain language ("to, among, or between" are said to imply a nonexclusive power; addition of "such of" or "any of" is said to negate this implication).

    ii. If nonexclusive, how much? If a nonexclusive power exists, then a second concept of illusory exercise becomes relevant—essentially asking whether so little was provided to a particular permissible appointee that it should not be respected at all. To avoid invalidity if a power of appointment is nonexclusive, required is an appointment to each appointee of a substantial and fairly proportionate amount in relation to the total fund. Given that requirement, if a donor truly wants the power to be nonexclusive it would be better to bequeath a certain amount to each intended beneficiary and not create the power at all, or give an exclusive power over amounts in excess of the minimum amount that the donor wanted each appointee to receive.

  b. Powers in trust (imperative powers). The second classification for nongeneral powers is whether the power is a "power in trust" or "imperative" power. Such a characterization applies, if at all, only to nongeneral powers with a very narrow class of permissible appointees and no default provision.

    i. Why classify a nongeneral power as imperative? This is a highly disfavored theory that is applied because—lacking both an effective exercise and takers in default—we don't know what to do with the appointive property on the powerholder's death. In the absence of an effective exercise or a default provision, normally the property would revert to the donor. To avoid that result when it is clear that a reversion is contrary to the wishes of the donor, regardless of the powerholder's failure to effectively exercise the power, the imperative label is applied to instead cause the property to go to the permissible appointees.

      ii.   Deceased permissible appointee. Cases go both ways on the question whether a deceased permissible appointee has a share that can descend—a share that is vested (subject to divestment if the power is exercised)—or whether only living appointees can take as the default beneficiaries of an imperative power.

 # EXAMPLES AND ANALYSIS

D devised Blackacre to S "with a power to devise Blackacre to such of my children as S may choose." If a power of appointment is deemed to exist and is not effectively exercised when S dies, then the issue is whether S's failure to exercise the power, combined with the failure of D to designate default takers, causes there to be a reversion to D—which may go to the children as takers of D's estate—or whether S has a fee simple absolute and the property passes with the balance of S's estate, which may not go to D's children. Alternatively, the power could be classified as imperative, which would guarantee that the children would receive the appointive property in default of S's effective exercise of the power. If so, and if one of D's children predeceased S, the additional issue is whether that child's successors would take her share.

      iii.   Objects take equally. The permissible appointees take equal shares in default of exercise if an imperative power exists, equality being the law's favor and a court not being willing to create different sized shares.

E.   FAILURE TO EXERCISE; NO DEFAULT BENEFICIARIES

Normally there is a reversion to the donor if there is no default provision and the powerholder fails to completely and effectively exercise the power. That always will be the case for general powers (unless the doctrine of capture applies, as discussed at page 365), and often for nongeneral powers as well. (The power in trust, or imperative power, classification discussed above is an alternative for dealing with the problem of what to do with property subject to a power that is not exercised and for which default beneficiaries were not named by the donor.)

1.   Implied Default Provision

If it is a nongeneral power with a class that is ascertainable and reasonably limited, and if the donor's intent appears to be that a reversion not apply, it may be reasonable to imply a default to each member of the class of permissible appointees, typically in equal shares with the right of representation. For example, in *Loring v. Marshall*, 484 N.E.2d 1315 (Mass. 1985), the testator did not provide for takers in default under a contingency that occurred, the powerholder did not exercise the power, and the permissible appointees were the powerholder's descendants. The court's best alternative recipients of the trust property were the testator's heirs (on the theory that, by not providing for default takers under the contingency that occurred, the testator effectively retained a reversion) or the powerholder's descendants (on the implied default theory that the testator intended to benefit the class of permissible appointees and a taker-in-default-of-exercise provision in their favor therefore should be implied). In part because intestacy is not favored, the court implied a gift in default of exercise to the permissible appointees.

F. CREDITORS' RIGHTS

The issue is whether the powerholder's creditors may reach property subject to a power of appointment on a theory that a powerholder should not be generous to appointees before being equitable to creditors.

1. Donor as Powerholder

If the donor is also the powerholder (a self-created power of appointment, which is not common but permissible), the general rule is that creditors of the donor may reach the appointive property, but only to the extent the donor is insolvent. This rule applies whether the power is general or nongeneral, exercised or not. (Curiously, with respect to creditors' rights, a power to revoke is given better protection—creditors usually cannot force exercise of a power to revoke. We cannot justify this disparate treatment of what appear to be similar powers, but recall the exalted status of powers to revoke with respect to spendthrift clauses in general (see Chapter 13) and in the context of the rights of a surviving spouse as against a funded revocable inter vivos trust (see Chapter 10)).

2. Third Party as Powerholder

If the donor is not the powerholder, the rights of the powerholder's creditors may depend on whether the power is general or nongeneral.

    a. Nongeneral powers. Property subject to a nongeneral power is immune to claims of the powerholder's creditors, even if the power is exercised, because the property subject to the power is not and never could be the powerholder's property. This result is fully consistent with the traditional view that the holder of a power of appointment is not the owner of the property but acts as an agent for the donor in exercising the power; under the relation back doctrine, any exercise of the power is deemed to relate back to creation of the power by the donor, and the property is viewed as having passed directly from the donor to the appointee, not from the donor through the powerholder to the appointee.

b. **General powers.** The traditional rule, still the law in most states, is that property subject to a general power created by a donor who is not the powerholder may be reached by the powerholder's creditors, but *only* to the extent the power is exercised and the powerholder is insolvent (which is to say that the powerholder's own property should be exhausted to pay creditors before appointive property is taken for that purpose). Illustrative is *Irwin Union Bank & Trust Co. v. Long*, 312 N.E.2d 908 (Ind. Ct. App. 1974), in which a debtor was the income beneficiary of a trust from which he also was given the right to withdraw up to 4% of the trust principal annually. The debtor's former spouse obtained a divorce related judgment against him and unsuccessfully attempted to reach the portion of the principal he could withdraw to satisfy the judgment. The debtor's right to withdraw principal from the trust was an inter vivos general power of appointment; the property subject to that power was not his and thus was reachable by his creditors only to the extent he exercised the power.

   i. **Modern rule.** Some states allow creditors to reach assets subject to unexercised inter vivos general powers to the extent the powerholder is insolvent, the notion being that the living powerholder could at any time seize these assets and her creditors should be able to reach them too. Inter vivos general powers are not common, except as a substitute for a mandatory distribution of a trust share (or in the form of a withdrawal right used in trusts for tax planning purposes), so this rule does not arise often except in cases in which we would regard the trust corpus as "belonging" to the powerholder anyway. The Federal Bankruptcy Code produces this result because the trustee in bankruptcy may exercise all the debtor's powers.

c. **Elective share of surviving spouse.** In most states, a powerholder's surviving spouse may reach appointive assets to satisfy an elective share claim (see Chapter 10) only to the extent the powerholder exercised a general power in favor of the powerholder's estate, or a concept known as "capture" applies, to which we turn shortly. (Under the UPC a surviving spouse's elective share may reach assets subject to an inter vivos general power that the decedent held immediately before death.)

G. CONTRACTS TO EXERCISE AND RELEASES OF POWERS

Occasionally, a powerholder will want to commit to exercise the power in a specified manner, or to not exercise the power at all.

1. Contracts to Exercise

A contract to exercise a power of appointment is the donee's agreement with a third party—a permissible appointee or otherwise—to exercise (or not to exercise) a power of appointment in a particular manner. In most jurisdictions contracting to exercise an inter vivos power is permissible but a contract to exercise a testamentary power is not enforceable. The different treatment relates to the donor's intent: the contract to exercise a testamentary power violates the second look objective of the donor by presently locking in an exercise that the donor wanted to be performed only in the future, at the powerholder's death.

a. **Remedy for failure to exercise.** The disappointed promisee of an unenforceable contract to exercise a power of appointment is not entitled to specific performance, nor to damages (because a damage recovery would act as an incentive to exercise the power in compliance with the contract, which the law wants to discourage), but restitution will apply for any consideration given pursuant to the contract.

b. **Exercise pursuant to contract.** The powerholder's voluntary exercise in compliance with the contract, however, is valid; it simply cannot be compelled by enforcement of the contract in any manner.

2. Release of Power

The release of a power of appointment acts like a renunciation: the powerholder essentially is saying that she will never exercise the power. A release of a power is permissible, even if the power is testamentary and even though, particularly with respect to testamentary powers, the release violates the donor's second look objective for giving the power.

a. **Compare to contract to exercise.** A release is acceptable but a contract to exercise is not, because a release amounts to an exercise in favor of the default takers, and this frustration of the donor's second look objective is permitted because the donor selected the ultimate (default) beneficiaries of the appointive property. That is not the case when the powerholder exercises under a contract (unless the contract was to not exercise the power and allow the appointive property to pass by default, or it was to appoint the property in favor of the takers in default). So the law addressing the two concepts differs in the results it is willing to accept.

b. **Exception if no default takers.** An exception to the rule allowing powers to be released applies if there is no default provision. Recall that the absence of default takers also is the circumstance in which an imperative power *might* be deemed to exist (although the two concepts may not overlap, because other requirements for application of the imperative power rule may not exist, such as a sufficiently small class of permissible appointees).

3. *Seidel v. Werner,* 364 N.Y.S.2d 963 (N.Y. Sup. Ct. 1975), *aff'd,* 376 N.Y.S.2d 139 (N.Y. App. Div. 1975), illustrates the difference between a permitted release of a testamentary power and an impermissible contract to exercise that power. In *Seidel* the holder of a testamentary power agreed to exercise it in favor of two of his four children, but failed to do so. Because by statute the contract to exercise the power was unenforceable, the claim was made that the contract was, in effect, a release of the power. The argument failed because the parties did not intend the contract to be a release, and because the effect of the promised exercise was substantially different than a release (e.g., a release would have resulted in all four children taking as default beneficiaries, not just two of them and, unlike the result under the default provision, the contract called for property to be held in trust for the two children until they reached majority, with the property to revert to the powerholder if they did not).

H. EXERCISE IN FRAUD OF A POWER

A powerholder's attempt to benefit nonobjects of a power of appointment usually results either in invalidation of the improper provisions of the appointment and the balance of the exercise being allowed to stand or, if those provisions are inseparable, in the entire exercise being void. An exercise in fraud of the power also is void if it is clear that the powerholder would not have exercised the power if the invalid attempt failed.

 # EXAMPLES AND ANALYSIS

Powerholder wants to benefit Surviving Spouse, but the power of appointment allows exercise only in favor of lineal descendants of Powerholder's grandparent (the donor who created the trust). So Powerholder elicits an agreement from a nephew—a permissible appointee—under which Powerholder will direct $150,000 to the nephew for his sole enjoyment and another $100,000 that the nephew will deliver to Surviving Spouse. A court might bifurcate the exercise, allowing the nephew to keep the $150,000 and invalidating the purported appointment of the other $100,000; more appropriately the court should invalidate the entire exercise, finding the provisions to be inseparable and tainted by the powerholder's motives and the nephew's participation in the fraud on the power. See *In re Carroll's Will*, 8 N.E.2d 864 (N.Y. 1937).

1. Not Applicable to General Powers

Although there can be nonobjects of a limited class general power of appointment, this doctrine is applicable only to nongeneral powers because the holder of a general power could appoint to her own estate and then leave the appointive property as she wanted.

2.   Motive of Powerholder When Exercise Is in Favor of Object

Generally, a powerholder's exercise in favor of a permissible appointee is valid without regard to the powerholder's motive for the exercise. Thus, a capricious or arbitrary exercise of a power of appointment is copacetic and the possibility of such an exercise should be considered by the donor in deciding whether to grant a power: the powerholder has the discretion to change the donor's plan to the extent the power is exercisable. Only a fraudulent exercise is not valid—i.e., an exercise subject to an agreement or understanding that property subject to the power will pass to a nonobject.

I.   EXERCISE OF POWERS

1.   Capacity and Formalities

The capacity of a powerholder and the formalities required to exercise a power are those applicable to the relevant medium for exercise. For example, testamentary capacity is required to exercise a testamentary power, and the capacity to deed—which generally is a little higher than the capacity required to execute a will—is required to exercise an inter vivos power over land by written instrument. Exercise of a power to appoint realty requires the same formalities required in the jurisdiction for a conveyance of realty (e.g., notarization).

2.   Donor Imposed Formalities

Most states permit the donor to impose *extra* formalities, which most often is done by requiring the donee to make specific reference to the power to validly exercise it. For example, review again the sample powers at pages 354 and 355: each testamentary power of appointment contains a specific reference requirement, designed to prevent inadvertent or "blanket" exercise of unknown powers by a broad residuary clause employing language such as: "I leave all the residue of my estate, *including all property over which I may have any power of appointment, . . .*"

3.   Blanket Residuary Clauses

Many wills contain a blanket exercise provision that purports to exercise all powers over which the testator may have control, even if the power is unknown to the testator. By it, even without knowledge of a particular power, the powerholder's will serves as a conclusive (nonrebuttable) exercise because the powerholder's intent to exercise is manifest on the face of the will. That will not be the case, however, if the donor conditioned exercise of the power on the powerholder making a specific reference to it in the powerholder's will.

   a.   **Average powerholder's intent.** Without doubt, the effect of exercise under either a statutory presumption applicable to a silent residuary clause or a blanket exercise provision is consistent with the intent of the average testator. Presumably a powerholder would desire that appointive assets pass to the objects of his or her bounty, rather than to those designated by the donor as takers in default of exercise or to the donor's successors if there is no default provision. Thus, assuming the groups of potential beneficiaries differ, exercise has the perceived advantage of substituting the powerholder's devisees for those who would receive in default of exercise of the power.

b. **Disadvantages of inadvertent exercise.** The unfortunate aspect of inadvertent exercise is that frequently it will result in the exercise of unknown powers that would be better left unexercised. By way of example, assume testator is unaware of the existence of a testamentary power of appointment of which she is powerholder; assume also that the default provision would dispose of appointive assets not effectively appointed to the powerholder's descendants living at the powerholder's death (which is a pretty common scenario) and that these descendants are the persons to whom the powerholder's estate passes by will. The powerholder's objectives might be equally well served in such a situation without exercise of the power. Yet, exercise could create some or all of the following problems:

i. **Pre-1942 general powers: estate tax.** First, if the power is a general power created before October 21, 1942, the assets subject to it will *not* be includible in the powerholder's gross estate for federal estate tax purposes *unless* the power is exercised. Thus, if the property is left to pass under the default provision, unnecessary taxes will be avoided. Naturally the incidence of such pre-1942 powers is dwindling; however, the older the power is, the more probable it is that the powerholder is unaware of its existence and that exercise therefore will be inadvertent.

ii. **Creditors' claims.** Second, as we saw earlier, under the common law creditors of the powerholder of a general power of appointment may reach appointive assets only to the extent the power is exercised and the powerholder is insolvent. This protection is lost through unanticipated exercise of unknown powers of appointment.

iii. **Exercise may fail.** Unintentional exercise of a power of appointment may cause the exercise to fail (e.g., the power of appointment may be nonexclusive or the donee may cause appointment in favor of impermissible appointees).

iv. **Violation of Rule Against Perpetuities.** Inadvertent exercise of a power also may run afoul of the Rule Against Perpetuities. This especially is true in light of the differing axioms governing when the period of the Rule commences with respect to powers of appointment. (See the Website for further information.) If unintended exercise violates the Rule, a state's *cy pres* statute may apply to reform the exercise. In such a case, however, litigation likely would be fostered, along with thorny administrative problems of segregation and marshaling of assets validly passing under the exercise to individuals whose interests do not violate the Rule. These complications are further compounded by the doctrine of capture (discussed below), applicable to any attempted exercise of a general testamentary power that is incurably invalid.

    v. **Delayed discovery of exercise.** All of these problems are exacerbated if the existence of a power of appointment is not discovered until some time after the powerholder's death, notwithstanding that the power was exercised unknowingly by the powerholder's will.

4. Marshaling

If a power has been exercised inadvertently, of greater significance is the potential liability of a powerholder's personal representative attributable to the doctrine of marshaling. Applicable only with respect to testamentary powers of appointment, the doctrine of *marshaling* (sometimes referred to as "allocation") may apply if exercise of a power is valid only in part.

    a. **Blending exercise.** The doctrine applies only to a "blending" exercise that treats appointive assets and the powerholder's own assets as commingled prior to distribution pursuant to the powerholder's will. Under the doctrine, appointive assets will be used to fund those dispositions that are valid under the will, while the powerholder's own assets will be applied to the invalid dispositions. The doctrine thus results in "saving" the exercise to the fullest extent possible.

    b. **Responsibility of personal representative.** If there is a blending exercise, it is incumbent upon a powerholder's personal representative to ascertain the extent to which appointive assets and the powerholder's own assets must be marshaled to the various interests created under the will, a virtual impossibility with respect to unidentified powers.

 ## EXAMPLES AND ANALYSIS

D devised her estate to T, in trust, income and principal being distributable in T's discretion to D's grandson, GS, for life. GS also had a nongeneral testamentary power to appoint the trust assets in favor of D's descendants. When GS died, the trust was valued at $1,000,000 and GS owned additional assets with a value of $1,000,000. GS devised "all property I own and have a power to appoint as follows: half to the Red

Cross and half to my descendants, per stirpes." GS was survived by one child, C. Because the trust assets could not be appointed to the Red Cross, the personal representative of GS's estate, PR, is required under the doctrine of marshaling to allocate GS's own assets to the Red Cross and the appointive assets to C. If PR was unaware of GS's power of appointment over the trust assets, however (which might be the case if, for example, GS was not receiving distributions from the trust when GS died), PR might distribute $500,000 of the assets in S's probate estate to each of the Red Cross and C. What happens when it later is discovered that GS possessed and exercised the power? Because the Red Cross is not an object of the power, presumably half of the appointive assets may not be distributed to it; in that case C receives more, and the Red Cross receives less, than they should have received. Or the exercise may fail with respect to half the appointive assets. Or the Red Cross may have a claim against either PR or C for the assets the Red Cross would have received if GS's own assets and the appointive assets properly had been marshaled. Only if PR neither knew nor reasonably could be expected to know of the trust and GS's power would PR escape liability.

5. Capture

The doctrine of capture may apply to the extent a powerholder makes an invalid or ineffective effort to exercise a *general* power of appointment. An attempt to exercise a general power is taken as an intent to "capture" the appointive assets, taking them out of the donor's plan and allowing the powerholder to dispose of them, even if exercise fails. Under this doctrine, a powerholder is deemed to have made an exercise to her estate by virtue of a failed attempt to appoint to someone else. Thus, to the extent capture applies appointive assets pass pursuant to the powerholder's estate plan, rather than under the power's default provision or, in the absence of a default provision, to the donor's successors. Capture applies only to general powers because the powerholder of a nongeneral power could not have appointed the property to her estate (i.e., could not have captured the property for disposition as a part of her estate).

 # EXAMPLES AND ANALYSIS

D devised her estate: "To T1, in trust, income to P for life, remainder to such person or persons, in trust or outright, as P appoints by will. To the extent P does not effectively exercise this power of appointment, remainder to the Red Cross." P's will provides: "I give the residue of my estate, and all property over which I have a power of appointment to T2, in trust, ..." Assume that the testamentary trust P attempted to create violated the Rule Against Perpetuities and failed (as discussed in the Website, the perpetuities period for measuring the validity of P's exercise of the power would begin to run at D's death, not at P's). The question is whether the trust assets should pass to the Red Cross, as the taker in default under D's will, or to P's heirs. Under the doctrine of capture, P's heirs take.

---

a. **Other causes of failed exercise.** The exercise of a general power can fail and trigger application of the doctrine of capture not only because of a violation of the Rule, as illustrated in the example, but also if the appointee predeceases the powerholder and antilapse does not apply (see the discussion of lapse below) or if the exercise is to a trust that fails for a reason other than a violation of the Rule, such as indefinite beneficiaries.

b. **Responsibility of powerholder's personal representative.** The powerholder's personal representative has the same fiduciary obligation to collect captured assets as with any other probate assets. Difficult as it is for the trustee of a power to know if the powerholder's will exercised a power (see the discussion above), there is no workable process by which the powerholder's personal representative may locate all powers the powerholder possessed and exercised. If the power was unknown to the powerholder, it presumably will be unknown to the personal representative as well (as it may be even if the powerholder knew of the power). Yet reasonable efforts must be made to identify any powers that may have been exercised.

c. **Method of attempted exercise; default clause.** Capture is applicable to either a blending exercise (as illustrated in the example above) or a nonblending exercise (e.g., "I leave the residue of my estate to A. I exercise any powers of appointment I may have as follows: . . ."). As also illustrated by the example, the presence of a default clause will not preclude application of capture.

d. **If exercise not attempted.** Capture will apply unless the powerholder of a general power over assets in trust fails to exercise or to attempt to exercise the power. The property will pass to the takers in default of exercise named by the donor only to the extent there is no attempted exercise; there will be a reversion to the donor or her successors to the extent there was no default provision and no attempted exercise.

6. **Exercise by Silent Residuary Clause**

Capture applies when a powerholder unsuccessfully attempts to exercise a general power (with a blanket or specific, blended or nonblended exercise). The question we now consider is whether a *silent* residuary provision in the powerholder's will exercises powers held by the powerholder. As a general rule, a silent residuary provision that makes no reference to powers (e.g., "all the residue of my estate") typically does not serve as an exercise. But if it can be established that the powerholder intended to exercise the power, a residuary clause in the powerholder's will does so even if it makes no reference to powers.

EXAMPLES AND ANALYSIS

D's will devised Blackacre to T1, in trust, income to P for life, remainder as P appoints by will, otherwise to D's descendants, per stirpes, to the extent P does not effectively exercise the power. P's will provides: "I give my entire estate to T2 in trust for X for life." P's will also includes provisions granting powers and directing T2 in the administration of the trust; among them is: "If X's child, C, desires to work on Blackacre, I request that T2 employ C to do so for as long as C desires." Under the general rule, P's silent residuary clause would not exercise P's power, but the reference to T2 employing C to work on Blackacre, the property subject to the power, indicates P's intent that the residuary clause exercise the power and it would do so.

a. **Proof of intent to exercise.** If the general rule applies, proof of intent to exercise is allowable to rebut the presumption, including factors such as (i) the disposition under the powerholder's will if appointment occurs; (ii) partial invalidity of the powerholder's plan if the power is not exercised (e.g., the powerholder's estate is $100,000; the trust assets over which the powerholder has a power are $500,000; the powerholder's will leaves $200,000 to X and the residue to Y; if the will does not exercise the power, X will get only $100,000 and Y will get nothing); and (iii) factors showing that the powerholder could have meant to exercise, including knowledge of the power, lack of reason not to exercise, that the residuary taker was a natural object of the powerholder's bounty, that the amounts involved were not inappropriate for the situation, and mistake by the powerholder or her attorney as to ownership of the appointive property or the necessity for express exercise.

b. **Minority rule #1: exception for general powers.** An exception to the general rule that a silent residuary clause—without evidence of intent to the contrary—will not exercise a power held by the testator is recognized in some states for *general* powers because the powerholder/testator may think of the appointive property as her own. Again, however, the question is one of the powerholder's intent—the silent residuary clause will not be deemed to exercise the power if it is proven that the powerholder did *not* intend to exercise. In *Beals v. State Street Bank &*

Trust Co., 326 N.E.2d 896 (Mass. 1975), the powerholder had treated the appointive property as her own, which led the court to treat a power that originally was a general power, but that had been cut back to a nongeneral power years earlier (probably for tax reasons), as having been exercised by a silent residuary clause; the jurisdiction treated silent residuary clauses as exercising general but not nongeneral powers.

c. **Minority rule #2: exception for nongeneral powers.** In a few jurisdictions, silent residuary clauses also exercise nongeneral powers if the devisees of the residuary clause are permissible appointees of the power (unless an intention of the powerholder not to exercise the power is proven).

J. CONFLICT OF LAWS AND POWERS OF APPOINTMENT

The question addressed here was at issue in *Beals*: if the donor died in state A and the trust is administered there, but the powerholder dies in state B, which state's law governs exercise of the power? The traditional rule is to apply the law that governs the trust administration, which usually was the donor's domicile. But because exercise issues arise under the powerholder's will, because we are most interested in whether the powerholder intended to exercise the power, and because the powerholder and her attorney presumably planned with respect to the law of the powerholder's domicile, the logical approach to this issue would be to apply the law of the powerholder's domicile. Although there is a modern trend to do so, only a very small number of cases so far have deviated from the traditional rule.

 ## EXAMPLES AND ANALYSIS

Assume that Donor died in New York, where Donor was a lifetime resident, and created a testamentary trust that grants Powerholder a nongeneral testamentary power to appoint the corpus of the trust. The trust now is administered by a California trustee for the benefit of beneficiaries located around the country. Powerholder's will, executed in Indiana where Powerholder was domiciled at death, fails to make any reference to the power, stating only that "the residue of my estate shall be distributed per stirpes to my descendants who survive me." Assuming for the sake of argument that Powerholder's descendants are all permissible appointees under Donor's power, the issue would be whether the New York rule that silent residuary clauses are effective to exercise nongeneral powers should apply. Also assume that Indiana follows the more traditional rule that a silent residuary provision does *not* exercise unspecified powers. Although it is possible that Powerholder or her attorney was aware of the New York rule and therefore found it unnecessary to state the intent to exercise the power, it is far more likely that they were acting on the basis of their understanding of Indiana law that governed all other aspects of Powerholder's will. Indeed, it may be that Powerholder did not know that the power of appointment was available.

Extrinsic evidence would be admissible to establish Powerholder's likely intent to exercise, but that endeavor would not be necessary if New York law applies to this case in the first instance and, under the traditional conflict of laws rule for this situation, New York law would apply. Modern cases would apply the law of Indiana. No case would select California on the basis of the simple situs for administration. See, e.g., *White v. United States*, 680 F.2d 1156 (7th Cir. 1982) (applying Indiana law in the hypothetical facts); *Toledo Trust Co. v. Santa Barbara Foundation*, 512 N.E.2d 664 (Ohio 1987) (Ohio trust with California powerholder, applying California law).

K.   POWERS OF APPOINTMENT AND LAPSE

If a testator devises property to someone who dies before the testator, and does not provide for that possibility, the gift is said to lapse (i.e., fail, unless the jurisdiction's antilapse statute applies). Generally, antilapse statutes apply if the devisee and the testator were related in a specified manner; if so, the predeceased devisee's descendants receive the devise by representation. See Chapter 8. What result applies if an appointee predeceases the powerholder of a testamentary power? Notwithstanding the fiction that a powerholder who exercises a power of appointment is an agent of the donor and that the exercise "relates back" as if the exercise terms were written in the donor's trust all along, the lapse rules can be problematic in the context of powers of appointment.

1.   Traditional Rule

The general rule has been that antilapse statutes do not apply to powers of appointment because the statutory representatives of the appointee (typically, the appointee's descendants) may be individuals who are not within the class of permissible appointees.

 ## EXAMPLES AND ANALYSIS

D devised her estate to T, in trust, income to C for life with C given a testamentary power to appoint the trust assets at C's death among C's siblings. C's will exercises the power and appoints the property to C's sibling, S, who was living when C executed C's will but who died before C. If the jurisdiction's antilapse statute applies, S's descendants would take even though they were not permissible appointees. For that reason (and because antilapse statutes on their face often apply only to devises by will), the traditional rule has been that antilapse statutes are not applied to exercises of powers in favor of appointees who predecease the powerholder.

a. **Exception for general powers.** Some courts will apply the jurisdiction's antilapse statute if the power is general, which is not necessarily copacetic if the class of permissible appointees of the general power is narrow (e.g., exercisable in favor of creditors of the powerholder's estate—which makes it a general power, probably desirable for tax purposes to avoid a generation-skipping transfer tax—and members of a narrow class of other designated persons, such as the donor's descendants).

2. Modern Rule

UPC §2-707(e) and Restatement (Third) of Property—Wills and Other Donative Transfers §18.6 allow antilapse statutes to apply and permit descendants of deceased objects to take directly—the theory being that the predeceased appointee, if alive, could have left the appointive property to those persons. A question under such modern statutes may be whether the predeceased appointee is within the class of beneficiaries covered by the antilapse statute. In applying such a statute, it is necessary to determine whether the appointee must be a relative of the donor or of the powerholder. Consistent with the relation back theory applicable to powers, is it relation to the donor that counts? It should not be; the sensible rule is that relation to the powerholder should govern, but don't expect to find unanimity on this issue.

EXAM TIP

Consider the following in analyzing power of appointment questions. Because general and nongeneral powers are treated so differently for a variety of reasons, first determine whether the power is general or nongeneral.

- If general, consider the following:

(a) If inter vivos, in some jurisdictions the powerholder's creditors may reach property subject to the power, regardless of whether the power was exercised; in most, however, they may reach such property only to the extent the power was exercised. If testamentary, the powerholder's creditors may reach property subject to the power only to the extent it is exercised.

(b) If exercised in favor of an appointee who predeceased the powerholder, does the jurisdiction's antilapse statute apply to cause the appointee's descendants to take? If so, must they be related to the powerholder or to the donor?

(c) In a minority of jurisdictions, a silent residuary clause in the powerholder's will is presumed to exercise the power (unless the donor required the powerholder to make specific reference to the power to exercise it). If such a presumption arises, is there evidence to rebut it?

(d) If ineffectively exercised, consider application of the doctrine of capture, under which the property subject to the power would pass as a part of the powerholder's estate.

(e) If not exercised, are default beneficiaries named to take the property? If not exercised and default beneficiaries are not named, there is a reversion to the donor or her successors.

• If nongeneral, consider the following:

(a) Creditors of the powerholder may not reach the property subject to the power regardless of whether it is exercised.

(b) Is the power exclusive or nonexclusive? The presumption is exclusive; is there sufficient evidence of intent to the contrary? If a nonexclusive, nongeneral power is exercised, is a sufficient amount appointed to each object to avoid an illusory exercise allegation?

(c) If the power is exercised, are the appointees permissible appointees?

(d) To the extent the power was not effectively exercised, were default beneficiaries designated by the donor? If not, is the class sufficiently narrow to warrant characterizing the power as imperative, or is there an implied gift to the permissible appointees, in either case causing the property to be distributed equally among the permissible appointees? If so and if one or more of them predeceased the powerholder, does the jurisdiction allow successors of the deceased permissible appointee to take her share?

(e) If the power is not effectively exercised and default beneficiaries were not designated, and if imperative power classification and an implied default to the objects are not appropriate, the property will revert to the donor or her successors.

(f) Is the power exercised as part of a plan to indirectly benefit a nonobject, in which case the exercise may be invalid altogether under the fraud on a power doctrine?

> • Whether general or nongeneral, if the power is exercised by a blending clause in the powerholder's will, would part of the attempted exercise be invalid? If so, can marshaling be applied to save the exercise in whole or in part?

REVIEW QUESTIONS AND ANSWERS

Question: Donor created a trust for spouse, S, for life and granted S a nongeneral testamentary power to appoint the trust property among the donor's grandchildren; takers in default were not named, and the donor's children were disinherited under the trust instrument. Donor died intestate, after which S died without exercising the power. Who takes the trust assets?

Answer: The grandchildren should take—the power should be labeled a power in trust (or imperative power) to prevent the children from taking in default of exercise. If the power is not classified as imperative, the property would revert on S's death to the donor's estate; because the donor died intestate, in most jurisdictions the children would take at least part of the property as the donor's heirs. There being a clear indication that the children were meant to be excluded, the power should be treated as imperative and the property distributed to the grandchildren; that result essentially implies a default provision in their favor.

Question: D's will devised her estate: "Half to T, in trust #1, income to A for life; at A's death, to such person or persons as A appoints by will, provided that A may not appoint to herself, her estate, or the creditors of either; to the extent A does not effectively exercise the power, to the Red Cross. The other half to T, in trust #2, income to A for life; at A's death, to such person or persons as A appoints by will, including A's estate; to the extent A does not effectively exercise the power, to the Red Cross." A's will provides: "I leave my entire estate to X." What disposition is to be made of the assets in trust #1 and trust #2 at A's death?

Answer: A has a nongeneral power over the assets in trust #1 because it is not exercisable in favor of A, her estate, or the creditors of either. A's power over the trust #2 assets is general because she may exercise it in favor of her estate. A's will does not expressly exercise either power. Except in a small minority of jurisdictions, the residuary clause in A's will does not exercise the power over the assets in trust #1, which will pass to the Red Cross as the taker in default of exercise of the power. In most jurisdictions, so too will the assets in trust #2, although in some states a silent residuary clause in a powerholder's will that makes no reference to powers is deemed to exercise general powers. In such a jurisdiction the assets in trust #2 would pass to X.

Question: In question #2, above, what result if X predeceased A and A's will had provided: "I exercise my powers of appointment over trusts #1 and #2 created by the will of D and appoint all property subject to such powers to X. I give my entire residuary estate to Y''?

Answer: The first question is whether an antilapse statute applies to the appointments to X. Most do not, but if an antilapse statute applied to powers, if X was related to A (or D, if the antilapse statute required the appointee to be related to the donor instead of to the powerholder), and if X was survived by descendants, these representatives would take. In the more likely circumstance of the antilapse statute not applying, the doctrine of capture would apply to cause the assets of trust #2 to pass through A's estate to Y, rather than pursuant to the default provision of D's will to the Red Cross. Absent application of an antilapse statute, the assets of trust #1 will pass to the Red Cross as the default beneficiaries; capture is not applicable to nongeneral powers.

Question: P had a general testamentary power to appoint the assets in a trust created by D. The taker in default is X. P's will left the residue of her estate—with no reference to powers—to a trust for A that failed under the Rule Against Perpetuities. At P's death, who takes?

Answer: The first question is whether the residuary clause in P's will exercised the power. Under the majority view it will not, absent evidence of an intent by P to exercise. In that case, X takes as the default beneficiary. In some states a silent residuary clause (like P's that makes no reference to powers) is deemed to exercise general powers. Such an exercise, however, would fail because the trust intended to receive the appointive assets itself failed due to the violation of the Rule. Because the power was general, however, P's attempted exercise might trigger application of the doctrine of capture, in which case the property would pass to P's heirs. Underlying the doctrine of capture, however, is the idea that a powerholder who ineffectively attempts to exercise a general power has expressed an intention to assert control over disposition of the appointive property that should cause it to pass pursuant to the powerholder's estate plan—because the powerholder would have exercised the general power for her own benefit had she known the exercise was invalid. In the case of a silent residuary clause that operates as an exercise because of state law there is no clear expression of intent by the powerholder to exercise control over the property subject to the power, and capture therefore might not apply. In that case, the property would pass to D's successors.

Question: D devised her estate to T, in trust, income to P for life, and gave P an unlimited general power of appointment—exercisable inter vivos or by will—over the trust assets. In default of exercise of the power by P, the property was to pass to D's descendants living at P's death per stirpes. P exercised the power by a provision in her will appointing the property to her sibling, S, but S died before P; one child of S (N) survived P. Who takes?

Answer: Most antilapse statutes will not directly apply to permit N to take. In such a jurisdiction it is likely that the default beneficiaries (D's descendants, per stirpes) would take. However, because P's power was general, and exercisable by P in favor of N, a court might apply the antilapse statute to cause N to take even without an antilapse statute that expressly dictates that result. (Note also that the power was exercisable inter vivos; in a variety of contexts the holder of a general inter vivos power is treated as the owner of the property subject to the power.) Modern antilapse statutes like UPC §2-707(e) apply to powers of appointment; the questions in such a jurisdiction would be whether the statute requires S to be related to the donor or to the powerholder for it to apply, and whether S has the required relationship to D or P. In any event, if the exercise fails, and antilapse is not extended to powers of appointment, this general power exercise would trigger the doctrine of capture and the property would pass to N if the antilapse statute includes P's siblings in its coverage. If so, it might make sense for a court to just apply the antilapse statute to the exercise directly. Alternatively, however, to avoid setting that precedent in other cases, the court might accomplish the same result with the capture doctrine and antilapse in P's estate distribution. Either way, N probably would take if the state law antilapse statute includes siblings in the class of beneficiaries to which it applies.

15

FUTURE INTERESTS: CLASSIFICATION, CHARACTERISTICS, AND CONSTRUCTION

CHAPTER OVERVIEW

- Virtually all trusts—whether inter vivos or testamentary—create future interests. Virtually all future interest questions arise because the instrument did not clearly address a contingency that occurred. Rules of construction help to give effect to the presumed intent of the settlor.

- This chapter addresses future interest classification and construction. Subjects covered include characteristics of future interests, distinguishing between vested and contingent future interests, whether the future interest holder must survive until the time of possession, and gifts conditioned on a beneficiary dying without issue or made to someone's heirs, descendants, issue, or children.

A. FUTURE INTERESTS IN A MODERN TRUSTS AND ESTATES PRACTICE

For many, "future interests" connotes archaic rules of English law that have little or no relevance to the modern practice of law. In fact, future interests are fundamental to a modern trusts and estates practice because trusts are commonly used and most of them are created to permit enjoyment of trust income and principal by one beneficiary or group of beneficiaries, followed by distribution to a different beneficiary or group of beneficiaries (e.g., income to my spouse for life, remainder to my children). Fortunately, the future interests that we encounter are relatively straightforward and much of the confusion of future interest law is reserved for busted plans—not the kind that you will draft. Indeed, our endeavor in this chapter is to highlight how to avoid common future interest drafting errors.

1. Legal vs. Equitable Interests

Future interests (and, for that matter, present interests) may be created with respect to the legal or equitable title to property. Historically, future interests typically were created for legal estates: e.g., a devise by D of "Blackacre to A for life, remainder to B." At D's death, A has a legal life estate in Blackacre (a present interest), B the legal remainder (a future interest). Today, the vast majority of future interests are created in trust: e.g., a devise by D of "Blackacre to T, in trust, for A for life, remainder to B." At D's death, A has an equitable life estate (again, a present interest), B an equitable remainder (a future interest). Our focus is on future interests in trust (equitable estates); the rules for future interests in legal estates usually are the same, but occasionally they may differ. For example, the Doctrine of Destructibility of Contingent Remainders (discussed below) only applies to legal estates. We will study it briefly only because it spawned rules that bleed over and affect future interests in trust.

2. Rules of Law vs. Rules of Construction

A rule of law controls without regard to intent. For example, if D devised property in trust for a period equal to lives in being at D's death plus 22 years, the devise violates the Rule Against Perpetuities without regard to D's intent. By contrast, most of the rules we study in this chapter are rules of construction that are needed because the controlling instrument was not properly drafted and did not address clearly the issue raised. In other words, if the instrument reflects the settlor's intent with respect to an issue about which a rule of construction applies, the settlor's intent—not the rule of construction—controls. To a significant degree we are studying this material to know how *not* to draft certain provisions. As you proceed through this chapter, consider how the issues you study could have been avoided by careful drafting.

3. "Future Interests" Is a Misnomer

A future interest is a presently existing property right or interest that may or will grant possession or enjoyment in the future. Enjoyment may be contingent (e.g., a devise by D: "To A for life, remainder to B, but if B does not survive A, remainder to C"; at D's death C has a future interest that may never vest in possession if A and B still are alive). But the interest presently exists; it is transferable, enforceable, and protectable.

a. **Unborns' interests** are supported by a relation back doctrine. Because the unborn cannot hold title to the future interest prior to birth, ownership is deemed to attach or fix at birth and relate back to creation of the interest. This explains the class opening and closing rules discussed in Chapter 8—the interest fixing and relating back as if always there, as each member of the class is born (and, if survivorship is required, as each dies).

 # EXAMPLES AND ANALYSIS

T has two children: A and B. B has children; A does not, and is not expected to in the future. T wants to divide her estate between A and B, but she wants what A does not use during A's life to be divided among B's children, if they reach 25 years of age. Thus, T leaves her estate half outright to B and the other half in trust for A for life, remainder to B's children who reach 25 years of age. T dies survived by A, B, and one child of B (C). The class of B's children who will share in the remainder does not close until A's death (if a child of B is at least 25 years old when A dies), or thereafter when a child of B reaches 25 years of age (if no child of B is at least 25 years old at A's death). If D is born to or adopted by B after T's death but before the class closes, D's interest fixes at D's birth or adoption and relates back to the date of T's death, as if D had a contingent remainder from that date.

B.   CLASSIFICATION IN GENERAL

When a transferor conveys a present interest in property, the future interest that follows it may be retained by the transferor or it may be conveyed to one or more other transferees (or it may be conveyed in part and retained in part). In the foregoing chart the interests that the transferor retained are in the left hand column, of which there are three types: two that follow defeasible fees (a possibility of reverter and a power of termination) and one that does not (a reversion). The names of these interests remain even if the transferor at some later date conveys the retained interest to a third party: what counts here is that the transfer creating the present interest did not also convey the future interest—it was retained and later transferred.

1.   Future Interests in the Settlor vs. in Third Parties

Note how the same "size" or "quality" of interest may be classified differently based on the side of this chart on which it appears (e.g., if the present interest holder has a fee simple determinable, the future interest will be a possibility of reverter if it is held by the transferor; it will be a shifting executory interest if it was created in a third party by the same conveyance that created the present interest). As we proceed through the materials in this chapter, note how such seemingly similar interests (except for the identity of the person holding the interest) may have different rights, attributes, and consequences.

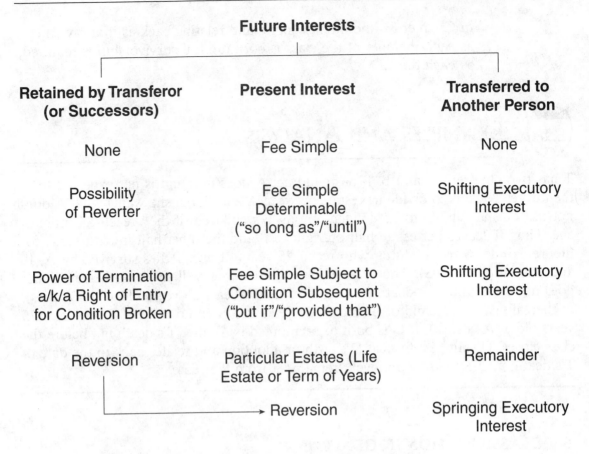

2. Executory Interests vs. Contingent Remainders

For most purposes there is no substantive difference between an executory interest and a contingent remainder, each of which is created in transferees when the present interest is conveyed. In each case, there is only a possibility that the future interest will become possessory: the contingent remainder or executory interest becomes possessory only if the required condition occurs. The difference in operation of the two estates is that—with one minor exception—an executory interest becomes possessory by divesting a preceding estate but a contingent remainder becomes possessory at the expiration of a preceding estate without divesting that estate.

 EXAMPLES AND ANALYSIS

G devised her estate: "To T, in trust, for A for life, remainder to B, but if B does not survive A, then remainder to C." As discussed below, because B's remainder is vested subject to divestment by a condition subsequent, C's estate is an executory interest rather than a contingent remainder. By contrast, if G's devise was: "To T, in trust, for A for life, remainder to B if B survives A, otherwise to C," surviving A is a condition precedent to B's remainder. B's estate is a contingent remainder, which makes C's interest an alternative contingent remainder rather that an executory interest. In each case C's future interest will become possessory only if B predeceases A. The operational difference between the two is that, in the first example, C's interest becomes possessory by divesting B; in the second, B's death before A causes C's contingent remainder to become possessory without divesting B. Should you care? The truth is—for most every purpose—*NO*. So, don't obsess about these historical and picky distinctions unless you have a case in which they matter for some unforeseen reason.

a. **Other consequences.** Whether a transferee's future interest is a contingent remainder or an executory interest usually will not affect it becoming possessory (if the applicable condition precedent or subsequent occurs), but it may in limited circumstances. For example, the Rule in *Shelley's Case,* Doctrine of Worthier Title, and Rule of Destructibility of Contingent Remainders (each discussed below) exempt executory interests but not contingent remainders; to the very limited extent these rules are still viable, they may allow extinction or merger of interests for modification or termination purposes, for different enforcement purposes, for marketability, and more.

 # EXAMPLES AND ANALYSIS

O conveyed property: "To T, in trust, to pay the income to A for life, remainder to B, but if B does not survive A, remainder to O's heirs." B's remainder is vested, subject to divestment; therefore, O's heirs have an executory interest, not a contingent remainder. Accordingly, the Doctrine of Worthier Title (if still applicable in the jurisdiction, which is not likely) would not apply to cause the gift to O's heirs to be treated as a reversion in O. (See the discussion below of the Doctrine of Worthier Title.)

Similarly, if O conveyed land: "To T, in trust, to pay the income to A for life, remainder to B, but if B does not survive A, remainder to A's heirs," A's heirs have an executory interest and the Rule in *Shelley's Case* (in the unlikely event that it still is applicable in the jurisdiction) therefore would not apply to cause the gift to A's heirs to be treated as a remainder in A. (See the discussion below of the Rule in *Shelley's Case.*)

Finally, assume O conveyed Blackacre: "To T in trust to pay the income to A for life, remainder to B, but if B does not graduate from law school before reaching 25 years of age, then to C if C graduates from law school before reaching 25 years of age." Also assume that A dies survived by B (age 20), and by C (age 18). C has an executory interest, not a contingent remainder; as a result, the Rule of Destructibility of Contingent Remainders (if still applicable in the jurisdiction, which also is unlikely) would not apply to destroy C's estate at A's death.

3.   Effect on Applicability of the Rule Against Perpetuities

Classification also is important because the Rule Against Perpetuities does not apply to vested interests and applies to contingent remainders and executory interests with different consequences. The Rule does not apply at all to any interest that the transferor retains, because they are not "transfers" that might "vest" outside the period of the Rule.

4.   Significance of an Interest Being Vested

Vesting is very important because it affects entitlement, the class opening and closing rules, tax liability, and more.

 # EXAMPLES AND ANALYSIS

O conveyed Blackacre to T in trust for A for life, remainder to B, and B predeceased A. If B's remainder is vested (e.g., "to A for life, remainder to B," and UPC §2-707 is not applicable—see the discussion below), at A's death Blackacre belongs to B and will be distributed to B's estate and pass through it to B's heirs or devisees. But if B's remainder is contingent (e.g., "to A for life, remainder to B *if B survives A*") and there is no alternative disposition, O has retained a reversion and, at A's death, Blackacre will revert to O for disposition to O's successors. In the first case B's estate will include the value of the remainder for estate tax purposes; in the second case O's estate will include the value of the reversion.

As an illustration of how vesting can affect class opening and closing rules, consider the following: O's gift is "to B's children who reach 25 years of age." B has two children, C (age 19) and D (age 10). C dies before reaching 25 years of age. C has a contingent interest and C's death before 25 years of age causes the class to remain open until D reaches 25 years of age. Thus, if E is born to B eight years after the gift is made (when D is 18), E will become a member of the class. But if the gift had been "to B's children, payable at 25 years of age," C's gift would be vested and the class would close no later than when C would have reached 25 years of age, six years later, regardless of whether C lives until then. As a result, E would be excluded from the class.

a.   **Taxes.** Transfer tax results may vary. If the holder of a transmissible interest (vested or contingent) dies, its value is included in her estate for estate tax purposes (but usually the contingency causes a contingent remainder or executory interest to have little or no value). On the contrary, a vested interest would be includible with a value that reflects only the delay attributable to deferred possession or enjoyment until the present interest ends. If the interest is not transmissible, it is not subject to estate tax at the owner's death, regardless of whether it is vested.

 EXAMPLES AND ANALYSIS

O conveyed Blackacre in trust, "income to A for life, remainder to B, but if B does not survive A, then to C." C has a transmissible executory interest because C need not survive A or B to take. If C predeceases A, C's executory interest passes to her heirs or devisees and its value is includible in C's estate (although the value of C's executory interest would be a small fraction of the value of Blackacre if A is elderly and in poor health and B is young and in excellent health at C's death). But B's interest (which is vested, subject to divestment) terminates if B dies before A; there is nothing for B to transmit to her heirs or devisees and nothing to be included in her estate for estate tax purposes. If the gift had been "income to A for life, remainder to B if living, otherwise to C," B's contingent remainder would have no value at B's death before A; for estate tax purposes, zero would be includible in B's estate.

    b. State law protection. State law rights to accountings and enforceability and the ability to enjoin actions or waste by the present interest holder may differ. Thus, a vested remainder is entitled to more effective current protection than a contingent one.

5. Effect of the Equities

Courts trifle with classifications to distinguish unwanted precedent: future interests is either a "wonderful calculus" or "a particularly low sort of cunning"—sometimes all in the same case—and care is required in every case in which the classification rules are applied to be sure the precedent is from a case that is similar in its inquiry (e.g., a case looking to avoid application of the antiquated Rule in *Shelley's Case* isn't likely to be persuasive in a current tax dispute) and is not skewed by the application of rules that were developed in response to doctrines no longer in force (e.g., the preference for early vesting or for vested over contingent remainders to avoid the Doctrine of Destructibility of Contingent Remainders, which no longer exists and never applied to equitable interests in trust).

C. FUTURE INTERESTS OF THE TRANSFEROR

Consult again the chart at the beginning of this chapter. The interests the transferor retained when the future interest was conveyed are:

1. Possibility of Reverter

A possibility of reverter is retained if a transferor conveys a fee simple determinable and does not provide for a third party to take if the fee is terminated. A fee simple determinable is a fee simple estate that is limited or defeasible. It often is identifiable by the use of words of duration, such as "so long as" or "until."

 ## EXAMPLES AND ANALYSIS

"To X so long as she remains in the Navy"; "to Y until zoning laws prohibit the current use"; "to Z so long as she does not remarry." Each of X, Y, and Z has a fee simple determinable. If the interest that follows theirs has not been conveyed, the transferor still owns it. As such, the transferor's interest is a possibility of reverter. If a year later the transferor died and it passed to A, it still would be regarded as a possibility of reverter.

    a. Alternative disposition. If the grant had provided an alternative disposition (e.g., "and if X leaves the Navy, to A") there would be no possibility of reverter. Instead, A would have the future interest—a shifting executory interest. See the right hand column of the chart at page 377. Same interest; different name (and a few differences in result).

2. Power of Termination

The power of termination (also known as a right of entry for condition broken) is retained when a transferor conveys a fee simple subject to a condition subsequent and does not provide for a third party to take if the fee is terminated. A fee simple subject to a condition subsequent also is a limited, defeasible fee. Words that imply the condition would look like: "but if" or "provided, however." For example, "To X, provided that she not leave the Navy"; "to Y, but only if the zoning laws do not change"; "to Z, but only if she does not remarry."

    a. Alternative disposition. If the transferor does not provide for disposition of the property to a third party if the condition subsequent occurs, the transferor has retained that interest (a power of termination or a right of entry for condition broken—same thing, different names). If the transferor had provided an alternative disposition (e.g., "but if X leaves the Navy, to A") there would be a shifting executory interest instead of a power of termination.

3. Possibility of Reverter vs. Power of Termination

Are powers of termination/rights of entry and possibilities of reverter the same interest, except for the semantics?

a. Differences. First, with a fee simple determinable, occurrence of the divesting condition that causes expiration of the fee automatically makes the transferor's possibility of reverter possessory. By contrast, an affirmative act is required for the transferor to reacquire possession under a power of termination/right of entry; the transferor may exercise her option to reacquire the property or choose not to. Second, at common law, the power of termination/right of entry could not be alienated and was destroyed if you tried. Not so with a possibility of reverter.

b. Acceleration of reversion. Each of a possibility of reverter and power of termination/right of entry can be used to accelerate the reversion.

 ## EXAMPLES AND ANALYSIS

If O conveys Blackacre to A for life and retains the balance of the fee, O has a reversion that will become possessory at A's death. If instead the grant is: "To A for life, but if A remarries, to O," O has a power of termination/right of entry incident to the reversion (as a condition cutting short A's life estate, which effectively accelerates the reversion). Similarly, a grant by O: "To A until the first to occur of A's death or remarriage," involves the retention by O of both a reversion and a possibility of reverter, with O's reversion accelerated by the possibility of reverter if A remarries.

c. No effect on transferee's interest. If creation of the defeasible fee is accompanied by the transferor's conveyance of the future interest to a third party as transferee (instead of the transferor retaining that future interest), the transferee's future interest is a shifting executory interest, regardless of whether the present interest is a fee simple determinable or a fee simple subject to condition subsequent, and these distinctions are meaningless. See the right hand column of the chart at page 377.

4. Reversion

Possibilities of reverter and powers of termination are seldom encountered in estate planning and estate and trust administration. Reversions are much more common, although well-drafted documents avoid them as well. A transferor who conveys less than what she owned retains whatever remains. If that interest follows a present interest, and if it cannot be a possibility of reverter or power of termination, it is a reversion. Reversions fill gaps in title, usually caused by the drafter's inadvertent failure to convey the full fee.

 # EXAMPLES AND ANALYSIS

In the following examples, identify the reversion:

- "To A for life." This is a pure reversion when A dies.

- "To A for life, then to such of A's children as survive A." The reversion at A's death will be cut off if any child of A survives A. (As discussed below, reversions always are vested; as this example illustrates, however, they may never become possessory.)

- "To B for life, and one year after B's death to E." The transferor has a reversion for the one year after B's death. E has an interest that will divest the transferor in actual possession and is known as a *springing* executory interest. In the chart at page 377 this is illustrated by the last line, showing the reversion in possession in the middle column and the springing executory interest in a third party in the right hand column.

- "To D for life, but if D remarries, to E." The transferor's reversion at D's death will be cut off if D remarries. Because the transferor will not be in possession at that time, D's interest is a *shifting* executory interest.

---

a. **Springing or shifting,** what's the difference? See page 377 and don't fret about the difference.

b. **Reversions always are vested.** Because reversions are retained and not transferred, the transferor is deemed to own a fully vested interest that is effective automatically—although it may be divested either before (e.g., the second and fourth examples above) or after (e.g., the third example above) it becomes possessory.

D. FUTURE INTERESTS OF TRANSFEREES

Most intentionally created future interests are created in transferees, rather than retained by the transferor. Transferees' future interests come in two forms: remainders (which may be vested or contingent) and executory interests (which may be shifting or springing).

1. Remainders

The most common future interest is the remainder, because it follows the most common intervening present interest, which is the life estate. Four technical requirements must be met for a future interest to qualify as a remainder: (i) it was created by the same instrument that created the present interest; (ii) it was created in another person (not retained by the transferor); (iii) it follows a particular estate (life estate, term of years, or fee tail—the first two of which are important but not the fee tail—see page 422); and (iv) it becomes possessory *immediately* upon the *natural* expiration of the preceding particular estate.

EXAMPLES AND ANALYSIS

O conveyed Blackacre to A for life. O conveyed O's reversion to B at a later date during A's life. B has a reversion, not a remainder. Retention of a future interest, followed by a subsequent transfer, does not create a remainder: "once a reversion, always a reversion." Remainders are created when a present interest is retained while transferring a future interest (e.g., the transferor transfers Blackacre to A following a reserved life estate), or when present and future interests are transferred at once.

G conveyed Whiteacre "to B for life, and one year thereafter to E"; E's interest follows the reversion in G that fills the one year gap, rather than following the life estate in B. As a result, E's interest cannot be a remainder; instead it is an executory interest. What result if the conveyance is "to B for life or until her prior remarriage, then to E"? Because remarriage is not regarded as a "natural" termination of B's particular estate, again E has an executory interest rather than a remainder.

a. **Other tests.** There are two easier tests for identifying remainders. First, would it be a reversion if the transferor had retained it? If so, it is a remainder. Mind you, if it *was* a reversion *because* the transferor *did* retain it, the interest remains a reversion even if the transferor later conveys it to a third party. Second, does it follow a particular estate (life estate, term of years, or fee tail) rather than a fee simple determinable or a fee simple subject to a condition subsequent? If so, it usually is a remainder.

b. **Vested or contingent.** Remainders may be vested or contingent. And just because a remainder is vested does not mean it will become possessory. For example, if D devised Blackacre: "To A for life, remainder to B, but if B dies before A, then to C," B has a vested remainder, but it is subject to divestment. If B dies before A, B's vested remainder terminates without ever having become possessory.

    i. **Significance.** Whether a remainder is vested or contingent has a variety of consequences: (i) The Rule of Destructibility of Contingent Remainders applies, if at all, only to contingent remainders. See pages 392–393. (ii) The Rule Against Perpetuities is concerned only with vesting (not possession): an interest that does not vest within the period of the Rule violates it. (iii) As illustrated by the example at page 380, whether an interest is vested or contingent may determine who is entitled to the property. (iv) Similarly, although whether an interest is subject to estate tax depends on whether it is transferable, rather than on whether it is vested, a vested interest is more likely to be subject to wealth transfer tax than is a contingent interest. See the example at page 381. (v) If a spendthrift clause does not preclude assignment or attachment, a vested interest has real value that creditors may seek to attach and beneficiaries may try to alienate. (vi) A future interest holder's ability to enjoin waste or other harmful activity by a present interest holder or the trustee and to recover damages is partially a function of the likelihood of the interest becoming possessory.

  c. **Vested remainders.** A remainder is vested if its holder is an ascertained person (e.g., an unborn cannot have a vested remainder, although an interest may attach at birth and relate back to original creation) and if the *only* condition precedent to it becoming possessory is the termination of one or more preceding estates. Vested remainders come in three flavors:

    i. **Indefeasibly vested:** "To A for life, remainder to B"; the traditional rule is that no condition of survivorship is implied if none is expressed, meaning that if B does not survive A, B's estate will take at A's death. (Compare the treatment of such a gift, if made in trust, that UPC §2-707 affords, under which B must survive A unless the document makes it clear that survivorship is not required, and provides anti-lapse protection if B does not. See pages 401–402.)

    ii. **Vested subject to open or to close:** "To A for life, remainder to A's children"; this vests as a class gift when A has a child, subject to open (meaning the class of takers will increase if A has additional children)—and subject to close if survivorship is required. (As stated, except under UPC §2-707 for gifts in trust, and unlike the common law implied condition of survivorship for *testamentary* gifts of present interests at the testator's death, a condition of survivorship is not implied for future interests.)

EXAMPLES AND ANALYSIS

O devised property: "To T, in trust, for A for life, remainder to A's children." At O's death A had two living children (B and C). B then died, after which a third child, D, was born to A. Unless UPC §2-707 applies, A's children are not required to survive A to take. Their remainder is vested at O's death, subject to open but not to close. Thus, at O's death B and C received vested remainders, subject to partial divestment, which occurs as a result of D's birth. At A's subsequent death, the property will be distributed ⅓ through B's estate to B's heirs or devisees, ⅓ to C, and ⅓ to D.

        iii.   **Vested subject to divestment:** "To A for life, then to B, but if A remarries, to C." B's remainder is vested, but it is divested if the specified condition subsequent occurs. Similarly, if D created a revocable inter vivos trust for D for life, remainder to D's child, A, the equitable remainder in A is vested, subject to divestment, because D may revoke or amend the trust to divest A. The same characterization would apply if the transfer were by O "to A for life, remainder as A appoints by will, in default of appointment to B"; A's exercise of the power might divest B's vested remainder.

    d.   **Contingent remainders.** A remainder that becomes possessory subject to a condition *precedent* is a contingent remainder. Whether a condition is precedent or subsequent may be purely a function of the language used in expressing the condition. For example, "to A for life, remainder to B if B survives A; if not to C" contains a condition precedent and creates a contingent remainder in B; but a gift "to A for life, remainder to B, but if B does not survive A, then to C" creates in B a vested remainder subject to divestment by a condition subsequent.

        i.   **Most common form.** Perhaps the most common form of contingent remainder is a gift to the surviving descendants of a life tenant: "To A for life, remainder per stirpes to A's descendants who survive A." The interest of a descendant of A will become possessory, if at all, only if the precedent condition of surviving A is satisfied. Further, the interest of any grandchild of A is subject not only to the condition precedent that the grandchild survive A, but also that the grandchild's parent who is a child of A must predecease A.

        ii.   **Heirs of a living person.** "To A for life, remainder to A's heirs"; assuming A is living when the transfer is made, this is contingent because, by definition, a prospective heir must survive A to be an heir of A—recall our discussion on page 4 that living persons do not have heirs. Difficult questions arise if the gift of the remainder is to the heirs of someone other than the life tenant. See pages 414–419.

iii. **Unborns.** If the gift is "to A for life, remainder to A's children" and A does not have children, the remainder is contingent until A has a child, at which time the remainder vests in the class; the first child's remainder is vested, subject to open (partial divestment) if additional children are born.

iv. **Contingent remainder or executory interest?** Consider a gift "to A for life, remainder to B unless B is not living, in which case to C if living." (There is a reversion if neither B nor C is living at A's death). Do B and C each have contingent remainders or is B's remainder vested, in which case C has an executory interest? There is a preference for vested interests over contingent ones, but also a preference for remainders over executory interests. Arguably the vested remainder/executory interest construction is preferable because it provides better protection and avoids potential Rule Against Perpetuities issues. For your purposes, although legal commentators dance with the angels on this pinhead, it really doesn't matter and most casual observers would say that B and C have alternative contingent remainders.

2. Executory Interests

Any future interest that is created in a transferee by the same document that created the prior present interest and that is not a remainder is an executory interest. As a matter of constructional preference, an interest is not executory if it could be a remainder.

a. **Divesting interests.** As a rule, executory interests become possessory by divesting a prior vested estate (e.g., "to A for life, remainder to B, but if B does not survive A, then to C"; B's remainder is vested, subject to divestment—if B does not survive A, C's executory interest becomes possessory by divesting B.) The one exception to this rule is an executory interest following a fee simple determinable that expires on its own, without being divested (e.g., "Blackacre to the City until it no longer is used as a park; then to X"; X's executory interest becomes possessory when the City's estate expires through discontinuation of use of the property as a park).

b. **Springing and shifting executory interests.** Generally, a future interest that may or will divest the transferor as the possessory interest holder is a springing executory interest; if it may or will divest a third party transferee in possession, it is a shifting executory interest. An exception: if the transferor retains a reversion and later conveys it away, it remains a reversion in the hands of the subsequent transferee and any future interest that divests it from the subsequent transferee is a springing executory interest.

 # EXAMPLES AND ANALYSIS

"To B for life, and one year after B's death, to E"; the transferor has a reversion that will become possessory at B's death. A year later, the transferor's reversion is divested; E has a springing executory interest. "To D for life, but if D remarries, to E," is a little trickier; the transferor has a reversion, conditioned on D dying without having remarried. If D remarries, the transferor's reversion is divested, which would indicate E's estate is a springing executory interest. E, however, has a shifting executory interest because, although it divests the reversion, it actually snatches possession away from D. (E's interest would be a power of termination incident to a reversion if held by the transferor.)

    i. Significance of distinction. For our purposes, it does not matter whether an executory interest is shifting or springing.

E. ORIGIN AND CHARACTERISTICS

The rules and constructional preferences for future interests originated in medieval English land law, when all land was viewed as being held by or through the king; when land was the predominant source of power, wealth, and social status; and when military protection and feudal duties were determined by land use. A legitimate question today is, given the change of context, which of these rules and constructional preferences are still justified. For example, we need to question the by-products of rules like the Destructibility of Contingent Remainders, the Rule in *Shelley's Case,* the Doctrine of Worthier Title, and the Statute of Uses, which all are of little or no currency. As we will see, some of the ancient rules and constructional preferences have gone by the wayside, others are alive and well, and still others are alive but their ongoing viability is in doubt.

1. Ongoing Importance

Future interests, almost always in trust these days, are used regularly in modern estate planning. Their characteristics and the rules of construction that apply when the transferor's intent is not stated or clear have continuing significance for us.

2. Transferability

Absent spendthrift prohibitions (see Chapter 13), future interests of both the vested and contingent varieties are transferable during life and at death. (Vested future interests always have been alienable; contingent remainders and executory interests were not alienable under old English law, but are alienable in a substantial majority of jurisdictions today.) Thus, future interests are descendible (i.e., to heirs by intestacy) and devisable (i.e., to devisees of a testate decedent), but only to the extent they survive the holder's death. And during the holder's life, again assuming no spendthrift prohibitions, future interests generally are alienable by the holder and attachable by her creditors.

EXAMPLES AND ANALYSIS

G conveyed "to A for life, remainder to B, but if B does not survive A, then to C." B's vested remainder is transferable during B's life; if B dies before A, however, B's remainder is terminated by occurrence of the condition subsequent (B's death before A) that divests B. Thus, there is nothing for B to transfer if B dies before A. In most jurisdictions, C's contingent remainder also is alienable, even during the joint lives of A and B. If C conveys the remainder to D and then B survives A, B takes the fee and the contingent remainder terminates. If B dies before A, however, C's remainder would vest and also would be descendible, devisable, alienable, and attachable.

---

a.   **Exception for the possibility of reverter and the power of termination.** At common law, these were not alienable, but they were attachable by creditors. Further, although not freely alienable, an attempt to do so might have been protected by estoppel, equitable assignment, or release. Today, possibilities of reverter and powers of termination are alienable in many jurisdictions but they are rarely seen in trusts.

3.   **Acceleration**

Future interests normally become possessory upon the natural expiration of one or more prior estates or the occurrence of a required condition precedent or subsequent. But in several circumstances a future interest may be accelerated into possession by other events.

a.   **Disclaimer.** In most jurisdictions (see, e.g., UPC §2-801(d)(1)), if a devisee of a life estate disclaims (see Chapter 2), she is treated as having predeceased the testator, which operates to accelerate the remainder. The effect can eliminate a contingent remainder of the life tenant's descendants. For example, *In re Estate of Gilbert*, 592 N.Y.S.2d 224 (1992), involved a son's renunciation of his life interests in trusts created by his father's will. The will provided for the remainder of the son's trusts at his death to be payable to his descendants but, when the renunciation was made, the son had no descendants. As a result, the other remainder beneficiaries took as if the son had predeceased his father, thus eliminating the contingent remainder in the son's descendants.

   i.   The alternative. As a practical matter, if the remainder was not accelerated, but the trusts instead were held intact until the son died, it would have been necessary to decide what to do with income during the son's remaining life (accumulate it, revert it to the father's estate, or distribute it to the presumptive next takers). The court properly avoided this issue with the acceleration result.

b.   Homicide. The same issue can arise in the context of a beneficiary being barred from inheriting by slaying the transferor. For example, assume that G's will devised Blackacre "to S for life, remainder to S's descendants, provided that if no descendant of S survives S, then to R," and S murdered G. Under UPC §2-803, R takes if S is barred from taking and S has no descendant, thereby cutting off future descendants of S, because G's estate passes as if S disclaimed S's interest (in which case S would be treated as having predeceased G and the contingent remainder in R would be accelerated).

c.   Elective share. The acceleration issue also can arise in connection with the exercise by a surviving spouse of the right to elect against the estate plan of a deceased spouse. For an example, see page 256.

4.   Protection

Future interests are entitled to protection. When the future interest is equitable (i.e., in trust), the beneficiary's remedies usually relate to the trustee's fiduciary duties, and are a matter of trust law (see the Website). The following is a brief summary of protections available to holders of future interests.

a.   Reinvestment. Sale and investment of the proceeds may be appropriate or necessary to preserve future interests.

b.   Waste. Generally, the holder of a present interest in property is entitled to its reasonable use and income; the future interest holder is entitled to possession and enjoyment only after termination of all prior interests. If a trustee or prior interest holders commit acts, or fail to take actions, that adversely affect the value of the corpus, however, they may be committing waste, which may be enjoined or actionable in damages. The nature and extent of the available remedy may depend on the nature of the future interest held.

   i.   Indefeasibly vested. The holder of an indefeasibly vested future interest may enjoin threatened waste or immediately recover damages for committed waste.

    ii. Contingent or defeasibly vested. The owner of a reversion or remainder, even if contingent or defeasibly vested, may enjoin threatened waste, but a successful suit for damages may result in the recovery being impounded pending resolution of the various contingencies. For executory interests, possibilities of reverter, and powers of termination, injunction and recovery should be allowed only if the alleged wrongdoing is (i) a wanton, unconscionable, or imprudent use, and (ii) there is a reasonable probability of the future interest becoming possessory.

  c. Security. Generally, the owner of a future interest in land may not require the present interest owner to provide security; the land itself, along with the remedies of injunction and damages for waste, are viewed as protection enough. The same would be true about personalty held in trust (although the trustee may be required to post a security bond), but if personal property is subject to a legal life estate, security—again in the form of a bond—may be available to protect the remainder beneficiary against invasions or exhaustion of the corpus.

  d. Practical limitations. Having rights to protection and being able to exercise them effectively may be two different things. For example, notice and accountings may not be available to the future interest beneficiary and, thus, it may not be possible to know what is happening. Further, representation of unborn or unascertained beneficiaries may be by "virtual representation," meaning that they are not represented at all. Instead, their interests are deemed adequately represented because another person—whose interest is similar to that of the unborn or unascertained beneficiary—is a party and that person, in protecting her own interest, is deemed to protect those of the unborn or unascertained beneficiary as well.

F. THREE ANCIENT DOCTRINES

The three doctrines discussed here have limited ongoing relevance.

1. Destructibility of Contingent Remainders

At common law, a contingent *legal* remainder in land would be destroyed by operation of law (i.e., this is not a rule of construction) if it did not vest at or prior to termination of the preceding estate.

 # EXAMPLES AND ANALYSIS

"To A for life, remainder to B's heirs." A and B are living. A has a life estate, B's heirs (who are unascertained because a living person cannot have heirs) have a contingent remainder, and the transferor has a reversion (which will become possessory if A predeceases B, because we cannot know who B's heirs are until B's subsequent death). If this was a legal interest in realty (the rule did not apply to personalty or to interests in trust, nor to any executory interest), vesting of the reversion in possession (because B is alive when A dies) would destroy the contingent remainder.

a.   **Current status.** This rule has been abolished in most (if not all) jurisdictions, being replaced with a construction of a life estate, a reversion in the transferor that is subject to divestment, and a springing executory interest. Historically, the rule had several collateral consequences, which is the only reason why it is important to us today.

　　i.   **Remainders preferred.** It contributed to the early development of the preference for remainders over executory interests at a time when the rule was in favor and destruction was desired so the property would revert and then pass through the transferor's estate, subject to feudal duties.

　　ii.   **Other doctrines.** The doctrine also spurred development of the Rule in *Shelley's Case* and the Doctrine of Worthier Title as alternative means of destroying remainders that the rule of destructibility did not reach.

　　iii.   **Vested preferences.** Later, when destructibility had fallen from favor, it contributed to the counterbalancing preference for vested over contingent remainders and the preference for early vesting.

2.   **The Rule in *Shelley's Case***

The second ancient property law doctrine with limited current applicability is the Rule in *Shelley's Case*. If the *Shelley* rule is applicable, a remainder purportedly given to the heirs of a life tenant is deemed to be a remainder in the life tenant rather than in her heirs. Then, not by the Rule in *Shelley's Case* itself, but made possible by it, there may occur a merger of the life estate and the remainder, yielding a fee in the holder of the life estate. The merger could be prevented by an intervening interest or a remainder made contingent for reasons other than being held by heirs of a living person.

 # EXAMPLES AND ANALYSIS

"To A for life, remainder to A's heirs." Under *Shelley*, the remainder is in A, not A's heirs. Because A would have the life estate and the remainder, a merger would occur, leaving A with the fee. But if the grant were: "To A for life, then to B for life, remainder to A's heirs," B's life estate would prevent a merger. The rule itself, however, still would apply—the remainder would be in A, rather than in her heirs. Compare "to A for life, remainder to A's heirs if A dies before reaching 25 years of age." The contingency—that A's heirs take only if A dies before the age of 25—not only avoids the merger, it also avoids application of the rule altogether. Thus, assuming A dies before reaching 25 years of age, A's heirs will take.

a.   **Requirements.** There are five requirements for application of the Rule in *Shelley's Case:* (i) the conveyance must be of realty; (ii) the transferee must have received a life estate (or a fee tail; see page 422); (iii) the conveyance must be a remainder to the heirs of the life tenant; (iv) the life estate and the remainder must have been created by the same instrument (typically, a will, trust instrument, or deed); and (v) both the life estate and the remainder must be legal or both must be equitable.

b.   **Rule of law.** Like the destructibility rule, the Rule in *Shelley's Case* is a rule of law, not of construction, if it is in effect at all. Thus, it applies notwithstanding intent.

c.   **Current status.** The Rule in *Shelley's Case* has been abolished in most states. If the grant "to A for life, remainder to A's heirs," were made in a state in which the Rule in *Shelley's Case* has been abolished, the interests created would be: (i) a life estate in A, (ii) a contingent remainder in A's heirs, and (iii) a reversion in the transferor or her successors (because there are no heirs of A until A's death). The rule is that the transferor has retained a reversion if a transferor conveys a life estate not followed by a vested remainder in fee.

3.   **Worthier Title**

The Doctrine of Worthier Title operates to convert what appears to be a remainder (or executory interest) in the transferor's heirs to a reversion in the transferor. Thus, if G conveyed "to A for life, remainder to G's heirs," G is treated as having retained a reversion rather than as having transferred a contingent remainder to her heirs.

a.   **Requirements.** The requirements for application of the Doctrine are similar to but not identical to the requirements for application of the Rule in *Shelley's Case.* The most significant difference between the two rules is that Worthier Title operates when a remainder (or executory interest) purportedly is conveyed to the *transferor's* heirs; the Rule in *Shelley's Case* applies when a remainder is purportedly conveyed to the present interest holder's heirs. Another difference is that, unlike the *Shelley* rule, the Doctrine of Worthier Title applies to personalty as well as realty, and applies if the present interest is a term of years or a defeasible fee, as well as if it is a life estate (or fee tail). Furthermore, unlike the *Shelley* rule, it does not matter whether the transferee's estate or the purported remainder in the transferor's heirs or both are equitable or legal for the Doctrine of Worthier Title to apply. Moreover, the Rule in *Shelley's Case* can apply to testamentary and inter vivos transfers, while the Doctrine of Worthier Title applies only to inter vivos grants. Like the *Shelley* rule, worthier title applies only if the transferee's estate and the purported remainder in the transferor's heirs were created by the same instrument.

b. Rule of construction. The Doctrine of Worthier Title is a rule of construction, not of law. Thus, the transferor's intent to create a remainder in her heirs will be given effect if it is established.

c. Current status. Like the Rule in *Shelley's Case,* the Doctrine of Worthier Title is disfavored most everywhere and it expressly has been abolished in many jurisdictions. Perhaps because it is a doctrine of construction and not a rule of law, however, statutory abolition of it has not been as widespread as that of the *Shelley* rule.

G. PROBLEMS OF CONSTRUCTION: INTRODUCTION

Construction issues are avoidable; they arise because a governing instrument does not adequately address a question. To be a good estate planner requires that you draft thoroughly and carefully, cover all contingencies, and use your knowledge of construction issues to anticipate problems based on prior drafters' mistakes. In this segment of these materials it is wise always try to think about how to draft to avoid the issues being addressed.

1. Settlor's Intent

Construction is a necessary evil in estate planning and trust administration, but keep it in perspective: often we are filling in a gap with a solution to a question that the settlor never even considered, much less formed an intent about. We should be careful not to manufacture intent when a provision should just fail and the property pass by reversion and, if necessary, by intestacy. We will see examples of this as we go along.

a. Precedent of limited benefit. Using cases to construe similar language is often like using nonsense to construe nonsense; like rules of construction, we need to keep precedent in perspective too.

b. No clear answers. The entire area is uncertain; black and white exist most often only in the treatises, not the actual decisions. You should not be distraught if it is hard to pin rules down and if you find that courts do equity while bending the rules to produce the result they want.

H. VESTED OR CONTINGENT

As discussed earlier in this chapter, whether an interest is vested or contingent is significant for a variety of reasons. In construing instruments under which vesting issues are raised, courts often employ preferences in favor of (i) early vesting, (ii) vested rather than contingent interests, and (iii) conditions subsequent rather than precedent.

 # EXAMPLES AND ANALYSIS

"To A for life, remainder to B if B attains 30 years of age." While B is under 30 years of age, her future interest is a contingent remainder and the transferor has a reversion. Attaining 30 years of age is a condition precedent to B's remainder becoming vested or possessory, meaning that B will not receive the fee until A dies and then only if B reaches 30 years of age. B's remainder will vest immediately if B is or attains 30 years of age during A's life, which will terminate the transferor's reversion. If B dies after reaching 30 years of age but before A dies, B's vested remainder will pass as a part of B's estate to B's heirs (if B dies intestate) or devisees (if B dies testate). B's successors will take the fee at A's death. If B is not yet 30 years of age when A dies, at common law the destructibility of contingent remainders rule would cause B's contingent remainder to be destroyed at A's death. Today, there would be a reversion to the transferor, with the property still subject to B's contingent remainder. If B reached 30 years of age thereafter, B would take from the transferor (or her successors); in essence, B's contingent remainder would then operate as a springing executory interest.

Let's try another one: "To X for life, remainder to Y, but if Y dies before X, to Z." Y's remainder is vested subject to divestment because it is subject to a condition subsequent. Z has a shifting executory interest because it will divest Y if it becomes possessory at all. Z need not survive to take; if Y predeceases X, and Z is not living at X's death, Z's estate will be entitled and Z's successors will take. By contrast, "To X for life, remainder to Y if living, and if not to Z," would give Y and Z alternative contingent remainders. Again, Z need not survive to take: Y's remainder is contingent on Y surviving X but Z's remainder is contingent on Y *not* surviving X—there is no contingency that speaks to Z's survival of anyone.

1. Twice Stated Age Contingencies

Before considering the following example that includes an age contingency that is stated twice, let's compare two other grants. First: "To A for life, remainder to B if B attains 30 years of age, and if B dies before then, to

C." Probably B's remainder is contingent, subject as it is to the condition precedent that B attain 30 years of age. In that case C has an alternative contingent remainder. By contrast, what if the language "if B attains 30 years of age" was not included and the grant was: "To A for life, remainder to B, but if B dies before reaching 30 years of age, to C"? Here, B's remainder is vested, subject to divestment; the condition on B taking—that B reach 30 years of age—is subsequent, not precedent. C has a shifting executory interest in that case because B's remainder is vested, subject to divestment.

 ## EXAMPLES AND ANALYSIS

"To A for life, remainder to B if B attains 30 years of age, but in the event of B's death before 30 years of age, to C." B's remainder is subject to an age condition that is stated twice, once precedent and once subsequent. Here we ignore the condition precedent and B receives a vested remainder subject to divestment. Why? One statement of the age condition is surplusage and we ignore the precedent condition at least in part because the law favors early vesting. Conditions subsequent are preferred over conditions precedent, which in the context of remainders is simply another way of saying vested remainders and their divesting executory interests are preferred over alternative contingent remainders.

   a.   **Why the classification matters.** It is important to know why the determination needs to be made, because the issue involved may affect the classification. For example, if the vested versus contingent remainder classification issue arises in connection with a Rule Against Perpetuities challenge, we would expect a construction favoring early vesting to save the gift. And if the issue were possible application of the rule of destructible contingent remainders, a vested construction again would be expected, to save the gift. But if the issue came up in connection with an attempt by a creditor of a beneficiary to reach the beneficiary's interest, and if the creditor's ability to do so would be reduced if the beneficiary's remainder was contingent, a court might reach a different result, depending on how it viewed the equities.

2.   **Remainder to Life Tenant's Children**

Poorly drafted language attempting to leave property to one person for life, with the remainder to her children, can raise a variety of construction issues.

EXAMPLES AND ANALYSIS

"To X for life, remainder to X's children, but if no child of X reaches 30 years of age, to Y." If X has no children at the time of the grant, the remainder is contingent until a child of X is born. Then it is vested in that child, subject to open (i.e., subject to partial divestment), but not to close (i.e., neither survivorship nor reaching 30 years of age is required, meaning that if, for example, X was survived by two children, one age 32 and the other age 25, the 25 year old's interest is vested without regard to whether she reaches 30 years of age). The remainder, however, is subject to divestment as a class, meaning that the remainder would be divested if no child of X reached 30 years of age. Note the difference between there being no survivorship requirement (the successors of a child of X who does not reach 30 years of age will take her share if at least one other child of X reaches that age) and the requirement that at least one member of the class must reach 30 years of age before any child may take.

Compare: "To X for life, remainder to such of X's children as survive X, and if any child fails to do so, that child's share shall go to Y." As in the prior Example, if X has no children at the time of the grant, the remainder is contingent until a child of X is born. It also appears that a child of X who predeceased X cannot take. But if the children's remainders are contingent on survivorship, how does a child who does not survive X have a share that can pass to Y? Arguably, therefore, the remainder is vested, subject to open (as additional children of X are born) and to divestment in favor of Y's shifting executory interest. Note that divestment is not the same as class closing. If a child of X dies before X, that child does not drop out of the class; rather, her remainder is divested in favor of Y's executory interest. In effect, Y is substituted as a class member for each child of X who predeceases X.

---

3. Effect of Powers of Appointment

A remainder may be vested, but subject to divestment by exercise of a power of appointment. For example, "to A for life, remainder to such person or persons as A shall appoint; in default of appointment in equal shares to A's children who survive A." The remainder is contingent until a child of A is born, at which time the remainder is vested subject to open to admit afterborns or afteradopteds, subject to close to reflect the survivorship requirement, and subject to divestment by A's exercise of the power. The transferor has a reversion that will become possessory if A dies without having effectively exercised the power and is survived by no child.

I. SURVIVORSHIP

A future interest is a presently existing property right or interest that will or may grant possession or enjoyment in the future. The question here is whether the holder of a future interest must survive until some future date (such as the death of a life tenant) to be entitled to take.

1. **Instrument Controls**

   The first place to look for the answer to that question is the governing instrument—it controls if it expressly addresses the issue. If not, the issue is one of construction.

2. **Traditional Rule**

   Absent an express requirement of survivorship, the traditional rule is that the law will not imply a condition of survivorship with respect to a future interest. Thus, if G conveys a life estate to A, remainder to B, B's remainder passes as an asset of B's estate to her heirs or devisees if B predeceases A, because B's remainder was vested—not conditioned on B surviving A.

   a. **Compare lapse and the law of wills.** This is the exact opposite of the common law implied condition of survivorship applicable to testamentary bequests at the testator's death: if T devises Blackacre to A without addressing the possibility of A dying before T, and if A does die before T, the gift will lapse and thus fail, unless saved for A's descendants by an antilapse statute. See Chapter 8. No such remedy is needed if the holder of a vested future interest dies before becoming entitled to possession: if survivorship is not required, the interest passes automatically to the future interest holder's successors. This difference in treatment is another illustration that using a revocable trust as the primary dispositive instrument in an estate plan may yield different results than using a will.

      i. *First Nat'l Bank v. Anthony,* 557 A.2d 957 (Me. 1989), is illustrative. The settlor of a revocable inter vivos trust retained a life estate in the trust corpus, with ⅓ of the remainder to a son who predeceased the settlor. Had the gift been made by will, it would have lapsed unless saved for the son's descendants by an antilapse statute. But because the son received a future interest upon creation of the trust, and because of the rule against implying a condition of survivorship when none is expressed, the son's remainder belonged to his estate for distribution to his heirs (if he died intestate) or devisees (if he died testate).

EXAM TIP

If you have studied rules and examples in terms of parties being designated by letter (e.g., A, B, C, X, Y, Z), don't be thrown off by fact patterns in questions that are stated in terms of persons' names. In *Anthony*, the grant at issue essentially was: "To A [the settlor] for life; then to B [the settlor's wife, who predeceased him] for life; remainder to C, D, and E [the son and his two siblings]." Viewed in that form, and in the context of the general rule that survivorship conditions will not be implied, the case is straightforward. Also, don't be reluctant to draw out or diagram the facts.

ii. **Testamentary trusts.** Lapse can apply in future interest cases but traditionally only in a *testamentary* trust and only if the future interest beneficiary predeceased the testator and not just predeceased the present interest holder.

 ## EXAMPLES AND ANALYSIS

D's will devised D's estate to T, in trust to pay the income to A for life, remainder to B. If B died before D, B's interest would lapse and might be saved by an antilapse statute. (See Chapter 8.) But if B survived D and died before A, neither lapse nor antilapse would apply under traditional principles. Rather, unless the instrument conditioned B's remainder on B surviving A, the traditional approach (now changed by UPC §2-707, discussed below) is not to imply such a requirement, meaning that B's interest is vested and B's heirs or devisees take the fee at A's death.

iii. **Application to inter vivos trusts.** Apparently because revocable inter vivos trusts are so commonly used as will substitutes, a few courts—including the lower court in *Anthony*—have applied the lapse rule if a beneficiary of such a trust who is to receive a distribution at the transferor's death predeceases the transferor. If a lapse rule is applied in such a context, however, so also should be the antilapse statute.

b. **Reasons for the traditional rule.** There are several justifications for the rule that the future interest holder's interest is vested, rather than subject to an implied condition of survivorship, if the instrument is silent with respect to whether the holder must survive to the time of possession (i.e., be alive when all preceding estates terminate).

i. **Early vesting.** Perhaps most important is the preference for early vesting, a relic of days when the doctrine of destructibility of contingent remainders was applicable but disfavored.

ii. **"Income vests principal."** In addition, if a gift of current income also is given to the remainder beneficiary, the "income vests principal" rule (see page 403) may support a finding that the interest vested without regard to survivorship to the time of possession.

iii. **Ultimate taker.** If survivorship was required and *all* the named takers predeceased the present interest holder, it would be necessary to determine who would take (or the entire remainder would fail).

iv. **Avoid intestacy.** If survivorship was required, and there was no gift over of the deceased taker's share (as often would be the case), presumably there would be a reversion to the transferor and a significant possibility of the property then passing to the transferor's heirs by intestacy. The law abhors an intestacy that is avoidable, especially at some time in the future.

v. **Holder's family.** If survivorship was required, the future interest holder's family—the members of which might be in need—would be excluded.

Notice that each of these concerns could be addressed by treating the holder's death before distribution as a lapse/antilapse issue, as the UPC does in §2-707, discussed below.

3. **UPC §2-707**

Unlike the traditional common law rule, a condition of survivorship is implied under UPC §2-707 if a gift of a future interest is made in trust (to a specific beneficiary or to a class) and the instrument is silent with respect to whether the present interest holder must survive until possession. If the beneficiary does not survive to possession, an antilapse concept is applied: if any descendants of the future interest holder survive to possession, they take by representation the share the holder would have received if living. Unlike the case when a testamentary gift lapses, the antilapse result under UPC §2-707 applies without regard to whether the holder of the future interest was related to the transferor. The consequences of the change made by UPC §2-707 can be significant.

a. **Who takes?** Under UPC §2-707, the future interest holder's descendants take. If there are none, there is a reversion in the transferor. Under the traditional approach, the holder's heirs or devisees take.

b. **Administration.** The traditional approach results in the property passing to the future interest holder's heirs or devisees by going through the holder's probate estate; under UPC §2-707 the property passes to the holder's descendants directly from the trust.

c. **Transfer taxes.** The traditional approach causes the future interest holder's interest in the trust to be includible in the holder's estate for estate tax purposes. Under UPC §2-707, the holder has no interest in the trust, nothing is transmissible to others, and the value of the interest is not includible in the holder's estate for federal estate tax purposes. (Although the estate tax consequence is more favorable under the UPC approach, for a large estate it may result in a generation-skipping transfer tax liability that exceeds any estate tax savings.) In addition, creditors of the holder's estate do not get to reach the interest.

d. **Flexibility.** The traditional approach affords the future interest holder complete flexibility to direct disposition of the trust assets. The UPC directs the disposition to the holder's descendants, a result many transferors (but not the future interest holder) may prefer. Those who want the holder to have flexibility to control the ultimate disposition of the trust assets—even if the holder dies before becoming entitled to distribution—may accomplish that objective (and avoid inclusion of the interest in the holder's probate or taxable estate) by giving to the holder a nongeneral power to appoint the future interest (see Chapter 14).

4. **Vested with Postponed Possession**

A 17th century English decision, *Clobberie's Case*, 86 Eng. Rep. 476 (Ch. 1677), is a source of the concept of vested ownership with postponed possession, and several vested versus contingent rules of construction that are still with us.

a. **"To A *at age* . . ."** If words of futurity are annexed to the substance of the gift (e.g., "to A at 30 years of age"), the traditional approach, not universally followed, is to treat the recipient's interest as contingent, to require survivorship to the specified age, and to postpone vesting. (Note that a gift "to A *if* A reaches 30 years of age" clearly would fail if A did not do so.)

    i. **"To A *when* A reaches 30 years of age."** Survivorship also is required if the gift instead was "to A *when* A reaches 30 years of age," under traditional rules, although this construction is not followed everywhere.

    ii. **Disposition if gift fails.** A's interest would fail if A in these hypotheticals dies before reaching the specified age and the traditional construction of treating the interest as contingent applies. The interest would *not* pass to A's successors; rather, it would pass to the transferor's successors by reversion.

b. **"To A, *to be paid* at age . . ."** The gift is not conditioned on survivorship if words of futurity are not annexed to the substance of the gift, but instead are annexed to enjoyment (e.g., "to A, to be paid at 30 years of age" or, "to A, payable when A reaches 30 years of age"). Thus, A's successors receive the property if A dies before reaching the specified age. This is a vested gift, with possession postponed.

c. **"To A at age . . . , *to be paid with interest.*"** A hybrid exists if the words of futurity are annexed to the subject of the gift but the transferee also is given income from the gift (e.g., "to A, at 30 years of age, to be paid with interest" or "income to A in the trustee's discretion, principal to A at 30 years of age"). Although the dispositive part of the provision looks like a gift for which vesting as well as possession is postponed, the income entitlement suffices to vest principal. Thus, even if A dies at 28 years of age, A's successors will take.

i. **Multiple beneficiaries.** However, this result may not apply if no single beneficiary is guaranteed sole current enjoyment of income or guaranteed distribution in the future of accumulated income.

EXAMPLES AND ANALYSIS

D's will devised the residue of her estate to T, in trust, for distribution "half to A at 30 years of age, the balance to B at 30 years of age, with income to be distributed to them in T's discretion or accumulated and distributed with the principal." A and B each survived D, A died at 28 years of age, and B later died at 29 years of age. Because A and B were not *entitled* to receive any portion of the income, the income vests principal rule may not apply. If not, A's ½ would pass by intestacy to D's heirs (probably at such time as A would have reached 30 years of age if A had lived, so that the fund would remain intact generating income for possible distribution to B) as a result of D's reversion. At B's subsequent death, D's heirs probably would take the remaining principal and accumulated income for the same reason they likely would take A's ½. However, B's successors could argue that the "income vests principal" rule should apply to B after A's death, because any income not distributed currently to B would be accumulated for distribution to B at 30 years of age. The problem with that argument is that it presupposes a different intent with respect to B than with A, and indeed a difference after A's death than before. As a result, we would not expect the argument to succeed, especially because no one could predict which of A or B would die first.

d. **Income rights not specified.** Assume a gift by D of $10,000 to A *at* 30 years of age. If the disposition does not direct what is to be done with the income from the $10,000 while waiting for A to reach 30 years of age, the income probably was retained by D and thus would be payable to D or D's successors. If the gift instead was to A, *to be paid when* A reached 30 years of age, the more likely alternative would be to treat the right to income as vested with the underlying corpus and to accumulate it for distribution with the $10,000 when A reaches 30 years of age, or to A's estate if A dies before reaching that age.

5. Acceleration

If a beneficiary whose interest is vested dies before reaching the required distribution age, the next question is whether the distribution should be made immediately to the beneficiary's successors, or whether it should be delayed until the beneficiary *would have* reached the age for distribution.

a. Income not distributable. If income from the fund was not distributable to the beneficiary, but was retained (expressly or implicitly) by the transferor, acceleration of the gift to the beneficiary's successors should not be made because doing so would deprive the transferor or her successors of the income in the interim.

b. Income distributable. If, however, income from the fund was distributable to the beneficiary, there would seem to be no reason to delay the distribution until the beneficiary would have reached the specified age (and delay is not favored). When only possession is being deferred— usually for reasons relating to immaturity—death eliminates the need to delay distribution and immediate termination would be favored.

c. Principal not vested. If a beneficiary dies before reaching the required distribution age, any interest that is not vested reverts to the transferor or her successors and the acceleration issue does not arise.

 # EXAMPLES AND ANALYSIS

The gift is of $10,000 "to A at 30 years of age"; A is 20 at the time of the gift, but dies at 23 years of age. The traditional construction (not followed in some jurisdictions) is that A's interest was contingent. A's premature death causes the interest to revert to the transferor or her successors. The absence of a provision for the income before A reaches 30 years of age probably means it was retained by the transferor in the form of a reversion, meaning that A would not be entitled to income even for the period before A's death.

The gift is of $10,000 "to A, payable at 30 years of age"; again there is no provision for income. A was 15 at the time of the gift, and dies at 18 years of age. A's interest is vested and, in the absence of a provision for income earned on the $10,000 before A reached 30 years of age, the income should be deemed vested with the underlying corpus. Because this gift is about postponement of possession, A's premature death should accelerate the gift to A's successors, because there no longer is any reason to postpone distribution.

6. Gifts of Future Interests to a Class

If a gift of a future interest is made to a class, the general rule (of construction only) is that the class is subject to open until distribution, but is not subject to close unless survivorship expressly is required (that is, there is no implied condition of survivorship).

 ## EXAMPLES AND ANALYSIS

Assume that D devised her residuary estate to T, in trust, income to A for life, remainder to D's siblings. D died survived by A; by a brother, B; and by a sister, S. B predeceased A, survived by one child (N). B devised his estate to his widow (W). At A's death, survived by N, W, and S, to whom is the trust estate distributable? S clearly will receive at least ½ of the trust assets. The question is whether B's death before A results in S taking the entire trust estate, or whether B's interest was vested so that B's successors take the share B would have received if B was alive. Generally, survivorship will not be implied in a future interest gift. As a result, B's remainder vested at D's death and passed through B's estate at B's death. Accordingly, W would receive ½ of the trust assets at A's death. (A different result would be reached under UPC §2-707, discussed above.) Note that, if another sibling of D had been born after D's death but before A's death, the new sibling also would share in the class gift; but any sibling born after A's death would be excluded from the class, which would close at A's death when distribution was required. See Chapter 8.

a. *Security Trust Co. v. Irvine*, 93 A.2d 528 (Del. Ch. 1953), also illustrates application of the general rule. James devised his estate in trust for two of his sisters, Martha and Mary, for their lives. At the second of their deaths the remainder was to be "equally divided among my brothers and sisters, share and share alike . . . the issue of any deceased brother or sister to take his or her parent's share." James was survived by Mary, Martha, and three other siblings but Mary was the last to die of all the siblings. Of the five siblings, two were survived by descendants who also survived Mary's death. If survivorship until possession was required the descendants of these two siblings would take everything; following the traditional rule, however (and the preference for early vesting upon which it is based), the court did not require survivorship. Rather, each of the five siblings had a vested remainder at James' death. The remainder of the two siblings who did not survive Mary but who had descendants who did was divested in favor of these descendants.

b.   If survivorship is required. The fortuitousness of death could generate inequity if survivorship until the time of possession was required for class gifts—the family of a class member who died one day before distribution would receive nothing but a class member who died one day after distribution could leave that share to whomever she wanted. Further, the gift would fail altogether if survivorship until the time of possession was required and no member of the class survived. The early vesting rule (under which survivorship until the time of possession is not required) avoids that result. (Note that, if a future interest devisee under a testamentary trust dies before the testator, the lapse rule and any antilapse statute avoids this problem and the preceding one as well. And UPC §2-707 avoids both problems by creating a lapse and antilapse regime for *all* future interests.)

c.   Single vs. multigenerational class. The general, no-implied-condition-of-survivorship rule applies to a future interest given to a class of single-generation members, but not to classes whose members are multigenerational. Thus, unless UPC §2-707 is in effect, survivorship typically is not required for gifts of future interests to children, first cousins, siblings, or nieces and nephews; by contrast, survivorship typically is required for future interest gifts to descendants, heirs, next of kin, or issue (if used properly to mean descendants).

   i.   Rationale for different treatment. One explanation for this is definitional: how do descendants, issue, or heirs take other than by representation of deceased ancestors? Another is that the inequality posed by an implied survivorship condition in a single generation class does not exist in a multigenerational gift with the right of representation.

7.   Conditions Unrelated to Survivorship

A future interest may be conditioned on an event other than survivorship. For example, a gift: "To A for life, remainder to A's children, but if A dies without children surviving her, then to B" conditions B's interest on A dying without living children. Survivorship to possession is not also required; it will not be implied as a condition *simply because the interest is otherwise conditional.* The majority view is that a remainder contingent on something other than survivorship is not also subject to an implied condition of survivorship simply because of the other contingency. Thus, B's successors will take if B dies before A, and A then dies not survived by any children, even though B is not alive to take.

a. **Vested subject to divestment.** The same result should obtain if the future interest is vested subject to divestment, such as by exercise of a power to revoke or to appoint, to distribute principal, or by occurrence of another condition subsequent. For example, if D created a revocable inter vivos trust, income to D for life, then income to S for life, then remainder to R, the remainder is vested in R from creation of the trust, subject to divestment if D revokes or amends the trust to reduce or eliminate R's interest. (See the discussion of *Anthony* above.) The fact that R's remainder is subject to divestment should not also imply a survivorship condition. Similarly, note that in *Irvine* (discussed above), the siblings' remainders were vested, subject to divestment if one died before the life tenant with issue, but that did not mean that their interests also would be divested if they died *without* issue before the life tenants.

b. **Rationale.** The same reasons for not implying a condition of survivorship when no other conditions are involved (see page 399) support not implying one when an interest is subject to another condition. In addition, the presumption when another condition is stated is that, because the transferor knew how to impose a condition, the absence of a condition of survivorship is intentional. Moreover, the absence of a gift over if the holder does not survive indicates that survivorship was not meant to be required, because we presume that the transferor wanted to avoid failure of the disposition.

8. **Express Conditions of Survivorship: Time to Which Condition Relates**

"Surviving" is a relative term: if a future interest holder is required to survive, what or whom must she survive? The usual rule is that a beneficiary whose interest is conditioned on the beneficiary "surviving" (what or whom must be survived is not stated) must survive all prior interests, or until the time for distribution, if later.

 EXAMPLES AND ANALYSIS

G devised her estate: "To T, in trust, income to my child (C) for life, remainder to C's surviving children." When G executed her will, C had two children (GC1 and GC2). C, GC1, and GC2 survived G. After G's death, GC3 is born to C. GC2 then dies, after which C dies. GC1 and GC3 survived C. Who takes? In most jurisdictions the requirement that C's children be "surviving" to take means that GC2's remainder will fail because GC2 did not survive C. GC1 and GC3 each will take ½ of the trust estate. Note that a typical antilapse statute will not save the gift because GC2 survived the testator, G.

a. **UPC.** As discussed at page 401, UPC §2-707 implies a survivorship condition on gifts of future interests, and substitutes for the predeceased remainder beneficiary her surviving descendants under an antilapse theory. As does the UPC in the context of lapse when a devisee predeceases a testator (see Chapter 8), UPC §2-707 requires more than limiting the takers to those who survive for antilapse not to apply. Thus, in the hypothetical above, under UPC §2-707, GC2's descendants, if any, would take the share GC2 would have taken if GC2 had survived C (unless there was affirmative evidence of G's intent to the contrary). That result also would have obtained under UPC §2-707 if the gift of the remainder had been to "C's then living children."

b. **Deviations from the general rule.** If a survivorship condition is imposed but what must be survived is not specified, the future interest holder must survive all prior interests, or until the time for distribution, if later. Deviations from this rule may occur in several circumstances. For example, if the income beneficiary also is a remainder beneficiary, the gift of the income will vest the principal (e.g., "income to my child, A, until she reaches 23 years of age; remainder to my surviving children"; if A dies at age 20, her right to income would have vested her share of the remainder without regard to her failure to survive to 23 years of age). The general rule also may not apply if surviving the life tenant was too unlikely to have been the settlor's intent (e.g., "to my surviving siblings at the death of all of my grandchildren"; for a sibling to take, it is likely that she need only survive *creation* of the trust rather than death of the last of the grandchildren).

9. **Effect of Limited Survival Requirements**

Consistent with the general rule that a survivorship condition will not be implied on a gift of a future interest, a limited condition of survivorship will be applied only as specified, and will not be treated as a general, broad, or global requirement.

 EXAMPLES AND ANALYSIS

G devised her estate "to A for life, remainder to A's children, but if any child of A dies leaving descendants, that deceased child's share to those descendants." G was survived by A and A's three children, B, C, and D. B and C died before A, B survived by one descendant (X), and C survived by no descendant. X and D survived A. A's children own vested remainders subject to divestment by dying before A leaving one or more descendants who survive A. That limited survivorship condition, however, does not create a survivorship requirement if a child of A dies before A without descendants. Thus, C's remainder was vested and was not divested (because C did not leave descendants who survived A); it passes through C's estate to C's successors. X (as B's divesting surviving descendant) and D each take the other ⅔.

Let's try another one:

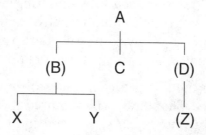

Here, assume again a gift from G "to A for life, remainder to A's children, but if any child of A dies leaving descendants, that deceased child's share to those descendants." Again, G is survived by A and by A's three children, B, C, and D, but for this example, assume that B and D die before A, that B is survived by two children (X and Y), both of whom survive A, and that D is survived by one child (Z), who predeceases A. The construction here is similar to that for a gift over if someone "dies without issue" (see page 411)—thus, we determine whether a child of A "dies leaving descendants" by whether a child of A dies leaving descendants who survive A. The result? B's vested remainder was divested by B's death before A, with B survived by descendants of B who survived A; thus, X and Y take B's share. C also receives a share. D's vested remainder was not divested, because D was survived by Z but Z did not survive A. Thus, D's share would be distributed to D's successors. That probably is not what you would expect.

---

i. *Irvine.* The limited survivorship condition rules are also illustrated by *Irvine*, discussed above, in which the remainder was given to siblings, with the issue of a deceased sibling to take the sibling's share. That limited survivorship condition did not prevent the deceased siblings with no descendants from taking.

ii. **Drafting.** A better way to express the most commonly misdrafted limited condition of survivorship is:

> To A for life, and on the death of A, remainder in equal shares to A's then living children, except that the then living descendants of a then deceased child of A shall take per stirpes the share the child would have received if living.

> **or**

> To A for life and, on the death of A, remainder per stirpes to A's then living descendants.

EXAM TIP

Consider the following for analyzing survivorship issues. First, the instrument will control if it addresses the issue, such as by requiring survivorship to a specified time and providing for a gift over to an alternative taker if the first taker does not so survive. The following survivorship rules are rules of construction that apply only if the instrument is silent as to survivorship.

If the instrument making the gift is a *will*, issues of lapse and the applicability of the antilapse statute (see Chapter 8) will be raised if (i) a devisee predeceased the testator, (ii) the gift was to a class, a member of whom predeceased the testator, or (iii) the gift was left to a testamentary trust, a beneficiary of which predeceased the testator. What if a gift under a will was left to a testamentary trust, a beneficiary of which survived the testator but died before being entitled to possession? Here, the issue should not be lapse. If a survivorship condition was not expressly imposed, generally one will not be implied, even if the gift is subject to some other condition. Survivorship is required, however, if UPC §2-707 is in effect: under it, if the beneficiary does not survive all prior interests, or to the time of distribution (if later), living descendants of the beneficiary, if any, will take under antilapse, regardless of the relationship of their predeceased ancestor to the testator.

If the instrument making the gift is an *inter vivos trust instrument*:

a. Lapse should not apply, even if the trust instrument is a revocable inter vivos trust that is being used as a will substitute. Such trusts typically will provide for the transferor to be a beneficiary for life (often the sole beneficiary); the beneficiaries designated to receive the trust estate at the transferor's death have future interests. If one of them dies before the transferor, the law of future interests should apply to determine who takes, not lapse or an antilapse statute. Some courts, however, have applied a lapse analysis in this circumstance, in which case the jurisdiction's antilapse statute should apply as well.

b. Assuming lapse and antilapse do not apply, the future interest survivorship analysis would be similar to that outlined above for a gift under a will. Thus, if the instrument addresses the survivorship issue, it will control. If it requires survivorship but does specify who or what must be survived, survivorship of all prior interests, or to the time of distribution (if later), normally will be required. If the instrument does not require survivorship, such a condition normally will not be implied, even if the future interest is subject to some other unrelated condition. But if UPC §2-707 is in effect, survivorship until the time of possession is required; if the beneficiary does not survive, living descendants of the beneficiary, if any, will take under antilapse, regardless of the relationship of their predeceased ancestor to the transferor.

J. DEATH "WITHOUT ISSUE"

A gift by G: "To H for life, remainder to A, but if A dies without issue, to X" raises three basic issues. Before looking at these, please note first that this is *not* a gift "to A, but if A dies without issue, to X": as discussed below, the rules differ if the distribution is immediate and outright rather than involving a future interest. Also note that the term "issue" is a terrible one to use (because some folks assume it means children, when in fact it means descendants) but we are going to use it here because this is how the legal question usually is framed. Please don't take this as an endorsement of that poor terminology.

1. **Definite or Indefinite Failure**

   Does "if A dies without issue" mean a definite or indefinite failure of A to have issue? That is, it can be read to mean: (i) X takes only if A never had issue; (ii) X takes if A has no living issue at some definite time (definite failure of issue); or (iii) X takes whenever the line of A's issue runs out—an indefinite failure of issue that is certain to occur sometime, however remote in the future. Definite failure is the favored construction. Indefinite failure may violate the Rule Against Perpetuities if followed by a remainder or executory interest. Never had issue simply is not what we know the average person would have intended.

2. **When Must There Be No Issue?**

   Assuming the definite failure of issue construction is applicable, the second issue is when does "dies without issue" mean; what is the definite time at which we look to see if A has died and there are no issue of A living to determine whether X takes? The possibilities include the time of death of the settlor (G), the life tenant (H), the named taker (A), or anytime before the death of the alternative taker (X). This issue is at the heart of this and numerous other construction questions. As discussed below, the preferred construction is that X takes if neither A nor any issue of A is living at the time of H's death.

3. **Must the Alternative Taker Survive?**

   The third issue is the survivorship issue we have examined above: if A does die without issue, must X be alive (or in existence, if X is not a natural person) to take? The general rule is that there is no implied condition of survivorship: if A dies without issue, X takes (actually X's heirs or devisees take) even if X is deceased. The exception we saw above may apply if the gift over is to a multigenerational class (e.g., if X is "descendants of Y"). Also, under UPC §2-707, X must survive to take; if X did not survive, X's descendants, if any, would take under the antilapse provisions of UPC §2-707.

4. **The Favored Construction** of the "dies without issue" hypothetical is: life estate to H, vested remainder in fee subject to divestment in A, shifting executory interest in X if neither A nor any issue of A is living at H's death.

This favored approach keys taking to the time of termination of all prior interests; title is certain at H's death. If A is then living, A takes; if A is not then living, but any issue of A is then living, A still takes—meaning the remainder passes through A's estate to A's heirs or devisees. Only if neither A nor any issue of A is living at H's death does X take.

5.   Problems with Other Constructions

Consider why the other constructions do not make sense.

a.   **Death of the settlor or before the alternative taker.** Because distribution is not made until the end of the life estate, a construction referring to death of the settlor is silly. It also is senseless to ask whether A dies without issue at any time before X's death. For example, nothing would support a construction that X should take if A survived H and then died survived by issue, but all of A's issue died before X.

b.   **Named taker not survived by issue.** Many (no, MOST) people want to read the hypothetical as saying that X takes if A is survived by no issue, whenever A dies. Thus, for example, they want X to take if A survived H and—on A's subsequent death—no issue of A survive A. That is, these readers would say that the word "dies" in "dies without issue" obviously refers to the natural termination of A's physical life. Notice, however, that nothing ties the word to a "logical" application or interpretation and that this is only one of several possible meanings of when the word "dies" is meant to apply. The problem with this reading is that it gives A what is essentially a life estate with alternative contingent remainders to X or to whoever takes after A's death with issue surviving (which would be A's heirs or devisees, as if A had a testamentary power of appointment). More accurately, if A is survived by issue, A had a fee (albeit a defeasible one), and A could dispose of the property to whomever A chose. Moreover, we wouldn't say that A has a fee subject to a condition subsequent because A is sure to die and the divestment does not cut A short unnaturally. A divesting condition must cut short a prior interest unnaturally, and this does not. Thus, the proper construction is not to regard this as a fee in A subject to divestment by a condition subsequent. With a natural termination of A's interest at death "without issue," the future interest would be a remainder and the present interest in A therefore would be a life estate.

c.   **Not settlor's intent.** To construe this as a life estate in A creates a conflict when we consider that the settlor knew how to create a life estate. H has a life estate, by clear language; if the same were to be true for A, wouldn't the same language be used? For example, "to H for life, remainder to A for life." Notice that the law assumes that, if the same intent exists (to create life estates in both H and then in A), the same language will be used.

d.   Construction preference. The favored construction is sensible because it is the only one that does not have the foregoing problems and it accelerates determination of who ultimately takes (i.e., we know we must delay determination of the ultimate taker until the death of H, but the favored construction does not make us delay that determination further until the death of A). If your conclusion is that the favored construction does not make sense, then the lesson to be learned is that words and phrases don't always mean what you think they do, making the drafting of future interests a far more challenging chore than the casual observer or practitioner might expect.

6.   Compare to Outright Gift

What if G's devise to A had been an immediate one, instead of a future interest following another life estate: "To A, but if A dies without issue, to X"? Here, the majority rule is different than the favored construction when the gift involves a future interest; the preferred construction is that A has a fee subject to divestment if no issue of A is living at A's death (before or after G). Thus, title is not certain until A's death: A's fee becomes indefeasible if A dies after G survived by issue; X (or X's successors if X is not then living) take if A dies after G and no issue of A survive A.

a.   Transferor's intent? Quaere whether this is what the average testator would intend; would they want A to take a fee simple absolute if A survives G, even if A later dies without issue?

b.   If A predeceases G. And the more difficult questions are what happens if A predeceases G, either survived by issue or not?

  i.   If A and A's issue predecease G. What if A predeceases G with issue alive, but they all also predecease G? A cannot take, because A predeceased G; the gift to A lapses (and because no issue of A survived G, A's gift cannot be saved by an antilapse statute, even if one otherwise would apply; see Chapter 8). A's issue do not take—they were not named as takers and they predeceased G anyway. X may not take either; the condition on X taking was that A die without issue, which did not occur. X not taking in this circumstance, however, seems contrary to G's likely intent, which was that X take if A (or, perhaps, A's issue) did not. It would have been easy enough to say that, however, and G did not; the devise to X was not conditioned on A not taking—it was conditioned on A dying without issue. Perhaps, however, a court would imply a gift to X in this circumstance. (See pages 188–192.) If not, a reversion would occur and G's residuary beneficiaries would take, unless this is a gift of the residue, in which case G's heirs would take by intestacy.

ii. **A predeceases G; issue of A survive G.** Finally, assume again the same outright gift: "To A, but if A dies without issue, to X," but here assume that A predeceases G survived by issue who survive G. Who takes? A cannot; A predeceased G and the gift to A lapsed. A's issue arguably cannot take (directly, at least)—they were not named as takers. X cannot take because A did not die without issue. If the relationship between G and A is such that the jurisdiction's antilapse statute applies, A's issue should take under the statute. If not, perhaps a court would imply a gift to them—because it appears likely G intended them to take in this circumstance. Otherwise, the property apparently will pass to G's residuary takers or, if this is a residuary gift, to G's heirs by intestacy.

K. GIFTS TO HEIRS

A gift under a will or trust instrument to someone's "heirs" raises a number of construction issues. Consider a gift: "To A for life, remainder to B's heirs." Determining the "heirs" of B who will take at A's death requires the answer to three questions:

1. Spouse Included?

First, does "heirs" include the designated individual's spouse, or is it limited to blood relatives? If the spouse is not taking a statutory forced heir share, usually the spouse is included as an heir (e.g., UPC §2-711). But this is not a universal nor predictable result; as with other construction issues, the drafter should anticipate this question.

2. Governing Law

Second, heirs is to be determined under the law of what jurisdiction, in effect at what time?

a. **Choice of law.** If the subject of the gift is real estate, the law of the jurisdiction in which the real estate is located governs the determination of heirs. If not, the choices are the law of the testator's domicile, or the law of the domicile of the designated ancestor (i.e., the person whose heirs are being determined) at her death. The cases go both ways.

b. **In effect at what time?** If the intestacy law of State A governs, what if its intestate succession statutes have changed over time? Do we apply the law in effect at execution of the document? When the document became irrevocable? When the designated ancestor died? Or when distribution is to be made? The most likely candidates are the law in effect at the designated ancestor's death and the law in effect when the document became irrevocable (i.e., the transferor's death for a gift under a will or revocable inter vivos trust, or the date an irrevocable inter vivos trust was created). Quaere whether the normal individual would want the law she knew or the law as the legislature amends it to apply. The likely answer is the former, but that creates the problem of having to go back and ascertain the law at that time, which could have been decades ago.

c. **Time for determination.** Third, if the designated ancestor is not the beneficiary immediately before distribution, when do we determine the heirs? For example, in *Estate of Woodworth*, 22 Cal. Rptr. 2d 676 (Cal. Ct. App. 1993), Harold devised the residue of his estate in trust for his wife, Mamie, for life, remainder to his sister, Elizabeth, if living, otherwise to Elizabeth's heirs. Elizabeth died before Mamie. At Mamie's death, the question was whether Elizabeth's heirs were to be determined at the time of Elizabeth's death (in which case the successors of her husband, who survived her but predeceased Mamie, would receive a share) or at the time of Mamie's death (in which case her predeceased husband would not be her heir). The usual rule, followed in *Woodworth*, is to determine heirs when the designated ancestor dies, because "heirs" means those persons who inherit from an intestate decedent. But these people all may be deceased by the time for distribution.

3. Designated Ancestor Still Living

Consider again a gift: "To A for life, remainder to B's heirs." What if B survives A? At A's death, B has no heirs to take (because a living person can have no heirs; see page 4). If the destructibility of contingent remainders doctrine applied (which, as discussed above, is unlikely), the remainder in B's heirs would fail and the property would revert to the transferor (which might have disadvantageous transfer tax effects). If the destructibility rule is not in effect, another possibility would be for the property to revert only until B's death, at which time the remainder to B's heirs would kick in. Still another possibility would be to accelerate the determination of B's heirs to A's death by making the determination as if B had died at that time. Whichever way you look at it, this if poor drafting.

4. Remainder to Transferor's Heirs

What if the gift of the remainder is to the transferor's heirs, and one of them is the life tenant? For example, assume a gift by G: "To A for life, remainder to G's heirs." G has four children: A, B, C, and D. Each of G's children has two children (A1 and A2; B1 and B2; C1 and C2; and D1 and D2). The order of deaths is: D, then G, then B, then A. When A finally dies, A is survived by C and by all eight of the grandchildren. Who takes at A's death? (Note that, if the Doctrine of Worthier Title, discussed above, is applicable, there is a reversion in G rather than a remainder in G's heirs, meaning that G's devisees would take if G died testate. As that doctrine's ongoing validity is limited, we will assume it is not applicable for this example.)

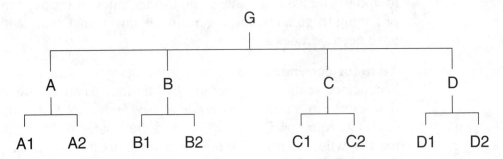

Order of deaths: Child D; Grantor G; Child B; Child/Life Tenant A. C still is alive.

a.   **Problems with application of general rule.** Under the usual rule, G's heirs would be determined at G's death—assuming no surviving spouse, that would mean A, B, and C each would have a vested remainder in ¼, which would become possessory at A's death; the other ¼ would belong to D1 and D2, as representatives of D and heirs of G. Note the problems and questions this construction raises. For example, distribution is not to be made until A's later death. At that time, B is not living; must B's estate be reopened for this interest to pass through to B's successors? Also, at G's death A's remainder in ¼ would become vested; would it merge with A's life estate to give A a fee in ¼ of the property? Does it make sense that G would leave A both a life estate and a part of the remainder?

b.   **Alternative times for determination.** There are several alternatives to the usual rule of using G's date of death as the date for determining G's heirs in a case like our example above:

   i.   **Irrevocability of instrument.** One is to determine heirs at the time the instrument became irrevocable, which would be G's date of death if the gift is made under G's will and which would not address the problems discussed above if the gift is by inter vivos trust.

   ii.   **Require survivorship to take.** Another is to determine heirs at the traditional time, but require survivorship to take. In our example, this would mean that any child of G who survived G but died before A would not take. This method would be unfair to those who do not survive the life tenant, and would raise the question of what to do if an heir of G who died before A (B in our example) was survived by descendants who survived A. In addition, this method creates the possibility of the gift failing altogether if no heirs determined at the traditional time (G's death) are alive at distribution (A's death).

iii. **Exclude life tenant.** A third possibility is to determine heirs at the traditional time (G's death) but simply exclude the life tenant (A) to prevent a merger problem; that, however, does not address the other problems, is unfair to A's family, and may be contrary to G's intent.

iv. **Treat life tenant as having predeceased.** A fourth alternative would be to determine heirs at the traditional time but treat the life tenant (A) as having predeceased the determination (G's death). This still requires reopening B's estate.

v. **Time of distribution.** Finally, we could determine heirs at the time for distribution (A's death) as if the designated ancestor (G) had died at that time. This is the sensible result because it avoids the merger problem and creating a share for any then deceased heir (as was necessary in *Woodworth* for Elizabeth's predeceased husband). Meanwhile, there is no delay while waiting for the designated ancestor (G) to die (e.g., if in our example the gift was inter vivos and A died before G, we would determine G's heirs at the time of A's death as if G had died then). Finally, no line of descent is cut out, nor is any line benefited if there is no one therein still alive to take. Despite its virtues, however, this approach is *not* the favored result—death of the transferor (G) would be the favored time for the determination.

5. Transferor's Intent

Remember, we are engaged in construction and rules of construction give way to a transferor's contrary intent. How would we show an intent of the transferor that the designated ancestor's heirs are to be determined at the life tenant's death rather than at the designated ancestor's death? There are several possibilities:

a. **Life tenant is sole heir.** If the life tenant is the sole heir at the time the gift is made, it is likely the transferor did not intend for heirs to be determined until the life tenant's death. (See Review Questions and Answers below.) Under the *rule of incongruity*, in some jurisdictions heirs are not determined until the life tenant's death if the life tenant is an heir, even if not the sole heir, because it is presumed that the transferor would not have intended to give the life tenant both a life estate and a remainder. If the life tenant is the sole heir, there is a greater likelihood that this rule would be followed.

b. **Alternative contingent remainders.** If there are alternative contingent remainders, heirs arguably were not intended to be determined until we know which alternative is going to be met. For example, assume a gift by G: "To A for life, remainder to B's heirs if A dies unmarried or in equal shares to the heirs of A and the heirs of B if A was married at death." Here, B's heirs and A's heirs have alternative contingent remainders. Arguably, G did not intend for B's heirs to be determined until A's death, when we know which of the contingent remainders will take. (Note that, if B survives A, we have the added problem discussed at page 415.)

c. **Delayed determination.** If the determination is going to be made so long in the future that it is unlikely any heir determined in the traditional manner still would be alive, the transferor arguably intended the determination to be made at the time of the determination.

EXAMPLES AND ANALYSIS

F and G (age 80) are siblings. F's only descendant is a grandchild, GC (age 8), who is in good physical health but has diminished mental capacity. G has one child, age 60, two grandchildren, and two great-grandchildren. F's will leaves the residuary estate in trust for GC for life, remainder to G's heirs. G's life expectancy is relatively short; it is likely that G's only heir will be G's child, but it is unlikely that G's child will survive GC to take the remainder at GC's death. F probably intended for G's heirs to be determined at GC's death, in which case the usual rule of determining heirs at the death of the designated ancestor (here, G) should not apply.

d. **"Atom bomb" provision.** Wills and revocable inter vivos trusts frequently provide for the testator or settlor's property to pass to a surviving spouse. If there is no surviving spouse, such instruments commonly leave the probate or trust estate to or in trust for descendants. In such cases, a question is what disposition should be made if there are no descendants who survive the testator or settlor, or if property is left in trust for descendants and they all die before the trust terminates. (And, if other persons are named as beneficiaries, they also are not living.) The drafting solution is to provide for an ultimate contingent beneficiary to whom the property can be distributed: one choice is charity; perhaps the more common one is the testator or settlor's heirs. Consider the following provision:

> SECTION *:   If upon the death of the survivor of my spouse and me, or at any time thereafter but prior to complete distribution of the trust estate, there is no living descendant of mine, the trust property then

held under this article and not vested or effectively appointed shall be distributed to my heirs at law determined according to the laws of the state of [**] as if I had died at that time.

   i.   Choice of law; time for determination. Note that this provision establishes what law governs the determination of heirs and when the determination is to be made.

L.   GIFTS TO DESCENDANTS, ISSUE, OR CHILDREN

In Chapter 2 we studied the alternatives for distributing the portion of an intestate decedent's estate passing to her descendants. Here, we consider how property left to "descendants," "issue," or "children" by a will or trust instrument is distributed.

1.   To "Descendants" or "Issue"

Technically, "descendants" and "issue" are synonyms. "Issue," however, is not a good alternative for "descendants" because too many courts and drafters think it means only children. In *Irvine*, for example, the will provided for "the issue of any deceased brother or sister to take his or her *parent's* share." The UPC once did but no longer uses "issue." A gift by will or trust instrument to a person's "descendants" (or "issue") raises at least three questions.

   a.   Per capita or by representation. First, do grandchildren or more remote descendants share if an ancestor who also is a descendant of the designated ancestor survives? For example, if Grandparent devises Blackacre to "descendants," and Grandparent is survived by one child, A, and one grandchild, B (who is a child of A), does A receive Blackacre or do A and B receive it? Absent some indication of intent to the contrary, "descendants" are determined by representation; in this example, A alone would take.

   b.   Method of distribution. Second, which of the three methods—discussed in Chapter 2—of distributing an intestate decedent's estate among descendants (classic per stirpes, per capita, and per capita at each generation) is to be applied if the instrument does not specify how to make the distribution?

      i.   Intestacy statutes, Restatement, and UPC. In many jurisdictions property left to descendants or issue will be distributed among them in accordance with the method used for intestate succession. Under the Restatement (Second) of Property—Donative Transfers, the distribution is to be made in accordance with the per capita method, even if that method is not used for intestacy, unless the gift is to issue or descendants "per stirpes," in which case the classic per stirpes method applies. The UPC approach follows the jurisdiction's intestacy statutes unless the gift is to descendants or issue "per stirpes," in which case the classic per stirpes system controls. The best solution? Provide in the instrument how property left to descendants is to be divided among them.

c. **Adopteds and nonmaritals.** Third, do adopted and nonmarital descendants take? Generally, a gift to "descendants," "issue," or "children" includes adopteds and nonmaritals under the same conditions as for intestacy (see Chapter 2).

   i. **Stranger-to-the-adoption.** Historically, under the stranger-to-the-adoption rule an adopted child would not share in a class gift to "children," "descendants," or "issue" unless the transferor was the adopting parent. Statutes in most jurisdictions have rejected that rule; the significant issue that remains is whether such a statutory change applies to an instrument that became irrevocable before the statute was enacted. In some jurisdictions such legislation is not retroactive; as a result, the stranger-to-the-adoption rule may still be followed for older instruments that were irrevocable before the statute reversing the rule was adopted.

   ii. **Adoption of adults.** In most jurisdictions a person adopted as an adult will share in a class gift to "descendants," "issue," or "children" in the same way as a person adopted as a child, regardless of the reason for the adoption. The minority view is that an adult who was adopted to allow her to take under another person's dispositive instrument will not be allowed to do so. For example, in *Minary v. Citizens Fidelity Bank & Trust Co.*, 419 S.W.2d 340 (Ky. Ct. App. 1967), a testator's son who had no descendants adopted his wife of 25 years in an effort to allow her to share in a trust his mother had established that was to be distributed to the mother's heirs at the son's death. Despite statutes allowing adults to be adopted and adopteds to inherit like natural borns, the court held that, to allow the wife to take as an adopted adult, would "be an act of subterfuge which in effect thwarts the intent of the ancestor whose property is being distributed and cheats the rightful heirs."

      (a) **UPC.** Under UPC §2-705(c) adopted adults do not share in class gifts made by someone other than the adopting parent unless the adopted adult lived while a minor as a regular member of the adopting parent's household.

EXAMPLES AND ANALYSIS

GP's will leaves her estate in trust for A for life, remainder to A's descendants. A married S, who had a child (C) who lived with A and S. A adopts C, but not until

C is an adult. C will share in the distribution of the trust established by GP at A's death, if the UPC applies and C was a minor when she began living with A as a regular member of A's household. In most non-UPC jurisdictions, C would share in the trust distribution in all adoption situations. In a jurisdiction following the *Minary* approach, C might not share if the adoption was made to confer on C trust beneficiary status. But even in such a jurisdiction, if C and A had developed a parent/child relationship—especially if they did so while C was a minor—C might share in the trust distribution without regard to whether A adopted C for the purpose of allowing C to do so.

---

      iii.   **"Adoption out."** In some jurisdictions the adoption of a person severs the parent/child relationship with the natural parent (and thus any status as a member of the natural parent's family), even if the adoption was made by a step-parent after the natural parent's death. The result can be to exclude the adopted child from membership in a class of "descendants" or "issue" of an ancestor of the deceased natural parent. In such a case, the adopted child is said to have been "adopted out" of the inheriting class.

 EXAMPLES AND ANALYSIS

GM's will leaves her estate in trust for her spouse, GF, for life, remainder to GM's descendants by representation. C is GM's child who predeceased GF. A child of C (GC) survived C but C's surviving spouse (S) married SP, who adopted GC. The question is whether GC shares in the trust when GF dies. Under the UPC, the answer would be yes. This "adoption out" issue essentially is the same as we saw under intestacy. See Chapter 2. In non-UPC states, the answer might be no—which is not the likely result GM would want if she had considered the situation, nor is it the right result based on policy grounds.

---

      iv.   **Nonmaritals.** In most jurisdictions today, nonmarital descendants share in class gifts made by will or trust instrument with descendants born during the marriage of their parents—just as they share under intestacy. See Chapter 2.

2. Gifts to "Children"

A question with gifts to "children" is whether the descendants of a deceased child will take their parent's share. For example, assume that G devised her estate in trust for S for life, remainder to G's "surviving children." G was survived by two children, A and B, but B predeceased S. However, one child of B (GC) survived S. Will GC share in the distribution of the trust estate at S's death?

a. **Descendants of deceased children excluded.** Taken literally, "children" means just that, in which case A takes all and GC is excluded. Note that a traditional antilapse statute will not save the gift, because B did not predecease G. In addition, if this was not a testamentary trust the antilapse result could not apply in most jurisdictions. And in most jurisdictions the "surviving" condition makes the remainders of A and B contingent on surviving S; because B did not do so, B's interest would fail and not pass to B's heirs or devisees.

b. **Clarify transferor's intent.** Did G intend that A should take to the exclusion of GC in this situation, or did the drafter of the instrument mistakenly use "children" when "descendants" is what G intended (or would have intended, if the question had been asked during the estate planning interview)? If the intent was to exclude grandchildren and more remote descendants, the way to avoid this issue is to say something like: "remainder to G's surviving children, without regard to whether a predeceased child of G is survived by any descendant who survives S."

3. **Rule in *Wild's Case***

Wild's Case, decided in 1599, interpreted a devise by T "to A and A's children." The possible interpretations include:

a. **If no children of A.** The first resolution in *Wild's Case*: if there are no children of A at T's death, A would take a fee tail. The traditional method for the creation of a fee tail was a devise: "To A and the heirs of his body," meaning that the property would pass to A and then descendants of A until A's line of descent ran out. Generally the fee tail estate is not recognized today. In many jurisdictions it is converted to a fee in A, although in some of these jurisdictions A is divested if A dies without descendants. In other jurisdictions A is treated as receiving a life estate, with a remainder in fee simple absolute in A's descendants. If a devise were made by T today: "To A and A's children," and A had no children at T's death, the likely result would be a fee in A, perhaps subject to partial divestment if A should have children.

b. **If A has children.** The second resolution in *Wild's Case*, followed in some jurisdictions today: A and A's children alive at T's death take as equal tenants in common. Afterborn children of A are excluded because the class would close under the rule of convenience at T's death. This is what the Restatement (First) of Property—Donative Transfers said was the accepted approach. An alternative if A has children at T's death is the so-called Pennsylvania rule, also followed in some jurisdictions today: life estate in A, remainder in A's children with the class not closing until A's death. This probably is the better interpretation because afterborns are not cut out; the Restatement (Second) of Property—Donative Transfers favors this approach.

    i. Individual and class gift. Still another alternative is to treat the gift as ½ to A and a class gift of the other ½ to A's children. Under this approach, A and A's children would take as tenants in common, with A's interest being ½, and A's children dividing the other ½ equally.

  c. Drafting alternatives for a gift to a testator's spouse and children, or descendants, would include:

    i. Spouse and each child take equal shares; per capita among children:
As many equal shares as necessary to distribute one share to each member of a class consisting of my spouse and my children who survive me, with no share for any class member or their descendants who do not survive me.

    ii. ½ to spouse and ½ to children; per capita among children:
Half to my spouse and half in equal shares to such of my children as survive me, with no share for any class member or their descendants who do not survive me.

    iii. Spouse and each child take equal shares; per stirpes distribution:
Per stirpes to my then living descendants [and, for purposes of division, treating my spouse as if she were a child of mine].

    (This may be appropriate for a second marriage situation.)

4. "In Equal Shares to the Children of A and the Children of B"

The construction issue here is whether there is a single gift to a class consisting of the children of A and the children of B, or whether there is a class gift of ½ to the children of A and a second class gift of the other ½ to the children of B. For example, if A had one child and B had two, does each child receive ⅓, or does A's child receive ½ and each of B's children ¼? Is the most likely construction a single class gift that, in the example, would result in each of the children receiving ⅓, or do you perceive that the transferor intends what in effect is a per stirpes distribution? Clear drafting would resolve this issue.

REVIEW QUESTIONS AND ANSWERS

Question: G conveyed Blackacre: "To A for life, remainder to A's children who graduate from college by the time they reach 25 years of age." At the time of the grant, A had two children, B and C. At A's death two years later, B was age 14 and C was age 4. (This conveyance would violate the common law Rule Against Perpetuities, but likely would be accompanied by a savings clause that would avoid such a violation. See the Website.)

a. What interests were created by G's grant?

b. What effect, if any, does A's death have?

c. What will happen if B graduates from college at age 22 and C is then living, but has not graduated from college?

d. What will happen if C does or does not graduate from college before reaching age 25?

Answers:

a. G's grant creates a life estate in A, a contingent remainder in B and C (subject to open if A has more children), and a reversion in G (which will become possessory after A's death if no children of A have graduated from college by the time they reach 25 years of age). The class of children is *not* subject to close based on survivorship—other than that a child must live long enough to graduate from college before reaching 25 years of age.

b. At A's death, G's reversion became possessory and the contingent remainders of B and C became springing executory interests that will divest G if either of them graduates from college before reaching 25 years of age. (At common law, the Doctrine of Destructibility of Contingent Remainders would have applied at A's death to destroy B and C's remainders, leaving G with the fee. Because the Doctrine has been abolished in most states and may no longer be applicable in any, B and C's remainders probably survive A's death.)

c. Upon B's graduation from college at age 22, with C still living but not a college graduate, B's executory interest will divest G. B will have a fee simple in Blackacre, but subject to partial divestment if C graduates from college before reaching 25 years of age.

d. If C graduates from college before reaching 25 years of age, C's executory interest (which will divest B and therefore would be regarded as a shifting executory interest rather than a springing one—which only divests the transferor or the transferor's successors in interest) will partially divest B: each of B and C will have a fee simple absolute in ½ of Blackacre. B's fee simple no longer would be subject to partial divestment if C reaches 25 years of age without having graduated from college (or dies before reaching 25 without a college degree).

Question: G's will provided: "I give Blackacre to T, in trust, for A for life, remainder to my heirs; I give the residue of my estate to Charity." G was survived by A (G's only descendant) and by a niece and a nephew, N1 and N2. A was G's only heir, but if A had predeceased G, N1 and N2 would have been G's only heirs. A dies testate, with a will devising A's estate to A's spouse, S; N1 and N2 survive A. At A's death, who takes Blackacre?

Answer: If the Doctrine of Worthier Title is in effect (doubtful, but possible), there would be no remainder in G's heirs, but instead a reversion in G, in which case Charity would take. If the Doctrine of Worthier Title is not in effect, the question is whether G's heirs are determined at G's death (the traditional rule) or at A's death. Under the usual rule of construction that determines heirs at the designated ancestor's death, A would have a vested remainder at G's death that likely would have merged with A's life estate to give A the fee. At A's subsequent death, A's devisee, S, would take. That rule, however, is one of construction only—it will give way to a contrary showing of G's intent. Arguably the fact that A is G's only heir indicates that G did not intend for G's heirs to be determined at G's death, as that result would give A the fee rather than the clearly intended life estate only. It appears more likely that G's intent was for G's heirs to be determined at A's death; thus, assuming the Doctrine of Worthier Title is not in effect, N1 and N2 should take.

An added issue would exist if either N1 or N2 is not alive at A's death; in that case determination of G's heirs at A's death would result in the survivor taking all if the deceased niece or nephew left no descendants.

Question: You represent Bank, a creditor of C. D, who was C's parent, created a revocable inter vivos trust in year 1, the terms of which called for D to receive the trust income for life; at D's death, the trust estate was to be distributed to C, who died in year 2, a month before D's death. Would Bank's ability to reach the trust assets be better if the jurisdiction had adopted UPC §2-707 (the future interest survivorship rule) or if the jurisdiction followed the traditional future interest no-survivorship rule? Explain fully.

Answer: The Bank would be better off if the jurisdiction followed traditional future interest law of not implying a condition of survivorship. Under that approach, C's remainder in the trust assets was vested upon creation of the trust in year 1; at C's death, the vested remainder was an asset of C's estate subject to the claims of creditors. By contrast, if UPC §2-707 were in effect, C's remainder would be subject to an implied condition of survivorship. Because C did not survive D, C's remainder would, in effect, lapse—any descendant of C who survived D would take; if there was no descendant of C, the gift would fail and pass to D's successors (probably D's heirs). That would require a determination of what "heirs" means—it would not include C because C predeceased D.

Question: D's revocable inter vivos trust provided: "Income to D for life, remainder ⅓ to D's nieces and nephews and ⅔ to D's descendants." When the trust was created, D had one niece and one nephew, N1 and N2, and two children, C1 and C2. N1 and C1 predeceased D; although each was survived by one child (GN1 and GC1), each died with a will devising their entire estate to Charity. At D's death, how are the trust assets to be distributed?

Answer: Under the traditional, no-implied-condition-of-survivorship rule, ½ of the ⅓ given to D's nieces and nephews would be distributed to N2 and the other ½ of that ⅓ would go to Charity (as N1's successor). By contrast, ½ of the ⅔ given to D's descendants would be distributed to C2 and the other ½ of that ⅔ would go to GC1; Charity does not take what C1 would have received because the multigenerational class gift to descendants results in an implied condition of survivorship. Because C1 did not survive D, C1 had no interest and the share C1 would have received if living passed to GC1 and not to C1's estate.

Traditional antilapse rules would not apply here because it is not a will and N1 and C1 take future interests—even though they are taking at D's death. Under UPC §2-707, however, survivorship *is* required for both gifts and the antilapse alternative disposition applies. As a result, Charity would not take. GN1 and GC1 take the shares N1 and C1 would have received if living.

Question: D devised her entire estate: "To T, in trust, income to A for life, remainder to A's child B, but if B does not graduate from college by 25 years of age, then to C." D died survived by A, B, and C; thereafter, C died survived by A and B. At A's death five years later, B was 26 years of age but had not graduated from college. Who takes?

Answer: B's remainder was vested subject to divestment; as a result C's estate owned a shifting executory interest. B's remainder was divested when B did not graduate from college by 25 years of age. The question is whether C's successors will take notwithstanding that C was not alive when B failed to graduate in time. The traditional view is that conditions of survivorship are not implied for future interests, and the majority rule is to that effect even if the interest is contingent on something else. Here, that means that C's successors will take because a condition that C survive A will not be implied even though C's interest was contingent on B not graduating from college by 25 years of age. If UPC §2-707 were in effect, an implied condition of survivorship would be imposed on C's interest; any descendant of C alive when B's interest is divested would take under the antilapse provisions of UPC §2-707 and only if there were none would D's heirs take—a reversion by intestacy.

Sample Exam Questions

Question: T, a single person, died leaving a two page handwritten will containing two dispositive provisions: section 1 contained a bequest of $50,000 "to each of my children, A, B, and C"; section 2 bequeathed "all of my stocks and bonds to B, to be used as we have agreed." Neither her home nor her tangible personal property, worth in the aggregate $150,000, were disposed of by the will. As found, A's name in section 1 had a pencil line drawn through it. On the bottom of page one, T had signed T's name. At the bottom of page two, T had dated the will, but did not sign it again. A and B, however, had signed their names at the bottom of page two as witnesses.

B is prepared to testify that T drew the line through A's name several years after executing the will because T wanted to disinherit A for marrying S. According to B, when T executed the will, B agreed with T that B would hold the stocks and bonds for C's care for the rest of C's life, after which any remaining stocks and bonds were to belong to B. C was partially incapacitated and died several months before T, leaving no surviving spouse or descendants. C's valid will left C's estate to a charity.

T died domiciled in New State. At T's death, T owned stocks and bonds with a total value of $200,000, and bank checking and savings accounts with a balance of $100,000. Relevant New State statutes provide as follows:

A. Except as provided in Section B, no will shall be valid unless it is in writing and executed in the manner hereafter stated. It shall be signed at the end by the testator, or by some other person in the testator's presence and by the testator's direction. The testator's signature shall be made or acknowledged by the testator in the presence of two or more witnesses present at the same time, and such witnesses shall attest and subscribe the will in the presence of the testator.

B. A will shall be valid if it is entirely written, dated, and signed by the hand of the testator.

C. All beneficial devises to a subscribing witness are void unless there are two other and disinterested subscribing witnesses to the will, except that if such interested witness would be entitled to any share of the estate of the testator in case the will were not established, he shall take such proportion of the devise or bequest made to him in the will as does not exceed the share of the estate that would be distributed to him if the will were not established.

How should T's estate be distributed? Discuss.

Answer: *Is the Will Validly Executed?* The first issue is whether the will is valid. Section A of the New State statute requires an attested will to be signed by the testator at the end. T signed T's two page will at the bottom of page one. Although some jurisdictions with an "at the end" requirement for the testator's signature allow the will to be signed at its logical end, the facts do not indicate a basis for making such an argument here. Accordingly, T's will was not executed in compliance with Section A.

In at least one jurisdiction, substantial compliance with will execution formalities is sufficient. If the other required formalities were complied with, arguably T substantially complied with the formalities despite having signed the will on page one rather than page two. The other formalities that Section A requires are that (i) the testator sign, or acknowledge the testator's signature, in the witnesses' presence, (ii) the witnesses be in each other's presence when the testator does so, and (iii) the witnesses sign in the testator's presence. The question does not include sufficient facts to determine if these formalities were satisfied. Under Section C of the New State statute, the fact that A and B were witnesses and beneficiaries of the will does not affect its validity; rather, as discussed below, the issue with respect to their being interested witnesses is whether the devises to them will be affected.

New State recognizes holographic wills that, under Section B, must be entirely written, dated, and signed by the testator. Attestation is not required. The facts indicate that the will was written, signed, and dated by T. Section B does not require the signature to be at the end of a holograph; consequently, T's signature on page one of the will should suffice. (There are no facts indicating that T did not intend T's signature on page 1 to execute the will, or that T's signature was not the complete act intended by T to validate the will.) The next issue is whether the signatures of A and B as witnesses to the will disqualify it as a holograph because of the requirement that a holograph be entirely in the writing of the testator. Signatures of witnesses to a will that otherwise is a valid holograph do not have dispositive or administrative effect on the testator's estate—they are surplusage—and thus should not be treated as the type of writing that will invalidate a holographic will. Accordingly, the will is valid, either under Section A as an attested will or under Section B as a holograph.

Finally, the attempted partial revocation of the will—the line drawn through A's name in section 1—does not evidence an intent to revoke the entire will, and thus is not an adequate act to revoke the will in its entirety, even if it is effective to partially revoke it.

If, contrary to this analysis, the will is determined to be not valid (and assuming T did not have a prior will that would be valid if this one is not), T's estate would pass by intestacy. All intestate succession statutes leave the entire estate of an intestate decedent who dies survived by one or more descendants, but not by a spouse, to the descendants, by representation. Because only two of T's children—A and B—survived T, and because C predeceased T with no descendants who survived T, the estate would pass equally to A and B if T's will is held invalid. In view of an often unarticulated preference of the law to treat children equally, this prospective result could influence a court to resolve close questions with respect to the validity of the will against validity.

A and B as Interested Witnesses. If, as appears likely, the will is a valid holograph but not a valid attested will, the devises to A—if not revoked—and to B will not be affected by their witnessing the will, because holographic wills are not required to be attested. If, on the other hand, the will is not a valid holograph—because not entirely in T's hand—but is a valid attested will because the formalities were substantially complied with, the devises to A—if not revoked—and to B will be void under Section C, except to the extent that A and B would have benefited from T's estate if the will had not been executed. We do not have sufficient facts to make that determination, because we do not know if T had a prior will that was revoked by this will. If so, A and B could take under the last will as much as they would have received under the prior will. If there was no prior will, the devises to A and B under the will would be limited to their intestate shares (half each).

If the will could be validated both as a holograph and an attested will, it is likely that the disinterested witness statute would not apply because witnesses are not required to validate the will as a holograph.

Attempted Partial Revocation. To revoke a will by physical act generally requires that the testator (or someone acting at the testator's direction and in the testator's presence) perform the act on the will with the intention of revoking it. Partial revocations by physical act are allowed in only some jurisdictions. Even in those they are not if their effect is to increase the devises other beneficiaries receive under the will (because such an increase would, in effect, be a testamentary gift accomplished without compliance with will execution formalities). Here, T's will did not include a residuary clause; thus, if A's devise was revoked, the effect would be to increase the property passing by intestacy, not to increase devises under the will. Accordingly, unless New State absolutely prohibits partial revocations by physical act, the devise to A likely will be treated as revoked if it can be established that T performed the revocatory act with the requisite intent to revoke.

The line drawn through A's name in section 1 of the will was made with a pencil. Some cases have held that use of a pencil indicates lack of finality of intent. With respect to the question whether T drew the line through A's name, a presumption would arise that T did so if the will was found in T's personal effects and T had exclusive access to it during T's life. In addition, although the credibility of the testimony of B concerning T's revocation of the bequest to A is affected by B's self interest (because B's share of the estate will increase if A's gift is revoked), generally declarations of a testator's intent with respect to a revocation are admissible. Finally, although capacity is required to have the requisite intent to revoke a will, there are no facts here indicating that T was suffering from a delusion or otherwise lacked testamentary capacity; disinheritance of a child may bear on a capacity determination if there is other evidence of lack of capacity, but it alone will not constitute the requisite showing.

Accordingly, T's drawing a line through A's name in section 1 of the will should be an effective partial revocation of the will as a cancellation that revoked the $50,000 bequest to A.

Effect of Disinheritance of A on Intestate Property. T died partially intestate even if T's will is valid, because the will did not dispose of all of T's cash, or T's home or tangible personal property. This property will pass by intestacy. A question raised is whether the revocation of A's $50,000 bequest affects the ability of A to share in the intestate estate as an heir. At common law, a will that states that an heir is not to receive any of the testator's property operates only to disinherit the heir from property passing under the will; intestate property passes by the intestate succession statute to the decedent's heirs, including the disinherited heir. That rule has been reversed by statute in some jurisdictions. If New State does not have such a statute, the revocation of A's bequest will have no effect on A's ability to receive half of the intestate property. If New State has such a statute, the issue is whether the cancellation of A's bequest should be construed as an expression of intent that A not share in the distribution of T's intestate property either. Although the cancellation, along with B's testimony of T's desire to disinherit A, arguably evidences T's intention that A not share in any of T's estate, it is unlikely that it would be construed to bar A from an intestate share, as T did not state an intention that A not receive any of T's property.

A as Pretermitted Heir. It is not likely that A will receive a share of T's estate passing under T's will as a pretermitted heir. First, the pretermitted heir statutes in most jurisdictions apply only to heirs born after execution of the will. Here, because T's will included a bequest to A, it clearly was executed after A's birth. Second, the cancellation of A's bequest indicates A was intentionally omitted from sharing in the property passing under the will. Moreover, typically any mention of a child in a will is adequate to negate operation of a pretermitted heir statute, even if that child is excluded from the will.

Bequest to C. T's will bequeathed $50,000 to C, but C predeceased T. In such a circumstance the gift lapses (i.e., fails), unless the will states an intention to the contrary. Here, there is no indication that the will did so. Accordingly, the $50,000 bequest will not pass to C's estate for distribution to C's heirs or devisees.

Most jurisdictions have antilapse statutes under which the gift to a predeceased devisee under a will may pass to the devisee's descendants if the predeceased devisee was related to the testator in a manner specified by the statute. Here, although C was T's child and thus clearly had the requisite relationship with T for the antilapse statute to apply, no descendants of C survived T and any antilapse statute thus would not apply. Accordingly, the gift to C fails. Because there is no residuary clause in T's will, the $50,000 that was bequeathed to C will pass by intestacy to T's heirs, A and B.

Trust for C. T's will left T's stocks and bonds to B, to be used as T and B had agreed. The will does not describe the terms of their agreement but, according to B, the stocks and bonds were to be used by B for C's benefit for C's life, with the remainder to B. The question is whether this is sufficient to create a valid trust. If so, B will receive the stocks and bonds as the holder of the trust remainder; if not, the attempted creation of an express trust for C, remainder to B, fails and the property becomes residuary estate that also passes to A and B by intestacy.

Such purported trusts sometimes are described as "semi-secret" trusts because the testator expressed an intent that the property be held in trust (and not received by the recipient beneficially), but did not express the terms that are to govern administration of the trust. Such trusts are invalid in some jurisdictions, the theory being that the disposition of a decedent's property is to be governed by the terms of a written will executed in accordance with the formalities for the valid execution of a will, not by an oral agreement. On that basis A would argue that the attempted oral trust fails and that a constructive trust of the stocks and bonds should arise in favor of T's estate to prevent B's unjust enrichment. Thus, the stocks and bonds then should pass by intestacy to A and B, equally.

B's argument will be that T's will was executed in accordance with the New State Wills Act, that T clearly intended a trust be created with the stocks and bonds, that extrinsic evidence is admissible to establish the terms of the trust, and that—even if the express trust fails—the constructive trust that arises should not be for T's estate, but instead should be for the intended beneficiaries of the trust. A difficulty with B's argument is that B, the person who will most benefit from the trust, apparently is the sole source of evidence of the terms of the oral trust. This factor, however, speaks to credibility and ought to be considered in the context of T's apparent intention to exclude A.

Conclusion. The most likely result is that the will is a valid holograph; that the interested witness statute does not affect the devises to A and B under the will; that A's $50,000 bequest was revoked; that the attempted oral trust of the stocks and bonds fails; and that the balance of T's estate will pass by intestacy equally to A and B.

Question: P executed a valid will that provided, in part: "I give my estate to my child, T. I request that T distribute half of it to C or C's descendants, if any, to provide for their best interests. In the meantime, I request that T distribute the income from that half to C, during C's life, and to C's descendants after C's death. It is my express desire that no creditors of C should be able to reach any of my property."

P had two children, T and C, both of whom survived P. C had a series of creditor problems during the years preceding P's execution of the will. Shortly after P's death C sent T a letter that provided, in relevant part, "I hold my interest in P's estate in a trust for my relatives by blood." Within a matter of months, C's spouse, S, filed for a divorce from C; that evening, C was driving home and negligently caused a traffic accident in which the driver of the other car, D, was seriously injured. Shortly thereafter, T and C had a conversation in which C requested that no distributions be made to C from P's estate until C had resolved any claims against C by S and D. Thereafter, C and S were divorced, S obtained a judgment against C for support, and D obtained a judgment against C to compensate D for injuries suffered in the car accident.

How will P's estate be distributed? May S or D reach assets of P's estate to satisfy their claims against C? Discuss.

Answer: *Gift to T; Trust for C.* P's will left P's estate to T with a "request" that T hold half of it for the benefit of C and any descendants C might have. Half of P's estate clearly is distributable to T; the question is what disposition is to be made of the other half. The word "request" is precatory language, which often is construed to create nothing more than a moral obligation or suggestion, rather that a legally enforceable mandate, with respect to disposition of the property as to which the precatory language applies. If such a construction applies here, T is the outright recipient of all of P's estate, in which case neither S nor D may reach any assets of P's estate.

Whether precatory language creates enforceable or moral obligations depends on the circumstances, as well as the language used. Here, despite the use of the precatory word, "request," P has manifested sufficient intent to impose enforceable duties on T to create a trust for C and any descendants C may have of half the assets received by T from P's estate. The factors evidencing such an intent are: (a) the definiteness of the property to be held by T—half of P's estate, as specified by the will; (b) the definiteness of the beneficiaries—the will is clear that C and any descendants of C are the only ones to benefit; (c) the relationships between the parties—C was a natural object of P's bounty, presumably on an equal footing with T, who was P's only other child; and (d) the financial situation of the parties and the motives that influenced P's disposition—C's financial difficulties presumably motivated P to dispose of C's share of P's property in such a manner as to be protected from creditors, as is manifested in the statement of intent included in the directions to T. In such circumstances, precatory words are construed as a polite command for the establishment of an enforceable trust; the trust property, beneficiaries, and purpose are ascertainable and P's intent is discernable. Thus, T should not be deemed to own all the property bequeathed to T to the exclusion of the rights of C and C's descendants in half of it.

Spendthrift Trust. Generally, the beneficiary of a trust may alienate the beneficiary's interest in the trust and the beneficiary's creditors may reach the beneficiary's interest in satisfaction of their claims. That is not the case if the settlor prohibits the voluntary or involuntary alienation of the beneficiary's interest; trusts subject to such provisions are protected from the claims of most creditors of the beneficiary, and are referred to as "spendthrift trusts." The rationale for allowing such trusts to benefit the beneficiary but not be reachable by the beneficiary's creditors is that the settlor's rights with respect to the property should include the ability to dispose of it for the benefit of such persons as the settlor chooses, subject to such restrictions or limitations as the settlor imposes. In addition, creditors of the beneficiary who extend credit to the beneficiary without ascertaining the ability of the beneficiary to repay the creditors are viewed as bearing responsibility for any resulting losses.

Here, P's will expressed P's "desire" that C's creditors not be able to reach the half of P's estate to be held in trust by T for C and C's descendants. If, as discussed above, P's use of the precatory word "request" does not preclude the creation of a trust for C and C's descendants, the "desire" with respect to C's creditors likely would be interpreted as a prohibition against C's creditors reaching the trust assets. In most jurisdictions, however, a spendthrift clause will not be valid unless it also prohibits the voluntary as well as the involuntary alienation of the beneficiary's interest. P's will does not expressly do so. In order to effect the apparent intent of P that the trust be a spendthrift trust, however, it is likely that a court would imply a prohibition against voluntary alienation of C's trust interest by C. If so, C's trust is a spendthrift trust, and C's creditors generally will be unable to reach it.

As a matter of public policy, however, courts have created exceptions to the normal rules under which spendthrift trusts are immune from claims of the beneficiary's creditors. Because of the nature of a support obligation, and the desire that divorced spouses not require public assistance for support, alimony or support claims in many jurisdictions are enforceable without regard to the presence of an otherwise enforceable spendthrift clause. Similarly, because a beneficiary's tort claimants generally cannot protect themselves by choosing not to extend credit to the beneficiary, arguably a spendthrift clause should not insulate the trust assets from the tort claimant's reach. Accordingly, the claims of both S and D against C may not be barred from reaching the trust assets by the trust's spendthrift nature (if it is deemed to be such).

Discretionary Trust. Protection of trust assets from the claims of creditors of a beneficiary may be afforded by a spendthrift clause or by the trust being discretionary. At common law, a trustee of a discretionary trust cannot be compelled by a creditor of a beneficiary to exercise its discretion to make a distribution. The theory underlying the rule is that the creditor of a beneficiary can have no greater rights to trust assets than the beneficiary—if distributions to a beneficiary are subject to the unexercised discretion of a trustee, the creditor is barred.

Further, only to the extent a trustee is found to have abused its discretion may a court interfere with its exercise. Here, S and D would have to show that, in not making distributions, T has abused T's discretion in deciding not to distribute principal to C. Given that C has not requested distributions from the trust, and that P's express intent is that no property be made available for C's creditors, this question of fact is one upon which S and D would appear unlikely to prevail. However, the equities of their claims make it at least possible that a court of equity would find T's agreement with C to make no distributions tantamount to an abuse of discretion by T, thus necessitating analysis of the question whether distributions, if ordered, could be reached by S or D.

Trust Income. C is entitled to receive distributions of trust income under P's will; they are not subject to T's discretion. If the trust is not a spendthrift trust S and D may reach undistributed trust income held by T. If the trust is a spendthrift trust, and the jurisdiction does not except support claims or tort creditors from the spendthrift bar the question is whether the spendthrift protection will extend to income that is distributable to C. In some jurisdictions S and D would be unable to reach the income—despite C's entitlement to it. The better view, however, is that spendthrift trust protection does not extend to trust assets the beneficiary is entitled to receive. Because of C's letter to T stating that C held C's interest in P's estate in an irrevocable trust for C's descendants, however, the question of the ability of S and D to reach trust income remains.

Creation of Irrevocable Trust by C. Creation of a valid trust, however, requires both a present trust corpus and identifiable beneficiaries. As to the former, interests that do not yet exist—such as profits to be earned in the future or an inheritance expected to be received from a living person—cannot be the corpus of a present trust.

Although C's interest in principal under the trust created by P's will is similar in some respects to property that does not exist, because there is no assurance that C will ever receive any principal from the discretionary trust, the better view is that equitable interests, contingent interests, and interests subject to divestment may be transferred to a trust. Further, C's right to receive income from the trust is not contingent or subject to divestment. Accordingly, C's interests in the trust created under P's will are sufficient trust property and there is no bar to a valid trust under this requirement.

As to the requirement that there be immediately identifiable beneficiaries, the question raised is whether C's "relatives" are identifiable. Although the term "relatives" generally does not describe a limited, defined class of persons, for this purpose it may be construed to mean "heirs." If not, the purported trust would fail for lack of identifiable beneficiaries. If so, the trust likely would fail anyway: as discussed above, if P's will is construed to create a spendthrift trust for C, as is likely, it is probable that the provision preventing C's creditors from reaching the trust assets will be construed also to prevent C from voluntarily alienating C's interest. Even if it did not, C as settlor cannot insulate C's own property from C's creditors in a spendthrift trust.

Consequently, any distribution by T to C, and any amounts of trust income T accumulates rather then distributes to C, would be subject to the claims of S and D. This factor likely would influence a court in weighing the issue discussed above whether T has abused T's discretion in making no distributions of principal to C. But as to current income and any distribution that T decides to make out of principal, S and D's claims likely may be satisfied.

Question. In Year 1, O, then age 67, single, and in good mental and physical health, created by Declaration of Trust an inter vivos trust described as the "O Trust." The trust instrument, which provided that O could revoke the O Trust at any time, designated O as the initial trustee and the sole beneficiary for O's life. Upon O's death, the instrument appointed O's child, C, to serve as the successor trustee, to terminate the trust by distributing its assets to C. At the time O created the O Trust O also executed a will under which O's estate was devised to the O Trust, and conveyed Blackacre and some stocks and bonds to the trust.

In Year 10, O married First Spouse (FS). Shortly thereafter, O executed an amendment to the Declaration of Trust. The amendment provided that, upon O's death, the successor trustee was to terminate the trust by distributing its assets half to FS and half to C, provided that if either of them predeceased O, all of the trust assets would be distributed to the other. In Year 11, O and FS were divorced, the decree including a property settlement under which they each received specified property in settlement of all claims of either to the property of the other.

By Year 20, O's mental and physical health was in decline. On occasion O was confused and disoriented about such matters as where O was and who were the people around O; at other times O had no such problems. O's physician told C that O was in the early stages of becoming senile. Because of O's physical problems, it also was becoming increasingly difficult for O to take care of O's daily living needs (bathing, dressing, preparing meals and eating, etc.). As a result, C arranged for N, age 50, to provide care for O in O's home. Within about six months, O and N had become very close and, over C's objection, married. The relationships between C and O, and between C and N, were very strained after the marriage, and C rarely saw or spoke to either of them.

Three months after the wedding, O executed a will (in compliance with all requisite will formalities and prepared by a lawyer who was representing N at the time in an unrelated matter) that provided, in relevant part, "I leave my entire estate to N." O died a month later, from natural causes, survived by N, C, and FS. At O's death, there were assets in the O Trust, and O owned other assets in O's individual name. O lived O's entire life in a noncommunity property state.

What claims do the facts suggest may be available to N, C, and FS with respect to the distribution of the assets in O's estate and in the O Trust? Discuss.

Answer: *Claim of FS.* FS is named as the remainder beneficiary of half of the assets in the O Trust at O's death. There is no indication that the Declaration of Trust was amended following the divorce of O and FS. Accordingly, FS may assert a claim to half of the assets in the O Trust. Most jurisdictions provide by statute that provisions in a testator's will in favor of a spouse are revoked by operation of law if the testator and the spouse divorce after the will was executed. The UPC and the statutes of some non-UPC jurisdictions provide that a divorce also revokes provisions in favor of the ex-spouse in instruments governing nonprobate assets, such as assets in a revocable trust. If the governing statute so provides, O's divorce from FS will have revoked the disposition in favor of FS under the Declaration of Trust.

If the governing statute does not expressly apply to dispositions in favor of a spouse under a revocable trust instrument, C and N nevertheless may argue that the will revocation statute should apply to revoke the disposition in favor of FS under the Declaration of Trust. First, the revocation-by-divorce wills statute reflects the presumed intent of the average testator—that he or she would not want a former spouse to share in his or her estate—and that presumption should be equally applicable to a revocable trust that serves as a will substitute. In this and some other contexts courts have held wills statutes applicable to revocable trusts, based in part on the revocable trust instrument being an integral part of a comprehensive estate plan (usually, as in this case, accompanied by a pour over will) for the disposition of the property of the settlor/testator at death.

A second, weaker argument available to C and N is that, although there is no indication that O's will expressly incorporated by reference the Declaration of Trust, O's will effectively did so by virtue of its dispositive provisions leaving O's probate assets to the O Trust for disposition under the terms of the Declaration of Trust. If so, the revocation-by-divorce wills statute may apply to the incorporated trust. Because the pour over will did not express an intention to incorporate the Declaration of Trust into the will (and doing so would not be advisable because the trust arguably would become a testamentary trust) an incorporation by reference argument likely would fail. Further, if O's second will was validly executed, the incorporation by reference argument would not even be available to C and N, because O's second will left O's estate to N, rather than to the O Trust.

C and N also may argue that the property settlement in the divorce proceeding operates as a waiver by FS of any claims to any property of O, including assets in the O Trust.

If under one or more of the theories described above the gift to FS from the O Trust is deemed revoked or waived, the next question is how the half of the O Trust assets that FS was to have received should be distributed. Under most revocation-by-divorce will statutes, the former spouse is treated as having predeceased the testator (or as having disclaimed the property devised to them, in which case the former spouse also is treated as having predeceased). The trust assets would be distributable to C if the governing statute so provides. If not, FS's half of the trust assets would be distributable under the law of the governing jurisdiction, perhaps to O's estate. If FS is deemed to have waived his or her claim to half of the trust assets in the divorce proceedings, C would argue that the waiver should be treated as a disclaimer, while N would argue that the Declaration of Trust did not dispose of the half of the O Trust assets that were to go to FS, but were waived by FS, and that they therefore should be held by C, the successor trustee of the O Trust, on a resulting trust for O's estate, to be disposed of to N under O's second will.

Validity of Second Will. If the second will was validly executed, N will receive the assets O owned individually as the devisee of O's entire probate estate. Without regard to the validity of the second will, there is no indication of a revocation of the trust by O. Accordingly, regardless of the validity of the second will, and thus regardless of how O's probate estate passes, the assets in the O Trust will pass under the terms of the Declaration of Trust to C, or C and FS (unless, as discussed below, N is able to make a successful elective share claim to part of these assets).

With respect to the validity of the second will, the facts state that O complied with the requisite will formalities in executing it. C may attack the validity of the will, however, on the grounds that O lacked testamentary capacity at the time O executed it, or that the will was the product of N's undue influence.

With respect to the issue of O's testamentary capacity, in most jurisdictions the burden of proof will be on C to establish that O lacked testamentary capacity (rather than on N to establish that O had testamentary capacity). The burden is a difficult one to meet, because the standard for testamentary capacity is low. To have testamentary capacity, which is necessary at the time of execution of the will, O must have had the ability to know and understand (i) the nature and extent of O's property, (ii) the objects of O's bounty (generally, those persons—such as close family members—who are close to O and who O ought at least to have in mind when planning a testamentary disposition), (iii) the disposition that O was making of O's property by the will, and (iv) the relationship of these factors to each other to create a plan for the disposition of O's estate.

Whether a testator had testamentary capacity at the time of execution of the will is a factual issue. The facts indicate several factors that would support a claim that O lacked testamentary capacity: O was approximately 90 years old; O died from natural causes a month after executing the will (indicating that O may have been in very poor health at the time of execution); less than a year before execution of the will O had periods of confusion and disorientation, sometimes not knowing where O was, or who the people around O were; and O's physician had concluded at that time that O was in the early stages of senility. Presumably, O's condition deteriorated further during the last year of O's life. Although these factors would lend strong support to a claim of lack of testamentary capacity, they alone likely would not be enough to establish it. Rather, testimony of witnesses who spent time with O around the time of the execution, and particularly O's lawyer (but not the witnesses to the will, who may not recant their attestation saying O was of sound mind) would be necessary for the fact finder to make the testamentary capacity determination.

Whether O executed the second will under the undue influence of N also is a question of fact for which additional information is needed. Generally, undue influence exists when the testator's free will is overcome by another such that the testamentary instrument executed by the testator reflects the desires and intentions of the influencer rather than the testator. Required is some element of coercion—usually not physical coercion, but a kind of mental coercion that results in the substitution of the influencer's testamentary desires for those of the testator. To be undue, the influence exerted generally must be directly related to the execution of the testator's will and must be intended by the influencer to result in a testamentary instrument that benefits the influencer or one whom the influencer wants benefited.

We do not have sufficient facts to determine whether O's second will was executed under the undue influence of N. Indeed, it often is impossible to prove undue influence directly—and the initial burden of doing so is on the contestant—because the testator has died and any influence exerted took place in private. Accordingly, many jurisdictions shift the burden of proof to the alleged influencer if the contestant shows that the testator was susceptible, the influencer had the opportunity to exert undue influence, and the influencer had the disposition or a motive to do so. Alternatively, a presumption of undue influence may arise if the contestant shows that the will benefits the drafter or a natural object of the drafter's bounty, or if the influencer was in a confidential relationship with the testator and participated in the procurement of the will.

Here, C may be able to shift the burden of proof to N by establishing: (i) that O was susceptible to undue influence by N (in addition to the factors discussed with respect to whether O had testamentary capacity, O was dependent on N for O's care); (ii) that N had the opportunity to exert undue influence; and (iii) that N had a disposition or motive to do so (the terms of the will leaving O's entire estate to N, which is more than N would have received but for the influence). Alternatively, a presumption of undue influence may arise if N participated in the procurement of the will (such as by arranging for O to meet with the attorney and participating in such meetings). In either case, C must overcome the general reluctance of courts to find undue influence exerted by one spouse over the other. But O's advanced age and poor mental and physical health, considered in the context of O's short-term relationship with N, O's dependence on N as O's caretaker, and the age differential between them may well overcome that reluctance (and lead a court to find a confidential relationship between O and N such that if N participated in the procurement of the will, the presumption of undue influence could arise).

If a presumption of undue influence arises or C otherwise succeeds in shifting to N the burden of proof, N likely would attempt to meet the burden of showing an absence of undue influence by showing that O had independent representation with respect to execution of the will. Because the attorney who drafted the will, however, was N's attorney, it is likely that O would not be found to have received independent representation.

Elective Share Claim by N. All noncommunity property states (except Georgia) provide the surviving spouse of a decedent with the right to elect to take a statutory share of the decedent's estate, in lieu of other provisions made for the surviving spouse by the decedent. If O's second will was not validly executed, O's estate would pass under the first will to the O Trust, for distribution with the assets already in the O Trust to C (or perhaps to C and FS). In such a circumstance, N would be entitled to elect to receive a statutory share of O's probate estate. Whether N's elective share also would reach the assets in the O Trust would depend on the jurisdiction's elective share law. Under the UPC (which provides for an elective share against the decedent's "augmented estate,") and in many non-UPC jurisdictions, assets owned by a decedent's revocable, inter vivos trust may be reached by a surviving spouse's elective share claim. In some non-UPC jurisdictions, however, the elective share does not reach assets in such a trust.

If O's second will was validly executed, N will be entitled to receive O's entire probate estate. In such case, N likely would not elect to take the statutory share (because doing so would be in lieu of the devise of the entire probate estate to N) unless the election would reach the assets in the O Trust and N's elective share of these assets, along with N's elective share of the probate estate, would exceed the probate estate (all of which N otherwise would receive under the will).

Glossary

Abatement is the situation in which a testator's estate is inadequate to finance all the bequests under the will, in which case the order of abatement specifies the gifts that will be funded first and those that will abate or fail to provide therefor.

Acceleration is an event that causes a future interest to become possessory, such as on disclaimer or application of a slayer statute.

Accessions are growth in assets, typically between execution of a will and the testator's death and then between death and distribution of the estate. The accessions rules govern who gets these extra assets.

Acknowledgement is a testator's affirmation that a signature is the testator's own and that the testator made it with the intent to validate a will or other document.

Ademption by extinction is the testate circumstance by which the subject of a specific bequest is not found in the estate at death and cannot be replaced.

Ademption by satisfaction is the testate counterpart to Advancement, involving a beneficiary's receipt during life of property or a bequest that was meant to be conveyed by the donor's will.

Administrative infinality is one of the fantastic presumptions under the Rule Against Perpetuities.

Administrator is the personal representative appointed by a court.

Administrator cum testamento annexo is an administrator with the will attached, meaning of a testate estate. Administrators may be appointed by the probate court because the will did not nominate an executor, or because the person appointed is not willing or able to act.

Administrator de bonis non is an administrator of goods not administered, which means a successor appointed because the predecessor executor or administrator was unable to complete the administration.

Adoption statutes regard adopted children as natural born, and allow children to inherit from and through their adoptive parents only (and vice versa), with certain exceptions in the case of step-parent adoptions.

Advancement describes an heir's receipt of property from an ancestor who subsequently dies intestate, the property being regarded as part of—it counts against—

the heir's ultimate inheritance. The testate counterpart is ademption by satisfaction.

Affinity means relationship by marriage.

Alien land laws relate to the right of a nonresident not a citizen heir to inherit real property in the United States, usually limited in the number of acres or the duration the property may be retained.

All-or-nothing rule under the Rule Against Perpetuities relates to class gifts, in which all members' interests must be valid or they all must fail.

Alternative contingencies doctrine is a Rule Against Perpetuities convention that attempts to validate a disposition if one set of facts would make it valid and another invalid.

Ambiguity comes in several versions: patent and latent, and latent ambiguity comes in three varieties: equivocations, misdescriptions, and inaccuracies. These usually raise the question whether extrinsic evidence may be used to resolve questions of intent.

Ambulatory means it does nothing until death. Wills are ambulatory during the testator's life.

Ancillary administration is probate administration in a jurisdiction other than the decedent's domicile.

Annuity is a contractual arrangement by which the issuer agrees to make certain payments, typically over the life of the annuitant, in exchange for consideration. It is a nonprobate asset.

Antenuptial agreements are the same as prenuptial agreements.

Anticipatory breach is possible in a will contract setting in which one party proposes to violate their agreement and it is discovered before that person dies.

Antilapse statutes override or preclude certain lapsed gifts and usually apply also to void gifts, in each case by substituting representatives in the place of a deceased named beneficiary.

Anti-netting rule precludes a fiduciary who invested imprudently from netting gains from prudent investments against losses from imprudent investments in an effort to avoid liability.

Apportionment usually is applied to describe the method by which a tax liability—typically the federal estate tax—is shared by the beneficiaries of an estate.

Assignment allows a potential heir to transfer an expectancy to a third party for consideration.

Assistance is a third party helping a testator with execution, such as guiding the hand through a signature. Compare Proxy signature.

Atom bomb provision directs distribution of property undisposed of in a trust when all the named beneficiaries are deceased.

Attestation is the formalities of signing the will. The witness signature procedure is referred to as the attestation and an attested will means the will was witnessed (as opposed to holographic).

Augmented probate estate is a Uniform Probate Code concept by which certain nonprobate property dispositions are regarded as part of the decedent's probate estate for purposes of computing and satisfying a surviving spouse's elective share entitlement.

Beneficial interest is the entitlement of a trust beneficiary.

Blending exercise of a power of appointment commingles the powerholder's own assets with the appointive assets.

Blockbuster will is a concept not yet accepted that a will should be able to make changes to the disposition of nonprobate property, such as to change the beneficiary of life insurance.

Cancellation is a form of physical revocatory act to a will that affects the words on the paper.

Capacity. See Mental capacity.

Capture is the consequence of an invalid attempt to exercise a general power of appointment.

Cessure provision is one form of spendthrift trust provision. Also known as a forfeiture provision.

Cestui que trust is a hugely outdated term for beneficiary of a trust.

Claflin doctrine refers to the existence of an unfulfilled purpose of the trust that would prevent voluntary termination of the trust, even with the consent of all trust beneficiaries.

Class gift is a disposition to a group of beneficiaries defined by a common characteristic, usually with each member of the class taking an equal share. Class closing rules relate to these gifts.

Collaterals are nonlineal blood relatives, including natural born, adopted, nonmarital, and half-bloods.

Commingling is the function of a fiduciary mixing fiduciary assets with its own, rather than clearly marking them as subject to the fiduciary relation. It is the converse of earmarking or segregation and constitutes a fiduciary breach of duty.

Community property is the system of intra-spousal property ownership that regards earnings from onerous activity during marriage as owned 50/50 by spouses.

Commutation is the process by which the value of a present and a future interest are determined and each is immediately satisfied by distribution of the underlying property in the proper proportions as between the two owners.

Concurrent ownership comes in several forms: joint tenancy, tenancy by the entireties, and tenants in common. It entails undivided mutual ownership of property, sometimes with probate avoidance and rights of survivorship at death, but not necessarily.

Conditional revocation is contingent on (non)occurrence of an event or fact. Basically the same as dependent relative revocation.

Conditional will is contingent on (non)occurrence of an event or fact to be intended as the maker's final wishes. "If I do not recover from surgery" would be a classic conditional will.

Conflict of laws describes the issue of which state law will be selected to resolve the substance of an issue, and which state's choice of law rules will be applied to make that selection.

Consanguinity means relationship by blood. The "degrees of consanguinity" is a method of determining how closely or distantly related an individual is to another.

Conservator is a court appointed fiduciary who represents an incompetent individual during life. Also known in some jurisdictions as a guardian.

Construction is the process by which a court construes a document, looking to discern intent. As compared to Interpretation this is more about what the maker meant to say, instead of the meaning of what the maker did in fact say. Sometimes referred to as "reading between the lines."

Constructive trust is a creature of equity, usually to prevent unjust enrichment.

Contingent beneficiary provision directs distribution of property undisposed of in a trust when all the named beneficiaries are deceased.

Convenience joint tenancy is created as a means of providing property management without intending to create property rights in the joint tenants, usually because the property owner did not know to use a durable power of attorney, and usually can be undone because of the lack of intent to make a gratuitous transfer of ownership rights.

Corpus is one name for the principal or res of a trust—the underlying property owned.

Curtesy is the largely antiquated and usually defunct common law entitlement of a surviving widower in the decedent's property, replaced in most jurisdictions with the elective share.

Cy pres refers to the authority to reform a trust, for example to avoid violation of the Rule Against Perpetuities, to comply with the likely intent of the settlor or prevent failure of a trust the purposes of which no longer are legal or achievable, or to generate a charitable deduction.

Dead hand refers to the prejudice of the common law to respect the wishes of the decedent who settled a trust for future generations. See the Rule Against Perpetuities.

Declaration of trust is a trust in which the settlor is also the initial trustee and "declares" that the settlor holds property as trustee, usually for the benefit of the settlor as well, at least until the settlor's death. A valid nonprobate property management and transfer device.

Deeds may serve as nonprobate dispositions if the property form used entails the right of survivorship.

Deferred compensation comes in many forms, such as qualified pension plans or stock option plans, that delay income taxation of salary or other forms of compensation for services, usually in a retirement benefit context. Often these are nonprobate assets, similar to insurance, annuities, and other contractual arrangements, and may constitute income in respect of a decedent if the employee dies before receiving the benefit.

Deficiency usually refers to diminished mental capacity.

Demonstrative bequest is one of a particular asset or source of funds but, if that source is inadequate, from other funds, such as "$100, to be satisfied first from the balance of my account at the XYZ bank." It is essentially a combination of Specific and General bequests.

Dependent relative revocation is a legal fiction that an act of revocation did not occur if an act or event upon which it is dependent is invalid (e.g.: "I revoke will 1 only if will 2 is valid").

Derangement usually refers to mental aberrations versus diminished capacity.

Disclaimer is a renunciation of property, and may be "qualified" by meeting certain requirements under the Internal Revenue Code.

Discretionary trust reposes authority in the trustee to choose among a group of beneficiaries in determining who will receive what amounts of income or principal.

Dispensing power under the Uniform Probate Code is authority for a court to admit a will to probate notwithstanding that it lacks certain formalities.

Divorce operates as a partial revocation by operation of law of dispositive provisions in favor of the former spouse and sometimes the spouse's relatives. It may revoke the entire document.

Doctrine of infectious invalidity is part of the result of violating the Rule Against Perpetuities that may invalidate otherwise valid interests that are closely tied to invalid interests.

Doctrine of worthier title converts a reversion to the heirs of the transferor into a remainder to the transferor.

Donee usually is the term used to describe a person receiving a gift of property, but in the context of powers of appointment it describes the person who may exercise the power, not the persons in whose favor the power may be exercised. See Objects or Permissible appointees, and Powerholder.

Donor usually is the term used to describe a person making a gift of property, and in the context of powers of appointment it describes the person who created the power.

Dower is the largely antiquated and usually defunct common law entitlement of a surviving widow in the decedent's property, replaced in most jurisdictions with the elective share.

Dry trust is one with no remaining corpus and that therefore will terminate.

Duplicate original wills are multiple copies each executed with the requisite formalities.

Durable power of attorney relies on the law of agency. Durable means that it survives the maker/principal's incapacity. The authorized agent is the attorney in fact. Durable powers may relate to property management or health care decision making, which might instead be called a health care proxy, health care directive, or medical directive. A living will is different.

Earmarking is the function of a fiduciary segregating fiduciary assets from its own and clearly marking them as subject to the fiduciary relation. It is the converse of commingling.

Elective share of a surviving spouse is the right in most jurisdictions to reject the decedent's estate plan in favor of a statutory entitlement. It exists only in the noncommunity property states and is their modern alternative to dower and curtesy.

Equitable election is the technique by which a testator leaves property to an individual by a will that at the same time purports to dispose of property that individual owns, putting the individual to an election to challenge the will and keep the individual's own property or to accept the validity of the will and the benefits it brings to the individual in exchange for permitting the will to dispose of the individual's own property. It also is used to describe the choice a surviving spouse must make between taking the elective share under state law or taking under the decedent's estate plan.

Equitable interest/title is what the beneficiary of a trust is deemed to possess. The fiduciary owns the legal interest/title.

Equivocation is a latent ambiguity that is an accurate description of more than one asset, person, event, etc. and creates ambiguity because it is not clear which of them was intended.

ERISA is the acronym for the Employee Retirement Income Security Act, largely tax rules that govern qualified deferred compensation retirement benefits.

Escheat is when the estate of an intestate decedent passes to the decedent's domiciliary state.

Executor is the personal representative appointed by a valid will.

Executory interest is the future interest created in the same document as a present interest and following any but a particular estate. The two varieties are springing and shifting executory interests.

Exoneration is the rule dealing with payment of a decedent's debts, usually with respect to realty in the probate estate.

Expectancy is what a potential heir expects to receive from a potential decedent.

Express trust is the standard issue variety, in juxtaposition to an implied (resulting or constructive) trust. Some varieties are living or inter vivos trusts, insurance trusts, funded and unfunded trusts, testamentary trusts, divorce and tort settlement, and employee benefit trusts.

Extrinsic evidence is alleged proof of intent, not within the "four corners" of a document.

Family allowance typically applies only for a limited duration, during probate administration of an estate, to provide support to surviving dependents.

Fertile octogenarian is one of the fantastic presumptions under the Rule Against Perpetuities.

Fictional eraser is a technique by which a court may ignore words in a document that create an ambiguity, in an effort to resolve the proper interpretation of the document. Usually applied in latent ambiguities of the inaccuracy and less often the misdescription variety.

Fiduciary is the term for any of a number of property owners who hold property for the benefit of others, such as trustees, guardians, conservators, and personal representatives (executors and administrators).

Forced election estate plan is the same as the widow's election.

Forced heir share is another term for the elective share or a pretermitted heir share.

Forfeiture provision is one form of spendthrift provision. Also known as a cessure provision.

Formalities are the rules for valid execution.

Four corners is the way of referring to a document and taking cues only from what actually was said "within the four corners" rather than implied or suggested by evidence extrinsic to the document.

Fraud is a will contest ground that entails deception. In the exercise of a power of appointment it involves an effort to appoint to an impermissible appointee.

Fraud in the execution relates to deceit regarding the terms or nature of a document.

Fraud in the inducement relates to deception in the facts underlying the testator's formulation of intent.

Funded trust means that the trust owns assets during the settlor's life, usually to provide asset management and probate avoidance, and is a valid nonprobate will substitute.

General bequest is one of an unparticular fungible asset, such as "50 shares of XYZ stock" or "$100" or "a pecuniary amount equal to the smallest sum needed to reduce my estate taxes to zero." Compare Specific, Demonstrative, and Residuary bequests.

General power of appointment permits the powerholder to appoint in favor of any one or more of the powerholder, the powerholder's estate, or creditors of either. Additional appointees are permissible but do not change the classification of the power. Compare Nongeneral, Limited and Special powers of appointment.

Guardian is a fiduciary who represents a legally incompetent individual, either because of lack of capacity or lack of legal age. There are guardians of the person and of the property, who may be and frequently are different people.

Health care proxy. See Durable power of attorney.

Heirs are determined at the designated ancestor's death as those who take by intestacy. Heirs apparent are certain to take if they survive the designated ancestor and heirs presumptive are first in line presently but could be displaced.

Holograph is a handwritten will that need not be attested. Not valid in the majority of states.

Homestead is personal residence property exempt from creditor claims.

Honorary trusts have no living person to enforce the trustee's duties and therefore frequently are regarded as invalid unless the trustee voluntarily chooses to comply. The most common is a trust for a pet.

Imperative power is one that the law treats the powerholder as having to exercise, usually because there is no default beneficiary. Failure may result in distribution to the permissible appointees in equal shares under an implied default provision. Also known as Power in trust.

Implied default is the equitable disposition of power of appointment property as to which there is no effective default provision. See Imperative power.

Implied gifts are an equitable device to fill gaps in a disposition to accomplish what a court believes the maker of the document meant to provide.

Implied trusts are a creature of equity, either resulting or constructive trusts.

Inaccuracy is a latent ambiguity that is an inaccurate description of only one asset, person, event, etc. Compare Equivocation and Misdescription.

Incapacity is the state of being unable to manage your own affairs, or lacking the mentality to validly execute a document.

Inconsistency in a subsequent instrument revokes the prior document to the extent the differences cannot be reconciled.

Incorporation by reference is one document treating another as if it was fully reproduced in the one. "Read the attached list as if it was a part of this will."

Independent legal significance implies that something else stands on its own—has its own independent legal significance—and is valid notwithstanding its indirect effect on a will.

In hand payment provisions require a trustee to make distribution directly to the beneficiary, constituting a form of spendthrift protection.

Insurance trust may own the policy of insurance or may be only the designated beneficiary of the death proceeds of the policy, and may be funded or unfunded during the insured's life. A valid nonprobate will substitute.

Integration is the coordination of multiple pages of a single document, which may include those validly executed at different times, such as a will and codicils to it.

Intent usually is associated with will execution or revocation. It also may arise in construction cases.

Interest or an interested witness means taking more under a document than if it was not signed or valid, such as because the witness is a beneficiary under a will.

Interpretation is the process by which a court seeks to translate or define what a document means. As opposed to construction, which is more about what the maker meant to say, this is about what it does in fact provide. Sometimes referred to as "reading the lines" instead of "reading between the lines."

In terrorem or "in terror of" is a provision that disinherits any beneficiary who contests a will.

Inter vivos power of appointment is one exercisable by deed or other instrument executed during the powerholder's life.

Inter vivos trust is the same as a living trust.

Intestate property is probate property not validly disposed of by a will. Dying intestate means to die without a valid will. "Partial intestacy" occurs if a will exists but does not validly dispose of all the decedent's probate property.

Joint and mutual will is one document serving as the will of several people, with reciprocal or mirror image provisions for each of them. It need not be contractual.

Joint tenancy is concurrent ownership by several owners/tenants who enjoy undivided entitlement to the property, typically with the right of survivorship at the death of any but the last tenant to die. It is a nonprobate asset.

Joint will is one that several testators sign. It is the will of each.

Lapse refers to failure of a gift because the named beneficiary is deceased. See Antilapse and compare Void.

Latent ambiguity is one that is not clear from the face of the document but only when the terms are applied to the facts at hand. These come in three varieties: equivocations, misdescriptions, and inaccuracies. Compare Patent ambiguity.

Legal list is a list of approved investments for fiduciaries.

Life in being for Rule Against Perpetuities purposes is someone who was alive when the transfer became irrevocable.

Life insurance is a contract by which the policy owner pays premiums to an insurer that agrees to pay a death benefit to a beneficiary upon the death of an insured. It is nonprobate property.

Limited power of appointment is the old term to describe a nongeneral power.

Lineals are ancestors and descendants in the blood line, natural born, adopted, non-marital, and half-bloods.

Living trust is the name of a trust created and typically funded during the settlor's life.

Living will is a very limited document that establishes the maker's wishes regarding end of life or heroic medical techniques, usually articulating the desire to be allowed to die. See also Durable power of attorney.

Marital property is used under the Uniform Marital Property Act to describe what would be community property in a community property state, and by the Uniform Probate Code to describe property of the surviving spouse that would be part of the augmented probate estate if it was owned by the decedent, and that counts against the elective share of the survivor.

Marshaling is the technique by which a blending exercise of a power of appointment as to which a portion is valid will direct appointive assets to the valid portions to the extent possible, such as to avoid violation of the Rule Against Perpetuities.

Medical directive. See Durable power of attorney.

Mental Capacity or Mentality usually is referred to as "of sound mind" for will or other document execution validity.

Merger is the legal combination of titles, either life estate or term of years with the remainder or legal and equitable titles, resulting usually in a fee simple entitlement and potentially causing a trust to terminate because the combination of legal and equitable titles destroys the nature of a trust.

Misdescription is a latent ambiguity that is an inaccurate description that could apply to more than one asset, person, event, etc. and creates controversy because it is not clear which is the intended reference. Compare Equivocation and Inaccuracy.

Mistake is an issue in execution, revocation, or understanding the law or facts as they relate to a document. Mistake of this last variety comes in four varieties: mistakes of law, of fact, in the inducement, and of omission. The common law said there was no remedy for mistake. See also Ambiguity.

Mortmain statutes are found in only a small number of states and relate to dispositions in favor of charity, usually under a will or codicil executed close to death.

Mutilation is one form of physical revocatory act to a will that affects the paper on which the will is written.

Mutual will is one with reciprocal or mirror image provisions. It need not be contractual.

Negative will does not dispose of property but, instead, merely disinherits an heir. Authorized only in a minority of jurisdictions.

Nongeneral power of appointment is the modern term for a limited or special power, meaning that exercise may not include the powerholder, the powerholder's estate, or creditors of either.

Nonmarital is the nonpejorative term used to describe a child born out of wedlock, also sometimes referred to as illegitimates or bastards.

Nonprobate property passes by operation of law pursuant to various will substitutes, such as a life insurance policy contract or retirement plan beneficiary designation, joint tenancy with right of survivorship or tenancy by the entireties, other payable on death arrangements, or pursuant to a trust.

Nuncupative is an oral will, recognized as valid in only a few states.

Objects of a power of appointment are the permissible appointees.

Obliteration is a form of physical revocatory act to a will that affects the words on the paper.

Oral trust may be invalid because it fails to comply with the Statute of Frauds.

Parentelic is a system of determining which of several collateral heirs is entitled to inherit in intestacy. Rather than the degree of consanguinity being determinative it is based on the relation of the nearest lineal ancestor in common with the decedent.

Particular estates are life estates, life estates per autre vie, and terms of years.

Passive trust is one with no unfulfilled duties and therefore that will terminate.

Patent ambiguity is one that is apparent from the face of the document. Compare Latent ambiguity.

Payable on death (POD) is a form of contract provision that creates an entitlement in a third party when someone dies. These usually are nonprobate assets.

Pennsylvania rule is one of the resolutions to the issue addressed by the Rule in *Wild's Case*.

Permissible appointees are those persons or institutions who are within the class of recipients of property under a proper exercise of a power of appointment. See also Objects.

Personal representative (either an Executor or Administrator) performs probate administration.

Per capita (or per capita at each generation) are two alternative systems of representation among descendants.

Per stirpes is the common law form of representation among descendants. There are classic and modified versions.

Plain meaning is the presumption that terms should be given their everyday meaning.

Possibility of reverter is the future interest retained by a transferor following a fee simple determinable.

Posthumous heirs are those conceived before the decedent's death but treated as alive at the time of conception if subsequently born alive.

Postnuptial agreement is a marital property contract that usually settles and waives elective share rights.

Pour back trust is a funded inter vivos trust that distributes at the settlor's death back to the settlor's probate estate.

Pour over will is a disposition in favor of a free standing trust, often unfunded during the testator's life, that contains the testator's primary estate planning provisions. The receptacle trust sometimes is known as a pour over trust.

Powerholder is the modern term for the holder of a power of appointment—historically called the donee of the power.

Power in trust is a power of appointment that the powerholder is regarded as obliged to exercise. See Imperative power.

Power of attorney is an authorization allowing an "attorney in fact" to act on behalf of the "principal" who is delegating the task or authority to act.

Power of termination is the future interest retained by a transferor following a fee simple subject to a condition subsequent. Also known as Right of entry for condition broken.

Precocious toddler is one of the fantastic presumptions under the Rule Against Perpetuities.

Prenuptial agreement is a marital property contract that usually settles and waives elective share rights.

Presence is a requirement of both execution and revocation, if a witness or proxy act is involved. Compliance may entail a line of sight test or a conscious presence standard.

Presumption of revocation exists if a will cannot be found, if the testator had exclusive control and access to it.

Pretermitted heir is an individual—usually a child or surviving spouse—who is not mentioned in the decedent's will and entitled to claim a statutory share of the estate. It is based on the assumption that the decedent "forgot" the heir and therefore differs from the elective share entitlement of a surviving spouse.

Principal is one name for the corpus or res of a trust—the underlying property owned. Also the person giving a power of attorney.

Probate means admitting a will to probate by proving the will is valid after the testator's death. The term also is used to refer to the property subject to probate administration (as opposed to nonprobate property that passes by operation of law or contract). The term also is a shorthand expression for probate administration.

Probate administration is the estate administration functions of marshaling assets, paying debts and expenses, and making distribution of the decedent's probate property.

Probate avoidance is the notion that delay, cost, and other disadvantages of probate administration should be avoided by use of will substitutes and nonprobate property devices.

Proxy signature is the testator authorizing someone to act on the testator's behalf to sign a will. Proxy revocation is the testator requesting that someone destroy the testator's will. Other forms of proxy refer to durable powers of attorney, such as a health care proxy.

Prudent investor/person rules are two versions of the standard to which a fiduciary will be held in investing trust corpus.

Publication is a testator's affirmation or declaration that the document being signed is a will.

Reciprocity statutes relate to the right of a nonresident not a citizen heir to inherit property if the law of her domicile would permit a citizen of our country to inherit from her decedent.

Relation back doctrine treats certain events, such as a disclaimer, as occurring at a previous time, such as when the transfer of an interest was made, when appointive property was placed in trust, or when a posthumous child was conceived.

Release allows a potential heir to receive early distribution of a share of a property owner's estate, in exchange for a release of the potential heir's expectancy.

Remainder is the future interest created in the same document as a present interest and following any particular estate.

Remarriage may restore or revive provisions or documents revoked by divorce.

Remedies usually are relevant in will contract cases involving breach. Specific performance is not an option.

Renunciation is another term for a disclaimer.

Republication by codicil is a means of (re)validating a will by subsequent execution of a codicil to that will.

Res is one name for the corpus or principal of a trust—the underlying property owned.

Residuary bequest is one of the residue of an estate. Compare Specific, General, and Demonstrative bequests.

Residuary clauses in a will dispose of property not specifically transferred under preresiduary provisions of the will—the residue. Absence or failure of a residuary clause causes that undisposed of property to pass by intestacy.

Residue is what remains in a probate estate after all debts, expenses, taxes, and prior preresiduary distributions have been satisfied.

Resulting trust is an equitable creature usually created to fill a gap in a trust document, the effect of which being to preserve the trust property for the settlor's benefit.

Retention statutes relate to the right of a nonresident not a citizen heir to inherit property if the law of her domicile will allow her to retain the property.

Reversion is the future interest retained by a transferor following any particular estate.

Reverter. See Possibility of reverter.

Revival is a fiction that a document previously revoked is restored in certain events, such as revocation of a second document that revoked the first document.

Revocable trusts are nonprobate property management and transfer devices that are not invalid as will substitutes.

Revocation by operation of law is automatic negation of a dispositive document or certain provisions in it under certain circumstances, such as divorce or murder.

Revocation by subsequent instrument usually involves a will or codicil that expressly or by inconsistency overrides a prior will.

Revocation, partial by physical act performed on only a portion of a will; not universally valid.

Right of entry for condition broken. See Power of termination.

Rule Against Perpetuities is the lives-in-being plus 21 years formulation that restricts the imposition of dead hand control.

Rule in *Clobberie's Case* addresses the question of required survivorship in a future interest.

Rule in *Shelley's Case* converts a remainder to the heirs of a life tenant into a remainder to the life tenant, which may be followed by a merger of the two interests.

Rule in *Wild's Case* addressed the meaning of a gift "to A and A's children."

Rule of convenience is a timing rule by which a class gift is determined by closing the class.

Rule of destructibility of contingent remainders is a now defunct preference treating remainder interests not yet vested when the preceding interest terminated as being invalid.

Satisfaction. See Ademption by satisfaction.

Savings clause is a provision, such as under the Rule Against Perpetuities, that attempts to make a disposition valid to the fullest extent possible or avoid invalidity to the fullest extent possible simply by stating the intent and calling for interpretation or application in a manner consistent with that intent.

Second look doctrine under the Rule Against Perpetuities tests the validity of a power of appointment or its exercise at the time the power is exercised or lapses.

Secret trust involves a transfer that on its face appears to be outright but that extrinsic evidence purports to show was meant to be restricted with fiduciary duties.

Self-proving affidavit is essentially a form of deposition, executed to avoid having to produce witnesses to affirm what they saw in a will execution.

Self-trusteed declaration of trust. See Declaration of trust.

Semi-secret trust is one that clearly is meant to be held subject to fiduciary duties but the nature of the trust or the identity of the beneficiaries is not disclosed.

Settlor is one name for the person who creates or settles a trust.

Simultaneous death is the circumstance when the order of several deaths cannot be established by proof. Seldom are they exactly simultaneous.

Small trust termination provisions permit a trustee to determine that continued administration of the trust will be uneconomic or counterproductive and collapse the trust with an outright distribution.

Special power of appointment is the old term to describe a nongeneral power.

Specific bequest is one of a particular asset or source of funds, such as "my watch" or "the balance of my account at the XYZ bank." Compare General, Demonstrative, and Residuary bequests.

Spendthrift provisions/trusts are those that protect a beneficiary's interest in trust from certain creditor claims.

Spousal annuity is the same as the survivor annuity under ERISA.

Spousal election is the same as the elective share.

Springing power is a durable power of attorney that by its terms does not become effective until a defined event, such as determination of the principal's incapacity.

Standing in a will contest context is the authority to prosecute the case because the contestant will be adversely affected by admission of the will to probate.

Statute of Frauds is that rule requiring agreements with respect to realty to be in writing.

Stranger to the adoption rule treated adopted children as natural born only vis-a-vis the adopting parent and not anyone—the stranger to the adoption—who was not a party to the adoption.

Substantial compliance in will execution is modern horseshoes: close is good enough.

Succession is the division of property among heirs, per stirpes, per capita, or per capita at each generation.

Superwill. See Blockbuster will.

Support trust is a trust providing for the beneficiary's support or maintenance.

Surcharge is one of several remedies to redress a fiduciary breach by holding the fiduciary personally accountable for any loss incurred.

Survivor annuity is the ERISA mandated entitlement of a participant's surviving spouse, also known as the spousal annuity.

Survivorship is the requirement that a named beneficiary must be alive at a certain time to take.

Takers in default are the beneficiaries who receive appointive property to the extent a power of appointment is not effectively exercised.

Testamentary power is a power of appointment exercisable by the powerholder's will.

Testamentary trust is one created by a will (testament).

Testate means there is a valid will.

Testator is the maker of a will.

Thelluson Acts relate to accumulation of income in trusts for the period of the Rule Against Perpetuities.

Tortious interference is a cause of action against anyone who intentionally and wrongfully influenced a decedent's making, revoking, or modifying a will.

Totten trust is a special form of bank account with payable on death provisions that essentially provides that the depositor is entitled to the funds during life and whatever remains at death is payable to a designated beneficiary. A valid nonprobate will substitute.

Trustee is the fiduciary who administers trust property.

Trustor is one name for the settlor who creates or settles a trust.

Trust pursuit rule permits beneficiaries to follow assets that were the subject of a fiduciary breach to recover them from whoever possesses them.

Unborn widow is one of the fantastic presumptions under the Rule Against Perpetuities.

Undue influence is one of several will contest grounds, meaning that the testator's free will was overcome and the will is that of the influencer, not the testator.

Unfunded trust means the trust has no corpus, or only a nominal corpus that just barely supports the legal existence of the trust, usually used in conjunction with life insurance or a pour over will.

Validating lives are individuals whose life or death might affect vesting for Rule Against Perpetuities purposes and are not the same as lives in being.

Virtual adoption permits a person who was not formally adopted to be treated as adopted in fact. This is a minority doctrine.

Void gifts are those that lapse because the named beneficiary predeceased the testator. Compare Lapse and see Antilapse.

Wait-and-see is the modern approach under the Rule Against Perpetuities that measures validity of interests not by the what-might-happen rule but by what in fact does transpire.

Widow's election can apply to a surviving spouse of either gender, and implies that the decedent put the survivor to an election, usually to give up property in exchange for benefits under the decedent's will, typically giving up a remainder in the survivor's property in trade for a life estate in the decedent's property.

Will is a document that may be handwritten by the testator (holograph), oral (nuncupative), or otherwise. It is revocable and ambulatory (it does nothing until death).

Will contest is an action challenging a will's validity.

Will contract is part of an agreement relating to terms or revocability of a document. Usually found with joint or mutual wills, but neither of these documents alone constitutes a contract.

Will substitutes are nonprobate forms of ownership that avoid the need for a will to convey ownership following a property owner's death. E.g., an inter vivos trust, or joint tenancy with the right of survivorship.

TABLE OF CASES

TABLE OF STATUTES

TABLE OF MODEL RULES AND UNIFORM ACTS

TABLE OF RESTATEMENTS OF THE LAW

INDEX